Sharing Knowledge, Transforming Societies

The Norhed Programme 2013–2020

Edited by
Tor Halvorsen, Kristin Skare Orgeret & Roy Krøvel

Published in 2019 by

African Minds
4 Eccleston Place, Somerset West, 7130, Cape Town, South Africa
info@africanminds.org.za
www.africanminds.org.za

and

UIB Global
PO Box 7800
5020 Bergen
http://www.uib.no/en/research/global

 Norad This book has been published with financial assistance from Norad.

The views expressed in this publication are those of the author(s) and should not be regarded as reflecting the views or position of Norad. When quoting from any of the chapters, readers are requested to acknowledge the relevant author(s).

ISBNs
978-1-928502-00-5 Print
978-1-928502-01-2 e-Book
978-1-928502-02-9 e-Pub

Copies of this book are available for free download at
www.africanminds.org.za and http://www.uib.no/en/research/global

ORDERS
For orders from Africa:
African Minds
Email: info@africanminds.org.za

For orders from outside Africa:
African Books Collective
PO Box 721, Oxford OX1 9EN, UK
Email: orders@africanbookscollective.com

CONTENTS

POSTSCRIPT

FOREWORD

The Ethiopian government has long recognised the vital importance of higher education and research for development. Ethiopia's Sustainable Development and Poverty Reduction Program envisages a key role for the universities. The number of universities in our country has increased dramatically, and the older ones have been overhauled. New graduate programmes have opened and specialised institutes have been launched on various campuses. From having only two universities for much of the 20th century, Ethiopia now has 50 public and over 170 private higher education institutions.

Following this achievement, we face challenges related to quality and relevance. A lack of adequate infrastructure and well-qualified staff, plus a scarcity of financial resources, means we still lag behind the swift changes in science and technology driven by globalisation. We need to improve the quality of our programmes and their graduates. The relevance of curricula needs to be improved to respond better to the demands of industry and other parts of the labour market as well as to the needs of society. Gender equity among academic staff and management as well as postgraduate students is another challenge facing the sector.

In essence, the question is how to balance expansion with quality and equity. The relevance and efficiency of all teaching and research must be guided by the principle of quality, and we must ensure equity in everything we do. To address these issues, Ethiopia is developing an educational roadmap that will lead the sector for the next 25 years.

It is clear that co-operation with a variety of partners has been highly instrumental in enhancing the quality and relevance of higher education and research in Ethiopia. In this, Norhed has been a key partner and support. With its South–South and triangular partnerships model that provides opportunities for scholars to share knowledge, experience and resources, the Norhed programme has facilitated effective capacity building that is enabling rapid and sustainable institutional development. The programme is helping partners to harness knowledge, create productive experiences and establish sustainable partnerships. Many academics across our universities have completed their PhDs with Norhed support.

In addition, the programme has made it possible for staff and other PhD students to conduct and publish research that is relevant to us in the South. Of particular benefit in this regard is the growing of awareness of the extent to which our problems are shared ones. Developing a common understanding of these, and obtaining wider access to available knowledge and experience related to them, makes South–South networking highly beneficial; it gives us knowledge relevant for tackling development problems as we see them.

In this way, South–South linkages are not only facilitating better networking within countries, as is the case in Ethiopia, but are also playing a role in regional integration by connecting universities across different countries. In particular, I would like to highlight that the Norhed programme has enabled universities in Ethiopia to engage closely with one another, and to share staff and other resources in ways that are contributing to enhancing the quality and efficiency of education and research.

Similarly, the triangular co-operation that links Norwegian institutions with multiple universities in the South has many benefits. The exchange of knowledge, based on a variety of experiences and the sharing of resources, has enriched all partners. Through staff exchanges, scholars from Norway have, I am sure, also gained much (as have we) from their experiences on our campuses. They have come to teach for a certain period, advise students on their theses, conduct research, hold seminars, participate in conferences and share their knowledge.

As one of the co-ordinators of a Norhed project (on capacity building in linguistics) run jointly by the University of Oslo, Addis Ababa University and Hawassa University, I witnessed these fruitful exchanges. The Norhed programme increased the capacity of scholars in Ethiopia to deliver high-quality education and relevant research.

As someone who has also been involved in Addis Ababa University at a senior management level, and now, as Minister of Science and Higher Education, I can strongly affirm that Norhed is playing a great role in supporting institutional development in Ethiopia: our capacity to deliver quality education and relevant research has increased. From my personal experience, I can see at least two ways in which the Norhed programme differs from other similar projects. First, the programme is highly gender sensitive. The programme works hard to ensure women's participation in projects and that gender issues are a central focus in research efforts. This contributes greatly to the empowerment of female academics – narrowing the gender gaps among PhD students and faculty members. Second, Norhed insists that all projects include a component on community engagement, thus ensuring that each pro-ject engages seriously with the question of what research is relevant to community development. It has been particularly rewarding for me to see how female PhD students benefit from this support by publishing their work, getting involved in research networks and participating in international conferences. This has helped many candidates produce better quality dissertations and is enhancing their chances of success in their chosen careers.

In my own development as an academic, I also benefited much from Norhed support. With my colleague at the University of Oslo, Elizabeth Lanza, who has become a life-long friend and collaborator, I had ten articles published in international journals. I was also able to present my research at several international conferences and thus became part of an international research network of linguistics and sociolinguistics scholars. Ultimately, these activities contributed to my being appointed as a professor in Addis Ababa University's Department of Linguistics and Philology, and enabled me to take on other roles such as joining the editorial committee of international journals and acting as an examiner for PhD candidates.

In general, therefore, I greatly appreciate Norhed and its work. I look forward to continued support from the programme, particularly with regard to the empowerment of women in higher education, and I hope Norhed will continue to adopt modalities in line with our experience in the South.

Her Excellency, Professor Hirut Woldemariam
Minister of Science and Higher Education,
Federal Democratic Republic of Ethiopia
July 2019

FREQUENTLY USED
ACRONYMS AND ABBREVIATIONS

AAU	Addis Ababa University
AIDS	Acquired Immune Deficiency Syndrome
AMR	antimicrobial resistance
AST	antimicrobial susceptibility testing
BA	Batchelor of Arts
BTVET	Business, Technical and Vocational Education and Training
CDRF	Capacity Development Results Framework, World Bank
CEDAW	Convention on the Elimination of All Forms of Discrimination against Women
CHUSS	College of Humanities and the Social Sciences, Makerere University
CIH	Centre for International Health, University of Bergen
DR Congo	Democratic Republic of the Congo
ELAM	Executive Leadership in Academic Medicine
EU	European Union
GrowNut	Growing Partnerships for Higher Education and Research in Nutritional Epidemiology
HE	higher education
HEI	higher education institution
HIV	Human Immunodeficiency Virus
HU	Hawassa University
IAMCR	International Association for Media and Communication Research

ICM	International Confederation of Midwives
ICN	International Council of Nurses
ICT	information and communication technologies
IMF	International Monetary Fund
JEWEL	Jimma Executive Program for Women in Academic and Educational Leadership
KSPH	Kinshasa School of Public Health
LCB	linguistic capacity building
LIC	low-income country
LMIC	low- to middle-income country
LOITASA	Language of Instruction in Tanzania and South Africa
MA	Master of Arts
MPAM	Master's Programme in Public Administration and Management
MU	Makerere University
MUHAS	Muhimbili University of Health and Allied Sciences
NGO	non-governmental organisation
NOMA	Norad's Programme for Master Studies
Norad	Norwegian Agency for Development Cooperation
Norhed	Norwegian Programme for Capacity Development in Higher Education and Research for Development
NUFU	Norwegian Programme for Development Research and Education
OECD	Organisation for Economic Co-operation and Development
OSHA	Occupational Safety and Health Agency
OsloMet	Oslo Metropolitan University
PAS	Political and Administrative Studies Department (Chancellor College, Malawi)
PCK	pedagogical content knowledge
PhD	Doctor of Philosophy
RSF	Reporters Without Borders
RUIICAY	Network of Indigenous, Intercultural and Community Universities of Abya Yala
SACCADE	Strategic and Collaborative Capacity Development in Ethiopia and Africa

SDGs	Sustainable Development Goals
SEARCWL	Southern and Eastern African Regional Centre in Women's Law
SENUPH	South Ethiopia Network of Universities in Public Health
SoL	School of Law (Makerere University)
SPHMMC	St Paul's Hospital Millennium Medical College
SIU	Norwegian Centre for International Cooperation in Education
STEM	science, technology, engineering and mathematics
SUM	Centre for Development and Environment (University of Oslo)
SUZA	State University of Zanzibar
TB	Tuberculosis
TBA	traditional birth attendant
Transled	Transformation, Language, Education and Development
UAIIN	Autonomous Indigenous Intercultural University (Colombia)
UCINPI-AW	Indigenous Community Intercultural University of the Nationalities and Indigenous Peoples 'Amawtay Wasi'
UDSM	University of Dar es Salaam
UiB	University of Bergen
UiO	University of Oslo
UN	United Nations
UNAS	Uganda National Academy for Sciences
UNDP	United Nations Development Programme
UNEVOC	UN International Centre for Technical and Vocational Education and Training
Unesco	United Nations Educational, Scientific and Cultural Organization
URACCAN	University of the Autonomous Regions of the Caribbean Coast of Nicaragua
UNZA	University of Zambia
US / USA	United States of America
UWC	University of the Western Cape
UZ	University of Zimbabwe

VET	vocational education and training
WHO	World Health Organization
WLEA	Women and Law in Eastern Africa
WLSA	Women and Law in Southern Africa

PREFACE

Sustainable capacity development in higher education and research: Norad's approach

Jeanette da Silva & Douglas Tendai Phiri

Higher education has often been narrowly associated with development limited to economic benefits, but this perception conceals the broader and vitally important *socio*-economic benefits of higher education. The Norwegian Programme for Capacity Development in Higher Education and Research for Development (Norhed) (which is funded by the Norwegian Agency for Development Cooperation, Norad), moves beyond this by emphasising that sound, strategic investments in higher education and research in low and middle-income countries (LMICs) pay off in the form of strong academic institutions and their societal outreach.

For Norad, such investments have many benefits – not least the contribution they make to development of countries' intellectual resources, competent workforces, good governance, gender equality and human rights. In the longer run, investments in the higher education sector also contribute to the development and implementation of evidence-based policies and decisions that have the potential to enhance sustainable economic, social and environmental development (Norad n.d.).

Norhed's primary objective is to strengthen capacity in higher education institutions (HEIs) in LMICs. To achieve this, Norhed has adopted what it sees as a holistic approach to capacity development through South–South–North partnerships. Holistic in this context entails strengthening the capacity of HEIs through interlinked and interdependent programmatic interventions that encompass education, research, institutional development and administrative management. Drawing on lessons learned so far, Norhed deviates from programmes previously supported by Norway, which focused more on separate and isolated initiatives such as scholarships, the development of study programmes, and research projects.

It has been widely documented that HEIs in LMICs lost momentum in relation to the wider development agenda during the 1990s, largely because of the World Bank's publications on educational rates-of-return, and its policies that supported the reduction of funding to universities and research institutions in favour of primary education.[1] It is worth noting that Norwegian support for HEIs in LMICs was largely unaffected by this World Bank position and remained relatively constant throughout this period. This reflects Norway's relatively independent higher education policy that charted its own course (see Norwegian Ministry of Foreign Affairs 1999).

Here we offer a historical overview of Norwegian funding for capacity-development programmes in higher education and research, illustrating the learning that has occurred over time, and how this has enabled systems to evolve that have shaped and informed the development of Norhed and its funding policies. We argue that Norhed's approach, anchored in sustainability, fosters the kind of capacity within the higher education and academic sectors that is a prerequisite for LMICs to develop their own intellectual resources and build the knowledge base necessary for transformational development. We illustrate Norhed's novelty, and the intentions behind its design and interventions. We highlight the core characteristics of the programme, which include holistic institutional capacity building, mutual partnerships, ownership, relevance and flexibility. Then we explain how the principle of sustainability is built into both the aims and the processes of the programme. Finally, we offer some key reflections on the programme's learning process and outline some projections of the programme.

Capacity building through Norhed

Launched in 2012, Norhed is the Norwegian government's flagship programme on capacity development in higher education and research. Its partner institutions in Africa, Asia, Latin America and the Middle East are in countries registered on the list of official development-aid recipients drawn up by the OECD's Development Assistance Committee.[2]

Norhed has six sub-programmes, which, to a large extent, reflect Norway's political priorities, and indicate where Norway sees itself as having the potential to make specific contributions to strengthening the capacities of HEIs in partner countries. Five of these are relevant to national plans and priorities in the countries in which Norhed works. These are: education and training; health; natural resource management, climate change and the environment; democratic and economic governance; and the humanities, culture, media and communication. The sixth area focuses specifically on capacity development in South Sudan.[3]

For Norhed, the strengthening of HEIs can be measured in relation to 'producing more and better research relevant to the thematic areas of the sub-programmes' and 'producing more and better-qualified graduates, men and women, relevant to the identified sub-programmes' (Norad n.d.: 6). Interventions envisioned as contributing to developing institutional capacity include: developing new and/or revising existing bachelor, master's and PhD programmes to better suit the needs of specific LMICs; building staff competence through supporting fellowships at master's, PhD and postdoctoral levels; supporting joint research projects conducted by Norwegian and Southern scholars; as well as the strengthening and equipping of administrative services and related small-scale infrastructure such as ICT facilities, or specialised units within laboratories, libraries and teaching facilities.

At the time of writing in early 2019, Norhed is supporting 50 projects across 26 LMICs. These involve 60 academic institutions in LMICs and 13 institutions in Norway. All Norhed projects are funded after competitive open calls and rigorous assessment processes that involve independent external review committees, as well as the Norwegian embassies in the respective countries and Norad's own thematic experts. Each project is funded for five years, with the possibility of a cost or no-cost extension.

Learning from previous programmes

Since early 1960s, the Norwegian government has supported various higher education and research initiatives in LMICs. Thus, Norhed has had the advantage of being able to build on the experience and learning gathered by the long-standing programmes and initiatives that preceded it. In this section, we discuss the lessons and learnings from previous programmes that have contributed to shaping the distinctive approach of the Norhed programme.

The Norad Fellowship Programme, initiated in 1962, was one of the first forms of Norwegian assistance to LMICs. At that time, many African countries were on the verge of achieving independence from colonial rule, and the fact that many of their citizens had been prevented from obtaining a sound education was considered a major obstacle to development. Norwegian policy was to offer training in areas where Norway had clear and cutting-edge competencies to share, and the Norad Fellowship Programme offered scholarships to students in LMICs which made it possible for them to undertake further study at Norwegian HEIs. The intention was for African students to obtain relevant and practical knowledge that they could put to use when they returned to their countries and thus replace foreign technical consultants (expatriates). It is estimated that 9 000 students benefited from short courses and attained diplomas or master's degrees in Norway with scholarships during the programme period 1962 to 2005 (Nordic Consulting Group 2005). However, while the early phase emphasised professional skills development with a strong vocational element, the focus gradually shifted towards academic capacity building and institutional co-operation.

During the 1970s, financially disadvantaged students from LMICs were enrolled at Norwegian universities and supported through the Norwegian State Educational Loan Fund's Section on Developing

Countries (*u-landsparagrafen*). Eventually, this evolved into a programme known as the Quota Scheme. Every year between 1994 and 2016, the Quota Scheme offered access to full scholarships, primarily at master's and PhD levels, to approximately 1 100 students from LMICs (including Central and Eastern Europe and Central Asia). The Quota Scheme's objectives were twofold. On the one hand, the programme aimed to provide relevant education that would be of benefit to students' countries when they returned home. On the other hand, the programme intended to promote internationalisation within HEIs in Norway.[4]

During the 1990s, Norwegian universities focused increasingly on internationalisation. By 2003, this culminated in the introduction of the Quality Reforms, which radically reformed Norway's whole higher education system in line with the Bologna Process. In other words, the old system of Latin degrees was replaced by the internationally recognised bachelor, master's and PhD system, with credits and gradings changed to comply with the European Credit Transfer System. In addition, while projects linked to capacity development in academic institutions in LMICs has always fallen under the Norwegian Ministry of Foreign Affairs, the Ministry of Education and Research also had a policy on development collaboration as a part of its internationalisation strategy. This is highlighted in the ministry's action plan for development collaboration on higher education and research (Norwegian Ministry of Education and Research 2006).

So-called quota students played a vital role in internationalisation. Several master's programmes were developed in English, and these were given a more global thematic focus so that course content responded more appropriately to the needs of quota students. Eventually, these same courses were offered to the broader pool of students as well. Hence, the Quota Scheme contributed not only to the internationalisation of study programmes in Norway, but also to making the composition of the classrooms more international.

The closure of the Quota Scheme in 2016 generated a public debate in which several Norwegian HEIs argued that the termination of the programme would lead to less diverse classrooms, and that African students, in particular, would be under-represented.[5] However, it is expected that the number of students from LMIC countries will gradually increase as the Norwegian Partnership Programme for Global Academic Cooperation (Norpart) is upscaled. Established in 2016, one objective of Norpart is to enhance the quality of higher education in Norway and LMICs through institutionalised academic collaboration and mutual student mobility, both South–North and North–South (DIKU 2018).

In an example of using programme design to address specific challenges, Quota Scheme scholarships were designed to avoid the brain-drain problem that often troubles international scholarship schemes. Accordingly, part of the students' funding was given in the form of a loan that was cancelled once the students returned home. An evaluation conducted in 2014 found that over 70 per cent of scholarship recipients from LMICs returned home after completing their studies (Damvad Analytics 2014). Although the Quota Scheme benefited many individuals who might not otherwise have had access to quality higher education, the 2014 evaluation also pointed to a lack of systematic linkages relevant to LMICs and their own universities.

As noted, the initial focus of Norad's Fellowship Programme and the Quota Scheme was on individual scholarships, and on students being given funding to study in Norway. Limited attention was directed to HEIs in LMICs or to cross-institutional collaboration. A turning point was the Norwegian Programme for Development, Research and Education (NUFU), which ran from 1991 to 2011. NUFU's main objective was to enhance the capacities and competencies of researchers and research-based education institutions in ways that were relevant to the national needs of LMICs. This was to be achieved via co-operation between universities and research institutions in Norway and partner countries. Primary focal points were research collaborations and the training of PhD candidates. NUFU also introduced and developed the South–South–North collaboration model. This proved highly successful in joint research and knowledge production, and in providing partner institutions in LMICs with international exposure and access to international research networks. Although the programme has been criticised for not focusing enough on strengthening institutions, and of over-prioritising individual researchers, NUFU nevertheless initiated several research projects that laid the foundations for subsequent collaborations, including several institutional partnerships that are vital to some of Norhed's current projects (COWI A/S 2009).

Alongside the attention NUFU was giving to PhD candidates, Norad's Programme for Master's Studies (NOMA) was established in 2006 to develop and run master's programmes in LMICs. This was done by creating close collaborations between HEIs in Norway and in partner countries. Thus, the NOMA programme represented a significant shift whereby capacity-building activities began to take place in the South and were facilitated by partnerships between HEIs.

An evaluation of NOMA and NUFU carried out in 2009 highlighted that both programmes had contributed significantly to capacity building in the South and in Norway as well to some extent (COWI A/S 2009). However, the programmes were assessed as highly supply driven. That is, the relationships between the Norwegian and partner-country institutions were considered asymmetrical, with the Norwegian institutions remaining the leading partners even though the capacity-building activities were taking place mainly in the LMICs.

Building partnerships and collaborations based on mutual interests and common understandings of the importance of higher education and its institutions takes time. As noted, Norway's commitment to the higher education and research sectors has remained a priority since the early 1960s. While the World Bank and governments worldwide reduced funding to higher education in the 1990s (Hydén 2016), Norway countered this by launching a strategy aimed at strengthening research and higher education in LMICs with which Norway had relationships (Norwegian Ministry of Foreign Affairs 1999).

This strategy underlined the crucial role played by HEIs in the long-term economic, social and cultural development. Further, the strategy emphasised the need to strengthen universities' role as institutions of knowledge production and knowledge dissemination, and promoted efforts to ensure a holistic perspective in Norwegian development policy which acknowledges the pivotal role that research has to play. The importance of research for generating new knowledge on key development issues is also highlighted by research programmes on development that are funded through the Norwegian Research Council.

This is the foundation on which the Norhed programme is built. The long-term relationships built through previous programmes and collaborations have evolved into sound, long-standing partnerships that take time to establish. This should not be taken for granted. Nor should the commitment and dedication of individual researchers, who have invested considerable time and effort in nurturing academic networks and partnerships, be underestimated. Many Norhed projects build on their work and, in fact, several of the current project co-ordinators were once recipients of scholarships awarded via NUFU, NOMA or the Quota Scheme. What this demonstrates is how programmes evolved – from focusing on offering scholarships to individual students, to fostering institutional partnerships that enhance research and capacity building – so that many are now managed by institutions in the LMICs. This shift was made possible through the long-term commitments made by both the Norwegian government and Norway's academic institutions to the strengthening of higher education institutions and the expansion of research across the world.

The development of Norhed

As noted, when Norhed was founded in 2012, it was able to benefit from the strong and long-standing collaborations between academic institutions in LMICs and in Norway. Besides accepting the recommendation to merge NUFU and NOMA into one programme, Norhed was designed to build on the experiences of previous programmes. It was therefore important that it addressed some limitations identified in relation to earlier initiatives, such as the separation of education and research into different programmes and the asymmetrical, supply-driven arrangements that were prevalent in some cross-institutional collaborations (COWI A/S 2009).

The challenge was to develop a model that would, on the one hand, best meet the priorities and needs of HEIs in a range of highly diverse LMICs and, on the other hand, satisfy the demands of Norwegian development policy as set out in the Report to the Storting No. 13 of 2008–2009 (Norwegian Ministry of Foreign Affairs 2009). Accordingly, ten guiding principles were identified as the foundation of the new programme:

- Create flexible mechanisms that can be adjusted to the prioritised needs of partner countries and cover all levels of higher education, from undergraduate to postdoctorate;
- Be more directed by the priorities of the partner countries than NUFU and NOMA were;
- Promote long-term capacity and sustainability;
- Allow for thematic or geographic foci;
- Connect with Norwegian HEIs;
- Build on mutual partnerships between researchers and institutions;
- Make quality research a key objective;
- In addition to building capacity in education and research, allow for institutional development, including the enhancement of infrastructure and the upgrading of administrative skills;
- Put efficient and cost-effective administration procedures in place, and choose the administrative model *after* the programme design has been selected;
- Systematically promote South–South collaboration.

Four core characteristics of the Norhed programme

Researcher initiated

While Norhed was being established, three models for programme design were considered. In 2010, the models were presented to central stakeholders in Norway and potential partner countries via an open consultation process. In the first model, higher education and research collaboration was to be defined by university-based *researchers* who would define and design proposals for North–South partnerships based on their mutual research interests. In the second model, collaborations were to be defined by *institutions* in the South. This mirrors the model used by the Swedish International Development Cooperation Agency (SIDA), where selected HEIs in the South define proposals for their respective institutions based on their own institutional needs and priorities (see Hydén 2016). In the third model, collaboration was to be defined by the *authorities* in the LMICs (mirroring the system then followed by the Dutch agency Nuffic), and would hence be more closely connected to national needs and priorities.

In the debates about each model that followed, the first was considered to have a stronger research focus while the second and third were considered more likely to emphasise educational and institutional capacity building. Furthermore, models two and three were expected to have a stronger focus on long-term planning linked to institutional and national priorities, while model one was seen as more likely to include the notion of mutuality in partnerships as well as regional South–South collaborations. Overall, model one was preferred, based on its emphasis on research and the greater possibilities it offers for facilitating South–South–North partnerships. This model was also considered likely to be most attractive to Norwegian partners, given their interests in mutually beneficial and collaborative research. Consequently, the decision supported by key stakeholders, via a hearings process, recommended that Norhed proceed with a researcher-led model rather than one that is directed at an institutional or governmental level.

This bottom-up approach, with its emphasis on research-initiated projects and academic freedom, is well worth noting as it represents the very core of the thinking behind the Norhed programme, and thus the foundation of Norwegian support to higher education and research in general. This approach is supported by the design of the programme, which issues open and competitive calls for proposals that emphasise the quality of research and teaching. Support for research-initiated projects includes direct support for public institutions in the South. This differs strongly from Norad-funded initiatives in other sectors such as primary education and health, where funding is increasingly channelled through multilateral organisations and global funds. Of the total Norwegian development budget for 2018, only 4 per cent was channelled directly to public institutions in recipient countries.[6]

The gravitation towards a stronger demand-driven orientation – that is, with activities being directed by the priorities of partner countries – is another vital element of the Norhed model. This not only aligns Norhed with the 2005 Paris Declaration and the 2008 Accra

Agenda for Action, but also with contemporary Norwegian policies on development collaboration. Furthermore, this approach helps to sustain the internationalisation of Norwegian institutions to some degree even though this is not a major priority of the programme.

Ownership and relevance led by the South

An evaluation of Norwegian support for capacity development (Norad 2015) shows that the ownership of interventions is a key factor in successful projects. LMIC partners being in the driver's seat is therefore seen as essential for institutional capacity development. In this context, ownership translates as drafting project proposals and assuming full responsibility for implementing and managing projects, including the co-ordination of partners and reporting to donors. Even more important here is ownership of knowledge production. This includes decision-making about what is taught and how, as well as the defining of research topics and research objectives (see also Mamdani, this volume).

By supporting this kind of ownership, Norhed is helping facilitate processes that support the decolonisation of knowledge, as partners in the LMICs increasingly define the substance and relevance of what is taught and researched in institutions. In many LMICs, knowledge production involving local researchers is very limited. In 2015, for example, *The Guardian* reported that Africa produced only 1.1 per cent of global scientific knowledge and estimated that the continent had only 79 scientists per million inhabitants. In Brazil and the USA, this figure stood at 656 and 4 500 scientists respectively.[7] In this context, Norhed is fostering capacity within African HEIs in relation to the production of research and knowledge. In this regard, Norhed support also provides a crucial means for amplifying the voices and perspectives of researchers in LMICs who are under-represented in global research production.

Relevance and ownership are closely related. For Norhed, the relevance of knowledge production to sustainable development is key. In this, the programme intends to be responsive to the priorities of the higher education sector in partner countries. Ideally, the needs and priorities identified by partner institutions should be linked to government policies and priorities at national and/or regional level. In

addition, projects are expected to enhance the sustainability of economic, social and environmental development in the partner countries.
Relevance therefore refers to how academic institutions are responsive
to both strengthening the higher education sector *and* having a positive
impact on society at large. For Norhed, being relevant in highly diverse
countries, and in contexts that have different needs and priorities,
means that flexibility in its range of interventions is key. For this reason, the Norhed model allows for a certain flexibility which project
partners have the latitude to convert into contextually relevant research
and education outcomes of high quality.

In Norhed, support for capacity development in higher education in
the South is based on co-operation between universities in Norway and
its partner countries. The North–South model has been continued
from previous programmes, with the asymmetrical relations typically
of previous programmes (whereby the Norwegian institutions often
took the leading role) having shifted to emphasise mutual partnerships
led by partner institutions in the South. The model has also expanded
to encompass a stronger emphasis on South–South partnerships. This
is adding impetus to inter-regional collaborations between LMICs,
where such networks are increasingly helping to improve the relevance
and quality of higher education and knowledge production.

As the main partners, institutions in the South carry primary
responsibility for project management, co-ordination and financial
accountability. This also means that they have the latitude to influence
the competency-strengthening components and the research agendas
of joint projects. In dialogues between institutional partners, research
agendas are established in ways that facilitate knowledge production
based on the needs and interests of all partners. Similarly, in projects
that focus on skills and capacity development in institutions in the
South, the Southern partner is defined as the lead institution and this
is embedded in the partnership model.

This is a major shift from previous programmes, where the
Norwegian partner would always assume the leading role. This
approach also stands out as different from those adopted by other
donor agencies such as the Finnish National Agency for Education
(Edufi) which invariably places the Northern partner in the lead. The

intention behind this shift is to empower and secure ownership of projects by the Southern institutions. The model is built on the realisation that, after decades of collaboration in the higher education sector, it is time to pass the baton over to the Southern partners. The goal of any donor funding is for support to become surplus to requirements over time. To achieve this, Southern institutions must develop the capacity to manage international academic projects and to secure future funding both nationally and internationally.

By positioning the Southern partners as lead institutions, and emphasising the mutuality of partnerships, it is hoped that asymmetrical power relations will gradually level out. At the same time, the benefits to be derived by institutions across the North–South divide from jointly shaping research priorities and sharing perspectives are increasingly evident and acknowledged. Unlike the predominantly unidirectional transfer of knowledge and capacity from North to South that seems to have characterised earlier programmes, Norhed is deliberately attempting to shift the discourse and the power balance towards an *exchange* of knowledge and skills.

Of course, it remains arguable whether asymmetrical power relations can be completely transformed simply by allocating project responsibility to Southern partners. After all, the Norwegian HEIs retain the advantage of proximity to Norad and to Norwegian development policy in general. In addition, Norwegian project co-ordinators tend to be more senior academics, even having acted as academic supervisors (at PhD or postdoctorate level) to project leaders in the South. Thus, the persistence of pre-established power relations is an issue. A further concern are the power relations that sometimes develop between partners in the South, whereby institutions that have more experience in the management of externally funded projects collaborate with less-established institutions that have relatively less capacity.

However, while the notion of 'equal partnership' is often highlighted as a goal in development collaborations, we question whether this is actually preferable, or even possible. As Nada Wanni, Sarah Hinz and Rebecca Day point out, 'a dynamic collaborative process between educational institutions brings *mutual* though not necessarily *symmetrical* benefits to the parties engaged in the partnerships' (quoted in

Ndaruhutse and Thompson 2016: 7–8). What we see in Norhed projects is that the different partners in a project contribute in different ways, depending on the context of the research being conducted, and the varied experiences and insights they have to offer. Similarly, activities undertaken at each partner institution vary for a range of reasons. For this reason, it should be possible for the 'lead partner' in a project to vary depending on the type of research or intervention being conducted. Hence, roles and activities might not be equal or symmetrical in any normative sense, but instead each partner has a specific purpose and reason for being involved in the project, and the benefits are mutual according to the context.

A holistic approach to capacity development

While Norad's earlier programmes tended to focus on offering scholarships, developing master's programmes, or on researcher and PhD training, Norhed takes a more holistic approach. That is, learnings from previous programmes indicate that sustainable capacity development is seldom achieved via isolated interventions. Instead, the various segments of institutions' core activities have to be seen as interrelated and interdependent. To improve the overall quality of graduates at a university, it is not sufficient only to establish new courses and teaching programmes. Rather, the research capacities of the academic staff have to be strengthened and then this has to be fully integrated into their teaching practice. Likewise, while improving institutional infrastructure, by providing or upgrading technical equipment and libraries is critically important, administrative systems related to procurement and financial accountability also need attention. By adopting a holistic approach, Norhed is attempting to boost institutional competencies related to infrastructural and administrative development as well as strengthen pedagogical and research skills.

Flexible and contextually adapted

To achieve the relevance alluded to above, Norhed was developed with the intention of being flexible and able to adapt to different contexts in line with the needs and aims of its Southern partners. In fact, it can be argued that flexibility in Norhed begins during the initial stages of project development, starting with the project concepts, the identification of partners and project proposals. Partners are free to team up with the institutions they find most relevant within a broad range of eligible partners and disciplines. Thus, flexibility applies to how partnerships are imagined and created, and is also clearly reflected in proposed research themes and the types of study programmes that are developed.

Norhed's programme design insists that the four core characteristics mentioned are incorporated into all projects. The applicability of each characteristic is wide and allows for flexibility as long as projects meaningfully contribute to defined higher education outcomes and have long-term relevance. This flexibility is reflected in the current project portfolio. Although all projects should reflect these core characteristics, how they do so does vary significantly from project to project, and even between partners in the same project. Hence, it can be argued that, although the programme is structured around predefined areas of intervention, these should not be considered straight-jackets but rather a foundation to which projects can add content and relevance.

Although the intention is to allow for flexibility, it has to be acknowledged that Norhed partners don't always experience Norad's results-based management requirements as particularly flexible. The results-based framework, with standard indicators to monitor project progress, together with detailed annual narrative and financial reports, requires that partners have a good understanding of the principles of effective and efficient monitoring and reporting. The potential gap between Norad's expectations and requirements, and the management capacity at the partner institutions can be a challenge and must be taken into consideration.

'Sustainable development' in higher education

The Norwegian approach to capacity development emphasises the crucial role that higher education and its institutions can play in achieving sustainable social, economic and environmental development. Although published in the late 1980s, the strongly ecologically focused report, *Our Common Future*, still offers the most commonly cited definition of sustainability as: 'development that meets the needs of the present without compromising the ability of the future generations to meet their own needs' (WCED 1987: 43).[8] Or as Filho (2000: 19) put it, sustainability is about long-term, systematic and 'durable development'.

In the context of higher education and research, sustainable development can be interpreted in different ways, but here too environmental concerns tend to be emphasised. This may involve the inclusion and integration of environmental literacy into curricula and course content, and of environmentally sound practices in relation to issues of waste, water and energy management into university operations and administration (Granados-Sánchez et al. 2012). However, HEIs also have valuable contributions to make to sustainable development in a broader social context. For this reason, Norhed's objective of capacity development in the university sector is based on an understanding that capacity development is not simply a goal in itself, but a means toward a higher goal – namely sustainability (Nossum 2016).

For Norhed, the role and benefits of a strong higher education sector in relation to sustainable development are multifaceted, broad and long term. Sustainability is seen as both a goal and a process. As a goal, Norhed's work is founded on the premise that sustainability has to be realised in three dimensions: social, economic and environmental. The thematic areas outlined above are thus aligned to focus on each of these three dimensions. For Norhed, higher education can help societies to enhance and deepen social development through strengthening social systems including in sectors such as health and education. Well-capacitated higher education systems have the resources to ensure social and gender equality as well as human rights more broadly – guaranteeing equitable access to resources, social justice and the practice of fundamental values including academic freedom, tolerance and respect for the dignity of all (Unesco 2018).

Although they have often been perceived as elitist and as entrenching inequality, strong HEIs allow for increased access including for marginalised groups by adopting open, inclusive and equitable policies. Furthermore, higher education can also strengthen governance, democracy and public service systems through ensuring that graduates who find work in public institutions are well-qualified, effective and competent. Relevant research and knowledge production carried out by universities and research institutions can also ensure that governments are able to base their policy decisions on evidence-based research, thereby making the decisions necessary for good governance and the attainment of sustainable, social, economic and environmental development. Environmental development can be attained through disseminating knowledge and raising awareness of the critical dependencies of human beings and our livelihoods on the existence and preservation of the environment. Hence, the notion of sustainability in Norhed is predicated on the long-term impact of project interventions that might lead to societal transformation.

As a process, sustainability has to be made to cut across all university activities, operations and missions. Norhed foregrounds environmental consciousness at partner institutions through the kind of research it supports, through curriculum updates, and through the strengthening of teaching capacity. That is, by supporting the updating of course content and the development of new study programmes that are relevant to national and institutional needs, by strengthening staff capacity through fellowships and research grants, as well as increased access to reading material and technical equipment, Norhed is contributing to the sustainability of academic institutions. In addition, the programme fosters capacity building by strengthening internal systems and reporting procedures for financial management, procurement, the training of administrative staff, and project management. In the long term, this contributes towards the development of partner organisations as strong and sound institutions that can secure funding, ensure prudent management, and contribute actively to development.

The glocalisation of higher education

For Norhed, relevance and ownership is anchored on the principle of local knowledge production. It is clear that when local knowledge informs evidence-based policy-making, local challenges are more likely to be resolved. Therefore, the ability of higher education institutions to respond to local challenges is a primary indicator of relevance. However, local challenges are increasingly entangled with global dynamics. Thus, while local relevance remains a starting point, the entanglement of local and global in response to the contemporary world order must be considered. For this reason, both global and local perspectives are critical in ensuring sustainable development and equipping countries to meet the demands of the fast-changing global knowledge economy. Globalisation has opened up linkages across different sectors and increased the need for a cross-pollination of perspectives on many issues. In this context, the notion of the 'glocal' emerged, and the challenge facing the academic sector is how to apply continuous learning and interdisciplinarity, the sharing of knowledge and best practice (Robertson 1995), across fields of learning in ways that address both local and global conditions.

As stated earlier, Norhed is underpinned by (some new and many long-standing) academic partnerships that cross a range of disciplinary and geographical areas. This creates space for interrogating local and global challenges from different disciplinary and geographical perspectives. Partnerships within Norhed offer unique opportunities for collaborations in the development of educational programmes, pedagogical approaches, interdisciplinary research and research protocols, joint publications, teaching and student exchanges, etc. These processes both challenge and empower academic institutions to respond better to the increasingly complex local and global challenges facing the world by producing more and better graduates and research. This transformation is even more critical, and it interrogates the traditional role of universities in the global development agenda.

Norhed and Agenda 2030

Norhed was established before the United Nation's Agenda 2030 and Sustainable Development Goals (SDGs) were launched in 2015. Therefore, achieving the SDGs was not one of Norhed's starting points. Nevertheless, the design of the programme is founded on the same principles, and Norhed concurs strongly with the SDGs on many levels. Arguably, higher education is given relatively little attention in the

SDGs, notwithstanding its strategic role and relevance to the achievement of all the goals. The complexity of sustainable development requires a cross-sectoral approach and a strong emphasis on the interface between policy-making and knowledge production derived from sound evidence-based research.

This further amplifies and underscores the need to support and nurture dynamic, transformational and interdisciplinary HEIs, capable of producing relevant knowledge and skills for innovation and sustainable development. Discourse on the role of higher education in achieving the SDGs is exerting pressure on the role traditionally played by HEIs, which confined them to teaching and research that was often theoretical and clearly separated from its application in the private and the public sectors. Increasingly, in discussions of higher education, its role in transformative development is seen to be located at the very core of achieving SDGs.

This has created not only a renewed interest in higher education but also a rethinking of how HEIs might transform into institutions that are capable of contributing to sustainable and multisectoral social, environmental and economic development in ways that benefit societies. This convergence of academia and development is increasingly highlighted in the agenda of development and donor agencies. While donor organisations can still be criticised as being supply-driven in nature, and for allowing the political interests of donor countries to overrule the interests of recipient partners (Koch and Weingart 2016), the SDGs reveal the multiplicity of arenas in which the interests of all should interact and overlap in mutually beneficial ways.

Reflections on Norhed's first programme period, 2013–2019/2020

In early 2019, the Norhed is in the final phase of its first programme period, from 2013 to 2019/2020. It is therefore pertinent for Norad to consider what has been learned from this first phase and the chapters in this book are important contributions to our reflection process.

In 2017, the Technopolis Group conducted an external mid-term review of Norhed, launching their final report in early 2018. The group reported that Norhed's programme design and thematic focus areas are highly relevant to the needs of partner countries and partner institutions. In addition, Norhed was found to be responding well to Norway's development priorities and to the SDGs. The South–South–North partnership model was emphasised as being particularly key in contributing to both capacity building and capacity exchange (Technopolis Group 2018).

The shift to making the Southern partner the 'agreement partner'[9] is highlighted as an important stepping stone to ensuring local ownership and relevance. Admittedly, in several cases, the learning process has been steep and some partners have struggled to comply with Norad's high expectations with regard to reporting and monitoring. The shift is therefore considered a great leap but it is acknowledged to carry some risks. Experience shows that the capacity of the agreement partner must be carefully assessed prior to project agreements being signed. In addition, despite Norhed's holistic approach to capacity development, the Technopolis report points out that institutional capacity-building interventions referring to systems strengthening, administration and management are still often seen as somehow de-linked from the academic activities. Thus, while capacity development processes have been closely linked to education and research activities in mutually reinforcing ways, support for administrative activities often receives less consideration. To achieve the intended impact and secure sustainability, future programme design must include additional mechanisms for strengthening institutional and administrative systems and training, as well as the relationships between different interventions areas in increasingly holistic ways.

Technopolis's final finding was that, despite the preference for research-initiated projects, some projects have remained rather isolated at a departmental level, without linkages to broader institutional priorities. In this regard, Norad is assessing and addressing ways to strengthen Norhed projects' institutional and national buy-in to ensure the long-term sustainable environmental, social and economic development impact.

Future directions

Norad is in the process of outlining Norhed's next phase. The key issue is to ensure the continuation of programme segments that have proven to be effective and relevant, and to strengthen segments that need further adjustment and development. As with previous programmes, Norhed's next phase must align with and/or balance the needs and priorities of LMICs on the one hand and Norwegian development policy on the other. While the two do not necessarily contradict or undermine one another, it is important that the intentions and objectives of the new phase are systematically considered and carefully aligned in relation to sustainable economic, social and environmental development.

Norway's development policy outlines some general directions. This includes the consolidation of Norwegian development co-operation to focus on fewer countries, as well as a clearer thematic focus and the co-ordination of initiatives across sectors within selected countries. The policy further emphasises the SDGs as the guiding framework for all Norwegian development co-operation (Norwegian Ministry of Foreign Affairs 2017).

This reinforces the intentions of Norad's newly established Knowledge Bank, in which Norhed's administration is located. The aim of the Knowledge Bank is to co-ordinate and strengthen institutional partnerships, as well as knowledge sharing and transfer on certain competencies in which Norway has particularly valuable or sought-after proficiency. Norhed's extensive experience not only of North–South but also South–South capacity building and knowledge sharing is key here. Synergies and co-ordination between different capacity-building programmes at country level will be essential as Norhed and its partners chart a way forward. Here too, the higher education sector can play a pivotal role by contributing skilled professionals, equipped with the skills to conduct evidence-based research and develop new knowledge.

In early 2018, reforms to the Norwegian development co-operation policy were announced by the Norwegian government. Included in this is an assessment of the organisation of Norwegian development co-operation. This will involve a review of the division of roles between the

Ministry of Foreign Affairs and Norad, with a view to ensuring knowledge-based and effective aid efforts. It is too early to know if or how the reform will impact on Norhed's next phase, but the programme will have to take this into careful consideration when it comes to both programme design and grant management.

* * *

As can be deduced from this preface, Norhed is both a product of, and a platform for, learning in relation to Norwegian development co-operation and its support for higher education programmes. Norhed has scored several successes and has demonstrated the need for further adaptations if such successes are to widen out and be made more sustainable. The SDGs present opportunities and challenges for Norhed as it plans for its next phase of development. They amplify how capacity development in the academic community goes together with, is a precondition for, and/or makes development possible. The chapters in this book are a valuable resource that will contribute to ensuring that Norhed is designed to respond effectively to the needs of HEIs, enhancing their capacity to respond to the clarion call of achieving the SDGs. Indeed, the book is a testimony to the importance of knowledge sharing and the value of interdisciplinarity.

About the authors

Jeanette da Silva is a senior adviser and co-ordinator of the Norhed programme in the Section for Research, Innovation and Higher Education within Norad's Knowledge Bank.

Douglas Tendai Phiri is an adviser in the same section within Norad.

Notes

1   For some information about the World Bank study, see Psacharopoulos (1985), and for a discussion of its impact see, for example, Hydén 2016.

2   For more information on this list, see http://www.oecd.org/dac/financing-sustainable-development/development-finance-standards/daclist.htm

3   When Norhed was launched, South Sudan had recently become an independent state (2011), and urgently needed a qualified workforce across all sectors. By creating a sub-programme focusing on capacity development in South Sudan, Norhed's intention was to strengthen the higher education sector as a key provider of the skills essential for building the country.

4   In the Quota Scheme, the concept of 'internationalisation' referred to giving HEIs in Norway access to the global knowledge market in the hope that wider exposure and partnerships would enhance the relevance and quality of curricula, broaden perspectives, attract international students and staff and enable these institutions to educate global citizens.

5   See, for example, Eva Tonnessen, Stadig færre studenter fra det globale sør i Norge, *Khrono*, 30 October 2017. Available online.

6   See the Norwegian Ministry of Foreign Affairs' grant portal at http://udtilskudd. regjeringen.no/#/en/country?year=2018

7   See Tom Kariuki's article, Africa produces just 1.1% of global scientific knowledge but change is coming, *The Guardian*, 26 October 2015. Available online.

8   This report is often referred to as the Brundtland Report in recognition of the role played by Norway's former prime minister, Gro Harlem Brundtland, who was chair of the World Commission on Environment and Development (WCED) when the report was researched, written and published.

9   The term 'agreement partner' is used within Norhed to refer to the main partner – that is, the HEI that enters into an agreement with Norad and takes overall implementation and administrative responsibility on behalf of project partners.

References

COWI A/S (2009) *Evaluation of the Norwegian Programme for Development Research and Education (NUFU) and of NORAD's Programme for Master Studies (NOMA)*. Evaluation Report 7. Oslo: Norad. Available online

Damvad Analytics (2014) *Evaluation of the Quota Scheme 2001–2012: Assessing Impact in Higher Education and Development*. Oslo. Available online

DIKU (Direktoratet for internasjonalisering og kvalitetsutvikling i høyere utdanning [Directorate for International Co-operation and Quality Enhancement in Higher Education]) (2018) *Evaluering av avviklingen av Kvoteordningen*. Oslo

Filho WL (2000) Sustainability and university life: Some European perspectives. In: WL Filho (ed.) *Sustainability and University Life*. Berlin: Peter Lang

Granados Sanchez J, Wals AE and Ferrer-Balas D (2012) Moving from understanding to action: Breaking barriers for transformation. In: M Barcelo, Y Cruz, C Escrigas, D Ferrer, J Granados Sanchez, F Lopez-Segrera and J Sivoli (eds), *Higher Education in the World: Higher Education's Commitment to Sustainability*. Basingstoke: Palgrave Macmillan

Halvorsen T and Nossum J (2016) (eds) *North–South Knowledge Networks: Towards Equitable Collaborations Between Academics, Donors and Universities*. Cape Town: African Minds. Available online

Hydén G (2016) The role and impact of funding agencies. In: T Halvorsen and J Nossum (eds), *North–South Knowledge Networks: Towards Equitable Collaborations Between Academics, Donors and Universities*. Cape Town: African Minds. Available online

Koch S and Weingart P (2016) *The Delusion of Knowledge Transfer: The Impact of Foreign Aid Experts on Policy-making in South Africa and Tanzania*. Cape Town: African Minds. Available online

Ndaruhutse S and Thompson S (2016) Literature Review: Higher Education and Development. A paper commissioned by the Education Development Trust for the NORHED Conference on 'Knowledge for Development', Oslo, 6–7 June

Norad (n.d.) *A Presentation of NORHED: The Norwegian Programme for Capacity Development in Higher Education and Research for Development*. Oslo. Available online

Norad (2015) *Evaluation of Norwegian Support to Capacity Development*. Oslo. Available online

Nordic Consulting Group (2005) *Evaluation of the Norad Fellowship Programme*. Oslo: Norad

Norwegian Ministry of Education and Research (2006) Handlingsplan for utviklingssamarbeid på utdannings- og forskningssektoren 2005-2007

Norwegian Ministry of Foreign Affairs (1999) *Strategi for styrking av forskning og høyere utdanning – I tilknytning til Norges forhold til utviklingslandene*

Norwegian Ministry of Foreign Affairs (2009) *Report No. 13 to the Storting, 2008–2009: Climate, Conflict and Capital, Norwegian Development Policy Adapting to Change*. Available online

Norwegian Ministry of Foreign Affairs (2017) *Report No. 24 to the Storting, 2016–2017: Common Responsibility for Common Future*

Nossum J (2016) Into the great wide open: Trends and tendencies in university collaboration for development. In: T Halvorsen and J Nossum (eds), *North–South Knowledge Networks: Towards Equitable Collaborations Between Academics, Donors and Universities*. Cape Town: African Minds. Available online

Psacharopoulos G (1985) Returns to education: A further international update and implications. *Journal of Human Resources* 20(4): 583–604

Robertson R (1995) Glocalization: Time-space and homogeneity–heterogeneity. In: M Featherstone, S Lash and R Robertson (eds) *Global Modernities*. London: Sage

Technopolis Group (2018) *Mid-term Review of the Norwegian Programme for Capacity Development in Higher Education and Research for Development (NORHED)*. Oslo: Norad

Unesco (2018) *Global Education Monitoring Report 2019: Migration, Displacement and Education, Building Bridges, Not Walls*. Paris. Available online

WCED (World Commission on Environment and Development) (1987) *Our Common Future*. Oxford: Oxford University Press

Introduction
The Norhed programme:
A laboratory for academic collaboration

Tor Halvorsen

Academic collaborations across borders are increasingly the norm (see Huang et al. 2014). In this process, areas of focus are shifting, established theories are being reconsidered, ingrained paradigms and disciplinary identities are being tested. For all these reasons, working across spaces and cultures is challenging, valuable and worthy of ongoing discussion and, in this context, Norhed has become a kind of laboratory for academic collaboration across national and regional borders. As of late 2018, around 250 scholars on several continents were involved in Norhed projects. As one of the Norwegian participants, I consider here what we are learning from this experiment. What knowledge are we gaining that otherwise would not be available to the world? In what ways is the experiment contributing to the development of knowledge, and for whom and to what is this knowledge relevant?

If modern universities can be said to constitute laboratories – in as much as they take resources to build, and without them, academic qualifications, or the testing of hypotheses and their interpretations that precede these, would be difficult to obtain – then Norhed can be seen as a laboratory for building academic independence. Its experiment crosses all kinds of borders and is seeking ways of entrenching academic capacity, deepening academic independence and ingraining local influence over knowledge production. The *means* being used are 'co-laboratory', and academics who receive funding define their research projects for themselves.

Participants in the experiment have accepted a number of assumptions. First, that human talents are distributed equally across the world and all social categories. What is not equally distributed are opportunities to use this talent. Second, that for co-operation between academics to be conducted on an equal basis, it has to be theory driven. Third, that knowledge and power are integrally linked, and that choices related to methodologies, research topics, theories, language and the interpretation of results all have the potential to express forms of domination. Fourth, that the vicious cycle of academic domination that is linked to contemporary knowledge and power relations can be transformed through mutual learning. Fifth, that academic knowledge (often known as science) can be exchanged across cultures, in mutually useful and beneficial ways despite differences in language, perception, interests and modes of thinking.

Taken together, these five assumptions make the case that what we know can be established through joint research and shared as inter-subjectively established *truths* that are worthy of respect from the academic profession as a whole. The problematic term 'truth' is discussed further below. However, I acknowledge at the outset that ideas accepted as true in any time or place are often a compromise between text and context, and they are expressed via conventions that tend to make context 'vanish' into text. For now, it is sufficient to note that without a strong belief in the validity of the five assumptions listed, the Norhed programme would be meaningless.

In what follows, this huge collaborative experiment is discussed in relation to: knowledge and power; space and place; epistemology and presuppositions; disciplines, decolonisation and/or neoliberalism; internationalisation, knowledge and development, as well as the UN's Sustainable Development Goals (SDGs). I conclude by briefly outlining the aim of this volume.

Knowledge and power

In framing the Norhed experiment, the most challenging issue for participants has been unpacking the relationship between knowledge and power. To help us reflect on this, a workshop was arranged (in March

2018) with academics from Germany and Denmark who have been part of similar experiments. At the workshop, we agreed that the complex interactions between knowledge and power can be analysed on many levels. These include: how knowledge shapes individuals and communities; how knowledge justifies, influences and legitimises politics; how knowledge and education affect the social or class structure of a society; and how knowledge is a productive force in any economy when it helps make organisations work effectively. The general consensus was that the power of knowledge is good for development, but not at all times and under any conditions. For example, where the 'power of knowledge' is too weak within an institution, the power of external experts deployed by donors and multilateral organisations can be overwhelming. It was therefore acknowledged that if Norhed is to deliver on its aim of *empowering* academics at the supported universities, the programme must succeed as both a social project and a knowledge project.

In their book, *The Delusion of Knowledge Transfer*, Koch and Weingart (2016) show how the sociologies of knowledge, power and politics are among the analytical tools needed to grasp how relations of knowledge and power shape societies. The sociology of knowledge reveals how knowledge is socially embedded in ways that shape its influence. This means that all professors are products of their time and place, and there is no such thing as neutral knowledge or a 'technical' expert. Regardless of experts' claims to objectivity, or agreement between scholars about what is true, no knowledge is the same in all contexts. In other words, the issues that influence the kinds of knowledge a society sees as 'objective' play a role in the knowledge that is seen as politically acceptable. There is thus a clear relationship between social power and forms of knowledge that pass as hegemonic truth.

In relation to state power, we have long talked about the co-production of knowledge and society (see Jasanoff 2004), and of how this co-production influences the resources that are mobilised for universities, locally, regionally and globally. In their book, *The Geography of Scientific Collaboration*, Agnieszka Olechnicka et al. (2019) analyse the hegemonic centres of knowledge, revealing the remarkable stability of the West in this regard, and the recent rise of China (to the level of the US) in some of the so-called STEM disciplines (science, technology, engineering and mathematics). Institutions located on the peripheries have their knowledge production assessed and valued by the hegemonic centres. Turning this around requires enormous effort. As Olechnicka et al. (2019: 177) put it:

> Research collaboration cements the long-term, hierarchical, core–periphery structure of the global distribution of research excellence. Top-notch research organisations tend to collaborate with each other. In effect, they gain additional advantage over scientifically less developed entities. Collaboration between more and less scientifically advanced organisations, places, or countries happens very often. However, the effects of such co-operation are not necessarily evenly distributed among partners. Although less scientifically advanced partners benefit – through the diffusion of knowledge – from relations with more developed collaborators, the latter profit even more because they are able to impose their paradigms, research agendas, and long-term objectives.

Norhed's goal of contributing to building academic capacity in the South has the potential to challenge this global hegemonic social structure. It also challenges the alliance between knowledge and power in cross-border academic collaborations that are constantly drawn into reproducing Western hegemony. However, for the Norhed experiment to succeed, it must be organised in ways that neutralise the sociological power of the West's influence over knowledge *without blocking access* to its academic centres (Koch and Weingart 2016).

In addition, the Norhed experiment has to secure enough support from society and the political sphere to be able to develop as a force in society and within politics. The disbursement of project funding to project leaders at universities in the South (who also determine projects' research agendas), is one strategy (and perhaps a precondition) for starting to transform this 'geography of inequality'. However, the sociology and political governance of knowledge make it clear that more is needed. If projects are to be embedded in the South (as Norad proposes), it is necessary to accept that they may also challenge established ideas about excellence and quality as determined by the hierarchies embedded in international journals, university ranking systems, citation indexes, big data, and 'big science'.

Norhed's basic principle is to hand over to the South, not only the power to determine and manage its own research agenda and capacity-building projects, but epistemological hegemony as well. This kind of collaboration requires us to be open to new understandings of our disciplines, new ways of working between disciplines, and even to the argument that the whole notion of disciplines, as developed in the West, creates 'black holes' that require some rethinking.[1] As discussed later in this chapter, disciplines are defined by social conventions that tend to resist being challenged by new contexts and experiences. Disciplines are not defined by theory, methodology, or a particular topic or object of study; they are the product of a socially guided 'disciplinary' process that help shape knowledge and power. It takes time to discover that even when disciplines seem similar in name and faculty-base, they can be perceived quite differently from region to region. Those entrenched in the STEM disciplines of the hegemonic North can find it challenging to learn about and engage with alternative ways of constructing knowledge, especially when this calls into question established knowledge–power relations. Likewise, because scholars are trained to look to the academic centres for confirmation of their relevance within their disciplines, it can be challenging to participate in developing new knowledge when academics from the periphery have the power to define what knowledge is relevant.

In other words, 'ownership' of research projects has to shift, but so do attitudes towards the South, along with concerns about all the 'losses' this may involve in terms of time, productivity, publishing opportunities, as reputation, status and 'academic legitimacy', if established disciplinary practices are not followed to the letter. Of course, this also entails challenging how projects are expected to report on their status and progress. Currently, reporting rules are among the tools that Western institutions use to entrench their position at the centre of academic innovation and scholarly networks. Norhed will succeed only if academics in the South are empowered, and if Norad's reporting requirements both presuppose, and allow for, some adjustments to what are considered acceptable forms and avenues of academic production. Without this, every Norhed project will feel the effects of the potential contradiction between Norad's power and Norhed's intentions.

The Norhed experiment is about creating *equal* partnerships, in the sense that researchers and academics from Norway, Nepal, Uganda, or any other co-operating countries, will find ways of agreeing on what is good, true, and relevant knowledge for the projects they are involved in. Thus, Norhed believes in the possibility of creating a 'power-free' space – where intellectual curiosity rules, collaborative work is carried out and academic spaces flourish through links with a partner or partners in Norway.

It is important here not to conflate *places* and *spaces* of co-operation. We see the universities, where funded research projects are located, as *places* of co-operation. As is evident from most of the chapters in this book, many of these are relatively weak institutionally. Transforming this reality is not a question of capacity building only (although this is Norhed's main raison d'être) but also of advancing the social strength of the academic profession more generally. Accordingly, we define the co-operation between the researchers and the many networks they are involved in as *spaces of co-operation*. Here, the academic resources drawn on and developed in project work can lead to the empowerment necessary for 'equal partnerships' to germinate and flourish. Of course, *how* spaces and places relate to one another is a big issue, but *that* they do is crucial if participants in the different projects are going to be able to turn away from 'feeding the centres' and focus instead on forming new knowledge nodes that are strong enough to draw from the research, teaching resources and energies of the centre and apply them on their own terms.

The establishment of Norhed reveals an optimism that is rare in our world. Debates about decolonising the universities seem to suggest that such co-operation inevitably reproduces the power relations that suit the North, both socially and epistemologically. Yet, at the March 2018 workshop referred to earlier, a group of Danish and African authors showed how 'place and space' can be linked in ways that counter Western hegemony. Similarly, in their book, *Higher Education and Capacity Building in Africa: The Geography and Power of Knowledge Under Changing*

Conditions, Adriansen et al. take as their point of departure the concept that 'knowledge production is one of the major sites in which imperialism operates'. Dedicating their book to the 'de-imperialisation of knowledge', they ask (as do I), how capacity-building projects at universities in Africa affect their knowledge production (2016: 32, 1).

The impression created in this book, and from input at the workshop, is that this group of authors found it difficult to collaborate on equal grounds just by changing attitudes and transferring decision-making powers over projects to the South. They argue that epistemology itself is so Westernised that new epistemologies will have to be built from other *places* of knowledge, and from those places, new *spaces* (where the research or renewing of knowledge goes on) will begin to create and promote new theories of knowledge. So-called indigenous knowledge counts as one point of departure here, but how indigenous knowledge can be transformed into academic knowledge in ways that challenge the academic centre is seldom debated. Yet, as Adriansen et al. (2016: 210) suggest, common ground for co-operation is the *space* of knowledge production into which 'Northern partners' must enter with a 'reflexive mind'.

Norhed's optimism makes the programme more open to how space and place relate to one another within common and potentially new epistemologies (as defined via project applications) despite huge differences in the power, social context and status accorded to knowledge production (via research and innovation) as well as reproduction (teaching). This is expressed via programme documents that reference, for example, human rights, the value of gender equality, the idea that the spread of knowledge might involve *translating* established hegemonic knowledge in ways that make sense in local conditions, thus enabling research partners to learn from each other without having to become like one another. This process of translation is crucial for preserving and respecting cultural perceptions and traditions with which local knowledge is so inextricably entangled, and is perhaps the most important reason why capacity building for independent research is so worthy of support. For Norhed, such translation is a prerequisite for independent knowledge development, and the building of independent academic cultures is a long-term project. Collaboration on equal terms requires a shift in power relations and a deep awareness of the sociology of knowledge, but neither of these presuppose a shift to an epistemology based solely on indigenous knowledge. The process of translation will always count. That's why building relations between Northern and Southern partners remains a fundamental principle in Norhed's overall strategy.

I now explore some of the issues raised above in relation to knowledge and power in a little more detail.

Space and place

As of early 2019, Norhed was supporting about fifty projects spread across different universities located in the South. In some institutions (such as Makerere University in Uganda), projects are more concentrated than others (see Chapter 5, this volume). The places are all in countries Norad considers worthy of development support, but this is less important than the academics involved. The crucial idea behind the Norhed experiment is that extending of the capacities of academics should be a major focus. Much of Norhed's support is directed towards improving master's and PhD programmes via cross-regional projects that combine teaching and research. Implicit here is the notion that the academics involved will discover ways of improving teaching and research at their universities through collaborating on a common project. The projects also assume that the academics involved will share (or be open to sharing) values, interests and identities that will help them overcome cultural and regional differences. Such values include: respect for academic freedom, truth seeking, speaking truth to power, cherishing the renewal of knowledge through research, and acknowledging the role of excellence in teaching, to name just a few.

While the teaching elements of these projects link them strongly to *place* (that is, the university, the classroom, the disciplines, where students live, etc.), their research aspects open up project *space* to a variety of networks. Disciplinary boundaries were established over time through a need to pass on an orthodoxy to students, and they tend to make disciplines fairly *place* bound. Disciplines are often also linked to professions that have a 'local' identity. For example, the field of law has a particularly national character, and the legal profession's ability to operate across national borders is limited in specific ways. However, free-roaming academic *space* is less discipline-bound. It is more driven by research, more willing to critique established knowledge and produce new knowledge – some of which might not yet have a place to discipline or empower it.

If we accept that Norway has more resources than many Southern academic institutions, and assume that the reversal of power relations made possible by local ownership works as intended, then giving Southern institutions links with Norway should be a good spatial move. Linked to this, the fact that Norwegian academics tend to be more willing to 'tap knowledge resources' for the sake of projects in the South, and are also interested in gaining entrance to broader networks that can be used for 'translation' means that Norwegians might conform less to the 'what's in it for me?' kind of academic than most. As Jeanette da Silva and Douglas Tendai Phiri point out in the preface, Norway values the expansion of interesting and rewarding research in ways that contribute little to any individual academic's personal status. Nevertheless, if we consider how the global centre values knowledge, Norway's achievements are undoubtedly noteworthy. A count of scientific papers published per million inhabitants (as one way of measuring knowledge power) ranks Norway as sixth in the world, after Switzerland, Denmark, Australia, Sweden and Singapore (Olechnicka 2019: 14).

Norhed's pairing of teaching and research in the projects it supports is another way in which the programme productively links space to place. This pairing helps reduce the global domination of Western knowledge by strengthening the academic profession both in the South and within a global alliance of knowledge solidarity. By including projects in the broader space of academic discourse, the process of translating or inserting international research into locally owned knowledge, in ways that help address the issue-based problems highlighted in project proposals, is made easier but also more pressing. If, as noted earlier, we accept that epistemological differences can be overcome, we must acknowledge that this process of translation will happen only if we think through how power is embedded in our theory of knowledge. In this regard, debates about 'post-colonial' knowledge have made us aware of how often Norhed projects can unintentionally fall into the trap of perpetuating intellectual imperialism.

Epistemology and presuppositions

Other research discussed at the March 2018 workshop included the work of the Austrian Partnership Programme in Higher Education and Research for Development (APPEAR), which documented 17 remarkable projects that focused on capacity building in higher education institutions in low- and middle-income countries (LMICs) (see Obrecht 2015). Overall, APPEAR highlighted epistemological commonalities as a basis for collaboration – that is, all 17 projects were driven by a 'common understanding of scientific enquiry'. This was supported by a shift in power relations similar to that being attempted by Norhed. As Andreas Obrecht put it,

> Allowing higher education institutions in the partner countries
> to also be able to guarantee full responsibility for the project
> and its financial aspect proved to be the right decision to guar-
> antee a future partnership of equals. (2015: 17)

The 'epistemic commonalities' evolved out of the global challenges facing our planet, and for which Western knowledge is largely to blame:

> The dawning realization that the consequences of modern,
> rationalist knowledge have brought the world's ecosystems and
> thus its people to the brink of global collapse is making us more
> sensitive to alternative knowledge systems and epistemologies.
> (Obrecht 2015: 20)

However, despite the fact that the Western 'worldview' is precipitating 'global collapse', it is still seen by many as crucial in determining what knowledge is relevant. In this case, it supports the notion that collaboration, across regions and within a common understanding of science, is necessary to address the global crisis. Obrecht thus alerts us to the fact that, as academics from different cultures who work together on projects, we have to be aware of our general presuppositions – that is, the frameworks or worldviews we think with, and that make our ideas about knowledge seem rational.

What such critiques of Western rationality or positivism underline, is what Norhed has adopted as its basic premise for projects it supports: namely that projects' theoretical underpinnings have to be clear. In other words, if co-operation between academics from different cultures is to succeed, project participants have to find ways of discussing how their presuppositions, which can sometimes be very different, guide their academic thinking and working methods. Until these are made explicit, any aspect of their work – from what constitutes a valid empirical observation to how to generalise findings – has to be open to question. When presuppositions remain implicit, hegemonic versions of 'rationality' tend to rule.

Jeffrey Alexander (1982) notes that our presuppositions guide our ideas about what we observe and how we interpret this. In an analysis of the scientific continuum, Alexander explains how research work involves going from observations to general presuppositions and back, but that general presuppositions direct our interpretations.[2] In discussing the same object of study, experts from different disciplines can allocate a wide variety of meanings or interpretations as they apply their own theories. As Alexander (1982: 33) puts it, 'Theoretical confrontation is, therefore, just as significant a factor in creating shifts in scientific commitment as empirical confrontation.'

For this reason, Norhed's view is that the struggle between general theoretical presuppositions should be at the heart of relations between academics across global power structures. An awareness of this struggle alerts us to how Western experts' implicit assumptions often justify theoretical domination, and encourage researchers to avoid confronting different interpretations of what might be seen as common empirical observations (Koch and Weingart 2016). Often, this hegemony masks what some researchers might see as their own disciplinary superiority (this can be likened to belief in the 'objectivity' of what is called 'positive proof') or superior rationality.

For example, one presupposition dominating the contemporary world is the belief that continual economic growth is both possible and necessary for global prosperity, even though, as Obrecht shows, this belief is leading directly to increasing inequality and the utter destruction of life on our planet.[3] An awareness of the massive challenges facing the world encourages the search for some different general presuppositions about what 'good development' means.

Western hegemony overlooks a basic insight from the foundations of the sociology of science – that a sound conceptual analysis should provide for the (re)construction of data (Koch and Weingart 2016: 40). Therefore, if the general presuppositions we carry with us *influence* how we theorise, the categories we use, the models we construct, and how we interpret evidence from the real world, we must, as Adriansen et al. (2016) suggest, consider these in self-reflexive ways. The word 'influence' is crucial here, since presuppositions do not necessarily determine *all other* levels of the scientific continuum. In other words, Norhed-type projects can work even if the researchers and professors have very different worldviews. We can discuss different, even conflicting, presuppositions about what constitutes good empirical evidence or good analytical models, and still find agreement about one or more of these relatively autonomous aspects of research. What is crucial to note, however, is that it is through these kinds of theoretical discussions and even confrontations that we can make our presuppositions explicit. By opening our assumptions up for scrutiny, we also open ourselves to new understandings of how theories are shaped in different contexts, and of how we can read reality together and still generalise very differently. As Alexander (1982: 35) notes:

> Science proceeds as surely by generalizing or 'theoretical logic'
> as it does by the empirical logic of experiment, and the positivist
> decision to focus on the latter alone must ultimately prove as
> self-defeating as reading one side of a double column of figures.

This challenge may not yet have been taken seriously enough by programmes like Norhed. To observe and reflect on how general presuppositions and empirical observations differ when researchers from widely different cultures meet will place extra demands on how joint projects are developed. In a paper titled, 'Negotiating scientific knowledge about climate change: Enhancing research capacity through PhD students', Lene Madsen and Thomas Nielsen (2016) try to show how much social science is still based on Western ethnocentric assumptions, conducting research through 'imperial eyes', and seeing Western theories as universally applicable, thus blocking the reflection necessary for opening up the debate around presuppositions. To counter this, Madsen and Nielsen take their lead from feminist studies, arguing that 'we as authors need to outline and engage in positionality' (2016: 148). Their general idea is that to reveal the complexity of research relations, it is necessary to address insider relationships explicitly. Following Edward Said (1978, 1994), who noted how the hegemony of Western epistemology excludes others, Madsen and Nielsen show how 'positioning' can lead to mutual reflection within a theoretical/empirical continuum.

However, when considering 'orientalism' as one aspect of Western hegemonic knowledge, Said praises Clifford Geertz's ability to make his presuppositions explicit, enabling others to see and understand his empirical approach while being sensitive to cultural variation in his analysis. Said's main point seems to be that if we are aware of how general presuppositions work on other levels of the knowledge-creation process, we may be able to communicate about knowledge that is good and true across contexts and cultures. If this is so, it should be possible to make this knowledge available to co-operating partners within, for example, Norhed's cross-national projects.

When we try to learn from Norhed's many projects, as the contributors to this book have, the degree of mutual reflection on these possibly different presuppositions becomes important to detect. In fact, a focus on the relationship between theoretical logics becomes a precondition for communication. As a result, we can argue that colonisation of the mind by Western hegemonic ways of thinking can be changed, not by blocking off the West, but by taking the time to clarify how often theory drives observation while also hiding the general presuppositions that make the theory valid *only for the context in which it was produced* rather than, as is often claimed, at a general level.

The fact that Norhed is theory driven – with project applications evaluated academically by peer review – is a good start. That is, both the project leaders and the Norhed evaluators acknowledge that different presuppositions can lead to very different ways of evaluating what kinds of knowledge can be considered good and relevant. This includes being sensitive to the histories of particular disciplines. There are many ways of telling the truth and Norhed-supported research, in particular, is likely to encounter problems with cross-disciplinary boundaries as we know them today, given that perhaps as many as 6 000 different disciplines exist across universities worldwide.

Disciplines and global knowledge

Typically, disciplines are what link teaching to a specific institution. Disciplines are how universities manage and mediate the orthodoxies of established truths. Research, on the other hand, is usually less linked to a particular place, fulfilling the notion that 'knowledge knows no borders'. In Norhed's *selection* of projects up to the end of 2018, cross-disciplinary research is foregrounded. Projects selected for funding were mainly by researchers who formed themselves into cross-disciplinary committees. However, a second focus area for Norhed is enhancing teaching, and thereby capacity building, through supporting master's and PhD programmes (with the help of spatially accessible networks). This element binds the whole programme in terms of both place and space.

The question asked in relation to funding research at any university is how to make the research link with teaching in mutually productive ways. If teaching is place and discipline bound but research easily wanders around in 'undisciplined' (or, at least, inter- or multidisciplinary) space, this question is also about how to link local commitments with global knowledge-needs via interactions within the academic profession that Norhed makes possible. In other words, the space and place categories overlap in terms of how disciplines reproduce themselves (by setting boundaries with other disciplines, certifying graduates, creating links with professional associations, etc.) and how the spaces in which new knowledge is produced through research are constructed. Of course, this does not mean that no new knowledge is produced in disciplines that are held together by teaching. Most of the research at universities has disciplinary renewal as part of its primary purpose and the strengthening of the academic profession as a central goal. In this, the academic profession holds place and space together, while watching over disciplinary quality.[4]

Norhed enters into this dialectic by supporting better master's and PhD education linked to solid research projects. Ideally, Norhed projects foster active research supervision of PhD and master's students based on ongoing research collaborations that strengthen the academic profession. Most disciplines in the countries where Norhed projects are located are shaped according to the disciplines of their Western colonisers. These, in turn, grew out of the combination of the Enlightenment and industrialisation eras and through the slow process of modernisation. Authors concerned about the 'historical origins of the knowledge economy' talk of the spread of the modern economy as the 'ultimate triumph of the Industrial Enlightenment' (Mokyr 2002: 288). (In the contemporary era, it is probably more accurate to reference the OECD than the West, as Mexico, Chile and a number of other LMICs wait in the wings to play a role as movers and shakers in this 'triumph'; see Halvorsen 2016.)

Less discussed is how much the industrial revolution's 'successes' depended on the division of labour between disciplines that had evolved in the universities, turning them into secular tools for the differentiation of society. Usually the peer system reproduces disciplines. Master's and even PhD programmes are still generally embedded in a single discipline. The Norhed programme faces the difficult dilemma of how to promote knowledge through disciplines, but more so through interdisciplinary work, or even through abandoning Western disciplinary divisions, as advocated by those who support decolonisation of knowledge, including those who are most repressed and discriminated against by so-called 'first-world people' (Smith 1999; see also Krøvel, Chapter 4, this volume).

Heilbron (1995: 269) argues that what holds the Western university model together are its disciplines:

> Disciplines in the modern sense thus became the central unit of
> the modern intellectual regime. What was previously ranked

under the common heading of 'natural philosophy' now became disciplined and led to a division in mathematics, physics, chemistry and biology. A similar transition occurred somewhat later from 'natural law' and 'moral philosophy' to different social sciences.

With growing interest in cross-disciplinary work, critiques of the detrimental consequences of the industrialisation have come to the forefront (see, for example, much of the work done by APPEAR mentioned earlier), along with many types of knowledge suppressed through disciplining (Bonneuil and Fressoz 2015). Intellectual imperialism is transformed into intellectual hegemony. This is due not only to the patent system and the Trade-Related Intellectual Property Rights agreement (the West's means of creating knowledge commodities) but mostly to the dominance of the West's 'worldview' of what knowledge is relevant.

Much of the debate about post-colonial knowledge has evolved in countries that adopted the university models of their oppressors, including their curricula, modes of teaching, ideas about socialisation, identity formation, and formation of the self (Mbembe 2017). In a study conducted for the United Nations University's World Institute for Development Economics Research, titled *Decolonizing Knowledge: From Development to Dialogue,* Frédérike Apffel-Marglin and Stephan Marglin (1996) challenge claims to the universality of modern forms of knowledge, noting that such claims serve to justify the exporting of the universities established by the colonial powers. Arguing that Cartesian rationality – 'the motor that has fuelled the Industrial Revolution' (1996: 2) – has colonised minds as well, they note that this has prevented other knowledge, on everything from farming methods and medicine to cosmology and how society functions best, from being recognised or respected. As a result, intellectual and cultural life are decimated and colonial administration systems are superimposed over social institutions to repress and undermine existing social values. Meanwhile, hegemonic disciplines from reputable universities, with their instrumental focus on specialised knowledge, ensure that a narrow set of 'international best practices' are imposed worldwide.

Apffel-Marglin and Marglin show how the economics profession, in particular, cleansed itself of all doubt about its universal value (even though Keynes himself warned against this so strongly).

Obrecht (2015) notes that in some fields, the costs of specialisation have been so high that Cartesian ontology has become counterproductive to the planet as a whole. As Mbembe argues (2017: 179) 'there is only one world', yet this understanding is somehow lost in the plurality of specialisations in the industrial world.[5] In fact, this argument was put forward by the UN University in 1996, twenty years before the adoption of the SDGs:

> It is not only animal and plant species that are becoming extinct at an ever-faster pace but human forms of life and thought. The latter can only be justified by a belief in progress, in the replacement of 'outmoded' ways of knowing and doing by more advanced ways of knowing and doing. The downside of progress and of development is creating a mood congenial to revisiting local forms of knowledge as well as to questioning the claims to universality of modern thought. What is happening in the world, whether the First or the Third, looks more and more like loss: loss of environmental integrity, loss of a diversity not only of plant and animal species but of human ways of doing and knowing. What only yesterday looked outmoded, today looks sustainable. (Apffel-Marglin and Marglin 1996: 2)

All this implies that other cultures, with different presuppositions about the mind–body relationship, the interdependencies between society and nature, and the relative values of intuitive and empirical knowledge, have the potential to inspire totally different kinds of disciplines and (probably more sound) relations between humans and the rest of nature. Norhed invites partners in the South to build on the knowledge in their own localities, and is open to the potential offered by cross-disciplinary work in which 'experiments' with forms of knowledge might be possible, even if these contradict the Cartesian divides (between mind and body, human and nature) and have the potential to create new disciplines. In addition, this creates the potential for reflection and learning, especially for Norwegian partners who tend to be submerged in Cartesian universalism (in the disciplines of medicine, economics and accounting, for example). But more importantly, this highlights how Norhed is involved in global debates about our shared world and its challenges, and is helping to legitimise and encourage stronger academic responses to global challenges. As part of the Norwegian state, Norad may indicate what knowledge is relevant but the work done by Norhed projects that are linked into this new global discourse may make us see things differently. Ownership of the programme is one thing, moral commitment is another, and to most academics the latter is what counts.

Decolonisation and neoliberalism

In their book on *The Shock of the Anthropocene*, Bonneuil and Fressoz (2016) discuss forms of knowledge that the West has suppressed in past decades, and then go on to describe novel combinations and new kinds of disciplines that are emerging out of 'there is only one world' thinking:

> The Anthropocene thus requires the substitution of the 'ungrounded' humanities of industrial modernity that adventures beyond the great separation between environment and society ... In the Anthropocene it is impossible to hide the fact that 'social' relations are full of biophysical processes, and that the various flows of matter and energy that run through the Earth system at different levels are polarised by socially structured human activities. (2016: 33)

In light of this, the debate about post-colonial knowledge that Norhed has embraced, and is contributing to via different projects, turns into a debate about how the (often poor) copies of colonial disciplines that were replicated in the Southern universities are gradually being transformed. Disciplines are changing, and the whole notion of 'disciplines' is being challenged because their basic presuppositions are open to question. Now that Western culture is no longer so much praised for its contributions to 'the good life' as it is critiqued for its devastating social and environmental consequences, the time has come for what Ngũgĩ Wa Thiong'o calls a 'globalectical imagination' (2012: 44). This is where Norhed has a major contribution to make. Decolonising the university has to be a global project, spreading from the South to the North, ensuring that we look anew at how disciplines discipline, what they open up and what they limit.[6]

Regardless of its own intentions, Norhed has no choice but to be involved in this period of heated debates about decolonisation and the need for us all to 'free our minds'. The debate seems to be about how to de-link established knowledge from Western 'ownership', as well as how to build local theory and develop a new academic language while putting global research networks to good use in the interests of this process. However, the discussion is also about the directions of development. Trust in local knowledge might lead to stronger democracies and economic independence (Koch and Weingart 2016). Thus, the debate about intellectual decolonisation has become a debate about the role of universities and the academic profession in relation to the global economy, academic capitalism and the ever-expanding use of the market as a tool for the distribution and sale of educational services.

The six different sub-programmes chosen by Norhed as focus areas can be seen as a concretisation of political priorities.[7] Reflecting Norad's own operationalisation of knowledge-needs for development, the focus areas prioritise the basics of health and education, but also make clear the crucial role of the humanities in promoting ethical values at a time when economic imperatives generally take precedence. In other words, the humanities, which are struggling for recognition and support almost everywhere else, have a central role in this programme. In addition, the way Norad constructs these fields of study within the Norhed programme covers most types of disciplines. Norhed is not, as is common in the development speak of our time, giving priority only to the STEM disciplines but rather showing that these are *as* necessary as narrative, analysis, interpretation and literacies (NAIL) (Higgins 2013). As such, Norad's Norhed programme has aligned itself with the basic values that underpin the academic profession.

The idea that economic development should be given priority (and that democracy usually follows economic growth) seems to have less support in Norhed (Norris 2012).[8] By contrast, much of the discourse on this in Western policy-making has been shaped by neoliberalism, in which the World Bank has such faith (Balsvik 2016; Norris 2012). But, as one of Norway's foremost political scientists, Johan Olsen argues:

> Reforms of universities have not taken much interest in the university as a democratic training ground for bureaucrats, political leaders, commercial actors, and citizens. Reforms have given priority to putting universities in the service of economic competitiveness and growth, and have largely ignored possible impacts on preparation for the duties of office and public life. (2007: 20)

It is important to highlight that this does not apply to how Norad shaped Norhed's focus areas for research and education, or to how the programme works as a whole. Norhed seems to have been shaped by actors who are at odds with much of this kind of thinking. Norhed's central concern is with the public good.[9] This is in line with the concerns expressed at the first World Conference on Higher Education, organised by Unesco in 1999. Since then, so-called borderless higher education has been seen as a way of 'bridging the knowledge gap' for the sake of the global common good. For some, this offers another pathway to the decolonisation of universities (see Bhambra et al. 2018).

However, this approach is refuted in many parts of the world where universities adhere to neoliberal thinking, claiming to be as colour blind as the market but reproducing and even strengthening colonial knowledge hegemony because of how knowledge and economics are related:

> These imperial projects – past and new – remain central to the financing of higher education in the West. Postcolonial scholars and anti-racist activists have made significant strides in bringing these issues to the fore. However, as numerous activists ... argue, the foundations of universities remain unshakeably colonial: there is as ever, more work to be done. (Bhambra et al. 2018: 6)

To decolonise the mind will require a new global economic order.

Norhed is, however, neither a student-catching machine to guarantee the collection of fees or brains (or talent, which is often mistakenly perceived to be a scarce resource), nor is it a way of opening up a market for Norwegian educational services. Of course, the programme can be read as one way of facilitating Norway's possible future entry into economic deals in partner countries, but not to a degree that influences the programme's focus areas or any of its projects' research interests. Similarly, no particular curricula are required in the way that the World Bank demands more focus on the study of science, technology, engineering and mathematics so as to build a knowledge economy that links into global markets (World Bank 2002). For Norhed, public values rule, and the programme aims to defend public university systems against pressures they face to transform in favour of market forces. As Marginson (2006) shows, these pressures threaten to tear the academic profession apart. Norhed intends to be part of promoting internationalisation through collaboration, rather than collaborating for the sake of market expansion.[10]

What type of internationalisation?

Norway is part of the hegemonic centre and also located on the periphery of a world driven by neoliberal policies. However, Norway is refusing to play the role currently being played by the previous colonial powers. In their study on *The Internationalization of the Academy*, Huang et al. (2014: 18) argue that in the present phase:

> In many developed countries, particularly English-speaking countries such as the United Kingdom, Australia, the United States, and other Western countries, internationalization of the academic profession is linked to commercial activities that are driven by an entrepreneurial spirit.

The former colonies, for their part, encourage the kind of internationalisation that Norhed supports. As Huang et al. (2014) put it:

Conversely, in the majority of developing countries in Asia, Africa and Latin America, internationalisation is more affected by academic factors, for example, dispatching faculty members abroad for advanced studies or research as part of the efforts to enhance the quality of their education and research activities.

For Norwegian academic centres, internationalisation is still embedded in strong links between the university sector and the state, not only for funding, but as argued above, for the sake of the public good. This is true at the global level as well as in the sense that internationalisation does not necessarily presuppose a de-linking between the state, higher education and research institutions in the way that the 'entrepreneurial spirit' of global academic capitalism is pushing for.

Given that for most universities in the LMICs most efforts made in support of internationalisation are about gaining access to the centre, working with more reputable universities, or securing the use of very expensive equipment and laboratories, the Norhed experiment is a unique one. John Higgins writes about South Africa and one of its investments in internationalisation, which has involved building a set of very expensive telescopes to attract the label of global 'excellence' to the South (Higgins 2016). While it is true that scientists from all over the world visit the facility, they then take their expertise back home with them. Bhambra et al. (2018: 5) insist that, in the neoliberal context, the hegemonic academic centres use internationalisation to perpetuate 'colonial plunder' and 'dispossession', thus cementing the infrastructure of empire. Dressing the South up in any number of telescopes will do little to stop this.

Norhed takes these debates seriously and is committed to preventing the West's hegemonic influence from continuing to dominate. For this reason, in a departure from previous programmes, a decision was taken to locate the ownership of Norhed projects within the academic communities based at universities in the South. Thus, ideally, both the content (or academic substance) of projects and their administration (including financial decision-making) is located in the South.

The general critique of existing forms of academic co-operation has been that theoretical frames and key project concepts are worked through and presented as parameters within which 'partners' in the South have to work.[11] This 'academic dependency' is often linked to intellectual imperialism that takes several forms, including dependencies on: ideas and the media through which they are accessible; educational technologies; financial aid for research and teaching; investments in education (Richardson, 2018: 240). This not only reproduces notions of mental and social inferiority, but also prevents researchers in the South from developing the ability to formulate theoretical reflections around what are seen as local challenges related to curriculum and research development, what we earlier referred to as 'black holes'.

One way to break down colonial hegemony is for responsibility for the academic process to shift completely to the South. Equally important is how crucial this is for (re)learning in the West as well; academics trained in the West need to reflect far more systematically on how our research concerns – and the content of what we teach – relate to the challenges of the South. Moving away from focusing so strongly on British and American literature in our curricula, we must seek links to other cultures of knowledge, to globalise and thus decolonise.

Despite all these inequalities, knowledge gaps, and Western influences, Norhed rests on the idea that university-based knowledge can be shared across cultures, language barriers, political interests and cognitive socialisation. If this was not so, the programme would have no meaning as a co-laboratory project (apart from a kind of 'money transfer').

Indigenous (local) knowledge presupposes knowledge of the contexts in which this knowledge has meaning. It is accepted that most academic knowledge has a fairly wide validity, despite its contextual preconditions. Thus, if Norhed's intentions are acted upon, some of the social barriers to indigenous knowledge becoming part of the global academic knowledge will be broken down. But this might not always be the case. The struggles of many indigenous groups (particularly those suppressed by Western culture) show how tough this battle is, particularly when the interests of the global economy are at stake.

In her book, *Decolonizing Methodologies, Research and Indigenous People*, Linda Tuhiwai Smith describes how indigenous knowledge and people have been repeatedly sacrificed to the market economy through treatises and other historical agreements and understandings. Smith argues that even when sanctioned by universities, claims to scientific knowledge and the power of truth matter little where powerful forces of globalisation are at play:

> Multinational companies have been given transnational free-
> dom that enables them ultimately to move labour across
> borders, to foster an intellectual property regime that has few
> ethical limits, to shape national laws and values at the expense
> of national identities, and to develop themselves in competition
> with governments. (Smith 1999: 221)

This logic works in relation to the global North/South dichotomy too. The battle to have local knowledge recognised as science, and as worthy of further study, is crucial, but even more necessary is for truth-tellers who are attempting to mediate this knowledge to be given space to communicate what they know. This is where internationalisation plays a vital role. The struggles of indigenous groups not only expose the black holes in the Western knowledge systems, they also remind us that academic networks must ensure that internationalisation brings to the centre those usually excluded by disciplinary hegemony and economic dominance. This is what Norhed is doing.

Knowledge can be said to be true when it reaches beyond linguistic or cultural identity and can be agreed upon and accessible to everyone. Science is not owned by anyone (or not until it is commodified by pat-ents and intellectual property rights). Norhed could not be the programme it is without believing that knowledge can be exchanged across Western and other barriers in line with general acceptance of what constitutes truth. Foregrounding local contextual knowledge does not have to block co-operation nor should it need to reproduce current forms of intellectual and cultural domination. Instead, space for partic-ipation in the academic community needs to be made wider and more open to information and generalisations from a variety of contexts. Altruism is also part of the story here. Norhed is firmly embedded in Norad's traditions and development priorities, which Koch and

Weingart classify as 'Type IV: example Norway', (2016: 63). Type IV organisations in their system are driven mainly by the values of 'solidarity/legitimacy'. By contrast, most other development aid is tied to the strategic interests of competitive states and often seeks to somehow privatise knowledge within the globalised market economy or use knowledge to secure some form of economic or political advantage.

The altruism that has been so important for academic collaboration is under pressure, however, even in Norway, given the growing role of Norwegian economic actors in LMICs (Sverdrup et al. 2012). In Norhed's upcoming second funding phase, more conflict between the values of competition versus global solidarity can be expected. That is, the ways in which development aid might benefit Norway's economic actors abroad might have to be publicly debated, despite the huge support in Norway for the SDGs (see below).

Knowledge and development: Disentangling 'capacity development'

Norhed's aims are to promote knowledge in the South via capacity building. The term 'capacity building' is development jargon; it is what many involved in development have seen as their primary goal over many years. However, for Norhed, capacity building is a knowledge-oriented goal that relates specifically to enhancing the capacity of academics.

Although less explicit, but equally embedded in Norhed's structure, is that behind capacity building is the need to decolonise knowledge, and for this to happen, project ownership must be located in the South. Thus, instead of delivering or receiving fixed theories, project partners in both the North and the South learn and theorise together, and learning occurs in a mutual and two-way process. This two-way learning might well turn out to be the most important consequence of the programme as a whole.

Koch and Weingart (2016) show that Western 'experts' justify their work in LMICs as 'knowledge transfer', implying that local people have no knowledge to begin with. Norhed seeks to diminish the need for these kinds of external 'experts' and aims to turn 'the delusion of knowledge transfer' into a two-way exchange. Norhed's tools for ana-lysing the relationship between politics and knowledge address the same issue. The programme's basic idea is that, in any country, devel-oping an independent knowledge base is important for development generally. Koch and Weingart show that when external experts prevent the locally situated experts from sharing their knowledge, local systems (in this case, Tanzania and South Africa) are fundamentally under-mined. That is, when local and contextually useful knowledge is side-lined by a need for 'technical expertise', scholars at local universi-ties and research institutions, whose knowledge of local realities could contribute to both better policies and better knowledge, are underuti-lised. As Koch and Weingart (2016: 78) explain:

> Framing advice as a technocratic exercise, however, not only disguises the impact of external experts on policy-making and governance in young democracies; it also makes it impossible to hold them to account for consequences of their advice, despite their considerable discursive power in the political realm.

Sheila Jasanoff (2004) usefully analyses the 'co-production of science and the social order'. This co-production presupposes that most citi-zens believe in the validity of science-based knowledge, and that trust exists between academics and students, and between academics and society outside the academy. Norhed sees this trust as an ideal, maybe even assumes it. However, it is important to understand that trust may not be present or warranted in every context.

As an alternative to co-production acting to reinforce mutually ben-eficial interchanges between knowledge production and society, trust breaks down when academics are (or allow themselves to be) misused for political purposes. In many contexts, the academic profession has become politicised, forming part (sometimes unwittingly) of systems that reproduce Western hegemony and the power of free-market eco-nomics instead of focusing on the excellence and independence of its knowledge production and dissemination. In such situations, rather than co-production, we are facing a process of co-destruction. The relationship between politics and knowledge should function in such a way that the influence of knowledge, and its ability to produce reliable, independent knowledge, presupposes a certain distance between the universities, the academic profession and other actors in society. When this distance is lost, the lack of academic independence undermines both the academic profession and academic freedom.

Norhed's capacity-building programme may thus also be an intervention in enhancing the relationship between knowledge and society in places where trust in and respect for academic knowledge has simply fallen too low.

Co-production at a societal level may have a long way to go, but co-operation at the micro level can also be crucial for growing independent academics and strengthening academic voices in society. In a number of contexts, this seems to be Norhed's role. A key question faced by the programme is to what degree can common (cognitive/ epistemological) ideas about truth exist despite vastly different social conditions and where the political interests involved either don't believe in the value of research-based knowledge or feel threatened by the independence of the academic profession?

By fostering an independent and theoretically self-aware academic community, Norhed is attempting to empower professional academics to interact with society as a truth-tellers.[12] This is idealistic, but worth trying. Trust-building processes must start from below and by enabling academics themselves to strengthen their voices. One may ask, who else if we still want universities? When the goal is truth-telling, how can Norhed funding help to secure academic freedom and institutional autonomy? Unlike so many programmes that are channelling support through state structures to institutional managers, Norhed's answer has been to focus on the academics, offering them the support they need to serve as independent voices in society.

Thus, Norhed focuses less on universities as organisations, with their mission statements and marketing strategies, and instead seeks to strengthen the academic community and the academic profession. The basic idea is that the academic profession, as well as the knowledge that academics mediate and try to constantly renew, must regain some social status. In its own view of development, Norhed see value in academics having a voice that other societal actors both value and trust.

Like all other professions, the academic profession depends on trust to be able to secure enough resources and influence to grow; that is, the academic community depends on its ability to make its academic values valued by society.

These values are a precondition for what Norhed asks of the academic community, namely: giving evidence-based advice, and being willing to be responsible to society. For Norhed, academics delivering on these roles is how the academic community gains respect as a knowledge authority, and can be held accountable for its work. This is also how local academics will be able to side-line so-called donor experts, who do not co-produce knowledge with society, yet still they have the right to impose policy templates for which they cannot easily be held responsible.

Norhed also offers academics the rare opportunity to learn about how interconnected the academic profession is, and to experience (despite huge divides) what a cross-national force of solidarity it can be, given the crises linked to global climate change. As Freidson discusses in his work on the sociology of professions, when universities and professionals confront the powers of the state or capital, they tend to come out as the weaker part. For this reason, he argues that state–capital alliances have transformed the academic profession in their image (Freidson 1994). The resulting weakness of the academic community makes professionalisation *across borders* a necessary countermove.

In many ways, Norhed projects answer some of the conclusions reached by Koch and Weingart (2016: 344), who, after analysing the failure of experts to transmit knowledge and relevant ideas for development, thereby undermining weak democracies, argue:

> It would probably be more constructive to use the available means to support the knowledge communities in developing countries so that these become able to produce a critical mass of local experts who qualify as producers and critical scrutinisers of expertise. This support does not need to (or should not) be delivered through conventional aid programmes since these are invariably affected by conflicts of interest and accountability pressures that undermine their actual objectives.

In response, calls for a new global academic solidarity have emerged, asking for new thinking about what knowledge is relevant, and how to link this to equitable and environmentally sustainable development. The UN's Agenda 2030 also presupposes that, to achieve the SDGs, knowledge inequality must be reduced, and, at the same time, a greater plurality of 'knowledges' is allowed to blossom. Agenda 2030 argues, as do Koch and Weingart (2016: 339) that there is 'no substitute for local knowledge' when it comes to the kinds of changes we all face at the global level.

The UN's agenda for sustainable development

The UN's 2030 Agenda calls for a transformative shift to meet the demands and threats facing our planet. This shift is seen by most of us to be on a scale equal or greater than the earlier shifts humanity has made from feudalism to capitalism, or from spiritualism to rationalism for example. When we reconstruct the discussion about how the 2030 Agenda and the 17 Sustainable Development Goals (SDGs) should, within a short space of time, lead to the changes that must happen, knowledge emerges as a critical factor. A second transformative shift – perhaps a new enlightenment – is now emerging out of the South, based on how those who were once perceived as the 'weakest links' in university networks are dealing with global challenges.

Obrecht (2015) describes how the APPEAR programme interacted with many global initiatives to move from the Millennium Development Goals (MDGs) towards the SDGs, and to make knowledge a driving force in solving these global challenges. One example is the establishment of the network of universities and other research organisations known as the Sustainable Development Solutions Network (SDSN). Obrecht illustrates how the purpose of knowledge development shifts towards a new but different common future. If economic development (measured by rising stock values and GDP growth) was also a measure of how society valued knowledge, we might now see a shift towards what UNRISD (2016) calls the 'social-solidarity economy', based on different measures and ideas of prosperity. As Obrecht argues, international discourse about 'development' is integrated directly into discourse around the SDGs:

The development policy implications of the SDGs mean that APPEAR, too, is at the center of a global discourse, the aim of which is an ecologically, socially, culturally and geopolitically more agreeable world. In this struggle to find sustainable mod- els for a future, which affords those born in the future no fewer life chances than we now enjoy, development research plays an essential role. Our efforts to create habitable living spaces in the future can only work on the basis of evidence-based and, ulti- mately, scientific research. (2015: 24–25)

If APPEAR is at the centre of the discourse around and the implemen- tation of the SDGs, Norhed is too. In addition, in the APPEAR project, as for Norhed, the issue of how Western knowledge is an active and willing contributor to global problems, is, in itself, a global challenge rather than part of the solution. If we seek a transformative shift wherein social and environmental issues determine our economic model (including acceptable kinds of product development and trade) rather than the other way around, we need an ecological approach – an eco-social paradigm shift. As indicated in the reports by APPEAR, knowledge has to transform if it wants to become part of the solution. If this doesn't happen, Western cultural presuppositions about what knowledge is valued will continue to direct future economic growth to those who already have the most, leaving little hope for the many already left behind.

This challenges Western views (*Weltanschauungen*) about how humans relate to the world. An important issue emerging here is the reality that humans are animals – perhaps not very different, and prob- ably not at all superior, to other creatures we share our world with. This challenges the subject–object dichotomy that undergirds so much of Western thought, justifying how we reflect on, study and exploit nature as a resource, and how the machine metaphor has shaped our knowl- edge priorities (Ellul 1954). As argued above, this subject–object, human versus nature, machine rationality and modelling, not only made industrialisation possible but justified the untold plunder, chaos, destruction and suffering caused by imperialism in all its historical forms and contemporary disguises.

Perhaps, for the future, our role is to detect and attend to this 'new enlightenment' as it emerges from the local contexts of those previously the most left behind. However, the need for 'transformative shifts' is subject to time constraints we have never experienced before. As Chabal (2009: 18) argues: 'It is the very legacy of Enlightenment that brought about imperialism and a social theory that devalues the particularly African, non-Western "other"' (see also Adriansen et al. 2016: 5). The global challenges we face do not allow this dichotomy between 'us and the other' to continue. After all, we have moved some way since the 1970s when Walter Rodney (1972) first explained how Europe underdeveloped Africa with the help of soldiers, followed quickly by missionaries and educators.[13]

When we are in it together, there is no 'other'.[14] The question then is how to build alternatives to Western hegemony that can succeed in generalising knowledge beyond its place of origin, not for the sake of domination but to legitimise alternatives and initiate meaningful theoretical confrontations. A focus on local knowledge is crucial here, and within this, the links between experience-based and scientific knowledge. By this I am not suggesting a break with the scientific in everyday language and experience but rather ways of establishing the *continuities* between different kinds of knowledge – an interchange between common sense and scientific work. Discussing topics in ways that bridge the common sense versus science cleavage is one basis for expanding alternative spaces of academic knowledge, and thus developing a variety of epistemologies that have relevance to the SDGs.

The SDGs call for development that 'leaves no one behind'. This is in stark contrast to the growing inequalities measured in access to knowledge. The SDGs appeal to the global academic profession to work together, to co-operate. This is a mandate to which Norhed can be said to have responded ahead of time.

To quote Obrecht again:

> The SDGs will not only deal with the interdependence of the social, ecological and economic realities, but also increasingly with the interdependence of the results of scientific research in a global context. In the transnational discourse about the

generation and exploitation of scientific knowledge, it becomes ever more self-evident that, in the future, priority must be given to the interlinking of scientific results rather than to the generation of individual scientific data, and that for this interlinking and meta-analysis that supports it, scientific co-operation will definitely become more important than scientific competition. (2015: 25)

About this book

On 6 and 7 June 2016, Norhed held a conference in Oslo on the theme, 'Knowledge for Development' in an attempt to shift the focus of the programme towards its academic content. This book follows up on that event. The conference highlighted the usefulness of presenting the value of Norhed's different projects to the world, showing how they improve knowledge and expand access to it through co-operation. What also surfaced at the conference was a wish for more meta-knowledge linked to the following questions. Is this way of co-operating contributing to the growth of independent post-colonial knowledge production in the South, based on analyses of local data and experiences in ways that are relevant to our shared future? Does the growth of academic independence, as well as greater equality, and the ability to develop theories different to those imposed by the better-off parts of the world, give rise to deeper understandings and better explanations? Does it, at least, spread the ability to translate existing methodologies in ways that add meaning to observations of local context and data, and thus enhance the relevance and influence of the academic profession locally and internationally?

Based on the contributions in this book, we cannot give a definite answer yet but our view is that Norhed is a step in the right direction.

The editors alone are, in the end, responsible for bringing forth the great variety of experiences and interactions that occur in Norhed's many projects. But we are also responsible for the quality of the book. Our greatest challenge has been to find a balance between variety, representability and quality, and this has led to publishing delays. In the end we hope challenging circumstances are tackled in thought-provoking and inspiring ways. We thank Norad for generously funding this book and for their inspiring co-operation during its production. Thanks also to our copy-editors, Mary Ralphs, Inga Norenius and Liz Mackenzie, as well as our exceptional publisher at African Minds, François van Schalkwyk, for helping us to stay on track during the long process of production.

Norhed is an attempt to fund *collaboration* within and between higher education institutions. We know that both the uniqueness of this programme, and ideas of how to better utilise the learning and experience emerging from it, call for more elaboration and broader dissemination before we can offer further guidance on how to do things better. This book is a first attempt.

About the volume editors

Tor Halvorsen is a senior researcher at the University of Bergen Global and SDG Bergen, as well as at the Fafo Institute for Labour and Social Research, Oslo. He can be contacted via e-mail at Tor.Halvorsen@uib.no

Kirsten Skare Orgaret is a professor in the Department of Journalism and Media Studies at Oslo Metropolitan University, Norway. She can be contacted at kristo@oslomet.no

Roy Krøvel is a professor in the Department of Journalism and Media Studies at Oslo Metropolitan University, Norway. He can be contacted at royk@oslomet.no

Notes

1   Disciplinary power over knowledge is part of what makes both interdisciplinarity and the building of disciplines that run counter to the hegemonic centre such an uphill battle; see the *Oxford Handbook of Interdisciplinarity*, edited by Robert Frodeman (2017), particularly the chapter by Thomas Köning and Michael E Gorman titled, 'The challenge of funding interdisciplinary research: A look inside public research funding agencies' (513–524).

2   Alexander defines the components of this scientific continuum as including: general presuppositions, models, concepts, definitions, classifications, laws, complex and simple propositions, correlations, methodological assumptions, and observations.

3   Hans Rosling is one example of an academic who took this approach. If we agree that facts are what we strive to present, Rosling delivers statistics to show that

health and general well-being of human beings in the contemporary era are general-ly better than they were in the past (Rosling et al. 2018). From within this paradigm, Western knowledge and the capitalist division of labour are seen as having driven this general upswing in human progress. These are then used to validate Western knowledge and labour practices, as well as the model of infinite economic growth being both possible and essential. As Rosling et al. (2018: 220) put it: 'Let's be real-istic about what the five billion people in the world who still wash their clothes by hand are hoping for and what they will do everything they can to achieve. Expecting them to voluntarily slow down their economic growth is absolutely unrealistic. They want washing machines, electric lights, decent sewage systems, a fridge to store food, glasses if they have poor eyesight, insulin if they have diabetes, and transport to go on vacation just as much as you and I do.'

4   As Victor R Baker (2017: 88) observes, 'scientific careers increasingly depend on positive outcomes from peer reviews of grant applications and successful editorial decisions on manuscript submissions to highly cited journals. Judgements by pro-motion committees, department heads, and deans depend on standards developed within established disciplines. Spreading one's professional activities across multi-ple disciplines leaves one open to charges of doing science that is "soft", "lacking in depth and/or rigor" or "spread too thin" and thereby deficient in demonstrating the scholarship expected for accountability standards of accomplishment and expertise. Thus, the young scholars who stray from disciplinary standards risk being perceived by colleagues as engaging in mere "dilettantism", that is, treating important matters of science in an amateurish manner.'

5   Mbembe's literary skill captures this better than many social scientists do (many of us have lost language through years of one-sided discipline-based training). He writes: 'It is therefore humanity as a whole that gives the world its name. In confer-ring its name on the world, it delegates to it and receives from it confirmation of its own position, singular yet fragile, vulnerable and partial, at least in relation to the other forces of the universe – animals and vegetables, objects, molecules, divinities, techniques and raw material, the earth trembling, volcanoes erupting, winds and storms, rising waters, the sun that explodes and burns, and all the rest of it. There is therefore no world except by naming, delegation, mutuality, and reciprocity' (Mbembe 2017: 180).

6   As Turner (2017: 19) argues, 'Each of the advantages of disciplinarity comes with limitations: the need to service students, the intellectual coercion that results from the disciplinary hierarchy that comes from the market exchange of students, the constraints on communication resulting from common training and norms, and the exclusion and limitations that go with them. Each limitation and exclusion produces an alternative unpopulated space, often involving practical problems, that' belong'

to no discipline and cannot be easily addressed by any of them. The difficulties, however, are commensurate with the opportunities.'

7 As noted in the previous chapter, these are: education and training; health; natural resource management, climate change and environment; democratic and economic governance; the humanities, culture, media and communication; and a special capacity development programme in South Sudan.

8 Pippa Norris was employed by the UNDP for many years and is now a professor at Harvard University and the University of Sydney. In her book *Making Democratic Governance Work: How Regimes Shape Prosperity, Welfare, and Peace* she explains that the World Bank's policies that promote economic growth first, and promise that the market will democratise societies 'in the long run' create false ideas about how markets work in society. She argues that, in fact, prioritising democratisation is better at creating peace, social welfare and prosperity. She then shows that the combination of democracy with a well-functioning state is what secures the kind of development that benefits the widest range of people in any population. Universities can contribute here by ensuring that states have a skilled workforce to recruit from (to counter donor experts, for example) and by operating according to democratic values in ways that equip the independent thinkers and academics that democracies and bureaucracies need.

9 Simon Marginson (2006) argues that since Thatcherism and public-choice theory as used by the World Bank (see Chapter 2 in this book), it is hard to say what 'the public' is when the global market rules.

10 To those who argue that Norway *always* goes for collaboration and has invariably supported Unesco's work for the global public, a reminder is necessary: following US-led demands from the World Trade Organization for South Africa to open up its education sector for trade in educational services (as other African countries have been pressured to do), Norway was among partnering countries that placed pressure on South Africa. This was withdrawn only after Kader Asmal, then South Africa's minister of education, visited Norway in October 2003 where he shamed Norway at an SIU conference for attempting to turn South Africa's public higher education system into a marketplace that would quickly become dominated by the private sector (Halvorsen 2005).

11 To this critique it must be added that, at a policy level at least, Norway has been an exception to this way of working since 1986, when universities initiated this North–South collaboration in the NUFU programme (see the previous chapter, this volume). In her overview of Norwegian aid policies, Randi Rønning Balsvik insists that NUFU actually favoured research that was prioritised in the South: 'From its start, the programme was meant to favour research topics that came from the South, and often this was the case' (2016: 141, my translation). As discussed in Chapter 1, however, capacity building related to this research was generally weak.

NUFU projects were of high quality but perhaps worked best to create free-floating intellectuals rather than institutionally embedded academics or institutions that were well equipped to conduct high-quality research. Eventually, the programme was moved to Norad, partly in an effort to remove bottlenecks linked to project administration; see also Skauge (2005).

12   In *Alternativa fakta* (2017), Åsa Wickforss notes how fast belief in academic knowledge is vanishing globally as knowledge is increasingly perceived as relative. This is partly because of the influence of contemporary politics and partly because of how academics have responded to political influence.

13   In Rodney's chapter titled, 'Education for underdevelopment', he writes: 'The main purpose of the colonial school system was to train Africans to help man the local administration at the lowest ranks and to stall the private capitalist firms owned by Europeans. In effect, that meant selecting a few Africans to participate in the domination and exploitation of the continent as a whole' (1972: 292). Science and engineering seldom reached schools in Africa during the colonial era, and ever since, vast numbers of school pupils, in *both* Africa *and* Europe (until very recently) learned that the British discovered Mount Kenya and that Cecil Rhodes more or less created Africa.

14   Rebecca Solnit's work on how even divided societies co-operate when faced with catastrophe is useful here. An insight into her thinking can be found in the interview with Solnit by Mark Karlin, *Truthout*, 29 January 2013. Available online.

References

Adriansen HK, Madsen LM and Jensen S (2016) *Higher Education and Capacity Building in Africa: The Geography and Power of Knowledge Under Changing Conditions*. New York: Routledge

Alexander JC (1982) *Positivism, Presuppositions and Current Controversies: Theoretical Logic in Sociology, Volume 1*. Los Angeles: University of California Press

Apffel-Marglin F and Marglin SA (1996) *Decolonizing Knowledge: From Development to Dialogue*. A study prepared for the World Institute for Development Economics Research at the United Nations University. Oxford: Clarendon Press

Baker VR (2017) Interdisciplinarity and the earth sciences: Transcending limitations of the knowledge paradigm. In R Frodeman (ed.) *The Oxford Handbook of Interdisciplinarity*, 2nd edn. Oxford: Oxford University Press

Balsvik RR (2016) *Norsk bistandshistorie*. Oslo: Samlaget

Bhambra GK, Gebrial D and Nisancioglu K (2018) *Decolonising the University*. London: Pluto

Bonneuil C and Fressoz J-B (2016) *The Shock of the Anthropocene: The Earth, History and Us*, trans. D Fernbach. London, New York: Verso

Chabal P (2009) *Africa: The Politics of Smiling and Suffering*. London: Zed and UKZN Press

Ellul J (1954/1964) *The Technological Society*. Toronto: Vintage

Freidson E (1994) *Professionalism Reborn: Theory, Prophecy and Policy*. Cambridge: Polity Press

Frodeman R (ed.) (2017) *The Oxford Handbook of Interdisciplinarity*, 2nd ed. Oxford: Oxford University Press

Halvorsen T (2016) South Africa, OECD and BRICS. In: E Braathen et al. *Poverty and Inequality in Middle-Income Countries: Policy Achievements, Political Obstacles*. London. Zed

Halvorsen T, Mathisen G and Skauge T (2005) *Identity Formation or Knowledge Shopping? Education and Research in the New Globality*, SIU report Series R3

Heilbron J (1995) *The Rise of Social Theory*. Cambridge. Polity Press

Higgins J (2013) *Academic Freedom in a Democratic South Africa: Essays and Interviews on Higher Education and the Humanities*. Johannesburg: Wits University Press

Higgins J (2016) The first philosophers were astronomers: Curiosity and innovation in higher education policy. In: T Halvorsen and J Nossum (eds) *North–South Knowledge Networks: Towards Equitable Collaboration Between Academics, Donors and Universities*. Cape Town: African Minds. Available online

Huang F, Finkelstein M and Rostan M (eds) (2014) *The Internationalization of the Academy: Changes, Realities and Prospects*. New York: Springer

Jasanoff S (ed.) (2004) *States of Knowledge: The Co-Production of Science and the Social Order*. London and New York: Routledge

Koch S and Weingart P (2016) *The Delusion of Knowledge Transfer: The Impact of Foreign Aid Experts on Policy-Making in South Africa and Tanzania*. Cape Town: African Minds. Available online

Madsen LM and Nielsen TT (2016) Negotiating scientific knowledge about climate change: Enhancing research capacity through PhD students. In: HK Adriansen, LM Madsen and S Jensen (eds) *Higher Education and Capacity Building in Africa: The Geography and Power of Knowledge Under Changing Conditions*. New York. Routledge

Marginson S (2006) The Anglo-American university at its global high tide. *Minerva* 44(1): 65–87

Mbembe A (2017) *Critique of Black Reason*. Durham: Duke University Press

Mokyr J (2002) *The Gifts of Athena: Historical Origins of the Knowledge Economy*. Princeton: Princeton University Press

Norris P (2012) *Making Democratic Governance Work: How Regimes Shape Prosperity, Welfare and Peace*. New York: Cambridge University Press

Obrecht AJ (2015) *APPEAR: Participative Knowledge Production through Transnational and Transcultural Academic Co-operation*. Vienna: Böllau Verlag

Olechnicka A, Ploszaj A and Celińska-Janowicz D (2019) *The Geography of Scientific Collaboration*. New York: Routledge

Olsen JP (2007) The ups and downs of bureaucratic organization, Working Paper 14, Arena Centre for European Studies, University of Oslo. Available online

Richardson WJ (2018) Understanding Eurocentrism as a structural problem of undone science. In: GK Bhambra, D Gebrial and K Nisancioglu (eds), *Decolonising the University*. London: Pluto

Rodney W (1972/2018) *How Europe Underdeveloped Africa*. London: Verso

Rosling H with Rosling O and Rosling Rönnlund A (2018) *Factfulness: Ten Reasons We're Wrong About the World and Why Things Are Better Than You Think*. London: Sceptre

Said EW (1978/1994) *Orientalismen: Vestlige oppfatninger av Orienten*. Oslo: Cappelen

Skauge T (2005) Co-operation for knowledge as alternative to marginalization by market. In: T Halvorsen, G Mathisen and T Skauge *Identity Formation or Knowledge Shopping: Education and Research in the New Globality*, SIU Report, Series R3

Smith LT (1999) *Decolonizing Methodologies: Research and Indigenous Peoples*, 2nd edn. London: Zed

Sverdrup U, Ulstein JH, Pedersen MF, Leira H and Ulriksen SU (2012) *Norske interesser: Sett fra utestasjoner*. Oslo: NUPI

Thiong'o NW (2012) *Globalectics: Theory and the Politics of Knowing*. New York: Columbia University Press

Thiong'o NW (1986) *Decolonizing the Mind: The Politics of Language in African Literature*. New York: James Currey

Turner S (2017) Knowledge formation: An analytical framework. In R Frodeman (ed.) *The Oxford Handbook of Interdisciplinarity*, 2nd ed. Oxford: Oxford University Press

UNRISD (United Nations Research Institute for Social Development) (2016) *Policy for Transformative Change: Implementing the 2030 Agenda for Sustainable Development*. UNRISD Flagship Report. Geneva

Wickforss Å (2017) *Alternativa fakta: Om kunskapen och dess fiender*. Stockholm: Fri tanke

World Bank (2002) *Constructing Knowledge Societies: New Challenges for Tertiary Education*. Washington DC

PART ONE
GLOBAL–LOCAL REALITIES

Introduction to Part One

Tor Halvorsen

Knowledge is often compared to light. When present, it travels the world and enlightens everyone. Or, to use a metaphor from economics: new knowledge creates its own demand. However, both of these views mask the fact that the global knowledge society is very unequal. Knowledge often carries the values, norms and political orientations of the context in which it emerges. As we develop it at universities, knowledge is a cultural product and, as such, it shapes our selves and our identities. Knowledge is never divorced from the context of its creation, nor can it travel without causing disturbance given the influences it carries. And yet, knowledge does seem to travel easily – it can connect people across cultures and create mutual understandings that transcend the contexts in which it is created.

During the 1990s, knowledge for nation-state development was countered by a discourse affirming that internationalisation and globalisation were a must for progress. The most internationalised universities were (and still are) ranked the most highly. This seemed to suggest that 'global knowledge' is more important for scholars than knowledge of their own national contexts. Accordingly, the amount of knowledge produced by networks of scholars across national and regional borders is growing fast and, as contemporary debates about the UN's 2030 Agenda on Sustainable Development show, knowledge about the globe and its challenges is expanding rapidly.

Scholarly networks are driven by a variety of interests and themes. Many try to serve the global economy and are highly valued by university leaders who are concerned with reputation building and institutional advancement. Competition for income from externally funded programmes (and especially for those that will cover overhead costs) promotes links with an increasingly globalised economy. Meanwhile, the global economic centres remain hegemonic academic centres in terms of measures of quantity and quality, albeit that China as a relative newcomer has perhaps taken over as world leader in the science, technology, engineering and mathematics (STEM) disciplines. In parallel with globalisation that promotes alliances between universities, states and the business sector, an underworld of alternative knowledges is also thriving; (see, for example, debates about the decolonisation of academic curricula and research in Mamdani, this volume). The Norhed programme straddles these two realities; driven by ideas about academia as global public space, it has the potential to contribute to a linking of the global and the local in ways that make cultural variation a resource for all.

To some extent, the Norhed programme counters the dominant trend whereby donors aim to shape universities in the South. The so-called liberation of local economies (linked to the neoliberal politics promoted by multilateral organisations such as the World Bank, the IMF, the OECD etc.) has strengthened the *functional orientation* of higher education. Countries and nation-states are named 'knowledge economies', and the role of higher education is to make these economies as globally competitive as possible. Thus, the STEM disciplines are given priority in ways that detach them from the broader social, as well as academic and university context.

It has even been argued that the knowledge economy would be best served if higher education became a commodity within the global trading system. The World Trade Organization's agreement on Trade in Services promoted the notion that private universities should compete for students, professors and research projects in a global market for education services as regulated by the rules of 'free trade'. As in other service sectors, where private providers emerged, public institutions had to undergo reform in order to compete with the private sector. The general idea is that global competition between universities should produce 'better knowledge'. To succeed, institutions are encouraged to specialise – and be the best at something – and to build 'networks of *strategic* co-operation' to promote themselves in the global rankings.

This idea of a competitive knowledge economy has changed universities in low to middle-income countries (LMICs) far more than those in countries such as Norway for example. The World Bank, in particular, has driven the privatisation of what they call 'tertiary education'. In many countries, universities have not only had to establish themselves as private businesses, but also resolved to focus on research that can earn them an income through patents and intellectual property rights. For LMICs, the question might be, why grow research capacity at business schools if you can secure 'value for money' for students by importing and disseminating knowledge from a highly ranked school in one of the world's economic centres. In many LMICs, private universities now dominate (in terms of student numbers at least), and many of these are subsidiaries of universities in high-income countries.

Inevitably, this has raised the issue of decolonisation once more. In universities, this is primarily about how to acknowledge and transcend colonial influence, but also how to respond to the ways in which contemporary globalisation undermines academic public space. In essence, globalisation has created new forms of colonisation that cross North–South divides just like the old forms continue to do.

The current focus on the globe as a common space for humanity does seem to have opened up alternatives to the discourse of 'economic globalisation', including academic policies and practices embedded in a knowledge commons. The UN's Agenda 2030, with its 17 Sustainable Development Goals (SDGs), and the Paris Agreement on Climate Change both grew out of (often hidden) opposition to the consequences of the neoliberal push to liberate or 'denationalise' the global economy. Today, universities in the South, located in areas where the global challenges are most visible, have gained prominence as arenas for knowledge development that are the most relevant to all of us if we accept that humanity has transgressed the limits of our planet.

The Norhed programme builds on both the old idea that universities are important for independent development and the new insight that universities in the South must be strengthened so as to be able to give voice to the consequences of the global challenge we all face. Although these consequences are increasing 'risk' for all beings on the planet, they are felt most forcefully in the South partly due to its colonial heritage. That is, the challenges we face might have local consequences, but their causes are clearly global.

We tend to take for granted that academics use their freedom in the realm of research and teaching to secure justice and fairness for all citizens of the societies in which they work. However, as Roy Krøvel explains in Chapter 4, the nation-state project (as in becoming Tanzania or becoming Colombia) can be a very repressive project for those that fall outside of its hegemonic cultural sphere. Where universities form part of such nation-building projects, they normalise and justify forceful adjustment to the orthodoxies of the ruling elites. Those left behind suffer the most from the development risks taken. And as the ruling elites align themselves within the global economy, repression becomes ever more visible, as is the case for indigenous people in Latin America. To prevent this kind of mental and physical repression, cross-border networks of like-minded academics can create support for an alternative vision of the university that works in opposition to state power and/or market forces.

The Norhed progamme takes for granted that academics can engage with one another across geographic and academic borders in support of those 'left behind'. It accepts that none of us escape the cultural context within which our thinking develops but we can still communicate across the academic landscape about what we think is true and important, as well as what is common or public knowledge about injustice and inequality, fairness and sustainability. To promote knowledge as if it is a product in a global marketplace undermines this ability to create a common global public space, and thus also our chance to find solutions to the global challenges.

To follow are four chapters and an interview discussing knowledge issues in this interchange between the local and the global, the North and the South, the well-resourced and those 'left behind' by both the state and economic sectors.

In Chapter 1, Mahmood Mamdani takes us to two universities in East Africa, Makerere University and the University of Dar es Salaam. With a broad historical and sociological approach, he raises the issue of how universities can and should be arenas that help unite the two interdependent roles that every academic must play: that is, to be a scholar and a public intellectual. Mamdani explains that academics move between the global common pool of knowledge and the local context where knowledge is given meaning, and justified as relevant. He argues that, while 'standards of excellence' may be set at the global level (in the hegemonic centres) in ways that make them seem detached from any context, relevance is constructed in interaction with the local (political) society. The way to bring these two dimensions of academic work (the scholar and the public intellectual) closer together is for academics to draw clearer links between the global and the local. Perhaps this means that, as active public intellectuals, academics have to work harder to translate 'excellence' into relevance, and thus be the force that defines what relevance is?

In Chapter 2, the global health crisis related to antimicrobial resistance is discussed by a collective of 11 authors. The purpose of their collaboration was to build capacity in the health sector to manage this multifaceted issue. Although focused mainly on Malawi and Mozambique, this North–South–South partnership has local backing not only from the leadership of the partner institutions and the local health and education ministries, but is also feeding into global discourse via links with the World Health Organization's Regional Office for Africa. This project is an excellent example of how problem-oriented knowledge seeking and a well-integrated university collaboration can use the policy/knowledge interface to link global discourse with a range of influential local actors. What this chapter makes clear is that solving a problem requires more than understanding. For action to follow knowledge, sound institutional and political groundwork is critical.

In Chapter 3, William Tayeebwa and Kristin Skare Orgeret discuss some of the most burning issues of our time for the profession of journalism. New media is changing not only this profession, but also what constitutes 'news' and whose news to trust. This is both a global debate and an issue for every local media outlet and the space it occupies in society. What is the role of journalists in promoting a good society? What ethics should guide their work when truth is relativised, freedom of speech is threatened, and social-media bots are working to control what people see? In this chapter, the authors link journalism, as a profession with ethical commitments to both truth-telling and interpretation, with Unesco's role as a guardian of these professional values. In the context of Uganda and Nepal, they demonstrate the value of a capable and ethically sound journalistic profession in societal development. They also explain that transforming Unesco ideals into local practices is no easy task. That is, when global norms and ethics underpin one's journalistic skills, encounters with local experiences, norms and values can place journalists' professional integrity at stake.

In Chapter 4, Roy Krøvel shifts our attention to Latin America, an area relatively under-represented within the Norhed programme. This chapter raises crucial issues about how universities, culture and human representation are linked in ways that cannot be explained or subsumed under the nation-state umbrella as conceived in Europe or within Africa's liberation movements. Rather, the cultural cleavages between the indigenous people and the descendants of the conquerors who have ruled these countries since their independence – in most cases for over 150 years – must be acknowledged as a conflict in which the state remains a tool of oppression. Where indigenous people are admitted to a national university, they have little option but to learn the institutionalised knowledge of the oppressor. Krøvel shows how important indigenous knowledge institutions are to the survival of the human collective and the biosphere. He argues that their survival is crucial to the wider world gaining respect for their cosmology, their knowledge, and their ability to share knowledge through a form of solidarity of learning that is alien to Western individualism. Indeed, a global indigenous movement has emerged out of countless local struggles between states and indigenous organisations. In this process, two things have become clear. The first is the value of indigenous knowledge for the autonomy of indigenous groups. The second is how local movements (like some academic networks) have joined together to gain strength and, in the process, have learned to use 'globalisation' as a liberating force. In some cases, these transnational networks of solidarity have been effective in limiting state powers and enhancing respect for the territorial autonomy, knowledge and identity of indigenous groups.

The final chapter of this section is an interview with Edward Kirumira, a representative of Makerere University, which has long been considered a 'donor darling'. The university was associated with 14 projects in Norhed's first funding phase and, as principal of the College of Humanities and Social Sciences, Kirumira was at the centre of managing several of these. In the interview, he considers questions about what North–South and South–South collaboration have added to the university's academic culture, whether and how these have created new kinds of knowledge, more independent scholars and/or a stronger institution. Kirumira also responds to the question of whether donors should support research institutions in countries where academic knowledge does not seem to be respected or trusted, and where governments spend very little of their own resources on higher education. In relation to this, he responds to the idea of donors considering a tactical hiatus in relation to funding Makerere University in future.

1

Decolonising universities

Mahmood Mamdani

Institutions of higher education originated in different parts of the world in the premodern era, but it is only one particular historical experience – the Western – that became globalised during the modern colonial era. The modern university, as the name suggests, claims a universal significance as a site for the study of the human. Its graduates claim 'excellence' globally. This chapter draws on the experience of two universities, Makerere University and the University of Dar es Salaam, and the contribution of two intellectual figures, Ali Mazrui and Walter Rodney, to flesh out some key post-independence debates regarding the role of the university and the scholar. The first debate arises from the nationalist demand that the university be a site of 'relevance', and not just 'excellence'. The demand informed debates over curriculum, leading to a second debate over the relationship between two different roles: that of the public intellectual and the scholar, articulated as the difference between 'ideological orientation' (Rodney) and 'mode of reasoning' (Mazrui). The chapter closes with a discussion on language. In a context where colonial languages were given official status, developing them into dynamic languages of popular culture, high learning and scientific reasoning, the tendency was to freeze the languages of the colonised in a folkloric condition due to lack of recognition and resources. Two experiences in particular – that of Afrikaans and Kiswahili – pointed a way forward to social inclusion, creating internal institutional capacities and translation work to support African languages. It is my view that the cases discussed in this chapter are important not because they are representative, but because the questions they raise are of wider and general significance. The challenge in higher education, in Africa and elsewhere, is to be both responsive to the local and engaged with the global.

The importance of theory

Theory is born of comparison. Comparison is older than colonialism but it matures to its fullest in the colonial period. The Greeks made modest comparisons, first between cities such as Athens and Sparta. Later, they turned to larger contexts: Greece, Persia and Egypt. Then came Arabs and Berbers. The great Berber historian, Ibn Khaldun, and the Arab traveller, Ibn Battuta, compared the North African and the West African worlds. Others compared Arabia and lands to the east. But the most comprehensive comparative work was carried out during the European colonial project. It is that work which is of concern to us today as we seek to define the problem of decolonisation.

With the European colonial project, classification became global. In the heyday of European expansion, the eighteenth and the nineteenth centuries, European intellectuals – as far apart as Hegel, Marx, Weber, Durkheim, Maine and others – began comparing the European and the non-European worlds, asking: what was and is so distinctive about the West?

The production of knowledge begins with ordering phenomena. Comparing means classifying and mapping. Durkheim looked to chemistry as the master classificatory science. Marx looked to biology and its most elementary unit of analysis, the cell. Comparison requires a standard – the familiar – through which the not-so-familiar is understood, sometimes as not-quite-yet, at other times as an outright deviation. All ordering has a reference point. For those who did the classifying and ordering of everything around the world, the reference point was the West, the reality they knew and considered natural. Take the example of Jesuit priests who went to China looking for 'religion'. Non-Buddhist China has no scriptures, but plenty of ritual. But religion for Europeans had a particular definition – there could be no religion without sacred texts. So they concluded that China had no religion. In later years, they reached a similar conclusion in Africa, that it had no religion, only magic and superstition, practised by witches and witch-doctors.[1]

The problem is unavoidable: since we are part of that which we compare, how does one avoid the problem of being evaluative and subjective? You cannot avoid it; you can only be conscious of it, and thus limit your claims.[2]

Colonialism and the university

The *institutional form* of the modern African university did not derive from pre-colonial institutions; the inspiration was the colonial modern. The model was a discipline-based, gated community with a distinction between clearly defined groups (administrators, academics and fee-paying students). The model traces its origin to the University of Humboldt in Berlin, a new type of university designed in the aftermath of Germany's defeat by France in 1810. Over the next century, this innovation spread to much of Europe and from there to the rest of the world.

Not only the institutional form but also the *intellectual content* of modern social sciences and humanities is a product of the Enlightenment experience in Europe. The European experience was the raw material from which was forged *the category human*. However abstract the category, it drew meaning from the actual struggles on the ground, both within and outside Europe. Internally, the notion of the human was an alternative to that of the Christian. It was a Renaissance response to Church orthodoxy. The intellectuals of Renaissance Europe looked to anchor their vision in a history older than that of Christianity. They found this in pagan Greece and imperial Rome, and self-consciously crafted these into a foundational legacy for Europe. Externally, it was a response to an entirely different set of circumstances – not the changing vision of a self-reflexive and self-revolutionising Europe but that of a self-assertive Europe, reaching out and expanding, in a move that sought first to conquer the world, starting with the New World, then to conquer Asia and finally Africa, and then to transform and to 'civilise' this world in its own image. This dual origin made for a contradictory legacy. The modern European university was a site for the study of the human. In their universal reach for the human, the humanities and the social sciences both proclaimed the oneness of humanity and defined that oneness as sameness – from a very European vantage point.

My first point is that the modern university in Africa has very little to do with what existed on this continent before colonialism, and everything to do with what was created in modern Europe. We may find and study great examples of institutions of learning in the African world before European conquest – in Timbuktu, Cairo,[3] Tunis, Alexandria – but these did not shape the contemporary African university, whether colonial or post-colonial. The decisive influence was the European university. This is my second point.

The problem

The African university began as a colonial project – a top-down modernist project whose ambition was the conquest of society. The university was in the frontline of the colonial 'civilising mission'. Properly understood, this 'civilising mission' was the precursor, the original edition of the 'one-size-fits-all' project that we associate with Structural Adjustment Programmes designed by the International Monetary Fund (IMF) and the World Bank in the 1980s. Its ambition was to create universal scholars, men and women who stood for excellence, regardless of context, and who would serve as the vanguard of the 'civilising mission' without reservation, or remorse. For those of us who are inmates of the modern university, prisoners in an ongoing colonising project, at least in a metaphorical sense, I suggest we think of our task as one of subverting the project from within, through a series of acts which sift through the historical legacy, discarding some parts, and adapting others to a new-found purpose.

The first critical reflection on this colonial project took place in the nationalist movement. From the ranks of the nationalist movement emerged a different kind of intellectual, the public intellectual. If the hallmark of the global scholar was *excellence*, that of the public intellectual was *relevance*. Excellence was said to be universal, measured without regard to context; relevance, however, was necessarily contextual, place-specific. The contest between the two unfolded on two very different campuses in East Africa. Makerere University, established in

1922, was the paradigmatic colonial university. The University of Dar es Salaam (UDSM), established at independence in 1963, would soon emerge as the flag-bearer of anticolonial nationalism. The two universities stood for two contrasting projects: the colonial university as the turf of the universal scholar and the nationalist university as home of the public intellectual.

The different visions were articulated by two different academics: Ali Mazrui and Walter Rodney. Mazrui called for a university true to its classical vision, as the home of the scholar 'fascinated by ideas'; Rodney saw the university as the home of the public intellectual, a committed intellectual located in his or her time and place, and deeply engaged with the wider society.[4] One moral of the story I want to tell is that we resist the temptation to dismiss one side and embrace the other. However compelling, these contrasting visions were anchored in two equally one-sided notions of higher education: relevance and excellence. At the same time, each contained something of value. Rather than choose between them, I suggest we identify the kernel of value in each, through a dialectical approach.

Does place matter, as Walter Rodney claimed? Or do ideas matter, regardless of place, as Mazrui insisted? Obviously, place matters. If universities could be divorced from politics, if knowledge production were immune from power relations, then place would not matter. But we know that is not the case. At the same time, ideas also do matter. If they did not, why have a university at all? This is to say that politics is not all.

The debate began at Makerere University in the early 1960s, on the eve of state independence. The two sides to the debate lined up on familiar ground – one side mobilised in defence of academic freedom, the other calling for justice. The first round of change produced resounding victories for the broad nationalist camp, which called for limiting the autonomy of the university, and of the faculty in particular, so as to put an end to racial privilege. They said the university should be national not only in name but also in appearance. Without a strong role for the independent state in higher education, it would not be possible to undermine the disciplinary nationalism and institutional autonomy which propped up the authority of the expatriate staff.

Dismissing academic freedom as a codeword in defence of the status quo, they called for state intervention in the name of justice. It did not take long for the terms of the debate to change, and dramatically so. With the emergence of the single-party regime, the university turned into an oasis where the practice of academic freedom allowed free political speech for those who disagreed with the ruling power. Instead of viewing it as a defence of racial privilege, as at independence, many began to rethink academic freedom as the cutting edge of a critique of nationalist power.

It is in this context that Rajat Neogy founded *Transition*, a cross between a journal and a magazine, one in which public intellectuals wrote for a public that included both the gown and the town.[5] Those who wrote for it included writers such as James Baldwin, Langston Hughes, Nadime Gordimer and Chinua Achebe, and politicians like Mwalimu Nyerere and Tom Mboya. *Transition* made possible a conversation that was simultaneously national, regional and global. Paul Theroux (1967) wrote 'Tarzan is an expatriate', an understanding of Tarzan and Jane as the first expatriates. Ali Mazrui wrote 'Nkrumah, the Leninist Czar' (1966), an essay on authoritarianism with a socialist tilt and 'Tanzaphilia' (1967), of which I will have more to say.

In the decade that followed the launch of the Arusha Declaration in 1967, the debate on Tanzania was framed by two critics. If Ali Mazrui was the most important liberal critic of nationalism in power, Issa Shivji was its most important critic from the left. Two of his books, *The Silent Class Struggle* (1971) and *Class Struggles in Tanzania* (1976) proposed that nationalisation and socialism should really be understood as the language masking accumulation by a new state-based class.

Despite this intellectual *brassage*, the two institutions – Makerere and UDSM – continued along their distinctive paths. The main issue for reformers at Makerere was the deracialisation of the teaching body, whose leading lights were predominantly white. Newly qualified young academics were promoted under pressure from government-appointed senior administrators. Among these was the young Mazrui: freshly graduated with a doctorate from Oxford, he rose from lecturer to professor in the space of a few years. At UDSM, by contrast, the relevance of the curriculum itself was being called into question; there was also a growing demand for interdisciplinarity, especially by faculty who thought disciplinary nationalism was at the root of the university's increasing irrelevance to the larger discussion on social and political ills in the country. The developments at Makerere and UDSM did not take place sequentially, one after another. They took place side by side, generating a strong and spirited exchange between Mazrui at Makerere and Rodney at UDSM.

The University of Dar es Salaam: The question of relevance

Whereas the main issue at Makerere was deracialisation of academic staff, the mobilising concerns at the University of Dar es Salaam were the relevance of the curriculum and the demand for interdisciplinarity. The UDSM discussion unfolded in the context of rapid political change, triggered by a student demonstration (on 22 October 1966) protesting a government decision to introduce compulsory national service for all secondary school graduates. The government's response was drastic: accusing students of betraying the nation, the government withdrew fellowships from all 334 students and sent them home. A few months later, on 5 February 1967, President Julius Nyerere issued the Arusha Declaration, a clarion call for building a socialist society. A programme to nationalise key sectors of the economy followed. The university responded with a conference on the role of the University College, Dar es Salaam, in a socialist Tanzania. Held from 11 to 13 March 1967, the conference noted that 'various disciplines and related subjects [were not studied] in the context of East Africa's and particularly Tanzania's socio-economic development aspirations, concerns and problems'. It ended with a call for *relevance*, including a recommendation for a 'continuous curriculum review' (Kimambo et al. 2008: 147). The conference triggered vigorous debates among the academic staff and students on campus. Accounts of these discussions identify three different points of view. *Radicals*, mostly non-Tanzanian, wanted a complete transformation of both curriculum and administrative structure; above all, they wanted to abolish discipline-based departments. *Moderates*, who were the majority and included most Tanzanian members of staff, agreed

that there should be a radical review of the curriculum but not an aboli-
tion of departments. *Conservatives,* then a minority, resisted any radical
change in either curriculum or the discipline-based organisation of the
university.

Two rounds of reform followed. The first round began with the
introduction of an interdisciplinary programme in 'development studies'. But changes were ad hoc and contradictory: interdisciplinary
streams were introduced; at the same time, however, departments
remained. The response was mixed, and opposition was pronounced. A
professor in the law faculty, JL Kanywanyi, recalled 'political-rally-like
classes' where 'speakers were drawn mainly from outside the college'
including 'government ministers and other public figures of various
calling'. The course 'became unpopular among students' – indeed, students rejected the new curriculum in 1969 (Kanywanyi [1989][6] cited in
Kimambo 2008: 120). Perhaps the most acute observation came from a
sub-committee of the University Council, appointed in November 1970
to review the programme.[7] It began by noting that the compromise that
had introduced streams but retained departments was contradictory:
'some departments have departed drastically from the sub-stream
structure in their attempt to respond to the market situation'. The
resulting tension 'proved right the fears of those who were opposing
co-existence of streams and departments which has enabled disciplines
to reassert themselves at the expense of the interdisciplinary programme'. More importantly, the sub-committee asked whether a
problem-solving focus was likely to reduce the scholarly content of
higher education, producing 'technocrats' rather than 'reasoning graduates' (Kimambo 2003: 5, 7). The academic staff opposed to the changes
either voted with their feet or were booted out of the university.
Between June and November 1971, 28 academic staff resigned and 46
academic contracts were not renewed. Of 86 academics in established
posts, 42 per cent departed. In light of this, the Council sub-committee
called for 'careful preparation' and recruitment of new staff. Those who
think of interdisciplinarity as the key to a new world may want to
remind themselves that both World Bank teams and the various centres
for area study, such as African Studies, have been interdisciplinary from
the start. The history of the development of the social sciences and

humanities shows that disciplines have been the predominant site for the development of method. Like the call for relevance, the call for an interdisciplinary approach to university education may also prove one-sided.[8]

Round 2 began with a two-track institutional reorganisation. The Faculty of Arts and Social Sciences set up its own interdisciplinary core to be taught by its own faculty. The Institute of Development Studies was set up to teach an interdisciplinary core in all other faculties, including the sciences and the professions. The Institute hired over 30 academic staff between 1973 and 1990. Departments remained, but so did career streams and sub-streams. The curriculum was revised and a compulsory interdisciplinary curriculum was introduced at all levels. The interdisciplinary core in the Faculty of Arts and Social Sciences, known as EASE (East African Society and Environment), focused on the teaching of history, ecology and politics in the first year, taking 40 per cent of student class time (two of five courses). In the second and third years, the time devoted to the interdisciplinary core course was reduced to one course out of five, focusing on the history of science and technology in year two and development planning in year three.

The reform process at UDSM was sustained over years because it was not confined to formal processes at the university. Those who wanted change built their own structures; student activists launched key publications: first *Che Che* and then, when it was banned, *Maji Maji*. Activist students and academic staff came together in regular discussion groups. The formal group, known as the 'ideological class', deliberately met at 10am every Sunday. Its stated aim was to provide students and staff with an alternative to church attendance. The second was less formal but also organised. This comprised a range of after-class study groups that proliferated over the years. In 1975, I recall belonging to five university-based study groups, each with between two and eight members. Meeting once a week, each required a background reading of around 100 pages. These groups focused on five different themes: Das Capital; the three Internationals; the Russian Revolution; the Chinese Revolution and the agrarian question.

We were looking to glimpse the outlines of a new world beyond our own reality. This was a period of tremendous intellectual ferment, marked by two different trajectories, each represented by the work of two different authors. The first was Walter Rodney's (1970) *How Europe Underdeveloped Africa*. Written in the mode of dependency theory, its reasoning was very much in line with that of the Arusha Declaration. The second was Shivji's two books, *The Silent Class Struggle* (1971) and *Class Struggles in Tanzania* (1976), which contrasted the language and promise of the Arusha Declaration with the reality of internal social and political developments in the country. The publication of Shivji's books triggered a debate focused on imperialism and the state among academics at UDSM.[9]

This is the context in which a series of memorable debates were held between Walter Rodney and Ali Mazrui, first in Kampala, and then in Dar es Salaam. Rodney called on intellectuals to join the struggle to consolidate national independence in an era when, though colonialism had ended, imperialism reigned supreme. If Rodney focused on the outside of nationalism, Mazrui called attention to its inside. If Rodney called on intellectuals to realise the unfinished agenda of anti-imperialism, Mazrui called attention to the authoritarian tendencies of nationalism in power. The debate between the two mirrored larger societal processes, the tension between nationalism and democracy on the one hand, and state and popular sovereignty on the other. It also reflected a growing tension within the academy, between the 'nationalist' public intellectual and the 'universalist' scholar. From this latter group emerged the most important critics of nationalism in power: Ali Mazrui from among the liberal critics, and Issa Shivji from the left.

Tanzaphilia

Ali Mazrui's critique soon extended beyond one of nationalism in power to that of left intellectuals seduced by radical state nationalism. Among the memorable essays Mazrui wrote for *Transition* was one titled 'Tanzaphilia: A diagnosis' (1967). Mazrui defined Tanzaphilia as 'a political phenomenon ... an opium of Afrophiles ... the romantic spell which Tanzania casts on so many of those who have been closely associated with her', a condition 'particularly marked among Western intellectuals'. Mazrui chided left intellectuals, liberals and socialists, expatriates and locals for having succumbed to this disease. He claimed that, seduced by the language of 'socialism', they were caught in the drift to single-party rule, approaching power with timidity and soft hands: 'Many of the most prosaic Western pragmatists have been known to acquire that dreamy look under the spell of Tanzania' (1967: 20).

Mazrui had his eye on simple facts like the 'Committee of Nine' at the University of Dar es Salaam which he termed the 'super-left' (Tordoff and Mazrui 1972: 438). Citing the pressure from the 'super-left' to turn the University of Dar es Salaam into 'an ideological college', Mazrui suggested that 'a genuine university should not be monopolistic'. He argued that the university should be 'multi-ideological rather than uni-ideological ... permit[ting] maximum interplay between different interpretations of reality'. Mazrui cited Colin Leys, a left-wing British intellectual who had earlier been principal of the party ideology school in Dar es Salaam, Kivukoni College, and who had famously lamented that besides the three conventionally listed social ills – 'poverty, ignorance, and disease'– Tanzania was also suffering from a fourth: empiricism (Mazrui 1967: 30–31; see also Tordoff and Mazrui 1972: 443, 445).[10]

To those like Leys – and presumably Rodney – who thought of ideological orientation as everything, Mazrui pointed to a deeper epistemological reality that he called 'mode of reasoning'. Compared to intellectual acculturation, ideological orientation is both superficial and changeable: 'To be in favor of this country or that, to be attracted by this system of values rather than that, all are forms of ideological conversion. And under a strong impulse one can change one's creed. But it is much more difficult to change the process of reasoning which one acquires from one's total educational background' (1967: 30–31). As proof, he gave the following example:

> No amount of radicalism in a Western-trained person can eliminate the Western style of analysis which he acquires. After all, French Marxists are still French in their intellectual style. Ideologically, they may have a lot in common with communist Chinese or communist North Koreans. But in style of reasoning and the idiom of his thought, a French Marxist has more in

common with a French liberal than with fellow communists in
China and Korea. And that is why a French intellectual who is a
Marxist can more easily cease to be a Marxist than he can cease
to be a French intellectual. (1967: 31)

To bring the point home, he distinguished between a 'pro-Western'
attitude and a 'Western' mode of thinking: 'Applying this to Julius
Nyerere, we find that someone like him can more easily cease to be
"pro-Western" than he can cease to be "Westernised" in his basic intellectual style and mental processes. And it is the latter quality which has
often captivated Afrophile Western intellectuals' (1967: 31).

Was Mazrui implying that his interlocuters from the left – this time
not just Nyerere but also Rodney – needed to go beyond changing
phrases, beyond a mere ideological facelift to an epistemological shift?
Mazrui called for a shift of focus, to use his own language in
'Tanzaphilia', from 'ideological orientation' to 'mode of reasoning', or
'intellectual acculturation' and 'style of analysis'. The year was 1967. If
Mazrui evokes Foucault for the reader, let us keep in mind that Foucault
would write about 'discursive formations' in *The Archaeology of
Knowledge* two years later, in 1969.

The development of higher education in Africa is basically a post-independence phenomenon. Except in South and North Africa, the
number of universities founded in the colonial period can be counted
on two hands. There was only one university in Nigeria, with 1 000
students at the end of the colonial period; by 1990, Nigeria would boast
31 universities with 141 000 students (Bako 1993). East Africa had a
single institution of higher learning, Makerere, during the colonial
period. Today, it has over 30. Having a national university was considered as much a hallmark of national independence as having a flag, an
anthem, a central bank and a currency. If Makerere was the quintessential colonial university, UDSM stood as the hallmark of nationalist
assertion. The fortunes of the African university dipped with the fiscal
crisis of the African state and the entry of Bretton Woods institutions,
which claimed to bail out countries in financial trouble in return for
subjecting their public budgets to a strict disciplinary regime. In this
era of structural adjustment, too, Makerere was the model university.

The World Bank took control of Makerere's planning in the late 1980s, at around the same time that the IMF took charge of the Ugandan treasury. The bank proposed a threefold reform, premised on the assumption that higher education is a private good. First, it argued that since the benefit from higher education accrues to an individual, that individual should pay for it by way of fees. Today, nearly 90 per cent of students at Makerere are fee-paying. Second, the bank argued that the university should be run by autonomous departments and not by a centralised administration. This was done by a simple formula: by requiring that 80 per cent of student fees went to the student's disciplinary department or faculty, the bank managed to starve the central administration of funds. Third, the bank said that the curriculum should be revised and made market-friendly and more professional. To give two examples of the changes ushered in at this time: the Department of Geography began to offer a BA in Tourism, and the Institute of Linguistics began offering a BA in Secretarial Studies, whereby a student would be equipped with secretarial skills in more than one language. The Makerere model was exported to other universities in the region and around the continent over the next decade. So it was not a surprise that fees were rising around the same time as 'independence' – transition to majority rule – in South Africa. Nor was it a surprise that expanded entry of black students into 'white' universities was followed by an expanded exit of more and more of the same students, because they were failing either to pay fees or to maintain good academic standing. When more and more of these students looked for explanations for their predicament, the discussion pointed to rising fees and a curriculum which bore little relationship to their life experiences, or family and community histories.

To the distinction Mazrui drew between ideological orientation and mode of reasoning, Rodney had no answer. Mazrui's point was, of course, that though Rodney (like Nyerere) may have had an ideological critique of the West, he was speaking from inside that same Western tradition. Mazrui was right, but then Rodney was not alone in sharing this insider-outsider position. Frantz Fanon was in a similar position. To stay with Mazrui's distinction between 'mode of reasoning' and 'ideological orientation', we may pose a question: is there an intellectual mode of reasoning we can term African, the way Mazrui spoke of a 'French' or a 'Western' mode of reasoning? And by this I mean not a mode of reasoning genetically or ancestrally African, but a discursive tradition constituted by a set of engagements and debates communicated in a common language, weaving a coherent intellectual community into a long-term historical formation.

The language question

Most of us who have come out of colonialism speak more than one language. One of these is the language of colonialism, inevitably a language of science, scholarship and global affairs. The other is a colonised language, a home language whose growth was truncated because colonialism cut short the possibility of the development of an intellectual tradition in the languages of the colonised. As a result, our home languages remain folkloric, shut out of the world of science and learning, high culture, law and government. There are of course exceptions, as always. In East Africa, the exception is Kiswahili, today a language of both popular interaction and culture, and a language of official discourse. Kiswahili is a language of primary and secondary education, but not of university education. At the university level, Kiswahili functions more like a foreign language, with its own department of Kiswahili Studies, *Idara Ya Taasisi Ya Kiswahili*. Not surprisingly, Kiswahili is also not the bearer of either a scientific or a scholarly tradition.

The difference becomes clear if we look at the example of Afrikaans. One needs to recall that Afrikaans – what used to be called kitchen Dutch – developed from a folkloric language to be the bearer of an intellectual tradition in less than half a century. That development would not have been possible without a vast institutional network – ranging from schools and universities to newspapers, magazines and publishing houses, and more, all resourced through public funds. This vast affirmative action programme lifted Afrikaans from its status as a folkloric language to become a language of science and scholarship, high culture and legal discourse in a very short time span. It is no exaggeration to say that Afrikaans represents the most successful decolonising initiative on the African continent. Not only did this happen under apartheid, the great irony is that it was not emulated by the government of independent South Africa.

Many think that the Afrikaans experience is not relevant when it comes to the plurality of African languages. Why? Because it is said that this continent is plagued by extreme linguistic heterogeneity. Numerous studies claim this: from Lord Hailey's 1938 tally of over 700 languages in Africa, to Grimes's more recent 1996 count that upped the number to over 2 000! The point, however, is that the count depended on the definition used to distinguish a language from a dialect.

Let us turn to the neighbourhood for some examples. Is Arabic a single written language, *fusa*, or a federation of multiple spoken dialects? Is Chinese a single written language or also a federation of different spoken dialects? Of course, Arabic is both a single written language and a family of a large number of spoken dialects. And the same goes for Chinese. Dr Jacob Nhlapo, the editor of the *Bantu World* in the 1940s and 1950s, led an untiring campaign to develop two core languages out of the cluster of spoken vernaculars in Nguni- and Sotho-group spoken vernaculars. Dr. Nhlapo was a pioneer who inspired others in the decades that followed, among them Neville Alexander of the University of the Western Cape, and Kwesi Prah of the Centre for the Advanced Study of African Societies in Cape Town.

Ngũgĩ Wa Thiong'o, who talks of the importance of decolonising history, memory and language, has argued that the starting point of decolonisation is language, not geopolitics (1986). Let us return to the problem as I defined it at the beginning: the African university began as a colonial project – a top-down modernist project – its ambition being to transform society in its own image. Add to this the fact that this project was unilingual, it was an English or French or Portuguese language project, and it acknowledged a single intellectual tradition, the Western tradition. At the same time, it aimed to create an apartheid society, one that shut the vast majority of the colonised out of the common discourse of humanity. What would it mean to decolonise such a project?

The East African experience suggests the following: first, socialise the cost of university education, so as to make it more inclusive. In every African country that I know, independence was followed by attempts to socialise spending on health, education, housing and so on.

South Africa is the exception. In practical terms, this means reducing fees – indeed, fees must fall, as demanded by the South African student movement in recent years. I was at the University of Cape Town from 1996 to 1999, in what I thought of as the post-independence era, and was amazed that fees were rising! Second, the decolonising project necessarily has to be a multilingual project whose purpose should be not only to provide Westernised education in multiple languages but also to provide the resources to nurture and develop non-Western intellectual traditions as living traditions with the capacity to sustain public and scholarly discourse.

The challenge is one of inclusion on every level. In South Africa, this is to acknowledge that affordable higher education must become a reality if the end of apartheid has to have meaning for the youth. In a university context, this calls for the establishment of a centre for the study of Nguni and Sotho languages and life traditions, and of associated translation units, which will translate the best of the literature – global, African and South African – into these languages. To broaden our referential world, we need to stop looking to only the West and start getting to know our neighbourhood by investing resources in developing academic units that can study and teach non-Western intellectual traditions. But that study should not be a superficial gloss, a homage to some new fashion. It needs to begin with the understanding that if you want to access a different intellectual tradition, you have to learn the language in which the tradition historically has been forged.

Theory cannot be developed without reference points – and our objective must be to develop new and multiple reference points. Give up the obsession of comparing with the West – the world is larger than we have known. The Sanskrit scholar, Sheldon Pollock, of Columbia University, has fruitfully compared Indian and Chinese worlds (Pollock 2015). The Chinese scholar, Kuan-Hsing Chen, has written a book, *Asia as Method*, calling for comparative studies across Asia (2010). The Senegalese scholar, Souleymane Bachir Diagne, wrote a book on the Urdu poet and philosopher, Muhammad Iqbal (2011). Perhaps the best example of intellectual labours that have gone into rethinking received categories of thought, and formulating new categories adequate to understanding and valorising particular histories and experiences, is the work of Nigerian historians of the University of Ibadan and Ahmadu Bello University. I am thinking of the work on the oral archive for the writing of a history of the premodern, and that on the historicity of ethnic identity by historians from Kenneth Dike to Abdullahi Smith and, above all, Yusufu Bala Usman.[11]

Colonialism brought not only theory from the Western academy but also the assumption that theory is produced in the West and the aim of the academy outside the West is limited to applying that theory. Its implication was radical: if the making of theory was a truly creative act in the West, its application in the colonies became the reverse, a turn-key project that did no more than operationalise theory. This was true on the left as well as on the right, whether student effort was going into the study of Marx and Foucault or of Weber and Huntington. One student after another learned theory as if learning a new language – some remarkably well, others not so well. As they stutter in translation, these others give us an idea of what is wrong with the notion that to be a student is to be a technician whose learning stops with applying a theory produced elsewhere. The unfortunate outcome of such an endeavour is to produce high-cost caricatures, yet another group of mimic men and women for a new era. The alternative is to rethink our aspiration, not just to import theory from outside as another developmental initiative, but to aim differently and not just higher: to theorise our own reality.

The process of knowledge production is based on two distinct but related conversations, local and global. The scholar needs to balance two relationships in the process of knowledge production: one with the society at large, and the other with the scholarly community globally. The local conversation is with different social forces, their needs, their demands, their capacities and their visions. The global conversation is the product of an ongoing global debate within and between disciplines, a debate where geopolitics is of little obvious relevance. The local conversation makes for a public intellectual who is very mindful of political boundaries; the global conversation calls for a scholar who transgresses boundaries. Our challenge is to acknowledge that the public intellectual and the scholar are not two different persona but two sides of a single quest for knowledge. To pursue this quest is to bridge and close the gap between the public intellectual and the scholar.

About the author

Mahmood Mamdani is professor and director, Makerere Institute of Social Research, Kampala and Herbert Lehman Professor of Government, Columbia University, New York City. This chapter is adapted from the 2017 TB Davie Academic Freedom Lecture given at the University of Cape Town, South Africa.

Notes

1   For a fuller discussion, see Pollock (2006) and also Pollock (2015).
2   The point was made generally by Yusufu Bala Usman with reference to the relation between the subjectivity of the writer in relation to the 'objective' reality the writer seeks to understand. See Usman (2006a and 2006b).
3   See Gubara (2013).
4   See Karioki (1974), African scholars versus Ali Mazrui. For Ali Mazrui's response, see Mazrui (1974).
5   Rajat Neogy was jailed by Milton Obote on sedition charges in 1968. *Transition* was revived in Ghana in 1971, and its editorship was taken over by Wole Soyinka in 1973. It folded in 1976 for financial reasons, and was then revived in 1991 by Henry Louis Gates Jr, who brought it to the WEB Du Bois Institute for African and African-American Research at Harvard University where it continues to be based, dislocated both in terms of its vision and its place.
6   JL Kanywanyi (1989) The struggles to decolonize and demystify university education: Dar's 25 years' experience focused on the Faculty of Law, October 1961–October 1986. *Eastern Africa Law Review*, p. 15.
7   Unless otherwise specified, the details in this and the next paragraph are drawn from Kimambo et al. (2008: 124, 125, 118).
8   The interdisciplinary PhD programme in Social Studies, introduced at the Makerere Institute of Social Research (Makerere University), required students to combine a set of interdisciplinary core courses with a major and a minor in two disciplinary specialisations: political economy, political studies, historical studies and cultural studies. See Mamdani (2013).
9   The 'debate' began with a set of critical comments on the writings of Dani Wadada Nabudere and Shivji, but soon turned acerbic, with a series of interventions. Led by

Karim Hirji, they turned the 'debate' into a sharply political exchange devoid of any significant scholarly or even political merit. See Nabudere (1976) and Tandon (1979).

10 In an article that was an earlier version of this chapter, I had mistakenly assumed that Colin Leys had been the principal of Kivokoni College at the time Mazrui wrote 'Tanzaphilia'. Leys wrote a letter to the editor of the *London Review of Books*, pointing out that he had been principal from 1961 to 1962, a year before the University of Dar es Salaam opened its doors. Leys also claims that Kivukoni was not 'the ruling party's ideological school' as I had characterised it but 'a local version of Ruskin College, created by a Ruskin graduate, Joan Wicken'. Leys forgot to add that Wicken was then also Nyerere's principal private secretary. Leys also complained that my article focused on the part and ignored the whole: 'the Cold War context, which conditioned Nyerere's efforts to chart a path out of neocolonialism and avert the risks of the kind of civil conflict that would later cause devastation in so many African countries, including Uganda (it was this, not an abstract idea of what an African university should be that preoccupied most of the left academics at Dar)'. I do not disagree. The article I wrote was admittedly about the university ('the part') and not about Nyerere's rule ('the whole'). Leys accurately describes the frame of mind of the 'left academics at Dar' (among whom I was one). In defining the vocation of the intellectual as predominantly political, they ran the risk of divorcing the public intellectual from the scholar and turning the university into the left wing of the party state. See Mamdani (2018) and Leys (2018).

11 For a brief discussion, see Mamdani (2012), chapter 3.

References

Bako S (1993) Education and adjustment in Nigeria: Conditionality and resistance. In: M Mamdani and M Diouf (eds) *Academic Freedom in Africa*. Dakar: Codesria

Chen K-H (2010) *Asia as Method: Toward Deimperialization*. Durham, NC: Duke University Press

Diagne SB (2011) *Islam and Open Society: Fidelity and Movement in the Philosophy of Muhammad Iqbal*. Dakar: Codesria

Gubara DEM (2013) Al Azhar and the orders of knowledge. Unpublished PhD thesis, Graduate School of Arts and Sciences, Columbia University

Karioki JN (1974) African scholars versus Ali Mazrui. *Transition* 45: 55–63

Kimambo IN (2003) Introduction. In: IN Kimambo (ed.) *Humanities and Social Sciences in East and Central Africa: Theory and Practice*. Dar es Salaam: Dar es Salaam University Press

Kimambo IN (2008) Establishment of teaching programmes. In: IN Kimambo, BBB Mapunda and YQ Lawi (eds) *In Search of Relevance: A History of the University of Dar es Salaam*. Dar es Salaam: Dar es Salaam University Press

Kimambo IN, Mapunda BBB and Lawi YQ (eds) (2008) *In Search of Relevance: A History of the University of Dar es Salaam*. Dar es Salaam: Dar es Salaam University Press

Leys C (2018) Letters: The African university. *London Review of Books* 40(15). Available online

Mamdani M (2012) *Define and Rule: Native as Political Identity*. Cambridge, MA: Harvard University Press

Mamdani M (ed.) (2013) *Getting the Question Right: Interdisciplinary Explorations at Makerere University*. MISR Book Series No. 1. Kampala: Makerere Institute of Social Research

Mamdani M (2018) The African university. *London Review of Books* 40(14): 29–32

Mazrui A (1966) Nkrumah, the Leninist Czar. *Transition* 26: 8–17

Mazrui A (1967) Tanzaphilia: A diagnosis. *Transition* 31: 20–26

Mazrui A (1974) Africa, my conscience and I. *Transition* 46: 67–71

Nabudere DW (1976) *The Political Economy of Imperialism*. Dar es Salaam: Tanzania Publishing House

Pollock S (2006) *The Language of the Gods in the World of Men: Sanskrit, Culture and Power in Premodern India*. Oakland, CA: California University Press

Pollock S (2015) Big comparisons: China, India and methodological cosmopolitanism. Mimeograph. Lecture, Department of Comparative Literature, Brown University, New York, 24 February

Rodney W (1970) *How Europe Underdeveloped Africa*. Dar es Salaam: Tanzania Publishing House

Shivji I (1971) *The Silent Class Struggle*. Dar es Salaam: Tanzania Publishing House

Shivji I (1976) *Class Struggles in Tanzania*. New York and London: Monthly Review Press; also published as Shivji I (1976) *The Class Struggle Continues*. Dar es Salaam: Tanzania Publishing House

Tandon Y (1979) *Imperialism and the State in Tanzania*. Dar es Salaam: Tanzania Publishing House

Tordoff W and Mazrui AA (1972) The left and the super-left in Tanzania. *The Journal of Modern African Studies* 10(3): 427–445

Theroux P (1967) Tarzan is an expatriate. *Transition* 32: 12–19

Thiong'o NW (1986) *Decolonizing the Mind: The Politics of Language in African Literature*. London: James Currey

Usman YB (2006a) History, tradition and reaction. In: *Beyond Fairy Tales: Selected Historical Writings of Yusufu Bala Usman*. Zaria: Abdullahi Smith Center for Historical Research

Usman YB (2006b) The problem of ethnic categories in the study of the historical development of the Central Sudan: A critique of MG Smith and others. In: *Beyond Fairy Tales: Selected Historical Writings of Yusufu Bala Usman*. Zaria: Abdullahi Smith Center for Historical Research

2

Antimicrobial stewardship and conservancy in Africa

L Middleton, F Lampiao, T Zimba, SN Muzime,
GS Simonsen, L Smabrekke, J Musaya, V Solomon,
F Suleman, A Sundsfjord & SY Essack

The Arabic proverb 'If you want to reap once, plant rice; if you want to reap ten times, plant an apple tree; if you want to reap a thousand times, educate people' succinctly summarises our capacity-building project in Malawi and Mozambique targeting antimicrobial resistance (AMR), which is a complex and escalating global public health problem. Effective antibiotics are a cornerstone of preventive and curative modern medicine and the escalation of multidrug-resistant pathogenic bacteria, combined with a lack of new antibiotics, is a true health threat facing humankind. 'Without harmonised and immediate action on a global scale, the world is heading for a post-antibiotic era in which common infections could once again kill' (WHO 2015: vii).

Low- and medium-income countries (LMICs) are likely to develop the highest rates of AMR because the burden of communicable diseases is high and health systems are under resourced. For instance, community-acquired bloodstream infections are a dominant cause of mortality and morbidity in sub-Saharan Africa (Reddy et al. 2010). The long-term trends linked to AMR in bloodstream bacterial infections in a large urban hospital in Malawi reveal a situation '*that is effectively impossible to treat*' (Musicha et al. 2017: 1042, emphasis added).

Aims, objectives and outcomes of the project

In the context of AMR, our project had the overarching aim of human and research development so as to enable optimal management of infections in the context of antimicrobial stewardship and conservancy in Malawi and Mozambique. In particular, the project intended to:

- Strengthen research, curriculum development and pedagogical skills among Mozambican and Malawian academics and health-care professionals in the area of antibiotic stewardship and conservation through the design and implementation of online and research-based postgraduate training programmes.
- Advance optimal management of infections in Mozambique and Malawi by conducting research to generate knowledge and evidence on the nature and extent of antimicrobial resistance with a view to designing context-specific interventions for its containment.

To achieve these project objectives, we framed project outcomes for each country, with project specific indicators to monitor and measure progress as shown in Table 2.1.

Table 2.1 Planned project outcomes with illustrative result indicators

Project outcomes	Illustrative result indicators
Strengthening higher education institutions in Malawi and Mozambique	Year-on-year increase in: • The number of postgraduate programmes • The number of postgraduate students, specifically women, who graduate • Research outputs, specifically with women as first authors
Strengthening health systems in Malawi and Mozambique	Optimising the management of infections and infectious diseases by the development and piloting of models for: • A reference laboratory • Surveillance of antimicrobial use and resistance to inform treatment guidelines and formularies • Establishing antibiotic stewardship and/or infection prevention control and/or Pharmacy and Therapeutics Committees centrally or within institutions

Project outcomes	Illustrative result indicators
Enhanced research capacity/competency	Year-on-year increase in: Research output, in the form of dissertations, theses, publications, monographs, conference presentations, specifically by women Number of postgraduate students supervised and graduated, specifically by women faculty
Human capacity development	Year-on-year increase in the number of faculty and/or healthcare professionals promoted to higher levels, specifically women Co- and cohort supervision, specifically of and by women faculty, jointly instituted between partners
Context-specific knowledge generation to inform policy and practice	Generation of evidence-based policy briefs on issues such as health and higher education; guidelines and/or formularies for the management of infections
Increased participation and stature of women in education, research and policy-making	Increasing numbers of women recruited for postgraduate training, as well as programme development and management

Project implementation and stewardship approach

Following a collaborative approach, partners from the South – the University of Malawi's College of Medicine (UNIMA), Mozambique's Instituto Superior de Ciências de Saúde (ISCISA) and South Africa's University of KwaZulu-Natal (UKZN) – and the North – the Arctic University of Norway (UiT) – implemented the project plan in three non-linear phases. Phase one included a situational and gap analysis of antimicrobial use and AMR in Mozambique and Malawi. This informed subsequent research and capacity-building initiatives. Phase two involved the establishment of relevant infrastructure, including reference and research laboratories in Mozambique and Malawi, as well as the development of an e-learning master's programme that targeted but was not limited to antimicrobial use and resistance as well as stewardship theory and practice. Phase three focused on capacity development using the WHO One Health approach (encompassing humans, animals and the environment) (WHO 2015) to recruit an interdisciplinary and gender-balanced cohort of master's and PhD students. In addition, cohort supervision teams were assembled – including biomedical engineers, environmental biologists, nurses, pharmacists, physicians, and veterinarians – and a structured approach to research supervision was agreed to.

Three principles underpinned project governance and our approach to building technical capacity. These were: collaboration, equity in decision-making, and the continual alignment of project activities with existing strategic and operational plans in each country (Holmarsdottir et al. 2013). In addition, at one of the first project meetings, all partners endorsed the notion that the project should be mutually and reciprocally beneficial. That is, we tried to maintain horizontal relationships based on an agreement that, even in the presence of asymmetrical technical, financial resources, South–South–North partnerships must balance the interests of all partners and strive for symmetrical engagement in project activities (Besharati et al. 2015, 2017).

Considering the complexity of the AMR-problem and the need to adopt the One Health approach, the project involved multiple sectors in each of the partner countries. Furthermore, the project steering committee included key representatives from the health and education ministries in Malawi and Mozambique as well as from the WHO Regional Office for Africa. These bodies collectively helped to inform decision-making processes and to ensure the alignment of project activities with country strategies and resources already allocated to dealing with AMR. This close and sustained co-operation between academia and government created a solid foundation for the implementation of the One Health approach, with some government and academic partners noting that 'this is the first time we have ever met' and 'it helps now we know who to contact'. Moreover, the participation of high-level delegates from the ministries in the steering committee was decisive in anchoring the project politically, and thus ensuring national ownership and long-term sustainability.

Global forces shaping the project

As the project was being rolled out in 2014, AMR, and specifically antibiotic stewardship for the conservation of antibiotics, was simultaneously gaining political momentum globally. AMR features in several international resolutions such as the International Health Regulations, the Global Action Plan on AMR (WHO 2015) and the 2016 adoption by the UN General Assembly of the Political Declaration on AMR, to which both Mozambique and Malawi are signatories. As shown in Table 2.2, this project advanced the compliance of these two countries with the international resolutions. As our project's principal investigator from Malawi remarked, the project also gave effect to Malawi's own 'One Health Roadmap', and responded to the findings of the *Situation Analysis and Recommendations on Antibiotic Use and Resistance in Mozambique* (GARP-M 2015), which was a precursor to Mozambique's 2016 National Action Plan on AMR.[1]

Table 2.2 Global resolutions on AMR and country responses

Global resolutions	Malawi	Mozambique
WHO Assembly Resolutions 58.3 of 2005 and 65.23 of 2012 adopted the International Health Regulations. These require all member states to develop and implement national action plans to build or strengthen their capacities to detect, assess and report public health events (WHO 2016).	Malawi endorsed the WHO Resolutions and established a One Health Committee that has been strengthened through project support.	In 2016, Mozambique underwent a Joint External Evaluation using the WHO IHR tool. Priority actions identified include a comprehensive implementation of the One Health approach across the public health sector and government, as well as further investment in related human resources, infrastructure and maintenance.
WHO Assembly Resolution 68.7 requires member states to have national action plans in place to address AMR by May 2017 (WHO 2015). In 2016, the UN General Assembly adopted the Political Declaration on AMR, endorsed the WHO resolution and required national action plans to be aligned with the WHO's Global Action Plan on AMR.	In 2016, as part of the project, Malawi completed a comprehensive situational analysis of AMR to inform government policy and strategy. In 2017, the health ministry led the development of the government's AMR Strategy 2017–2022. In 2018, this strategy was submitted for approval as the Malawian National Action Plan on AMR.	In 2012, the health ministry developed a national policy to protect citizens against the ravages of antibiotic resistance. In 2015, GARP-Mozambique produced its first situational analysis and recommendations on antibiotic use and AMR to inform a national action plan (GARP-M 2015). In 2016, the country's National Action Plan on AMR was finalised.

Our approach to technical assistance, capacity building and partnership

Following the principle of mutual benefit for partners in this project, we mapped the technical and capacity-building needs and capabilities of each institution relative to agreed project outcomes. Both UKZN (the main Southern partner) and UiT (the Northern partner) already had a strong research focus on AMR and were able offer a wide range of technical assistance and capacity-building expertise linked to the project objectives, specifically in the areas of AMR research, research supervision and the mentoring of faculty members. For partners at UKZN and UiT, the project provided new insights into the complexity of project implementation in a new LMIC context.

UKZN's School of Health Sciences has a well-established Antimicrobial Research Unit that delineates the nature, extent and molecular epidemiology of antibiotic resistance in human, animal and environmental health, and uses the One Health approach to inform evidence-based strategies for AMR monitoring, prevention and containment. The university also hosts the South African Research Chair in Antibiotic Resistance and One Health. When the incumbent chair agreed to act as principal investigator (PI) to this project, access to national, regional and international AMR networks immediately expanded. For this reason, UKZN took the lead on postgraduate and educational infrastructure development for this project, leading the establishment of the online master's programme, including curriculum design, content development and training in online pedagogy and assessment. UKZN also revised its existing online Master of Health Sciences to include modules in antibiotic stewardship and conservancy. In the first year of the Norhed grant, faculty from Mozambique and Malawi enrolled in this programme. In this way, the project developed a set of academics and researchers in AMR who could then support project implementation in the field.

Similarly, UiT had developed strong interdisciplinary research and educational capacity within AMR in partnership with the University Hospital of North Norway (UNN). The main research activities include mechanisms related to resistance development, the molecular epidemiology of AMR, human–microbe–drug interactions, antibiotic-prescription epidemiology and intervention studies, as well as antibiotic drug design and development. UNN and UiT also host the Norwegian Organization for Surveillance of Antimicrobial Resistance and the Norwegian National Advisory Unit on Detection of AMR, and are partners in multiple national and international AMR-related research networks, including the European Commission's Joint Programming Initiative on AMR. In this project, UiT took the lead on optimising Malawi's and Mozambique's reference laboratories so that they can function as national hubs for knowledge and expertise in the performance and interpretation of antimicrobial susceptibility testing (AST). These laboratories were also a crucial element in creating the infrastructure necessary for enabling microbiology-related MSc and PhD studies within the project. In addition, UiT played a leading role in the theoretical and practical training of students and faculty in AST, as well as in basic statistical and epidemiological methods. Both UiT and UNN participated in research-proposal development, organised via interactive workshops and student mentoring.

For ISCISA, having access to this regional and international expertise in AMR expedited project implementation, specifically in relation to the development of new postgraduate programmes in AMR, and being able to conduct research in AMR priority areas. The upgrading of the Mozambique's national reference laboratory was crucial in helping ISCISA address key issues linked to the challenges of AMR in Mozambique. At the same time, by relying heavily on intersectoral collaboration, the project operationalised existing relations between research units focused on human, animal and agricultural health, as well as between the university and national health and laboratory services. That is, by leveraging this national pool of diverse capacity development, technical resources and expertise in AMR, the project was able to offer postgraduate programmes in the field of AMR for the first time at this institution.

Similarly, at the College of Medicine at UNIMA, having access to this expertise accelerated the growth of their own suite of long-standing postgraduate and PhD programmes so that the institution was able to offer its first online interdisciplinary master's degree in health sciences with a focus on AMR research.

Knowledge and gender gains in Mozambique and Malawi

Overall, as shown in Table 2.3, the AMR partnership facilitated the strengthening of higher education institutions and health systems in Mozambique and Malawi, enhancing academics' research and professional skills, generating knowledge to inform best practices in AMR containment, and, to some extent, increasing the participation of women in science.

With respect to the latter two areas, knowledge generation is emergent, as is evident from the range of postgraduate research topics, and from the results of the national situational analyses of AMR and national AMR research priority setting. The research priority-setting exercise yielded 16 research-domain clusters with 108 topics in Malawi, and 20 research-domain clusters with 76 topics in Mozambique. The research clusters were similar for both countries, spanning areas such as: laboratory studies, sources of supply, environmental reservoirs, animals and agriculture, AMR in specific diseases, the burden of AMR, health-worker competencies, community practices, policy and legislation and indigenous knowledge. Research topics covered by the first cohort of master's and PhD students aligned both with these clusters and with global AMR research priorities. Topics included: the epidemiology of AMR in hospitals and the community; the prevalence of AMR in the food chain; studies of antibiotic use, supply and expenditure; and knowledge and attitudes related to antibiotics and AMR among students, healthcare workers and patients.

Globally, more women are pursuing careers in the health sciences but a gender gap remains visible, expanding at PhD level and peaking at postdoctoral level, with women constituting only 28.4 per cent of the world's scientists working in research and development in 2013 (Unesco 2015). In the partnership, Norway ranks highest (6th) on the gender equality index for 188 countries, followed by South Africa (90th),

Table 2.3 Project outcomes and illustrative gains for Malawi and Mozambique

Project outcomes	Illustrative gains	
	ISCISA	**UNIMA**
Strengthened higher education institutions	Master's in Health Sciences (online programme) approved by relevant authorities	
	E-teaching and learning platforms installed and IT personnel trained	
	Developed and introduced the first Master's in Health Sciences (Research) with an AMR focus; 14 students from health, agriculture and veterinary services enrolled	Master's in Philosophy (AMR Research) introduced, with 10 students proposed for enrolment
Strengthened health systems	Established and launched the first national reference laboratory and provided training in AST	Refurbished, equipped and launched the national reference laboratory and provided training in AST
Enhanced research capacity/ competency	Ongoing training in research proposal development, data analysis, scientific writing, and research supervision	
Staff development	Exchanges of technical staff, faculty and students in various areas, including molecular epidemiological laboratory work, online teaching pedagogies, IT, qualitative data analysis	
	10 faculty members, 70 per cent of whom are women, are undertaking postgraduate study with an AMR focus	8 faculty members, 37 per cent of whom are women, are undertaking postgraduate study with an AMR focus
Context-specific knowledge generation to inform policy and practice	National situational analysis on AMR was conducted using the One Health approach in partnership with government ministries (health, education, agriculture and veterinary services) professional councils and associations, and a report was submitted to the Ministry of Health	
	National consensus was reached on priority research areas for the optimal management of infections in the context of antimicrobial stewardship and conservancy. This was developed across sectors including health, veterinary medicine, and agriculture/environment	
Increased participation and stature of women in education, research and policy-making	Increasing participation of women in project leadership roles and in postgraduate programmes, but overall women constitute only 36 per cent (21 out of 58) of project participants in 2016.	Participation of women significantly improved, especially with respect to project leadership, with women constituting 89 per cent (28 out of 53) of project participants in 2016.

Mozambique (139th) and Malawi (145th) (UNDP 2016). Noting that women are disproportionately under-represented in certain areas of health services and education (among physicians and faculty, for example) and over-represented in others (such as nursing), a concerted effort was made to ensure at least 50 per cent of project participants at master's and PhD level were female. Overall, the participation of women in the project improved from 34 per cent in 2014 to approximately 43 per cent in 2015 and to 60 per cent in 2016. Mozambique, in particular, made great strides in gender equity, with women constituting 89 per cent (28 out of 53) of project participants in 2016.

Sustainability

In the context of this project, we defined sustainability as the continuation of the project goals, principles and efforts to achieve desired outcomes. As the project period ended, it was clear that the project was well-established. The project team therefore assessed the programme in relation to its initial goals and planned for the future. A summary of this assessment is provided below

At UNIMA's College of Medicine

The antimicrobial stewardship programme at the College of Medicine, UNIMA is likely to be sustained for several reasons. Firstly, there is a very strong buy-in from the institution's top management because of the close alignment of the project activities with the College's development plan. Senior leaders in the College willingly support the activities of the project and, through regular monitoring, ensure that the team delivers in the interests of the institution and the project.

Secondly, project stewardship processes and structures have been systematically embedded within the College structure, assuring their continuation beyond the funding period. For instance, the project's PI is also deputy dean of the Faculty of Biomedical Sciences, while the co-PI who is responsible for overseeing education and research is also dean of postgraduate studies and research. Having people in such key positions in the College increased awareness of the project within and beyond the College and improved project implementation.

Thirdly, the programme is pioneering the introduction of online teaching in the College. This aligns with the institution's long-term vision and strategic development plan, which means the College will continue supporting the project after the funding period lapses.

Fourthly, the project involved key national stakeholders, including the Ministry of Health, which sees antimicrobial stewardship as a priority area. Reasons for this include the fact that Malawi is listed among the world's least developed countries, and drug resources in most of the country's health facilities are extremely limited. This makes AMR an even bigger threat here than it is in more prosperous countries. In addition, the health ministry and mission hospitals support the project because it ensured that their staff received much-needed training and their reference laboratory infrastructure and equipment was upgraded. Ongoing collaboration between the health ministry and the project is crucial for project sustainability. Already, the health ministry has enabled key staff members to join the postgraduate programme and has taken responsibility for supporting the reference laboratory. Through their membership of the project's national steering committee, senior members of the ministry helped shape the direction of the project, and were kept informed of project activities to ensure the alignment of the project with the interests of the ministry and the university.

Finally, the project has a working understanding of, and good relationships with, other projects in the College. For example, the Africa Centre of Excellence in Public Health and Herbal Medicine, which has indicated a willingness to fund students with limited resources who wish to pursue the MSc offered by the project. This intra-project goodwill ensures that sufficient numbers of students enrol in the programme each year, thus helping to ensure the sustainability of the project.

At ISCISA

Five key factors support the sustainability of the AMR stewardship programme at ISCISA. Firstly, the ministries of health, agriculture and the environment, as well as GARP-Mozambique, see AMR as a top priority in their respective action plans. ISCISA formulated and reached collaborative agreements with these partners, to address AMR using the One Health approach within the project context. Secondly, through the project, the abovementioned multisectoral group developed and finalised the country's National Action Plan, operationalising the country's commitment to containing AMR and preserving antibiotics. Thirdly, the new reference laboratory increases not only the health system's capacity but also the capacities of the ministries of agriculture and the environment with regard to AST for AMR containment. The health ministry has undertaken to ensure a continuous supply of reagents and the maintenance of equipment in the laboratory. Fourthly, the solid South–South–North bonds established during this project set the foundation for ongoing collaboration and technology transfer. Finally, as noted, ISCISA launched its first ever master's programme in 2016, in the area of antimicrobial stewardship and conservancy. Over time, this programme will help create the critical mass of health workers that the country needs to address this public health threat.

Conclusion

To sum up, the project facilitated compliance with national, regional, and international commitments, advanced the mobilisation of formal collaborations between government ministries around the common goal of AMR containment, and generated knowledge from research to inform country-specific policy and practice using the One Health approach.

Although the project exceeded its objectives in several ways, it also faced substantive, albeit not insurmountable, challenges. The main challenges included finding ways to address the intractable issue of gender inequality, some over-reliance on UKZN and the UiT partners and hesitancy from UNIMA and ISCISA to assume full ownership of the project in the penultimate project year as had been planned.

The project continues to tackle gender inequality through the targeted recruitment of women to its postgraduate programmes, through outreach programmes targeting schools that encourage girl children to choose science subjects, and through participating in national discussion forums on gender equality. In terms of project ownership, joint sustainability planning exercises, drawing on the principles of mutual benefit and symmetrical engagement, cleared the path for the transfer of powers and responsibilities.

Key to the project's successes were the fact that this South–South–North partnership was committed to national capacity building that would address the global AMR challenge. In addition, we had a strong Southern institutional partner with long-term experience in addressing the specific challenges related to African health and higher education, and a well-resourced Northern partner committed to sharing its theoretical and practical knowledge and experience in AMR and to supporting the Southern institutions to adapt this knowledge to their local context. Importantly, anchoring the project leadership at high institutional level, and recruiting key representatives from the ministries of health and education on to the steering committee, were imperative for creating local ownership and sustainability. Collectively, all partners contributed to the development of national capacity in AMR in the South through the training of high-calibre graduates at master's and PhD level who will continue to generate and disseminate local evidence for reducing AMR, train local clinicians in AMR stewardship practices and be prepared to take on leadership positions in academic and government health and laboratory services.

About the authors and the project

L Middleton is based at the Department of Pharmacy, School of Health Sciences at University of KwaZulu-Natal (UKZN), South Africa

F Lampiao is based at the Department of Physiology, College of Medicine at the University of Malawi (UNIMA), Malawi

T Zimba is based at the Instituto Superior de Ciências de Saúde (ISCISA) and Maputo Central Hospital, Mozambique

GS Simonsen is based at the Department of Medical Biology at UiT The Arctic University of Norway (UiT), and Department of Microbiology and Infection Control at University Hospital of North Norway (UNN)

L Smabrekke is based at the Department of Pharmacy at UiT

J Musaya is based at the Department of Pathology, College of Medicine at UNIMA

SN Muzime is based at the Instituto Superior de Ciências de Saúde (ISCISA), Mozambique

V Solomon is based at the Department of Pharmacy, School of Health Sciences, UKZN

F Suleman is based at the Department of Pharmacy, School of Health Sciences, UKZN

Arnfinn Sundsfjord is based at the Department of Medical Biology at UiT and
Department of Microbiology and Infection Control, UNN
SY Essack is based at the Department of Pharmacy, School of Health Sciences, UKZN

Project title: Antimicrobial Stewardship and Conservancy in Africa
Partner institutions: University of KwaZulu-Natal (South Africa), Arctic University of
Norway (Norway), College of Medicine, University of Malawi (Malawi) and the
Instituto Superior de Ciências de Saúde in Mozambique (ISCISA)

Notes

1   At the time of writing, the 2016 plan was still being approved; this occurred in early
2019 but the plan has yet to be disseminated.

References

Besharati N, Moilwa M, Khunou K and Rios O (2015) *Developing a Conceptual Framework
for South–South Co-operation.* NeST Africa working document, University of the
Witwatersrand, School of Governance, available online
Besharati N, Rawhani C and Rios O (2017) *A Monitoring and Evaluation Framework for
South–South Co-operation.* NeST Africa working paper, University of the Witwatersrand,
School of Governance. Available online
GARP-M (Global Antibiotic Resistance Partnership, Mozambique Working Group) (2015)
Situation Analysis and Recommendations: Antibiotic Use and Resistance in Mozambique.
Washington, DC and New Delhi: Center for Disease Dynamics, Economics and Policy
Holmarsdottir HB, Desai Z, Botha LR, Breidlid A, Bastien S, Mukoma W, Nomlomo V et al.
(2013). Compare Forum: The idea of North–South and South–South Collaboration.
Compare 43(2): 265–286
Musicha P, Cornick JE, Bar-Zeev N, French N, Masesa C, Denis B, Feasey NA et al. (2017).
Trends in antimicrobial resistance in bloodstream infection isolates at a large urban
hospital in Malawi, 1998–2016: A surveillance study. *The Lancet Infectious Diseases*
17(10): 1042–1052
Reddy E, Shaw AV and Crump J (2010) Community-acquired bloodstream infections in
Africa: A systematic review and meta-analysis. *The Lancet Infectious Diseases*, 10(6):
417–432
UNDP (2016) *Human Development Report 2016: Human Development for Everyone.* New
York
Unesco (2015) *Unesco Science Report: Towards 2030.* Paris

WHO (World Health Organization) (2015) *Global Action Plan on Antimicrobial Resistance.* Geneva

WHO (2016) *Joint External Evaluation Tool: International Health Regulations, 2005.* Geneva. Available online

3

Bridging gaps, building futures: Global journalism and local practices

Kristin Skare Orgeret & William Tayeebwa

Introduction: A global journalism?

In this chapter, we discuss central understandings from the Norwegian Programme for Capacity Development in Higher Education and Research for Development (Norhed) project, 'Bridging Gaps, Building Futures: Strengthening Media in Post-conflict Societies through Education and Research', a collaboration between institutions offering journalism education in Nepal, South Sudan, Uganda and Norway. We explore journalism education in these countries, noting that all the South partners were considered to be post-conflict societies at the outset of the project. In line with the principles of the Norhed programme, these curricula were developed partly through a collaboration between researchers in the three South countries and Norway, and involved both a South–North and a South–South type of knowledge interaction.

The project was particularly sensitive to how global norms and ethics underpin the journalist's meeting with local experiences, norms and values. Our starting point is that the ultimate goal of journalism education, regardless of its provider, is to empower not only the student but journalism itself (Berger and Foote 2017). In other words, its goal of strengthening the role of journalism in democratic societies, such as to provide information about people's rights, to uncover illegal activities, to function as a two-way channel between those who govern and the governed and to shape social identity (see e.g. Orgeret and Tayeebwa 2016), is as important as its goal of training journalists. The quality of journalism education will impact on the quality of citizenship and society. Hence journalism education educates not only practitioners, but the public as well (Berger and Foote 2017). This echoes Unesco's statement that journalism education is essential 'for the underpinning of key democratic principles that are fundamental to the development of every country' (Tibbitts 2007: 5).

It is often argued that although media systems and journalistic cultures may differ widely, the changes and challenges facing journalism education around the world are largely similar, and thus would benefit from a 'global' approach (see e.g. Deuze 2006). This is also a principle of the current Unesco curriculum model, which is globally developed, rich in content from different settings, and attempts to set standards based on good practice internationally, in this way providing a resource on which stakeholders around the world can draw in order to improve the quality of journalism education in their countries. Previous cross-national work in the field, such as that offered by Frohlich and Holtz-Bacha (2003) signal an ever-increasing international formalisation and standardisation as a fundamental feature of developments in journalism education worldwide. Many of these central standards stem from Europe and North America, and increasingly, lately, it has been argued that there is a continuous need to focus on decolonisation or de-Westernisation of the academic field – journalism included.

In this chapter, we discuss some of the key experiences from our project and whether professionalisation of journalism education in South Sudan, Uganda and Nepal may be seen as part of a modernisation project, or, rather, as shaped by values stemming from local settings and adjusted to local needs? Or is it both? The South–South dimension of our project is highlighted and we also discuss the need for journalism to reflect the constantly changing demands of the media industry while focusing on larger political and social issues. In doing so, the aim of this chapter is to participate in a broader discussion on transnational co-operation and processes that Roland Robertson (1992), in a somewhat convoluted way, referred to as the 'universalisation of the particular and the particularisation of the universal' – in other words, globalisation seen as both sameness and diversity.

Journalism and global norms

Journalism training in the global South, particularly in sub-Saharan Africa, borrows extensively from the Unesco model curricula for journalism education (Unesco 2013). Our Norhed project was no exception. While reviewing curricula under the Norhed project, we found that the Unesco model curricula provided a ready tool to be adopted and adapted to local training settings in Nepal, Uganda and South Sudan. Within the Unesco model curricula for journalism education, several pertinent themes relevant to global South settings are proposed, including community radio journalism, humanitarian journalism, reporting on human trafficking and media sustainability. Other relevant themes proposed in the model curricula are data journalism, science journalism, gender and journalism, as well as global and intercultural journalism (Unesco 2013). Challenges that came with the 2008 economic crisis amid technological changes within the media, coupled with an increasing immigration crisis that posed both real and imagined security threats are relevant themes, for the global North as well as the global South, that the curricula explore. Eric Freedman and Richard Shafer (2010) argue that the Unesco model offers a valuable, welcome springboard for discussion of effective, pragmatic ways to improve journalism education. It provides a multinationally endorsed, credible leverage point for educators to promote curricular modernisation in their own countries and universities. Freedman and Shafer also stress that 'working effectively to improve the quality of journalism education in a wide range of national settings and under a wide range of media and academic environments will require educators and professionals to eschew what Brislin calls belief in "the universal portability of Western values"' (2010: 35).

It is commonly argued that since the birth of modern journalism in Europe in the seventeenth century, some standardised values have become central to the profession (Deuze 2006; Weaver 1998). Even though researchers agree that certain values of journalism have universal application, there are legitimate differences in journalistic culture from one country to another that are of interest to issues of professional ideology (for example see Hanitzsch et al. 2011). The concept of objectivity is one where the universalism and difference discussion becomes particularly relevant. Alternative 'journalisms'[1] or press systems, such as development journalism and peace journalism, are not given detailed discussion in the Unesco model, perhaps because peace journalism and development journalism are more closely connected to advocacy, which clashes with the objectivity ideal of the universal model of journalism. When objectivity is contrasted with advocacy, it primarily connotes neutrality and detachment. 'Objective reporting' conjures up the distinction between facts and values, typically in journalism between news and opinion genres. The norm of advocacy, by contrast, is loaded with values and adherents of advocacy are often explicit about these values. Advocacy journalism and its central principles, such as closeness, empathy and social commitment may challenge the notion of objectivity (Krøvel, Orgeret and Ytterstad 2012). We believe our project gained from having specialists on peace journalism and development journalism in the Norhed network to fill in the gaps of the Unesco model, thus strengthening our project. In particular, peace journalism, as proposed by Johan Galtung (2002) includes practical methods for correcting the bias towards war journalism, by allowing society at large to consider and value non-violent and often local responses to conflict. The inclusion of peace journalism as an important element of our project added to and also challenged the universal journalistic model.

The very first PhD thesis coming out of our project, Gerald Walulya's 'Hybrid journalism' (2018) illustrates this powerfully, as hybrid journalism is a mixture of what might be called professional and unprofessional journalism, and highlights the tension between universal professional ideals such as objectivity, and the activism of local realities. Analysis of the press coverage of elections in the one-party-dominant states of Tanzania and Uganda reveals that the African realities described do not really fit the instruments developed elsewhere. Walulya's discussion offers a clear indication of the tensions and shows that agenda-setting theory, for instance, is not applicable to the situation in Uganda and Tanzania. Methodologies developed in another context may not cater for some of the local professional particularities, such as the 'underground markets of journalism' in Uganda and Tanzania, where bribes and corruption are widespread during election periods (Walulya 2018).

Neocolonialism, post-colonialism and the Norhed project: Turning the tide?

Anthea Garman advises that we must 'never forget that most of the theory and methodology we use in media and communication studies did not come out of Africa, and that much of it has ambiguous histories of alliance with colonial power' (Garman 2015: 17). Along the same lines, Last Moyo and Bruce Mutsvairo argue that 'all scholars must realise and acknowledge their physical location in relation to the global power structure of colonial modernity in terms of the geopolitics and biopolitics of knowledge production' (2018: 22).

For most African scholars in this field and other disciplines, Europe is generally perceived as the source of theory, while Africa can only provide case studies for testing Western theory (Comaroff and Comaroff 2012). This dependence has traditionally been exacerbated by the global political economy of publishing. And, of course, a lot of the literature is still produced in the North. Thus a very positive outcome of the Norhed project is that new journalism scholarship is being produced within the network, including by local scholars in South Sudan, Uganda and Nepal. Some of it explicitly problematises the universality of existing theories and methods, not only drawing their agency from local history and experiences, but also critically engaging with reigning epistemologies. All of the published work will make important additions to local, and hopefully also global, reading lists. Whereas the first Norhed anthology (Orgeret and Tayeebwa 2016) was published by an open access Northern publisher with global outreach (Nordicom), the second anthology will be published by *The Journal of African Media Studies*. The 2016 anthology on post-conflict journalism focuses on both the role of journalism in the period after conflicts and the tension built into the vocation of the journalist. The chapters seek to probe the contradictory character of the journalist's vocation: to report on conflict but also to build consensus on the way out of it.

What, in this context, is the meaning of mediation and reconciliation? Are journalists external to the conflict? Can they be objective or should they recognise their own limitations, thereby reporting all sides of the conflict? What are the moral dilemmas faced by a war journalist as opposed to a peace journalist, since the former is more likely to turn into an official mouthpiece? The questions are addressed in a variety of contexts drawn from those directly involved in the Norhed project – Nepal, Norway, South Sudan and Uganda – as well as from Afghanistan, Colombia, Libya and Syria.

Carr (2003: 133) identifies three core issues in the debate about curriculum: purpose, form, and content. Curriculum research, Carr argues, walks a fine line between identifying 'which potentially objective kinds or forms of knowledge and understanding are appropriate for inclusion', and taking into consideration the cultural, historical and geographical factors that determine educational value for the particular social constituency involved. This balancing act was indeed experienced in the joint work on the curricula within our project. Contrary to positivists' claims of objectivity, we found that both research and journalism are processes that are manifestly ideological, cultural and political. Thus although there are very good reasons to develop strong frameworks to guide researchers, educators and journalists, there can never be only one critical way of thinking about or presenting phenomena. As Chakrabarty reminds us, all research is always deeply embedded in the power relations between the knower and the known and produces theory that is inherently limited since it cannot 'transcend places of [its] origin' (2000: 12). Hence, to adjust to local needs was an important outcome for our project, specifically so that new and relevant research material would be produced, highly relevant for teaching (discussions of teaching methods are also core here). According to Priyamvada Gopal (2017), *decolonising* the *curriculum* means, first of all, the acceptance that education, literary or otherwise, needs to enable self-understanding. This, she argues, is particularly important for people not used to seeing themselves reflected in the mirror of conventional learning or in the mainstream media. Decolonising should also be about including more women's voices, thus increasing the percentage of female contributors was also an explicit aim of our project. This was a good reason for making sure that at least half of our project's PhDs were women; in addition, one of the PhD projects focused specifically on the role of women journalists in Nepal. Samiksha Koirala's (2018) 'Gender representations in the Nepali press during pre-conflict, conflict and post-conflict periods' explores post-colonial feminism, which points to the lack of racial diversity in Western feminists' understanding and representations of gender and rejects the universalising tendencies of mainstream feminist ideas. Koirala's doctoral thesis also demonstrates how women, despite having been active in the revolution, are seldom given any power when it is redistributed and how each conflict and post-conflict situation has unique traits, specific to local realities.

The changing face of journalism practice

When Marshall McLuhan (1964) pronounced his widely quoted dictum that 'the medium is the message' as well as the term 'global village' to explain the rise of television as a mass medium in the North America of the 1960s, he surely had no idea that a few decades later the internet would indeed make his satirical observations a reality. Yet, the emergence of new media tools and technologies, heralded by what Manuel Castells (1996) described as the 'network society' and the 'information age', is most ubiquitous in a phenomenon variously referred to as 'social media' or 'social networking sites' (Kaplan and Haenlein 2010). One PhD thesis emerging from our project, Florence Namasinga's 'Sourcing in converged media spheres', analyses the use of social media for sourcing information, and the extent to which social media sources are used in newspaper articles in Uganda, in order to provide a better understanding of how online social networks influence journalistic sourcing practices, reportage and professionalism. The study is premised on the assumption that newspaper journalists deploy social media sources heavily in published articles – more heavily than they acknowledge, out of a conviction to maintain professional norms and practices. Social media – Twitter, Facebook, Instagram, YouTube and others – have already changed the face of journalism practice in many ways, presenting journalists and their sources with opportunities such as improved access to online resources and instantaneous sharing of information, but also with professional challenges such as the potential for dissemination of unsubstantiated information that often turns out to be outright false or defamatory (see e.g. Tandoc et al. 2018).

Whereas the responsive journalism institutions have exploited the opportunities that social media offer by creating online platforms that can be used as a source of news and as distribution channels, those that remain cautious and timid will most likely be left in the ruins of history (Reese and Cohen 2000). Even for countries in the global South, the internet, particularly as accorded by mobile telephones, has opened up opportunities for communities to source news content and provide it directly to interested audiences without the traditional gatekeepers and agenda-setters in newsrooms (Wiik 2009).

According to scholars such as Ganaele Langlois (2011), social media have made it possible for anyone with access to technologies such as a smartphone and/or any other forms of technology-mediated communication to gather, process and disseminate information to others. In the electronic media world of radio and television, whoever has such facilities can make their own broadcasts, and by doing so assume the job of the conventional journalist. Authors such as Abdelhay (2012) and Bibuli (2014) have noted how social media sites rival traditional media such as newspapers and television as sources of news and information, and by doing so, also diminish the role of traditional journalists. Others, such as Naughton (2013) and Kirkpatrick (2010), have noted the increasing power of Twitter and Facebook as effective news-sharing outlets, to become de facto 'global newswires'. Nonetheless, scholars such as Hujanen (2017) remind us that the phenomenon of social media ought not to take away the values and principles on which journalism as a profession is founded. Such principles – truthfulness and accuracy, balance and fairness, objectivity and impartiality, neutrality and detachment, for example – are inviolable norms (Rich 2009).

While social media afford ease of access to and distribution of information, it is the function of conventional journalism to ensure that the information to be disseminated adheres to the norms of the profession, and to the ethical principles that media houses define in codes of conduct so as to safeguard the well-being of the public. The new media tools may take away the role of the journalist as the first chronicler of events, but they should not take away the role of journalists and editors in checking that the news provides credible information and adheres to the professional values of quality (Reese and Cohen 2000). Clearly, therefore, traditional ways of educating journalists remain relevant in order to safeguard the sacrosanct values of the profession. This traditional approach operates alongside the move towards the deployment of new media tools in response to the changing dynamics of the profession and the various local realities in which journalists work.

New dynamics and journalism professional needs

Most, if not all, journalism training institutions realise the changing face of the profession due to advances in technology. Whereas the Unesco model curricula are not particularly strong on, for instance, online journalism or even what has been referred to as multimedia journalism, the compendium still recognises the new media tools afforded by the computer and the various software applications as concomitant to the training of the 21st century journalist. For instance, in the discussion on community radio journalism, the model curriculum proposes that 'the internet and other "new media" technology' are a good 'source of information to enrich community radio broadcasting, and as a distribution channel for community radio' (Unesco 2013: 79). The curriculum further notes the 'use of technology such as internet streaming and mobile-phone-based broadcasting' such as SoundCloud (2013: 80). The revisions of the 'multimedia journalism' and 'online journalism' curricula in Uganda, South Sudan and Nepal under the Norhed project, however, were fully cognisant of the new dynamics and therefore new professional training needs, and heavily incorporated social media as new tools for the field. In 2018 Unesco launched an additional handbook for journalism education and training, *Journalism, 'Fake News' and Disinformation*, which includes topics such as the transformation of the news industry and social media verification (Unesco 2018).

Of particular interest to journalists in the global South is the fact that the use of social media or social networking sites provides an improved opportunity for them to circumvent draconian media regulatory regimes that are often not adapted to the new technologies. According to the 2017 World Press Freedom Index by Reporters Without Borders (RSF), each of the project countries is ranked poorly, with South Sudan the worst, ranked at 145 of the 180 surveyed countries, followed by Uganda at 112, and Nepal at 100. For South Sudan, the report notes that 'harassment, arbitrary detention, torture, or execution-style murder is the price that journalists pay for not censoring themselves' (RSF 2017). About the situation in Uganda, the report notes that 'acts of intimidation and violence against journalists are an almost daily occurrence' (RSF 2017). In Nepal, the report notes, 'there was also an increase in arrests of outspoken journalists in 2016'. In June, the authorities issued a directive restricting online media freedom and free speech. Inter alia, it allowed them to block websites arbitrarily for content deemed to be immoral or 'without authoritative source or creating misconceptions among the public' (RSF 2017). According to the key to the global map on the RSF Press Freedom Index for 2017 website, journalists in Uganda and South Sudan are judged to be working under a 'difficult situation', while those in Nepal work in conditions that are a 'noticeable problem' (RSF 2017).

While authoritarian regimes always try to restrict online media freedom and free speech as the above cases demonstrate, it is also true that networks such as Twitter, Facebook, YouTube and others based in the West would not agree to requests by African regimes to delete a post by a journalist who has reported on human rights abuses. Such is the power that social media platforms afford to journalists in dictatorship countries, although physical harassment of the journalists who openly criticise those regimes, even online, remains rampant.

Coupled with equipping journalism students with new media technology competences, the Unesco model curricula, on which the Norhed project partners relied heavily in the review of their curricula, emphasise other aspects relevant in global South settings. One particular focus is the issue of 'safety and security of journalists', which includes 'digital safety' (Unesco 2013: 195–207). In South Sudan, the RSF (2017) report notes that nine journalists have been killed since 2011. Further, a 2016 Unesco report, *Safety of Journalists and the Danger of*

Impunity, noted that there was a 'sharp increase in the number of online journalists killed in 2015'; 'local journalists by far were the most affected by killings'; and 'most killings occurred in countries where there has been armed conflict' (Unesco 2016: 18–19). The Unesco report further noted a worrying trend where the reported cases had not been resolved by the concerned state authorities: 'For the remaining 333 cases (or 40 per cent of all cases) for which information was received, either a police or judicial enquiry is still underway, or the cases have been archived or are unresolved' (2016: 30).

To strengthen the component of 'security and safety of journalists', in November 2017 a team commissioned by Oslo Metropolitan University (OsloMet), the Northern project partner, was sent to train a dozen journalists from Uganda and South Sudan in safety issues. The team of trainers was composed of a mix from the global North (Norway), the Middle East (Egypt) and South Sudan. Moreover, throughout the duration of the project period (2014–2019), professors from OsloMet offered courses in 'war, peace and conflict reporting' as well as in 'science journalism and communication' at Makerere University. A winter graduate course offered to Norwegian and international students drew participants from the three global South project partners. The course, together with the visiting professorships, supplemented the internationalisation efforts of the project through joint research and publications by Southern and Northern colleagues (Orgeret and Tayeebwa 2016). The focus on 'war, peace and conflict reporting' as well as on 'security and safety of journalists' responds to the objectives of Sustainable Development Goal (SDG) 16 on 'peaceful and inclusive societies'.[2] In addition, researchers and PhD students from all the Southern countries gave presentations at each of the annual Safety of Journalists Conferences held at OsloMet from 2015 to 2019.

Cross-cutting issues for journalism education: Gender and environment

The major cross-cutting issues of the project remained gender and the environment. In all aspects of the project, gender considerations were paramount, not just in the tokenism of balancing numbers between females and males, but also in mainstreaming gender issues within the reviewed curricula. The first project book, *Journalism in Conflict and Post-conflict Conditions: Worldwide Perspectives* (Orgeret and Tayeebwa 2016), dedicated two chapters to the discussion of gender, in keeping with the spirit of the fifth United Nations SDG on gender equality.

As the title of her chapter suggests, Samiksha Koirala (2016) discusses the experiences of female journalists in post-conflict Nepal. The chapter shows how 'women often take over non-traditional roles brought on by the changes and transformations during the conflict' and illustrates that 'despite the popular discourse of women being naturally inclined toward peace making, in Nepal such stereotypes were defied as women assumed active roles, either as negotiators or as party cadres and guerrillas, in the ten-year armed conflict of the Maoist war' (Koirala 2016: 20). Koirala also explores the participation of women journalists in Nepali media, including their reporting during the war.

Additional discussion about gender is provided by Kristin Skare Orgeret in her chapter titled 'Women making news: Conflict and post-conflict in the field', in which she explores 'what challenges and opportunities women journalists face when covering conflict-related issues either at home or in a foreign context where gender roles may be very different from those of their home country' (2016a: 21). In the chapter, she argues 'that female journalists' conditions of employment, including aspects of safety, can serve as a pointer of democratic development, freedom of expression, civil rights and media freedom in general' (Orgeret 2016a: 21).

On the second cross-cutting issue – the environment – which is in keeping with the SDG 13 on climate action, Goretti Nassanga has completed research, with the support of the Norhed project, on climate change discourse in both African media and global South journalism more generally (Nassanga 2013; Nassanga et al. 2016). The massive environmental challenges facing the world is one of the transnational issues where journalists need to co-operate across national borders in order to cover the issue in a satisfactory way, similar to how global climate changes require the building of 'universities of democracy' (Halvorsen 2016). Addressing the issue of global environmental challenges is an important part of the master's course in Global Journalism at OsloMet, which Norhed students from Nepal, South Sudan and Uganda participate in every second year, as well as the master's course in Science Journalism provided at Makerere University, also part of the Norhed programme.

The implications of intercultural interactions within the project

According to the Unesco model curricula for journalism education, intercultural journalism includes aspects such as 'identity introspection', 'mediatisation of social domains' and 'social legitimisation' among others (Unesco 2013: 55). Some of the specific topics proposed for discussion within such a course include: 'Journalism – a vector of embodied conceptions, conquerors and converts of culture?'. In this strand, the class would discuss for instance: 'Colonial conceptions of cultural confrontation, from French-style negation and levelling universalism to British cosmopolitanism' (2013: 59).

Within the second strand, the curriculum proposes a discussion of 'the scientific stigmatisation of "racialism", "trans-cultural diffusion" and other forms of "false evolutionism"' as well as the 'anthropological promotion of "cultural relativism"' (2013: 59). Further, 'the "arts of doing and making" of indigenous peoples; tactics used against the coercion of the dominant powers' (2013: 60) is another strand proposed for discussion.

The Norhed journalism education project had as its overarching objective, and as a subtitle, 'Bridging Gaps, Building Futures in Uganda, South Sudan, Nepal and Norway'. Clearly, the project brought together three main cultural traditions, namely: European (Norway), African (South Sudan and Uganda) and Asian (Nepal). Inevitably, there was mutual intercultural learning on issues ranging from the gender focus, where the subjectivity of women in African settings is still wanting and yet extremely advanced in Norway, to issues of accountability and time management. The event of the #Metoo campaign also showed that Norwegian female journalists share some of the challenges experienced by their colleagues in Nepal or Uganda, as shown in papers that Florence Namasinga, Gerald Walulya, Aisha Sembatya Nakiwala, Samiksha Koirala, Trond Idås and

Kristin Skare Orgeret presented during the fourth annual conference on the Safety of Journalists at OsloMet in November 2018.[3]

Building bridges alludes to co-operating in research endeavours, but also to building bridges between academia and society at large. Part of the work of the Norhed project was to establish contact with practitioners in the journalism field in order to discuss issues related to the challenges of journalism in post-conflict situations, including the safety of journalists. The latter issue saw both media houses and other actors, such as the International Federation of Journalists, working to ameliorate the situation in the field.

Questions of how to teach norms and values in journalism in contexts that in many ways are radically different from one's own were of pedagogical interest to all lecturers involved in the programme. All the scholars involved in the project seemed to agree that 'who teaches whom' is a perennial question as the teacher learns a lot from the students and their contexts too. This is a Facebook post from Professor Rune Ottosen after teaching War and Peace Journalism at Makerere in 2018:

> The last few days I had the pleasure of teaching master's students at Makerere University in Kampala on my favourite subject, War and Peace journalism. The students are well informed and interested in the subject. We have interesting discussion. They are engaged and ask me provocative questions. More than my Norwegian students, I must say. But I love it. This is real communication. In the last lecture I had problems hearing my own voice because there is a campaign for students elections outside the window. Hundreds of students are rallying for their candidates in democratic elections. Loudspeakers are dominating the campus and I have to raise my voice. Even if I am a bit disturbed I am happy. What engagement – what enthusiasm. Returning to my hotel room I watch CNN. Trump has fired his Secretary of State on Twitter. The Norwegian news media are preoccupied with our minister of law who has published a provocative statement on Facebook hoping this will help her anti-immigrant agenda. I ask myself if the hope of our future is just here. I hope the students of Makerere represent our common future. (Ottosen 2018)

Sometimes the cross-cultural exchange was much more challenging, as when diving into topics in which the cultural and political differences were great and worldviews collided. A case in point, in which conflicting values between the journalism education institutions on three different continents became very clear, was the controversy over the acceptance of homosexuality. Norway, Nepal, South Sudan and Uganda have very different political and historical trajectories, and represent highly divergent views on homosexuality. This had consequences for both discourse and cognition within the co-operation. Some Norwegian colleagues felt that OsloMet should not co-operate with actors in countries not adhering to the UN's Declaration of Human Rights, and believed that 'all academic contact with Uganda should be cut short as a clear message to the Ugandan government' (Orgeret 2016b: 250).

The discussions around homosexuality represented a thorny subject in the collaboration, but were also educational, shedding light on how journalistic concepts that appear to be globally shared – like 'objectivity' – are actually highly polysemic, with varying definitions across and within geographical regions. Furthermore, the fact that the Nepalese PhDs shared their experiences of the 'third gender' with their colleagues from Uganda and Norway was seen as particularly valuable, as they were not part of what could be read as a 'Western frame of understanding'. Much of the pressure for both strict religious laws and LGBTI rights in Uganda has its origins in the West, and many argue that the topic of homosexuality is yet another ideological struggle that 'the West' is fighting on African soil. Input from another 'South partner' certainly had its own value, as it was not part of the old 'patronising discourse of the West'.

Clearly, mainstreaming gender in curricula – an important part of the project in respect of the fifth SDG on gender equality – involved knotty intercultural aspects, which manifested not only in the discussions but, on a more physical plane, in the classroom when it became necessary to consider female graduate students with children, for instance. It was initially culturally shocking to Ugandan students to see their South Sudanese female colleagues bring babies to class. Mechanisms had to be developed to ensure the babies were taken care of so as to ensure that the female students could concentrate on their studies.

The South–South dimension of the partnership opened the space for particularly interesting discussions about journalism in relation to issues ranging from post-conflict situations and democratisation, to climate change, human rights and sexualities. Furthermore, on a more personal level, solidarity in the South–South dimension was strong when the Gorkha earthquake hit Nepal, killing nearly 9 000 people and injuring some 22 000 in April 2015. Due to the aftershocks, our partners in Kathmandu had to sleep outside for several nights in a row, and the partners from Uganda shared their own experiences of similar circumstances during the Ugandan war. This happened again when, not long after, MA students from Juba, in their turn, had to install their families in refugee camps as the unrest in South Sudan increased.

On a more conceptual and theoretical level, it was interesting to see the legacy of efforts that have been made to formulate genuine African journalism models over the past decades[4] in discussions about how to include ingrained African cultural values, such as 'community participation, consensus building, widespread communal consultation, and religious belief systems' (Tayeebwa 2016, 2017). It was argued that an appreciation of Afrocentric media values found within 'ubuntu-journalism' – such as 'co-operation and consensus, patience and moderation, reconciliation and forgiveness, humanness, communal justice, communal harmony' (Murithi 2008; Tayeebwa 2016, 2017) – could, over time, improve how the global South is framed, particularly the African continent, where dehumanising frames of people as disease-ridden, perpetually malnourished and barbaric killers are frequently used. Devoted journalism professionals may be critical of such blurring of professional boundaries, just as they are critical of the 'prescriptive' nature of peace journalism (e.g. Loyn 2007), and it may be argued that more activist forms of journalism such as ubuntu run the risk of being misused for political purposes (Fourie 2010). The idea of interventionism, which points to the extent to which journalism should actively advocate change in society, has characteristics similar to the journalism referred to as 'alternative' earlier in this chapter, posing a threat to the notion of objectivity. At the same time, that idea that journalists are unbiased and should keep their values and beliefs out of their work might, as several scholars have stressed, be connected to a 'myth of objectivity' (Zelizer 2008). These interesting discussions feed into what has been referred to as an 'epistemic liberation', which aims to critique and challenge basic assumptions and themes of knowledge from the global North. The focus of these normative discussions is primarily set on ideal-type journalism rather than actual journalism practice, but may in turn give directions for journalistic practice, not least through the education of journalists that the Norhed project was involved in. In this respect, our project gained much from the combination of the theoretical and the practical in the PhD projects.

Final reflections on sustainability and impact indicators

The Norhed programme and the project described in this chapter were designed before the UN SDGs were adopted in 2015. Nevertheless, the programme is founded on the same principles of sustainability and echoes the SDGs on many levels. Our project also took national development plans as well as the research agendas of the respective academic institutions into consideration. Given this focus, the impact with respect to trained students and the knowledge created through research will be felt for the foreseeable future. For instance, the Norhed project provided multimedia equipment to the three Southern partner institutions that became central in the training of journalists and communication specialists. This enables them to deploy the new media technologies as well as the vast array of online platforms.

Underlying the research collaboration that brought together Northern and Southern researchers, and across the graduate cohorts of doctoral and master's students was a model that ensured horizontal and vertical academic growth within the project. Joint publications between Northern and Southern partners featured works of faculty staff but also of graduate students. Further, collaboration between Northern and Southern researchers ensured internationalisation and de-Westernisation of knowledge and epistemologies, as discussed above.

There are numerous examples in our network of the project's mutual benefits and of knowledge travelling in many directions, not at all only from the North to the South, as old-fashioned knowledge transmission theories and modernisation paradigms would predict. In the course of workshopping our Norhed group's first joint anthology (Orgeret and Tayeebwa 2016), it became clear to several of the Norwegian colleagues how much there was to be learned from partners in the South, particularly in the aftermath of the Oslo and Utøya terror attack of 2011, when discussing the role of journalists and trauma, crisis journalism and the safety of journalists (Frey 2016). The strength of multiple perspectives is also time and again reflected within our network – in scholarly discussions about the role of journalism in transformative development, democratic and economic governance, for instance. We have seen how many of the universal global journalistic ideals are both challenged and acquire new relevance when applied in a local context – in the true spirit of 'glocalisation'.

Yet, it is important to also remember that younger generations learn better from each other and experiential learning is one of the best means of doing so. While the Norhed project model was very successful in promoting North–South collaborations in research and teaching, as well as the movement of Southern graduate students to the North, the project afforded hardly any movement of Northern students to the global South to allow for intercultural experiential learning. It is such exchanges within younger generations that will break cultural barriers and bring about what Unesco refers to as the search for a 'new humanism' based on 'interculturalism as an adherence to a set of common values, potentially fed by each cultural expression' (2013: 61).

Nevertheless, the Norhed project certainly achieved its overarching goal of 'bridging gaps and building futures' between North and South, and South and South through the training of a new generation of journalists who are equipped with skills and competences that respond to the demands of the current (dis)information age. The project has created opportunities for new theoretical considerations questioning Western-centric media values (Tayeebwa 2016, 2017) while simultaneously reflecting on the relevance of the sacrosanct norms of the profession (Reese and Cohen 2000; Rich 2009). It is our hope that we will see more North–South student exchange included in future projects, to continue the building of knowledge exchanges and to continue strengthening journalism education in ways that undermine threats against the freedom of expression and academic freedom core to our democracies.

About the authors and the project

William Tayeebwa is a lecturer in the Department of Journalism and Communication at Makerere University, Uganda

Kristin Skare Orgeret is a professor in the Department of Journalism and Media Studies at Oslo Metropolitan University, Norway

Project title: Bridging Gaps, Building Futures: Strengthening Media in Post-conflict Societies through Education and Research

Partner institutions: Makerere University (Uganda), College of Journalism and Mass Communication (Nepal), University of Juba (South Sudan) and Oslo Metropolitan University (Norway)

Notes

1   Alternative journalism can refer to a more participatory mode of journalistic practice, to the subject matter being covered or to the positions of its producers outside of dominant media channels.

2   For further information on the Sustainable Development Goals, see https://sustainabledevelopment.un.org/?menu=1300.

3   These papers are listed in the appendix to this chapter.

4   See Skjerdal (2012) for an overview.

Appendix

Papers presented at the 4th Annual Conference on the Safety of Journalists, Oslo Metropolitan University, 5–6 November 2018

Idås T and Orgeret KS (2018) #Metoo and the chilling effect of unwanted sexual attention on journalists

Koirala S (2018) Why self-censorship? Nepali journalists and freedom of expression

Nakiwala AS (2018) Perceptions of risks and mitigation mechanisms among Ugandan female journalists working in contexts of political demonstrations

Namasinga F (2018) Journalists' safety in the age of social media: The case of Uganda

Walulya G (2018) Defending the watchdog: How journalist organisations foster safety and security of media workers

References

Abdelhay N (2012) The Arab uprising 2011: New media in the hands of a new generation in North Africa. *Aslib Proceedings* 64(5): 529–539

Berger G and Foote J (2017) Taking stock of contemporary journalism education: The end of the classroom as we know it. In: RS Goodman and E Steyn (eds) *Global Journalism Education in the 21st Century: Challenges and Innovations.* Austin, TX: Knight Center for Journalism in the Americas, University of Texas at Austin

Bibuli J (2014) *The Elephant in the Room: Social Media and News Conveyance in Uganda.* Available online

Carr D (2003) *Making Sense of Education.* London: Routledge

Castells M (1996) *The Rise of the Network Society, the Information Age: Economy, Society and Culture* vol. 1. Cambridge, MA: Blackwell

Chakrabarty D (2000) *Provincialising Europe: Postcolonial Thought and Historical Difference.* New York: Princeton University Press

Comaroff J and Comaroff JL (2012) Theory from the South: Or how Euro-America is evolving toward Africa. *Anthropological Forum* 22(2): 113–131

Deuze M (2006) Global journalism education: A conceptual approach. *Journalism Studies* 7(1): 19–34

Fourie PJ (2010) African ubuntuism as a framework for media ethics: Questions and criticism. In: SJA Ward and H Wasserman (eds) *Media Ethics Beyond Borders: A Global Perspective.* New York: Routledge. pp. 105–122

Freedman E and Shafer R (2010) Ambitious in theory but unlikely in practice: A critique of Unesco's model curricula for journalism education for developing countries and emerging democracies. *Journal of Third World Studies* 27(1): 135–153

Frey E (2016) Improving post-conflict journalism through three dances of trauma studies. In: KS Orgeret and W Tayeebwa (eds) *Journalism in Conflict and Post-conflict Conditions: Worldwide Perspectives.* Gothenburg: Nordicom

Frohlich R and Holtz Bacha C (2003) *Journalism Education in Europe and North America: An International Comparison.* New York: Hampton Press

Galtung J (2002) Peace journalism: A challenge. In: W Kempf and H Luostarinen (eds) *Journalism and the New World Order* vol. 2. Gothenburg: Nordicom

Garman A (2015) Making media theory from the South. *African Journalism Studies* 36(1): 169–172

Gopal P (2017, 27 October) Yes, we must decolonise: Our teaching has to go beyond elite white men. *The Guardian*

Halvorsen T (2016) International co-operation and the democratisation of knowledge. In T Halvorsen and J Nossum (eds) *North–South Knowledge Networks: Towards Equitable Collaboration between Donors and Universities.* Cape Town: African Minds

Hanitzsch T, Hanusch F, Mellado C, Anikina M, Berganza R et al. (2011) Mapping journalism cultures across nations. *Journalism Studies* 12(3): 273–293

Hujanen J (2017) Renegotiating the journalism profession in the era of social media: Journalism students from the global North and South. *Journalism and Mass Communication Educator* 7(3): 282–292

Kaplan AM and Haenlein M (2010) Users of the world unite! The challenges and opportunities of social media. *Business Horizons* 53(1): 59–68

Kirkpatrick D (2010) *The Facebook Effect: The Inside Story of the Company that is Connecting the World*. New York: Simon and Schuster

Koirala S (2016) Experiences of female journalists in post-conflict Nepal. In: KS Orgeret and W Tayeebwa (eds) *Journalism in Conflict and Post-conflict Conditions: Worldwide Perspectives*. Gothenburg: Nordicom

Koirala S (2018) Gender representations in the Nepali press during pre-conflict, conflict and post-conflict periods. PhD thesis, University of Oslo

Krøvel R, Orgeret KS and Ytterstad A (2012) Objectivity and advocacy in global warming journalism. *Asia Pacific Media Educator* 22(1): 15–28

Langlois G (2011) Social media, or towards a political economy of psychic life. In: G Lovink and M Rasch (eds) *Unlike Us Reader: Social Media Monopolies and the Alternatives*. Amsterdam: Institute of Network Cultures

Loyn D (2007) Good journalism or peace journalism? *Conflict and Communication Online* 6(2): 1–10

McLuhan M (1964) *Understanding Media: The Extension of Man*. Cambridge, MA: MIT Press

Moyo L and Mutsvairo B (2018) Can the subaltern think? The decolonial turn in communication research in Africa. In: B Mutsvairo (ed.) *The Palgrave Handbook of Media and Communication Research in Africa*. Basingstoke: Palgrave

Murithi T (2008) African indigenous and endogenous approaches to peace and conflict resolution. In: DJ Francis (ed.) *Peace and Conflict in Africa*. London and New York: Zed Books. pp. 16–30

Namasinga F (2018) Sourcing in converged media spheres. PhD thesis, University of Oslo

Nassanga GL (2013) African Media and the Global Climate Change Discourse: Implications for Sustainable Development. Open Science Repository Communication and Journalism. Available online

Nassanga GL, Eide E, Hahn O, Rhaman M and Sarwono B (2016) Climate change and development journalism in the Global South. In: K Risto, E Eide, M Tegelberg and Y Dmitry (eds) *Media and Global Climate Knowledge: Journalism and the IPCC*. New York: Springer

Naughton J (2013, 14 September) Twitter and the transformation of democracy. *The Guardian*. Available online

Orgeret KS (2016a) Women making news: Conflict and post-conflict in the field. In: KS Orgeret and W Tayeebwa (eds) *Journalism in Conflict and Post-conflict Conditions: Worldwide Perspectives*. Gothenburg: Nordicom

Orgeret KS (2016b) Dialogues and difficulties: Transnational co-operation in journalism education. In: JF Hovden, G Nygren and H Zilliacus-Tikkanen (eds) *Becoming a Journalist: Journalism Education in the Nordic Countries.* Gothenberg: Nordicom

Orgeret KS and Tayeebwa W (eds) (2016) *Journalism in Conflict and Post-Conflict Conditions: Worldwide Perspectives.* Gothenburg: Nordicom

Ottosen R (2018, 14 March) The last few days ... Post to Facebook page created for the project, Bridging Gaps, Building Futures. Available online

Reese SD and Cohen J (2000) Educating for journalism: The professionalism of scholarship. *Journalism Studies* 1(2): 213–227

Rich C (2009) *Writing and Reporting News: A Coaching Method,* 6th edn. Boston: Wadsworth

Robertson R (1992) *Globalization: Social Theory and Global Culture.* Thousand Oaks, CA: Sage

RSF (Reporters Without Borders) (2017) *World Press Freedom Index 2017.* Available online

Skjerdal T (2012) The three alternative journalisms of Africa. *The International Communication Gazette* 74(7): 636–654

Tandoc E, Wei Lim Z and Ling R (2018) Defining 'fake news': A typology of scholarly definitions. *Digital Journalism* 6(2): 137–153

Tayeebwa W (2016) In quest of Afro-centric media values: Inspirations from the ubuntu philosophy. In A Lahjomri (ed.) *L'Afrique Comme Horizon de Pensée.* Rabat, Morocco: Academy of the Kingdom of Morocco

Tayeebwa W (2017) From conventional towards new frames of peace journalism: The case of Uganda and Burundi. In: LK Tukumbi and J Gahama (eds) *Peace, Security and Post-Conflict Reconstruction in the Great Lakes Region.* Dakar: Codesria. Available online

Tibbitts F (2007) *Curriculum Development and Review for Democratic Citizenship and Human Rights Education.* Paris: Unesco/Council of Europe/Office for Democratic Institutions and Human Rights of the Organization for Security and Co-operation in Europe/Organization of American States. Available online

Unesco (United Nations Educational, Scientific and Cultural Organization) (2013) *Model Curricula for Journalism Education: A Compendium of New Syllabi.* Paris. Available online.

Unesco (2016) *The Safety of Journalists and the Danger of Impunity: Report to the Intergovernmental Council of the IPDC.* Paris. Available online

Unesco (2018) *Journalism, 'Fake News' and Disinformation: Handbook for Journalism Education and Training.* Paris. Available online

Walulya G (2018) Hybrid journalism: An investigation into press coverage of elections in East Africa's one-party dominant states of Tanzania and Uganda. PhD thesis, University of Oslo

Weaver D (ed.) (1998) *The Global Journalist: News People Around the World.* Cresskill, NJ: Hampton Press

Wiik J (2009) Identities under construction: Professional journalism in a phase of destabilization. *International Review of Sociology* 19(2): 351–365

Zelizer B (2008) *Explorations in Communication and History.* London: Routledge

4

Indigenous and communitarian knowledges

Roy Krøvel

As we were planning the project application for the Norwegian Programme for Capacity Development in Higher Education and Research for Development (Norhed), I was reading an article by Eduardo Viveiros de Castro titled 'Cannibal metaphysics: Amerindian perspectivism' (partially reprinted in *Radical Philosophy*). According to Peter Skafish in his introduction to the article, de Castro shows that 'what falls under the domain of "social" and "human" relations for ... Amazonian peoples' is very broad. In fact, 'animals, plants, spirits are all conceived as persons' so that 'modern distinctions between nature and culture, animals and humans, and even descent and marriage ties are effectively inverted' (Skafish 2013: 15).

At the same time, I had been reading a biography of Arne Næss (Gjefsen 2011). No one has influenced Norwegian thinking on matters such as philosophy of science more than the philosopher Næss. For decades, virtually all Norwegian students had his textbooks on philosophy and research methodologies on their reading list. However, in the 1950s other philosophers, such as Hans Skjervheim, began to view the textbooks on research methodologies as too narrowly focused on methodologies developed in the natural sciences, ignoring methodologies coming from the humanities. The critique led Næss to rewrite the textbooks to include chapters on hermeneutics and other methodologies from the humanities. Næss seemed to agree with his critics that methodologies imported from the natural sciences alone were not adequate to study human society. Subsequent developments in disciplines such as history and cultural studies seem to build on and underline this notion of *difference* between studying nature and studying society.

My development as an academic took place within these debates. I was trained in research methodologies grounded in this supposed difference between studying society and studying nature. But what if indigenous peoples of the Amazon and elsewhere are right? How can research methodologies be developed where students do not take 'modern distinctions between nature and culture, animals and humans, and even descent and marriage ties' for granted?

According to Koch and Weingart (2016), research methodologies can never be 'transferred' from one locality to another. Instead, methodologies are sampled, mixed and socially reconstructed. In this chapter, I take a reflexive approach to sampling, mixing and socially constructing research methodologies. I consider what happened during the Norhed project process and what this can tell us about encounters between Norwegian traditions of education and research and indigenous people's perspectives on education and research. I try to shed light on this process by analysing what I see as a series of key moments. Ultimately, I hope to explain how and why indigenous and communitarian universities in Latin America are different from most universities participating in the Norhed programme.

Literature

According to Julian Baggini, 'by gaining greater knowledge of how others think, we can become less certain of the knowledge we think we have, which is always the first step to greater understanding' (2018: 6). Unfortunately, the philosophy most North American and European students encounter at university is 'based entirely on canonical Western texts ... [and] is presented as the universal philosophy, the ultimate inquiry into human understanding'. Baggini, however, is convinced that 'we cannot understand ourselves if we do not understand others' (2018: 4).

Northern scholars such as Arturo Escobar, Eduardo Gudynas and Maristela Svampa are increasingly turning to indigenous peoples, indigenous organisations and indigenous knowledges in Latin America for inspiration and guidance. Arturo Escobar (2018) believes that 'African, Asian, and Latin American nations can and should put forward alternatives to development that incorporate non-Western concepts of what constitutes a thriving society':

> With a firm footing in the worldviews of indigenous peoples, Buen Vivir embraces the inseparability and interdependence of humans and nature. In the current development debates, Buen Vivir has informed critiques of the prevailing development model, confronting basic assumptions about progress, competition, consumerism, and materialism. It rejects anthropocentricism and critiques capitalist and socialist forms of development because both, albeit in different ways and to different degrees, are destructive of both humans and ecological systems. The ethos of Buen Vivir centers on fostering harmony between humans and nature, quality of life, and conviviality. (Escobar 2018: 3–4)

A generation of radical thinkers such as Escobar has found the Zapatista notion of 'pluriverse' particularly useful to imagine 'alternative worlds'. The pluriverse is 'a world in which many worlds fit' built on the concept of diversity within a whole 'Earth system'. It is a world that accepts and celebrates diversity. 'The concept of the Pluriverse pushes us to think in terms of many possible worlds as well as the circularity of life, a perpetual flow and "radical interdependency" of all living things' (Escobar 2018: 5–6). For the indigenous Zapatista rebels of Chiapas, Mexico, the concept 'pluriverse' arose from the struggle for dignity and recognition of diversity after 1994. It helped put into words the demand not only for dignity and respect, but also for the right to autonomy and self-governance.

From a different perspective, Koch and Weingart (2016) have raised concerns about the praxis of 'transferring' knowledge from the North to the South in development work. After reviewing a large body of development reports, evaluations and so on, Koch and Weingart had to conclude that such knowledge transfer does not exist. Knowledge cannot simply be transferred from one locality to another. In a similar vein, Adriansen et al. (2015) argue that knowledge production is always influenced by the local context. Koch and Weingart suggest that the weakness of African states and their inability to withstand pressure from the global North is a danger to the social construction of national identities. The answer, in this conundrum, is most likely 'to use the available means to support the knowledge communities in developing countries so that these become able to produce a critical mass of local experts who qualify as producers and critical scrutinisers of expertise' (Koch and Weingart 2016: 344).

The indigenous and communitarian universities discussed here have been moulded in these debates. The emergence of indigenous and communitarian universities can best be understood as an attempt to establish self-organised and self-governed institutions able to produce, as Koch and Weingart suggest, 'a critical mass of local experts who qualify as producers and critical scrutinisers of expertise'. However, indigenous perspectives on 'states' and 'countries' as key agents in the production of 'local experts' would normally be very different from those presented in the literature on higher education in Africa. In general, indigenous organisations in Latin America do not have high expectations as to what governments and state institutions can and will do to promote autonomous indigenous higher education (see RUIICAY 2017). Instead, most autonomous indigenous higher education initiatives have been met with responses ranging from suspicion, opposition, resistance and obstruction to outright confrontation. The very term 'post-colonial' looks different from the perspective of indigenous organisations struggling for autonomy. In Latin America, indigenous peoples have experienced 200 years of existence in 'post-colonial' states established after independence from (mostly) Spain and Portugal in the early 1800s. Most of the independent states eagerly sought to create homogeneous masses of subjects, minions and underlings. Since the late nineteenth century, nationalist ideologies in most Latin American states have been built on the 'powerful myth' that the country is homogeneous and its citizens are the product of 'mestisaje' between indigenous peoples and Spaniards (Gould 1998). Mignolo et al. (1998: ix) comment: 'In this telling, Nicaragua's native peoples no

longer exist and Nicaragua's advance into the modern world of capitalism and nationhood depend on this disappearance.' After independence
from colonial powers, internal groups wanting to establish new 'colonial' relations soon enough captured the states. This time, however, the
colonial relations were designed for internal exploitation of indigenous
peoples, minorities and others generally on the periphery of the state.
State independence from European colonial powers hardly meant an
end to colonial relations in Latin America.

'Autonomy' is a key concept for understanding indigenous initiatives for higher education in Latin America. Article 4 of the UN
Declaration dealing with indigenous governance states that 'indigenous
peoples, in exercising their right to self-determination, have the right
to autonomy or self-government in matters relating to their internal
and local affairs, as well as ways and means for financing their autonomous functions'.[1] Historically, indigenous autonomy has emerged out
of indigenous people's struggles 'to preserve and strengthen their territorial and cultural integrity through self-government units practising
participatory democracy' (López y Rivas 2013). Building institutions of
higher education has been seen by indigenous organisations not only
as a way to produce 'a critical mass of local experts' but also as a pivotal
part in the struggle 'to preserve and strengthen' autonomy and integrity through self-governance and participatory democracy. More often
than not, these struggles have pitted indigenous organisations against
state and capital, keen to extract the rich natural resources often found
within indigenous territories.

In short, the global indigenous movement has emerged out of
countless local struggles between states and indigenous organisations
over indigenous autonomy. Using transnational networks of solidarity
has, at times, proved quite effective in limiting state powers and
expanding indigenous territorial autonomy (Brysk 2000; Leyva-Solano
2001). The universities discussed in this chapter are members of the
Network of Indigenous, Intercultural and Community Universities of
Abya Yala[2] (RUIICAY). RUIICAY is an example of a transnational network uniting forces in the struggle to build and defend locally
self-governed institutions of higher education.

Histories of indigenous struggles

Three members of RUIICAY took part in the Norhed project discussed here. The Pluriversidad Amawtay Wasi in Ecuador and the Universidad Autónoma Indígena Intercultural (UAIIN) in Colombia were both founded by indigenous organisations with roots going back to the early 1970s. The Regional Indigenous Council of Cauca (CRIC) had emerged in this violent region of Colombia in 1971. Cauca was, and continues to be, among the regions most affected by the civil war between leftist guerrilla organisations such as *Fuerzas Armados Revolucionarias de Colombia* (FARC) and *Ejército de Liberación Nacional* (ELN) and the Colombian army and right wing paramilitaries. For several years (1984–1991) an indigenous insurgent group (Quintin Lame Armed Movement) operated in the Cauca region, with the declared aim of defending indigenous communities against violence unleashed by the army and armed groups (Palechor et al. 1995). Peace negotiations led to the adoption of a new constitution in 1991, which enshrined important rights for indigenous peoples, such as the right to protection of communal lands, recognition of the ethnic and cultural diversity of the Colombian nation and the right to bilingual education. Building a system of education is defined as one of the central axes of CRIC's political struggle, seeking 'an education that promotes the recovery of our identity, our territory and cultural practice, that values and recognises the importance of our native languages'.[3]

CRIC emerged in a context of extreme violence and danger. According to reliable estimates, over 400 members of CRIC were killed during the first 30 years of the organisation (Gow 2008). The number of those killed has since increased significantly. This violence shaped and formed the political struggle of the indigenous peoples in the region.

Similarly, the Pluriversidad Amawtay Wasi is closely connected to the Confederation of Indigenous Nationalities of Ecuador, more commonly known as CONAIE. As in Colombia, the indigenous movement in Ecuador has passed through a lengthy series of popular mobilisations and direct actions, such as the famous indigenous uprisings of 1990, 1994, 1997 and 2005 (Uzendoski 2010).

The third member of the project is the University of the Autonomous Regions of the Caribbean Coast of Nicaragua (URACCAN). The Nicaraguan context is different from the ones in Ecuador and Colombia briefly described above. In Nicaragua, the civil war after the Sandinista revolution (1979) prompted negotiations between the Sandinista government and (mainly) indigenous and Afro-Caribbean peoples on the Atlantic coast. The violence on the Atlantic coast came to an end when a new constitution was adopted in 1987 after a long struggle. The constitution recognises the fact that Nicaragua is a multicultural country and defines the Atlantic Coast regions as 'autonomous'.

The common trait in the historical context of these three institutions is that indigenous peoples and minorities have gained rights and autonomy only over the last three decades, and only after protracted and violent struggles. However, the struggle to build autonomous systems for higher education continues and has been an ongoing issue throughout the course of the Norhed project.

Methodology

As mentioned in my introduction, I have chosen a reflexive approach to my analysis of the encounter between Northern perspectives on knowledge and research methodologies and those of the Latin American partners in the project. The approach is based on 'a less instrumental, more constructivist, relational and social theory of learning, which, through a process of reflective dialogue, engages the learner in a critically reflective construction of meaning' (Doyle 2003). Taking a 'reflexive approach' means considering what is happening during the research or learning process. In the instance discussed in this chapter, the process is not simply a research process, although elements of research certainly have been a part of the process, but rather a process involving local institutions for higher education and research in the co-production of knowledge.

I build on the work of Sheila Jasanoff (2004), who sees 'co-production' of knowledge as 'simultaneous processes' through which modern societies form their epistemic and normative understandings of the world. The concept of co-production can be used to understand the production of scientific knowledge in most areas and disciplines. Concerning indigenous peoples, however, the concept should be defined more narrowly as a 'process where people intentionally try to collaborate on equal terms to develop a more collective wisdom, which can become a basis for making the quality of life "better"' (Romm 2017: 49).

Adopting a reflexive approach means that my focus will be on 'interpreting one's own interpretations, looking at one's own perspectives from other perspectives, and turning a self-critical eye onto one's own authority as interpreter and author' (Alvesson and Sköldberg 2000: vii). To achieve this, I draw on and refer to important debates and discussions from the workshops where we co-produced the application for funding (thereby choosing the future research subjects), as well as on discussions with students and the papers they handed in during the course of the project. I also analyse some of the outcomes of the project, mainly the research manuals, public declarations and books on pedagogy and philosophy of science published at the indigenous and community universities. These key documents are, in the order in which I discuss them:

- The journal *Revista Ciencia e Interculturalidad*, Volúmen 23, Núm. 2, Julio–Diciembre, 2018, which contains 20 articles written by graduate master's students on intercultural communication from indigenous and communitarian perspectives.
- A manifesto produced by 50 invited participants from ten Latin American countries at a pre-conference to the International Association for Media and Communication Research (IAMCR) 2017 annual conference in Cartagena, Colombia, titled 'Manifesto: Minga of thought "Communication and indigenous peoples"'.
- A jointly produced documentation of indigenous science and research methodologies titled 'Base Document for Cultivation and Nurture of Wisdom and Knowledge'(CCRISAC).
- The final document I discuss is also the result of a long and participatory process. Ten indigenous researchers jointly authored an introduction to the pedagogy of the indigenous university of Ecuador: *Kapak Ñan Pedagógico: Filosófico de la Pluriversidad*

'*Amawtay Wasi*' (*The Great Road of Learning: The Philosophy of the Pluriversity 'Amawtay Wasi*').

In order to consider what was happening during the research or learning process, I connect the discussion to five key moments that have been helpful in prompting me to look at my 'own perspectives from other perspectives', and to turn a self-critical eye onto my 'own authority as interpreter and author', as Alvesson and Sköldberg (2000) suggest.

Key moments and documents in the reflexive process

El bastón de mando will always be here

In April 2015, at a conference held in Popayan, Colombia, the CRIC indigenous leader in charge of education gave the opening speech: 'I am here today, but someone else will represent us the next time. Thereafter someone else will come. But the *bastón de mando* will always be here. It is the *bastón de mando* that leads us. We are only passing through.' (I have translated from Spanish to English.)

The *bastón de mando* is a ceremonial stick that represents the authority installed in elected leaders of indigenous communities in the region of Cauca, Colombia. The anonymous leader wanted to instil a sense of communality into the audience by underlining the insignificance of individual leaders. In fact, CRIC is collectively led by nine leaders, each elected for two years to represent different parts of the region. At both regional and local levels, leadership rotates regularly between trusted persons. The rotations reflect the difficult security situation of the region. It is dangerous to be a leader. Significantly, however, the system of frequent rotations also reflects a scepticism about all forms of specialisation. Therefore, the university founded by CRIC, Universidad Autónoma Indígena Intercultural (UAIIN), does not have a rector. Instead, a 'co-ordinator' is appointed for two or three years to lead the UAIIN before being 'rotated' to another position in the indigenous structure of governance. In addition, across the spectrum of staff at the university, teachers, researchers and directors are required to have a broad range of experience of all aspects of communal life.

Who am 'I'?

The indigenous students have a sense of belonging to a collective that seems to be different from mine. The divergent perceptions of belonging to a collective surfaced numerous times during lectures and workshops. A few months after the first batch of master's students had graduated, we held a workshop on academic writing with the aim of publishing a special issue of a scientific journal based entirely on their master's theses (the first 'key document' mentioned earlier). As we were reading and discussing first drafts, it struck me that the former master's students were using the word 'we' frequently. One wrote 'We, the Nasa people decided to …'. Another wrote, 'We, the people, feel that …'. To my Norwegian academic ear, the liberal use of 'we' sounded strange. One of my teachers on a PhD course I attended many years ago even forbade us to use the word 'we' in this way. Therefore, I tried to explain why an academic audience in the global North probably would not appreciate statements such as 'We, the people, feel …'.

As a compromise, I suggested using 'I' instead of 'we'. I even argued that a reflexive approach needs a human subject – an 'I' – that is willing to turn 'a self-critical eye onto one's own authority as interpreter and author'.

The graduate students protested and tried to convince me that 'I' without 'we' is an illusion born out of modernism and 'individualisation'. My counter argument was to present the ideal of 'transparency' in academic writing. An author should, I argued, be open about his or her evaluations and judgements, so that readers, too, could turn a critical eye onto the authority of the author as interpreter. For the sake of transparency, you should make your personal judgements visible where appropriate, I argued. In the end, I did not get much support for the view that an individual author was making the evaluations and judgements. It seemed that my former students were more concerned with the fact that individual authors are embedded in cultures consisting of norms, values, traditions, and so on that in effect, make evaluations and judgements for them.

Re-reading the articles as they have been published in *Revista Ciencia e Interculturalidad*, it becomes clear that these master's graduates are in the process of constructing a culture of academic writing that is not willing to submerge itself in the hegemonic cultures of academia. A similar issue (which I will mention only briefly here) is related to the style and structure of academic arguments. An academic article, for instance, typically follows a linear path from introduction, question or problem, theory and methods, to results, discussion and conclusion. Following this pattern helps most readers to understand what the author is trying to convey. However, as Joanne Rappaport so elegantly has demonstrated, indigenous Nasa storytelling follows different patterns and structures (Rappaport 1990). The Norhed project put much energy into enabling students to communicate with hegemonic academic cultures, including the ability to read and write European- or North American-style academic papers. However, there is no reason to expect that Northern norms of academic writing are universal or are the only useful way to communicate science. Building local institutions, as Koch and Weingart recommend, will lead to the construction of a multiplicity of academic worlds in Latin America.

Some academics worry that such a pluriverse of science will be a threat to higher education and universities (Saugstad et al. 2018). A more pressing concern is how to make 'the many worlds' enrich one another.

Making a manifesto at La Minga
(collective work for the common good)

It is not possible to translate 'Minga' into other languages without losing some of the meaning of the word. In Norwegian, 'Minga' is best translated as 'dugnad'. In English, it is probably best to explain the concept as a form of collective work for the common good. A Minga could be many things – a march, a demonstration, collective work on communal land or intellectual work at a workshop.

Some 40 students and researchers from the three indigenous and communitarian universities involved in the Norhed project attended the 2017 IAMCR conference in Cartagena, Colombia. Attending a conference by presenting a paper and receiving a few comments before retreating to your offices to complete an article appeared to be a rather

meaningless academic exercise for those coming from the communitarian and indigenous universities. It somehow represented the zenith of
individualised knowledge production. Instead, the communitarian and
indigenous universities wanted some 'real collective work' to be done
and invited participants to join a 'Minga of thought' (a 'pre-conference',
to use the language of IAMCR). In the call, the organisers wrote:

> For the indigenous people, 'Minga' means to circulate, making
> every physical and spiritual force meet in the Minga. Minga
> means to construct unity from the vision of the people. It means
> looking for ways to improve communication, food autonomy
> and to revitalize the mother tongue, always seeking dialogue
> between human beings and Mother Nature in order to remain
> in harmony and balance. In the Nasa tradition, Minga is 'pi' txya
> or pi 'txyuwe', an invitation from a person or community to
> others to work for a day in partnership to carry out different
> tasks such as planting corn. In indigenous agriculture, work is
> demanding and many hands are needed. As a result, indigenous
> peoples use the Minga to create unity and as a strategy of solu-
> tion. This Minga is the MINGA OF WORK.[4]

As a Minga is a space for open dialogue, there were no calls for papers.
Instead, the organisers invited people to come and 'help produce a
result in the form of a text or declaration that corroborates the power
of indigenous communication in the contemporary world'. The value of
meeting and discussion would be manifested in a collective document
that could be used to focus energy and direct future collective efforts.

Close to 100 participants at the IAMCR conference came to take
part in the collective work. Discussions were held in plenary sessions
before participants were divided into groups to discuss specific issues.
A long day's work ended with plenary sessions to construct a manifesto
based on reports from the various groups. For the indigenous participants, this was a very familiar methodology, well-tested at numerous
indigenous conferences. Most non-indigenous participants had little
experience with such collective efforts.

The manifesto, the second of the above-mentioned key documents, was later published by openDemocracy, an independent global media platform covering world affairs, ideas and culture that 'seeks to challenge power and encourage democratic debate across the world'.[5] The manifesto began:

> We, the Originary Peoples and Afro-descendants of Abya Yala have been walking for years in processes of struggle and resistance in defence of our collective rights and ancestral territories. This struggle once again vindicates the maintenance of knowledges, know-hows, wisdoms and ancestral practices, together with the recognition of our own systems of communication, organisation, production, health, justice and education.

The manifesto goes on to list seven issues that need to be resolved if indigenous peoples and Afro-descendants are to achieve self-governance in higher education. The first issue reveals much about the priorities of the communitarian and indigenous universities:

> First: We demand that states and society in general recognise, respect and guarantee the systems of self-education that Indigenous Peoples have been able to build and consolidate through intercultural universities, pluriversities and community education projects as legitimate places for the transmission and reproduction of ancestral knowledges, know-hows, wisdoms and practices that are essential to face the civilization crisis looming over the world, by integrating the ancestral wisdom of the grandmothers and grandparents of the Indigenous and Afro-descendant peoples in Abya Yala. (RUIICAY 2017)

As much as producing a list of demands on behalf of indigenous peoples and Afro-descendants was the purpose of the Minga, so, too, its purpose was to introduce scholars from the global North to indigenous ways of producing collective knowledge. Post-conference essays by the master's students make it clear that many saw the Minga as a small act of civil disobedience or a silent subversion of typical forms and procedures of academic work at academic events. One student wrote: 'You wanted to introduce us to the academic world of communication and media scholars. We wanted to make sure that the academic world was introduced to *our* ways of producing knowledge' (unpublished document).

Equality versus diversity?

During the Norhed planning process, we met in Nicaragua to write up the application. We needed to find the right words to capture the meanings and intentions of all parties. The Norwegians were eager to use the concept of 'equality' to describe the type of partnership we wanted to build. However, as I have described more fully elsewhere, the indigenous university leaders did not share the Norwegian fondness for the concept 'equality' (see Krøvel 2018). On the contrary, they received the proposal to use 'equality' to describe the nature of the partnership with some suspicion.

'Liberty, Equality, Fraternity' was a much-used slogan during the French Revolution. In the history of Norwegian trade unionism, the call for 'equality' has been a central part of the discourse. 'Equality' is a word with numerous positive connotations for most Norwegians. For indigenous leaders, however, the word is closely related to a particular discourse of governance that has sought to produce a more homogeneous body of subjects. Nationalist ideologies in most of Latin America continue to promote the 'powerful myth' that the country's citizens in reality are the product of a 'mestisaje' between indigenous peoples and Spaniards. Many indigenous leaders have come to see 'equality' as meaning 'integration', 'incorporation' and even 'annihilation as peoples'. Instead, they wished to build the application to Norhed around concepts such as 'diversity'. As the rector of Pluriversidad Amawtay Wasi explained, they did not seek to become 'equal'. The university ('pluriversity') was built to ensure that indigenous peoples could remain different, thus helping safeguard continuing cultural diversity.

Norwegian philosopher Arne Næss has also pondered the relationship between socal justice and diversity. In 'The Deep Ecology Platform', co-penned with George Sessions in 1984, the first two points read:[6]

1. The well-being and flourishing of human and nonhuman life on Earth have value in themselves (synonyms: inherent worth, intrinsic value, inherent value). These values are independent of the usefulness of the nonhuman world for human purposes.
2. Richness and diversity of life forms contribute to the realization of these values and are also values in themselves.

For Næss, 'richness and diversity of life forms' includes diversity of human life forms. Yet, what appears to be 'diversity of social and cultural life forms' can prove to be cultural or social hierarchies. Elsewhere, Næss has argued for 'extreme caution towards any overall plans for the future, except those consistent with wide and widening classless diversity' (Naess 1973: 97). At the workshop held to write the Norhed application, Næss's warning that plans need to be consistent with 'widening classless diversity' provided the cultural translation I needed to understand the indigenous participants' scepticism about the equality discourse. Similarly, indigenous and communitarian universities in Abya Yala are sceptical about 'multiculturalism'. The 'multiculturalism' of Latin American cities, for instance, is understood as resulting from processes of inclusion, integration and incorporation that celebrate a superficial 'diversity' while diversity in fact is being reduced as minorities are forced to adapt to life under neoliberalism and the dominance of the Spanish language. Instead, to promote 'widening classless diversity', the indigenous and communitarian universities promote 'interculturalism' in much the same sense as Martha Nussbaum (1997) and Ali Rattansi (2011). According to Rattansi, interculturalism could be a more fruitful perspective than multiculturalism from which to view different ethnic groups co-existing in mutual understanding and civility. Nussbaum understands interculturalism as a recognition of common human needs across cultures as well as dissonance and critical dialogue within cultures. For the RUIICAY network of universities, 'interculturalism' signals a conscious effort to create dialogue between cultures free of deep-rooted power relationships and social/political hierarchies.

An indigenous feminism?

Concern about social and cultural hierarchies and discrimination against particular groups within indigenous cultures led me to ask the master's students to write essays on internal discrimination. I asked them to use the online learning platform established for the project to discuss discrimination based on gender and sexual orientation. The assignment led to a very heated debate, but not for the reasons I had anticipated. In fact, the debate soon came to revolve around me as a foreign professor asking questions about internal discrimination.

The first to take issue with me was a very experienced and eloquent male student from an urban indigenous community. He posted a polite message that nevertheless managed to make it clear that the assignment was 'inappropriate' as long as 'the indigenous communities are involved in a battle to survive as peoples'. Others agreed. 'First things first'. However, a more helpful stream of posts quoted numerous internal documents and manifestos highlighting the struggle against gender discrimination. All the universities had plans and strategies to improve gender balance and to end discrimination based on gender, religion and ethnicity. It seemed that the debate was less about disagreement over the issue of discrimination than over disagreement about discussing these issues with an outsider such as me.

In hindsight, I realise that I had moved too fast, asking intimate questions before having managed to establish trust between the master's students and me as a foreign professor. Additionally, my way of formulating the question revealed that I had transferred concerns based on European experiences of how discrimination functions in Northern contexts to indigenous contexts without the cultural sensitivity needed. In fact, even those students who pointed me towards documents discussing discrimination (primarily) against women, were reluctant to accept my premise for the debate. Even self-proclaimed indigenous feminists made efforts to explain why discrimination in indigenous communities is not the same as the discrimination described by 'occidental feminism'. In keeping with the injunction made by Koch and Weingart, it seems that not even knowledge of discrimination can be transferred from the global North to the global South.

*'Base Document for Cultivation
and Nurture of Wisdom and Knowledge'*

The five moments just described help explain why it was necessary to
organise a series of workshops to formulate indigenous research methodologies and pedagogical philosophies. As Viveiros de Castro (2013)
and Escobar (2018) remind us, indigenous worldviews are different
from dominant (European and North American) ways of understanding
the world. It would therefore be strange if indigenous and communitarian philosophies of science and research methodologies turned out to
be mere copies of those found in the North.

The 'Base Document for Cultivation and Nurture of Wisdom and
Knowledge' (CCRISAC) gives us a glimpse of what indigenous science
could look like (Gutiérrez et al. 2018). First of all, it shows that indigenous and communitarian universities envisage the production of
knowledge more as 'cultivation' and 'nurturing' than as 'dissection'.
Knowledge 'grows' and 'flourishes'. CCRISAC intends to (re)construct a
decolonised episteme that has the strength to 'wake up' wisdom, cultural expressions, knowledges and praxis. CCRISAC defines 'eight
principles' for indigenous and communitarian research in order to
avoid reductionism. The principle of *relationalism* holds that all the
elements that make up Mother Earth are intimately related. The principle of *communality* promotes participatory processes where collective
construction takes priority over the individual. The principle of *reciprocity* means that mutual sharing motivates construction and
evaluation of knowledge and wisdom. The principle of *complementarity*
implies the necessary presence and participation of the other.
Spirituality is considered as the forms of relationship that help achieve
physical, mental, emotional and spiritual balance and harmony between
all persons and communities that make up Mother Earth. *Intraculturality
and interculturality* is appreciated as the process of strengthening internal manifestations of the cultures and identities of all peoples. The
principle of *bioethics* involves exteriorising love of life in order to live in
harmony with Mother Earth. Finally, the principle of *flexibility* means
embracing the permanent possibility of making use of all the 'different

ways' and the 'different ways of walking' as part of the cultivation and nurturing of knowledge and wisdom.

For a professor trained in Norway, the most thought-provoking moments of CCRISAC were those when spirits and spirituality were discussed as part of the research methodology. For instance, one of the first things a researcher is advised to do when investigating a particular issue in a community is to listen, feel and sense the community. This includes the spiritual level. Spirituality is accepted as one way of producing knowledge. As Skafish (2013) explains, it is the responsibility of the shamans to negotiate with the supernatural beings when balance and harmony has been broken. Collective knowledge produced by shamans and religious leaders is part of the tradition of indigenous knowledge the researcher is expected to use.

The great road of learning: A philosophy of pedagogy

The CCRISAC deals with the relationship between worldviews (*cosmovisión*) and research methodologies. The language of the text reveals how life as small farmers informs the ways in which indigenous and communitarian universities envisage that knowledge is produced. Knowledge will grow, flow and flourish if the researcher allows it to. The book *Kapak Ñan Pedagógico: Filosófico de la Pluriversidad 'Amawtay Wasi'*, meanwhile, sets out to explain the philosophy of the indigenous university as it has emerged from struggles to resist the obliteration of the peoples it serves (Sarango 2017). By doing so, the document places the university firmly within the ongoing social and political struggles of Ecuador:

> The arrogant, hegemonic and destructive (*avasallador*) system of education of the occident ... has as its prime motive to maintain the world as a market and to extinguish culturally original peoples because we are an obstacle to achieving their goals ... Now, the system lacks the moral authority to push through their goals. It is not a question of becoming more like them. We are already demonstrating that the nature of humanity is to be *distinct* ... we come from a different matrix of civilization. We

are only similar in the condition of being *humans*. Nothing more.
(Sarango 2017: 16)

Within this framework, education is not necessarily a good thing: ' the occidental school is a perfect domesticating space for manipulation. It is where the deceiving death of cultural identity begins, the ethnocide of originary peoples' (2017: 16). Historically, higher education and science are seen as having played a pivotal role, together with the Catholic Church, as guardians of scientific truths. The current epoch, however, is dominated by the 'globalisation of capital' (2017: 20). Therefore, science and higher education have become 'responsible for producing efficient, effective and competitive products' thus '"quality" is measured in terms of mercantile parameters'. Universities are 'capitalism's most cherished creature used to impose its regime of truths' (2017: 23). The role of the pluriversity is no less than to help 'recuperate the feeling of belonging to a community'. Indigenous peoples need to 'change the system of economic, social and political organisation of society' and replace it with an alternative (2017: 29).

The *Kapak Ñan Pedagógico: Filosófico de la Pluriversidad 'Amawtay Wasi'* resonates with some 'occidental' perspectives on science. The *pluriversidad* itself sees similarities between 'action research' and the ways in which the *pluriversidad* envisages research and community. Some define action research as research initiated to solve an immediate problem or as a reflective process of progressive problem-solving led by individuals working in teams or as part of a 'community of practice' (Stringer 2007). It could also be seen as an example of the co-production of knowledge, in Jasanoff's sense of the concept.

From this framing of the role of higher education, the indigenous university describes how new elites emerged in the post-colonial states after independence to reproduce colonial exploitations internally. The new elites constructed new forms of identities, such as Mexicans, Nicaraguans, Colombians, and so on. That is, 'they planted a tree without roots' (Sarango 2017: 30). The elites used those newly created 'imagined communities' to 'de-indianize' indigenous peoples. However, as Sarango correctly notes, the elites could hardly have succeeded in 'de-indianizing' indigenous communities without the help of indigenous teachers and other indigenous community leaders. It is not surprising, then, that the text reserves some fierce criticism for those within the indigenous communities who think and behave 'as if they were North Americans' (2017: 55). In many ways, Sarango echoes Franz Fanon when describing how 'shame' (of being indigenous) becomes a driving force in the homogenisation of cultures when people prefer not to speak their language outside the home (2017: 54).

The reader might be forgiven for thinking that this line of reasoning will lead to a collective form of what Gregory Smithers and Brooke Newman have dubbed 'stubborn and at times self-destructive isolationism' (Smithers and Newman 2014). However, this would be a misunderstanding. The *pluriversidad's* curriculum is remarkably outward looking, more so than at most European universities. Sarango (2017) describes the 'Chakana curriculum/Cycles to achieve intercultural learning'. The first three semesters are reserved for 'traditional knowledges' (*conocimiento originario*). The following three semesters are dedicated to 'occidental and other knowledges' (*shutak yachaykuna*). The most advanced stage, however, is the last four semesters, the cycle of 'the dialogue of knowledges' (*yachaykunapura*).

The three cycles of intercultural learning do not indicate a backward-looking project determined to preserve and conserve culture as it is imagined to have been, although concepts such as 'revitalisation', 'reawakening' and 're-enchantment' are in frequent use. Instead, the curricular design is geared towards reconquering at least some agency over rapid-paced changes currently affecting communal life. The eagerness to learn from outsiders is further demonstrated by the frequent citation of 'occidental' scholars such as Paolo Freire and José de Souza Silva.

Abya Yala is not Africa

I believe the experiences of working with indigenous and communitarian universities can inform debates about the possibility of 'knowledge transfer' and about development support for local education and research institutions on several levels. To begin with, because RUIICAY provides us with a case that would appear to be significantly different from the experiences of projects in Africa or the Middle East. Based on the RUIICAY experience, I believe it is worth revisiting ideas of the 'post-colonial' or 'de-colonial'; the role of the state in emancipatory knowledge production; the use of concepts such as 'nation' and 'nation-state', and also to reconsider the often taken for granted role of education and higher education in improving well-being and *buen vivir*.

As the heading for this section states, Abya Yala is not Africa, an obvious difference being the fact that Latin American states gained independence from the European colonial powers some 150 years before most African states did. Existing literature on knowledge production, transfer of knowledge and indigenous knowledge in Africa emphasises historical colonial relations and new forms of colonial hegemonies when discussing 'local' knowledge production. Resolving the problematic relationship between the 'global North' and the sovereign African states is depicted as the key to building a critical mass of local knowledge. Indigenous scholars, meanwhile, are much more concerned with the state as a problem in itself. For them, the crucial issue is not North–South colonial relations but the internal colonial relations between dominating groups that use state institutions to further their own interests at the cost of indigenous peoples and other minorities.

Learning from indigenous peoples' struggles in Latin America could translate into a more critical attitude to the potentialities and limitations of state-centred thinking in higher education programmes such as Norhed, as well as thinking in academic research on knowledge production and knowledge transfer. So far, there is little evidence to suggest that most states in Africa, the Middle East or Latin America have been part of the solution if the problem is to construct education systems capable of supporting well-being, *buen vivir* or emancipation, as put forward by De Sousa Silva, Freire and Escobar.

I also believe the experience of the indigenous and communitarian universities should inspire both donor communities and researchers to reconsider the often cavalier use of concepts such as 'nation' and 'nation-state'. The modern idea of the 'nation-state' was born in a particular historical context (Europe and national struggles for independent states in the 1800s). Proponents claimed that each 'nation' had the right to an independent state. However, the so-called nation-states always consisted of more than one nation. Peoples such as the Sami rightfully felt excluded from the imagined community of the 'nation' in Scandinavian countries, for example, and were subjected to policies designed to minimise cultural diversity. As a concept, the 'nation-state' travels badly when used to analyse relationships between states and peoples and nations in Africa, Asia and Latin America. Instead, researchers and donor communities alike should be keenly aware of the historical fact that governments and states have employed the idea of the 'nation' (by creating an imagined community) to subjugate minorities. Formally, at least, most Latin American constitutions today accept the fact that their states are multinational. Nevertheless, donors and researchers continue to transfer concepts such as 'nation-state' uncritically from one historical context to another.

The final issue where I believe learning from indigenous and communitarian universities could enrich academic debates on higher education, is their deeply rooted sceptical attitude towards institutions of higher education and research. The experience of indigenous peoples reminds us that we cannot take for granted that higher education and research will play a positive role in human emancipation.

These issues are not limited to Latin America, of course. However, I would argue that the issues become more salient in the Latin American context because indigenous peoples in Abya Yala have succeeded in building autonomous institutions for higher education and research. These autonomous institutions provide us with what Koch and Weingart call 'a critical mass' of local experts capable of challenging knowledges 'transferred' from the outside and, in addition, construct alternative readings and narratives of history.

Becoming less certain of the knowledge we think we have

The purpose of this chapter has been to reflect on the experience of working with indigenous and communitarian universities in Abya Yala by 'looking at one's own perspectives from other perspectives, and turning a self-critical eye onto one's own authority as interpreter and author' (Alvesson and Sköldberg 2000).

One issue has concerned me more than anything during the process: the role of spirits and spirituality in the research methodologies. As Skafish (2013: 15) explains, for indigenous peoples 'modern distinctions between nature and culture, animals and humans ... are effectively inverted'. Trees, plants and animals can speak. Spirits and spirituality interconnect all the interrelated beings in the world.

I have referred earlier to Arne Næss and in particular to eco-philosophy as one 'occidental' perspective that could help non-indigenous researchers better understand indigenous philosophies. Næss was profoundly influenced by Baruch de Spinoza (1632–1677). However, it has rightly been said that Næss, while drawing heavily on Spinoza, quietly chose to ignore the important aspects of spirituality in Spinozism. Other eco-philosophers, meanwhile, such as George Sessions, see de-spiritualisation as a key problem:

> Western society has been diverted from the goal of spiritual freedom and autonomy ... modern Western society has arrived at the opposite pole of anthropocentric 'absolute subjectivism' in which the entire non-human world is seen as a material resource to be consumed in the satisfaction of our egoistic passive desires. (Sessions 1977: 481)

In my case, I did find the re-spiritualisation of science challenging for reasons related to the history of the community where I was born (Volda). Drawing on Sheila Jasanoff's notion of science as 'co-produced', it is fair to say that modern science 'came to' and was 'co-produced' in my community by a group of young and radical journalists in the 1880s. With some higher education, they set out to publish new radical ideas of the time in the local newspaper *Vestmannen*. Radical ideas inspired by Darwin, Marx and Kropotkin were met with fierce resistance from the clergy as well as those speaking with the authority of 'traditional knowledge'. Rereading the newspaper some 130 years later, it becomes clear that 'co-production' of scientific knowledge happened through numerous struggles over issues such as what to include in the curricula at local schools: science or religion; Darwin or the Bible? Another contentious issue was the introduction of new scientific methods in farming that embraced animal welfare in the pursuit of improving the well-being of animals. New methods emanating from newly established institutions for research and education collided with traditional knowledges and local (indigenous?) ways of doing things.

Those young, radical journalists were my idols while I was growing up. I still sympathise with their belief in an emancipatory science building on the 'radical humanist message of the Enlightenment' (Chomsky 2014). In the social and political context of the time and place, turning to 'scientific methods' originating from the natural sciences of the day was an appropriate answer to challenges and difficulties the community had to meet. However, it did lead the young radicals into conflict with tradition, the clergy, the elders of the community and with traditional knowledge.

My concern over issues such as spirituality has diminished considerably over time. As Luis Fernando Sarango, rector of Pluriversidad Amawtay Wasi has explained on numerous occasions, indigenous people's knowledges are characterised by a great deal of pragmatism, as illustrated by the principle of flexibility documented in CCRISAC. 'Flexibility' embraces the permanent possibility of using all the 'different ways' and all the 'different ways of walking' as part of the cultivation and nurturing of knowledge and wisdom. Additionally, Sarango assures me, the end goal is not agreement, but preserving the greatest classless diversity possible.

What would be the benefit, then, of scientific co-operation, if not to find an answer all could agree on? As the CCRISAC document eloquently argues, it is impossible to understand and respond to most problems that affect local communities today without communication on a global scale (RUIICAY 2014). Mutual understanding across borders and cultures is essential. Indigenous peoples have become important actors in international communication and negotiation on issues of global reach, such as global warming. However, attempts at mutual understanding on issues such as global warming will be fruitless unless everyone involved makes an effort to understand, for instance, indigenous people's worldviews and knowledges.

Also, as Baggini (2018: 4), rightfully says, 'we cannot understand ourselves if we do not understand others'.

About the author and the project

Roy Krøvel is a professor in the Department of Journalism and Media Studies at Oslo Metropolitan University, Norway

Project title: RUIICAY-HIOA Intercultural Communication Linkage Programme?
Partner institutions: The Pluriversidad Amawtay Wasi (Ecuador), the Universidad Autónoma Indígena Intercultural (Colombia), the University of the Autonomous Regions of the Caribbean Coast of Nicaragua, and Oslo Metropolitan University (Norway)

Notes

1   See https://www.un.org/development/desa/indigenouspeoples/wp-content/up-loads/sites/19/2018/11/UNDRIP_E_web.pdf
2   Indigenous name for Latin America.
3   CRIC, *Programa Educación*, http://www.cric-colombia.org/portal/proyecto-cultural/programa-educacion/
4   For a description of the conference and call for proposals, see https://cartagena2017.iamcr.org/static/pre-conferences/minga-of-thought/
5   See https://www.opendemocracy.net/en/about/
6   See http://www.deepecology.org/platform.htm

References

Adriansen HK, Madsen LM and Jensen S (eds) (2015) *Higher Education and Capacity Building in Africa: The Geography and Power of Knowledge under Changing Conditions.* Abingdon: Routledge

Alvesson M and Sköldberg K (2000) *Reflexive Methodology: New Vistas for Qualitative Research.* London: Sage

Baggini J (2018) *How the World Thinks: A Global History of Philosophy.* London: Granta

Brysk A (2000) *From Tribal Village to Global Village: Indian Rights and International Relations in Latin America.* Stanford, CA: Stanford University Press

Chomsky N (2014) *On Anarchism.* London: Penguin

Doyle M (2003) *A reflexive critique of learner managed learning. British Education Index.* Available online

Escobar A (2018) Farewell to development: Interview with Allen White, *Great Transition Initiative*, February. Available online

Gjefsen T (2011) *Arne Næss: Et liv.* Oslo: Cappelen Damm

Gould JL (1998) *To Die in This Way: Nicaraguan Indians and the Myth of Mestizaje,* 1880– 1965. Durham, NC: Duke University Press

Gow DD (2008) *Countering Development: Indigenous Modernity and the Moral Imagination.* Durham, NC: Duke University Press

Gutiérrez N, Perera F, Paiz G, Flores CM, Mejía M, Treminio X, Sarango F et al. (2018) *Base Document for the Nurture and Cultivation of Wisdoms and Knowledges: CCRISAC,* 2nd edn. Managua: Universidad de las Regiones Autónomas de la Costa Caribe Nicaragüense

Jasanoff S (2004) *States of Knowledge: The Co-Production of Science and the Social Order.* London and New York: Routledge

Koch S and Weingart P (2016) *The Delusion of Knowledge Transfer: The Impact of Foreign Aid Experts on Policy-Making in South Africa and Tanzania.* Cape Town: African Minds

Krøvel R (2018) Indigenous perspectives on researching indigenous peoples. *Social Identities* 24(1): 58–65

Leyva-Solano X (2001) Neo-Zapatismo: Networks of power and war. PhD thesis, University of Manchester

López y Rivas G (2013, 7 January) *Latin America: Autonomic Processes of Indigenous Peoples in the Neoliberal Transnationalization.* Louvain-La-Neuve: CETRI. Available online

Mignolo W, Silverblatt I and Saldívar-Hull S (1998) About the series. In: JL Gould (ed.) *To Die in This Way: Nicaraguan Indians and the Myth of Mestizaje,* 1880–1965. Durham, NC: Duke University Press

Naess A (1973) The shallow and the deep, long-range ecology movement: A summary. *Inquiry* 16: 95–100

Nussbaum MC (1997) *Cultivating Humanity: A Classical Defense of Reform in Liberal Education.* Cambridge, MA and London: Harvard University Press

Palechor NBC, Mera JJF and Carvajal VAS (1995) *El Movimiento Armado Quintin Lame: Autodefensa, guerrilla y desmovilización.* Cali: Pontificia Universidad Javeriana

Rappaport J (1990) *The Politics of Memory: Native Historical Interpretation in the Colombian Andes.* Cambridge: Cambridge University Press

Rattansi A (2011) *Multiculturalism: A Very Short Introduction.* Oxford: Oxford University Press

Romm NRA (2017) Researching indigenous ways of knowing-and-being: Revitalizing relational quality of living. In P Ngulube (ed.) *Handbook of Research on Theoretical Perspectives on Indigenous Knowledge Systems in Developing Countries.* Hershey, PA: IGI Global

RUIICAY (2017) *Manifesto: Minga of Thought 'Communication and Indigenous Peoples'.* Available online

Sarango LF (2017) *Kapak Ñan Pedagógico: Filosófico de la Pluriversidad 'Amawtay Wasi'.* Quito: Pluriversidad Amawtay Wasi

Saugstad J, Frøland SS, Madsen K, Matlary JH, Sirevåg R and Preus IN (2018, 14 August) Avkoloniseringsideologien truer universitetene (The decolonizing ideology threatens the universities). *Aftenposten*

Sessions G (1977) Spinoza and Jeffers on man in nature. *Inquiry* 20(1–4): 481–528

Skafish P (2013) Introduction. *Radical Philosophy* 182(Nov/Dec): 14–15

Smithers GD and Newman BN (eds) (2014) *Native Diasporas: Indigenous Identities and Settler Colonialism in the Americas.* Lincoln, NE: University of Nebraska Press

Stringer ET (2007) *Action Research.* London: Sage

Uzendoski M (2010) *The Napo Runa of Amazonian Ecuador.* Champaign, IL: University of Illinois Press

Viveiros de Castro E (2013) Cannibal metaphysics: Amerindian perspectivism. *Radical Philosophy* 182(Nov/Dec): 17–28

5

A view of Norhed from the South

Edward K Kirumira interviewed by Tor Halvorsen

Edward K Kirumira was a professor of sociology and former principal of the College of Humanities and Social Sciences at Makerere University (MU) in Uganda, a position he held for five years. Before that he was Dean of MU's Faculty of Social Sciences for eight years. Kirumira studied at Makerere and Exeter Universities, as well as the London School of Hygiene and Tropical Medicine. He was awarded his PhD by Copenhagen and Harvard Universities. His own research has focused on population and reproductive health, and he has conducted extensive interdisciplinary research on HIV/AIDS, emerging diseases and international health issues. He is a fellow and former treasurer of the Uganda National Academy of Sciences, and chairs the Academy's forums on health and nutrition and on the prevention of violence against children. Kirumira has years of experience in working with donors and donor-funded programmes. While at MU, he was involved in how the university managed its relationship with Norhed, as well as in the Norhed-supported Water and Society Project, WaSo, which involves collaborative research across eleven partner institutions, four each in Africa and Asia and three in Europe. This interview took place in South Africa in December 2018, just before Kirumira took up the position of director of the Stellenbosch Institute for Advanced Study.

Tor Halvorsen (TH): In this interview, I would like us to focus on the Norhed programme, and the kind of university co-operation it tries to enable. I want to draw on your experiences at MU and in Norhed projects run from that institution. With a total of 14 Norhed projects, MU has been among the most successful institutions in obtaining support from Norhed. I know you have been closely involved in two of these projects; I am interested in how you see the Norhed programme generally and how you assess the value of the programme for MU in terms of knowledge development. Can we start with your own experience? Please explain why MU was awarded so many projects and say what you think the institution has gained from them?

Edward K Kirumira (EK): To start with a broader perspective, MU has been supported by the Norwegian government for quite some time. We were beneficiaries of both the NOMA and NUFU programmes (described in the preface to this volume). So, in a way, MU was well positioned when Norhed was set up. One of the conditions set by Norhed was that applying institutions had to have a Norwegian partner. From working on the NUFU programme, a number of us had quite extensive networks with Norwegian universities and that helped us a lot. For other institutions, finding partners in Norwegian universities was actually a bit of a problem. But MU's history with NUFU, and our work on the Nile Basin Research Programme that was funded by the Norwegian Ministry of Foreign Affairs, probably made it easier for MU to submit competitive proposals. In fact, MU won 13 out of the 46 projects that were offered, and was also part of one more that was co-ordinated by Khartoum University. So, yes, in total, we secured Norhed support for 14 projects.

The fact that we got several projects also allowed us to invest a bit in a central co-ordinating platform. Although this ran into some difficulties later, initially it enabled projects to develop a conception of a broader, more meaningful connection with the university, and its administrative system. So, right from the start, those involved in the Norhed projects got a sense that they were part of a process of institutional capacity building rather than simply recipients of individualised project support.

TH: If we look at the basic idea of the programme: the money was to go to the South, and the Southern partner had to find a partner in the North with whom to develop an application. You mentioned that some projects found it difficult to find a partner, but MU had a long-term relationship you could build on. Do you think this new way of giving the Southern partners the power to decide on both the content and budget allocations of projects worked? That is, did this allow MU to apply to create the kinds of projects that the institution saw as relevant? And did you find Northern partners were able to work well within this new system, or did project partners tend to fall back into the old ways of working?

EK: I think in the case of Uganda the new system worked to a great extent. But having gone through the experience and had time to reflect on it, I can see there are some inherent weaknesses in the approach. First, it assumes that the Southern institutions will find a Northern partner. However, this can be difficult if relationships haven't already been established, as applicants had a fairly short time in which to respond to Norhed's call for proposals. Indeed, some of MU's own projects faced this challenge and therefore couldn't submit proposals.

Second, it assumes that Southern institutions have the capacity to competitively evaluate a large and diverse body of proposals – to self-evaluate in a way. However, self-evaluation, especially in a competitive environment, tends to be a bit dicey because, often, the people who are applying are also part of the evaluation process in some way.

In the case of MU, certain sensitive moments occurred in which one could feel that the self-evaluation process had simultaneously become part of a competitive process. So, the extent to which you can have a truly objective self-evaluation system within a Southern institution is potentially risky. This is especially true because Southern institutions are operating in such resource-constrained environments. Virtually everyone in the institution would like to be able to gain access to the funding stream, and, in some instances, the adjudication committee included people who had not been able to qualify to compete in the call for proposals themselves. In fact, I think this tension has existed within the MU–Norhed Institutional Development and Implementation Committee since Norhed was established, and this might have limited the effectiveness of that committee.

TH: Are you saying that the academic selection committees that Norad set up to evaluate the applications for the Norhed programme created some contradictions locally because projects were evaluated according to criteria that were different to those MU would have used if the institution had set up its own selection committees?

EK: I think so. I think the situation created contradictions. For me, the lesson is that the Southern universities have to build more robust grant-management capacities, and ensure that they have relatively senior people to take part in institutional self-evaluation processes. Instead, the MU–Norhed Institutional Development and Implementation Committee included some relatively junior people who still needed to benefit from this funding stream. They were asked to withdraw from funding applications if they agreed to join the Committee. So, yes, the process created some tensions between applying for and being part of the projects versus being part of their administration.

TH: Should we rather be giving donor money to organisations like research councils that are located and governed in the South, and which could have committees to evaluate projects like those that Norhed wants to support? Would that be a better way of empowering the South? In the current system, as you indicate, control suddenly shifted back to Oslo. That is, Norad set up the selection committees to evaluate projects using a mix of criteria that were determined partly by Norad and partly by academic requirements. But ultimately the committees were controlled by Norad's programme committee.

EK: I think what you suggest would be better in Uganda. As you know, MU has helped to build capacity to establish other universities – the country now has about six public universities and some very strong private universities are emerging. This means we can start to set the stage for some kind of national research council that would make it possible to shift the selection of projects to the South in a more fundamental way. As things work now, we are still more or less dependent on the existence of good relationships between academics or academic institutions in Uganda and Norway.

Uganda's National Council for Science and Technology tends to be more of a regulatory body, and has not yet had a funding component. However, I am not sure if this organisation should be turned into a national research council because regulatory and funding functions probably need to be kept separate. Nevertheless, a similar organisation would enable us to transcend the institutional politics that would occur were it to be placed within that institution. Perhaps we need to consider working with both the National Council for Science and Technology and the Uganda National Council for Higher Education, and creating a body that is inbetween the two. The challenge is, I don't know whether we have created enough capacity to manage such an entity and prevent it from being 'captured', if we can use that expression. However, we and our donors definitely need to think about a possible shift in this direction.

TH: Institutional capture by certain interests is, of course, a danger anywhere, not only in Uganda, but if such a council had existed, MU would not have needed a Norwegian partner. But let's go back to the rule that you had to have a Norwegian partner, do you think that influenced the nature of the projects in any way?

EK: I know of at least two, maybe three, projects on which this rule really had an impact – it actually transferred the project back to the Norwegian partner institution. For the majority, however, I think there were, and are, tremendous gains to be made from building the capacity of the Southern partners to manage not only the research process but also the budgeting and administrative components.

My project experience was special in this regard. The WaSo Project in which I am involved had an institutional administrative office at MU – the MU/UiB office – through which we had already developed close ties related to common projects. So, in a way, our Northern partners were able to operate very easily in the 'South'; they had a platform at MU, and through this platform we could work with them. I see this as an ideal model for long-term collaboration between universities. For projects without this advantage, I am sure it became 'convenient' to have the co-ordinating office in the North. In other words, project administration is a challenge in Norhed-funded projects, but it is something worth focusing on as part of the empowerment of the South.

TH: Do you think any academic 'recapturing' took place, or were project leaders in Uganda and at MU able to use their Norwegian links without being transformed by them so to speak? In other words, is the old story still operating or, if we talk about decolonising knowledge, is this the way to go?

EK: Well, an unintended consequence was that, unlike NUFU projects, not many Norhed projects had strong research components. For this reason, younger Norwegian researchers did not find the project attractive and few young Norwegian scholars took part. Instead, a good measure of older scholars were involved who were, so to say, more open to letting the Southern academics lead. Many of these older scholars had worked in the South themselves, and were less inclined towards 'academic recapturing'. Instead, they saw themselves playing a facilitative or mentorship role. This was really unintended so one cannot say that the programme, in itself, led to a shifting of power to the South. And, actually, I think among the Norhed programme's major problems so far is that it lacks a strong research component and that so few younger Norwegian scholars took part in it.

That said, however, some projects did express frustration with the Norhed model. This was especially so for projects that had relatively few partners – say one or two partners in the South and one partner in the North. Where projects had several partners, the frustrations seemed to be more diffuse. For example, the WaSo Project had three partners in the North and eight in the South. The only way we could manage was to share and distribute power relations everywhere. In cases where just one Norwegian university works with several Southern universities, the tendency is to rotate around the Northern partner; in those situations, power has not shifted.

TH: So, are you saying that stronger South–South links give you a bigger network, and this helps transfer the research focus to issues relevant to the South? And have your experiences of South–South networking been good?

EK: Yes, we have had very good experiences with this. Even in problematic situations like South Sudan, or the occasional challenges that arise in partner institutions in the South, we were able to distribute the problem across the partners and, in a way, find solutions in the South. For example, we could send PhD students to Kenya or Uganda, or even Sri Lanka, Bangladesh or Cambodia, so you could actually distribute and increase capacity building efficiency. This would have been slightly more difficult if our project had involved only MU, Juba [University in South Sudan] and a university in the North.

TH: Do you think Norhed should drop the requirement that a Norwegian partner be included?

EK: Norwegian partners are beneficial. Our Norwegian partners came in handy when we had challenges with internal university systems, especially with procurement. But there are several reasons why I think it would be nice to continue to have such partnerships. Many universities in the South undervalue our own home-based graduate training. And unfortunately, scholars who are wholly trained in the South are often expected to prove themselves unduly in terms of the quality of their education. In this context, Northern partnerships help add legitimacy and, more importantly, they provide avenues for greatly needed networking.

TH: Of the 90 MU professors we interviewed, I think only one or two of those who have a PhD had received it wholly from MU.

EK: That is correct. My wife earned all three of her degrees at MU, but, in the process, she worked with three other universities, two in Europe and one in the US. It more or less works so that when you get to a point where you are ready to sit and write, you can go somewhere where you have better access to literature and senior scholars and such things. To say that your degree, or part of your degree, was at such and such a place abroad is still seen as prestigious. So, I think the continued inclusion of Norwegian partners is good but should not necessarily be a precondition for funding.

TH: But you also mentioned that it was good for procurement and for 'development aid' kinds of things. This implies a combination of Norad and Norhed; or rather, a combination of academic partnership with development assistance. The combination seems to work well in this case. However, it is still important to ask: do you feel that the development logic has been too strong in any way? That is, has Norad pushed too many of its own ideas about what its support should lead to in terms of development? Take this idea of capacity building, for example: what kind of capacity are we talking about?

EK: I think there has been a tension on several levels. One was the tension between the NOMA and NUFU conceptualisations of the Norhed support. Another is the appreciation of capacity building: are we talking about institutional capacity building so that our institutions are more relevant to society or the more traditional building of an individual's capacity where the emphasis is on increasing the number and quality of PhD and master's graduates?

The reporting structure for Norhed projects has changed over time. Initially, reporting was done on the assumption that projects should show how they were building capacity that would enable the university to be more relevant to society. However, the focus of the projects often ended up being on enhancing PhD or master's programmes, which kept bringing the projects back to the traditional idea of academic capacity building. Given that MU was asked to support the University of Juba, I think the emphasis tended to revert back to building the capacity of individuals and maybe a bit of South–South mobility. But even then, South–South mobility was structured around PhD and master's students rather than on broader institutional development or societal institution-building through what you could call an educationalisation.

TH: I agree that the research component, in the sense of research as a product you can make relevant for actors in society is downplayed a bit. But, isn't the strengthening of academics crucial for enabling them to later have more influence on society? Or how do you solve the chicken and the egg question here?

EK: Yes, if there is one thing the Norhed programme can lay claim to, it is the establishment of platforms and networks of academics that then have more impact in sort of a second phase or third phase. In a way, now that we have project partners as far away as Sri Lanka, for example, we have all these Norhed-crafted groups and multidisciplinary teams of academics in the South working with all these different themes, sub-themes, such as Democratic and Economic Governance; Health and Equity; Education and Training; and Natural Resource Management, Climate Change and Environment.

So, I think the issue was that we assumed that the influence on society would happen during the three or four years of the programme's life. But if we acknowledge that the aim of the programme was to enhance the capacity of institutions in the South to be able to do [rather than just do], then the Norhed programme has definitely been successful. However, in the reporting structure, you find yourself having to account for 'how has this impacted on national politics and policies' for example, and you really have to struggle to find evidence!

Very strong intra-institutional thematic areas have developed as a result of the Norhed programme, and a critical mass of interdisciplinary academics, or different disciplines working together, can now actually engage. I think the capacity for Southern universities to engage in knowledge creation/provision for policy has definitely improved. The question, for me, is how we can maintain this momentum. When you look, for example, at the level of publications produced over the three or four years of the Norhed programme, it has been low because the emphasis has been more on the supervision of PhD and master's and undergraduate students.

If Norad is thinking of a second phase, I suggest it should be structured around using the capacity and the platforms built so far to enable academics to engage beyond the university, rather than focusing only on building capacity through more PhD and master's programmes. A bit of this is still necessary, such as where MU is supporting other public or private universities, but I think there would be more value for money if projects are now supported to move beyond the current programme. A good critical mass has been developed and now needs to be, for lack of a better phrase, 'empowered to engage' and to produce knowledge in accordance with this engagement.

TH: So are you saying that this idea of having these two dimensions – a research component and another one focused on giving evidence-based advice, as Norad and Norhed put it – has not really taken off?

EK: Where it was achieved, it was in accidental or ad hoc ways. For example, with the WaSo Project, it started when the project was challenged by the number of people applying for fellowships from the marginalised category. We then reached out to Uganda's Ministry of Water and Environment. This 'accidental' action started a relationship with the ministry, which has become so strong that the project has been invited to be on the advisory committee for the ministry's efforts to set up and operationalise a Water Resources Institute. Such linkages, or expectations thereof, were not explicitly built into the project, and they were not funded by either the university or the project. These efforts depended very much on personal initiatives, but the gains we made via that relationship have been huge and really tremendous.

TH: You've also mentioned the successes you've seen with interdisciplinary work. The Norhed programme is very open to, and encourages, cross-disciplinary linkages, perhaps more than ordinary university-based or research-council funded projects. Could you talk about this a bit more?

EK: I think Norhed's funding model has promoted strong interaction across disciplines. When I look at almost all the projects, I don't see any that have not achieved a significant measure of cross-disciplinary work. Even the journalism project, which was quite focused, led to the flourishing of sub-disciplines within journalism to the extent that they are starting at least two additional master's programmes in various genres of journalism.

TH: I'm asking about this because cross-disciplinary work is always difficult when combined with teaching. In straight research it might be easier to initiate, but teaching at master's and PhD level is often very discipline-based.

EK: Yes, if you emphasise research, it can be much easier to achieve a cross/multidisciplinary objective. But it is going to be very difficult if we don't invest sufficiently and efficiently enough in research to develop stable cross-disciplinary work that changes disciplinary curricula over time, or even leads to new disciplines that are more in line with our knowledge demands. In other words; a shift towards more independent knowledge development – the post-colonial shift we are struggling with now – is supported, in theory at least, by being open to a multidisciplinary approach. This is also an argument for a link in the Norhed programme between research and teaching. However, as argued above, too little space exists in the research dimension to make this a resource for curriculum change. Too much curriculum is still imported without being properly translated so that it is relevant to our own knowledge culture.

The terrain in the South also is problem-solving / problem-oriented to a great extent. Established theories (that are often imported orthodoxies) seem to lack good tools with which to understand and possibly solve the problems we experience in the South. A multidisciplinary approach helps to puzzle together something new and more relevant. The grounds for cross-disciplinary research are also very fertile as we are dealing with multifaceted social problems – a world of complex social, environmental and economic interconnections that are more challengingly integrated than anywhere else in the world. To draw on some observations from my own field, I think this complexity is why, for example, research into public health is currently rapidly gaining ground.

So, yes, I think that, as academics and researchers, we should not be shy to assert ourselves in defining or determining the frameworks within which we are often asked to express ourselves – disciplinary, multidisciplinary, developmental or any combination of these. We need to be at the centre of the debate on academic freedom so that we do not end up being either apologetic or confrontational. We always say that national governments should invest in research and commit a certain percentage of GDP to research funding. The question is how much are we involved in shaping that debate? For example, in Uganda, we have struggled to set up a national AIDS Trust Fund for I don't know how many years. We have now started what we call the 'One Dollar Initiative', which is trying to encourage the private sector to contribute to the national aids programme. The One Dollar Initiative is based on the idea that all private-sector employers should contribute at least one dollar for every employee they have into this Trust Fund as a way of mobilising national ownership. Even this is difficult in resource-constrained environments, yet we to continue to push policy-makers to prioritise research, and to invest in evidence-based policy making. In their defence, quite a number of them do appreciate evidence-based policy making, but I think they have not got to the level of investing in the process of producing the evidence. They would rather come to you to give them evidence-based advice and hope that somebody else has already paid for this evidence to be created. To be able to produce relevant evidence, cross-disciplinary flexibility is essential. This again, presupposes the strengthening of research driven curricular and disciplinary development.

In terms of Norwegian development aid, we can envision a situation where Norad says, 'we will give you this amount of money but MU must match every shilling we put in'. And we can imagine MU being established enough to say 'okay, we will match it' or strong enough to be able to convince our government to do the matching. Although this will be very difficult for institutions like MU, some successes have been recorded. For example, with the funding of Uganda's National Response to HIV, TB and malaria, the Central Coordination Mechanism Board convinced the government to match every dollar given by the Global Fund, and they are doing so. So, I think perhaps national government needs a bit of nudging through its bilateral agreements.

TH: At present, as you indicate, MU is reproducing the donor trap. So, if there is another phase of Norhed funding, would you suggest that Norhed gives US$100 million only if the Ugandan government promises to come up with the same amount over, say, a five-year period? And, yet, in the past, you have said that you doubt that the government has enough interest in knowledge to come up with their share. Should you, therefore, risk dropping all funding for a while?

EK: I think we might have to take that risk. What we could do is to push for national government funding to increase annually over a certain number of years as a precondition for continued funding. We would like to see at least 20 to 30 per cent year on year increases from government. Financing higher education is expensive, and one can easily use that as a bargaining tool to say 'we are lifting 80 per cent of your load, so put in your 20 per cent'. I think that the bilateral conversations that the Norwegian government has with national governments in low- to middle-income countries are critically important because, once a bilateral framework is in place, it becomes easier for Norhed to work. One of the challenges is that the academic community, including its most senior and prominent members, have not been present in those conversations even though they could play important roles. Instead, we wait passively to become recipients. I think it is about time for us academics to be present at the bilateral negotiation table.

TH: In a way, that is what we are trying to do with this book: we want to raise these kinds of issues. It is very strange, to me at least, to see how easily the Ugandan government employs consultants instead of calling on much cleverer people at the university that we have spent millions supporting over the years. In my view, in such situations, support for higher education should be put on hold until governments like yours start to understand how much they are undermining their own academic community.

EK: I think that MU, for example, is in the very privileged position of having trained almost everyone in government. But at the same time, MU, and, for that matter, all the other higher education institutions in the country are conspicuously absent from the bilateral negotiations that provide frameworks for subsequent support. I think it is critically important that people from MU are strategically chosen to be part of setting that agenda.

It might even be that, when the Norwegian government is having discussions with the Ugandan government, you suggest that it would be wise to invite one or two people from the universities 'who understand us' and all these different issues. I think that is probably part of the missing link. We saw this when we started engaging with the Ministry of Water and Environment, for example. We could see that, sometimes, the people in the ministry were surprised to realise that they actually have resources right here in their own higher education institutions. 'Where have you been?'

If Norhed is thinking of a second phase, rather than saying, 'now we are stopping funding', it might be beneficial to first invest in a middle phase, a transition phase, that would be about negotiating the framework for, and within which, a second phase could work. An example of the start of such a conversation happened in 2018, during the Swedish International Development Cooperation Agency's annual review. At the meeting, SIDA spoke quite frankly and said, 'Look, we have been here since 2003. That is so many years. We think SIDA will not continue to support MU in this way.' Unfortunately, the media interpreted this as SIDA saying they would stop funding MU completely.

So, Norad might want to consider investing in that transitional phase, because then we won't just continue into the next phase in a business-as-usual mode. I think institutions and governments in the South need a 'shock phase', if we can put it that way. This shock or transition phase could be critically important in [re]defining Norwegian support for capacity development in higher education and for research for development. Some of us would really be keen to participate in this.

TH: So, a shock or transition phase would include ensuring that the university is represented in the negotiation process and making demands on Southern governments to gradually match donor funding. But there is still another problem: few academics in the South are really standing up and ensuring that value is placed on what they see as valuable and relevant knowledge.

EK: That is true. I think it is partly because the mode of much of the support received has tended to be given to an individual, either in terms of supporting their PhD or another research project. The need to demonstrate relevance was not part of the process. Instead it was all geared towards moving individuals from one phase of their career to the next – moving from assistant lecturer, to lecturer, to senior lecturer and finally to professor. This mode not only perpetuated the alienation of the university from the public, but also made academics a bit reclusive. One of the few times they are forced to justify themselves publicly is in defence of their PhD (and, even then, it is very seldom that anyone outside of the academic world would be present, so we are not talking about a public defence in the real sense of the word).

Going forward, I think that any academic or researcher's public standing should be part of the architecture of programme support. MU has the advantage of having many senior professors, some of them now retired, who could play an important role making the institution stand on its own. Norhed could consider asking how best to invest in these people. These are academics who have trained almost everybody in government and as senior professors, they are beyond competition and do not need to publish an extra article to get promoted. As things stand now, when these academics retire at 65 or 70 years of age, the private universities are taking them in and they continue to teach.

I think this should also be included in this shock phase. You see my worry is that, with less government investment in research and higher education, MU is becoming so inward looking that it risks becoming destructive. I mean, some very unhealthy competition is evident – everybody wants to be a head of something or a member of senate or council. Everybody wants to be inside these little enclaves where they think they will be in a position of power so they begin to eat at each other. We need to expand horizons of academic staff in higher education institutions.

TH: Part of what we hoped to include in this book is how Norhed-supported research and capacity development programmes could help to really strengthen the academic profession and academic values. For example, something we hoped would emerge from research conducted in this first phase was a sense of what we can call 'objective knowledge' or knowledge that withstands objections. Norhed also aimed to strengthen teacher-driven research as a means of driving curriculum change and updating curriculum content. Another aim for Norhed was to strengthen links between PhD students and their supervisors. Do you think these would be useful avenues to pursue further?

EK: These avenues are crucial. The way Norhed went about things was different. For example, if you look at WaSo, the approach was to contribute to existing programmes and curricula, and improve their quality. We have had significant success, with input into 12 programme curricula offered by WaSo's network of universities in Africa and Asia. In addition, Norhed helped other projects to start completely new programmes. That was very hard because these programmed had to deal with the university system of accreditation and those kinds of things.

I think one needs to be a bit creative, and one area where Norhed could gain more mileage would be to focus more on improving existing programmes rather than starting new ones. It is important to note that an inherent weakness (or missing link) was the assumption that a body of research, or an engagement with research, would feed into the process of curriculum development. But how could Norhed assume a goal of research-based teaching and then decide not to fund a research component in the programmes they supported? There seems to be a bit of a disconnect between the assumption and the practice. What we did in WaSo was to draw on the 11 universities in our broader network, and select the best elements from existing programmes across these universities. Essentially, we relied on existing research and teaching material.

Among the challenges most Southern universities face is that curricula have not changed for years; many still replicate what was taught in Western universities long ago. Part of the curriculum in higher education institutions thus still bears the hallmark of the post-independence intention of 'training' the civil service. Now, we have to do something else, yet many of the graduates we are producing are still destined either for civil service or to stay in academic institutions. Either way they lose out: neither the civil service nor the universities are recruiting except to fill vacated posts. So, we need to shift and say that the urgent need is to invest in curriculum review and curriculum development. But, this time, curricula must be research-based. Uganda's National Council of Higher Education says universities need to review curricula every three to five years but, so far, curriculum reviews have been desk based. To change this, it could be useful if, in Norhed's second phase, tracer-studies look at graduates of MU and other higher education institutions, to find out what are they doing, what did they not learn that they should have learned and so on. These tracer-studies should inform curriculum reviews and curriculum development rather than be done for their own sake.

TH: So, to create curricula that are more flexible and locally relevant, Southern universities must make administrative changes and shift the way research is channelled into curriculum development?

EK: Yes, and of course traditional universities like MU always struggle with these things. You know some people insist that disciplines must be seen as sacred. But then the people you produce are not sacred. Especially now that MU is not the only university in Uganda, I think our role and mode of curriculum delivery must be redefined. Right now, I worry that we have become too insular, to the extent that if this continues we could very easily become irrelevant. You can hear this in the political corridors, where people are saying 'Maybe we should put money into Kyambogo or Mbarara University of Science and Technology'. If Norad does invest in a second phase, which I hope they will, then a little break that shocks people might be a good idea, even if the break lasts only three to six months, and Norad is still present on campus, but in a negotiating mode.

TH: Returning to the issue of relevance, are you saying your country's oldest university might be becoming irrelevant due to its conservative or historical legacy? But who decides what is relevant knowledge in Uganda now? Who would you say is crucial in this process and where are they? You have said elsewhere that the World Bank tells you what is relevant and that you think this is unfortunate as they seem to think the STEM disciplines (science, technology, economics and mathematics) alone are important. What are people inside Uganda saying?

EK: In Uganda now, it is very difficult to know who decides what is relevant. Unfortunately, politicians are trying very hard to make these decisions and, of course, they have been captured by the World Bank/STEM narrative. But you can also find pockets and platforms, some of which we have not paid very much attention to before, that are interrogating this question and some of these are very powerful. For example, the Uganda National Academy for Sciences (UNAS) and other professional bodies are looking at this question, albeit often from a regulatory perspective. In fact, as a platform for discussing and debating what is relevant, UNAS have a number of forums dealing with governance and leadership, climate change, economic development, health, education, partner violence and violence against children, vaccine and vaccination, antimicrobial resistance, biotechnology and biosecurity [see http://www.unas.org.ug/]. They have also started a forum on urbanisation and urban planning, bringing together professionals in public health, architecture, the social sciences and planning. UNAS is still struggling to establish itself, and it is certainly one platform that is utilising senior academics and senior professors. The current president is Nelson Sewankambo, former principal of MU's College of Health Sciences. Then people such as Frederick Kayanja (former vice-chancellor of Mbarara University of Science and Technology), Mary Okwakol, (vice-chancellor of Busitema University) and Livingstone Luboobi (former vice-chancellor of MU who got an honorary doctorate from University of Bergen), all chair various UNAS forums. So, that is somewhere we could look to find platforms for discussing the question of relevance.

TH: What about Uganda's public universities, do the vice-chancellors get together to discuss?

EK: There is the Vice-Chancellors' (VC) Forum.

TH: Does that provide any academic guidance?

EK: Not quite. Unfortunately, they seem to spend most of their time engaging with the government on issues of finance. But the problem with that structure is the way vice-chancellors are elected and appointed. The process is becoming increasingly bruising, not just at MU, but in all the public and private universities. This is a problem because it ends up undermining the legitimacy of the incumbents. But, yes of course, if the VC forum could shift focus away from the urgent concerns of financing and student unrest, it could perhaps become more engaged in the relevance debate. Another platform to consider is the East African Association of Universities that brings all the universities in East Africa together.

Norad could look at these platforms that have all tended to stay kind of silent in the past and decide that one of its strategies will be to invest in them. They could say, okay, we have funded individuals and universities in the past, now let's look at the national, regional, continental structures.

TH: Yes, my impression is that the academics see themselves as being in a very weak position when it comes to saying what is relevant. That is, they don't really stand up or stand together as academics. Of course, this has a lot to do with history and the whole way projects are funded and all that, and so we come full circle. A question that remains is, since Norhed is trying to approach things differently, how would you describe it in relation to other programmes?

EK: The first difference I see is that I think Norhed made a conscious attempt to enhance institutional capacity-building using a networking perspective and to support training and student mobility essentially within a South–South framework. So, although MU got support for many projects, Norad was not supporting the university per se, but rather a bunch of institutions in the South and giving MU the responsibility for institutional co-ordination. Now, I don't see any other donor programmes that engage two, three or four universities on an equal basis with a partnership agreement. SIDA's current programme created a localised version of this model, whereby MU was funded to work with other universities in Uganda such as Kyambogo, Busitema, Mbarara and Gulu. In that model, MU retained the power and supported the others. So, I think that Norhed has been on a unique journey in terms of establishing partnerships within the South.

The second difference is that the majority of the projects Norhed supported were cross-disciplinary, and universities were requested to work within the four themes; so the organisation was thematic rather than disciplinary. I think that that was really a good thing. Of course, it assumes that academics are embedded strongly enough in their own disciplines to be able to work in interdisciplinary ways.

The third one was to, at least, attempt to shift the donor–recipient power relations. Sure, in some instances it worked and in other instances it did not, but at least the construction of the programme was such that power could shift to the South. I think that was a very good thing as far as the programme was concerned. The fourth difference was that the programme came with various kinds of institutionalised support, such as [partial] support for PhD fellowships.

And another really crucial one is how Norhed supported the operationalisation of South–South mobility. In my own case, without the Norhed programme, I doubt I would ever have considered going to Cambodia or Sri Lanka or Bangladesh to do anything. But this kind of horizontal mobility is *really* critical. It opened doors in higher education institutions and allowed us to begin to see what internationalisation could mean from a South–South perspective.

So, those are some of the things I see as characteristic of Norhed, and different from other funding streams. I think one challenge was that there were many different ways of doing things within the Norhed programme. Perhaps we could have invested more than we did, but it was an experiment so people didn't want to jump into the deep end.

South–South mobility for PhD students has been such a huge thing. We are creating this new cadre of PhDs. You know, reflecting back on my own training, I wish I'd had that opportunity. For these candidates, by the time they settle at MU, they will have people in academia, a community of scholarship that can allow you to move to the next level.

This is really good, because in earlier years, the university would send PhD candidates to Bergen, or somewhere like that, full time. After some years, they would come back and they would be a Bergen person. In contrast, South–South mobility issue is really very nice. I remember when we went to Cambodia and we thought, wow, there are some really solid scholars here, people that we can work with. That was a really good experience.

So, to varying degrees, this aspect of shifting the power to the South opened up opportunities for us to co-ordinate with others, and to put into practice academic co-ordination in the South. We realised that this South–South co-ordination involves a lot of work, and the extra is not tagged or articulated within your programme or reporting system, but it is really good, it is really worthwhile; it gives you something more.

TH: That brings me to my last question. When you report back on your programmes, you report into a system that Norad developed, and might even be evaluated by Norad. This system is, again, based on pretty traditional ideas of what constitutes academic output and so on. I don't think any of the things you mentioned as hugely important characteristics of the Norhed programme are part of the standard reporting systems. Instead, these count the number of articles in important journals and how many fellowships are awarded, which already presuppose that academics have networks in the academic centres. Meanwhile, crucial aspects of South–South co-operation – such as creating new knowledge through interdisciplinary collaboration and learning to use the power you have in the South to promote and disseminate knowledge based on research you value (whether or not this is published by international peer-reviewed journals) – is often not counted, and becomes somehow invisible. How should future Norhed programmes change this?

EK: I think part of the solution is to make South–South co-operation an integral part of the expectations linked to programme support. Put a value to this, so that it becomes attractive to do rather than just a nice to have. I mean you can even ask projects to quantify it by saying how many research networks they involved in the project and how they worked with them. Similarly, you can ask institutions how many universities they worked with, where and how. This would turn these aspects around and make them into expectations rather than so-called synergies. You know the current reporting format; such kinds of things might feature in terms of the synergies a project has created. This is so vague and it means that project teams report on them in equally vague ways. For example, we would say, 'we have established a network with the environment ministry' or something like that.

Much more important is the qualitative value that programmes add, and unless we pay attention to the qualitative values of programme outcomes, true institutional capacity building in the South is going to be very difficult to achieve. If you look at the universities in the North, they are, to a great extent, built on values, rather than their outputs. To put it another way, it is their values or ethos that drive their outputs. Their values determine and push you to publish. Their values push you to be accountable.

For me, the experience of being part of co-ordinating the Norhed project, the value that I placed on accountability to others, including other institutions, increased tremendously because I had to be conscious of Prof Francis Mutua at the University of Nairobi and of the environment in which he is operating. I had to learn to appreciate the workings of Addis Ababa University in Ethiopia, and the conditions at the University of Juba in South Sudan, where it was hugely difficult to get anything done yet we managed to do a lot anyway. This awareness also fed into my understanding and appreciation of my own university, and perhaps made me a bit more patient with my institution. And the more we can give Southern academics and researchers an experience of different universities in this way, the more the quality of our institutions will improve.

PART TWO
THE ECO-SOCIAL PARADIGM SHIFT

Introduction to Part Two

Tor Halvorsen

In this section we present examples of projects engaging with questions of eco-social relations, which lie at the centre of debates about our future on the planet. The challenges for knowledge institutions, given the Paris Agreement and the adoption of the SDGs, is how to encourage humans to live, work and be *for* rather than *against* nature. How can our social and natural worlds interact in ways that do not destroy the biosphere we depend on? How can we secure fairness and equality among humans, and promote production and consumption that respects the limits of planetary resources? An eco-social paradigm that is capable of guiding politics is clearly necessary but will not evolve by itself. To light the way, universities have both ideas and knowledge to contribute. As Baker (2012) suggests, a 'green theory of value' that prioritises healthy environments and balanced ecosystems would be a common (and global) good.

Low- to middle-income countries (LMICs) are experiencing the worst of the consequences arising from how humans and nature have interacted so far, both locally, at points of pollution and poison, and as global environmental transformations take effect (see, for example, Durant et al. 2017 and Held et al. 2013). It is therefore particularly important that we attempt to both understand and mitigate the impacts of these consequences, and also show how humans and nature can work together for a more sustainable future. Knowledge is impor-tant, politics may be crucial, but in the end, the imagination and work of those hit hardest might provide some of the clearest solutions, hopefully supported by contributions made possible by some of Norhed's projects (Redcliff and Woodgate 2010).

A cross-disciplinary turning point

Academic history is marked by a cleavage between the natural and human sciences. What both have in common, however, is a conviction that humans are somehow separate from, and in mortal combat, with nature. This view dominates the cultural dynamic of the West and has gradually pervaded much of the rest of the world (Huber 1989). In addition, both of these main epistemological traditions have in common a constant cleansing or silencing of knowledge that reveals the consequences of human activities both for ourselves and the biosphere (Bonneuil and Fressoz 2016). As shown by these two French historians, academics arguing for human/nature interactions (to be preserving both), were quickly side-lined. Instead, in the academic world, the cleavages, not only between the two branches of natural and human science but also between disciplines within each branch, were growing as specialisation became the most rewarded way of organising knowledge. Specialisation secured growth both in science and in society and, after the Second World War, these ideas of growth merged in what the OECD called the new 'growth paradigm' – the measure of GDP. GDP is still the main measure of economic prosperity, despite being critiqued since the 1970s (by the Club of Rome among others) for failing to acknowledge the costs to society and to nature (Schmelzer 2016).

The end of growth? The Anthropocene

As Bonneuil and Fressoz argue (2016: 33):

> The Anthropocene (thus) requires the substitution of the 'ungrounded' humanities of industrial modernity by new environmental humanities that adventure beyond the great separation between environment and society. Environmental history, natural anthropology, environmental law and ethics, human ecology, environmental sociology, political ecology,

green political theory, ecological economics, etc., are among the new disciplines that have recently begun to renew the human and social sciences, in a dialogue with the science of nature. They sketch a new environmental humanities that goes beyond the two cultures' fissure and puts an end to the jealous division of territories.

Along with the eco-social paradigm, demand for knowledge that reveals the integration of nature and society is growing. Both sides must reflect on one another and on their 'disciplining' while new types of disciplines and ways of working in practical research must develop. In the *Oxford Handbook of Interdisciplinarity*, Valdir Fernandes and Arlindo Philippi (2017) have a chapter on 'Sustainability sciences', inspired by the fact that citations of cross-disciplinary work, such as that published by our two French historians, have increased from just one in 1974 to thousands today.

Numerous debates about how to make disciplines work together, and how to create new disciplines across nature/society divides, have emerged. One such debate led to agreement on the importance of opening up Western rationality to ritualised (but not scientised) human/nature knowledge – that is, to the experience of those whose knowledge has been excluded from systematic research in the West over a long period because of the West's hegemonic approach to rationality – what Joseph Huber calls 'promodal thinking' versus the (in scientific terms) suppressed anamode (Huber 1989: 207, my translation). New ways of linking the social and natural sciences thus challenge knowledge hierarchies as well as links between codified and non-codified knowledge as pursued so far in our more and more specialised fields.

The Sustainable Development Goals (SDGs)

With the coming of the SDGs, the nature/society duality turned into a triad with 'the economy' as its third point. The focus is now on the social and environmental consequences of economic actions. Increasingly, we need to know how to assess the likely social and environmental consequences of all economic activities (Sachs 2015). The role played by states as regulators and redistributors is no longer enough. At all levels, from the investments made by local businesses to the long-term planning by global companies, social and environmental 'conditionalities' must guide decisions. As noted by the UN-driven Sustainable Development Solution Network of universities and think tanks, this is a formidable challenge for the way we develop knowledge across disciplines:

> We aim to accelerate joint learning and promote integrated approaches that address the interconnected economic, social, and environmental challenges confronting the world.[1]

A programme for the eco-social paradigm

Norhed is very serious about adopting the eco-social paradigm and prioritises funding for projects that are willing to accept this challenge. As noted in the Preface to this volume, one of Norhed's sub-programmes is on Natural resource management, climate change and environment, and all the chapters in this section describe projects in this sub-programme. Several other sub-programmes could potentially be linked to the eco-social paradigm and, in future, more should perhaps be done to build upon the synergies that this could create between projects.

It is noteworthy that the Norad committee, who choose which projects to support from among the many applications received, is made up of academics from a rare mix of disciplines and university backgrounds, from the US to Thailand. The nature/society cleavage is challenged head-on by the composition of this committee which includes sociologists, anthropologists, engineers, scholars who are combining disciplines in new kinds of departments and in their research, as well as a person with years of experience in the development field. Whereas most donors have project selection committees in which disciplinary interests prevail, Norhed's aim of promoting of interdisciplinarity is met from the outset. It is difficult to see how this could have been the case if the programme had been organised within the established norms for university/research funding, where peer-review processes are often organised in ways that reinforce and reproduce disciplinary specialisation.

As noted, this cross-disciplinary orientation is both a challenge and an opportunity. The sub-programme on natural resource management, climate change and environment can thus be seen as an opportunity for testing and experiencing the value of cross-disciplinary research in practice. We talk a lot about integrating nature/society/economy in our research but we still do not quite know how to do it successfully as the discourse around 'resilience studies' shows. On the other hand, we also seem to agree that we have no alternative but to try. Those who had hoped for 'ecological modernisation' seem to have reached a cul-de-sac. As the UN argued when launching the SDGs, ecological modernisation will not secure the 'formative shift' we need, the institutions we work in must not only be modernised but also transformed.

This sub-programme is the largest in terms of the number of projects approved and funds allocated. The knowledge and experiences gained from these projects is expected to be of crucial importance to everyone on the planet. As the renowned Swedish historian and sociologist, Sverker Sörlin, pointed out, 'In fact, people in developing countries have even more to gain if the entire world can formulate a less dualistic and more integrated view of nature and society' (Sörlin 2011: 252).

Today we see this is true, in the sense that, while people in LMICs suffer the most from environmental shifts and societal inequalities, there is no longer any doubt that the higher income countries are as exposed to threatening and destructive change. These projects are globally relevant precisely because they are developmentally relevant (Benjaminsen and Svarstad 2017).

In Chapter 6, on the management of coastal resources in Tanzania and Zanzibar, Pius Z Yanda, Ian Bryceson, Haji Mwevura, Wahira Othman, Betsy Beymer-Farris, Chris Maina Peter, Emma Liwenga, and Faustin Maganga explain why a transdisciplinary approach is vital to understanding the vulnerabilities and resilience of coastal eco-social systems.

In Chapter 7 Mesfin Tilahun, Stein Holden and Julius Mangisoni, from within the economics departments of their respective universities, outline their project's focus on 'climate-smart natural resource management' in Ethiopia and Malawi. Despite their seemingly similar disciplinary backgrounds, they explain the importance of using a multidisciplinary approach for understanding the dynamic processes unique to eco-social systems. They also emphasise the importance of curriculum change across *all* disciplines in line with the principles of sustainability.

In Chapter 8, Claire Armstrong and Nguyen Thi Kim Anh focus on marine ecosystem management in Vietnam and Sri Lanka. This project run by the University of Nha Trang and the Arctic University of Norway also illustrates how the eco-social paradigm inspires and requires a multidisciplinary approach. Their experiences of working out how to link teaching and research, and what curriculum reforms are needed, offer valuable insights into what it takes to create and conduct inter/multi/cross-disciplinary curricula and research.

Notes

1   See Sustainable Development Solution Network (n.d.) 'Vision and organisation', http://unsdsn.org/about-us/vision-and-organization/.

References

Baker S (2012) Climate change, the common good and the promotion of sustainable development. In: J Meadocroft, O Langhelle and A Ruud (eds) *Governance, Democracy and Sustainable Development: Moving Beyond the Impasse*. Cheltenham: Edward Elgar

Benjaminsen TA and Svarstad H (2017) *Politisk Økologi: Miljø, mennesker og makt*. Oslo: Universitetsforlaget

Bonneuil C and Fressoz J-B (2016) *The Shock of the Anthropocene: The Earth, History and Us*, trans. D Fernbach. London, New York: Verso

Durant RF, Fiorino DJ and O'Leary R (2017) *Environmental Governance Reconsidered: Challenges, Choices, and Opportunities*. London: MIT Press

Fernandes V and Philippi Jr A (2017) Sustainability sciences: Political and epistemological approaches. In: R Frodeman (ed.) *The Oxford Handbook of Interdisciplinarity*, 2nd edn. Oxford: Oxford University Press

Held D, Roger C and Nag E-M (2013) *Climate Governance in the Developing World*. Cambridge: Polity Press

Huber J (1989) *Herrschen und Sehnen: Kuturdynamik des Westens*. Basel: Beltz

Redcliff MR and Woodgate G (2010) *The International Handbook of Environmental Scociology*, 2nd ed. Cheltenham: Edward Elgar

Sachs J (2015) *The Age of Sustainable Development*. New York: Columbia University Press

Schmeltzer M (2016) *The Hegemony of Growth: The OECD and the Making of the Economic Growth Paradigm*. Cambridge: Cambridge University Press

Sörlin S (2011) Exiting the environmental trap: Knowledge regimes and the third phase of environmental policy. In: S Helgesson (ed.) *Exit: Endings and New Beginnings in Literature and Life*. New York: Rodopi

6

Building capacity
for the management of coastal resources
in Tanzania and Zanzibar

Pius Z Yanda, Ian Bryceson, Haji Mwevura, Wahira Othman,
Betsy Beymer-Farris, Chris Maina Peter, Emma Liwenga
& Faustin Maganga

Setting the scene

Coastal ecosystems have supported human livelihoods for thousands of years. In many parts of the world, the abundant resources that often form part of coastal ecosystems have attracted high concentrations of people into coastal areas who depend on the local ecosystem services for their livelihoods (Church et al. 2019).[1] Population growth and climate change have already compromised coastal ecosystems worldwide, undermining community livelihoods in various ways (Case 2006). A deeper understanding of the interactions between climate variables and anthropogenic stressors is critical if we hope to learn to better predict and mitigate the ecological impacts of climate change for coastal ecosystems (Hewitt et al. 2016).

Our main goal in this chapter is to share our experiences and findings from an ongoing research-through-capacity-building project focused on the coastal areas of mainland Tanzania and the island of Zanzibar, where the appropriate use of ecosystem-based adaptation strategies offers a valuable and effective tool for present-day manage-ment. The project is investigating issues of vulnerability and resilience linked to coastal ecosystems and community livelihoods. We aim to generate knowledge and information that promotes the conservation and maintenance of coastal systems, encourages adaptation to climate change, and enhances the resilience of coastal communities.

Our main activities include: the development of a Master's of Natural Resources Management and Climate Change at the State University of Zanzibar; enhancing the existing master's and PhD pro-grammes on Climate Change and Sustainable Development at the University of Dar es Salaam; putting infrastructure and facilities in place to enhance the capacities of the newly established Centre for Climate Change Studies at the University of Dar es Salaam; creating a unit to host a new master's programme at the State University of Zanzibar; and building the capacity of staff at these centres through collaborative research in four major areas. These are:

- Understanding the climatic impacts of global warming on the integrity of coastal ecosystems in the regions studied.
- Institutional and legal frameworks for coastal resource govern-ance and management.
- Social systems and their inter-linkages with communities' vulner-ability to the impacts of climate change and coastal ecosystems integrity.
- Community responses to climate change impacts and their impli-cations for coastal resource use.

The question of how best to ensure that outreach and information sharing are foregrounded in all four areas.

The rest of the chapter has three sections. The first outlines our understanding of the concepts of vulnerability and resilience, and explains why we see transdisciplinary approaches as best suited to the study of ecosystems and biodiversity.[2] The second describes how we see the links between social and ecological systems in the areas studied. The third sums up what we have learned from our research.

Key concepts

Vulnerability and resilience

Vulnerability is defined by the Intergovernmental Panel on Climate Change as the 'propensity or predisposition to be adversely affected'. In relation to the dynamics of socio-ecological systems, vulnerability encompasses a variety of concepts and elements, including sensitivity or susceptibility to harm and a lack of capacity to cope and adapt. Likewise, the notion of resilience is often applied to socio-ecological systems, to highlight their non-linear dynamics, thresholds, uncertainties, surprises, how periods of gradual change interplay with periods of rapid change and how such dynamics interact across temporal and spatial scales (Adger et al. 2005). We use the notion of resilience as a lens that helps us understand the dynamics of socio-ecological systems. This is an attempt to challenge the dominant view which is based on the notion of stable equilibrium.

Although the concepts of resilience and vulnerability are approximate opposites in meaning (Janssen and Ostrom 2006), as Callo-Concha and Ewert (2014) point out, the two concepts overlap and augment one another in various ways. For example, both concepts are used to assess the risks associated with the physical, social and economic aspects and implications of a system's ability to cope with change (Proag 2014a, 2014b). Interestingly, the concept of resilience has its roots in ecology and the natural sciences (Holling 1978) while notions of vulnerability are rooted in the social sciences, and particularly in political economy (Wisner et al. 1994). In our experience, the various analytical approaches to the two concepts are complementary and strengthen both concepts (Miller et al. 2010).

Transdisciplinarity

The introduction of the concept of ecosystem services has sparked a vast amount of research but limited progress has been made in putting this knowledge to use in relation to the sustainable use of such services. In addition, although a number of studies have been conducted, much of the research has addressed single variables or hypotheses, rooted in one or two disciplines, and the human dimensions of these questions are seldom accorded the weight they deserve. Our project therefore adopted a socio-ecological systems model, which allows for the characterisation of human–nature interactions in an integrative way (Berkes and Folke 1998).

Although coastal systems provide a wide variety of regulating, provisioning, supporting, and cultural services (MEA 2005), they have, as noted earlier, been heavily altered by human activities, with climate change constituting just one of many pressures they are facing. Human systems' impact on coastal ecosystems include the built environment (such as housing settlements, water systems, drainage, as well as transportation infrastructure and networks), human activities (such as tourism, aquaculture, fisheries), as well as formal and informal institutions (such as policies, laws, customs, norms, and culture). Together, human and natural systems form a tightly coupled socio-ecological system (Berkes and Folke 1998; Hopkins et al. 2012). From an academic viewpoint, the importance of transdisciplinary approaches in studying complex systems is clear: this is the approach that is most likely to produce information that takes into account the diversity of stakeholders' interests in complex social-ecological systems such as coastal environments.

Bennett et al. (2015) argue that the scope of research into ecosystems services can be broadened if it sets out to answer three key questions: how are ecosystem services co-produced by social-ecological systems; who benefits from the provision of ecosystem services; and what are the best practices for the governance of ecosystem services? Given the transdisciplinary nature of our project, we have found Bennet's questions useful for guiding research in ways that allow for the integration of different perspectives.

A case-study approach has been used as a means to understand socio-ecological systems for this study to investigate place-based issues. Three areas in mainland Tanzania (Pangani, Mafia-Rufiji, and Mtwara-Lindi) and one area in Zanzibar were sampled for field studies. The research was conducted by PhD and master's students in the four major thematic areas already mentioned and included a focus on gender dynamics, outreach and information sharing. Faculties also conducted supplementary studies in these areas. In line with our transdisciplinary approach, the graduate students who were recruited into the project come from a range of disciplines.

Coastal ecosystems in Tanzania

No single definition for coastal zones or areas exists but most consider coastal ecosystems to consist of land areas affected by their proximity to the sea, and marine areas that are influenced by their closeness to land. In relation to exposure to potential sea level rise, the low-elevation coastal zone refers to areas of up to ten metres above sea level (Vafeidis et al. 2011). In addition, coastal systems are conceptualised as consisting of both natural and human systems. The natural systems include distinct features and ecosystems such as rocky coasts, beaches, barriers and sand dunes, estuaries and lagoons, sea grass meadows, mangrove forests, deltas, river mouths, wetlands, and coral reefs. Such elements help define the seaward and landward boundaries of the coast.

Globally the climate is changing, and African countries, including Tanzania, are among the most vulnerable to the impacts of climate change. A lack of capacity for adequate adaptation planning, low levels of economic wealth, and low institutional capacity are contributing to this vulnerability (IPCC, 2007). Indeed, climate change has the potential to undermine and even undo the current socio-economic status of communities in these countries. Obviously, the negative impacts of climate change are being exacerbated by other factors, including widespread poverty, poor healthcare, and high population density. As long ago as 2007, the IPCC estimated that unless drastic changes are made, the demand for food, water, and land on which livestock can forage would double over the next 30 years (IPCC 2007).

According to Wong et al. (2014), coastal systems are particularly sensitive to three key drivers related to climate change: sea level or beach erosion, ocean temperature, and ocean acidity.

In Tanzania, the data on sea-level rise is contested. On the one hand, Woodworth et al. (2007) argue that although sea-level is rising on a worldwide basis, this is not the case along the Tanzanian coast due to tectonic shifts which are causing the land to rise as well. They argue that beach erosion is mainly due to sand extraction from beaches, river beds and near-shore areas, in addition to the construction of groynes and damming of rivers. On the other hand, URT (2007), Kebede et al. (2010) and Pallewatta (2010) suggest that sea-level rise *is* evident in the rate of beach erosion, particularly in Dar es Salaam, Bagamoyo, and Pangani. They also note that coastal communities in Bagamoyo are abandoning springs and wells that have long served as a source of fresh water because seawater is seeping into the groundwater. It is possible, however, that salt intrusion into near-shore aquifers is related to the increasing number of wells being drilled and the rate of water extraction rather than to sea-level rise.

In contrast, coral bleaching and loss of species can be clearly attributed to rising temperature and levels of acidity in the ocean. For many other coastal changes, the impacts of climate change are difficult to tease apart from human-related drivers of change such as changes in land use, coastal development and increasing pollution.

Linking social and ecological systems

Our research confirms that the dynamics of coastal ecosystems are being severely compromised by human development, with population increases leading to increasing demand for ecosystems goods and services. These findings are supported by Marchant and Lane's (2014) work, which also focused on East Africa. Future demand for ecosystems goods and services is likely to significantly undermine the integrity of the region's coastal ecosystems as well as community livelihoods (Hamerlynck et al. 2011). In saying this, we acknowledge that trade-offs between resource use and conservation are inevitable. However, when demand is not checked and no effective ecosystems management strategies are in place, trade-offs become increasingly lopsided until natural systems fail and can no longer sustain local communities (Berkes et al. 2009).

The management of coastal ecosystems is complicated by the complex, non-linear dynamics already mentioned (see also Rosenzweig et

al. 2011), and by the presence of multiple management goals, the competing preferences of stakeholders, and the social conflicts these create
(Hopkins et al. 2012). In many instances, coastal adaptation can be
characterised as a 'wicked problem' (Rittel and Webber 1973).
Agreement about exactly what the problems are is rare, while uncertainties and ambiguities about what adaptations might be effective are
common (Moser et al. 2012). Our own research shows that some adaptation measures deepen the degradation of ecosystems. For example, in
the Rufiji Delta, extreme dry periods led local people to clear mangrove
forests to make way for wetland agriculture.

Several studies demonstrate the role of well-managed mangrove
forests in protecting coastal shorelines. Thus, adaptation measures
based on the protection and restoration of natural coastal systems,
such as mangroves (Schmitt et al. 2013), reefs (Beck et al. 2011), and
salt marshes (Barbier et al. 2011), are seen as no- or low-regret options
to be encouraged irrespective of climate change (Cheong et al. 2013).
However, further work is needed to provide reliable quantitative estimates of the capability of such ecosystems to reduce the impacts of
sea-level rise such as wave and storm surges, as well as cost-benefit
analyses of how these measures compare to interventions designed and
driven by civil-engineers.

Based on studies of social and ecological resilience and vulnerability,
Plummer and Armitage (2007) argue that adaptive management is
being widely recognised as the most scientific approach to management
of natural resources. This approach is also increasingly being incorporated into international development programmes (Chapin et al. 2009).
Adaptive management was developed as a scientific concept by Holling
(1978) and Walters (1986). Initially focused on fisheries management,
this approach has since been expanded to natural resources more
broadly.

Considered unorthodox by leaders who think of management in
terms of command and control, adaptive management takes the view
that resource-management policies should be treated as 'experiments'
from which managers, users and scientists must continually learn. The
process is information and learning intensive, requiring continual and
active collaboration with the communities and other stakeholders who

are most affected by policies. It is also based on inductive reasoning, thus relying on comparative studies that combine ecological and social theory with constant observation and verification. Adaptive management is co-evolutionary, and involves two-way feedback between management policy and the state of the resource or ecosystem. It recognises the non-linear nature of resource management, and it focuses on the importance of scale, time and space, as well as cross-scale interactions between adaptive cycles.

Lessons learned from our research

MSc and PhD programme development and implementation

Research students from diverse disciplines have worked together to address research questions using a transdisciplinary approach. This has enabled them to gain a range of skills and knowledge on ways of studying complex social-ecological systems while still maintaining their own disciplinary specialisations. This approach has generated data and information relevant to addressing the challenges of managing coastal social-ecological systems. Furthermore, the knowledge acquired by young faculty members through their research is equipping them to teach others about ecosystems using transdisciplinary perspectives. Thus, they are enhancing their teaching and research skills through fieldwork-based study and by being required to review a variety of literature. This should ensure that their teaching will no longer be purely theoretical, but rather based on what they have learned from conducting their own rigorous fieldwork.

The approach used in most studies has been participatory, whereby stakeholders are engaged in the process right from the inception phase. This has made it possible for researchers to modify their research tools based on stakeholders' input. Likewise, information gathered has been presented to stakeholders for validation. This not only ensures that stakeholders develop a sense of ownership over the information, but also helps to increase their uptake of recommendations as well as their feedback on how well these are working.

A number of theses, dissertations, journal articles and chapters in books have already been published, with many more in preparation. It is through such publications that the knowledge generated throughout research will be widely shared. The information will also be packaged into policy briefs. Researchers have conducted several forums to influence knowledge uptake by various stakeholders. In this way, findings from fieldwork have been disseminated to governmental, non-profit and other policy organisations associated with marine and coastal resources, gender, and climate change. Furthermore, a documentary film has been produced in Kiswahili and English as a means of disseminating our findings to non-specialist audiences.

Through all these processes, capacities have been built at different levels. Institutionally, the programme has significantly improved and strengthened the research laboratories at the two universities. Also, seven young faculty members in the two universities have been supported to pursue their PhDs in climate change and sustainable development. Meanwhile 35 students at the University of Dar es Salaam and 24 students at the State University of Zanzibar have been supported in their master's degrees.

To conclude, the project has demonstrated the importance of inter-disciplinary approaches in studying complex systems. This approach is producing relevant information that considers the diversity of stakeholder interests in complex social-ecological systems such as the coastal environment. Information generated using this approach helps develop integrated perspectives relevant to addressing challenges on the ground. At an institutional level, the programme significantly improved and strengthened the research laboratories and capacities of young faculties in the two Southern universities.

Challenges, opportunities and future scenarios for coastal and marine resources

Almost all our research confirmed that Tanzania's coastal and marine resources are highly vulnerable to climate change and are already being notably affected. These impacts include a decrease in average rainfall and changes in rainy season patterns. Salt intrusion and coastal flooding is affecting rice farming in coastal lowlands. While climate change can be clearly associated with the degradation of coastal and marine resources, our studies confirmed that several non-climatic factors, such as poverty, inadequate education and poor levels of awareness, weak governance, and deforestation are accelerating the crisis. The research also found that communities have adopted some coping mechanisms and made some efforts to adapt to the social-ecological degradation they are experiencing but their adaptive capacity is low and they are very unlikely to be able to arrest the process.

The deployment of scholars from diverse disciplines in our research projects enabled us to investigate issues in a more integrated and holistic manner, and to translate the data into a range of meaningful messages relevant to different stakeholders. However, disagreements between the specialisations can create communication challenges, as well as contestation over how to understand and interpret information collected.

For future sustainability to be made more secure, stakeholders from a diverse range of related social systems and sectors, that are currently fragmented, have to appreciate that marine and coastal resources require their co-operation and collaboration. Sectoral co-ordination will create synergies capable of resolving some of the existing governance problems. The introduction of regular monitoring and data collection will provide the long-term data that are vital to climate change studies. At the time of writing in late 2018, such data are scarce, unrelated and have such notable gaps that they limit meaningful analysis of trends related to climate change and its impacts on coastal and marine resources. Ideally, an inclusive approach to monitoring will be established, with a well-defined framework that facilitates full participation from a range of sectoral stakeholders so that contributions from as many disciplines as possible are included and acknowledged as valuable. This must include traditional knowledge from the community. In addition, mechanisms will be set up so that the information gathered via these monitoring processes is appropriately packaged and disseminated.

About the authors and the project

Pius Z Yanda is vice-chair of the IPCC Working Group II and Professor of Physical Geography at the Institute of Resource Assessment, University of Dar es Salaam, Tanzania

Ian Bryceson is a professor in the Department of International Environment and Development Studies at the Norwegian University of Life Sciences in Ås, Norway

Haji Mwevura is a senior lecturer in environmental analytical chemistry at the State University of Zanzibar, Tanzania

Wahira Othman is a lecturer in natural resource management at the State University of Zanzibar, Tanzania

Betsy A Beymer-Farris is director of the Environmental and Sustainability Studies Program at the University of Kentucky, USA

Chris Maina Peter is a professor at the School of Law, University of Dar es Salaam, Tanzania

Emma Liwenga is a senior lecturer at the Institute of Resource Assessment, University of Dar es Salaam, Tanzania

Faustin Maganga is an associate professor at the Institute of Resource Assessment, University of Dar es Salaam, Tanzania

Project title: Vulnerability, Resilience, Rights and Responsibilities: Capacity Building on Climate Change in Relation to Coastal Resources, Gender and Governance in Coastal Tanzania and Zanzibar

Partner institutions: University of Dar es Salaam and the State University of Zanzibar (Tanzania); Norwegian University of Life Sciences (Norway)

Notes

1   The concept of ecosystem services has become mainstream as a way of expressing the monetary value that can be assigned to functions performed by ecosystems (such as water filtration, carbon sequestering, crop pollination, etc.) based on what these would cost if they had to be managed by mechanical or other artificial means (see Bennett et al. 2015).

2   The concepts of vulnerability, resilience, multi-/inter- and transdisciplinarity are highly context dependent (Costache 2017). For the purposes of this chapter, we are using them with reference to complex social-ecological systems.

References

Adger WN, Hughes TP, Folke C, Carpenter SR and Rockström J (2005) Social-ecological resilience to coastal disasters. *Science* 309(5737): 1036–1039. Available online

Barbier EB, Hacker SD, Kennedy C, Koch EM, Stier AC and Silliman BR (2011) The value of estuarine and coastal ecosystem services. *Ecological Monographs* 81(2): 169–183

Beck MW, Brumbaugh RD, Aroldi L and Carranza A (2011) Oyster reefs at risk and recommendations for conservation, restoration and management. *BioScience* 61(2):107–116

Bennett EM, Cramer W, Begossi A, Cundill G, Díaz S, Egoh BN, Geijzendorffer IR et al. (2015) Linking biodiversity, ecosystem services, and human well-being: Three challenges for designing research for sustainability. *Current Opinion in Environmental Sustainability* 14: 76–85. Available online

Berkes F and Folke C (eds) (1998) *Linking Social and Ecological Systems: Management Practices and Social Mechanisms for Building Resilience.* Cambridge: Cambridge University Press

Berkes F, Kofinas GP and Chapin FS (2009) Conservation, community, and livelihoods: Sustaining, renewing, and adapting cultural connections to the land. In: FS Chapin, GP Kofinas and C Folke (eds) *Principles of Ecosystem Stewardship: Resilience-Based Natural Resource Management in a Changing World.* New York: Springer. Available online

Callo-Concha D and Ewert F (2014) Using the concepts of resilience, vulnerability and adaptability for the assessment and analysis of agricultural systems. *Change and Adaptation in Socio-Ecological Systems* 1(1): 1–11. Available online

Case M (2006) *Climate Change Impacts on East Africa: A Review of the Scientific Literature.* WWF. Available online

Chapin FS, Kofinas GP and Folke C (2009) *Principles of Ecosystem Stewardship: Resilience-Based Natural Resource Management in a Changing World.* New York: Springer

Cheong SM, Silliman BR, Wong PP, Van Wesenbeeck B, Kim CK and Guannel G (2013) Coastal adaptation with ecological engineering. *Nature, Climate Change* 3: 787–791

Church JA, Aarup T, Wilson WS and Woodworth PL (2019) Sea-level rise and vulnerable coastal populations. Available via ResearchGate

Costache A (2017) Conceptual delimitations between resilience, vulnerability and adaptive capacity to extreme events and global change. *Annals of Valahia University of Targoviste, Geographical Series* 17(2): 198–205. Available online

Hamerlynck O, Duvail S, Vandepitte L, Kindinda K, Nyingi DW, Paul J-L, Yanda PZ, Mwakalinga AB, Mgaya YD and Snoeks J (2011) To connect or not to connect? Floods, fisheries and livelihoods in the Lower Rufiji Floodplain Lakes, Tanzania. *Hydrological Sciences* 56(8). Available online

Hewitt JE, Ellis JI and Thrush SF (2016) Multiple stressors, nonlinear effects and the implications of climate change impacts on marine coastal ecosystems. *Global Change Biology* 22(8): 2665–2675. Available online

Holling CS (1978) *Adaptive Environmental Assessment and Management*. New York: John Wiley & Sons

Hopkins TS, Bailly D, Elmgren R, Glegg G, Sandberg A and Stottrup JG (2012) A systems approach framework for the transition to sustainable development: Potential value based on coastal experiments. *Ecology and Society* 17(3). Available online

IPCC (2007) *Climate Change: Impacts, Adaptation and Vulnerability*, Fourth Assessment Report of Working Group II's Contribution to the Intergovernmental Panel on Climate Change. Cambridge: Cambridge University Press

Janssen MA and Ostrom E (2006) Resilience, vulnerability, and adaptation: A cross-cutting theme of the International Human Dimensions Programme on Global Environmental Change. *Global Environmental Change* 16: 237–239

Kebede AS, Brown S and Nicholas RJ (2010) The Implications of Climate Change and Sea-Level Rise in Tanzania: The Coastal Zones, a synthesis report submitted to the Stockholm Environmental Institute

Marchant R and Lane P (2014) Past perspectives for the future: Foundations for sustainable development in East Africa. *Journal of Archaeological Science* 51: 12–21. Available online

MEA (Millennium Ecosystem Assessment) (2005) *Ecosystems and Human Well-Being: Synthesis*. Washington, DC: Island Press

Miller F, Osbahr H, Boyd E, Thomalla F, Bharwani S, Ziervogel G, Walker B, Birkmann J, Van der Leeuw S, Rockström J, Hinkel J, Downing T, Folke C and Nelson D (2010) Resilience and vulnerability: Complementary or conflicting concepts? *Ecology and Society* 15(3): 11

Moser SC, Williams J and Boesch DF (2012) Wicked challenges at Land's End: Managing coastal vulnerability under climate change. *Annual Review of Environment and Resources* 37: 51–78

Pallewatta N (2010) Impact of climate change on coastal ecosystems in the Indian Ocean region. In: D Michel and A Pandya (eds) *Coastal Zones and Climate Change*. Washington DC: Hendry L Stimson Center

Plummer R and Armitage D (2007) A resilience-based framework for evaluating adaptive co-management: Linking ecology, economics and society in a complex world. *Ecological Economics* 61(1): 62–74. Available online

Proag V (2014a) Assessing and measuring resilience. *Procedia Economics and Finance* 18: 222–229. Available online

Proag V (2014b) The concept of vulnerability and resilience. *Procedia Economics and Finance* 18: 369–376. Available online

Rittel HWJ and Webber MM (1973) Dilemmas in a general theory of planning. *Policy Sciences* 4(2): 155–169

Rosenzweig C, Solecki WD, Blake R, Bowman M, Faris C, Gornitz V, Horton R, Jacob K, LeBlanc A, Leichenko R, Linkin M, Major D, O'Grady M, Patrick L, Sussman E, Yohe G and Zimmerman R (2011) Developing coastal adaptation to climate change in the New York City infrastructure-shed: Process, approach, tools, and strategies. *Climatic Change* 106: 93–127

Schmitt K, Albers T, TT Pham and SC Dinh (2013) Site-specific and integrated adaptation to climate change in the coastal mangrove zone of Soc Trang Province, Vietnam. *Journal of Coastal Conservation* 17: 545–558

URT (2007) National Adaptation Programme of Action. Dar es Salaam: Vice President's Office, Division of Environment, Tanzania

Vafeidis A, Neumann B, Zimmermann J and Nicholls RJ (2011) *MR9: Analysis of Land Area and Population in the Low-Elevation Coastal Zone*. London: Foresight Project, Government Office for Science

Walters C (1986) *Adaptive Management of Renewable Resources: An Overview of an IIASA Book written by Carl Walter*, IIASA Executive Report 12. Available online

Wisner B, Blaikie P, Cannon T and Davis I. (2004) *At Risk: Natural Hazards, People's Vulnerability and Disasters*. New York: Routledge

Wong PP, Losada IJ, Gattuso J-P, Hinkel J, Khattabi A, McInnes KL, Saito Y and Sallenger A (2014) Coastal systems and low-lying areas. In: CB Field, VR Barros et al. (eds) *Climate Change 2014: Impacts, Adaptation, and Vulnerability. Part A: Global and Sectoral Aspects*, Contribution of Working Group II to the Fifth Assessment Report of the Intergovernmental Panel on Climate Change. Cambridge: Cambridge University Press

Woodworth PL, Aman A and Aarup T (2007) Sea level monitoring in Africa. *African Journal of Marine Science*. Available online

7

Capacity building for climate-smart natural resource management and policy in Malawi and Ethiopia

Mesfin Tilahun, Stein T Holden & Julius H Mangisoni

Among Norhed's six main focus areas are natural resource management, climate change and environment. Our project is part of this focus area and involves three universities, Mekelle University in Ethiopia, Lilongwe University of Agriculture and Natural Resources (LUANAR) in Malawi, and the Norwegian University of Life Sciences (NMBU) in Norway. The core role of the project is to support academic and research staff. Our aim is to strengthen understanding of the interdependence of socio-ecological systems, and of the behavioural aspects of human responses to environmental and related policy changes. Hence, the project is in line with the eco-social paradigm shift outlined in the introduction to this section of the book.

Issues related to natural resource management, climate change and the environment are among the most critical concerns facing humankind. Over the last 30 000 to 40 000 years, humans have thrived partly because of our ability to restructure the ecosystems we live in and depend on in ways that suit us. We use fire to alter where trees and plants grow, we domesticate animals, and harness a whole range of energy sources (Young et al. 2006). Consequently, we are now experiencing a 'no equivalent' state. In other words, human actions have driven major planetary support systems beyond the bounds of what is observable in the paleo-climatic record (Crutzen and Stoermer 2000; McNeill 2000; Steffen et al. 2004).

The fact that human activities around the world now inevitably affect *all* natural ecosystems means that it is now best to view the environment as a social-ecological system. This requires an integrative research approach that bridges the biophysical and socio-economic domains to reveal the dynamic processes driving these systems (Collins et al. 2011). In other words, the formulation and implementation of environmental policy for the sustainable management of socio-ecological systems *requires* the integration of cross and multidisciplinary knowledge. In this context, understanding human responses to environmental and/or policy change is as critical as understanding the socio-ecological systems and the outcomes they produce (Smajgl et al. 2011).

Human-induced environmental changes are now also global in scale. These include soil degradation, biodiversity loss, changes in hydrology, and changes in climate patterns resulting from anthropogenic greenhouse gas emissions. All of these changes are already having detrimental effects on human well-being and that of the biosphere we are part of; thus the scientific community has a renewed responsibility to support policy formation that can lead to a more sustainable future. By this we mean a society that can help 'meet the needs of the present without compromising the ability of future generations to meet their own needs'.[1] According to Dasgupta (2018), sustainable development requires that, relative to their respective demographic bases, each generation should bequeath to its successors at least as large a productive base as it inherited. Cortese, in his 2003 paper 'The critical role of higher education in creating a sustainable future', poses a number of interesting questions related to envisioning a sustainable future, and asks what critical role higher education should play to help us realise this vision. Cortese goes on to call for higher education institutions to design their curricula so that the educational experience of *all* students (regardless of discipline) is aligned with the principles of sustainability. To achieve this, the content of all learning programmes will have to cover interdisciplinary systems thinking, dynamics and analysis. In this context, expanding teaching and research capacity in the higher education system worldwide, and particularly in low- and middle-income countries (LMICs), is crucial for generating cross- and/or multi-disciplinary scientific knowledge on environmental and developmental issues to support policy-makers at a local, national, regional and global level.

Background to the collaboration and its focal points

The goal of reducing poverty and improving the welfare of poor people necessitates, and is driving, various initiatives to spur growth in the economies of the world's poorer countries. However, because economic growth can be achieved in various ways, the search for sustainable development remains an important challenge for academics and policy-makers. Sustainable development requires the prudent use, management, and valuing of natural resources. In addition, climate change is acknowledged to be a real problem, affecting most poor people through persistent droughts, floods and emerging diseases even though poor communities have contributed very little to causing these disasters.

Ethiopia and Malawi are implementing a number of interventions to address the degradation of natural resources, food insecurity and poverty, and to mitigate the impact of climate change. It is crucial to evaluate the impacts of these interventions and to search for policy options that have the potential to create win-win situations whereby viable policies reduce poverty and improve the sustainable management of natural resources. All of these activities, from designing and evaluating interventions to policy formulation, require expertise. All areas of natural resource management, climate change and environmental studies require skilled and knowledgeable individuals who can undertake advanced and innovative research as well as deliver research-based education to increase knowledge and its effective use in policy and decision-making.

In this context, the three partners designed the project with the aim of improving expertise and capacity for evidence-based research, analysis and policy implementation in climate-smart and sustainable natural resource management. The project partners first attempted to assess the national situations and highlight the major challenges facing

Ethiopia and Malawi. They also evaluated what had been learned from previous collaborations and applied this to both the design and implementation of the project and its educational and research activities.

In *Ethiopia*, poverty eradication is the main development challenge emphasised in the country's successive five-year *Growth and Transformation Plans* issued since the early 1990s. Agriculture and rural development invariably feature strongly in these plans, highlighting the need to encourage smallholder agriculture, reduce water scarcity as well as improve natural resource conservation and management (see for example FDRE 2010). The government has also adopted 'the development of a green economy' as a strategic direction in addressing climate change and other environmental issues (FDRE 2011).

At the same time, the expansion of the higher education sector is listed in Ethiopia's priority areas in terms of social sector development (FDRE 2010). Consequently, the size of the student population in higher education has increased enormously. Although (or perhaps because) the participation of women in the higher education system is low, all universities in Ethiopia are facing an acute shortage of qualified teaching and research staff. Existing staff are overburdened by huge administrative and teaching loads and have almost no time for research. Although Ethiopia's public universities have established postgraduate programmes, including at PhD level, capacity in Ethiopia's higher education institutions to educate candidates to PhD level in the economics of natural resource management (or any other specialisation in economics) is extremely small, and the Department of Economics at Mekelle University is no exception.

In *Malawi*, erratic rainfall patterns are creating droughts and floods, while higher temperatures are forcing farmers to switch to short-season hybrid crop varieties that tend to be more expensive to grow. This is steadily eroding farmers' assets and leaving them more vulnerable to disasters. In addition, droughts and floods are leading to an increase in the incidence of diseases such as cholera and malaria. This means that women, in particular, have less time to spend working their fields as they are often responsible for looking after the sick. Fortunately, the government has embraced the management of natural resources and climate change as priority areas in its medium-term plan for accelerating the country's economic development (GoM 2012, 2017). However, LUANAR's Department of Agricultural and Applied Economics is very small and needs far more staff capacity in the fields of climate change, natural resource management and environmental studies.

Essentially, the demand for academic staff with PhDs and postdoctoral experience is very high in Ethiopia and Malawi, not only at Mekelle University and LUANAR but also at other public universities.

Building on previous partnerships

Before the CLISNARP partnership began, the three universities had already worked together to build capacity at master's level under Norad's NOMA and NUFU programmes.[2] Through this long-standing collaboration, the three partner institutions established various databases to facilitate research-based teaching and build research capacity related to climate change, natural resource management and food security. The CLISNARP project will build on and expand these databases, focusing on the identification and assessment of local climate-smart development strategies, policies, institutions and technologies.

Research themes and outputs, 2015–2018

The project identified 'economic analyses of climate-smart natural resource management and policy in Ethiopia and Malawi' as its theme. This includes assessing the use of climate-smart technologies in the Farm Input Subsidy Programme and studies related to interventions in natural resource management for climate change adaptation, mitigation and resilience. The project is supporting 19 PhD students whose research topics are linked to these issues (see Appendix 1). The project co-ordinators at NMBU and LUANAR are supervising most of these PhD candidates. In addition, postdoctoral researchers from Mekelle University and the project co-ordinator from NMBU are collaborating on several related research projects (see Appendix 2), several of which involve working with researchers outside the project.

The long-term nature of the partnership between the three universities, and the team spirit between the researchers in the respective departments, have been instrumental in ensuring the success of the project, providing a lived experience of how cross-national, cross-disciplinary and gender-oriented capacity-building research can work.

Gender empowerment

The project has taken the problem of gender disparity in our departments seriously and tried to address this by offering scholarships across the higher education system – from bachelor and master's degrees to PhD and postdoctorate levels. At the project's inception in 2013, the plan was to allocate close to 100 per cent of scholarships at bachelor and master's level and up to half of all PhD scholarships and postdoctoral fellowships to females, with the aim of increasing the female participation in the host departments of the Southern universities. In practice, we almost reached the target at bachelor and master's levels but securing competent female candidates for PhD and postdoctoral positions has been a major challenge and we are still far off target. As of late 2018, the project had awarded scholarships to six female PhD candidates, three at NMBU and three at LUANAR.

To address this, we used a number of strategies, including appointing more academic staff, and inviting employees from public institutions that have links with the host departments to apply for scholarships. As a result, the number of female academics employed by the Department of Economics at Mekelle University increased from one to twelve, eleven of whom were employed after the project's inception. This has increased the percentage of female academic staff in the department from 2.5 to 30 per cent.

Project outcomes

Researchers supported by the project have worked exceptionally hard towards achieving output targets set when the project was designed. In addition, the project co-ordinators have worked closely with their respective university managements and Norad to find solutions to challenges the project has encountered. Communication between and the reporting of progress by the project co-ordinators has been accurate and regular, as has communication between scholarship holders, their PhD supervisors and the project co-ordinators. This has contributed to the exceptional number of publications and conference presentations by project participants (see Appendix 3).

One reason for the project's strong focus on publications and conference presentations is because a major aim of the project is to provide policy-makers with evidence-based scientific data so that they can make informed decisions. In this regard, several of our research outputs have already had an impact. For example, one of our studies was cited in Future Policy's Global Award for 2017 in which Ethiopia's Tigray Region won the Gold Award for combatting desertification and land degradation.[3] In addition, in April 2016, the African Ministerial Conference on the Environment decided to honour a report generated by the project called *The Economics of Land Degradation in Africa* (Tilahun et al. 2015). Decision 4/SS6 records the ministers' intention to use the study as a vehicle for creating new data and generating policy-relevant information that links the biophysical aspects of land degradation with the economic drivers of change.

Conclusions

The CLISNARP project has achieved a number of research and capacity-building outcomes, in line with Sustainable Development Goals (SDGs) 1, 2, 4, 5, 8, 13 and 15. The research outputs of the project are already influencing policy-making processes in Ethiopia and Malawi. Moreover, the scope of the research activities carried out is relevant not only to the natural resource, environmental and developmental problems of the two Southern partners, but also to other countries in Africa and Asia.

The project has encountered a number of challenges, including securing competent candidates (particularly female ones) for PhD scholarships, a shortage of funds for fieldwork and for the wider communication and dissemination of research outputs. Funds have been lost because of the depreciation of the Norwegian kroner against the US dollar and the currencies of Malawi and Ethiopia, particularly from 2014 to 2016.

Based on the experience we have gained from this project we recommend the following for Norhed's next funding phase:

- Gender disparity has been rife historically and remains stark in most countries. For this reason, further investment in empowering women at bachelor and master's levels of the higher education system will help ensure that more high-calibre candidates are available to fill the gaps at PhD level and beyond.
- In designing five-year projects, project designers and Norad should try to allow for the likely impact of fluctuating exchange rates and ensure that adjustments can be made where necessary. Similarly, when exchange rates are favourable, project implementers need to report the relevant increase in income to Norad and make clear recommendations about what additional activities this could cover.
- In the first phase, no age limit was set for scholarship applicants and very few younger candidates applied, especially for PhD programmes. We recommend that an age limit of 35 years should apply to PhD scholarships. This will encourage younger candidates to apply and ensure that, after graduating, these candidates can serve their home universities and the academic profession for longer than candidates who are more advanced in age.

Appendix 1: PhD research

1   The Economics of Climate Change Adaptation Behaviours of Farm Households in Developing Countries: Field Experiment Evidence
2   Economic Implication of Animal Feed Scarcity on Animal Farm Intensification, Food Production and Consumption; Empirical Evidence from Tigray, Ethiopia
3   Climate Change, Technology Adoption and Common Pool Resource: Evidence from Tigray, Northern Ethiopia
4   Four Empirical Essays in Development Economics
5   Land Certification, Rental Markets, Commercialization and Technology Adoption in a Semi-Arid Area of Northern Ethiopia
6   Impact of Public Programmes on Livelihoods of Rural Households: The Case of Ethiopia's Productive Safety Net and Land Certification Programs

7   Sharecropping Contracts and Efficiency in Northern Ethiopia

8   Farmers Behaviour and Investment Decisions in Developing Countries

9   Environmental Shocks and Intra-Household Child Nutrition: Evidence Using Anthropometric Indicators in Ethiopia

10   The Economics and Policy of Irrigation Water Management in the Awash Basin of Ethiopia

11   The Impact of Small-Scale Irrigation on Households Income Inequality and Food Security

12   The Issue of Land Tenure Security in Peri-Urban areas of Northern Ethiopia; Does Geographical Proximity to Growing Cities Distort the Effective Implementation of Land Policies and Programmes?

13   Climate-Smart Agriculture in Malawi: Uptake and Opportunities in the Face of Climate Change.

14   Governance of Agriculture Land, Land Markets and Agriculture Productivity in Malawi

15   Beekeeping and its Impact on Livelihoods in the Mzenga and Mpamba Extension Planning Areas of Nkhatabay District, Malawi

16   Determining the Economic Value of Surface Irrigation Water and Farmers' Willingness to Pay for Irrigation Service Fees in the Shire Valley of Southern Malawi

17   Environmental and Economic Benefits of Pigeon Pea Production in the Thyolo and Mulanje Escarpments of Southern Malawi

18   Impact of Climate Change on Yield, Yield Variability, and Crop Profits in Malawi

19   Analysis of Smallholder Maize Farmers Behaviour Under Climate Risk in Malawi

Appendix 2: Research collaborations at postdoctoral level

1   Landless youth, livelihood opportunities and environmental conservation

2   Rural-land rental markets and land registration as well as land-tenure policy

3   The economics of land degradation: Forest restoration through community participation and the devolution of forest-use rights to communities

4   A valuation of forest ecosystem services and the conservation of protected forest areas

Appendix 3: Publications and conferences

Articles in peer-reviewed journals

Fisher M, Holden ST, Thierfelder C and Katengeza SP (2018) Awareness and adoption of conservation agriculture in Malawi: What difference can farmer-to-farmer extension make? *International Journal of Agricultural Sustainability*

Hadush M (2017) Implication of animal feed and water scarcity on labor allocation, food production and per capita food consumption in Tigrai Region, Ethiopia. *Journal of Economic Development*

Hadush M (2018) Impact of improved animal feeding practice on milk production, consumption and animal market participation in Tigrai, Ethiopia. *Problems of Agricultural Economics*

Hadush M (2018) Understanding farmers seasonal and full year stall feeding adoption in Northern Ethiopia. *Review of Agricultural and Applied Economics*

Holden ST, Fisher M, Katengeza SP and Thierfelder C (2018) Can lead farmers reveal the adoption potential of conservation agriculture? The case of Malawi. *Land Use Policy*

Holden ST and Tilahun M (2018) The importance of Ostrom's design principles: Youth group performance in Northern Ethiopia. *World Development*

Katengeza SP, Holden ST and Fisher M (2019) Use of integrated soil fertility management technologies in Malawi: Impact of dry spells exposure. *Ecological Economics*

Katengeza SP, Holden ST and Lunduka RW (2018) Adoption of drought tolerant maize varieties under rainfall stress in Malawi. *Journal of Agricultural Economics*

Tilahun M, Birner R and Ilukor J (2017) Household-level preferences for mitigation of Prosopis juliflora invasion in the Afar region of Ethiopia: A contingent valuation. *Journal of Environmental Planning and Management*

Tilahun M, Damnyag L and Anglaaere LCN (2016) The Ankasa Forest Conservation Area of Ghana: Ecosystem service values and on-site REDD+ opportunity cost. *Forest Policy and Economics*

Tilahun M, Maertens M, Deckers J, Muys B and Mathijs E (2016) Impact of membership in frankincense co-operative firms on rural income and poverty in Tigray, Northern Ethiopia. *Forest Policy and Economics*

Tilahun M, Vranken L, Muys B, Deckers J, Gebreegziabher K, Gebrehiwot K, Bauer H and Mathijs E (2015) Rural households' demand for frankincense forest conservation in Tigray, Ethiopia: A contingent valuation analysis. *Journal of Land Degradation and Development*

Reports

Holden ST, Bezu S and Tilahun M (2016) *How Pro-poor are Land Rental Markets in Ethiopia?* CLTS Report No. 1/2016, Centre for Land Tenure Studies, Norwegian University of Life Sciences

Signh A, Barr JE, Lund HG, Tovivo K, Tilahun M, Apindi E, Giese K and Nyamihana C (2015) *Rwanda State of the Environment and Outlook Report 2015*

Tilahun M, Mungatana E, Singh A, Apindi E, Barr J, Zommers Z and Lund G (2015) *The Economics of Land Degradation in Africa: Benefits of Action Outweigh the Costs.* ELD Initiative and UNEP. Available online

Tilahun M, Singh A, Kumar P, Apindi E, Schauer M, Libera J and Lund HG (2018) *The Economics of Land Degradation Neutrality in Asia: Empirical Analyses and Policy Implications for the SDGs*. Available online

Working papers

Between 2016 and 2019, the project contributed significantly to the valuable CLTS Working Paper Series published by Centre for Land Tenure Studies, Norwegian University of Life Sciences. These include No. 6 in 2016, Nos 2, 3, 5 and 6 in 2018 and Nos 1, 2, 3, 4, 5, 7, 10, 11 and 13 in 2017. The series is available at https://www.nmbu.no/en/faculty/hh/research/centers/clts/research/working-papers

National and international conferences at which research papers were presented

30th International Conference for Agricultural Economics, Vancouver, Canada. 28 July–2 August 2018

6th World Congress of Environmental and Resource Economists. Gothenburg, Sweden. 25–29 June 2018.

19th World Bank Conference on Land and Poverty, Washington DC, USA. 19–23 March 2018.

International Conference on Sustainable Agricultural and Natural Resource Management under Changing Climate in Sub Saharan Africa (SANCCSSA-Malawi), Lilongwe, Malawi. 16–18 October 2018.

Bergen Economics of Energy and Environment Research Conference, Norwegian School of Economics, Bergen Norway. 11–12 April 2018.

UNCCD-COP13, Ordos, China. 11 September 2017.

Research Dissemination Conference for National Commission for Science and Technology, Mangochi, Malawi. 28–29 September 2017.

16th NORDIC Conference on Development Economics, Gothenburg, Sweden. 12–13 June 2017.

2017 World Bank Conference on Land and Poverty in Washington DC, USA. 17–24 March 2017.

National Conference on Economic Research for Development, Mekelle University. June 2017.

Ethiopian Economic Association and the International Food Policy Research Institute's International Conference on the Ethiopian Economy, Addis Ababa, Ethiopia. June 2017.

Nordic Annual Environment and Resource Economics Conference, Helsinki University, Finland. 17 April 2017.

European Association of Environmental and Resource Economists, Athens University, Greece. June 2017.

5th International Conference of African Association of Agricultural Economists (AAAE), Addis Ababa, Ethiopia. 23–26 September, 2016.

Australasian Development Economics Workshop (ADEW), Melbourne. 2016.

6th Special Session on African Ministerial Conference on Environment (AMCEN), Cairo, Egypt. 16–19 April 2016.

NORHED Conference on Knowledge for Development, Oslo, Norway. 6–7 June 2016.

About the authors and the project

Mesfin Tilahun is based at the Department of Economics, Mekelle University, Ethiopia and the School of Economics and Business, Norwegian University of Life Sciences in Ås, Norway

Stein T Holden is based at the School of Economics and Business, Norwegian University of Life Sciences in Ås, Norway

Julius H Mangisoni is based in the Department of Agricultural and Applied Economics, Lilongwe University of Agriculture and Natural Resources in Malawi

Project title: Capacity Building for Climate-Smart Natural Resource Management and Policy (Norhed-CLISNARP)

Partner institutions: Department of Economics at Mekelle University in Ethiopia and the Department of Agricultural and Resource Economics at Lilongwe University of Agriculture and Natural Resources in Malawi, in partnership with the School of Economics and Business at the Norwegian University of Life Sciences in Ås, Norway

Notes

1   This well-known definition of sustainable development is from the Brundtland Report (WCED 1987).

2   See the Preface to this volume for more on this.

3   See Tigray's conservation-based agricultural development-led industrialisation at *Future Policy.org* (n.d.).

References

Collins SL, Carpenter SR, Swinton SM, Orenstein DE, Childers DL, Gragson TL, Grimm NB, Grove JM, Harlan SH, Kaye JP, Knapp AK, Kofinas GP, Magnuson JJ, McDowell WH, Melack JM, Ogden LA, Robertson GP, Smith MD and Whitmer AC (2011) An integrated conceptual framework for long-term social–ecological research. *Frontiers in Ecology and Environment* 9(6): 351–357. Available online

Cortese AD (2003) The critical role of higher education in creating a sustainable future. *Planning for Higher Education* 31: 15–22

Crutzen, PJ and Stoermer EF (2000). The 'Anthropocene'. *IGBP Newsletter* 41: 17–18

Dasgupta P (2018) Foreword. In: S Managi and P Kumar (eds) *Inclusive Wealth Report 2018: Measuring Progress Toward Sustainability*. Abingdon: Routledge

FDRE (Federal Democratic Republic of Ethiopia (2010) *Growth and Transformation Plan*. Addis Ababa: Ministry of Finance and Economic Development

FDRE (2011) *Ethiopia's Climate-Resilient Green Economy Strategy*. Addis Ababa: Environmental Protection Authority

GoM (Government of Malawi) (2012) *The Second Malawi Growth and Development Strategy (MGDS II) 2012–2016*. Lilongwe

GoM (Government of Malawi) (2017) *Malawi Growth and Development Strategy (MGDS III) 2017–2022*. Lilongwe

McNeill JR (2000) *Something New Under the Sun*. New York: WW Norton

Smajgl A, Brown DG, Valbuena D and Huigen MGA (2011) Empirical characterisation of agent behaviours in socio-ecological systems. *Environmental Modelling and Software* 26: 837–844

Steffen W, Sanderson A, Tyson PD, Jager J, Matson PM, Moore III B, Oldfield F, Richardson K, Schellnhuber HJ, Turner II BL and Wasson RJ (2004) *Global Change and The Earth System: A Planet Under Pressure*. New York: Springer

Tilahun M, Mungatana E, Singh A, Apindi E Barr J, Zommers Z and Lund G (2015) *The Economics of Land Degradation in Africa: Benefits of Action Outweigh the Costs*. ELD Initiative and UNEP. Available online

WCED (World Commission on Environment and Development) (1987) *Our Common Future*. Oxford: Oxford University Press

Young OR, Berkhout F, Gallopin GC, Janssen MA, Ostrom E and Van der Leeuw S (2006) The globalization of socio-ecological systems: An agenda for scientific research. *Global Environmental Change* 16: 304–316

8

Building research and educational capacity in Vietnam and Sri Lanka on the impacts of climate change on marine ecosystems management: Challenges, achievements and lessons learned

Claire W Armstrong & Nguyen Thi Kim Anh

Many of the major challenges facing the world today are multifaceted and complex, requiring input from many disciplines to describe, understand and potentially resolve (Stock and Burton 2011). Climate change is one such challenge. The natural sciences can explain some of its physical, chemical and biological aspects, and suggest possible solutions. However, knowledge related to human behaviour is also necessary if we are to better understand the mechanisms driving ongoing carbon emissions, and identify strategies that are likely to reduce or mitigate these. Inevitably, the two sciences, natural and social, are entangled in both the description of the problems and possible solutions.

Most scientists agree that climate change is occurring with such speed that humanity's need for broader and deeper scientific knowledge is urgent. They also agree that climate change is human-made (IPCC 2014) and a function of human behaviour. The environmental consequences of this behaviour tend to be focused on by the natural sciences, while socio-economic consequences are examined by applying the social sciences. Hence, for humans to be able to respond to climate change, it is imperative that the scientific community interacts in a multidisciplinary or, even better, in an interdisciplinary fashion. Active interaction across disciplinary boundaries is critical to the formulation of relevant research and knowledge.

The eco-social paradigm adopted by our project (and others in this volume) is well-grounded in the United Nations Sustainable Development Goals (SDGs). The SDGs also require that we transcend traditional disciplinary approaches to be able to clearly observe human–ecological interactions and drivers of change. In our view, this paradigm is foundational to finding the solutions to many of the world's most pressing problems. It is also the basis of the capacity-building project we describe in this chapter.

Our project focuses on building capacity in relation to climate change in marine environments, especially with regard to impacts related to fisheries and aquaculture in Vietnam and Sri Lanka. Nha Trang University in Vietnam leads the project, with the University of Ruhuna, Sri Lanka being the central South partner. These two institutions selected two universities in Norway to collaborate with – the University of Bergen and UiT, the Arctic University of Norway. As we illustrate, capacity development is challenging, but can also be contagious and move in directions not always envisaged when planning projects. In the development process, the need for new and different kinds of capacity became clear.

Exposure to climate change

In low- to middle-income countries (LMICs), many of which are located closer to the equator, climate change may be occurring more slowly than at the poles (Serreze and Francis 2006; Zhang 2005). However, poverty and weak governance means that the vulnerability of populations in such countries to the impacts of climate change is often greater than that of people living in more affluent regions. Arctic communities are often shown to be culturally vulnerable to climate change as their lifestyles and cultures depend on cold climates (Nymand Larsen and Fondahl 2014). However, these communities are less economically vulnerable, because, for the most part, they are based in industrialised countries with well-developed economies. At least in economic terms, they should be more resilient to climatic events (Adger et al. 2005). The same cannot be said for the many LMICs that figure prominently on a multitude of different climate-risk indices (Kreft et al. 2014).

Moreover, when it comes to coastal populations in LMICs, the potential for crisis is even stronger. In many cases, coastal communities are among the poorest of the poor. Indeed, in most coastal areas, fishing, both artisanal and industrial, is often an occupation of 'last resort'. This, together with the fact that fisher communities are often inherently poor, has been known since the 1950s, with the seminal work by H Scott Gordon (1954). Gordon showed how the potential 'super-profits', which 'free' natural resources such as fisheries provide, attract effort. Unless this effort is checked, it increases to such an extent that overfishing occurs, thus reducing the super-profits fisheries can generate. In recent decades, some countries have managed to tackle this problem, but in many parts of the world, the lack of fisheries management means that overfishing continues (Hilborn and Ovando 2014; Jackson et al. 2001). Similarly, many of the newer industries in coastal zones, such as tourism and aquaculture, require the presence of a range of additional natural resources, such as clean beaches and water, seed and feed. When these human activities are uncontrolled, overexploitation, environmental degradation and conflict invariably ensue (Naylor et al. 2000; Oracion et al. 2005; Primavera 2006).

On adopting a multidisciplinary approach

In such settings, inter- and multidisciplinary knowledge is imperative to assess and address the environmental and the human issues. This is demanding for academics anywhere in the world, as disciplinary traditions are strong, incentives to cross disciplinary boundaries are limited, and the requirements of doing so are often daunting (Wätzold et al. 2006). Nevertheless, awareness of the need for interdisciplinary research is increasing worldwide, alongside some encouragement for such efforts in the form of targeted funding (such as the EU's Horizon 2020).[1] In LMICs, many academic institutions have low levels of funding, and most have great difficulty accessing external funds. Some are still developing their competence at a disciplinary level, which can be both a challenge and a blessing. In many cases, a solid disciplinary base is vital for doing robust inter- or multidisciplinary science. Yet, in some situations, lower levels of familiarity with long-standing disciplinary traditions can make academics freer to explore, and more open to non-traditional inter- or multidisciplinary scientific endeavours. Either way, the actual meeting of different disciplines requires time and effort to get to grips with specialised terminologies and methodologies. As a result, this kind of research is costly and seldom rewarded via career incentives. Likewise, creating inter- or multidisciplinary educational programmes also requires heavier investments of time and effort (Ciannelli et al. 2014), as scholars from different disciplines have to collaborate to adjust their teaching styles and focus on specific topics, such as climate change.

In running this project, we have found that the delivery of a multi-disciplinary postgraduate course to mature graduates from diverse backgrounds necessitates an andragogical rather than a pedagogical slant for the conveying of information. This is so because our students enter the programme with their own experiences, knowledge, perceptions and beliefs. One appropriate method for capturing students' interest in the course material is through the inclusion of their existing knowledge whereby students share their own experiences with others through dialogue and classroom demonstrations.

In our experience, postgraduate students are more likely to inject their life experiences into the learning environment and rely less on the need for verification via the literature. For example, such students are likely to express their views without trying to promote any particular theory of climate change. There is no reason to discard information conveyed in such non-conventional forums. Instead, we suggest lecturers develop ways to ensure its inclusion. In a sense, lecturers act more like facilitators and must be ready to apply a multidisciplinary approach to analyse real-life experiences. Major constraints are the lack of time, and the shortage of instructors with multidisciplinary backgrounds and whose knowledge base spans both the social and natural sciences. Academics who have received strongly focused disciplinary training tend to be unwilling or insufficiently patient to participate in this kind of work. Multidisciplinary teaching requires making time to think through and apply different knowledge streams from a range of disciplines so as to be able to construct a context for an orderly assimilation of ideas.

Adopting a multidisciplinary approach made us rethink our curricula, and we divided our curriculum into two parts. The first part consists of a set of courses that focus on securing a shared multidisciplinary knowledge base. The second part includes courses run jointly by two or more lecturers from different disciplines, in which the students participate by developing case studies on ecological systems, natural resources and the socio-economic dimensions of climate change using a multidisciplinary approach.

One difficulty of sharing knowledge from different sources is that the information gathered requires different kinds of validation. At present, sources of climate-change data are diverse and not all of it, especially from the domain of social science, is based on solid evidence. Though experiential learning is important in teaching adults, the information source must be trustworthy and more than anecdotal. Hence, sources of information must be verified and issues must be investigated from within a sustainability framework – that is, it is important to teach students about climate change and its impacts in ways that acknowledge that that the global problems we face are both natural and societal in nature, and that disciplinary interdependence is not an optional extra but a fundamental principle. Indeed, the interconnectedness of our planetary biosphere, as revealed by climate change, underlines the need for global interaction and collaboration as seen in this project.

Ecosystem approaches to fisheries and aquaculture management in Sri Lanka and Vietnam

Capacity development in the project occurs along three main axes. The first is an English-language multidisciplinary master's programme in Marine Ecosystem-based Management and Climate Change that aims to develop capacity in the partner universities. The second is a research project on climate change in the marine environment; this funds PhD candidates and postdoctoral research in both natural and social sciences. The third is a gender-mainstreaming programme that focuses on mentoring female academics in career advancement in the partner universities. In addition, care is taken to ensure that a gender lens is applied to educational and research efforts undertaken by the project.

As mentioned, to provide for the complexities of climate change in marine environments, the project consists of academics from both the natural and social sciences. The different disciplines offer their own distinctive perspectives on the problems at hand, but all participants acknowledge that the development of a broader understanding and the formulation of possible solutions (be these for mitigation and/or adaptation), require a combination of approaches. As requirements for a PhD degree usually demand strong disciplinary approaches and methods, the multidisciplinary aspect of the project is more evident in the master's programme. By bringing together teachers from different disciplines to focus on a particular topic, we give students the tools to understand and assess climate change, as well as some ideas on how to tackle this global problem.

Students in our master's programme come from all kinds of disciplines, spanning the natural and social sciences as well as the humanities. Some already work for public institutions or private enterprises in the marine environment. Furthermore, we have had students from ten different countries in the programme, spanning Africa, Asia and Europe, while the lecturers have come from several Asian countries, the US, Australia and Norway. Supervisors cover an even wider geographic area because when students choose thesis topics that focus on their home countries, we attempt to secure additional local supervisors for them. This has created a very rich and stimulating learning environment for both students and lecturers, and has ensured that knowledge sharing is mutual, from North to South, South to North, and South to South.

Interactions between students and professors conducting research in their own local areas allow them to develop theories based on their experiences. Hypotheses to be tested embrace environmental as well as societal concerns and are, therefore, more meaningful to the researchers and the intended end-users of the research. The introduction of new ideas into the process invigorates the investigators in their search for answers to perceived problems. For example, in Kenya, where we had a student conducting research on students', parents' and teachers' knowledge and perceptions of climate change, much excitement arose when the research began. Survey questions and interviews sparked enormous interest among the local respondents in the climatic events resulting from climate change. Once answered, the research questions generate results that will be immediately useful to society, and the students will be able to share their experiences via seminars, workshops and other media. This is extremely important in areas where awareness and information on climate change is sadly lacking.

Our mentoring programme provides academic mentors for female academics who aspire to advance their careers. Several workshops have provided input for both mentors and mentees, allowing them to share experiences and develop institutional goals and processes that will facilitate career development for female academics.

PhDs candidates and postdoctoral fellows have spent some time at the Norwegian partner institutions to complete certain courses and start their research. While they were in Norway, we encouraged these scholars to build relationships with one another so that when they return to Vietnam and Sri Lanka, they can continue to learn from each other, and encourage further knowledge sharing and research partnerships. Here too, while Northern supervisors teach methods and approaches for assessing climate change issues in the South, they also learn a lot about climate issues and consequences in the South. This knowledge is hugely beneficial to them as they continue with research, teaching and supervision in the North, as they acquire a deeper and wider understanding of the challenges facing the globe, rather than learning only about issues relevant to the scientific community in the North.

Challenges

A number of issues are especially challenging in relation to projects such as these. First, as mentioned earlier, bridging the eco-social chasm, familiar to most Northern researchers, is also challenging in the South, and has naturally impacted on our project. It is worth noting, however, that this divide may take on a multitude of forms, and have different causes and effects in the South, requiring different approaches to bridge the gap (Green 2014). In our case, there is a clear difference between how our two Southern partner universities focus on the social sciences. In Vietnam, hard-core economics is strongly prioritised, while in Sri Lanka, the other social sciences are more prevalent.

Second, the most interdisciplinary aspect of the programme is its teaching programme, and specifically within the master's programme. In both Northern and Southern contexts, it seems to be easier to educate students in a multidisciplinary way, than for individual academics to *be* multidisciplinary or to work in interdisciplinary ways. The hope is that the upcoming generation of academics will have a broader range of vision than the current generation, and that projects like these create forums for ongoing cross-disciplinary and collaboratory engagements between scientists.

Third, gender is a central part of our project, and we have a strong focus on issues related to women in academia. In the project, female PhD candidates have experienced a number of problems related to the timing of the project. The project period is short and the budgetary delays are often long. The PhD students are part of a kind of 'sandwich' system, in which they spend half their time at the Norwegian universities, and the other half at their home university. This is economically beneficial for the project, in that it secures stronger connections with (and economic contributions to) the Southern universities than when PhD students study only in the North. However, when female PhD students returned home to begin their research, support from local institutions has been less forthcoming. In addition, upon returning home, female PhD students with families are expected to take on household and familial responsibilities that absorb much of their research time. Some research projects require researchers to spend a significant amount of time away from home. This is especially difficult for female students (who are in the majority in the project) as they are unable to spend long periods away from their families.

Similarly, female postdoctoral students experience challenges in reconnecting with their local programmes and continuing to focus on their research when they return home. Because staff shortages are often acute in Southern universities, many have been allocated teaching and other administrative work despite having been promised that they would be released from such duties.

Such practical and economic challenges are common in most research projects. In this case, however, cultural challenges are also present. For instance, female faculty members had a difficult time finding suitable mentors, as most of the qualified persons were male. The use of male mentors for female mentees is culturally challenging, as this kind of engagement between two academics of the opposite sex is not necessarily seen as acceptable because the whole concept of mentoring is not yet well-rooted in all academic contexts.

Some of the challenges experienced were expected to a certain degree, but most were not, so we had to find pragmatic solutions and compromises. For example, the laboratories and other facilities necessary for conducting experiments were not as ready as initially understood, and the process of establishing these required monies unavailable locally. Furthermore, in the second year of the project the Vietnamese government drastically reduced funding to its universities. This reduced the amount of matching funds that Nha Trang University had available to put towards the development of facilities. In addition, limited access to good background data is often a problem for robust scientific work in LMICs. This is especially the case in relation to fundamental natural and societal data and statistics that are systematically collected in wealthier nations. The collection of this data requires funding not only for its collection, but also for complex and costly analytical infrastructure. Likewise, access to social data at community or individual level in LMICs is hampered by limited resources as well as cultural and political obstacles.

Some challenges related to the very nature of the project. One such is the issue of time. Climate change is a long-term phenomenon but such projects are short term. In some cases, climate-change events manifest as too much rainfall. In other cases, snow might fall in highly tropical areas, or heat and drought might afflict temperate zones. Short-term observations tend to result in erratic data, spreading confusion and even causing some policy-makers to doubt the causes of climate change. Longer-term observation processes generally produce more meaningful results. Our students attended classes for a maximum of two years.

A related issue is that experiences of climate change vary for the individuals witnessing and recording the changes. Some have shorter memories while younger researchers have less life experience on which to draw. Consequently, many past events and weather patterns don't form part of their memories or those of the people they survey. Ultimately, data generated in the short run, focused on recent climate events and the circumstances surrounding them, challenged us to avoid over-emphasising certain aspects of weather events that occurred during our teaching programmes.

Interestingly, and this was embarrassingly unexpected, we also found that climate change, or at least weather events, created great challenges for us in relation to accessing respondents and in carrying out experiments. An unusually large typhoon hit Vietnam in November 2017, impacting all aspects of our research and teaching there. The typhoon disrupted both commercial and research-related aquaculture production. Infrastructure was demolished and people in rural areas were displaced. Research facilities stopped functioning and much data was lost. The natural scientists had to start their experiments all over again. Individuals conducting social science research encountered difficulties contacting communities they were working with who suffered substantial displacement and economic losses. Some villagers were no longer willing to answer questions about climate change, preferring to forget the terrible experience they had just survived. Climate change or at least a climate event clearly impacted our project.

Ultimately, however, challenges create additional learning opportunities. Some may claim that problems with the sandwich system, for instance, justify changing it. However, it can be argued that the difficulties that PhD students and postdoctoral researchers experience upon returning to their home institutions highlight the need for research time, acceptable laboratories and other working conditions that these institutions must address. Facing these questions has the potential to improve research conditions not only for project members, but also within these institutions more broadly. Experiences regarding gender, the lack of basic data, and so on, also increase the understanding and knowledge of researchers from the North, thereby enhancing their awareness in relation to future North–South interactions.

Achievements and lessons learned

Although still in process, the project has already contributed much to developing competence and knowledge related to climate change in the marine environments studied. In this section, we discuss some of the perhaps less visible yet very important contributions.

The limitations of available local data, combined with the fact that data collection is imperative in a project like this, means that academic work done by master's and PhD students as well as postdoctoral researchers has largely involved collecting primary data. In the social science context, many data are collected from the coastal communities to better understand their perceptions of climate change and adaptation. An underlying respect for the perceptions and knowledge of stakeholders living in and off the marine environments we are studying pertains to this work. Nevertheless, we encounter a multitude of issues – from legal limitations to limited awareness of what climate change means – that challenge our research outputs. The meeting point between public perceptions and scientific output can help informing the authorities about where and how to interact with the communities to better meet both their aspirations and the SDGs.

SDG 14 (Conserve and sustainably use the oceans, seas and marine resources) is highly relevant to our project. The goal includes a central statement outlining its focal aspects, namely: 'Careful management of this essential global resource is a key feature of a sustainable future.'[2] We believe Norad could contribute directly to this goal by focusing more on competence and capacity development by reaching out not only to the universities, but also to marine management institutions. These organisations are often hampered by scarce resources and employees who have little or rather dated knowledge. Providing scholarships or partial funding for the further education of these employees could directly and rapidly enhance marine conservation and sustainable management. Moreover, rather than focusing only on students who have to then enter these institutions in junior positions, educating senior employees within these institutions could help to ensure a more rapid incorporation of climate change knowledge and modern management principles. Indeed, in expanding meeting points between scientists and non-scientists, this strategy would potentially also open the project to more transdisciplinarity. We are not suggesting the educating of marine management staff alone. Rather, we suggest that a mix of students, with and without management experience, would be advantageous for all. This would also make more hands-on management insight available to both lecturers and fellow students, while providing more input into the education and research process on real-world challenges faced by marine management institutions.

The SDGs emphasise the need to incorporate a societal perspective, including issues of equity. In the Vietnamese and Sri Lankan contexts, this means highlighting issues related to poor coastal communities, and the most marginalised in these communities, who are often women. The gender profile of our researchers and lecturers at all levels is predominantly female. This encourages and enables a stronger focus on gender issues, regarding the situation of women both in the communities studied and in our project. As academics, we have in the past tended to sometimes overlook gender issues and prioritise our disciplinary expertise, but we admit to having learned important lessons from incorporating gender mainstreaming into this project. The mentoring programme has foregrounded several issues that female academics face in their careers. The identification and sharing of these issues has been valuable, and has helped us to create a more balanced academic environment. That this balance will have long-term impacts is beyond doubt, and adds another wonderful (though unexpected) facet to the sustainability of the project.

The students attracted to the master's programme were drawn from an unexpectedly diverse pool both in terms of their countries of origin and their range of occupations in the marine sector. Having such a range of students means that the project is making a significant contribution to enhancing competence not only in the partner universities, but also within the sector more generally. The fact that Vietnam attracted students from countries as far away as Africa was unexpected, and has increased our awareness of the potential for postgraduate programmes in economically attractive hubs such as Vietnam.

Norad's requirements related to the sustainability of projects carried is challenging because the themes and issues defined by Norad do not always fit exactly with the local situation or the main strategies of the Southern universities. What we realised, however, is that sustainability comes in many shapes and forms. It is not solely about ensuring that programmes carried out in the project period live on beyond this time. Sustainability is also about the afterlife of project contributions. Clearly, specific programmes will have limited lifespans, and it might not be possible or even be useful to extend these after the project period is over. Nonetheless, if the capacity-development processes built into projects are successful, the projects will continue via the different but related programmes that follow on. For instance, Nha Trang University might have limited funding to continue offering master's programmes in English such as those funded by the current project. However, the competencies developed through the project are very likely to result in the development of new research, education programmes and courses in Vietnam and Sri Lanka with a clear focus on climate change. In addition, the dissemination of knowledge via the students, who are spread across different enterprises and marine management institutions all over the world, will ensure sustainability far beyond the project's original aims, as well as secure a multitude of small steps towards meeting the SDGs.

About the authors and the project

Claire W Armstrong is based at UiT, the Arctic University of Norway
Nguyen Thi Kim Anh is at Nha Trang University in Nha Trang, Vietnam

Project title: Incorporating Climate Change into Ecosystem Approaches to Fisheries and Aquaculture Management in Sri Lanka and Vietnam
Partner institutions: Nha Trang University (Vietnam), University of Ruhuna (Sri Lanka), University of Bergen and UiT, the Arctic University of Norway (Norway)

Notes

1   See 'What is Horizon 2020?', https://ec.europa.eu/programmes/horizon2020/what-horizon-2020.
2   See http://www.un.org/sustainabledevelopment/oceans/.

References

Adger WN, Hughes TP, Folke C, Carpenter SR and Rockström J (2005) Social-ecological resilience to coastal disasters. *Science* 309(5737): 1036–1039

Ciannelli L, Hunsicker M, Beaudreau A, Bailey K, Crowder LB, Finley C, Webb C, Reynolds J, Sagmiller K, Anderies JM, Hawthorne D, Parrish J, Heppell S, Conway F and Chigbu P (2014) Transdisciplinary graduate education in marine resource science and management. *ICES Journal of Marine Science* 71(5): 1047–1051

Gordon HS (1954) Economic theory of common-property resources: The fishery. *Journal of Political Economy* 62: 124–142

Green I (2014) Ecology, race, and the making of environmental publics: A dialogue with Silent Spring in South Africa. *Resilience: A Journal of the Environmental Humanities* 1(2). Available online

Hilborn R and Ovando D (2014) Reflections on the success of traditional fisheries management. *ICES Journal of Marine Science* 71(5): 1040–1046

IPCC (Intergovernmental Panel on Climate Change) (2014) *Climate Change 2014: Synthesis Report*, Contribution of Working Groups I, II and III to the Fifth Assessment Report of the IPCC. Geneva, Switzerland

Jackson JBC, Kirby MX, Berger WH, Bjorndal KA, Botsford LW, Bourque BJ, Bradbury RH, Cooke R, Erlandson J, Estes JA, Hughes TP, Kidwell S, Lange CB, Lenihan HS, Pandolfi JM, Peterson CH, Steneck RS, Tegner MJ and Warner RR (2001) Historical overfishing and the recent collapse of coastal ecosystems. *Science* 293: 629–638

Kreft S, Eckstein D, Junghans L, Kerestan C and Hagen U (2014) *Global Climate Risk Index 2015: Who Suffers Most from Extreme Weather Events? Weather-Related Loss Events in 2013 and 1994 to 2013.* Berlin: Germanwatch

Naylor RL, Goldburg RJ, Primavera JH, Kautsky N, Beveridge MCM, Clay J, Folke C, Lubchenco J, Mooney H and Troell M (2000) Effect of aquaculture on world fish supplies. *Nature* 405: 1017

Nymand Larsen J and Fondahl G (2014) *Arctic Human Development Report: Regional Processes and Global Linkages.* Copenhagen: Nordisk Ministerråd

Oracion EG, Miller ML and Christie P (2005) Marine protected areas for whom? Fisheries, tourism, and solidarity in a Philippine community. *Ocean and Coastal Management* 48(3): 393–410

Primavera JH (2006) Overcoming the impacts of aquaculture on the coastal zone. *Ocean and Coastal Management* 49(9): 531–545

Serreze MC and Francis JA (2006) The Arctic amplification debate. *Climatic Change* 76(3): 241–264

Stock P and Burton RJF (2011) Defining terms for integrated (multi-inter-trans-disciplinary) sustainability research. *Sustainability* 3(8): 1090

Wätzold F, Drechsler M, Armstrong CW, Baumgärtner S, Grimm V, Huth A, Perrings C, Possingham HP, Shogren JF, Skonhoft H, Verboom-Vasiljev J and Wisse C (2006) Ecological-economic modelling for biodiversity management: Potential, pitfalls, and prospects. *Conservation Biology* 20(4): 1034–1041

Zhang J (2005) Warming of the arctic ice-ocean system is faster than the global average since the 1960s. *Geophysical Research Letters* 32(19). Available online

PART THREE

UPSKILLING AND PROFESSIONALISATION

Introduction to Part Three

Kristin Skare Orgeret

In this part of the book, we aim to shed light and reflect on how Norhed projects balance traditional ways of educating professionals with more modern ones, and we examine the differences between these systems in relation to developing students' attitudes towards their own fields of study. I use the term 'field' in the Bourdieusian sense, drawing on his *Outline of a Theory of Practice* (1977) in which he argues that separation is a hidden condition behind all academic activity, and that each field is a setting in which agents and their social positions are located.

Hence, the question of how modern concepts are adapted to specific local contexts is core. For this reason, we begin this section by revisiting the theories about modernisation that constitute the first theories of development. The term 'modernisation theory' covers a whole range of ideas that emerged in the 1950s. That decade, characterised by the start of the Cold War and growing momentum of anticolonial independence movements, saw a new interest in studies of the economic, cultural, social and political development in the low- and middle-income countries (LMICs).

Modernisation theory is related to both evolutionism and structural functionalism, and posits definite stages of development through which every country has to pass in order to develop from a traditional into a modern society (see Rostow 1960). Inspired by the distinction between 'traditional' and 'modern', well-established in classical sociology and Weber's ideal models, modernisation theory's solution to underdevelopment is simple: by following in the footsteps of the West, the LMICs should go through the same stages of development, just faster. The modernisation paradigm sees economic development as unidirectional, mechanistic, deterministic and uniformly positive, in which growth is inevitable and universal.

Modernisation theory accorded particular importance to the role of media as a tool for development. For supporters of this view, the role of 'development communication' was essentially to convey the views of external experts in a vertical, authority-based, top-down process. This is exemplified by Daniel Lerner's work, *The Passing of Traditional Society: Modernizing the Middle East* (1958), which still plays an important, if unacknowledged, inspirational role in many development projects.

Analyses of the impact of higher education on societies in LMICs emerged alongside post-colonial discourse and modernisation theories. Research generally focused on how governments could use higher education to train a small elite in the skills needed to ensure forms of governance that would ensure economic growth. The academy in this context was regarded as being as irrelevant to local communities as local communities were to the academy. Vocational training was largely run by the state (Thomson 2008). At this time, aid to higher education focused primarily on providing scholarships for graduate training in donor countries (Varghese 2010).

Dama Mosweunyane (2016) notes that few African universities have contributed meaningfully to the intellectual, economic, political, social or environmental culture of their countries or their continent. He suggests that this is because they rely too heavily on Western concepts and this undermines this development. Mosweunyane points out that imported research methods and agendas limit the inventiveness and creativity of African academics and that they draw too heavily on the work of scholars from the West, ignoring the work of fellow African scholars and the wisdom of local communities.

Although strongly criticised from various quarters, notions of modernisation have played an important role in much of the thinking behind development projects for many decades, and it can be argued that traces of modernisation theory are still present in the programmes run by many donor agencies today. In this context, Norhed is attempting to take a radically different approach. As noted in the introductory section, the strengthening of higher education institutions in the

South and supporting collaborative research is its central objective. In line with what Mahmood Mamdani (2007) proposes, Norhed sees research capacity building at universities as an integral function of higher education, particularly in countries with a colonial history. We also believe that universities play a key role in delivering the knowledge requirements for development. What is revealed in the following chapters are some of the tensions and productive differences that often arise between traditional and modern approaches to professions, and when different cultures meet.

In their chapter, 'Promoting professionalisation in nursing and midwifery', Alfred Maluwa, Margaret Maimbolwa, Clara Haruzivishe, Patricia Katowa-Mukwato, Jon Oyvind Odland, Babil Stray Pedersen, Ellen Chirwa, Midion Chidzonga and Address Malata describe their work with nursing and midwifery practitioners and educators in Malawi, Zambia and Zimbabwe. Nurses and midwives comprise the overwhelming majority (90 per cent) of health workers in these three countries, and the aim of the project is to contribute to training a critical mass of professionals who are capable of responding to current and emerging health challenges, thus improving the quality of patient care. The author team show how traditional and modern midwifery practices operate side by side and examine how the nursing and midwifery profession has been modernised in response to political, social and epidemiological shifts as well as in relation to shifts in state health policies. The authors explain why Western models are not always appropriate in Africa and argue that systems developed in the West need to be validated locally prior to being applied.

Arne Rohnny Sannerud expounds on society's need for vocational training and describes the collaboration between Kyambogo University in Uganda and the Oslo Metropolitan University in Norway to develop appropriate vocational pedagogy. In his chapter, he explains the challenges of establishing action-oriented research and other research tools within the project and the activities that helped build capacity among academic staff at Kyambogo University. He also explains why the sustainability of vocational training programmes relies on the participation of both internal and external stakeholders and argues that securing this participation is an essential part of such projects.

In a chapter on teacher training in Ethiopia, Ahmed Y Ahmed, Meskerem L Debele, Haftu H Gebremeskel, Dawit A Getahun, Dawit T Tiruneh and Dereje T Wondem discuss the launching of master's programmes at Bahir Dar University on the teaching of mathematics and science. The aim of this project is to strengthen the skills of lecturing staff at Ethiopia's colleges of teacher education where primary-school science and mathematics teachers receive their training. The authors of this chapter argue that if the Ethiopian government's vision of strengthening the teaching of science and technology is to be achieved, primary and secondary schools require more competent teachers and relevant in-service teacher training programmes that support students' learning. The perception that good teaching relies primarily on advanced content knowledge remains strong in Ethiopia and the introduction of courses focused on pedagogy was initially met with some resistance and misunderstanding. The authors outline how they first had to face the challenge of breaking down the existing academic culture among teachers and teacher educators which prioritised content knowledge and paid almost no attention to helping teachers assess how to convey their content knowledge or check the effectiveness of their teaching. This made teachers' need for a framework that would help them integrate technology, pedagogy, and content knowledge into their own teaching and materials development very clear. The author team then describe their efforts to design training programmes for mathematics and science educators that blend technology and pedagogy.

The training of mathematics teachers is also the focus of the last chapter in this section. Here, Mercy Kazima and Arne Jakobsen focus on the project they are part of in Malawi. They argue that transformation is necessary if educators are to improve the quality of mathematics here – the quality of education is generally poor and mathematics education is particularly weak. Acknowledging that this will involve changing norms and values as well as institutions and structures (Jha 2016), Kazima and Jacobsen stress the importance of 'understanding the context of the targeted society' and of retaining the beneficial elements of traditional approaches to teaching. The authors explain how their project therefore first attempted to study and understand mathematics education in Malawi before implementing a professional development programme for trainers of mathematics teacher educators. They recommend that the benefits of traditional concepts and teaching methods should be identified and retained in ways that enable teachers to adopt and adapt additional or alternative teaching methods and content in contextually relevant ways.

As a whole, the contributors to this section discuss the challenges experienced when different cultures meet, and reveal some of the implications of this for teacher training at this point in time. All of the chapters tackle critical questions, such as: what should happen to traditional education as we attempt to improve teaching practices? Can different systems operate side by side in ways that strengthen one another? How is project implementation challenging our existing concepts of training?

References

Bourdieu P (1977/2013) *Outline of a Theory of Practice*. Cambridge: Cambridge University Press

Jha A (2016) Impact of modernisation on education. *International Journal of Advance Research and Innovative Ideas in Education* 2(2): 1885–1889

Mamdani M (2007) *Scholars in the Marketplace*. Dakar: Codesria

Mosweunyane D (2016) Panjandrums in African universities: Inapt scholars for African development. *English Language Teaching* 4(1): 1–8

Rostow WW (1960) *The Stages of Economic Growth: A Non-communist Manifesto*. Cambridge: Cambridge University Press

Thomson A (2008) *Exploring the Relationship Between Higher Education and Development: A Review and Report*. Brighton: Guerrand-Hermes Foundation for Peace

Varghese NV (2010) Higher education aid: Setting priorities and improving effectiveness. *Journal of International Cooperation in Education* 13: 173–187

9

Promoting professionalisation in nursing and midwifery

Alfred Maluwa, Margaret Maimbolwa, Clara Haruzivishe,
Patricia Katowa-Mukwato, Jon Oyvind Odland,
Babil Stray Pedersen, Ellen Chirwa,
Midion Chidzonga & Address Malata

Academics in Malawi, Zambia and Zimbabwe have formed a consortium to train adequate numbers of nurses, midwives, educators and researchers in each country who will be capable of addressing existing and emerging challenges in child and maternal health, as well as improving the availability and quality of patient care. In this chapter, we describe how nursing and midwifery practices have evolved in the three countries in response to local and international political, social and cultural trends, as well as to government policies. We also provide a summary of the consortium's activities and achievements from 2015 to 2018.

Background

Basic health indicators in Malawi, Zambia and Zimbabwe are among the poorest in the world (see Table 9.1). Maternal mortality rates are high, and although 90 per cent of the health workers in these countries are nurses and midwives, nurse-to-patient ratios are distressingly low. The World Health Organization's recommended minimum nurse-to-patient ratio is 1:1 000 (WHO 2006) but, as shown in Table 9.1, of the African countries in this consortium, only Zimbabwe is even close to achieving this target. The ratio of midwives per 10 000 women of child-bearing age in each country is similarly alarming. Consequently, mothers and infants in all three countries are dying from treatable pregnancy and birth-related complications, with maternal and neonatal morbidity and mortality rates further compounded by the incidence of HIV and AIDS.

Table 9.1: Basic health indicators in Zambia (2014), Malawi and Zimbabwe (2016)

Health indicator	Malawi	Zambia	Zimbabwe
Maternal mortality per 100 000 live births	439	398	651
Neonatal mortality per 1 000 live births	27	24	29
Infant mortality per 1 000 live births	42	45	50
Child mortality (under 5 years) per 1 000 live births	63	75	69
Nurse–patient ratio	1:2300	1:1864	1:1136
Qualified midwives per 10 000 women of child-bearing age	3	7	10
Percentage of women who deliver their babies at home	7%	53%	20%

Sources: Malawi: NSO (2017); Zambia: CSO and MoHZ (2014); Zimbabwe: Zimstat (2016)

The high maternal and child mortality rates highlight the need for new nursing and midwifery training that is more competence- and evidence-based, and that can rapidly deliver a significant number of well-trained nurses and midwives. In addition, existing nursing and midwifery training programmes are not adequately addressing the challenges facing graduates once they qualify. Part of this project's aim, therefore, is to improve curricula by making them more evidence- and competency-based.

In addition, the nursing midwifery profession in the three countries has been adversely affected by brain drain. Many of the most qualified and experienced nurses and midwives have migrated to high-income countries in search of better wages. Studies have shown that increased availability and better training of nurses and midwives in their own countries can mitigate this problem. Since the inception of the project in 2014, none of the nurses/midwives trained within the programme is reported to have emigrated.

The degree of professional autonomy granted to nurses and midwives has long been debated. In the formal health sector, nurses earn professional certification when they pass examinations based on curricula that, in addition to basic epidemiology and patient care, cover issues such as professional standards, codes of ethics, and cultural and social skills. In midwifery, however, levels of professionalisation can vary depending on the role and status of the midwife and on where they work. In addition, the term 'midwife' is sometimes used interchangeably with 'nurse', hence it is useful to define both roles and clarify the differences between them.

The International Confederation of Midwives (ICM)[1] defines a midwife as a person who:

- has successfully completed an education programme based on the essential competencies for basic midwifery practice within the framework of their own Global Standards for Midwifery Education;
- is recognised in the country in which they work;
- has acquired the requisite qualifications to be registered and/or legally licensed to practise midwifery and to use the title of midwife; and
- demonstrates competency in the practice of midwifery.

The ICM further defines midwifery practice as the work of a recognised, responsible and accountable professional who works in partnership with women to: give the necessary support, care and advice during pregnancy, labour and the postpartum period; take responsibility for assisting women during childbirth; and provide care for newborn infants. This includes preventative care, the promotion of normal deliveries, the detection of complications in mother and child, assessing the need for medical care or other assistance, and taking emergency measures if necessary. The ICM also sees midwives as playing an important role in providing health counselling and education not only to parents, but also to the wider family and community. This includes antenatal education and preparation for parenthood, and extends to educating women about sexual and reproductive health as well as basic infant and childcare. They also acknowledge that midwives can practise in any setting, including homes, clinics and hospitals.

Nurses, on the other hand, must complete a programme of basic general nursing education and be authorised by the appropriate local or national regulatory authority to practise. Nursing education is a formally recognised programme of study that allows students to first obtain a broad foundation in the nursing sciences for the general practice of nursing. Those who wish can study further for a leadership role or pursue various specialisations in advanced nursing practice.

In general terms, formal nursing training emphasises the biomedical model of disease and the authority of doctors, while in midwifery training, patient wellness and practitioner autonomy are focus points. However, in Malawi, Zambia and Zimbabwe, midwives are first expected to complete their nursing training and can only enrol for midwifery as a post-basic programme.

As part of the Norhed project, academic institutions in the consortium were able to change this situation. As shown in Table 9.2 Malawi and Zambia introduced a direct-entry four-year midwifery degree. Malawi now also offers an integrated four-year nursing and midwifery programme that allows students to graduate as a nurse/midwife. Meanwhile, Zimbabwe introduced a three-year BSc in midwifery that is open to midwives who already have a diploma. In addition, all three countries now offer postgradudate programmes in midwifery and nursing.

Table 9.2 Degree programmes developed by academic institutions in the consortium as part of the Norhed project

Qualification level	Malawi	Zambia	Zimbabwe
BSc (Midwifery) direct-entry four-year degree	✓	✓	
Integrated four-year nursing and midwifery programme	✓		
BSc (Midwifery) three-year degree, open to students with a midwifery diploma			✓
Postgraduate Diploma in Midwifery, open to students with a BSc (Nursing)			✓
Master's and PhD degrees in midwifery	✓	✓	
Master's and PhD degrees in nursing	✓	✓	✓
PhD in nursing and midwifery			✓

Note: In all three countries, this training is guided and regulated by the respective Nurses' and Midwives' Councils. These councils are, in turn, guided by the ICM, the ICN and the WHO.

A brief history of nursing and midwifery training in the three countries

Gelfand (1988) observes that every nation in the world has a 'midwifery' tradition, albeit known by different names. Traditionally, midwives were and still are seen as powerful and caring, and are highly respected and trusted in their communities. In the past, in general, these women learned their skills through a practical apprenticeship and later mentored others. Licensing was not always seen as necessary – families knew who to go to when a woman was pregnant and the time for delivery had come (Gelfand 1988).

In the mid nineteenth century, when European missionaries settled in what is now Malawi, Zambia and Zimbabwe they introduced nursing and midwifery. Some had medical training and others were accompanied by doctors and/or nurses. Thus, while they saw evangelising as their primary role, they offered Western-style education and medical care as a means of winning over the local communities (Benkele 2011; UNFPA 2007). As they built clinics and hospitals, they recruited local men and women to assist as wound-dressers, orderlies and cleaners (Benkele 2011). In 1857, the missionaries introduced nursing and midwifery training in these (mostly rural) mission hospitals and clinics; the training was open only to women (Mbeba et al. forthcoming).

In Zimbabwe, in the early 1950s, the training of midwives became the prerogative of the state. The authorities set up training programmes in urban hospitals such as Mpilo Hospital in Bulawayo and Harare Central Hospital in Harare. In 1964, the first nursing college was opened in Kitwe, Zambia, and in 1965, a nursing college was established in Blantyre, Malawi (Benkele 2011). Prior to this, Zambian and Malawian nurses had to go to Zimbabwe or South Africa for training. Once these state-run nursing colleges were established, the mission stations and other private hospitals aligned their training programmes with the state-run system. Subsequently the training of midwives was rolled out to provincial and district hospitals.

From the start, formal midwifery training was open only to nurses who had already completed basic nursing training, and had at least two years of practical nursing experience. Competition for a place on midwifery training programmes was always intense because very few midwifery schools existed. Often nurses with up to five years of work experience were still waiting for admission to a midwifery programme. All three countries were formerly British colonies; consequently, all nursing and midwifery training programmes were based on the British curriculum. However, since the 1990s, curricula have begun to include elements from American, Canadian, Swedish and Norwegian programmes. Increasingly, the British system is being adapted as the ICN (for nurses) and the ICM (for midwives) standardise nursing and midwifery training and practice worldwide in collaboration with the WHO.

The introduction of formal nursing and midwifery training and practice gradually led to the institutionalisation of medical care and childbirth (UNFPA 2007), but given the lack of adequate facilities and staff, some women in rural areas have resisted this paradigm shift and continued seeking the services of traditional healers and traditional birth attendants (TBAs) when sick or in childbirth (Butrick et. al. 2014). As shown in Table 9.1, approximately 7 per cent of all births in Malawi occur in village households (NSO 2017); in Zambia, 53 per cent of women deliver at home (CSO and MoHZ 2014); and in Zimbabwe, 20 per cent of women deliver at home (Zimstat 2016). In effect, traditional and modern midwifery practices operate side by side in all three countries. While official health policy encourages all pregnant women to attend antenatal clinics, and have their babies in clinics or hospitals, stating that this has been proven safer for both the mother and child (CSO and MoHZ 2014; NSO 2017; Zimstat 2016), few women in rural communities have easy access to well-resourced clinics or specialised care. The services of traditional healers and TBAs are still widely used (Butrick et al. 2014).

Factors affecting the training and practice of nursing and midwifery

Economic challenges

The economic structural adjustment programmes implemented in many African states in the 1980s heralded an array of deep social challenges for African countries, involving the rapid decline of state-run services, including the health sector (Herbst 1990). For health workers, salaries decreased in real terms and working conditions worsened, resulting in strikes in some cases. In response, governments introduced laws prohibiting providers of essential services from participating in strike action. For nurses, this led to much frustration and eventual burnout, with many opting to leave the public sector and seek employment elsewhere. Although nurses and midwives established unions to bargain for better pay, low wages remain prevalent, particularly in the public sector.

Consequently, many nurses now work in private institutions, while even greater numbers emigrated to countries such as the UK, Australia and Canada (Dovlo 2007).[2] In the southern African region, as in other countries, nurses and midwives form the backbone of healthcare delivery. The large-scale emigration of nurses with specialised skills (including midwifery) has left Malawi, Zambia and Zimbabwe with a skeleton staff of less-experienced nurses struggling with exceptionally heavy workloads. The impact of all this on the provision of healthcare is obviously hugely negative (MoHM 2017; MoHZ 2013).

Abel Chikanda (2007) examines the emigration of health professionals from Zimbabwe in the face of that country's economic and political crisis. Drawing on data from selected health institutions, he shows that at the time of his study, the rate of emigration of health professionals was increasing and showing no sign of slowing. Most emigrants indicated that economic factors were the major push factor. This outflow negatively affects all users of the health system, but particularly the poor who cannot afford the services of better-staffed and well-equipped private clinics, and consequently resort to traditional or faith healers.

The governments of Malawi, Zambia and Zimbabwe all responded to the crisis by trying to recruit and train more nurses and midwives. Malawi implemented its Emergency Human Resources Programme between 2005 and 2011 (MoHM 2011). In Zambia, the government developed a programme to scale up the enrolment of trainee nurses by building new colleges, reopening colleges that had been closed and introducing new programmes for pre-service certified midwives as well as a pre-service post-basic nursing degree. These programmes included the introduction of e-learning for both in-service and pre-service trainees. Other measures included the opening of new private schools, increased budgetary allocations for health-worker salaries, increasing the number of nursing posts in the public sector, and putting some pressure on newly qualified government-sponsored candidates to fill these vacancies (Zimstat 2012, 2016). However, this strategy created a pool of junior and inexperienced nurses and midwives, and reduced the number of students who went on to complete more specialised studies. In Zimbabwe, in 2008, the number of nurses required in all the posts was 19 379 but the vacancy rate stood at 28 per cent (Kararach and Otieno 2016). In all three countries, a locum system became a kind of stopgap – basically, nurses and midwives who are employed in either public- or private-sector posts do locums in other hospitals or clinics when they should be off duty.

The recognition of midwives as practitioners in their own right

There is no separate register for midwives in Zimbabwe; they are registered as nurses with a midwifery qualification, thus skewing the number of nurses in the system. However, the Zimbabwe Confederation of Midwives is calling for a separate register. In Malawi and Zambia, separate registers do exist for the nurses and midwives, and are held at the respective nurses and midwives councils.

The impact of HIV and TB

HIV has increased morbidity and mortality rates among mothers and infants in all three countries. Even though the prevalence of HIV and AIDS in the region is declining,[3] incidence remains high and accounts for significant morbidity and mortality. In addition, the HIV pandemic has led to an increase in the prevalence of TB. According to the WHO (2017), TB accounts for 1 in 5 of HIV-related deaths globally and people living with HIV are 29 times more likely to develop TB than people in the same country without HIV.

Integrating traditional and Western nursing and midwifery practices

Although moves to encourage women all over the world to have their babies in hospitals were intended to eradicate traditional birthing practices and TBAs, this has not happened. In the early 1980s, the fact that mothers worldwide were still consulting TBAs (sometimes by choice and sometimes not) led the United Nations Population Fund to fund training programmes for TBAs to try to help reduce maternal and infant mortality and morbidity rates (UNFPA 2007). Consequently, by 2007, the health ministries in all three countries had redefined the roles of TBAs.

At a policy level, the role of TBAs is defined as helping with antenatal care and, where they identify problems, referring pregnant women to formal healthcare facilities for assistance (Butrick et al. 2014). However, state clinics and other facilities remain inaccessible to many rural women because they are located far from where they live; if transport is available it is expensive.

In more urban areas, TBAs increasingly work hand in hand with clinic staff, including nurses, midwives, doctors and gynaecologists. The magnitude of support given to mothers by TBAs is seldom quantifiable because many are given recognition only in so far as they help pregnant women get to hospitals or clinics for antenatal care and childbirth, and not when they assist women to deliver their babies (Choguya 2014).

While the health policies of all three countries in our study recommend that all maternal and infant care should be facility-based, several constraints make this impossible. These include: the critical shortage of formally trained nurses and midwives already mentioned; limited national health budgets and a lack of basic infrastructure; high levels of poverty and/or illiteracy among parents; the reportedly negative attitudes of health personnel, especially midwives, towards women who attend clinics when they are pregnant or ready to give birth; and cultural practices and religious beliefs linked to childbirth. In this context, the facility-based models developed in the West are perhaps not the most appropriate. The reality is that it is difficult for many pregnant women in the region to get to clinics or hospitals, whereas they can more easily obtain support and assistance from locally based TBAs.

Despite health policy recommendations that women should register for antenatal care in their first trimester, many women wait until they reach their second or third trimester before they do so. One reason for this is that, in African culture, pregnancy is traditionally not announced early. Another reason is that staff shortages create huge workloads for midwives, and they tend to be more concerned with near-to-term mothers than those in their first trimester. In addition, the number of antenatal visits recommended internationally is unclear. In the 1970s, one visit per month was recommended. In 2002, this changed to four visits over the pregnancy (Baffour-Awuah et al. 2015; WHO 2002). In 2016, the recommendation changed again to a minimum of eight visits over the pregnancy (WHO 2016).

Similarly, recommendations concerning the breastfeeding of infants have shifted in recent decades. In the 1980s and 1990s, mothers were encouraged to bottle feed or at least supplement breastfeeding with bottle feeding. However, since the HIV pandemic, breastfeeding is widely recommended again (Muchacha and Mtetwa 2015). For mothers living with HIV, the so called option B+ (breastfeeding plus enrolment in a prevention of mother to child transmission programme) is recommended (WHO 2014). In practice, this conflicting information has led to a range of breastfeeding practices, and the uptake of option B+ has proven difficult to monitor in low- to middle-income countries (LMICs) (Chanda et al. 2018). In our experience, women are taught and encouraged to breastfeed but there are no follow-up mechanisms to verify what happens in practice. What is apparent is that when healthcare policies come from the West, and are adopted without any baseline assessment of their suitability in local contexts, conflict and confusion arises in relation to their implementation.

To an extent, it can be argued that traditional and Western concepts of midwifery and nursing are in conflict with one another. For this reason, it is crucial that all health practitioners acknowledge that cultural norms, practices and attitudes preserved in communities remain a vital factor in childcare (Marinda et al. 2017). In addition, robust information campaigns are urgently needed across healthcare systems

– from specialist facilities to community clinics and families – to ensure that families, and mothers in particular, are informed about the range of healthcare support available to them and how this can be accessed (Marinda et al. 2017).

The Norhed project

The Norhed project aims to expand the provision of training for nurses and midwives in Malawi, Zambia and Zimbabwe, and address gaps in research capacity linked to this field. Using an innovative competence and evidence-based approach to curriculum development for nursing and midwifery at MSc and PhD levels, the project leaders are working with mentors from the Arctic University of Norway and the University of Oslo. By working together, faculty members across all three African countries are able to provide enough supervision and mentorship to build the required capacities in their universities. The three countries complement each other, deepening their areas of strength, exchanging teaching staff, and sharing the load when it comes to clinical supervision.

The aim of the project is to ensure that graduates will be equipped to address both current and emerging challenges in the health sector, and improve the quality of nursing and midwifery in in their countries in the long run. It is hoped that this training programme will serve as a model that other LMICs can adapt and scale up. The project's specific objectives are to reinforce the capacity of higher education institutions to: produce more and better research in priority areas to increase and improve levels of research undertaken in Malawi, Zambia and Zimbabwe, thereby improving knowledge production and dissemination in each country; and to produce better-qualified graduates, thus growing the skilled workforce and enabling evidence-based policy and decision-making.

Outcomes of the project to date

Research capacity has been strengthened among faculty members and students in the consortium. Joint training of supervisors in research methodology, research management and supervision has enabled the project to build a pool of faculty members that are skilled not only in conducting a multi-centre studies, but also in supervising BSc Nursing and Midwifery students at master's and PhD level.

Students have received courses in research methodology run by experts from all three countries, and mentorship from staff at the Norwegian institutions. All their research is focused on the priority area of child and maternal health and midwifery. The PhD programme accepted 15 candidates, most of whom graduated in 2018. Furthermore, researchers in the programme published over a hundred articles on child and maternal health in the three countries between 2015 and 2018. This publication record reflects the increase in, and improving levels of, research and knowledge within each country.

After graduating, most of the PhD candidates plan to teach in local universities. That is, the postgraduate training made possible by the Norhed project has significantly increased the number of lecturers with MSc and PhD degrees who are able to train others. In addition, the project helped consolidate a South–South collaboration that is enabling the universities in the three countries to share resources when it comes to teaching, external examiners, quality assurance and staff promotion processes. These networks and collaborations are likely to last long after the current project is phased out. Furthermore, the North–South collaboration, whereby Norwegian institutions provided technical backup and mentorship to the Southern institutions, will also continue after the current project ends. Throughout this process, the project has helped develop capacity in the Southern universities when it comes to applying for competitive research grants in nursing and midwifery, as well as project management, budgeting, accounting and reporting. This has helped the Southern institutions to attract additional partners that are willing to fund other studies. That is, the Norhed project has ena-bled consortium members to leverage further research funding and knowledge generation. This too should continue into the long term.

The universities in Malawi, Zambia and Zimbabwe have taken own-ership of the project by building their own capacity in curriculum development. This will enable the staff across the institutions to revise and/or develop new curricula as conditions change. Using the curriculum-development model used by the Norhed project, they will be able to ensure that courses are well structured, user-friendly and context-appropriate, thus increasing the likelihood that new or revised curricula are suitable for adoption across all three countries.

Impact

The Norhed project has started to demonstrate how improving research capacity in nursing and midwifery improves practice, and that networking and collaboration can create positive results that impact on society. The project has encouraged intra- and inter-faculty collaboration on teaching and research, and faculty members have gained valuable experience through staff exchanges. Similarly, the exposure of students and staff to international research collaborations has been enriching. Students now engage in peer-to-peer knowledge exchange in their academic work, including their theses, which is an effective means of knowledge transfer. Teaching and learning materials and facilities that have been procured by the project are enhancing the quality of teaching, learning, research and examinations. The articles published in peer-reviewed journals have the potential to impact on nursing and midwifery practice worldwide.

The Norhed project is mindful of the Sustainable Development Goals (SDGs) and sees itself as contributing directly to SDG 3 (good health and well-being). With increasing numbers of nurses who wish to upgrade their qualifications to degree level, universities have become crucial in training health workers. This project is promoting good health, through increasing the number of highly trained university-based trainers in the fields of nursing and midwifery. By the end of the project, over 2 000 nurses or midwives will have been trained. In addition, by improving the quality and scope of research linked to nursing and midwifery and training, the project aims to contribute to good birth outcomes as well as reduce maternal and child mortality in the sub-Saharan region. That is, nurse educators as well as health-sector administrators and research specialists equipped with master's or doctoral qualifications will return to their stations with the skills to cascade their knowledge and expertise across district and provincial levels.

A critical assessment of the Norhed model

Norhed support to the higher education sector in LMICs began with scholarship programmes through which students from Africa and other countries were given scholarships to study in Norway (see Da Silva and Phiri, this volume). Besides contributing to the brain drain, students who participated in these scholarship programmes developed their skills in conditions very different from their local settings. Those who did return home had difficulty applying what they had learned. It seems hardly necessary to point out that working conditions for nurses and midwives in Norway and Africa are very different. Africa's disease burden is very high; Norway's is low. Africa's health sector has severe staff shortages and resources are often very limited; such conditions are not prevalent in Norway.

The current Norhed project has learned from the limitations of the scholarship programmes and is now focused on deepening teaching and research capacity in higher education institutions *in* the LMICs. This approach is likely to be more sustainable because the training is more locally relevant, and when students train locally, they often choose to work locally too. The current project is also more cost (and carbon) effective because less is spent on moving and accommodating large numbers of students overseas. Available funds have instead been used to build the requisite capacity for higher education research and training in the region. We therefore recommend that Norhed continue implementing this programmatic approach in the longer term as fundamental change takes time, and its real impact at local level will be revealed over time.

About the authors and the project

Alfred Maluwa is associate professor of research at Malawi University of Science and Technology

Margaret Maimbolwa is associate professor of midwifery at the University of Zambia's School of Nursing

Clara Haruzivishe is associate professor of midwifery at the University of Zimbabwe's College of Health Sciences

Patricia Katowa-Mukwato is a senior lecturer in nursing at the University of Zambia's School of Nursing

Jon Oyvind Odland is a professor of community medicine at the Arctic University of Norway

Badil Stray Pedersen is a professor of medicine at Oslo University

Ellen Chirwa is professor in nursing and midwifery at the University of Malawi's Kamuzu College of Nursing

Midion Chidzonga is professor of medicine at the University of Zimbabwe's College of Health Sciences

Address Malata is professor of nursing and midwifery at Malawi University of Science and Technology

Project title: Development of a Novel Nursing and Midwifery Graduate and Postgraduate Training Programme in Malawi, Zambia and Zimbabwe

Partner institutions: University of Malawi's Kamuzu College of Nursing, Malawi University of Science and Technology (Malawi), University of Zambia's School of Nursing (Zambia); University of Zimbabwe's College of Health Sciences (Zimbabwe); Arctic University of Norway; University of Oslo (Norway)

Notes

1   All information about ICM noted here is from their website, https://www.internationalmidwives.org/, accessed in late 2017. The WHO takes the lead in monitoring ICM standards at country level through the local health ministries. However, the scope of practice and the number of years of training and work experience required before midwives can be licensed is still defined at country level and linked to local conditions.

2   A shortage of nurses in several higher-income countries led to recruitment drives aimed at nurses from regions such as southern Africa. The UK, for example, eased visa requirements for immigrants with specialised nursing skills, and for some, their new employers even covered travel and resettlement costs (Dovlo 2007).

3   In Malawi, prevalence declined from 14 per cent in 2010 to 8.8 per cent in 2016 (NSO 2017). In Zambia, the rate was 16 per cent in 2000/2001 and went down to 13 per cent in 2013/2014 (CSO and MoHZ 2014). In Zimbabwe, the rate declined from 15 per cent in 2010 to 13.5 per cent in 2016 (Zimstat, 2016).

References

Baffour-Awuah A, Mwini-Nyaledzigbor P and Richter S (2015) Enhancing focussed antenatal care in Ghana: An exploration into perceptions of practicing midwives. *International Journal of African Nursing Sciences* 2: 59–68

Benkele RD (2011) *The Development of Nursing: Professional Practice.* Available online

Butrick E, Diamond-Smith N, Beyeler N, Montagu D and Sudhinarased M (2014) *Strategies to Increase Health Facility Deliveries: Three Case Studies.* San Francisco: UCSF Global Health Group. Available online

Chanda B, Likwa R, Zgambo J, Tembo L and Jacobs C (2018) Acceptability of Option B+ among HIV positive women receiving antenatal and postnatal care services in selected health centres in Lusaka. *BMC Pregnancy and Childbirth* 18: 510. Available online

Chikanda A (2007) Medical migration from Zimbabwe: Magnitude, causes and impact on the poor. *Development Southern Africa* 24: 47–60

Choguya (2014) Traditional birth attendants and policy ambivalence in Zimbabwe. *Journal of Anthropology.* Available online

CSO and MoHZ (Central Statistical Office and Ministry of Health, Zambia) (2014) *Zambia Demographic and Health Survey, 2013–2014.* Rockville, ML: ICF International

Dovlo D (2007) Migration of nurses from sub-Saharan Africa: A review of issues and challenges. *Journal of Health Services Research* 42(3): 1373–1389

Gelfand M (1988) *Godly Medicine in Zimbabwe: A History of Medical Missions.* Harare: Mambo Press

Herbst J (1990) The structural adjustment of politics in Africa. *World Development* 18(7): 949–958

Kararach G and Otieno R (2016) *Economic Management in a Hyperinflationary Environment. The Political Economy of Zimbabwe, 1990–2008.* Oxford: Oxford University Press

MoHM (Ministry of Health, Malawi) (2011) *Final Evaluation Report of the Emergency Human Resources Programme, 2004–2009.* Lilongwe

MoHM (2017) *Health Sector Strategic Plan for Malawi II (HSSP III), 2017–2022.* Lilongwe

MoHZ (Ministry of Health, Zambia) (2013) *National Training Operational Plan, 2013–2016.* Lusaka

Marinda P, Chibwe N, Tambo E, Lulanga S and Kwayeka-Wandabwa C (2017) Challenges and opportunities of optimal breastfeeding in the context of HIV option B+ guidelines. *BMC Public Health* 17: 541. Available online

Mbeba M, Sagawa S and Gunda M (forthcoming) *The History of Nursing and Midwifery in Malawi.*

Muchacha M and Mtetwa E (2015) Social and economic barriers to exclusive breastfeeding in rural Zimbabwe. *International Journal of MCH and AIDS* 3(1): 15–21

NSO (National Statistical Office) (2011) *Malawi Demographic and Health Survey 2010.* Zomba: IHF

NSO (2017) *Malawi Demographic and Health Survey 2015–16*. Zomba: NSO and ICF

Smith JJ (1994) Traditional birth attendants in Malawi. *Curationis* 17(2): 25–28

UNFPA (2007) *Maternal Mortality Update 2006: Expectation and Delivery, Investing in Midwives and Others with Midwifery Skills*.

WHO (World Health Organization) (2002) Major causes of maternal mortality and morbidity in pregnancy and childbirth: New WHO model is effective and cheaper. *Progress in Reproductive Health Research* 56. Geneva

WHO (2006) *The World Health Report 2006: Working Together for Health*. Available online

WHO (2014) Infant and Young Child Feeding: Fact Sheet 342. Geneva

WHO (2016) New guidelines on antenatal care for a positive pregnancy experience. *Sexual and Reproductive Health Programme*. Available online

WHO (2017) *Regional Response Plan for TB and HIV, 2017–2021*. Geneva

ZimStat (2012) *Zimbabwe Demographic Health Survey, 2010–2011*. Harare

ZimStat (2016) *Zimbabwe Demographic and Health Survey: Final Report, 2015*. Harare

10

Vocational pedagogy

Arne Rohnny Sannerud

Vocational education and training (VET) aims to prepare people for work in a wide variety of careers, from retail and office work, to hospitality and food technology. This is the educational sector where the technical skills needed in building and other heavy industries – from welding and casting to plumbing and instrument maintenance and repair – are passed on. Vocational schools or colleges are educational institutions specifically designed to provide VET, usually through a combination of theory and practical work. Vocational education can be pitched at the post-secondary school level, also known as further or higher education and, in many countries, VET providers interact with national apprenticeship systems. Although the purpose of vocational education is quite similar in all countries, VET systems can vary quite substantially.

It is useful to note that the acronym VET is probably the most widely used, followed by TVET (technical vocational education and training) and BTVET (business and technical vocational education and training). Moreover, while the terms might reflect slight differences between vocational education systems in different countries, all VET, TVET and BTVET practitioners should be able to demonstrate theoretical and technical mastery of their fields and have some practical experience of the world of work; they should also have strong pedagogical skills and be interested in constantly improving how they share their knowledge with their students.

In Uganda, the term BTVET is probably the most used. Here the education ministry acknowledges that the system needs to change and improve if it is to be able to deliver skills that help graduates meet the requirements of the world of work now and in the future. To this end, in 2012, the education ministry introduced a strategic plan called *Skilling Uganda* (MoES 2012). The plan calls for a paradigm shift regarding skills development in the country, and for the VET field to emerge from its relegation as a neglected educational sub-sector to begin to deliver a comprehensive skill set targeted at ensuring graduates' employability, productivity, and growth potential (MoES 2012). The following are noted as essential elements of the plan:

- Reforming the business, technical and vocational education and training (BTVET) system, including its funding and institutional base;
- Expanding BTVET in the country's priority national development sectors;
- Strengthening existing BTVET institutions;
- Training more BTVET instructors;
- Expanding the scope of Uganda's Vocational Qualifications Framework;
- Establishing comprehensive public–private partnerships;
- Expanding and improving agricultural training;
- Expanding and improving productivity in the informal sector; and
- Creating a unified body for skills development.

In a similar vein, *Uganda Vision 2040*, approved by Cabinet in 2007, articulates how the government intends to 'operationalise Uganda's vision statement', which is to transform 'Ugandan society from a peasant to a modern and prosperous country within 30 years'.

> Vision 2040 is conceptualized around strengthening the fundamentals of the economy to harness the abundant opportunities around the country. The identified opportunities include: oil and gas, tourism, minerals, ICT business, abundant labour force, geographical location and trade, water resources, industrialisation, and agriculture among others that are to date considerably under-exploited.[1]

The views of the Ugandan authorities regarding the need for vocational qualifications have been echoed by its emerging oil industry. The news media also frequently point out that VET has the potential to increase levels of innovation and success in Ugandan industries (see Olema 2017 for example). However, while Ugandans are generally well aware of the importance of vocational competence, many see VET as catering mainly for academically weaker students, and see university degrees as the only route to secure employment and social prestige. Some of the scepticism about vocational education is probably justifiable. At the time of writing, many of Uganda's VET schools are poorly built and maintained; they lack necessary equipment and learning materials, and as currently delivered, the skills that graduates obtain don't really meet employers' requirements. The education authorities, as well as the management and educators in VET schools, need to act urgently to improve and update their institutions, curricula and pedagogy.

In this context, a master's programme in vocational pedagogy that is being developed at Kyambogo University (KyU) in Uganda has the potential to improve the quality of education delivered in VET institutions, thereby equipping graduates with the skills companies need now and in the future. In this chapter, I describe the role that this research-based master's programme aims to play in helping develop a sustainable vocational education system in Uganda. In particular, I discuss the following:

- The importance of vocational education globally and in Uganda;
- The use of action research and other research tools;
- The building of capacity among academic staff at KyU and among students on their master's programme; and
- The importance of anchoring of the project in ways that enhance synergies between internal and external stakeholders and to achieve sustainability.

Since vocational pedagogy is not a 'commonly' used term, and is used mainly by those working in the VET sector, it is perhaps appropriate to clarify how I see it: vocational pedagogy is interested in understanding how people learn best in fields of knowledge oriented towards the trades (plumbers, electricians, mechanics, welders, etc.) as well as the technical and service professions, and in developing appropriate teaching methods and curricula.

Global support for vocational education

Since the turn of this century, the centrality of vocational education and training to global and national economic and social development has been acknowledged in several important forums. In 2002, for example, the European Commission issued the Copenhagen Declaration on enhanced European co-operation in vocational education and training within Europe (European Commission 2002). In 2012, the Third International Congress on Technical and Vocational Education and Training issued the Shanghai Consensus, which emphasises the importance of vocational education, competencies and skills. And in 2015, the World Education Forum called for inclusive and equitable quality education and lifelong learning for all, highlighting the need for professional and vocational skills development as well as quality vocational education and training (Unesco 2015).

Furthermore, in 2014 an important conference held by Unesco's International Centre for Technical and Vocational Education and Training (Unevoc) defined the mission of VET as being to ensure that individuals and enterprises acquire the skills they need to increase productivity and income. With approximately 200 participants from 65 different countries in five regions,[2] the conference focused on vocational pedagogy – what it is, why it matters and how teachers can put it into practice. One outcome of the conference was that it became clear how remarkably consistent views about vocational pedagogy are across different contexts and cultures. The conference called on educators and policy-makers worldwide to urgently engage in making VET more relevant to productivity development and economic growth, to increase the quality of skills provided and widen access to VET institutions, to improve the efficiency of VET managers and organisations, and to expand the resources available for VET (Unevoc 2014a).

Vocational education in Uganda

Uganda has three VET systems – formal, informal and private.[3]

In the *formal* education system, three levels overlap: *technical schools* (which include farm schools, vocational training centres and community polytechnics) offer craftsperson training; *technical colleges* offer technical level training and *universities* offer graduate engineering degrees.

To access this system, students must complete seven years of primary schooling, and can then either proceed to lower secondary school or move to a technical school. Those who choose the latter embark on a three or four-year training as craftsperson (community polytechnics four-year training).

Those who complete this training earn a Uganda Certificate of Education (UCE) and then can choose one of four further avenues if they wish to pursue further education and training. That is, they can enroll in a two-year advanced course at a technical institute, join a two-year primary teacher training programme in primary teachers' colleges or join any of the government departmental training institutes that offer a variety of technical and professional courses under different ministries. Through these avenues, they can also access the advanced education that leads to the Uganda Advanced Certificate of Education (UACE).

Private VET providers are a strong part of the sector: in 2011, over a thousand institutions represented approximately 81 per cent of all VET providers. The Ugandan government supports private providers in the sense that they can access all the support schemes offered to TVET institutions, and can apply for public subsidies if they invest in under-served regions and supply training in priority occupations.

The *informal* sector is a stronghold of job creation in Uganda, accounting for 58 per cent of non-agricultural employment in 2011. The TVET system has largely neglected the training needs of the informal sector, and offers no systematic skills development for people in or seeking to enter the informal sector. Much of the training on offer is not based on market assessments and tends to simply imitate formal-sector training but at very basic levels. Sometimes, highly effective programmes are not replicated because of a lack of information and resources. Acknowledging the importance of the informal sector for economic growth and employment generation, the Ugandan government plans to establish regional support centres to expand the training that is available as well as facilitate communication, co-ordination and support so that that this becomes an integral part of Uganda's TVET system.

The 'new' master's degree in vocational pedagogy

In 2009, under the Norwegian government's NOMA programme, KyU in Uganda, the Upper Nile University in Sudan and OsloMet in Norway collaborated in the development of a master's programme in vocational pedagogy.[4] The master's course was established to improve knowledge about VET and build capacity for research and development in the sector. Overall, the programme was successful; 58 students from Uganda and Sudan graduated, and considerable capacity was built among the academic staff who delivered the programme. Indeed, graduates of the programme have already been instrumental in improving the VET system in both the public and the private sector.

However, a number of the master's theses produced by graduates of the NOMA programme highlighted the need for updated training in the VET system, and for stronger collaboration between education institutions and employers. Similarly, Habib and Nsibambi (2014, 2017) have reported on the urgent need for change and improvement within Uganda's VET system. Thus, in 2013, under the Norhed programme, funding was made available to run the master's programme again, this time using an action-research and development-oriented approach. The 'new' master's programme spans three and a half years of part-time study, and is being funded by Norhed for four years, so three cohorts of students will complete the course during the project period. The focus of the degree is on vocational didactics, theories of learning and science, as well as on research methodologies that are appropriate to human, environmental and gender development in Uganda. Besides having to submit various assignments and reports, students have to present a research-based dissertation.

Acknowledging that the quality and relevance of VET depends on solid collaboration between VET institutions, employer organisations and universities, and that establishing such collaborations in Uganda is a huge challenge, this has become a major focus of the project. Accordingly, our funding application emphasised the need to strengthen KyU in the area of vocational pedagogy and in its capacity to collaborate with vocational schools and employers.

Project implementation

The project aims to establish a sustainable master's programme in vocational pedagogy that will lead to a qualitative improvement in the vocational training offered in Uganda. This means that the project has several important elements. First, besides revising and renewing the previous master's programme to ensure that it is more action oriented, we are seeking to establish a strong network of VET institutions, employers, universities, the education authorities, etc. so that graduates will be able to enter into robust co-operation and collaboration with employers and other stakeholders whenever they design and run training courses. This network also provides a crucial aspect of the infrastructure needed to support teaching and learning using ICT-based communication, blended learning and simulation programmes. Second, academic staff are deepening their knowledge of pedagogy and research methods. For this purpose, academic staff have been organised into communities of practice (Wenger 1998) to explore teaching and mentoring practice, fieldwork practice, and methods of conducting vocational action research in co-operation with schools and employers. All academic staff involved in the master's programme are expected to participate in and present seminars, as well as publish in relevant forums. Third, both academic staff and students were trained to use ICT more effectively to support their own teaching and learning.

Outreach to employers and VET institutions

From the start, it was clear that the master's programme would have a limited value without the involvement and ownership of employers and VET institutions. For this reason, a series of activities were organised to enhance their participation. In early 2013, two breakfast meetings were held on the theme of linking VET to the world of work.

These were attended by major companies, the educational authorities, as well as academic staff and management of KyU. The outcome of these meetings was very clear and can be summarised as follows:

- KyU should co-operate with selected industries to start pilot projects in workplace-based research.
- KyU should set up 'centres of excellence' for specific trades, and establish an action-research centre based on the needs of key industries.
- Forums should be established to bring industry, VET institutions and other stakeholders together on a regular basis.
- Processes should be put in place to deliver demand-driven curricula which industries help to plan, and which make it possible for VET students to obtain relevant hands-on experience as part of their studies.

KyU subsequently held meetings with a range of other educational, commercial and industrial stakeholders. Again, the views expressed were clear: all stakeholders want both VET and higher education to include a stronger practical component and orientation, and for tertiary education to be made more relevant to the competencies employers need. The need for collaboration between the university and external stakeholders emerged very clearly, and real breakthroughs were achieved in terms of building trust between the university and the private sector.

In 2015 and 2016, two symposia were held that represented another step towards establishing strong and formalised co-operation between VET providers and employers. The First Annual Vocational Pedagogy Symposium (2015) was organised by KyU in partnership with OsloMet. Input from the labour market was limited to plenary presentations, and here they repeated their message to the educational institutions: co-operation between education and the labour market must be strengthened and the training provided by VET and other tertiary education institutions must be in line with labour market needs. The second symposium in 2016 aimed to promote direct collaborations with employers and to generate further discourse on the links between work and learning. The second symposium was also organised by the Faculty of Vocational Studies at KyU and OsloMet, but this time several strategic partners came on board as well. These included the Nakawa Vocational Training Institute (a state-owned formal VET provider), the Uganda Investment Authority (state-owned but semi-autonomous), the Uganda Manufacturers' Association, the Uganda Small Scale Industries Association and the Federation of Uganda Employers. The symposium attracted 216 participants from government, the private sector, education institutions, development agencies and civil society organisations, as well as academics, students, journalists and exhibitors. Eight papers were presented followed by discussion from participants. In summary, the issues and action points raised significant concerns that require the urgent attention of the various stakeholders in order to realise the required improvement in the quality of VET in Uganda. The need for stronger collaborations between all stakeholders emerged as pertinent to giving VET students opportunities to obtain relevant skills from learning experiences at schools and workplaces during their training.

Training academic staff at Kyambogo University

Based on the outcome of the meetings and symposia, several internal workshops were held to build action-oriented research capacity among academic staff in the Faculty of Vocational Education at KyU. Action research is relatively new to Uganda. Since it is completely different from ethnographic studies, action research is generally perceived positively. That is, it is seen as moving away from scholarly traditions that find it acceptable to conduct research *on* issues of concern, towards ways of doing research *with* people impacted by such issues (Sannerud 2003; Svensson 2002).[5]

Staff from OsloMet facilitated most of these workshops but Ugandan academics also contributed. In particular, staff who were part of the earlier NOMA project were able to draw from that experience to enrich this programme. Various research tools, methodologies and philosophies of science were introduced in the workshops along with a variety of action-learning processes. Activities varied from presentations, discussions, and group work, to training on practical tools such as work-process analyses and running future workshops (see below). In addition, the participants conducted mini 'real life' research as they extended their own ICT skills and were trained to use computer-based learning management systems. In addition, both students and staff learned to use Lego Mindstorm for practical skills training.[6]

In the first workshops, participants discussed several types of research and research tools. While most staff had experience in con-ducting interviews, on-site observations and the like, few were familiar with tools such as work process analysis or future workshops. These tools are useful, if not crucial, for improving BTVET as they offer meth-ods for the collection of other qualitative and quantitative data as well as practical analytical instruments.

Work-process analysis takes actual vocational practice (that is, the technical operations and the organisational context) as the starting point for all VET. Through careful analysis of actual work and produc-tion processes, the competencies needed to perform work are defined, and when competencies are clearly defined, defining the learning pro-cesses needed to achieve them becomes easier (Gessler and Howe 2015; Sannerud and Harlem 2014). However, if used in isolation, work-pro-cess analyses can be somewhat technical and instrumental, and deflect focus from the human, empowering and progressive values that consti-tute the point of doing the research in the first place. The 'future workshop' tool was introduced to address this gap.

A *future workshop* is a process that enables a group of people to develop new ideas or solutions and is particularly suited to groups that have little experience of creative decision-making processes. Very briefly, the method was developed by Robert Jungk and Norbert Müller in the 1970s (Jungk and Muller 1989); they were inspired mainly by critical theory – as developed by the Frankfurt School led by philo-sphers such as Theodor Adorno and Max Horkheimer, and later Jürgen Habermas, Oscar Negt and others (Negt 1981). The workshops involve participants in a process of working out solutions to an existing situa-tion by asking them to draw on basic values, such as dialogue, transparency, equity and democracy. The method enables participants' to use their intuitive and analytical skills for thinking about problems and seeking solutions. In Norway and other countries, such workshops have been used to develop successful work-based learning programmes and to improve school curricula.

Based on the Frankfurt School's critical theory mentioned above, OsloMet's Faculty of Education and International Studies (Department of Vocational Teacher Education) developed what it calls 'vocational pedagogical principles' to help promote the values of democracy and empowerment in all its teaching, learning and research activities (Sannerud and Holmesland da Silva 2009). Strongly rooted in experiential learning (Kolb 1984), these principles are a fundamental part of capacity building among academic staff, and of the design of learning activities and research projects for students. Having acquired skills in applying this combination of research tools, learning processes and basic values, the academic staff at KyU are now similarly able to equip their students with useful knowledge and skills, and to guide them in conducting their own action-research projects.

Teaching and learning activities for students

As noted, the master's programme is structured as a three-and-a-half-year part-time course. Students gather for three face-to-face training sessions each semester. Between times, the students work at their own workplaces, and conduct the practical aspects of their action research projects. The students in the current cohort were recruited from within the university, from among teachers at VET institutions, and from the staff of education authorities and private companies. The programme generated great interest, and Norhed is supporting 62 students on the master's programme, of whom 23 had already graduated by the time of writing in late 2018.

Inspired by the work of John Dewey (1916), a major feature of the master's programme is the active participation and input from the students themselves, with capacity building integrated into all activities. Accordingly, students are divided into groups of about seven students and each group is allocated two mentors (from among the academic staff). All students are encouraged to create a learning log to encourage them to reflect on their own progress and deeper learning. The students share their reflections with one another and with their mentors.

The desired long-term effect of the master's programme is to increase opportunities for youth and adults to create sustainable livelihoods for themselves, and to reduce the gap between the VET that is provided and the skills that graduates require at work. Working with collaborating institutions that include VET institutions, employers, government departments and social partners, students and staff involved in the master's programme carry out research projects that should prepare them to design and conduct their own action research related to VET.

Synergies and sustainability

Before the master's programme in vocational pedagogy was established in Uganda, much work was required to explain and convince those academic staff and university management who were not directly involved in the project that giving students the tools to teach VET effectively would help to improve job skills in the country as a whole, and thus had the potential to drive job creation and enhance economic well-being. Securing the support of employers and the education authorities was an important aspect of winning over these sceptics. As noted, extensive work was done to win the support of external stakeholders, give them a sense of ownership over the project and attempt to ensure their ongoing commitment to the project's sustainability. Many small breakthroughs occurred that were crucial in ensuring ongoing co-operation with employers – hands-on workshops on modern technology being just one example of this.

The potential of a huge breakthrough presented itself when Victoria Engineering and Yabimo A/S approached KyU and OsloMet and asked us to help establish a project to train welders to the international standards required by the oil industry. There is a great need for welding expertise in Uganda and in neighbouring countries. Any company that wants to carry out fabrication/welding in the energy or transport industries has to employ welders who have international certification. To date, no organisations in Uganda are able to certify that their welding training complies with international standards.

Although a project at this scale could have made a major contribution to convincing any remaining sceptics about the value of vocational education, and teaching and learning practices could have been monitored and documented by the university, the initiative stalled.

The aim of the programme was to recruit trainee welders, and give them six months of school and workplace training, like an apprenticeship. In addition, trainees were to be given lessons at KyU in topics such as health and safety, the working environment, work ethics, the theory of welding, plus relevant science, mathematics and technical language skills. The plan therefore was to involve a range of actors from the university to VET schools and the companies mentioned.

The first candidates were to be recruited from Victoria Engineering. Subsequently there would have been space to recruit external candidates who already had some welding experience, and where their prior learning would be validated as a basis for acceptance into the training programme. Victoria-Yabimo would employ trainees or they could apply for jobs in other companies.

This project emerged from the trust that had been built between KyU and large companies such as Victoria-Yabimo. The idea for the project was a direct consequence of the Norhed master's programme. As such, it was designed to fully integrate all aspects of the VET system – from the workplace, to VET schools, to the training of VET practitioners via ongoing action research.

The project application was submitted for funding under the programme 'Building skills for jobs', which is administered by Norad and the Norwegian Centre for International Cooperation in Education (SIU) and which aims to support partnerships between businesses and education institutions that promote vocational training in low- and middle-income countries (LMICs). Unfortunately, the application was rejected even though a solid team of partner organisations were prepared to collaborate to develop a training intervention that is greatly needed in Uganda. The funders' record of decision notes the following:

> *Strengths*: The project is relevant to the needs in the labour market within the given sectors. The quality of the partnership is good. The close co-operation between the education and

private sector will provide a good combination of theoretical and practical skills, and should secure that the training delivered is directly transferable to relevant and different sectors.

Weaknesses: The partners are strong, but it is not clear how they will contribute. The proposal is rather brief on risk analysis and cross-cutting issues. Some information about other providers of the same skills in the region should have been included in the proposal. Although it is explained why, the budget is too high for training only 90 students.[7]

We could have responded and clarified some of the weaknesses that the funders identified. For example, Uganda had no other providers of these skills at that time. In fact, applicants were given no opportunity to provide further clarification or to highlight the potential that such 'substantial' projects have to contribute to an entire educational field and/or local economic sector. In this case, the project could have contributed substantially to improving the relationship between business, VET providers and VET-related training and research in Uganda. While donors' administrative systems tend to consider these sectors separately, in practice, stakeholders aspire to more interaction and co-operation. I raise this in the hope that, in future, Norad will attempt to address this issue.

Sustainability

Throughout the establishment of the master's programme, great efforts have been made to ensure its sustainability. This can be measured in various ways. First, the future of the master's course is partly dependent on the degree to which the programme is approved by necessary national certification agencies and the extent to which a relevant literature base remains accessible to both staff and students. Both of these requirements are in place.

Second, sustainability can be assessed in terms of the number of academics from the faculties of education, engineering and vocational studies at KyU, and the number of staff at the Directorate for Industrial

Training and the Nakawa Vocational Training Institute, who have received training through the project. In addition, some faculty members from KyU have already completed a number of PhD-level courses in vocational pedagogy at OsloMet, and a further four faculty members have been accepted into the full PhD programme. This bodes well for the delivery of PhD-level courses at KyU in the near future.

Third, in terms of infrastructure, a learning-management system has been established that will facilitate the registration and monitoring of future students. In addition to this, a computer laboratory and the Lego Education laboratory are vital components that contribute to practical training and make the visualisation of advanced processes possible.

Fourth, from day one, the project had the support of the university management, staff and students, as well as Uganda's educational authorities, VET providers and employer organisations. The master's programme is also monitored by a range of stakeholders in various ongoing ways.

Nevertheless, the university management has many priorities to attend to and does not necessarily think about how they can support the project. Nor do they necessarily respond readily to private-sector initiatives requesting that the university curricula take companies' needs into account. This is a critical issue and has the potential to undermine the sustainability of the master's course. One way of addressing this would be for the faculty to establish a centre for vocational education and lifelong learning on campus. At this point, they have the buildings, the ICT facilities, enough skilled staff, a range of useful and relevant industry and other networks, as well as the international contacts necessary to make such a facility into a centre of excellence in the region when it comes to teaching, learning and research in co-operation with employers and VET institutions.

Reflections and conclusion

The adoption of the Sustainable Development Goals (SDGs) has brought issues of skills for development and the transformation of VET to the fore. Among other things, scholars Simon McGrath (2012) and

Lesley Powell (McGrath and Powell 2016) have questioned what skills development is for, and what skills best support development that is sustainable for individuals, communities and the planet, while also promoting social justice and reducing poverty. McGrath and Powell discuss a number of topics relevant to VET, such as sustainable development, green skills, green jobs, and the green economy, and argue that VET needs a human development focus in which skills for life are as important as skills for work.

It is possible to argue that the master's programme described here includes both content and practices that comply with McGrath and Powell's approach. The content, organisation and learning methods of the master's course, in which 'doing' is a fundamental element, helps to develop a 'doing attitude' among both staff and students. Course content focuses on didactics that take work processes in an organisational context as their starting point. This ensures a focus on skills relevant to work. Meanwhile, the future workshop methodology promotes democratic processes, empowerment, transparency and creativity, which are arguably all related to human development.

The collaboration of individuals from Norway and Uganda in this project has created both challenges and opportunities. The challenges relate to our different bureaucratic cultures and academic traditions which tend to work against the strongly pragmatic focus that workplace-based learning demands. The opportunities lie in the fact that Ugandan academics who have Norwegian-European partners and vice versa can help each other to gain access to international and local companies where trust is a crucial factor.

Despite a number of challenges, graduates of the master's programme have qualifications that will contribute to the gradual development of VET. As a result, skills levels in key economic sectors in Uganda, such as tourism and agriculture will also develop.

Finally, perhaps the most significant contributions made by the master's project, and the work done to establish it, is the fact that it has created awareness of the value of action research and encouraged attitudes among all who were involved with it that continual improvement is both desirable and possible. In addition, it has enhanced relations between the university, employers and the VET institutions.

About the author and the project

Arne Rohnny Sannerud is a professor in the Faculty of Education and International Studies in Oslo Metropolitan University's Centre for Vocational Research and Development

Project title: An Action-oriented Master's Degree in Vocational Pedagogy, in Collaboration with Vocational Training Institutions and the World of Work

Partner institutions: Kyambogo University (KyU) (Uganda) and Oslo Metropolitan University (OsloMet) (Norway)

Notes

1   See https://www.gou.go.ug/content/uganda-vision-2040
2   Of those attending the online event, 44 were in Africa, 58 were in Asia and the Pacific, another 58 were in Europe and North America, 34 were in Latin America and the Caribbean, and 6 were in the Arab states (Unevoc 2014a).
3   The information and statistics in this section are derived from Unevoc's *World TVET Database: Uganda* (Unevoc 2014b).
4   For more information about NOMA, see Da Silva and Phiri, this volume. Given the political unpredictability in South Sudan, and the that fact that the anchoring built up via the NOMA project was no longer in place there, we considered it too challenging to include South Sudan in this project.
5   See also Gibbons et al. (1994) whose work highlights how social trends impinge on the relationships between knowledge production, the application of knowledge, and learning and work.
6   Lego Mindstorm is a set of tools for hands-on, cross-curricular training in science, technology, engineering and mathematics that gives students the resources to design, build and programme their creations while helping them develop essential skills such as creativity, critical thinking, collaboration, and communication.
7   Decision: Building Skills for Jobs project, BSFJ-2016/10009 (author's own copy).

References

Dewey J (1916/1944) *Democracy and Education: An Introduction to the Philosophy of Education*, revised ed: New York: The Free Press
European Commission (2002). The Copenhagen Declaration. Available online
Gessler M and Howe F (2015) From the reality of work to grounded work-based learning in German vocational education and training: Background, concept and tools. *International Journal for Research in Vocational Education and Training* 2(3): 214–238

Gibbons M, Limoges C, Nowotny H, Schwartzman S, Scott P and Trow M (1994) *The New Production of Knowledge: The Dynamics of Science and Research in Contemporary Societies.* London: Sage

Habib K and Nsibambi C (2014) The potential of vocational pedagogy in vocational education and training education. *International Journal of Vocational Education and Training* 22(1): 25–36

Habib K and Nsibambi C (2017) The potential of vocational pedagogy in vocational education and training education: Part II. *International Journal of Vocational Education and Training* 24(1): 92–106

Jungk R and Muller NR (1989) *Håndbog i fremtidsverksteder.* København: Politisk Revy

Kolb DA (1984) *Experiential Learning.* Englewood Cliffs: Prentice Hall

McGrath S (2012) Vocational education and training for development. *International Journal of Educational Development* 32(5): 623–631

McGrath S and Powell L (2016) Skills for sustainable development. *International Journal of Educational Development* 50: 12–19

MoES (Ministry of Education and Sports, Uganda) (2012) *Skilling Uganda: BTVET Strategic Plan 2012/3–2021/2.* Kampala

Negt O (1981) *Sociologisk fantasi og eksemplarisk indlæring.* Kurasje

Olema V (2017, 27 May). Vocational education can be a game changer in Uganda. *Daily Monitor.* Available online

Sannerud AR (2003) *Interaktiv forskning: Utfordringer i interaktiv forskning.* Høgskolen i Akershus

Sannerud R and Harlem E (2014) *Mesterkvalifikasjonen: HiOA rapport.* Oslo

Sannerud AR and Holmesland da Silva I (2009) Can practice-based learning foster knowledge creation? Experiences with practice-based learning within technical and vocational teacher education. *Annual Conference Proceedings, 2009.* Brussels: ATEE

Svensson L (2002) *Interaktiv forskning: För utveckling av teori och praktik.* Stockholm: Arbetslivsinstitutet

Unesco (2015) *World Education Forum 2015: Final Report.* Available online

Unevoc (Unesco International Centre for Technical and Vocational Education and Training) (2014a) *Vocational Pedagogy: What it Is, Why it Matters and How to Put it into Practice.* Report of the Unesco-Unevoc Virtual Conference, 2014, Bonn. Available online

Unevoc (2014b) *World TVET Database: Uganda.* Bonn: Unesco-UNEVOC International Centre for TVET. Available online

Wenger E (1998) *Communities of Practice: Learning, Meaning and Identity.* Cambridge, MA. Cambridge University Press

11

Teacher education in Ethiopia: Reshaping the training of science and mathematics teacher educators

Ahmed Y Ahmed, Meskerem L Debele, Haftu H Gebremeskel,
Dawit A Getahun, Dawit T Tiruneh & Dereje T Wondem

Since 2010, Ethiopia's government has strongly emphasised the role of science and technology in driving economic development. Consequently, in its two Growth and Transformation Plans (GTP I and GTP II), science and technology are accorded central roles in leading the nation towards becoming a middle-income country by 2025 (see MoFED 2010 and NPC 2015). In this chapter, we argue that the success with which science and maths educators are able to teach school students matters for achieving this vision.

Many countries now promote the integration of the so-called STEM subjects (science, technology, engineering and mathematics) to prepare their citizens for the modern world. Good STEM education is essential to help learners move beyond memorising facts and formulae, and ensure that they gain an understanding of the principles of science and mathematics that underlie so much of contemporary engineering practice and technological development. These principles are also critical to the development of problem-solving and thinking skills.

In line with this, in 2008, the Ethiopian government adopted a policy for higher education institutions, whereby departments that teach in the STEM fields accept 70 per cent of students and the social sciences absorb the remaining 30 per cent (MoE 2008, 2010). To give effect to this policy, and enable the government to achieve its goal of producing innovative citizens, the training of quality science teachers at all levels has been emphasised. In particular, support for primary and secondary teachers is seen as crucial to the fostering of school students who are both confident and capable of mastering the fields of science, mathematics, engineering and technology.

Consequently, a number of strategic activities have been initiated with the aim of improving the quality of science and mathematics education nationally. These derive from the Ministry of Education's guiding policy document, *The Education Sector Development Programme V, 2015/2016–2019/2020*, which makes improving the quality of education a top priority at all levels (MoE 2015). The policy advances a number of strategic goals and activities to guide efforts towards improving the quality of science and mathematics education (MoE 2015). Major projects linked to this include the preparation of new STEM education policies and strategies, the revision of pre-service teacher education programmes, the establishment of STEM centres in teacher training colleges and the provision of new in-service training programmes for science and mathematics teachers.

No one would argue that the quality of primary and secondary science and mathematics teachers depends on the ability of teacher-training institutions to deliver relevant and high-quality programmes that combine research and innovation. However, effective teacher training depends, in turn, partly on the quality of teacher educators. Teacher educators must be able to explain and model innovative pedagogical approaches and, in this way, enhance the instructional capacities of their students.

With regard to pre-service teacher training, attempts have been made since 2008 to reorient objectives, content and learning approaches in the curricula taught to both primary and secondary teachers (MoE 2009; MoE 2013). More reflective and innovative approaches to teaching are being adopted, and teacher education is being better integrated with what the school curricula actually cover. That is, the importance of content knowledge and the principles of pedagogical integration are being highlighted in new teacher education programmes. In all of this, the role of teacher educators is seen as crucial.

Currently, after completing their own secondary schooling, aspiring primary school teachers have to complete three years of teacher education. Those training to be secondary school teachers have to first obtain a university degree and then a one-year postgraduate teacher education qualification. Teacher education curricula for both primary and secondary teachers emphasise the need for strong content knowledge and professional pedagogical skills. Moreover, the alignment of effective teaching methodologies with specific content or thematic areas of the syllabi has become a guiding principle of teacher training. This results in more credit hours being allocated to pedagogical content knowledge (PCK) in teacher training curricula. For instance, in the primary teacher curriculum, PCK takes up eight credit hours[1] compared to the two credit hours previously allocated. It is now also mandatory for the primary and secondary school syllabi, teacher guides and textbooks to be used as references for PCK and general education courses. This ensures teacher trainees become familiar with the content and pedagogy of the subjects they will teach.

Ethiopia's teacher education curricula identify teacher educators as key players in ensuring quality teachers (MoE 2003, 2009, 2015). This assumes that, by demonstrating good practice and commitment, teacher trainers will model to their students the essential skills and dispositions required of a good teacher. Importantly, it asserts that the reform of teacher education curricula can be realised when teacher trainers are convinced of the need for reform and can demonstrate their commitment to its implementation. To realise such reforms, however, it is necessary that teacher trainers go through the appropriate professional preparation.

Cognisant of this, the present teacher education programme clearly specifies minimum requirements for teacher training. For example, given the emphasis on PCK, teacher educators require not only a mastery of their subject areas, but also the ability to integrate content knowledge with appropriate pedagogy. In this context, priority is given to teacher educators who have master's and PhD degrees in *teaching* specific subjects rather than in the pure subject areas alone. In contrast to what was accepted before, the current curriculum requires teacher trainers to demonstrate an in-depth knowledge of how to integrate school curricula with pedagogical skills, and become role models for their students.

Statement of the problem

Despite these shifts, the programmes currently used to train teacher educators in science and mathematics appear to be ineffective. Concepts of quality and effective teaching still seem to be equated with subject-area mastery. Consequently, students judge training programmes based on the weighting of subject-area courses relative to professional pedagogy courses. In addition, although teacher training programmes include courses on pedagogy and content knowledge, the two domains are usually treated separately rather than in an integrated manner. Thus, while subject area courses try to help trainees become experts in their fields, courses on pedagogy offer fairly generic teaching skills related to classroom management, assessment, lesson planning etc. Few teacher training courses are therefore designed to help trainees learn how to *teach* the core concepts relevant to specific subject areas.

Moreover, many academics in the teacher training colleges are subject-area specialists rather than specialists in pedagogy. They, too, are products of an educational culture that considered subject mastery to be the main foundation of quality learning and teaching. Of course, subject mastery can give teachers more options when it comes to providing 'multiple explanations' for particular concepts (NCATE 2008), but it offers no guarantee that they will know how to use this to help their students grasp the real essence of a concept. Even so, at national workshops we took part in, we often heard appeals for more courses on subject mastery.

Such thinking is prevalent in other parts of the world too. According to Mishra and Koehler (2006), content knowledge was long considered teachers' main knowledge base. Subsequently, a shift of focus highlighted the importance of pedagogy, but the two knowledge bases were still considered dichotomously. Shulman (1987) proposed PCK to address the dichotomy to go beyond isolated consideration of the two. As Mishra and Koehler (2006: 1021) put it: 'PCK represents the blending of content and pedagogy into an understanding of how particular aspects of subject matter are organised, adapted, and represented for instruction.' What we see in Ethiopia's teacher training centres is a complete contrast to this.

Based on the conviction that we can improve the quality and relevance of science and mathematics education in primary and secondary schools by convincing teacher educators to change the ways in which they prepare primary school teachers to teach mathematics and science, Bahir Dar University (BDU) in Ethiopia, the University of Juba in South Sudan and the Norwegian University of Science and Technology (NTNU) in Norway initiated a five-year partnership supported by Norhed.

In this chapter, we focus on activities related to this project at BDU, where we launched master's programmes in the teaching of mathematics and science with the aim of building the skills and knowledge of academic staff in the teacher training colleges. First, we outline our efforts to design master's programmes using a PCK framework, through which we aim to give teacher educators a direct experience of a formal and evidence-based teacher preparation programme. We then discuss the challenges we have faced in attempting to balance the emphasis on content knowledge with an equal focus on pedagogy and related skills.

The needs assessment

Prior to launching the master's programmes, a comprehensive needs assessment was conducted with the aims of understanding the current status of science and mathematics education in Ethiopia, identifying the gaps in the preparation of primary school teachers and teacher educators, and developing a master's level curriculum relevant to the teaching of mathematics and science. During the needs-assessment study conducted in February 2017, 37 participants (ten deans and vice-deans, ten department heads, six teacher educators, two experts, two policy-makers, and seven previous graduates) were selected from five teacher education colleges, two universities and the education ministry's Science and Mathematics Subject Improvement Centre. Data were collected using semi-structured interviews and focus group discussions. Relevant secondary sources linked to education planning and outcomes in Ethiopia were also referred to. These include results from the National Learning Assessments (run by the Ministry of Education from 2000 to 2016), documents linked to the Education Sector Development Programmes (MoE 2010, 2015), the government's national growth plans (GTP I and GTP II) (MoFED 2010; NPC 2015), as well as various curriculum documents and other reports.

When asked about teacher educators' competence with regard to content knowledge, several participants noted that they have sufficient content knowledge to teach. For instance, a college dean and a department head said:

> I believe that there is no subject matter knowledge gap on the part of teacher educators to teach their respective subjects. (Dean, interview)

> I agree that teacher educators have sufficient subject matter knowledge to train teacher candidates. (Head of Mathematics Department, focus group)

However, our own assessment revealed that teacher educators in the selected colleges of education have limited mastery of PCK. The perception that good teaching relies primarily on advanced content knowledge, regardless of its relevance to the levels at which they teach, remains strong. Almost all the teacher educators we spoke to hold degrees that affirm their subject knowledge but include no pedagogy courses. In addition, they insisted that pure subject-area courses should be included in the new master's programme we were planning, with some suggesting that these should comprise 50 per cent of the course load. Participants maintained this argument despite admitting to having felt some confusion about how to 'lower' their teaching standards to the level of their students when they were 'promoted' from teaching science and mathematics in preparatory schools to offering these subjects in teacher training colleges. In the preparatory schools, they taught high-achieving Grade 11 and 12 students, while at the teacher training colleges, few of their students have achieved a pass in the national examinations for Grade 10. This implies that such educators are not yet equipped to offer pre-service teachers the skills to teach science and mathematics to primary school children in ways that cater to their cognitive, psychosocial, and academic needs. In one focus group session, we asked teacher educators if they cover child-friendly teaching techniques (such as using plays, music and art to teach mathematics and science) in their teacher training programmes. They responded as if such approaches had never crossed their minds.

In general, we found a mismatch between the training that teacher educators receive and the roles they are expected to play in training pre-service primary school teachers in the teacher training colleges. This informed the design of the master's curriculum so that it emphasises the integration of technology and pedagogy with the content knowledge (TPCK) relevant to primary school mathematics and science. Increasing access to computers and internet in schools has created opportunities to use such technologies for instructional purposes and hence to promote TPCK.

Academic programme development

Based on the needs assessment, our approach to programme development and course design changed in at least two major ways. First, TPCK was acknowledged as a major knowledge base for programme development. Second, we decided to focus on ensuring that students who complete the master's programme are equipped to teach science and mathematics in ways that are relevant to their pupils' everyday lives.

Integrating knowledge bases

During round-table discussions between the project team and their Northern partners, a question was raised about whether the course content for educators who are being trained to teach teachers should coincide with primary school science and mathematics syllabi or be more advanced. Based on results from the needs assessment and wider consultation with partners we agreed to use the primary school curriculum as a basis for designing the courses that make up the master's programme. That is, instead of broadening trainees' personal disciplinary knowledge, it was agreed that it is more useful for them to be acquainted with the primary school curriculum so that they can contextualise their teaching to the training of primary school teachers.

Effective teaching also requires a clear understanding of the complex relationship between technology, pedagogy and content knowledge, as well as the ability to develop relevant and contextualised representations of concepts (Mishra and Koehler 2006). As a guiding framework for curriculum development, TPCK offered us a means of aligning the competencies of teacher educators with their own teaching roles and responsibilities. That is, TPCK is a useful means for specifying what teacher educators need to know and an important conceptual tool to guide the processes they will use to achieve the required competencies.

With this in mind, curriculum development was anchored in situated learning, and courses were designed around the primary and secondary school curricula using the kinds of technologies available in the local context. What sets this apart from previous educator training is the specificity of our articulation of the relationship between content, pedagogy and technology, which highlighted specific knowledge that is applicable to teaching in the domains of science and mathematics. This means that teacher educators who complete this programme will develop knowledge that differs from that of disciplinary experts (mathematicians for example) and also from the general pedagogical knowledge shared by experienced teachers across different disciplines. As one experienced teacher educator put it:

> Teacher educators should pass through a training programme that focuses on primary and secondary school curricular contents and that creates opportunities for them to integrate content, pedagogy and technology; and teacher candidates should be trained on what and how they will teach in schools. (Interview)

The programme design also emphasised the constructive alignment of curricula with instruction and assessment to meet the overarching goal of making the training strongly practice-oriented.

Teaching science and mathematics for everyday life

The ability to draw on students' personal and everyday experiences to teach them science and mathematics, and to make teacher training more practice-oriented, is highly emphasised in the design and delivery of the master's programme. The programme promotes the use of inquiry-based learning in the classroom and provides candidates with experiences of real educational problems in schools and challenges them to find solutions to these through the learning process. Thus, the design and provision of opportunities for teaching linked to pupils' experiences is an attempt to connect inquiry-based learning with the actual problems schools face.

The ability to use both concrete and virtual simulations add value in terms of making learning more meaningful. Moreover, the programme connects theory with practice by providing a supervised practical module in which candidates are involved in the systematic design, development, implementation and evaluation of science and mathematics lessons in collaboration with other teachers and teacher educators. A major focus of the master's programme is to provide students with opportunities to apply their knowledge and skills in actual instructional settings.

Challenges in implementing the programmes

While stimulating great discussion and debate, the design and implementation of the new master's programme has not been smooth. Conflicts arose in relation to the design of traditional teacher education curricula, rigid conceptions of disciplinary boundaries, and students' confusion about their professional identity. These issues are explained in a little more detail below.

Traditional versus new curricula

The basis of the master's programme, which uses TPCK as a course development and organisation framework, challenged the traditional oil-and-water approach of the undergraduate and graduate programmes that preceded the introduction of our course. In BDU's previous curricula, subject-specific courses were provided by the corresponding academic departments (biology, chemistry, physics, mathematics, etc.). General pedagogical and methodology courses were run alongside these, but with no contextualisation of pedagogical tools in relation to any specific discipline. That is, while a methodology course was allocated to each disciplinary field (Subject Methods in Biology, Subject Methods in Physics, etc.), these courses focused on the early history and philosophy of the field rather than on specific models, knowledge and skills for effective teaching of the subject. Indeed, as undergraduate students, most of the current academic staff at the university, both in the College of Education and in the College of Science, completed these kinds of courses before specialising in either in the pedagogical or subject-related streams.

While faculty members of the College of Education and Behavioural Sciences became increasingly convinced of the appropriateness and the urgency of using the TPCK framework to develop more integrated teacher training programmes, some of their colleagues in the College of Science saw little need for change. The idea that teacher educators should acquire more discipline-focused knowledge (such as the calculus) rather than professional teaching skills (such as theories of learning in mathematics) led to a prolonged debate between the two colleges. Issues of programme ownership, the nature of collaboration in course delivery (team teaching), and the very nature of teaching as a profession were questioned. Despite the findings of our own needs assessment, and an awareness of international practice, some colleagues in the College of Science resisted the idea of hosting an integrated programme in the College of Education. Their assumption was that, since subject methodology courses had previously been delivered by the specific departments at the College of Science, the new programme should follow suit. They also insisted that separate and advanced subject-matter courses be in included. Dealing with this issue meant that it took the project team a long time to get the new curriculum approved.

Crossing disciplinary boundaries

The culture of delineating rigid disciplinary boundaries between academic programmes, and creating increasingly narrow specialties at both undergraduate and postgraduate levels, is directly contrary to the interdisciplinary and collaborative principles we set out to follow. In this regard, course offerings were developed based on ongoing discussions, needs assessments and validation workshops in which experts from both colleges were involved, alongside other relevant stakeholders such as representatives from teacher training colleges, the national education ministry and the regional education bureau. This participatory approach to programme development is not usual at the university where territorial mindsets tend to dominate. In addition, a truly integrated approach also demands that professors discuss and agree on course content and delivery methods. This approach challenges the concept of 'team teaching' at BDU which tends to mean little more than assigning course components to different professors.

It will take time for new practices to replace the prevailing ones. However, these issues created a level of conflict that created opportunities for debate. For example, faculty members were invited to reflect on the place of teaching as a profession and on how committed they are to improving the quality of schooling in the lower grades. They had to consider how willing they are to really understand primary school children, and question the extent to which existing practices were effective in inculcating caring and nurturing values in would-be primary school teachers. At the very least, the debates helped some candidates who are interested in the project's PhD programmes to decide whether or not to 'shift' their professional identities from 'mathematician' or 'scientist' to 'teacher educator'.

Students' confusion about their professional identity

An experience at the College of Science highlighted a level of confusion in some of the master's students. Many of the candidates targeted for the master's programme had qualifications in subject areas such as biology, chemistry, mathematics and physics, obtained mainly from the teacher training colleges that train primary school teachers. When these candidates were informed that they had been accepted for the master's programme and wanted to register, many went to departments within the College of Science to do so. For example, a candidate who had majored in physics at a teacher training college went to the head of the university's physics department to ask about registration. Similar situations occurred in other departments as candidates attempted to hold onto the disciplinary identity they had formed during their under-graduate training and had to be redirected to the education faculty.

Cognisant of possible confusion among the candidates, the project team provided an orientation course to give them a full picture of the degree programme. Questions raised during these orientation sessions also showed the extent to which trainees were clinging to their discipli-nary identity and were concerned about possible 'detachment' from their disciplinary focus. Some of the questions raised included:

> What are we going to teach after we graduate and go back to our colleges?

> Are we going to teach our major subject area or pedagogy?

> After graduating, can we apply for jobs in university science departments?

Even after the course began, some students expressed frustrations about the interdisciplinary nature of the programme, noting that the courses were not direct extensions of their undergraduate studies. For example, a course on integrated science focused on cross-cutting issues such as natural resources, theories of population development and political ecology, as well as on how to teach children about demographic transitions and natural resources by drawing on pupils' lived experi-ences of demographic change and through outdoor excursions. The students taking the course argued that these topics fit into the field of geography and kept reminding the lecturers that their degrees in biol-ogy, chemistry or physics made them feel they did not belong in the course. We had to repeatedly remind them that the aim of the master's programme was not to equip them with advanced knowledge and skills in science that would enable them to work in scientific laboratories. Instead, the aim was to enable them to give their future students at the teacher training colleges the basic knowledge and skills they would need when they in turn had to teach their own pupils the general environmental science in the primary school curriculum.

This mismatch of expectations was serious enough to lead some students to consider dropping out. For example, early in the programme one student called the project co-ordinator and informed him that he would be leaving. At a meeting with the course co-ordinators, the student noted that when joining the master's programme he had expected to be able to take advanced courses in analytical chemistry, and since that was not going to happen, he wanted to leave. The programme co-ordinators then explained what is expected from a teacher educator and how the education ministry sees career development for academics in teacher training colleges. They also outlined his prospects in science education, including the option of researching science education in Ethiopia (which is chronically under-researched). The student was informed that if he wanted to become a 'pure scientist', he should find another course, but if he wanted to serve in a teacher training college, the current programme was indeed appropriate. The co-ordinators left him to decide and, later on the same day, the student informed them that he would continue with the course.

Project sustainability

Sustainability refers to the continuation of a project's goals, principles and efforts towards desired outcomes (Riggs 2012). Various indicators point to elements of sustainability in any project. These include developing new capacities among staff, creating relationships that continue after a grant or a project ends, the implementation of new policies or practices, and new or revised academic programmes being independently handled by funding recipients. However, one of the most challenging tasks in grant-funded academic programmes is ensuring their continuation after the funded project period is over. With this understanding, in addition to a careful assessment of needs and resource allocations, as well as the development of clear objectives and implementation timelines, exit strategies were a key aspect of this project. Clear exit strategies were developed and linked to three project phases: before, during and after implementation. These are elaborated below.

Exit strategies built into the development of the project

From the beginning, attention was given to programme sustainability and a variety of strategies were built into the design of the project to ensure that it will continue to have an impact beyond the grant and the project period. For instance, the development of academic programmes at both the master's and PhD level were participatory and included relevant academic staff from all partner institutions. In addition, all relevant stakeholders, inside and outside BDU, who were likely to have a direct or indirect impact on the success of the academic programmes, were involved. The development of the academic programmes followed the proper processes for curricula that work across disciplinary boundaries, and major efforts were made to use the knowledge and skills of experts in Ethiopia. In particular, potential employers of our graduates, from the national education ministry, to regional education bureaus, to teacher training institutions and NGOs were invited to engage fully in the process. We believe these efforts will have a hugely positive impact in sustaining the academic programmes.

Second, candidates were carefully screened to ensure that those enrolled will benefit from the support provided in the programme and are likely to graduate. Moreover, experienced academic staff members who fulfilled the university's requirements were given an opportunity to audit or enrol in the master's programmes to help reduce the staff shortage. For example, one staff member who enrolled in the programme is simultaneously serving as a teaching assistant. Similarly, stringent procedures were followed in selecting the first cohort of PhD candidates who will enrol at NTNU, with selections made in collaboration with the partner universities' professors. The main aim of the PhD programme is to train academics to take over and revise classes initially given by colleagues from NTNU. By running courses jointly, NTNU and Ethiopian professors have had opportunities to work together and share experiences. Team teaching will be further strengthened by ongoing collaborative research, which, along with institutional capacity building, is seen as one of the project's key pillars. Moreover, a course-management system (such as Moodle) is being developed. This will include a database of reference works and teaching materials used by NTNU professors, thus significantly addressing the shortage of reference materials. The system will not only support students directly, but also help to transfer knowledge and sustain the academic programme.

Exit strategies during project implementation

Excellence in programme implementation, clear results and evidence of positive change all contribute to the sustainability of academic programmes. That is, as long as the education faculty at BDU maintains the quality of these academic course offerings, their reputation will help ensure their sustainability. During the project implementation phase, the academic programmes are being carefully monitored. Co-ordinators are assigned to each master's course; they are responsible for ensuring the quality of the programme as a whole but also for helping any candidates who might need extra help. To help maximise the success of the programme, a co-ordinator has been assigned to focus on encouraging and empowering female candidates. Moreover, regular discussions are held with students to identify implementation problems.

Strategies to monitor the ongoing impact of the programme

Strategies planned for after the project period include, but are not limited to: conducting a tracer study to track the whereabouts and competencies of graduates; revising the academic programmes based on feedback from alumni; encouraging the future PhD graduates to take ownership of the programme; strengthening institutional relations between the project partners; and creating an alumni network.

Sustainability strategies require ongoing project assessments, so key stakeholders will meet to revise the existing strategies and develop new ones before the project ends. At that point, the academic programmes will be formally evaluated and key findings of this evaluation will be presented to policy-makers and stakeholders to make sure that the programmes have achieved their goals. The evaluation process and report should give all stakeholders an understanding of the intervention evidence (that is, the problems the academic programmes have addressed). This should, in turn, help to sustain the programmes.

In addition, in 2017, the Federal Ministry of Education designated the College of Educational and Behavioral Sciences (CEBS) at BDU as one of four centres of excellence in teacher education and educational leadership based in higher learning institutions in Ethiopia. This new role gives the Centre a mandate to run other similar programmes using this project as a starting point. The naming of the College as a centre of excellence should contribute to the sustainability of its entire academic programme, including this project.

Other government initiatives related to STEM education in Ethiopia

As mentioned in the introduction to this chapter, Ethiopia has a number of ongoing strategic activities aimed at improving the quality of science and mathematics education nationally. These include the preparation of new STEM education policies and strategies, new in-service training programmes for existing science and mathematics teachers, the establishment of STEM centres in the teacher training colleges, and the revision of pre-service teacher education curricula.

In 2016, the Federal Ministry of Education launched the *Strategic Policy for National Science, Technology and Mathematics Education*. The policy capitalises on the critical role of science and technology in realising the country's vision of becoming a middle-income country by 2025. The need to improve the quality of science and mathematics education from pre-school to university level is highlighted. In this regard, the policy identifies teachers' roles as 'indispensable' in enhancing the quality of education, transforming classroom instruction and ensuring students' learning. To this end, the policy commits the government to implementing several strategies, including recruiting competent science and mathematics teachers, revisiting pre-service teacher education at all levels, and institutionalising an ongoing CPD system in the schools.

To strengthen the work of the education ministry, they have undertaken to open regional mathematics and science training units in teacher training colleges in each region (MoE 2015). At the time of writing in late 2018, about 36 teacher training colleges were spread across Ethiopia's 11 regions; with at least one college in each region. The policy also gives the colleges the additional role of supporting in-service teacher development programmes in schools. In particular, they are expected to collaborate with schools in their region and support the development of science and mathematics teachers in these schools. This requires reorienting the teacher training colleges and building the abilities of teacher educators to provide in-service training and support to teachers in schools. In this regard, the Norhed programme will make a significant contribution to building the capacity of the teacher educators in these colleges.

The basic challenge for the sustainability of current efforts linked to improving STEM education in Ethiopia is a lack of qualified people at different levels in the education system (including in the teacher training colleges and universities) who can take over the initiative and continue to develop and implement them. To help address this, the programme is offering professors at NTNU and BDU opportunities to collaborate in providing courses and supervising PhD students. It is hoped that this will enhance the ownership of the programme at BDU and that this will, in turn, enhance its impact and sustainability. The project also plans to reach schools through offering in-service training to mathematics and science teachers, thereby extending existing capacity development and research components in ways that improve the quality of STEM education in Ethiopia. It is hoped that this will enable teacher training colleges and universities develop additional capacity to research the appropriateness and impact of our initiatives and come up with viable recommendations and new initiatives. This should lay the foundation for the ongoing improvement and quality of STEM education in the region.

About the authors and the project

Ahmed Ahmed is a lecturer in the Department of Educational Planning and
Management at the College of Education and Behavioral Sciences, Bahir Dar
University, Ethiopia

Meskerem Debele is an assistant professor in the Department of Teacher Education and
Curriculum Studies at the College of Education and Behavioral Sciences, Bahir Dar
University, Ethiopia

Haftu Gebremeskel is an assistant professor in the Department of Teacher Education at
the Institute of Pedagogical Sciences, Mekelle University, Ethiopia

Dawit Getahun is an associate professor in the Department of Psychology at the College
of Education and Behavioral Sciences, Bahir Dar University, Ethiopia

Dawit Tiruneh is an assistant professor in the Department of Teacher Education and
Curriculum Studies at the College of Education and Behavioral Sciences, Bahir Dar
University, Ethiopia

Dereje Wondem is a lecturer in the Department of Teacher Education and Curriculum
Studies at the College of Education and Behavioral Sciences, Bahir Dar University,
Ethiopia

Project title: Advancing Quality in Education in the Primary and Lower Secondary
Schools in Ethiopia and South Sudan

Partner institutions: Bahir Dar University (BDU) (Ethiopia), University of Juba (UJ)
(South Sudan), Norwegian University of Science and Technology (NTNU) (Norway)

Notes

1   In the Ethiopian higher education system, one credit hour is equivalent to 16 contact hours per semester.

References

Craft A (2000) *Continuing Professional Development: A Practical Guide for Teachers and
Schools*, 2nd edn. London: Routledge

Mishra P and Koehler MJ (2006) Technological pedagogical content knowledge: A framework for integrating technology in teachers' knowledge. *Teachers College Record*
108(6): 1017–1054

MoE (Ministry of Education, Ethiopia) (2003) *Teacher Education System Overhaul:
Handbook*. Addis Ababa

MoE (2008) *Annual Intake, Enrolment Growth and Professional Programme Mix of Ethiopian Public Higher Education: Strategy and Conversion Plan, 2001–2005.* Addis Ababa

MoE (2009) *Postgraduate Diploma in Teaching: Curriculum Framework for Secondary School Teacher Education Programme in Ethiopia.* Addis Ababa

MoE (2010) *Education Sector Development Programme IV: 2010/2011–2014/2015.* Addis Ababa

MoE (2013) *Curriculum Framework for Primary Pre-service Teacher Education Programme in Ethiopia.* Addis Ababa

MoE (2015) *Education Sector Development Programme V: 2015/2016–2019/2020.* Addis Ababa

MoFED (Ministry of Finance and Economic Development, Ethiopia) (2010) *Growth and Transformation Plan (GTP).* Addis Ababa

NCATE (National Council for Accreditation of Teacher Education, USA) (2008) *Professional Standards Accreditation of Teacher Preparation Institutions.* Washington, DC

NPC (National Planning Commission) (2015) *The Second Growth and Transformation Plan (GTP II): (2015/16–2019/20).* Addis Ababa: Democratic Republic of Ethiopia

Riggs K (2012) Strategies for sustainability of grant-funded programs. *Families and Communities,* October, Co-operative Extension, Utah State University. Available online

Shulman LS (1987) Knowledge and teaching: Foundations of the new reform. *Harvard Educational Review* 57(1): 1–22

12

Improving the quality and capacity of mathematics teachers in Malawi: A collaborative project between the University of Malawi and the University of Stavanger

Mercy Kazima & Arne Jakobsen

In this chapter we discuss a project whose overall goal was to improve the quality of mathematics teaching and learning in Malawi schools. The project aimed to achieve this by improving the quality of mathematics teacher education since good teachers are key to quality teaching and learning. In designing activities to achieve its intended outcomes, the project expected the professionalisation of mathematics teacher educators to generate some degree of transformation in mathematics education in Malawi. A process of sociocultural transformation is necessary when aiming to improve the quality of teaching in a country such as Malawi where, in general, the quality of education is low and the quality of mathematics education, in particular, is poor. Since transformation involves changing norms and values as well as institutions and structures (Jha 2016), it is important to understand the social context and prevailing norms that need to be addressed. Although many societies could benefit from changing traditional modes of thinking and acting, some traditions remain beneficial and are important to retain. Thus, before we began designing or implementing any professional development programme for mathematics teacher educators, our project set out to study and understand the mathematics education context in Malawi.

Since the early 2000s, three new concepts have influenced the field of mathematics teacher education. The first is mathematical knowledge for teaching (MKT) (Ball et al. 2008), which describes the different forms of knowledge that mathematics teachers need in order to teach effectively. The second is the mathematical discourse in instruction (MDI) framework (Adler and Rhonda 2017), which illustrates what constitutes a successful mathematics lesson in terms of students' learning. The third is lesson study (LS) (Lewis and Hurd 2011), which is a way of studying teachers' teaching and their own learning about their students' learning. Our project aimed to introduce these three concepts into the field of mathematics teacher education in Malawi in such a way that they could be integrated with traditional ways of teaching and build on students' existing knowledge. That is, we expected the process of change to be relative to Malawi's own context. That is, we encouraged teachers to adopt these new ideas and related teaching methodologies to the extent they found them useful, and in ways that identified and retained the benefits of traditional knowledge.

Some background about Malawi

In 1994, free primary education for all was introduced in Malawi. While this was a big step forward for the country, it created many challenges for the education sector. Student enrolment in primary schools increased by 65 per cent in the first year – growing from 1.9 million students in 1994 to 2.9 million in 1995 – and almost doubled by 1996 (Kazima and Mussa 2011). This solved the problem of access to primary education for children but very few schools had enough facilities and teachers to handle this massive increase in enrolment. In an attempt to cope with the demand for additional teachers, the Malawian government employed many unqualified teachers and introduced fast-track teacher training for primary school teachers.

One consequence of this is that quality of teaching in general, and of mathematics teaching in particular, has fallen. This can be seen in achievement levels in mathematics at both primary and secondary level, as evidenced from national examinations and international assessments. For example, in 2016, Malawi's National Examinations Board reported pass rates of less than 50 per cent for the Malawi Schools Certificate of Education examinations for the previous ten years (MANEB 2016). Furthermore, evaluations (such as the Early Grade Mathematics Assessments and those carried out by the Southern and Eastern Africa Consortium for Educational Quality) have shown that primary school children in Malawi perform below the levels expected by the national curriculum (see Brombacher 2011; Hungi et al. 2010).[1] Since a good knowledge of mathematics is crucial for social and economic development, these findings must be acknowledged and the factors leading to such low achievements must be addressed. As Kazima (2014) shows, one of the main factors contributing to this problem is the poor quality of teachers in primary schools.

With this background, our project was implemented with the overall goal of improving the quality of teaching and learning mathematics in Malawi's schools through improving the quality of mathematics teacher education at the University of Malawi and at primary teacher education colleges. It was expected that by improving the quality of mathematics teacher education, the quality of teachers who graduate will also improve, and that this will, in turn, improve the quality of mathematics teaching and learning in schools in the long term.

The project and its achievements

The project was a collaborative effort between the University of Malawi and the University of Stavanger, and comprised a team of ten academic staff – six from the University of Malawi and four from the University of Stavanger. The project had five components, each with intended outcomes which together feed into the goal of improving the quality of mathematics teacher education. The five components were: a PhD programme, a master's course, a professional development programme, research, and infrastructure development. In each one, at least one of the three key concepts (MKT, MDI and LS) was introduced. As described in more detail below, most of the project's intended outcomes had been achieved by the end of 2018.

The PhD programme

Before the project, the University of Malawi offered a general PhD in education but had no PhD programme in mathematics education or the mathematical sciences. Our project designed and established one PhD programme specialising in mathematics education and another in mathematical sciences. When the project offered fellowships to University of Malawi staff, three staff members opted for the former and one chose the latter. Supervision of these students (two females and two males) started in 2014 and ended in 2018, and was carried out jointly between the two universities.

As part of the PhD in Mathematics Education, we developed a module on 'Theories in the teaching and learning of mathematics'. This included readings and discussions related to mathematical knowledge for teaching. In addition, all PhD students focused their research and expanded their knowledge and abilities in relation to MKT. The topics selected by these three PhDs students are: i) An exploration of mathematical knowledge for teaching geometric proofs, ii) Investigating pre-service secondary school teachers' mathematical knowledge for teaching equations, and iii) Assessing student teachers' development of MKT through their initial primary teacher education. All three studies greatly informed the project, and by the end of 2018, two candidates had completed and graduated.

Having faculty members study MKT at PhD level has made them very knowledgeable about contemporary teacher education and of the importance of offering student teachers opportunities to develop all the forms of teacher knowledge necessary to teach mathematics effectively. This increased the number of staff at the University of Malawi with PhDs in Mathematics Education, thus enabling us to meet a key project objective.

The master's course

Before the project started, the Faculty of Education at the University of Malawi ran a Master's of Education programme that included some courses in mathematics and science education. However, to run a specialised master's programme in mathematics and science education, the faculty was required to create one additional course. Until our project was established, limited staff capacity had prevented this course from being offered.

Our project therefore soon developed a course on the history and pedagogy of mathematics suited to master's students. Initially, the content was adapted from a course run by the University of Stavanger and was taught by the project team from that university. This made it possible for the University of Malawi to offer a new master's programme focused on mathematics, which was a significant achievement. By 2018, a total of 23 candidates had been recruited for the degree in two cohorts. By the end of 2018, ten had successfully completed their studies.

In fact, we were aiming to recruit a total of 24 students in three cohorts. Since 23 had already been recruited in the first two cohorts, we exceeded this target when the third cohort of six students was recruited in September 2018. For this cohort, staff from the University of Stavanger and the University of Malawi jointly delivered the History and Pedagogy of Mathematics course. That is, PhD candidates who have graduated through the project are already helping to teach master's students. This has ensured that the specialised master's programme continues to be offered at the University of Malawi after project life. The fact that University of Malawi staff have completed their PhDs as part of the project, and begun teaching alongside experienced staff from the University of Stavanger, has been of great benefit to the University of Malawi and has helped to ensure that the project achieves its objective of increasing the capacity of the education faculty to offer specialised master's programmes.

Professional development

Mathematics teacher education in Malawi is provided via two categories of institution; that is, teacher education colleges train primary school teachers and universities train secondary school teachers.

Our project designed and developed a professional development programme on the teaching of mathematics for primary school teacher educators. The project worked with all eight public teacher education colleges for primary schools in Malawi and offered all mathematics teacher educators a professional development course. The course began in 2016 and was offered for three consecutive years.

The course began in May of each year, with a three-day workshop during which teacher educators were introduced to LS and MKT related to multiplication and fractions. Then the educators worked together to develop mathematics lesson plans for LS at their own colleges. After the workshops, and until November of each year, the educators conducted their own LS, recording the lessons and their discussions of these on video. Each November, the teacher educators attended a follow-up workshop where they reported back on the LS they conducted, and discussed what they had learned.

In addition, teacher educators were introduced to the MDI framework (see Adler and Rhonda 2017), and encouraged to use this to critically evaluate their lesson plans and textbooks. The MDI framework was developed in under-resourced mathematics classrooms in public schools in South Africa and helps teachers to identify what matters in a mathematics lesson regardless of the resources available in the classroom. Although the framework is applicable globally, we found it particularly relevant because Malawi schools are so under-resourced.

The topic of mathematical knowledge for teaching was also covered briefly during the November workshops. Like the students who enrolled for the PhD programme, the mathematics teacher educators involved in this development programme grew professionally. We expect that this professional growth to expand the skills levels of teacher educators as well as their values and ideas about teaching mathematics.

In terms of our aims, we hoped that at least 48 mathematics teacher educators would have completed the professional development course by 2018. In fact, we exceeded this number quite considerably. By the end of 2018, 89 mathematics teacher educators had completed the course. The skills acquired by teacher educators will stay with them long after the project ends, and we hope that many will share their skills with all the new teachers that they train, thus ensuring that our project has a lasting effect.

Research

Research is integrated into all project activities and can be divided into that carried out by our doctoral and master's students and that conducted by the project team. The latter involved collaborative work across the two universities.

By late 2018, we had initiated 22 research studies on issues related to teaching and learning mathematics in both primary and secondary schools – three PhD dissertations, 15 master's theses and four collaborative studies by members of the project team.

Our research findings have strongly informed the project and the mathematics education community in our universities. The research process has also improved the capacity of staff and students of the University of Malawi to design and carry out research linked to mathematics education. Research linked to teaching mathematics in Malawi had a great influence on the project. That is, studying and understanding our context was prioritised and this enabled us to apply modern teaching methods in ways that are appropriate to this context.

Infrastructure development

This component involved developing a mathematics room at the University of Malawi; that is, refurbishing an ordinary classroom into a room that is well-equipped for teaching and learning mathematics. Decisions made about what to include in the room were based on our research findings as well as the insights and experiences we gained from running the professional development programme. All of the teaching and learning materials developed for the mathematics room were made locally to ensure relevance and sustainability.

By the end of 2018, the room was completed and is now being used for teaching mathematics, mathematics education, and also for professional development courses for mathematics teachers. Locating this room at the University of Malawi is also helping to ensure that the project's objectives continue to be met even though the project itself has ended.

Collaboration between North and South

As noted, the project was a collaboration between the University of Stavanger in Norway and the University of Malawi. Norway and Malawi are very different contexts with very different cultures. We were all aware of these differences as we conceptualised the project, and realised that developing some common understandings would be important in facilitating our ability to work together effectively. For example, Norwegian and Malawian colleagues had very different understandings of what constitutes a typical primary school mathematics classroom. This included every aspect from the number of students, the kinds of furniture, the resources available to the students and the teacher, to what teachers should do in a lesson.

For this reason, the entire Norwegian project team visited Malawi at the start of the project to experience the reality of Malawi's schools, teacher education colleges, the University of Malawi and the general social context. This was very helpful when it came to planning and implementing project activities in Malawi. For the same reason, we revisited these institutions whenever Norwegian colleagues came to Malawi as this deepened their understanding of what is possible when it comes to the teaching and learning of mathematics here.

Similarly, we made sure that the project team in Malawi had an opportunity to understand the Norwegian context by visiting Norway and some Norwegian institutions. Recognising the differences between the Norwegian and Malawian contexts was useful to all project team members and helped us to appreciate each other's views.

Our two countries have different cultures and systems related to schooling and university that shape our administrative and approval processes and impact on levels of efficiency. Since the project was based in Malawi, we relied more on Malawi's systems and we could see how challenging it was for the Malawian team not only to perform effectively within the constraints of the system, but also to get the Norwegian team to understand those constraints. For example, procurement processes at the University of Malawi take so long that even though we anticipated delays, these took even longer than expected.

Similarly, obtaining approval for the new master's course on the history and pedagogy of mathematics took much longer to be approved than we expected, and meant we had to postpone the recruitment of our first cohort of master's students. At the beginning, the Malawian team struggled to explain these delays and the Norwegian team battled to understand the extent of the challenges. However, once the Norwegian colleagues became part of the faculty in Malawi and were helping to deliver the master's course in Malawi, our awareness of each other's cultures made the project team appreciate one another more.

In all, the collaboration worked well and quickly sparked another programme that has two components. The first component began in 2014. Since then, two Stavanger University students have visited Malawi for a month each year to conduct research for their master's theses. Staff at the University of Malawi supervise them during this period. By late 2018, ten students had participated in this programme. While the focus is on mathematics education, fields such as special needs education are also covered. The second component involves student teachers from the University of Stavanger who can opt to do a four-week teaching practice in Malawian schools, supervised by the Department of Education and Sports Science at the University of Stavanger and the Department of Curriculum and Teaching Studies at the University of Malawi. By late 2018, six Norwegian student teachers had made use of this opportunity.

Although independent of our initial project, these additional collaborations have enriched it greatly. Research done by University of Stavanger students increased understandings of Malawi's schooling system in general and its mathematics classrooms in particular. This was very useful for creating shared understandings between members of the project team.

New versus traditional ways of teaching mathematics

Traditionally, mathematics teachers in Malawi explain a concept and demonstrate how to use the concept to complete exercises. They then give students exercises to work out for themselves. This approach teaches children what to do and how, but not why. Consequently, students learn procedures without understanding the mathematical reasoning for them or how they can be applied to practical problem-solving in the real world. Many students then memorise the procedures without engaging with the mathematical principles, and are unable to apply what they know in any meaningful way.

Our project sought to shift this traditional way of teaching and encouraged teachers to explain and justify the mathematical principles and skills that they teach. Furthermore, we encouraged teachers to create opportunities to discuss and explain to students how and why they do mathematics. When students are taught mathematics in ways that help them understand mathematical reasoning, they tend to find the subject more interesting, are more motivated to learn, they develop more skills and gain confidence in their own abilities. For teachers to be able to do this competently, they need a range of content knowledge and pedagogical skills.

Bringing the concepts of LS, MKT and MDI into mathematics teacher education in Malawi was interesting. On the one hand, the Malawi mathematics teacher educators could relate to these concepts and engage in discussions at levels expected of mathematics teacher educators anywhere in the world. This shows that, when the focus is on mathematics, and the teaching of mathematics, academic and professional skills are similar across different contexts. However, primary school teacher educators were accustomed to following a handbook that provides details of how to teach each topic. This handbook is a recommended text prepared and provided by the Malawian Ministry of Education. This made it challenging for teacher educators to put newly learned theories into practice and change their way of teaching.

The project was very aware of the need to help the teacher educators make the 'transition' from the traditional to new ways of teaching. The professional development course we offered included a workshop on evaluating mathematics textbooks using the MDI framework. Through hands-on activities, the teacher educators evaluated their own teaching materials, the handbook and other textbooks they use. This helped the teacher educators to see how they can apply MDI theory. Perhaps most importantly, it made teacher educators realise that following any text too systematically limits their thinking about possible examples, activities and explanations that could encourage students to participate more fully in the lessons. The MDI framework encourages teacher educators to think about these elements in every lesson. Furthermore, inviting teacher educators from different colleges to engage in discussions with one another about their teaching provided an opportunity for them to learn from each other and share ideas about how to improve their practice.

The tradition of closely following recommended textbooks and teacher guides provided by the Malawi Ministry of Education is also prevalent in Malawi's primary schools. Similar to the teacher educators' handbooks, the teacher guides contain detailed suggestions on how to teach every topic, and provide examples and exercises for students. In this way, very traditional ways of teaching mathematics are encouraged and student teachers learn to emulate their own lecturers who also tend to follow these texts. However, as teacher educators learn to use these texts differently, student teachers will follow. Soon, neither student nor qualified teachers will see textbooks and teacher guides as prescriptive, but rather as tools that they can modify to suit their lessons and students.

We must note that Malawi's education ministry does not dictate that handbooks and teacher guides must be systematically followed. However, the ministry has also not clearly indicated that suggested examples, tasks and activities are optional or open to modification. The professional development workshops we ran included participants from the education ministry's department of teacher education, and we are hopeful that having these officials participate in discussions and evaluations of teaching materials will increase the chances of uptake of MDI ideas in official circles.

Having said this, attempts to change teaching practice in Malawi must be understood in the context of local schools where the average class size in primary schools is 88 students to one teacher. It is not uncommon for teachers to have over a hundred students in a class. Improving practice in such contexts requires careful reflection and the modification of teaching methods to suit the context. It is also important to consider which aspects of traditional teaching do work and to merge these with new alternatives. This is something that the project team has taken into a subsequent Norhed project titled, 'Strengthening numeracy in early years of primary education through the professional development of teachers in Malawi'.

In our view, three traditional methods still have some value in certain contexts. The first is that it is fine for under-and newly qualified teachers, who are not confident or able to design an effective lesson by themselves, to follow the handbooks and teacher guides. The second is the teaching of mathematics by demonstrating an example on the chalkboard and giving students exercises to work out using the example as demonstrated. This method remains effective in very large classes where space for teachers and students to move around in is very limited. The third is checking what students can or cannot do in order to evaluate the effectiveness of lessons. Although limited, this does allow for a quick assessment of each lesson and for follow-up action to be taken in the next lesson. Thus, given the current educational context in Malawi, completely replacing traditional teaching methods with ideas developed elsewhere could be unwise. Instead, this must be done slowly and with caution so as not to risk losing methods that do have some value.

Situating the project in relation to the Sustainable Development Goals

The project objectives were in line with the United Nations Sustainable Development Goals (SDGs), in particular SDGs 4, 5 and 17. SDG 4 aims to 'ensure inclusive and equitable quality education and promote life-long learning opportunities for all'. Our project's overall goal clearly supports this. Furthermore, the project reached all public teacher colleges which means it has made an impact on improving teaching in rural and urban schools, thus promoting inclusivity and equity.

SDG 5 aims to 'achieve gender equality and empower all women and girls'. In Malawi, most mathematics teachers are male, so having good female mathematics teachers has real potential to encourage girls to study mathematics and follow mathematics-related careers. The project contributed to this by making sure that both genders were represented at different levels in the project. That is, the project team included both male and female faculty members from both universities. In addition, the project recruited two male and two female PhD students, and the project encouraged female students to register for the master's programme by offering eight scholarships to women. Our hope is that these female teachers will in turn encourage more girls in the schools where they teach to pursue mathematics.

Furthermore, while the professional development programme targeted all mathematics teacher educators across all eight teacher training colleges, regardless of gender, we realised that the colleges employ very few female mathematics staff. As noted, by the end of 2018, 89 teacher educators had completed the programme; only 17 of these were female. In response to the very low representation of women, the project held a meeting and workshop for all the female participants in the project with the aim of encouraging and empowering them within the male-dominated departments in their colleges. We hope that female mathematics teacher educators will continue to draw on this and support one another. Confident female teacher educators can be important role models for female student teachers who, we hope, will, in turn, encourage and empower girls in schools.

SDG 17 focuses on partnership and aims to 'enhance international support for implementing effective and targeted capacity-building in developing countries to support national plans to implement all the sustainable development goals, including through North–South, South–South and triangular co-operation'. In the collaboration described here, the University of Malawi's capacity to educate more teachers (and teacher educators) has increased.

In addition, the project ensured its own sustainability in several ways. The first was by ensuring that project activities and benefits could continue after the project ended. Four of the five components of the project, that is, the PhD programme, the master's course, the mathematics room and various research initiatives that have been institutionalised by the University of Malawi will continue into the future. The second is that the capacity building that occurred among University of Malawi staff is enabling them to continue offering the master's degree and supervising postgraduate students. Finally, in terms of the professional development programme aimed at mathematics teacher educators, our hope is that sustainability is ensured in the sense that the teacher educators we trained acquired new knowledge and skills that they will continue to use in their ongoing teaching practice.

About the authors and the project

Mercy Kazima is a professor at the University of Malawi
Arne Jakobsen is a professor at the University of Stavanger in Norway

Project title: Improving the quality and capacity of mathematics teacher education in Malawi
Partner institutions: University of Malawi (Malawi) and the University of Stavanger (Norway)

Notes

1   See also the Southern and Eastern Africa Consortium for Monitoring Educational Quality (SACMEQ), in particular, the 2006 SACMEQ II Project Results regarding pupil achievement levels in reading and mathematics available at www.sacmeq.org

References

Adler J and Ronda E (2017) Mathematical discourse in instruction matters. In J Adler and A Sfard (eds) *Research for Educational Change. Transforming Researchers' Insights into Improvement in Mathematics Teaching and Learning.* London: Routledge

Ball DL, Thames MH and Phelps G (2008) Content knowledge for teaching: What makes it special? *Journal of Teacher Education* 59(5): 389–407

Brombacher A (2011) *Malawi Early Grade Mathematics Assessment (EGMA): National Baseline Report 2010.* Blantyre: USAID and Ministry of Education, Malawi

Hungi N, Makuwa D, Ross K, Saito M, Dolata S, Cappelle F, Paviot L and Vellien J (2010) *SACMEQ III Results: Pupil Achievement Levels in Reading and Mathematics.* Available online

Jha A (2016) Impact of modernisation on education. *International Journal of Advance Research and Innovative Ideas in Education* 2(2): 2395–4396

Kazima M (2014) Universal basic education and the provision of quality mathematics in Southern Africa. *International Journal of Science and Mathematics Education* 12(4): 841–858

Kazima M and Mussa C (2011). Equity and quality issues in mathematics education in Malawi schools. In B Atweh, M Graven and P Valero (eds) *Managing Equity and Quality in Mathematics Education*. New York: Springer

Lewis CC and Hurd J (2011) *Lesson Study Step by Step: How Teacher Learning Communities Improve Instruction*. Portsmouth: Heinemann

Malawi Institute of Education (2006) *Initial Primary Teacher Education Programme Handbook*. Domasi: Malawi Institute of Education

MANEB (Malawi National Examinations Board) (2016). Chief Examiners' Reports for Malawi Senior Certificate Mathematics Examinations. Unpublished

MoE (Ministry of Education, Malawi) (2013) *Education Statistics 2013*. Lilongwe: Education Planning Division

PART FOUR

KNOWLEDGE, IDENTITY, CULTURE

Introduction to Part Four

Roy Krøvel

These chapters have been assembled under the heading 'knowledge, identity and culture' for a number of reasons. Knowledge and the possibility of knowledge transfer are hotly debated topics in the so-called development literature. Discourse on 'knowledge transfer' after the Second World War typically focused on the transfer of *technological* knowledge. More recently, however, the World Bank and others have become more sensitive to the challenges of 'combining local knowledge with the wealth of experience' from around the world, as Koch and Weingart (2016) put it. Instead of 'knowledge transfer', many now prefer to speak of 'mutual learning' based on the recognition of knowledge derived from local traditions, cultures and languages.

According to Koch and Weingart, Western scientific and local knowledges interact in many ways, from 'dominance all the way to innovative adaptation and mixing'. We thought that a section on projects dealing specifically with issues related to culture and language would be helpful for teasing out the patterns of interaction between scientific and local knowledges in the Norhed project. We wanted to explore the extent to which we could talk about 'adaptation and mixing' when Northern European and Southern local knowledges met as part of the Norhed programme.

Whose knowledge?

A document providing a short introduction to Norhed refers to the term 'knowledge' 12 times in the course of 22 pages (Norad 2015). To contribute to 'increased knowledge' by 'strengthen[ing] capacity in higher education institutions in LMICs [low and middle-income countries]' is defined as a key purpose of Norhed. To 'contribute to improved documentation, access to information, knowledge transfer between institutions and individuals' is given as a rationale (Norad 2015: 4). But what is 'knowledge'? Who defines what is 'knowledge' and what is not? Thousands of books and peer-reviewed articles have tried to define and explain 'knowledge'. Still, 'knowledge' is a hotly disputed topic, especially when used in development discourse.

The debates on 'knowledge' are relevant for Norhed partnerships. First, as feminist scholars such as Haraway and Harding argue, knowledge can be seen as situated (Haraway 1988; Harding 2016). Situated knowledge is knowledge specific to a particular situation. Those who support this view are critical of the idea that researchers are neutral observers of reality. In contrast, they aver that knowledge is 'situated': it is produced in a context, and with a point of view. If knowledge is situated, this raises questions about the possibility of transferring knowledge from one situation to another.

A second debate of relevance to the Norhed programme concerns scientific knowledge and other forms of knowledge. Historically, many philosophers of science have held that knowledge must be justified by evidence (see Kirkham 1984). The 'scientific method' sought to provide evidence by collecting data, through observation and experimentation, in order to test the validity of hypotheses that had been formulated. In the global North, the scientific method became the hegemonic way of producing 'knowledge'. More recently, however, the hegemony of the scientific method has been challenged from various perspectives. According to one Unesco paper, 'Sophisticated knowledge of the natural world is not confined to science. Human societies all across the globe have developed rich sets of experiences and explanations relating to the environment they live in' (Nakashima and Bridgewater 2000: 11).

A third debate of relevance here is the question of indigenous knowledges and decolonising education. An almost global movement has gathered around the call to 'decolonise education'. The movement seeks to unsettle colonial structures, systems and dynamics in educational contexts by showing the impact that colonialism has had on education. From this perspective, knowledge produced by the scientific method and the right to define what knowledge is or is not has been intrinsically linked to colonial structures. Thus merely intending to 'transfer' knowledge from the North to the South would be yet another round of colonisation.

Overview of the chapters in this section

The chapters in this section deal with very different topics, yet there are many parallels and connections between them.

José Luis Saballos Velásquez tells the story of trying to build up a system of indigenous and communitarian higher education in the opening chapter of this section, 'Intercultural communication and autonomy in Latin America'. Many Afro-descendants' and indigenous peoples' organisations in Latin America believe it necessary to use the mother tongue not only to teach in primary and secondary schools, but also to educate teachers, do research and educate researchers, in addition to developing alternative research methodologies and paradigms. As might be expected, the attempts to build an indigenous and communitarian educational system extending from primary school to higher education has been met with confrontation from governments, who see indigenous autonomy as a threat to state sovereignty and 'national identity'.

The chapter on linguistic capacity building in Ethiopia, by Derib Ado Jekale, Binyam Sisay Mendisu and Janne Bondi Johannessen starts with the observation that many languages used as mother tongues in Ethiopia are not developed for writing. The authors see this as a problem for instruction in the education system as well as for the practice of democracy, as 'large groups of people do not get necessary information concerning their civil rights'. The chapter makes the connection between democracy, civil rights and the possibility of studying and learning in one's mother tongue, thus highlighting some of the important challenges for ethnic minorities.

In her chapter on the academic and cultural perceptions of foreign students at Makerere University in Uganda, Elizabeth Kaase-Bwanga highlights important challenges that need to be confronted by universities hosting foreign students. These include the need to ensure adequate communication and to establish clear communication channels between project co-ordinators, professors and students, as well as the necessity for a high degree of project management skills among project co-ordinators.

Birgit Brock-Utne reflects on two different models of co-operation between a university in Norway and two universities in Africa. The chapter is an autoethnographic report based on thirty years of experience with university collaborations. Brock-Utne concludes that, so far, Norhed's TRANSLED project has produced few results, and observes that 'most of the teaching we have done could have been done locally, provided money had been allocated for that purpose. For me as the initiator of the TRANSLED project, there has been no professional benefit from the project and it has so far led to a lot of frustration.'

The delusion of knowledge transfer?

These chapters are relevant for ongoing debates on North–South relations and the role of higher education in 'development' and 'aid'. To begin with, most of them employ a reflexive approach similar to the one employed by Adriansen, Madsen and Jensen (2015) in exploring how 'capacity building affects scientific knowledge production' in the (for lack of a better word) global South. The authors of the chapters in this section benefit from being able to draw on their direct experiences of participating in capacity-building projects, in addition to drawing on more traditional methodologies such as interviews, observations, measurements and so forth.

While there are quite a number of peer-reviewed articles referring to reflexive approaches, the term seems to have various meanings, sometimes depending on discipline and theoretical perspective. However, it is generally agreed that a reflexive approach is a less instrumental, more constructivist, relational and social theory of learning. A reflexive approach should involve 'interpreting one's own interpretations, looking at one's own perspectives from other perspectives, and turning a self-critical eye onto one's own authority as interpreter and author' (Alvesson and Sköldberg 2000: vii). Others stress that 'adopting a "reflexive approach" means considering what is happening during the research process in which you are implicated: during the choice of subject, during the fieldwork and finally during the analysis' (Guillermet 2008: 7). A reflexive approach would seem to be appropriate when using lived experience to analyse knowledge production, knowledge transfer, language and culture. A particular challenge in these chapters is that most are reflections of not only one person's interpretations of a set of experiences, but more likely a negotiated account of various reflections made by the various team members.

One cross-cutting issue of concern in all Norhed projects is gender. However, while all projects sought to include gender issues as an integral part of education and research, knowledge about gender also appears to be a good example of situated knowledge that is not easily 'transferred' from one place to another, let alone from Norway to the global South. Gender will always have to be interpreted and hopefully understood in the local context. Place and space play crucial roles when knowledge about gender is being produced (Adriansen, Mehmood-Ul-Hassan and Mbow 2015).

Taken together, these chapters also illustrate a few differences (and disagreements?) regarding the use of concepts (and heuristic devices) for the analysis of knowledge production and higher education. For Adriansen, Mehmood-Ul-Hassan and Mbow (2015) 'local' and 'local knowledge' are useful concepts. The authors juxtapose the concept 'local' with the concept 'foreign' in order to underline power imbalances, issues related to financial strength, administrative capacity, problems of legitimacy and so on. According to Koch and Weingart (2016: 22), the importance of local expertise rests with having 'first-hand knowledge of the country's problems and needs and how to meet them'.

The Latin-American partners (or rather the partners from 'Abya Yala') in Saballos Velásquez's chapter would agree on the importance of producing indigenous knowledges suited to local needs. However, framing the argument as local versus foreign, or as seen from the perspective of 'the country', would make it rather more difficult to transfer from one place (Africa) to another (Abya Yala). Instead, the preferred framing would be to contrast the 'indigenous' with the 'occidental'. Instead of 'state sovereignty', the preferred concept would be 'indigenous autonomy'.

This difference in discourse reflects differences between Africa's and Abya Yala's experiences of colonialism and post-colonial order over the last 200 years. In Africa, colonialism is intrinsically linked to experiences with European colonial systems. It is more seldom used to describe one group's dominance of other groups within the same state. In Latin America, however, European colonial powers withdrew some 200 years ago and local elites formed a system of independent states.[1] Seen from the perspective of indigenous peoples in Abya Yala, the transfer of power from Spanish and Portuguese colonial masters to local elites did not end colonialism. The colonialisation (and exploitation) of indigenous peoples continued, albeit now by elites placed geographically much closer. Decolonising education has come to mean defending indigenous peoples' autonomy over education against state intrusion. Interestingly, when indigenous peoples have won rights to autonomy and protection against human rights abuses, it has seldom come from processes within sovereign states. More commonly, such advances have been outcomes of international process led by, for instance, the United Nations[2] or as part of an inter-American human rights process, limiting the sovereign powers of the individual states.

Unsurprisingly, then, the network of indigenous and communitarian universities in Abya Yala (RUIICAY) does not see defending state sovereignty as part of the solution, possibly in contrast to the analysis of Koch and Weingart (2016). A place-based historical approach might help us understand why concepts such as 'state', 'state sovereignty', 'colonialism' and 'post-colonialism' take on such contradictory meanings. Similarly, talk of the 'Africanisation' of curriculum (Adriansen, Madsen and Jensen 2015) would stir up gloomy memories of 'mestisaje' among the indigenous educators of the RUIICAY. As Sarango (2017) explains, elites ruling the sovereign states in Latin America set out to construct a national and cultural identity. The process of turning indigenous peoples, peoples of African descent and others into 'Nicaraguans', 'Guatemalans', 'Colombians', 'Brazilians' and so on is often referred to as 'mestisaje'. Producing a 'national identity' (*mestizo*) made sense from the perspective of the state. From the perspective of indigenous peoples, however, it meant losing identity, language and culture. As Saballos Velásquez explains, only recently, and after long struggles, have governments in Latin America come to accept that their states consist of many nations.

Perhaps the case of Abya Yala can be used to 'obtain variance in data' by serving as a comparative case study (Koch and Weingart 2016: 26). Being able to learn in your own language is of importance for all of the Sustainable Development Goals related to education. Language is fundamental to all learning processes. Yet many pupils and students from minority groups in Africa are being denied the possibility of learning and studying in their mother tongue. Analysis of the role of knowledge and higher education in African contexts could conceivably benefit from the critical perspectives that indigenous and communitarian universities put forward on the 'state'.

Differentiating knowledge and the political economy of knowledge transfer

A brief afterthought on the political economy of higher education co-operation between the global North and South is needed. None of the chapters in this section deal directly with the political economy of knowledge transfer and knowledge production but, taken together, a few emerging trends are worth mentioning, given that the Norhed projects are part of much larger ongoing development of knowledge transfer and production.

Koch and Weingart (2016: 14) rightly point out that knowledge needs to be differentiated: 'Simple standardised technical solutions to problems such as installing water pumps are much more easily transferred to a community with little technical knowledge than complex design of, for example, an effective and just tax system.' The underlying economic and social knowledge needed for the latter is abstract and also requires the input of local knowledge.

The World Bank optimistically expected that knowledge was like light and could travel the world. If any knowledge today could be said to resemble light and to have travelled the world, it must be the ever-present cell phones, computers, and the internet with all their underlying programmes and applications. The digital divide is still a real phenomenon, of course. But the projects discussed in this section illustrate the importance of digital technological solutions such as online libraries, computer laboratories and cell phones for higher education and knowledge production, whether in Abya Yala, Africa, Asia or the Middle East.

These chapters show the 'power of identity' (Castells 1997) and underline the need to pay close attention to local knowledges, culture and language as we get to understand that knowledge is not merely transferred, but adopted, modified, mixed, challenged, destabilised. Still, digital technology is (almost) always present. It is already 20 years since Castells (1997) said that the internet has become the 'fabric of our social life'. Indigenous peoples in Colombia, for instance, have learned to use 'occidental' technologies to organise and educate themselves in the struggle for autonomy. Others use digital technology to recuperate indigenous languages and technology. Minorities around the world employ technological solutions to adapt and mix knowledge to their own ends.

However, not all knowledge production is of equal *exchange* value. It would be tempting to treat computers, applications, programs, computer languages, the internet and so on as simple and standardised technical solutions, similar to water pumps, with little or no social and cultural impact. However, that would be misleading on many levels. The point here is that this type of knowledge – operating systems, program language, programs, applications and so on – is not 'adapted', 'mixed', 'challenged' or 'destabilised' in the proper sense of these terms. It is more accurate to say that this type of knowledge is 'transferred' or 'imported' or 'incorporated' or even 'bought' and used without much local capacity to modify or mix.

That leads us to the political economy of knowledge transfer and knowledge production. First, because this type of knowledge production is creating new dependencies and structures of inequality in the world. As a group, those who have the knowledge to produce operating systems, programs, applications and so on are growing increasingly rich. As recently as the year 2006, the ten largest (by market capitalisation) companies in the world were mainly from the extractive industries: ExxonMobil was estimated as the largest (market capitalisation) closely followed by Gazprom, Royal Dutch Shell, BP and PetroChina, apart from a few banks and General Electric. Ten years later, the face of the richest of the rich had changed dramatically, with Apple in the first place, followed by Alphabet (Google) in second place, and Amazon, Microsoft, Facebook, China Mobile all on the top ten list (*The Economist* 2016). Similarly, the Forbes list of the richest persons on the planet also leaves a clear impression of where money is piling up. Jeff Bezos (Amazon) tops the list before Bill Gates (Microsoft) with the men behind Facebook and Google not far behind. Digital technology and communications technology have replaced oil, mining and energy as the biggest money-making machines in the world.

Second, because this has happened at the same time as inequalities between rich and poor in the global North have reached a historical high. Capital is also increasingly concentrated within a few companies. According to *The Economist*, in a special report on companies, 'The McKinsey Global Institute calculates that 10 per cent of the world's public companies generate 80 per cent of all profits.' The same report reveals that the share of nominal GDP generated by Fortune's 100 biggest companies in America has risen significantly, from about 33 per cent in 1994 to a hefty 46 per cent of GDP in 2013 (*The Economist* 2016: 2).

Perhaps it is time to re-imagine what colonialism looks like. The 'old' extractive industries also had global reach, but were place-based raw-material production sites that tended to make the corporate structures less flexible, less capable of fluidity. Today, however, corporate networks are growing increasingly complex as technology makes it possible to construct impenetrable webs of ownership across borders while profits are rapidly and massively moved between countries and continents.

What might be the consequences when computers, the 'net', 'apps' and cell phones become the underlying grammar of social life that we depend on to communicate and interact, to get access to knowledge, and to adapt and modify knowledge? All forms of social and commercial activity online will continue to generate enormous incomes for those who own and control the underlying infrastructure.

Hardt and Negri are concerned with the so-called 'data-mining' and 'data-extraction' businesses: 'The metaphors of "data mining" and "data extraction" paint an image of unstructured fields of social data that are available for capture by intrepid prospectors, just like oil or minerals in the earth – and indeed there is today a digital gold rush to rival California and the Yukon' (Hardt and Negri 2017: 168).

New possibilities and new dependencies

The Norhed projects serve to produce optimism about knowledge production, adaptation and mixing as well as local capacity, the local knowledge base and local ability to assimilate knowledge. It would appear that Norhed has helped local knowledge communities to produce a 'critical mass of local experts who qualify as producers and critical scrutinisers of expertise' (Koch and Weingart 2016: 344).

At the same time, the projects indicate that new dependencies on Northern/occidental technological solutions are emerging. Transfer of technological knowledge continues to produce a steady outflow of capital from the global South. While we rightly should celebrate the emergence of a critical mass of local experts, it is equally important to note the emergence of new dependencies.

Notes

1   The US has, of course, played a dominating role in shaping regional policies ever since. But, at least formally, the norm has been that governments formed by local elites have ruled independent states.

2   See, for example, the ILO's Indigenous and Tribal Peoples Convention, 1989.

References

Adriansen HK, Madsen LM and Jensen S (eds) (2015) *Higher Education and Capacity Building in Africa: The Geography and Power of Knowledge Under Changing Conditions.* Routledge Studies in African Development. Abingdon, Oxon: Routledge

Adriansen HK, Mehmood-Ul-Hassan M and Mbow C (2015) Producing scientific knowledge in Africa today: Auto-ethnographic insights from a climate change researcher. In HK Adriansen, LM Madsen and S Jensen (eds) *Higher Education and Capacity Building in Africa: The Geography and Power of Knowledge Under Changing Conditions.* Abingdon, Oxon: Routledge

Alvesson M and Sköldberg K (2000) *Reflexive Methodology: New Vistas for Qualitative Research*. London: Sage

Castells M (1997) *The Power of Identity*. Oxford: John Wiley and Sons

Guillermet E (2008) Reflexivity, a tool for the anthropologist. An example: The fieldwork of a French PhD student. *AntropoWeb* 1: 16–21. Available online

Haraway D (1988) Situated knowledges: The science question in feminism and the privilege of partial perspective. *Feminist Studies* 14(3): 575–599

Harding S (2016) *Whose Science? Whose Knowledge? Thinking from Women's Lives*. Ithaca, NY: Cornell University Press

Hardt M and Negri A (2017) *Assembly*. New York: Oxford University Press

Kirkham RL (1984) Does the Gettier problem rest on a mistake? *Mind* 93(372): 501–513

Koch S and Weingart P (2016) *The Delusion of Knowledge Transfer: The Impact of Foreign Aid Experts on Policy-Making in South Africa and Tanzania*. Cape Town: African Minds. Available online

Nakashima D and Bridgewater P (2000) Tapping into the world's wisdom. *Unesco Sources* 125: 11–12

Norad (2015) *A Presentation on the Norwegian Programme for Capacity Development in Higher Education and Research for Development (Norhed)*. Available online

Sarango LF (2017) *Kapak Ñan Pedagógico: Filosófico de la Pluriversidad 'Amawtay Wasi'*. Quito: Pluriversidad Amawtay Wasi

The Economist (2016, 17 September) *Special Report: Companies*. Available online

13

Intercultural communication and autonomy in Latin America: The journey of the RUIICAY-HIOA Intercultural Communication Linkage Programme

José Luis Saballos Velásquez

Introduction

In Latin America, indigenous peoples and Afro-descendants continue their struggle for real citizenship and inclusive, equitable and intercultural development within national and regional contexts that perpetuate discrimination and racism, and consequently social exclusion, marginalisation and impoverishment. A widely cited definition states that

> indigenous communities, peoples and nations are those which, having a historical continuity with pre-invasion and pre-colonial societies that developed their territories, consider themselves distinct from other sectors of the societies now prevailing on those territories, or parts of them. They form at present non-dominant sectors of society and are determined to preserve, develop and transmit to future generations their ancestral territories, and their ethnic identity, as the basis of their continued existence as peoples, in accordance with their own cultural patterns, social institutions and legal system. (Martinez Cobo, cited in OHCHR 2013: 6)

In the case of Afro-descendants, their diverse histories, experiences and identities comprise a heterogenous group resulting from the trans-atlantic slave trade, slavery or migrations (UN 2017). Beyond externally imposed or universally agreed definitions, there is an ample recognition of these peoples' right to self-identify and self-define themselves. The United Nations Declaration on the Rights of Indigenous Peoples (article 33) states their right to determine own identity or membership in accordance with customs and traditions and the ILO Convention No. 169 also grants self-identification rights. Both international instruments have been important in prompting governments around the world to embrace the recognition and rights of indigenous peoples and Afro-descendants.

Since the late 1980s, the national constitutions of Latin American countries have recognised the multicultural and multi-ethnic nature of their societies, acknowledging in this way the existence of indigenous peoples and Afro-descendants. Nevertheless, most higher education by-laws to acknowledge indigenous and Afro-descendant people's existence and rights are still pending. Indigenous, intercultural and community universities have been founded yet, faced with barriers posed by higher education regulatory and accreditation bodies, political systems and ruling elites, still struggle for autonomy in developing quality and pertinent study, research, social and community linkage academic programmes.

The Network of Indigenous, Intercultural and Community Universities of Abya Yala (RUIICAY, acronym in Spanish) brings together universities that result from the struggle of indigenous and Afro-descendant peoples for recognition and effective exercise of rights in the field of higher education. These universities incorporate indigenous and Afro-descendant peoples' cultures, worldviews, spirituality, wisdoms and knowledge systems in their education, research and outreach activities as a means to strengthen self-reliance and autonomy. The RUIICAY-HIOA Intercultural Communication Programme, a project of the Norwegian Programme for Capacity Development in Higher Education and Research for Development (Norhed) is particularly emblematic in fostering autonomy at three RUIICAY member universities: the University of the Autonomous Regions of the Caribbean Coast of Nicaragua (URACCAN) in Nicaragua, the Indigenous Community Intercultural University of the Nationalities and Indigenous Peoples 'Amawtay Wasi' (UCINPI-AW)/Pluriversity 'Amawtay Wasi' (PAW) in Ecuador and the Autonomous Indigenous Intercultural University (UAIIN-CRIC) in Colombia.

In this chapter I shed light on whether this, the only Latin American Norhed project, has developed the institutional capacities of these universities to fulfil their social and communitarian responsibilities as generators of autonomous knowledge, research and intercultural communication education (URACCAN et al. 2013). Several questions frame my analysis: have institutional capacities been augmented? Has RUIICAY advanced? What constraints were faced? And finally, has autonomy been strengthened?

Main issues

Indigenous peoples, Afro-descendants and higher education

In Latin America, the recent inclusion of indigenous peoples and Afro-descendants in national statistics still lacks completeness and reliability. As of 2010, there are an estimated 111 million Afro-descendants in the different countries, representing 21.1 per cent of the region's total population (CEPAL 2017). Other estimates set the Afro-descendant population at 125 million people (Del Popolo 2017). This population is predominantly urban (89.2 per cent). The total indigenous population is estimated at 44.8 million people distributed in 826 different ethnic groups, which is 8.3 per cent of the total Latin American population (Del Popolo 2017). See Table 13.1 for recent estimates. Since 2010, self-identification as Afro-descendant or indigenous has improved in the national censuses of most countries. Nevertheless, some countries reflect considerably low estimates (Ecuador, Bolivia and Chile) – the result of census shortfalls and cultural and ethnic self-adscription problems (rejection or fear of, or discomfort with being labelled), derived from a history of marginalisation and mistrust.

Table 13.1: The presence of indigenous peoples and Afro-descendants in Latin America

Country and year of data collection	Total population	Afro-descendant population	Afro-descendants (%)	Indigenous population	Indigenous people (%)
Argentina 2010	40 117 096	149 570	0.4	955 032	2.4
Bolivia 2012	10 059 856	23 330	0.2	6 216 026	62.2
Brazil 2010	190 755 799	97 171 614	50.9	896 917	0.5
Chile 2012	---	---		1 805 243	11.0
Costa Rica 2011	4 301 712	334 437	7.8	104 143	2.4
Cuba 2012	11 167 325	4 006 926	35.9	---	---
Ecuador 2010	14 483 499	1 041 559	7.2	1 018 176	7.0
Honduras 2013	8 303 772	115 802	1.4	536 541	7.0
México 2010	112 336 538	1 348 038	1.2	16 933 283	15.1
Panamá 2010	3 405 813	300 551	8.8	417 559	12.3
Uruguay 2011	3 251 654	149 689	4.6	76 452	2.4
Venezuela 2011	27 227 930	936 770	3.4	724 592	2.7
Colombia 2010	46 448 000	4 877 040	10.5	1 559 852	3.4
El Salvador 2010	6 218 000	8 083	0.1	14 408	0.2
Guatemala 2010	14 334 000	5 734	0.04	5 881 009	41.0
Nicaragua 2010	5 813 000	29 065	0.5	518 104	8.9
Perú 2010	29 272 000	585 440	2.0	7 021 271	24.0
Total	**527 495 994**	**111 083 648**	**21.1**	**44 795 758**	**8.3**

Source: (CEPAL 2017; Del Popolo 2017)

Colonisation and slavery left a long-standing heritage of racism, inequality and structural and institutionalised discrimination against indigenous and Afro-descendant peoples in Latin America. As a result, compared to the rest of the population, indigenous and Afro-descendant peoples are affected by a high degree of severe, accumulated impoverishment and vulnerability. The poverty gap for the indigenous and Afro-descendant population is 38 per cent to 300 per cent higher than the national average in Latin American countries (CEPAL 2017). Their living conditions are characterised by inadequate housing, sanitation, drinking water, health, employment and education. Indigenous and Afro-descendant women, children and youth tend to be the most affected by poverty and exclusion. Such privations in well-being potentiates and adds to the existing vicious cycle, including unequal access to opportunities and to the exercise of rights, autonomy and self-determination.

Education is a key area where disparities exacerbate indigenous and Afro-descendant peoples' impoverishment and vulnerability in the present and probably for the foreseeable future. The education deficits worsen as school-aged children and youth grow older. The coverage and access gap for indigenous and Afro-descendant children and youth aged 6 to 11 years is not significant in total national statistics, but increases for the 12- to 17-year-old group, and even more for the 18 to 24 years age group, with females in rural areas at a greater disadvantage (CEPAL 2017). At post-secondary or higher education level, the indigenous and Afro-descendant population aged 20 to 29 years experiences the worst deficits in coverage and access in most countries, females having higher access and graduation rates than males (CEPAL 2017). The exceptions are Argentina, Honduras, Nicaragua and Panama. In higher education, indigenous and Afro-descendant peoples experience a greater breach in the exercise of citizen education rights, becoming an important and strategic battleground for the defence, further recognition and advancement of rights.

The struggle of indigenous and Afro-descendant peoples toward real citizenship, social justice, equality and inclusive development has seen important milestones in international legal frameworks, such as the Universal Declaration of Human Rights (1948), the ILO 111 covenant against discrimination (1958), the International Convention on the Elimination of All Forms of Racial Discrimination (1965), the International Covenant on Civil and Political Rights (1966), the International Covenant on Economic, Social and Cultural Rights (1966), the International Convention on the Supression and Punishment of the Crime of Apartheid (1973), the ILO 169 covenant about indigenous and tribal peoples (1989), the United Nations Declaration on the Rights of Indigenous Peoples (2007) and the American Convention on Human Rights. These are important international instruments for indigenous and Afro-descendant peoples, which have impacted on national consti-tutions and laws. Other milestones include international conferences, such as the Regional Higher Education Conference of 2008 (CRES 2008), which highlighted the struggle for the rights of indigenous and Afro-descendant peoples in higher education.

In Latin America, over the last 30 years multiculturality and pluri-ethnicity have finally been acknowledged in most national constitutions. Among a total of 20 countries, 15 national constitutions include such recognition, particularly also of indigenous peoples (CEPAL 2014; Saballos Velásquez 2016). Of these, 13 establish non-discrimination and equality precepts, but only four countries explicitly recognise Afro-descendant peoples: Bolivia, Ecuador, Brazil and Colombia (CEPAL 2017). Afro-descendants are acknowledged as either a people or a community, which have different legal and political implications in these countries. In higher-education laws and by-laws, however, indigenous and Afro-descendant peoples are practically invisible. Only three countries explicitly open higher education to cultural diversity, and consequently interculturality (Saballos Velásquez 2016). Nonetheless, interculturality has recently gained a certain momentum in indigenous and Afro-descendant peoples' discourses, organisations and initiatives.

Interculturality

The recognition of multiculturality and pluri-ethnicity in national constitutions has created opportunities for fighting structural discrimination, racism, exclusion and inequality, promoting at the same time inclusive democracy, citizenship and development with identity. In this sense, interculturality embraces the goals of a decent life through breaking the history of dominance, subordination and prejudice, establishing instead a permanent process of communication and learning, based on tolerance, respect, empathy, reciprocity and solidarity between culturally different peoples and their knowledge, values and traditions (Córdova 2003; Etxeberria 2003). For indigenous peoples and Afro-descendants, interculturality is a road towards self-determination and self-affirmation in various well-being dimensions.

Education is considered a fruitful ground for interculturality. Intercultural education is defined as a set of activities strategically guided to regulate – within schooling settings – conflictive inter-ethnic social relations that are based on the logic of power and social dominance (Baronnet 2013). By strengthening the struggle against structural discrimination, racism, exclusion and inequality and through the revitalisation of culture and identity, intercultural education offers a road forward, towards empowerment, autonomy and peaceful, respectful co-existence. This is why intercultural education incorporates history, culture, language, knowledge, values and aspirations as key components in curriculum design, knowledge (re) production and teaching and learning-assessment practices. Curriculum design is flexible, customised to accommodate local needs and potentialities, and incorporates alternative methodologies and conceptual and analytical frameworks, thus contributing to unity in cultural diversity while enhancing the wealth of ancestral knowledge and wisdoms (Hooker Blandford 2015). Besides being sociocultural and ethical, intercultural (higher) education is deeply dialectical and political. According to Gasché (2014), the solidarity, reciprocity values and resistance praxis of indigenous peoples are the essence of what is needed for the restoration of an active democracy for the whole of society.

University autonomy

Autonomy – both external and internal – is a key concept in intercultural higher education institutions. University autonomy refers to an institutional capacity to decide, act upon and lead to the realisation of the university vision, mission and academic model, according to the agreements and by-laws established by the university community. The activities of indigenous, intercultural and community universities, however, are constantly hampered by the racist attitudes and behaviours of government officials and higher education regulating bodies, by rigid academic and administrative procedures, inflexible evaluation criteria for recognition and accreditation, as well as by inadequate financing and political-party interference (Mato 2016). Power contests between different groups combine to further weaken these universities. The most important underlying factor in this devaluation of university autonomy is the non-compliance of relevant government organisations and agencies with the rights of indigenous peoples and

Afro-descendants as enshrined in national constitutions, laws, by-laws and ratified international instruments.

The year 1918 represents a momentous milestone for higher education in Latin America. It is the year in which what is called the Cordoba Reform instituted university autonomy in the region, leading to the democratisation of access to higher education, a large increase in public university enrolment and a move away from elitist, colonialist education models (Rama 2006). But the democratisation of higher education systems has entailed neither a departure from the hegemony of Eurocentric, modernist representations and institutions as aspirational, nor a move towards the recognition of multiculturality and pluri-ethnicity, and away from institutionalised racism (Mato 2008). For a vast majority of indigenous peoples and Afro-descendants in today's Latin America, the dream and benefits of higher education are dependent on further and profound higher education reform, including full support for indigenous and Afro-descendant peoples' own universities.

RUIICAY: The thinking behind the network

RUIICAY is the main regional platform for the advancement of indigenous, Afro-descendant and other vulnerable peoples' higher education rights and institutions, including recognition by the national states. Three universities established RUIICAY in 2008: the Autonomous Indigenous Intercultural University (UAIIN-CRIC) from Colombia, the Indigenous Community Intercultural University of the Nationalities and Indigenous Peoples 'Amawtay Wasi' (UCINPI-AW) from Ecuador and the University of the Autonomous Regions of the Caribbean Coast of Nicaragua (URACCAN). Today, ten universities from eight countries constitute this network, including the three indigenous universities of Bolivia (UNIBOL Aymara 'Tupak Katari', UNIBOL Quechua 'Casimiro Huanca' and UNIBOL Guarani y Pueblos de Tierras Bajas 'Apiaguaiki Tupa'), the University of the Peoples of the South (UNISUR) from Mexico, the Ixil University from Guatemala, the Intercultural Higher Education Institute 'Campinta Guazu Gloria Perez' (IESI) from Argentina and the Indigenous Peoples Office of the University of Panama (OPINUP).

RUIICAY integrates universities established by the state, indigenous and Afro-descendant organisations and/or leaders as part of an effective exercise of the right to pertinent, quality higher education and the struggle for autonomy, intercultural citizenship and decolonisation. The aims of RUIICAY are, among others, to establish a regional intercultural higher education system, to strengthen indigenous, intercultural and community universities in each country and to promote appropriate recognition and accreditation in accordance with their particular undertaking (RUIICAY 2017). The undertakings of these indigenous, intercultural and community universities break away from the social underpinning of the hegemonic mainstream higher education institutions, providing alternatives.

These universities are spaces for the development of local resilience and the capacity for self-determination, for ethnic and cultural revitalisation; spaces where intercultural dialogue and community-based organisations can be nurtured, building consensus for collective action and advocacy that will advance human and citizen rights. The intergenerational cultivation and transmission of ancestors', elders' and Mother Earth spirits' wisdom and practice is another important dimension of RUIICAY member universities' work. Education, research and outreach activities are substantiated by dialogue about knowledge, grounded in the principles of epistemic equality and inspired by indigenous and Afro-descendant peoples' knowledge systems (PAW 2017). The academic offer tackles the local brain drain, what is needed for sustainable development and good living, and the formation of new leadership. RUIICAY's academic offers are international, and include various master's programmes on issues such as intercultural public health, development with identity, worldviews on good living, and intercultural communication. The International Master's Programme in Intercultural Communication with a Gender Focus is part of the Norhed project.

Methodology

This chapter is guided by the Base Document for the Cultivation and Nurture of Wisdom and Knowledge (CCRISAC), developed collectively by the academic staff of the three Latin-American partner universities in the Norhed RUIICAY-HIOA Intercultural Communication Linkage Programme. CCRISAC is a research approach that articulates the main elements of indigenous peoples' knowledge-generation systems and the partner universities' accumulated experience of intercultural community research and particular pathways in Ecuador, Colombia and Nicaragua. The approach seeks to understand reality on the basis of own (ancestral) practice and wisdom in a dialogue with Western or scientific knowledge (RUIICAY 2015). Its ultimate goal is to foster a decolonising, intercultural and inter-epistemic dialogue for the revitalisation and strengthening of identity, autonomy and well-being, especially that of indigenous and Afro-descendant peoples.

CCRISAC comprises three methods for carrying out research work: i) the Chakana, ii) the experiential-symbolic-relational and iii) the creation and recreation of knowledge, wisdoms and practices. The experiential-symbolic-relational method is the basis of the present work. This method views learning as the result of fully experiencing praxis through combining reason, intuition and senses in an individual–collective relationship in order to generate meaning. Using this method, three moments are completed: living and experiencing, observing and recovering, and giving meaning.

Living and experiencing

The various activities during the project provided fertile ground for generating valuable information and comprehension. Among them, two activities were particularly fruitful:

- The ninth encounter of the International Master's Programme in Intercultural Communication with a Gender Focus, held in Ecuador from 13 to 23 November 2017, covered the topic 'journalism and intercultural communication for good living and the exercise of intercultural citizenship' presented by Oslo Metropolitan University's (OsloMet) Professor Andreas Ytterstad. As part of this course, the students used the research questions that Ytterstad raised for a paper on the topic to prepare and carry out interviews with the project's stakeholders (universities' rectors, teachers and project leaders). The interview reports contributed to the paper's main findings, outcomes and results.

- In Ecuador, the RUIICAY second annual meeting (20 to 23 November 2017) and the international forum 'Indigenous, Afro-descendant peoples and higher education in Latin America and the Caribbean: Toward intercultural higher education' (24 November 2017) were important events that complemented the master's encounter. These events provided both spaces for interviewing the various university rectors, teachers and project leaders, and a valuable source of information about the current state of indigenous, intercultural and community universities.

Observing and recovering

As part of learning, there is a need for reflexive observation during the experiencing of events and situations. In this sense, four years of Norhed project implementation has been a fruitful journey involving active observation, open dialogue and communication, reciprocal sharing of knowledge and wisdom, complementarity and partnership building among the participants of partner universities. The experiences, reflections and comprehensions derived from being immersed, as part of the project-leaders team, in such a unique space of cultivating and nurturing knowledges and wisdoms are an important source of information.

Giving meaning

Ultimately, attaining the capacity to make words, concepts, events and experiences generate meaning provides the basis for deep understanding. The accumulated experiences of leading this Norhed project participation allowed me to assess readily available information, best practices and lessons learned in order to develop institutional capacities at RUIICAY partner universities for the generation and strengthening of autonomous education.

Main findings

Development of institutional capacities

Norhed's HIOA-RUIICAY Intercultural Communication Linkage Programme has made important contributions to the development of institutional capacities at URACCAN, UAIIN and UCINPI-AW/PAW for the provision of quality education and research in intercultural communication. Among the various contributions are the following:

- The joint development of the International Master's Programme in Intercultural Communication with a Gender Focus, starting with curriculum design and continuing with teaching, supervision, thesis examination and the graduation of two cohorts of students. Online as well as in-person academic encounters were carried out in Colombia, Ecuador and Nicaragua. This study programme targeted mainly the academic staff of the three Latin-American partners, with the intention of contributing to the consolidation of high-quality teaching and research in intercultural communication. In the first cohort, 20 students graduated in 2016, including 12 females. In the second cohort, 25 students graduated in 2018, 15 of whom were female. For the most part, these graduates are actively involved in education and research duties in the partners' communication academic programmes.
- A doctoral scholarship programme that allowed three faculty staff to take part in relevant PhD programmes – two from URACCAN in Nicaragua, and one from UAIIN in Colombia. The aim of this programme is to contribute to the development of research, supervisory and educational competencies with a view to establishing a future own RUIICAY PhD programme in intercultural communication and media studies. In 2018, URACCAN – with the partnership of OsloMet in the curriculum design process – initiated its first PhD programme in intercultural studies. Of the 18 participants in the programme, five are from RUIICAY-affiliated universities.

- The Base Document for the Cultivation and Nurture of Wisdom and Knowledge (CCRISAC). This document articulates the best practices of URACCAN, UAIIN and UCINPI-AW/PAW in doing indigenous and intercultural community research. The document was developed as a guide to doing research, particularly master's students' thesis research. Currently, CCRISAC has been mainstreamed by UAIIN and is underway at URACCAN and UCINPI-AW/PAW, adapted to each unique sociocultural context and related careers. A second edition was developed in 2018 to guide relevant doctoral programme research.
- A body of knowledge contributing to inter-epistemic dialogue has been generated. The master's and PhD students' thesis research presents relatively deep insight into indigenous and Afro-descendant peoples' wisdom and knowledge systems, especially in the practice of own and intercultural communication that reinvigorates social and community cohesion, collective action and the struggle for autonomy. The research results also seek to strengthen the work of the universities' intercultural communication academics. These results have been shared in various conferences in Norway, Nicaragua, Colombia, Ecuador, Bolivia, Mexico and Paraguay. In addition, the academic articles have been disseminated, in printed and open-access formats, to the wider academic world.
- The establishment of intercultural communication laboratories in the three Latin-American partner universities. These laboratories enhance education, research and social-community linkage activities through ample production of audiovisual materials, making more visible indigenous and Afro-descendant peoples' reality and struggles, and university work. Students, faculty staff, community communicators and leaders are the main users of these live sociocultural dialogue and academic spaces.
- The partners' intercultural communication researchers and educators have also been linked to relevant global academic and educator networks by the Norhed project. During the lifespan of the project, the partner universities organised five conferences. The first international intercultural communication conference was held in Managua, Nicaragua, from 27 to 29 May 2015. The second, titled

'Global journalism and education: A diversity of voices', was organised by OsloMet in Oslo, from 5 to 6 October 2015. The third conference was the regional encounter 'Quality assurance of intercultural higher education: Toward building for institutional strengthening'. This Latin-American conference, held in Managua, Nicaragua, from 27 to 29 April 2016, focused on the accreditation of indigenous, intercultural and community universities. The fourth conference, the international forum 'Indigenous and Afro-descendant peoples and higher education in Latin America', was organised by UCINPI-AW/PAW and held in Quito, Ecuador, on 24 November 2017. The fifth conference was the second international intercultural conference held at UAIIN, Colombia, from 17 to 19 October 2018.

In addition, the partner universities' academic staff participated in the Norhed conference 'Knowledge for development' (Oslo, 6–7 June 2016), the International Association for Media and Communication Research Conference (Cartagena, Colombia, 16 to 20 July 2017), the Regional Latin America Higher Education Conference (Cordoba, Argentina, 11–14 June 2018) and the tenth Nordic Latin American Research Network conference (OsloMet, Oslo, 25–26 October 2018).

RUIICAY advancement

Since 2000, indigenous and Afro-descendant peoples have significantly improved inclusive higher education through the establishment of their own indigenous, intercultural and community universities. These universities are a very important milestone in the exercise of rights to education and the democratisation of access to higher education in Latin America. At the forefront of this breakthrough to inclusivity is RUIICAY, whose member universities have led the development of relevant careers and curriculum content, pedagogical and research approaches and methodologies to strengthen the autonomy and well-being of indigenous and Afro-descendant peoples. Table 13.2 summarises enrolment and graduation at RUIICAY universities for the period 2017–2018.

Table 13.2: Student enrolment and graduation at RUIICAY universities, 2017–2018

No.	University	Total careers	Student enrolment			Total graduates
			Total	Indigenous	Afro-descendant	
1	URACCAN	39	9 890	2 404	549	7 155
2	UAIIN	12	831	831	–	78
3	PAW	7	267	237	30	270
4	UNIBOL Quechua	4	500	500	–	420
5	UNIBOL Aymara	4	471	471	–	808
6	UNIBOL Guarani	4	545	545	–	250
7	UNISUR	5	200	150	50	300
8	Ixil University	3	112	112	–	35
9	IESI	3	800	800	–	388
10	OPINUP	216	63 091	12 000	–	166 656
	Total	**297**	**76 707**	**18 050**	**629**	**176 360**

Over the last few years, to complement a diverse career portfolio at bachelor degree level, RUIICAY has immersed itself in developing post-graduate studies. The joint RUIICAY academic platform has established an academic offer of five master's degree programmes: in intercultural health, in sexual and reproductive health, in development with identity, in worldviews on good living and in intercultural communication. These programmes have contributed to the development of education and research competences among member universities' faculty staff. A total of 123 students have graduated, including 71 females. In addition to faculty staff, these graduates include indigenous and Afro-descendant leaders from most Latin American countries. The Norhed project has contributed 45 graduates, through the International Master's Programme in Intercultural Communication.

As mentioned in the previous section, the Norhed programme co-ordinated five of the nine international conferences organised or participated in, together with RUIICAY. In addition, the rectors of RUIICAY-affiliated universities participated in the Regional Latin American Higher Education Conference (CRES 2018). A total of approximately 750 participants attended these conferences, the aims of which were mainly to share knowledge, to advocate for rights and recognition and to promote networking and strategic alliances. In the case of CRES 2018, the following acknowledgements in the final declaration (IESALC-Unesco 2018) are noteworthy:

- Education, science, technology and arts must be a means towards freedom and equality, without any distinction (ethnic or racial).
- Higher education systems ought to be 'painted in many colours', recognising interculturality as a way to equality and social upward mobility.
- Higher education policies and institutions must contribute proactively to dismantling all mechanisms that cause racism, sexism, xenophobia, and all other forms of intolerance and discrimination.
- It is mandatory to recognise and value the epistemologies, modes of learning and institutional arrangements of indigenous and Afro-descendant peoples.

RUIICAY also functions as a mutual academic, administrative and political support strategic alliance. Rectors and faculty staff constantly exchange best practices and lessons learned when tackling the need for institutional strengthening on issues such as intercultural curricular design, intercultural research approaches and methodologies, academic management, social and political advocacy, the praxis of an intercultural gender perspective, project financial management and international co-operation. Approximately 50 faculty staff have participated in various exchange and mutual support activities. The Norhed programme facilitated valuable opportunities for URACCAN to support UAIIN and UCINPI-AW/PAW. Being the first community intercultural university in Latin America, URACCAN plays a leading role in the institutional strengthening of partner universities, including the accreditation and certification of courses in Ecuador and Colombia. URACCAN has also lobbied higher education and accreditation agencies for the recognition of UAIIN and UCINPI-AW/PAW in these countries.

Constraints and challenges

In spite of the social innovation and impact of RUIICAY's work, member universities are continually antagonised in the majority of countries. There are noticeable examples. In Guatemala, the national constitution established the San Carlos University as the only public state university in the country. But the peace accords signed between the state and the guerrillas on 29 December 1996 included the recognition and strengthening of the Maya and other indigenous peoples' education systems, including higher education (Botón 2015). The fulfilment of the right to indigenous, intercultural higher education institutions is still pending. The Ixil Indigenous University, for example, is an initiative functioning without state recognition. Their degrees are accredited by foreign universities (Nicaragua).

Since 2007, UNISUR has experienced a similar struggle in Mexico for recognition in the Guerrero state. In contrast, the Mexican state has founded more than ten intercultural universities to attend to the demands of indigenous and Afro-descendant peoples for higher education. A major criticism of this initiative, however, is its disconnection from indigenous and Afro-descendant communities' self-development and good-living processes. In the case of Bolivia, the three indigenous universities (UNIBOL) were established in 2008 by indigenous President Evo Morales through a presidential decree. The major constraint of these universities is their sustainability, since they are not incorporated into the formal higher education system of the country. So far, President Evo Morales has not obtained the needed votes to reform higher education law.

During the lifespan of the Norhed project, partner universities in Ecuador and Colombia faced key challenges. In Ecuador, the Rafael Correa government (2007–2017) closed UCINPI-AW in 2014 through the Council for Evaluation, Accreditation and Quality Assurance of Higher Education (CEAACES). The external evaluation carried out by CEAACES excluded the intercultural factors, criteria and indicators required by the national constitution and relevant by-laws. The National Supreme Court of Justice declared the evaluation and its results unconstitutional. However, CEAACES did not re-open the university in compliance with the court decision. In 2017, Lenin Moreno was elected president of Ecuador and embarked on extensive dialogue with indigenous peoples. One important issue tackled was the re-opening of UCINPI-AW/PAW with adequate public funding, which is underway.

In Colombia, the Regional Indigenous Council of Cauca (CRIC) maintained the recognition of UAIIN, which had been a long-standing demand. In October 2017, CRIC organised a mass rally of resistance (*minga*) for territory, dignity and the fulfilment of agreements. Despite the violence it evoked, this rally managed to reach important agreements, which are contained in decree 1811-2017. Among the agreements are the recognition of UAIIN by the Ministry of Higher Education and that of 47 degree titles issued by URACCAN to UAIIN students. Significant progress towards such recognition was made during 2018. On the contrary, in Nicaragua, the sociopolitical crisis has meant a reduction of approximately 20 per cent in the state-provided budget to URACCAN. In all these instances, the social mobilisation capacity of indigenous and Afro-descendant peoples has been an active force in defending the legitimacy of these universities. International co-operation and support is also an important enabling factor for academic, advocacy and linkage activities.

Objections to indigenous and Afro-descendant peoples having or advancing their own universities are various. In the case of Bolivia's indigenous universities, former president Victor Hugo Cardenas considered that such initiatives reflected an ethnically ideologised discourse and that what is really needed is to fully open conventional universities to diversity (Vaca 2009). In the case of Colombia, Calvo and Garcia (2013) argue that the state – through the Ministry of Education – has used centralisation, regulation and normalisation to control the nature of resistance and social struggle inherent in indigenous and Afro-descendants peoples' higher education initiatives, even when linked to conventional universities. In doing so, the state segregates these initiatives, confining them to a small ethnic space that does not allow diversity to permeate into the whole higher education system.

Main outcomes and results

The HIOA-RUIICAY Intercultural Linkage Programme facilitated a notable journey towards strengthened autonomy for indigenous and Afro-desencant peoples. Autonomy is important for the achievement of a decent, good living, bounded to a collectivity, a territory, traditional health practices and pertinent, own education, permanently reaffirmed through resistance to hegemony and the defence of life and intercultural communication (Cuji 2017). In this sense, university autonomy is a first, key dimension to be strengthened. The development of institutional capacities has allowed URACCAN, UAIIN and UCINPI-AW/PAW to further realise their vision, mission and autonomous education model in accordance with RUIICAY strategic aims and the struggle of indigenous and Afro-descendant peoples. According to Baronnet (2013), an autonomous education produces pertinent sociocultural, economic and political contents and pedagogies. It does so by reproducing or revitalising historical memoirs, subjectivities, knowledge, wisdoms, values and collective aspirations that strengthen cultural identity and self-esteem, empower people to exercise their rights, and diminish cultural discrimination, racism and inequalities.

As a result of the Norhed project, URACCAN, UAIIN and UCINPI-AW/PAW have strengthened their autonomy as dynamic motors of cultural revitalisation and intercultural, collective empowerment. The syllabus of the International Master's Programme in Intercultural Communication with a Gender Focus is a good example. The academic modules, participating academic staff and academic encounters launched students into processes of discovering and recovering relevant local knowledge systems, spiritualities, collective values, relationships and practices. In the process, the classroom becomes a space where local and traditional knowledge is articulated and complemented by Western and Eurocentric knowledge in the pursuit of significant and useful learning. This is in line with contributing to an epistemological pluralism and the building of a just knowledge society.

Furthermore, CCRISAC was key in promoting a pro-active inter-epistemological dialogue among students, tutors, community leaders and wise men and women, and occidental perspectives and literature. To this end, every student was required to commit to participation in community work and traditions, harmonisation rituals and rallies (*minga*) as part of their research process (De la Cruz 2017). This helped to ensure a holistic, experiential and transcendent learning experience for students, based on the local realities and culture of indigenous and Afro-descendant peoples, and contribute to intercultural academia. For example, at UAIIN, the *Tul* – a space for the collective formation and generation of knowledge through dialogue led by spiritual leaders and elders – is mainstream in its institutional pedagogic approach and methodologies (Daquilema 2017). An ancestral, cultural practice of indigenous peoples, families use the *Tul* to transmit and generate knowledge through sowing different type of plants (Chocué 2017). In this way, the land and Mother Earth is cherished as a life giver.

A dialogue with and respect for the spirits of plants, nature and ancestors is developed through the *Tul*. The 'technicalities' and mathematics of plant cultivation is learned, including how plants are related to nutrition, healing, spiritual harmonisation and overall well-being. A wider understanding of the interconnectivity of life (material and spiritual) is taught, discussed and actively lived. In this ancestral teaching method, the use of different indigenous languages stresses prestige and pride in everyday life, whether in education spaces, communities or the outside world (Puama 2017). As a consequence, these universities are not forming selfish individuals, but autonomous collective beings committed to the common good and loyal towards indigenous and Afro-descendant peoples' culture and struggle.

The strengthening of URACCAN, UAIIN and UCINPI-AW/PAW, through the Norhed intercultural communication project, bolsters the present and future struggle of RUIICAY for the effective exercise of indigenous and Afro-descendant peoples' human and citizen rights in the various countries of the region. The 45 intercultural communicators who graduated are a vital asset in propagating the struggle for recognition, autonomy and well-being. Prepared to be educators and researchers in such transformational processes, the students were also politically prepared as potential present and future leaders for the advancement of autonomy. They learned about, conceptualised and re-conceptualised the rights, history and culture of indigenous and

Afro-descendant peoples, as well as best practices in the struggle for autonomy. This is consistent with a pedagogy of resistance and autonomy (Tenorio 2017). In addition, the intercultural and inter-epistemic dialogues established by the project through the different conferences paved the way for RUIICAY's increasing recognition, alliances and agreements. This was particularly the case in the network's participation in CRES 2018.

In some Latin American countries, autonomy is framed by a rich corpus of specific laws and by-laws. Nevertheless, the constraints imposed by political parties and local elites have resulted in conflicts, divisions, mistrust and disillusion among indigenous, Afro-descendant and other vulnerable peoples, severely weakening participation and unity in diversity (Calderón 2017; Velásquez 2017). RUIICAY's indigenous, intercultural and community universities have become strongholds of resistance and struggle for the exercise of rights and spirituality. The road to autonomy requires constant inner strength and building of harmony, and as spiritual spaces, the universities make it possible for spiritual leaders, traditional healers, elders and others to transmit their knowledge and wisdoms, guiding the new generations toward a life in harmony with Mother Earth and other human beings (Ruiz 2017).

Conclusion

In Latin America, indigenous, intercultural and community universities represent an important trend in the transformation of higher education. Never before has higher education been so closely linked to societal transformation needs, as proclaimed by the Cordoba Reform. The different academic models implemented by these universities seek to empower young, talented indigenous and Afro-descendant people to realise their dreams as a collectivity through appropriate careers, academic endeavour and activities that will directly and positively impact on the fulfilment of rights, autonomy and well-being for all in their communities (Garcia 2017). Authorities have been challenged to deviate from Eurocentric frameworks, procedures and instruments in the national recognition, quality assurance and accreditation processes, which have so far been a constraining force. The contribution of indigenous, intercultural and community universities, rather than their non-conformance to conventional and hegemonic academic models, is what really needs to be emphasised (Torrez 2017). It is only in this way that higher education can contribute to positive social change in accordance with constitutional precepts.

In advancing autonomy and rights praxis, intercultural communication plays a strategic and facilitating role. Intercultural communication, as an advocacy, inter-epistemic and dialogue possibility across cultures and ethnicities, contributes to an enabling public imaginary, collective action, unity in diversity and a virtuous cycle of autonomy building. Autonomy (or self-determination) is a road to a better life based on indigenous and Afro-descendant peoples' visions, aspirations, worldviews and (resilience) capacities (Reyes 2017). RUIICAY – through the Norhed project and URACCAN, UAIIN and UCINPI-AW/PAW work – has advanced significantly in developing academic competences (in education and research) in intercultural communication. This area intermingles with other academic areas to potentiate indigenous, Afro-descendant and other vulnerable peoples' struggle for recognition and rights.

About the author and the project

José Luis Saballos Velásquez is a project director at Norhed and Director for External Cooperation at the University of the Autonomous Regions of the Caribbean Coast of Nicaragua (URACCAN)

Project title: The RUIICAY-HIOA Intercultural Communication Linkage Programme
Partner institutions: University of the Autonomous Regions of the Caribbean Coast of Nicaragua (Nicaragua), the Autonomous Indigenous Intercultural University (Colombia), the Indigenous Community Intercultural University of the Nationalities and Indigenous Peoples 'Amawtay Wasi' (Ecuador) and the Oslo Metropolitan University (Norway)

References

Baronnet B (2013) La autonomía como condición para la educación intercultural. In: SE Hernandez Loeza, MI Ramirez Duque, Y Manjarrez Martinez and A Flores Rosas (eds) *Educación Intercultural a Nivel Superior: Reflexiones desde diversas realidades Latinoamericanas*. Puebla, México: Universidad Intercultural del Estado de Puebla

Botón S (2015, 9 March) Guatemala: Se levanta la Universidad Ixil, sobre cenizas de la represión militar. *TeleSUR*. Available online

Calderón N (2017) Autonomía regional desde los pueblos costeños en Nicaragua. Informe de entrevistas. Maestría Internacional en Comunicación Intercultural con Enfoque de Género, URACCAN, Quito, Ecuador

Calvo GF and Garcia Bravo W (2013) Revisión crítica de la etnoeducación en Colombia. *Historia de la Educación: Revista Interuniversitaria* (32): 343–350

CEPAL (United Nations Economic Commission for Latin America and the Caribbean) (2014) *Los Pueblos Indígenas en América Latina. Avances en el Último Decenio y Retos Pendientes para la Garantía de Sus Derechos*. Santiago, Chile: CEPAL

CEPAL (2017) *Situación de las Personas Afrodescendientes en América Latina y Desafíos de Políticas para la Garantía de Sus Derechos*. Santiago, Chile: CEPAL

Chocué A (2017) El Tul en los procesos de autonomía en la Universidad Autónoma Indígena Intercultural-UAIIN. Informe de entrevista. Maestría Internacional en Comunicación Intercultural con Enfoque de Género, URACCAN, Quito, Ecuador

Córdova P (2003) Interculturalidad y dialogismo. In: N Vigil and R Zariquiey (eds) *Ciudadanías Inconclusas: El ejercicio de los derechos en sociedad Asimétricas*. Lima, Perú: Pontificia Universidad Católica del Perú

Cuji M (2017) La autonomía de los pueblos indígenas. Informe de entrevista. Maestría Internacional en Comunicación Intercultural con Enfoque de Género, URACCAN, Quito, Ecuador

Daquilema I (2017) Situación actual de la educación superior intercultural de los pueblos indígenas en Colombia. Informe de entrevista. Maestría Internacional en Comunicación Intercultural con Enfoque de Género, URACCAN, Quito, Ecuador

De la Cruz A (2017) Elementos simbólicos comunicacionales del matrimonio ancestral. Informe de entrevista. Maestría Internacional en Comunicación Intercultural con Enfoque de Género, URACCAN, Quito, Ecuador

Del Popolo F (2017) *Los Pueblos Indígenas en América (Abya Yala): Desafíos para la igualdad en la diversidad*. Santiago, Chile: CEPAL

Etxeberria X (2003) La ciudadanía de la interculturalidad. In: N Vigil and R Zariquiey (eds), *Ciudadanías Inconclusas: El ejercicio de los derechos en sociedades Asimétricas*. Lima, Perú: Pontificia Universidad Católica del Perú

Garcia Y (2017) El proceso de lucha de la RUIICAY. Informe de entrevista. Maestría Internacional en Comunicación Intercultural con Enfoque de Género, URACCAN, Quito, Ecuador

Gasché J (2014) La motivación política de la educación intercultural indígena y sus exigencias pedagógicas ¿Hasta dónde abarca la interculturalidad? In: J Gasché, M Bertely and R Podesta (eds) *Educando en la Diversidad: Investigaciones y experiencias educativas interculturales y bilingües*. México: Paidos

Hooker Blandford AS (2015) Interculturalidad desde la perspectiva de la Red de Universidades Indígenas, Interculturales y Comunitarias de Aba Yala, RUIICAY. *Revista Caribe* 15(2): 8–11

IESALC (International Institute for Higher Education in Latin America and the Caribbean)-Unesco (2018) Declaración. Paper presented at the IIIa Conferencia Regional de educación Superior para América Latina y el Caribe, Cordoba, Argentina, 11–15 June 2018

Mato D (2008) Actualizar los postulados de la reforma universitaria de 1918. Las universidades deben valorar la diversidad cultural y promover relaciones interculturales equitativas y mutuamente respetuosas. In: E Sader, P Gentili and H Aboites (eds) *La Reforma Universitaria: Desafío y perspectivas noventa años después*. Buenos Aires: Consejo Latinoamericano de Ciencias Sociales

Mato D (2016) Educación superior y pueblos indígenas y afrodescendientes en América Latina. Interpelaciones, avances, problemas, conflictos y desafíos. In: D Mato (ed.) *Educación Superior y Pueblos Indígenas en América Latina: Experiencias, interpelaciones y desafíos*. Buenos Aires, Argentina: EDUNTREF

OHCHR (Office of the United Nations High Commissioner for Human Rights) (2013) *The United Nations Declarations on the Rights of Indigenous Peoples. A Manual for National Human Rights Institutions*. Geneva, Switzerland: OHCR and APF (Asia Pacific Forum of National Human Rights Institutions)

PAW (Pluriversidad 'Amawtay Wasi') (2017) *La Pluriversidad 'Amawtay Wasi'. El Gran Camino de los Aprendizajes*. Quito, Ecuador: PAW

Puama H (2017) El prestigio de las lenguas indígenas. Informe de entrevista. Maestría Internacional en Comunicación Intercultural con Enfoque de Género, URACCAN, Quito, Ecuador

Rama C (2006) La tercera reforma de la educación superior en América Latina y el Caribe: Masificación, regulaciones e internacionalización. In: Unesco-IESALC *Informe Sobre la Educación Superior en América Latina y el Caribe 2000–2005*. Buenos Aires, Argentina: Fondo de Cultura Económica.

Reyes L (2017) URACCAN es hija del proceso de autonomía regional en Nicaragua. Informe de entrevista. Maestría Internacional en Comunicación Intercultural con Enfoque de Género, URACCAN, Quito, Ecuador

RUIICAY (2015) *Cultivo y Crianza de Sabidurias y Conocimientos* (CCRISAC). Managua, Nicaragua: URACCAN

RUIICAY (2017) *Nuestro Camino Recorrido en la Construcción de la Educación Superior Intercultural*. Managua, Nicaragua: URACCAN

Ruiz S (2017) El camino de la autonomía desde los sitios sagrados. Informe de entrevista. Maestria Internacional en Comunicación Intercultural con Enfoque de Género, URACCAN, Quito, Ecuador

Saballos Velásquez JL (2016) La universidad y la efectividad del desarrollo comunitario. Hacia un modelo integral de promoción de la apropiación comunitaria en las regiones autónomas de Nicaragua. Doctorado Internacional en Estudios del Desarrollo Doctorado, Universidad del País Vasco, Bilbao, España

Tenorio D (2017) Hacia una pedagogía de pervivencia de los pueblos desde los procesos de formación, en el marco de la interculturalidad y la autonomía. Informe de entrevista. Maestría Internacional en Comunicación Intercultural con Enfoque de Género, URACCAN, Quito, Ecuador

Torrez D (2017) Los caminos del diálogo. Informe de entrevista. Maestría Internacional en Comunicación Intercultural con Enfoque de Género, URACCAN, Quito, Ecuador

UN (2017) *International Decade for Peoples of African Descent 2016–2024*. New York: OHCHR

URACCAN, OsloMet, UAIIN and UCINPI-AW (2013) *HIOA-RUIICAY Intercultural Communication Project*. Managua, Nicaragua: URACCAN

Vaca M (2009, April 13) Bolivia: Universidades sólo para indígenas. *BBC News Mundo*

Velásquez J (2017) Autonomía regional y desvalorización del sentido de comunitariedad. Informe de entrevista. Maestría Internacional en Comunicación Intercultural con Enfoque de Género, URACCAN, Quito, Ecuador

14

Linguistic capacity building in Ethiopia: Results and challenges

Derib Ado Jekale, Binyam Sisay Mendisu
& Janne Bondi Johannessen

In this chapter we describe our project and analyse its impacts from the perspective of a human development approach to linguistic citizenship. A large number of languages are used as mother tongues in Ethiopia, but many have not been sufficiently developed in written form. This is a problem for the education system (and goes against Unesco's advocacy for multilingual education since 1953) as well as for democracy, as large groups of people do not get necessary information concerning their civil rights. The problem also contradicts the Ethiopian constitution, which states that people have the right to learn in their own language.

The linguistic capacity-building (LCB) project was intended to increase the number of languages that can be used in schools and local administration in Ethiopia. The project attempted to contribute to the United Nations Sustainable Development Goals (SDGs), specifically via SDG 4 (quality education) and SDG 5 (gender equality). However, the use of mother tongue in communication between people and authorities is a basic and democratic issue, and has probably impacted positively on all the other goals, too. For example, it is vital that people can read and understand health information given by the authorities if SDG 3 (good health and well-being) is to be attained.

The chapter starts with a brief description of the sociolinguistic context of Ethiopia, followed by an explanation of the conceptual framework for the project and the methodology used. We then present the why and the how of our linguistic capacity-building activities, and the preliminary results. We had anticipated a number of challenges, and taken measures to meet them. However, unanticipated challenges influenced the project in various ways. The next section examines both the anticipated and the unforeseen challenges and how we dealt with them and this is followed by a discussion of how we have attempted to ensure sustainability. Our conclusion is framed by two questions:

- How relevant are the LCB project activities to the achievement of particularly SDGs 4 and 5?
- What can be learned from the implementation of the LCB project for future North–South and South–South co-operation?

Ethiopia's sociolinguistic context

Ethiopia, situated on the Horn of Africa, is home to several ethnic groups, between them speaking about 90 languages. From the thirteenth century until the fall of the Derg regime in 1991, the country covertly followed a monolingual language policy favouring Amharic (Cohen 2000; Getachew and Derib 2006; Zelealem 2012). The Ethiopian Peoples' Revolutionary Democratic Front (EPRDF), who took over power from the Derg, put in place a federal system built on ethnicity, with divisions based mainly on the languages that are spoken in the country. The constitution of the Federal Democratic Republic of Ethiopia (FDRE), ratified in 1994, gives all linguistic groups the rights to use and to develop their languages for whatever purposes they want.

Following the provisions of the constitution, several languages became official languages of the regional states. Afar, Harari, Oromo, Somali and Tigrinya became official languages of the regional states where they are primarily spoken. Amharic became the official working language of the federal government as well as of three heterogeneous regional states. Besides serving as the official language of the Amhara National Regional State, Amharic has remained the working language of the federal government, but is no longer a national or official language. The Education and Training Policy (FDRE 1994), promulgated in the same year as the constitution, stipulated that primary school children should be taught in their mother tongue, given the positive pedagogical implications. Since the introduction of the policy, about 50 languages have become either a medium of instruction, or are offered as subjects, or are serving both purposes in primary schools throughout Ethiopia (FDRE Ministry of Culture and Tourism 2015). However, only Amharic and Tigrinya had stable orthographies. Orthographies for all other languages in the education system had to be designed and textbooks prepared within a short period of time and with whatever human resources were available. Orthographies were thus designed in haste, with noticeable problems as a result.

Poor preparation, lack of resources and lack of trained personnel are the main challenges in employing mother-tongue education. In recent research conducted to evaluate the reading ability of students in primary schools in selected regions, it was found that more than half could not read at all, or their reading skills were below the minimum standard required (RTI International 2010). While there are several factors contributing to these poor results, one of them is the lack of mother-tongue teaching material and of people with appropriate skills in mother-tongue education.

The situation for Ethiopian Sign Language is worse. It is the only language that has been recognised by name in the constitution, yet there are no resources to help the deaf integrate in schools, in the workplace, or in public service. At the time of writing, the only BA programme in the country that offers training on Ethiopian Sign Language is at Addis Ababa University.

Conceptual framework and methodology

Poverty in Africa is associated with lack of successful 'development communication' which 'is closely linked to the language factor in education' (Wolff 2006: 54). Ekkehard Wolff (2006: 50) succinctly summarises the importance of the language factor: 'Language is not everything in education, but without language everything is nothing in education.' The importance of language goes far beyond education and identity. Language is seen as a means through which we view the world: 'all observers are not led by the same physical evidence to the same picture of the universe, unless their linguistic backgrounds are similar, or can in some way be calibrated' (Whorf 1956: 214). Yet the language policy of African countries has been influenced by politics, the economy and ideology rather than pedagogical and epistemological considerations (Ball 2010; Ferguson 2013). In multi-ethnic countries such as Ethiopia, language is a means of power and access to social and economic benefits.

Language is central to the well-being of individuals and societies. Article 3 of the Universal Declaration of Linguistic Rights (1996)[1] asserts that individuals have

> the right to the use of one's own language both in private and in public; the right for their own language and culture to be taught; the right of access to cultural services; the right to an equitable presence of their language and culture in the communications media; the right to receive attention in their own language from government bodies and in socioeconomic relations.

The main criterion for measuring the level of development of a nation is now considered to be the well-being of its people, rather than its income per capita, GDP or other resource-based computations:

> Human development is development of the people through the building of human resources, for the people through the translation of development benefits in their lives and by the people through active participation in the processes that influence and shape their lives. Income is a means to human development but not an end in itself. (UNDP 2016: 25)

According to an estimate made in 2012, 40 per cent of the world's population, that is, close to 2.3 billion people, do not have access to education in the language they know best. A recurring obstacle that is retarding Africa's progress towards achieving quality, access and equity in education is the language-of-instruction predicament. With its close to 2 000 languages, Africa is one of the most linguistically diverse regions of the world. However, this diversity and multilingualism are rarely reflected in educational systems across the continent. For the majority of African children who are enrolled in schools, the language used at home and the language used at school are different. This creates a disconnect between home and school, and then inhibits students from active class participation, learning and educational success. This in turn creates a major obstacle to learning and leads to high levels of repetition and drop-out.

In general, regionally dominant African languages and/or European languages such as English, French and Portuguese are languages of instruction employed in many primary schools in Africa. This puts children who have no or limited knowledge of these dominant languages at a great disadvantage as it seriously hinders learning. In addition, research has revealed that the detrimental effect of such policies and practices is twice as great for girls and economically and socially marginalised children as it is for others. Nonetheless, there are some African countries, such as Ethiopia and South Africa, that are actively promoting the use of many African languages in schools, which has yielded encouraging results. Even these countries have a number of challenges and need continuous support to meet the necessary targets, given that education is a complex process that requires long-term investment, preparation and political commitment.

Unesco recognised the importance of mother-tongue and multilingual education more than half a century ago with the publication of a monograph in 1953, clearly stating that

> it is axiomatic that the best medium for teaching a child is his mother tongue. Psychologically, it is the system of meaningful signs that in his mind works automatically for expression and understanding. Sociologically, it is a means of identification among members of the community to which he belongs. Educationally, he learns more quickly through it than through an unfamiliar linguistic medium. (Unesco 1953: 11)

Unesco reiterated its strong support for the relevance of mother-tongue education with the publication of another monograph in 2003: 'Education in a Multilingual World'. Alongside these high-profile, global recognitions, a great deal of evidence in support of aligning home and school language has been published by linguists and educators. Amidst all of this evidence and support, however, one problem persists: practice lags behind theory. After six decades of global recognition and scholarly support, the implementation of mother-tongue education is still either non-existent or in its infancy in several African countries.

Building the capacity of languages is clearly connected with strengthening the capacity of speakers to be informed, to preserve their cultural identity and to empower them in various ways. Thus, linguistic capacity building is directly related to empowering speakers to exercise their human rights. The capacity-building efforts in this project were therefore linked to the concepts of linguistic human rights and linguistic citizenship. We worked with the notion of linguistic citizenship as proposed by Stroud (2001, 2002) specifically to extend the concept of linguistic human rights, as the latter focuses more on the politics of recognition. Linguistic citizenship puts the issue of language at the centre of citizenship discourse and takes very seriously the material and economic implications of using languages in different contexts.

We consider capacity building to be a major means of developing human resources and contributing to overall human development, and language is a central element in achieving that. In a document prepared by the UNDP (2009: 1), capacity building is described as 'the process through which individuals, organisations, and societies obtain, strengthen and maintain the capabilities to set and achieve their own development objectives over time'. Since the LCB project was a South–North collaboration, we paid special attention to the ways in which the partnership between the two sides was forged and how responsibilities in building capacity were distributed. In this regard, it is worth noting that the way knowledge is used for development in North–South collaborations has always been controversial. As Koch and Weingart (2016: 10) state: 'The idea that the North could solve the problems of the South by exporting its expertise and technology seemed increasingly obsolete.' Some of the major issues in this debate include the role and place of local knowledge and expertise in such collaborations, and the much-needed shift from concepts such as 'knowledge transfer' to 'knowledge exchange'. Although a lot of improvement has been made in defining what a win-win partnership should look like, practice seems to lag behind. In relation to this, Koch and Weingart (2016: 11) write that 'the discursive shifts, however, have not (yet) substantially changed international co-operation – neither in terms of power relations nor with regard to the use of expertise'. We attempt to investigate the type of partnership built among the partners in the North and South in light of the issues raised above about the use of knowledge for development.

This chapter is mostly based on the reflections of the authors, as we were all involved in the planning and implementation stages of the LCB project. The major data for the activities are derived from the annual reports submitted to the Norwegian Agency for Development Cooperation (Norad) and observations recorded in the various fieldwork and networking workshops that the authors participated in during the period 2014 to 2017.

Project goals: Capacity building through collaboration

The desired long-term impact of the LCB project was that there should be increased resources and opportunities for all speakers of disadvantaged spoken and signed languages to use their mother tongue in Ethiopia. In order to achieve this long-term goal, a major goal of the LCB project was to capacitate higher education institutions (HEIs) to produce staff and students with the competence to implement language resources, and standardisation for marginalised languages – including sign language – for the benefit of Ethiopia and its people.

Transfer of knowledge through PhD and master's programmes

Since Ethiopia started expanding the policy of mother-tongue education introduced in the 1990s, training linguists in the country has become crucial in order to develop orthographies for languages without a writing system. There are few resources for literacy development in almost all languages introduced into the education system, except for the textbooks prepared by local experts who received no training in the field of materials development for literacy. This giant task of orthography and materials development could not be completed with the limited faculty staff at Addis Ababa University (AAU) and Hawassa University (HU) who are also involved in teaching and research. There was a dire need to train people who could work full time in this area and also those who could train such experts.

A core desired output of the LCB project was thus trained human power in the different sub-branches of linguistics, at MA and PhD level, in order to fill the gap in the human resources needed for language development tasks. The aim of the LCB's support for this training was twofold. On one hand, the subjects of study supported by the project were to be languages and sociolinguistic phenomena that had so far been given little attention – such as the grammatical descriptions that could be used as input in preparing pedagogical grammars for those languages. On the other hand, the trained linguists were to be involved in further training of linguists who would join the workforce of the regional education bureaus and research institutions to work full time in language development activities.

With these aims in mind, the two South partners – HU and AAU – collaborated to launch an MA programme in Linguistics and Communication at HU in 2014. Since the launch of the programme, more than 40 students have been enrolled and of these, so far 13 have been supported either fully or partially through the project. This support includes fees, subsistence, laptops and financial assistance for fieldwork. Staff from AAU participated in the development of the curriculum and in joint teaching of courses in the newly launched programme. AAU was also involved in the joint examination of the MA students. This South–South partnership was extended to include joint capacity-building training, joint networking workshops and joint publications. Knowledge exchange and capacity development between partners in the South was also key to nurturing linguistic capacity, as different institutions have different experiences and expertise and have much to learn from each other.

In addition, HU is now in the process of launching a PhD programme in Applied Linguistics, again with the help of AAU. The programme has been approved by the university but has not yet been launched due to the need to get a certain number of staff up to the level of associate professor. The result of the increased collaboration between the two universities fostered by the LCB project, this has become a model for South–South institutional collaboration.

For the past ten years, Addis Ababa University has been running the only BA programme in Ethiopian Sign language and Deaf Culture in the country. The AAU also has a BA programme in Linguistics, as well as an MA programme and a PhD programme in Linguistics. The AAU also wanted to launch a postgraduate programme in sign language linguistics, but has not yet been able to do so due to the lack of trained academic staff to handle the courses. The LCB project is now supporting four students who are working on different linguistic aspects of Ethiopian Sign Language at PhD level (in the AAU Linguistics programme), and who have supervisors at the Norwegian University of Science and Technology (NTNU) through the project. These four, and their work, when completed, will be of great importance to the deaf community as well as researchers, as they will constitute the staff necessary for the MA programme. Two of the PhD candidates have already been involved with the Ministry of Education in preparing textbooks in Ethiopian Sign Language from grades 1 to 12. This is a significant step that will need a lot of resources when the language is to be taught.

An MA programme in Sign Language Linguistics has been developed, but has not yet been ratified by the university body as there are problems related to the restructuring of graduate programmes and extended bureaucracy, as well as the above-mentioned problem related to staff. It is expected that the programme will be launched in the near future. It will be the only one of its kind throughout Ethiopia and will serve as a training ground for those who will be teaching sign language courses in higher institutions of learning. But the most important contribution of the programme will be the trained sign language linguists who will contribute to the study of Ethiopian Sign Language and the preparation of pedagogical resources for teaching the language as a subject, and its use as a medium of instruction at all levels of education. Above all, this will pave the way to reducing inequalities in access to education for the deaf, and improving the quality of their education.

A total of 13 students enrolled in the AAU PhD programme in Linguistics were supported by the LCB project. Gender mainstreaming was taken seriously: the project supported as many female candidates as possible and made every effort to integrate gender issues in all project activities, including the research conducted by students. Of the 13 PhD candidates, five were female – a step towards increasing the number of female academics with PhDs in the country. In terms of specialisation, candidates worked on Ethiopian Sign Language, for which no linguistic description was available, as well as the description of less studied languages such as Aari, Enor, Muher and Nuer; on language contact and secret language; on discourse and on language standardisation. The topics that the candidates worked with were carefully selected to feed into the capacity-building work that was being done on the languages. Nearly all of the candidates were academic staff of three higher education institutions in Ethiopia, namely Addis Ababa, Hawassa and Kotebe Metropolitan universities. The selection of the candidates was done purposefully to build the capacity of Ethiopian universities.

The project's support for PhD and MA students took the form of money for fieldwork and the provision of laptops. PhD students were given online access to the University of Oslo (UiO) library, research visits to the UiO and co-supervision of their PhD dissertation. Such internationalisation of the PhD programme was quite limited before the LCB project started. PhD students had mainly one local supervisor and the graduate seminars irregularly prepared by the department were the only forum they had to present their research.

The students now have the benefit of a forum, created by the project, where they can present their research and even publish it. Such publication by PhD students is a new development and greatly enhances the quality of training given at AAU. Students also get support to participate in local and international conferences which would otherwise have been difficult to achieve, which also helps to build up academic quality. To mention a few examples, only those PhD students who were supported by the project were able to participate in the 46th North American Conference of Afro-Asiatic Linguistics held in the US in May 2018, and the 20th International Conference of Ethiopian Studies held in Mekele, Ethiopia, in October 2018. This shows the project's role in the internationalisation of the PhD programme.

The PhD students in the project had two supervisors each: one from the host institution, AAU, and one from Norway. A series of lectures by the staff of UiO both at both AAU and HU benefited staff and students. This is again another important aspect of the capacity-building process, since students and staff in both the South and the North are expected to benefit from this mutual learning and knowledge exchange. Students go on a research visit to the UiO or the NTNU to help them access resources that otherwise would have been difficult to find in Ethiopia, and to work on their dissertations with their Norwegian supervisors. Their dissertations will be published with support from the project, thus increasing the accessibility of the studies conducted to the wider public. The training of PhD students was one of the core capacity-building activities of the project and various attempts were made to make the capacity development effort sustainable. The fact that students were enrolled in universities in the South (rather than in the North) has been found to be beneficial in developing capacity at many levels, as it gives full recognition to academic institutions in the South and empowers their graduate programmes and their staff. It is obviously also more sustainable and less costly.

Exchange of knowledge through collaborative projects

Two types of collaboration exist in the LCB project: North–South and South–South. The North–South collaboration focuses on the creation of speech and text corpora, whereas the South–South co-operation focuses on training local experts and creating resources such as dictionaries and primers that can be used directly by educators and the target population.

Work on grammatical descriptions, primers and dictionaries benefits greatly from speech and text corpora. They are reusable and once created, they provide low-cost access to linguistic information. At UiO, there is a lot of experience and expertise in developing speech and text corpora and using them in linguistic research. The University developed the corpus search engine called Glossa (Johannessen et al. 2008), which is used for Scandinavian languages, such as for the Nordic Dialect Corpus (Johannessen et al. 2009). AAU, however, despite its strong linguistic programmes had never developed a corpus or used corpora for linguistic research. The LCB project created a platform whereby AAU engaged in corpus development in close co-operation with UiO. The collaborative corpus development started with UiO staff giving lectures on corpus development and the use of corpora, which then progressed into speech data recording and transcription by AAU. AAU and HU have linguists who can collect and transcribe data in the available orthography or in a writing system that is close to phonetic writing for those languages whose orthography is not ready for such work.

Preliminary speech corpora are now available for Hamar, Muher, Gumer, Oromo and Amharic on the UiO website and are accessible for free. Speech corpora for Haddiyyaa and Gamo are under preparation while annotation is continuing for all the speech corpora, which will be extended both within the project and afterwards. The speech corpora are also available for installation on local machines so that lack of an internet connection will not prevent researchers from accessing them.

Text corpora have been created for the four major languages of Ethiopia: Amharic, Oromo, Somali and Tigrinya. The corpora were built by crawling the web, which led to sizeable corpora, though with fewer text types than for many Western languages. Most of the texts are either political or religious, not from blogs and leisure texts. The creation of the text corpora was done in a collaborative effort between the LCB project and the Norwegian-Czech HaBiT project (financed by the European Economic Area), with the University of Masaryk of the Czech Republic taking a leading role (Pala et al. 2017), but with input by Ethiopians and Norwegians during a workshop in Brno in 2017. By joining the efforts of the two projects in this way, we were able to avoid duplication of effort and actually managed to complete creating the corpora well ahead of time.

Like the speech corpora, the text corpora can be accessed on the web and are available for free download. This gives researchers the opportunity to develop the corpora further and utilise them even when internet connection is problematic.

The text corpora have already been used for research purposes by project participants (Feda and Derib 2016). They are also being used in the teaching of a PhD course in lexicography. In the past, when these corpora were not available, students had to rely on corpora available in other languages, mainly English, which of course was not satisfactory when the goal was to study one's own languages. Because of the creation of the corpora, students now have the opportunity to work on Ethiopian languages while learning to make and evaluate dictionaries. Clearly, the LCB project outputs have contributed towards introducing technology, with far-reaching positive effects for future work in lexicography, linguistic research and the preparation of resources for mother-tongue education.

The creation and use of corpora were a new development for the South partners – a successful example of the transfer of knowledge from the North to the South. The South–South collaboration was also a very important component of the project. The collaboration took two forms: collaboration between the HEIs involved in the project (AAU and HU) for the training of MA and PhD students (elaborated in the previous section) and networking between the HEIs and the local authorities and experts (discussed in the next section).

Finally, since the LCB project started, orthographies have been developed for two languages, namely Aari and Hamar. Another orthography has been developed for a group of languages spoken in the Gurage zone of the Southern Nations, Nationalities and Peoples Regional State (SNNPR). These orthographies have been developed by members of the faculty of the two Ethiopian universities involved in the project. There are still more languages needing to be reduced to writing, so the effort continues.

Networking with local authorities

While researchers and teachers at a university can identify problems in a society, there is no more authoritative source for details about the real problem than those who are working on the ground. That is why the LCB project put networking with local authorities and experts at the top of its agenda. When the project was launched, the first task was to organise networking workshops with stakeholders. In these workshops, the objectives of the project were presented to the concerned local authorities and educators and they were asked to prioritise areas of interest and identify gaps that needed to be filled in terms of short-term training, studies and long-term training. These networking workshops resulted in identifying candidates to be trained at MA level at HU, and a series of lectures on the preparation and revision of orthographies, textbooks, primers and dictionaries.

The networking workshops opened the way to a win-win relationship between project members and local authorities. The workshops extended beyond project activities: project members were invited to evaluate primers prepared by local experts and grammars worked out by a third party, and they were invited to participate in the language and culture symposiums held annually. The project also offered special workshops for teachers teaching in deaf schools and short courses on Ethiopian Sign Language. With very few people trained formally in the language, these workshops aimed to develop the capacities of local experts to provide training in Ethiopian Sign Language.

The networking workshops were organised by each of the two South partner institutions in Ethiopia, alone or jointly. The project made continuous efforts to involve local stakeholders at every stage, since their involvement and insight was key to its success. As Koch and Weingart (2016: 10) note, integrating 'local knowledge into transformational processes' is indispensable. And in the context of language planning, 'neither elites nor counterelites are likely to embrace the language planning initiatives of others unless they perceive it to be in their own interest to do so' (Cooper 1989: 183).

It is only through projects such as the LBC that engagement with local experts and authorities becomes possible. Prior to the project, co-operation between universities and local experts and authorities had been very minimal and research decisions were based on the personal motivations of the staff of the two HEIs. The collaboration created by the LCB project has helped refocus research on local issues that have a direct impact on society.

Training local educators

Recognising the fact that the actual work of teaching and learning is done at the local level, the project set out to work with local experts who were involved in mother-tongue education. In order to address problems speedily, and because timely interventions boost social development at the local level, the project used a special training approach, engaging local experts directly and parallel to the formal training at MA and PhD level. The training was based on the needs assessment and prioritisation of tasks identified during the networking workshops discussed in the previous section. Local experts asked for training on textbook preparation, dictionary compilation and primer preparation. Teacher training in textbook preparation and curriculum development in the South Omo Zone of the Southern Nations, Nationalities and Peoples Regional State was instrumental in getting Aari, one of the disadvantaged languages in the project, introduced as a subject language in the two *woredas* (local administrative units) where it is spoken. Aari was introduced as a subject in two steps. First, model schools were selected and the curriculum was implemented in these schools. Based on learning from this experience, the language is now a subject in all 80 primary schools in the two *woredas*. There is a plan to assess the use of orthography, the materials prepared and the overall implementation of the mother-tongue education in Aari during the remaining project period.

In addition, during the project period, a manual on the teaching of Ethiopian Sign Language, written in Amharic, was published by one of the project participants (Pawlos 2015), who is a staff member at Addis Ababa University and a PhD candidate. The book was published thanks to the personal and professional commitment of the author and did not require any special support from the project. This is clear evidence that the support focusing on Ethiopian Sign Language is not just donor-driven but based on deeply felt real needs.

The fact that local educators and authorities had full ownership of introducing their language in the education system and led the initiatives can be explained conceptually, in terms of linguistic citizenship. The LCB project contributed to enabling people to learn their languages, which will pave the way for using their languages in domains where they have previously been unable to use them. This empowers them to become participants in the development and democratisation process.

New language resources supporting corpus planning of Ethiopian languages

Language is a vital issue in Ethiopia. The country's constitution provides for equal recognition of all its languages and the 1994 education and training policy stipulates mother-tongue instruction in primary education. As a result, Ethiopia has been involved in status, corpus and acquisition planning activities since 1991. Once the status of languages was determined, both corpus and acquisition planning activities became the focus of regional education bureaus as there was a need for codification of the languages before textbooks could be prepared. Yet, after more than 20 years, the process is still ongoing: there are still new languages that have to be reduced to writing, and dictionaries are not available for the majority of the languages that have been introduced in the education system.

The LCB project aimed to create resources that could be directly used by local experts as well as students in the mother-tongue education system, as a helping hand in the corpus planning activities. The development of paper-based resources such as grammatical descriptions using the local languages or English, primers and dictionaries for the educators, and electronic resources – mainly speech and text corpora – for the university researchers, were key project outcomes.

Grammatical descriptions: Grammatical descriptions have been created by PhD students and staff participating in the project. Thus the PhD training, apart from building the capacity of the individuals and the institutions they belonged to, helped to create resources that could be used after the project period was over. The grammatical descriptions will be used to prepare pedagogical grammars when the relevant languages are to be taught in the second cycle of primary schools and the secondary schools offering mother-tongue education. In the case of some languages, in which mother-tongue education has already started, courses are now being offered at secondary school level as well (in

Kambaata for example) and a few even at college level (such as Oromo, Haddiyya, Sidama and Wolaita). Descriptions for Aari, Enor, Ethiopian Sign Language, Hamar, and Nuer are in the making. The description of Enor has been done by a PhD student. She is now awaiting her PhD dissertation viva voce. The rest are in progress. When completed and disseminated, they will have a direct impact on the teaching and learning process, helping to enhance the quality of education and ensuring that the target population are able to exercise their linguistic human rights.

Orthographies: Except for the three languages Amharic, Tigrinya and Ge'ez, orthographies for more than 50 languages have been developed in the past 25 years. Most were developed without proper linguistic research and by people with no linguistic expertise. Thus, there was a need to look into these orthographies for issues that need attention. So far, researchers have suggested slight revisions of the orthographies of Sidama and Haddiyya, though the decision to accept the orthographies is that of the local administrations.

New orthographies have been designed for Aari and Hamar. The orthography for Aari has already been implemented as Aari has been introduced as a school subject in two *woredas* of the South Omo Zone where the language is spoken. The orthography of Hamar has been presented to the local administrators (Yigezu and Mendisu 2015) for their approval. These two orthographies are huge contributions to the empowerment of local communities and their overall development in the education system.

An Ethiopic script-based orthography for the Gurage languages was designed by two project members, and has been ratified by the Gurage Zone administration. The orthography was designed for use in several Gurage languages, but has not yet been adopted for use by any of them as the people preferred to use Amharic as a medium of instruction in their schools. Nevertheless, computer science specialists at Wolkite University developed fonts for some of the graphemes that are not supported by current systems. In addition, they even developed a prototype mobile application that helps people to learn Gurage languages.

Primers and dictionaries: Primers and dictionaries provide additional resources for children learning different Ethiopian languages. The primers were written by researchers in the project or by local experts trained by the project or by the joint efforts of both researchers and local experts. So far, the project has published two primers on Kambaata, written by the local experts in Kambaata Zone. A total of 4 000 copies has been handed over to the zone's administration. Further publications include an Aari-English-Amharic dictionary and *Our Voice: Guragina Grammar*. A primer and a dictionary in Gumer are in preparation. It is worth mentioning that the Aari multilingual dictionary was prepared and compiled by local experts in South Omo Zone, with technical support from LCB project academics. In this case, both the process and the output were used to develop local capacity.

While revision of orthographies and grammatical descriptions for disadvantaged languages could have been done without the LCB project, the input that the project has given to the work of language development has been indispensable. The publication of primers, grammars and dictionaries would have been unthinkable without support from the project, in terms of both financial and technical assistance. The grammars that are being produced now also have the additional advantage of being produced with input from the speech corpora that the students developed for these purposes. The forums at which the students present their papers create additional capacity to strengthen their work.

Electronic corpora: Electronic corpora are searchable collections of language, with ample opportunities for representing the results in different ways. Corpora are indispensable for modern linguistics. The LCB project has developed electronic speech corpora (with audio and transcription) for five disadvantaged languages, and written text corpora for four major Ethiopian languages. Work on grammatical descriptions, primers and dictionaries benefits greatly from speech corpora, since they make it possible for linguists other than those who did the recordings to investigate a language. There are now preliminary speech corpora available for Hamar, Muher, Gumer, Oromo and Amharic on the UiO website, and accessible for free. Speech corpora for Haddiyyaa and Gamo are under preparation while annotation is continuing for all the speech corpora, which will be extended both within the project and afterwards. The speech corpora were the results of collaboration between the text laboratory at UiO and the Department of Linguistics and Philology at AAU. Considering the fact that the internet connection in Ethiopia is not always reliable and researchers may not have access to an online corpus any time they need it, the corpora can also be installed on local machines, running on both Windows and Linux operating systems. The final goal is for the partners in the South to increase the size of the corpora and to create their own corpora in the future, using the system developed by the Northern partners.

Academic independence and quality standards

All the PhD and MA programmes are hosted and run in Ethiopia, at AAU and HU. As mentioned earlier in this chapter, the PhD programme in Linguistics has been running at AAU for more than ten years now. It was the aim of the LCB project to strengthen the PhD programme as it was the only one of its kind in the country and its outputs would support ongoing language development activities. In the past, before the launch of the PhD programme, some students who went abroad to study for their PhD did not return, resulting in a brain drain for the local institution. Since the launch of the programme, there is less risk of brain drain.

The LCB project has contributed to academic quality and independence by involving staff in joint PhD supervision and joint publication with staff from Norway. After the launch of the project, staff publication increased noticeably. All involved in the project published at least once with financial support from the project. A jointly edited volume (Binyam and Johannessen 2016) was published as a result of the North–South as well as South–South collaboration. Staff also published in a collective volume (Meyer and Edzard 2016) which was the result of their participation at the 19th International Conference of Ethiopian Studies held in Warsaw, Poland, in 2015. There are publications in progress from another panel at the same conference. The research outputs clearly show the capacity being built and the lasting effect on academic independence and quality standards.

The Norwegian partners gave seminars and public lectures on different topics each year. The seminars were related to the PhD courses offered and the research being conducted in the project. The major focus of the seminars was the use of the corpora for research, lexicography and dictionary preparation, for Semitic morphology and syntax, and for sign language.

The new MA and PhD programmes at AAU and HU will add further to the academic quality of Linguistics in Ethiopia.

Gender mainstreaming

One of the issues introduced by the LCB project was gender mainstreaming. The issue of gender has long been a catch phrase used by national and international agencies working on human resource development. Nevertheless, gender mainstreaming has been difficult to achieve on the ground. In the past ten years, since the PhD programme in Linguistics started at AAU, the number of female PhD graduates has been limited to four out of the 34 graduates. The emphasis given by the project enabled the recruitment of five female PhD candidates out of the 13 PhD candidates supported by the project. Compared to the previous participation of females in the PhD programmes, this was an achievement – a near 50 per cent participation of women. In addition, females were given priority in the MA programme supported by the project, and in cases where there was a shortage of female applicants, all the available female applicants were given a scholarship. A special support system ensured that females did not lag behind males in their studies.

Gender mainstreaming has been an agenda not only in terms of the number of participants, but also in terms of the subject matter studied. Among the PhD dissertations supported by the project, the issue of gender was the main subject of study for one thesis and gender was a variable in at least two of the theses. There are now also courses that focus on gender as an issue in the MA programme.

Challenges

We had foreseen certain challenges before the project started, but encountered others that we had not expected. Some of the anticipated risk factors were as follows:

- Local authorities might withdraw support from the projects. One risk that we had anticipated was that local language authorities would not accept the new orthographies or writing systems suggested by the project on the basis of linguistic research. To mitigate this risk the relevant groups in the project established networks with the relevant local authorities and educators. This had the positive effect of replacing distrust with trust and co-operation.

- Recruitment of females might be poor. We had foreseen that there would be poor recruitment of female students and staff. In Ethiopia, females account for about a quarter of the student population, and yet their attrition rate is higher: 25 per cent for females compared to 8 per cent for males (Abraha 2012). In the Department of Linguistics at AAU, out of the 28 academic staff, only three are female. Economic factors are a serious obstacle to female education in Ethiopia (Abraha 2012). We used MA grants to alleviate this problem, and now see an increase in the number of female students, in accordance with the UN's fifth goal for sustainable development.

- PhD students might leave Ethiopia. We had feared that PhD candidates might leave the project to settle in Norway. To counter this, we did not invite candidates to do their degree in Norway, nor were they invited to stay in Norway for long periods that might have given them personal ties. However, we did have a situation during a seminar in Norway, arranged by the project, in which two PhD candidates left, and were later discovered to have applied for political asylum.

There were four major issues that we did not foresee, but which turned out to delay the project. They are described below.

- A national state of emergency in Ethiopia: in the middle of the project period, Ethiopia introduced a ten-month state of emergency. This made it difficult, sometimes impossible, to conduct necessary fieldwork and workshops. As a result the project was severely delayed.

- We did not expect frequent changes of project co-ordinator. Change of project leaders (Färnman et al. 2016), or even main leadership of NGOs, be those of the North or the South (Ashman 2001), is one challenge identified in the aid literature. We could not have foreseen that the first three project co-ordinators would all get new work positions that forced them to leave their role as co-ordinator. The first leader was vice president of the university, some time later became the minister of culture and tourism, and is now minister of science and higher education. The second was offered a position as a programme officer at the Unesco International Institute for Capacity Building in Africa, after managing the project for three years. The third was a tenure position at the Langage, Langues et Cultures d'Afrique Noire laboratory in France. The fourth project leader will hopefully see the project to its successful end, but there is no doubt that the project lost some continuity and transfer of knowledge through these changes in leadership. Nonetheless, the fact that we managed to continue the main activities of the project also proves that it had a sound institutional basis, independent of the co-ordinators.
- Key staff were appointed to the Centre of Excellence in Norway. Four of the Norwegian staff who were supposed to have major teaching and supervision roles in Ethiopia instead found themselves as central members of the new Center for Multilingualism in Society across the Lifespan (MultiLing) at UiO. This led to a much smaller input from the Norwegians than had first been planned. In addition, one of the other Norwegians left academia, while another found that she was pregnant and felt it was impossible to continue with a role in Ethiopia. One important development in this regard was the role that the host AAU took as a collaborator in a programme opened at the partner institution HU, partly due to one of the Norwegian members retiring.
- The financial system at AAU is very complicated. We had not foreseen that it might be difficult to get money transferred to relevant parts of the project, as well as from Norway to Ethiopia. This delayed activities such as workshops and fieldwork.

It should be stated that some of the unforeseen challenges were due to positive developments for people or other projects, and should not be regarded as unwanted. For example, MultiLing arranged a number of summer, winter and spring schools for research students, and paid for travel, board and lodging for many of the PhD candidates in the project. All the same, they did create delays for us. We could therefore add a final challenge for the project: unforeseen delays. This could be alleviated with an extension of the project, and we are happy that Norad has now offered this opportunity to the project.

Sustainability

From the beginning, the LCB project was designed to be sustainable. Below we list the main factors for sustainability.

Education of and by local staff

Collaboration programmes are expected to be sustainable to the extent that the programmes are finally owned by the Southern partners (Holtland and Boeren 2006; Wield 1997). The LCB project was planned to be sustainable in line with Norad's and Ethiopia's interests. First, it focused on building the capacity of current and future staff of HEIs. Such capacity-building work has a lasting effect as the instructors trained by the project will be involved in training others in the coming decades. The programmes that were supported through the project are fully owned by the institutions of higher learning in Ethiopia and will continue with even better capacity to run them after the completion of the project. One of the problems in other project-supported programmes in HEIs in low- and middle-income countries is staff composition. When new programmes are launched, usually staff are drawn from the Northern partners. When the projects end, there are not enough local staff to take over and there is not enough funding to continue hiring expatriate staff. Thus programmes cease when the projects end. In the case of the LCB-supported programmes, almost all academic staff involved in teaching in these programmes were

Ethiopians. Thus there are no concerns about a shortage of human resources after the project is completed.

Project funding not supporting basic needs

A common problem with project-supported programmes is how funds are used. Programmes cease to run when apparently abundant funds are used to run every aspect of the programme and then suddenly run dry. The funds in the LCB project were not used for the basic aspects of running the programmes. The funds did not pay salaries for staff or fees for most of the students in the programme, nor did they cover basic costs such as stationery and other materials used to run the programme. The programmes existed even without the LCB project. What the project did was to give support that helped make them more effective, and that enabled them to provide higher-quality training. Financial support for fieldwork ensured that research conducted by students and staff would not to be constrained by a shortage of data. Likewise, financial support for participation in international conferences helped researchers get international exposure that encouraged them to think outside the box.

Networks with local authorities and educators

From the very beginning the LCB project arranged networking workshops with local educators and authorities. This helped to ensure that the resulting development of orthographies was well received and that local educators were equipped to develop teaching material. Local experts from the Kambaata Zone Culture and Tourism Bureau, who had not received training, approached the researchers for consultation on and evaluation of the materials that they had prepared with the result that the project extended its support to include them – a successful example of the TOT (train the trainer) model. Two primers, prepared by the experts from the bureau and evaluated by the project researchers, were published on behalf of the bureau for distribution to libraries in the primary and secondary schools as well as the College of Teacher Education in the zone.

The project helped introduce Aari as a school subject in two *woredas* of the South Omo Zone, ensuring that the orthography developed will stay in use. All related costs were covered by the local government. The training in textbook preparation and dictionary compilation received by the teachers increased their capacity and will serve them in the years to come as they keep on producing dictionaries of different types, writing primers and supplementary books.

The networking proved valuable in developing the necessary mutual trust between the groups involved in the LCB project, thus making it possible to implement the linguistic changes and outputs in the communities.

Project outputs become resources with lasting value

The orthographies developed in the project will have lasting value, as will the primers for education and the dictionaries. In addition, the language corpora developed for linguistic research are reusable, and both can and should be used by researchers of the relevant languages in the future. In addition, the education of 13 new PhD graduates and the development of two new MA programmes will ensure sustainable transfer of knowledge to new generations.

The North–South and South–South co-operation which commenced with the project continues, as many of the researchers in the project have started doing research together and co-publishing.

Finally, the gender mainstreaming that was a core part of the project has borne fruit. The fact that women were especially supported in the project at both PhD and MA level, and that there is now an increased number of female postgraduates, will have lasting results. As visible representatives of their gender's possibilities for success in academia, these women are role models who will inspire others.

Conclusion

In this chapter, we set out to explain the relevance of the LCB project activities in the context of achieving SDGs 4 and 5 and to identify the lessons learned from the implementation of the LCB project for future

North–South and South–South co-operation. We described how the LCB project supported the language planning activities in Ethiopia through an exchange of knowledge from North to South and from South to South. Democratisation, in the form of providing equal opportunities for citizens, begins with ensuring equal access to education and other services. We believe that the LCB project has impacted directly on the possibilities for social transformation in Ethiopia.

Our main goal was to contribute to a more democratic Ethiopia by using linguistic resources to improve the quality of education in the country. Mother-tongue education is central to learning, especially at the junior levels of education, but Ethiopia's 90 languages, including sign language, presented a challenge to the achievement of this goal. The linguistic capacity-building work that the project achieved is grounded in the concept of linguistic citizenship in which the right to use one's own language is put at the centre of citizenship discourse and is pivotal to the political, social and economic empowerment of speakers.

The project has contributed towards obtaining a higher degree of mother-tongue education by developing more knowledge about some languages through language descriptions, using fieldwork and developing research tools – in particular, spoken and written language corpora for a total of nine languages so far. Language primers and dictionaries, as well as orthographies, were developed for the most disadvantaged languages. Relevant MA programmes and a PhD programme were developed at two universities, and regular workshops were given to train local educators. The linguistic work was done mainly by staff and PhD candidates in Ethiopia, while the language technology tools were developed as a joint effort by the partners in Ethiopia and Norway, as well as external project partners in the Czech Republic.

The capacity-development efforts of the project were multilayered, with an emphasis on empowering local players and ensuring that responsibility and ownership lay with the partner in the South. One outstanding feature of Norhed projects is the fact that the institution in the South is identified as a project agreement partner. This is a major shift in the approach to development aid and Norad should be commended for this. If used properly, this approach has the potential to solve the imbalance of power so often noted in North–South partnerships. In this project, the partner in the South was fully aware of the responsibility that came with it and various attempts were made to maximise its benefits. In order to avoid the resistance and scepticism locals might feel towards ideas pushed on them from the outside, we arranged regular networking workshops with local educators and authorities – a strategy that worked to good effect.

Gender mainstreaming was an additional and perhaps ambitious goal in the project, but active support and recruitment of female PhDs and special MA grants for women made this less of a challenge than we had feared.

The LCB project has already yielded fruits. There are now better publication records at Addis Ababa and Hawassa universities, the orthography and primers developed are in use, and the graduates have joined their employers with increased capacity. The electronic resources are being used for research. We have gained higher participation of women, and we have better chances of sustainable results, given the workshops with local educators and authorities. Above all, we think that the long time span of the project, combined with multiple visits in both directions, have created good conditions for mutual respect and co-operation in the future.

About the authors and the project

Derib Ado Jekale is assistant professor in the Department of Linguistics at Addis Ababa University, Ethiopia, and co-ordinator of the the Linguistic Capacity-Building (LCB) project

Binyam Sisay Mendisu is programme officer for teacher education and curriculum development at Unesco's International Institute for Capacity Building in Africa and an associate professor in the Department of Linguistics at Addis Ababa University

Janne Bondi Johannessen is professor at the Center for Multilingualism in Society across the Lifespan and director of the Text Laboratory, Department of Linguistics and Scandinavian Studies, University of Oslo

Project title: Linguistic Capacity Building: Tools for the Inclusive Development of Ethiopia
Partner institutions: Addis Ababa University, Hawassa University (both Ethiopia) and University of Oslo (Norway)

Notes

1   See https://pen-international.org/app/uploads/drets_culturals389.pdf

References

Abraha A (2012) *Gender Inequalities in Tertiary Education in Ethiopia: Mediating the Transition to University Through the Development of Adaptive Competencies.* Global Scholars Program Working Paper Series No. 5, Centre for Universal Education, Brookings Institution. Available online

Ashman D (2001) Strengthening North-South partnerships for sustainable development. *Nonprofit and Voluntary Sector Quarterly* 30(1): 74–98. Available online

Ball J (2010) Educational equity for children from diverse language backgrounds: Mother tongue-based bilingual or multilingual education in the early years. Presentation to Unesco International Symposium: Translation and Cultural Mediation, Paris, Unesco, 22–23 February. Available online

Binyam S and Johannessen JB (eds) (2016) Multilingual Ethiopia: Linguistic challenges and capacity building efforts. *Oslo Studies in Language* 8(1): 1–8

Cohen GPE (2000) Identity and opportunity: The implication of local languages in the primary education system of SNNPR. PhD thesis, School of Oriental and African Studies, University of London

Cooper RL (1989) *Language Planning and Social Change.* Cambridge: Cambridge University Press

Färnman R, Diwan V, Zwarenstein M, Atkins S and the ARCADE consortium (2016) Successes and challenges of North-South partnerships: Key lessons from the African/Asian Regional Capacity Development projects. *Global Health Action* 9(1). Available online

FDRE (Federal Democratic Republic Government of Ethiopia) (1994) *Education and Training Policy.* Addis Ababa

FDRE Ministry of Culture and Tourism (2015) Executive summary of language development execution from 2010/11–2012/13. Presentation at the 2015 Annual Panel Discussion on the Day of Speaking in One's Mothertongue, Sekota Town, Amhara National Regional State, Ethiopia

Feda N and Derib A (2016) Visual recognition of graphic variants of Amharic letters: Psycholinguistic experiments. *Oslo Studies in Language* 8/1: 173–200

Ferguson G (2013) The language of instruction issue: Reality, aspiration and the wider context. In: H. McIlwraith (ed.) *Multilingual Education in Africa: Lessons from the Juba Language-in-Education Conference.* Manchester, UK: British Council

Getachew A and Derib A (2006) Language policy in Ethiopia: History and current trends. *Ethiopian Journal of Education and Sciences* 2(1): 37–61

Holtland G and Boeren A (2006) *Achieving the Millennium Development Goals in Sub-Saharan Africa: The Role of International Capacity Building Programs for Higher Education and Research*. Den Haag: NUFFIC

Johannessen JB, Nygaard L, Priestley J and Nøklestad A (2008) Glossa: A multilingual, multimodal, configurable user interface. In: *Proceedings of the Sixth International Language Resources and Evaluation Conference (LREC 2008)*. Paris: European Language Resources Association

Johannessen JB, Priestley J, Hagen K, Åfarli TA and Vangsnes ØA (2009) The Nordic Dialect corpus: An advanced research tool. In: K Jokinen and E Bick (eds) *Proceedings of the 17th Nordic Conference of Computational Linguistics NODALIDA 2009*. Northern European Association for Language Technology (NEALT). Available online

Koch S and Weingart P (2016) *The Delusion of Knowledge Transfer: The Impact of Foreign Aid Experts on Policy-Making in South Africa and Tanzania*. Cape Town: African Minds. Available online

Meyer R and Edzard L (eds) (2016) *Time in Languages of the Horn of Africa*. Abhandlungen für die Kunde des Morgenlandes Band 107. Wiesbaden: Harrassowitz Verlag

Pala K, Horák A, Rychlý P, Suchomel V, Baisa V, Jakubíček M, Kovář V et al. (2017) HaBiT System, issued 2017

Pawlos K (2015) *A Guide to Teaching Ethiopian Sign Language*. Addis Ababa: Addis Ababa University Press

RTI International (2010) Ethiopia Early Grade Reading Assessment. Data analytic report: Language and Early Learning. Addis Ababa: USAID Ethiopia

Stroud C (2001) African mother tongues and the politics of language: Linguistic citizenship versus linguistic human rights. *Journal of Multilingual and Multicultural Development* 22(4): 339–355

Stroud C (2002) Language and democracy: The notion of linguistic citizenship and mother-tongue programs. In K Legere and S Fitchat (eds) *Talking Freedom: Language and Democratization in the SADC Region*. Windhoek: Macmillan

UNDP (2009) *Capacity Development: A UNDP Primer*. Available online

UNDP (2016) *Human Development Report 2016: Human Development for Everyone*. New York. Available online

Unesco (1953) The Use of Vernacular Languages in Education: Monographs on Fundamental Education. Paris: Unesco

Whorf BL (1956) *Language, Thought, and Reality: Selected Writings of Benjamin Lee Whorf*. 2nd edn. Cambridge, MA: MIT Press

Wield D (1997) Coordination of donors in African universities. *Higher Education Policy*, 10(1): 41–54. Available online

Wolff HE (2006) Background and history: Language politics and planning in Africa. In: H Alidou, A Boly, B Brock-Utne, SY Diallo, K Heugh and HE Wolff (eds) *Optimizing Learning and Education in Africa: The Language Factor*. Libreville: Association for the Development of Education in Africa

Yigezu M and Mendisu BS (2015) The orthography of Hamar. *Studies in Ethiopian Languages* 4(1): 1–16

Zelealem L (2012) The Ethiopian language policy: A historical and typological overview. *Ethiopian Journal of Languages and Literature* 12(2): 1–60

15

Academic and cultural perceptions of foreign students: Implications for the sustainability of international partnerships

Elizabeth Kaase-Bwanga

Research on foreign students' experiences in universities in America, Finland, Japan, Spain and many other countries have focused on second language acquisition in general, and application of the second language in speech in particular. They identify classroom culture – especially interpersonal exchanges, the classroom environment, communication strategies that teachers use to correct students' mistakes, taking a personal interest in the students' progress and cultural issues, particularly those related to gender roles, as major factors that affected students' views and achievement (Brecht and Robinson 1995; Freed 1990, 1993, 1998; Koskinen and Tossavainen 2003; Lafford 1995).

The research described in this chapter focused on the academic and cultural perceptions of students of African origin in foreign universities during collaboration between the University of Juba in South Sudan and Makerere University in Uganda, under the auspices of the Norwegian Programme for Capacity Development in Higher Education and Research for Development (Norhed). The goal of the programme was to build higher education and research capacities in mainly low- and medium-income countries (LMICs), as a means to enhance sustainable conditions conducive to societal development and poverty reduction.

Makerere University was the main implementer in the partnership, with nine projects, six of which involved collaboration with the University of Juba. This attracted a sizeable number of students from South Sudan, all of whom had similar cultural backgrounds and experiences of civil strife. It also provided a sizeable cohort to study academic and cultural experiences of foreign African students in an African university. Geographically close neighbours, South Sudan and Uganda do not share the same culture or the same education system. The role of Makerere University was to receive funding from the Norwegian Agency for Development Cooperation (Norad), identify deserving students from South Sudan and provide a conducive academic and research environment for capacity building in Makerere University and the University of Juba. The students' role was to pursue programmes of study leading to specific academic awards on completion. The overall objective of this research was to examine the academic and cultural perceptions of the South Sudan students at Makerere University. The research focused on the students' socio-economic background, the academic and cultural environment at Makerere University, the students' first impressions of Makerere University, their perceptions of academic stress, including self-assessment of their English language proficiency, their family life and its effect on their academic progression, their experiences with the local community in Uganda, and what all these factors implies for the Norhed collaboration.

A review of the literature

Available literature on foreign students' experiences focuses on students' perceptions mostly at American, Japanese, Spanish and Chinese universities, some involving collaborative and partnership arrangements. Forstat (1951), Lee and Rice (2007), Miller (1993), Power et al. (2015) and Poyrazli and Lopez (2007) note that higher education partnerships have the potential to improve the quality and relevance of higher education. However, they also observe that it can be very difficult for such partnerships to deliver successfully, due to imbalances in resources, insufficient funding to sustain the partnership after its initiation, poor monitoring and evaluation, issues related to cultural divide and general lack of confidence in the weak research capacity. Zimmermann (1995) studied perceptions of intercultural communication competences and international student adaptation to an American campus, pointing out that studying in foreign countries was not limited to simply taking classes. Students needed to adapt or adjust to a sociocultural system different from their own.

Koskinen and Tossavainen (2003) observed that student exchange was being used increasingly in nursing education throughout Europe, as a method of acquiring intercultural sensitivity. In the host country, each foreign student was assigned a personal tutor to enhance learning. Their study describes tutor–student relationships between Finnish nurse teachers and British exchange students, from the tutors' perspective. The tutoring relationship was pastoral and clinical rather than academic. The pastoral aspect of the relationship was essential in assisting the students to adjust to the stress of studying in a foreign country, although tutors were unable to help all the students overcome their culture shock. Although they found their role pleasant, tutors were uncertain about it, and did not integrate Finnish culture or practice into theory. The study found that a dialogic tutor–student relationship was important for learning intercultural sensitivity, and recommended tutoring strategies to assist students' adjustment to the differences in the host culture and to encourage their reflection on personal, experiential and scientific cultural knowledge during their study abroad.

Kim (2008) pointed out that cross-cultural adaptation was an interactive process that involved both the newcomers and the host environment as well as the interplay of acculturation (adapting to the new culture) and de-acculturation (discarding some of the old culture) to come up with a neutral culture. Huang and Brown (2009) investigated Chinese students' academic experiences in North America and identified six issues causing students to feel discomfort: the disconcerting classroom behaviour of North American students; the professorial focus on discussion rather than lecture; a lack of organisation; the fact that lecturers did not follow the textbooks; the emphasis on group work and the fact that there were no lecture summaries. Above all, they did not have any common interests (e.g. sports, religion) with their North American counterparts.

Spenader (2011) investigated the relationship between acculturation and language learning during a one-year study-abroad programme at pre-collegiate level. The study focused on the experiences of four Americans studying in Sweden, specifically selected as case studies because they had no prior knowledge of the target language. The researcher compared descriptions of the students' acculturation and a measure of their acculturative outcomes to their language development as measured by an unofficial oral proficiency interview, first after five months and later, after ten months. The results indicated that higher levels of acculturation were associated with higher levels of proficiency in Swedish and that the host culture was not associated with lower levels of proficiency. However, Spenader recommends study-abroad programmes that support language learning.

Sun and Chen (1997) studied the difficulties mainland Chinese students encountered in the United States. They reported lack of English proficiency, cultural differences, the unfamiliar foreign classroom environment and university facilities as the major obstacles in the academic and social lives of the students. Yan and Berliner (2009) examined stressful aspects of Chinese international students' academic experiences in the United States. Most students experienced a high level of academic stress, including ineffective interactions with foreign lecturers, their lack of English proficiency and educational disparities between their countries of origin and the foreign universities. Huang (2006) investigated the academic listening skills of Chinese students at an American university and found that most of the students were confident of their reading ability and grammar. Their challenges were their speaking and listening skills, their lack of vocabulary, their writing skills and they had very little confidence about their pronunciation.

Li and Stodolska (2006) explored the leisure experiences of Chinese graduate students in the United States. It was noted that Chinese students recognised the importance of leisure and enjoyed the feeling of relaxation. However, their leisure behaviour and habits were constrained due to their limited social networks, heavy study- and workloads, and visa restrictions. Most Chinese students were not satisfied with their leisure life in America and felt strongly homesick for their life in China.

Guntermann (1995) studied language proficiency in Spanish among Peace Corps volunteers who were typically American students. The author assessed Peace Corps training and service in the field and evaluated the Spanish production of several volunteers in the official Foreign Services Institute. Oral interviews were used to study the impact of study abroad on idiomatic usage, especially on second-language use of the words 'por' and 'para'. It was noted that the accuracy of the use of these words improved to 90 per cent after a year in service. The Peace Corps training and service provided a unique set of conditions for language learning, the details of which were continually evaluated and revised on the basis of proficiency outcomes as well as efficiency of practices. However, little evidence was found that classroom study abroad, prior to Peace Corps training, had made a major difference. The study found that formal instruction, in conjunction with an immersion setting such as a home stay in a country where the target language was spoken, could provide adults with the necessary preparation for successful acquisition. Students seemed to learn the necessary strategies and skills for continuing to learn independently.

Wang and Mallinckrodt (2006) examined the relationship between psychological attachments and the acculturation of Chinese international students from the perspective of their home culture. It was reported that students with a high level of attachment avoidance and attachment anxiety were more likely to experience sociocultural adjustment difficulty and psychological stress than students with attachment security (low attachment avoidance and low attachment anxiety). Students who adapted to Western values and lifestyles adjusted more successfully to the American environment. Wei et al. (2007) observed that acculturative stress was positively associated with depression among Chinese students at Midwestern University. Students who experienced high maladaptive perfectionism (the difference between expectations and actual performance) were more vulnerable to depression. The students' length of time in America, together with acculturative stress and maladaptive perfectionism, were significant predictors of depression.

Although available literature is limited to cultural and academic experiences, it adequately informs this research as it highlights the different dimensions of stress and related factors that affect foreign students' academic achievement. It specifically acknowledges that although partnerships can be very beneficial, it may also be difficult to deliver the desired outcomes successfully if these stressors and related factors are not taken into account.

Theoretical frameworks

Various scholars have advanced theories to explain the cultural and academic experiences of students studying in foreign universities. The theoretical framing of this research is a combination of cultural fusion theories, each with its own perspective. These include the uncertainty reduction theory advanced by Berger and Calabrese (1975), Kim and Ruben (1988) and Zimmermann (1995); the stress-adaptation-growth model by Kim and Ruben (1988); Kim's cross-cultural adaptation theory (2008); the anxiety/uncertainty management theory proposed by Gudykunst (2005); De La Garza and Ono's (2015) theory of differential adaptation; and the cultural fusion theory as discussed by Croucher and Kramer (2017).

Croucher and Kramer (2017) point out that the newcomers acculturate into the dominant culture and maintain some aspects of their minority culture. The dominant or host culture also absorbs some aspects of the newcomer's culture into the dominant culture, thus creating a fused intercultural identity. De La Garza and Ono's (2015) differential adaptation theory postulates that migrants may adapt in a variety of ways that do not necessitate consenting to pressures to assimilate or accommodate the culture of the larger society they have joined. The new immigrants may change the existing culture of the society into which they move.

Kim's (2008) cross-cultural adaptation theory postulates that adaptation is a process of dynamic unfolding, with the natural human tendency to struggle for internal equilibrium when faced with conflicting environmental conditions. Multiple factors, including the environment, the ethnic and the personal exposure of the individual, simultaneously interact during the communication interface between the individual and the foreign environment. Some of the interactive factors may be more significant than others. In some cases, the adaptation process may be almost entirely due to the strength, openness, and positivity of the stranger's personality. In other cases, very little adaptive change is necessary in strangers whose ethnicity offers almost complete insulation from the challenges of the host culture. The author argues that the ability to communicate in accordance with the norms and practices of the host culture, and active engagement in social communication processes is central to the process of adapting to the host environment. Adapting successfully requires the acquisition of new cultural communication practices and a willingness to discard some of the old ones, proficiency in the host communication system and active participation in the interpersonal and mass communication processes of the local community.

Kim (2008) assumes that as we keep our focus on the goal of successful adaptation to the host society, we experience a gradual self-identity transformation, involving a subtle and smooth unconscious change that transforms us into an increasingly intercultural person – the process of acculturation. Due to the many unpredictable changes in the new life, we are challenged to step into a domain that reaches beyond our original cultural perimeters. Our old identity can never be completely replaced by a new one, but can be transformed into something that will always contain some of the old and some of the new culture existing side by side, to form a new perspective. This provides more openness to and acceptance of differences in people and a capacity to participate more deeply in the intellectual, aesthetic, and emotional experience of the host community. The onus is thus on foreigners to embrace change and decide what degree of change they are willing to undergo. If they decline to change, they minimise the adaptation process and may not fit into the new environment, and vice versa. This theory highlights the important role of communication between the newcomer and the host society, the importance of the newcomer's willingness to drop some of the home culture and norms in order to create room for the new culture in the adaptation process, as well as the important role of the host environment in facilitating or impeding the adaptation process. The individual is the primary 'mover', as well as the primary bearer of the 'burden' of adaptive change.

Kim and Ruben (1988), in their stress-adaptation-growth model, demonstrate that intercultural transformation is cyclic and continuous, taking on a 'draw-back-to-leap' pattern through which stress, adaptation and growth together define the internal dynamics of the newcomer's intercultural communication experience. Communication between the strangers and the host society is paramount. Kim (2008), too, noted that successful adaptation will only occur when the strangers' internal communication systems sufficiently overlap with those of the natives. Together with Gudykunst (2005), Kim and Ruben highlight the issues of change management and the adjustment process.

Berger and Calabrese (1975), Kim (2008), Kim and Ruben (1988) and Zimmermann (1995) advanced the uncertainty reduction theory. This theory assumes that when individuals experience uncertainty, they are motivated to seek information in order to reduce the ambiguity or increase their understanding about the behaviour of both themselves and others in the interaction. It is assumed that communication can help people accomplish their goals. In anxiety/uncertainty management theory, Gudykunst (1988, 2005) stresses that during intergroup or intercultural communication, there are always in-group members and out-group members (strangers). At the initial stage of interaction, strangers will experience both anxiety and uncertainty (a condition of not knowing how to behave or a state of indecision), and they will be hyperaware of differences. If the cultural gap widens, the strangers' level of anxiety and uncertainty increases. Moderate levels of anxiety and uncertainty may motivate people to better adjust to the host environment. Excessive anxiety and uncertainty may lead to failure to adjust and/or to communicate. This theory suggests that self-conceit, inadequate motivation to interact with the host, social categorisation of hosts, situational processes, inadequate connections with hosts, ethical interactions and changes in conditions in a host culture are some of the causes of uncertainty/anxiety management.

In view of the above, the process of providing academic and cultural experiences through international partnerships and collaborations is not an easy one. From the student perspective, it involves changes in environment, culture and language, as well as adapting to new rules and regulations and social relations that govern the partnership or collaborations. The change process is gradual, involving the internal dynamics of the newcomer's academic and intercultural communication experience, and depends almost entirely on the strength, openness, and positivity of the newcomer.

Methodology

The methodology was built on a data collection exercise from willing South Sudan students. They were drawn from projects under the Norhed programme at Makerere University that were willing to participate in the research: 'Increasing the capacity of mama-baby survival in post-conflict Uganda and South Sudan'; 'Regional capacity building for sustainable natural resource management and agricultural productivity under changing climate'; 'Capacity building in zoonotic diseases management using the integrated ecosystems health approach at the human–livestock–wildlife interface in eastern and southern Africa'; 'Strengthening media in post-conflict societies through education and research – bridging gaps, building futures in Uganda, South Sudan, Nepal and Norway'; 'Institutional capacity building in water management and climate change adaptation in the Nile Basin'; 'Ecology and management of the Sudd Wetlands, South Sudan' and 'Improving weather information management in East Africa for effective services provision through the application of suitable ICTs'.

A questionnaire was developed, focusing on the cultural and academic experiences of the students sponsored under the programme. This was augmented by in-depth interviews with them and secondary data from the results of the 2017 Norhed Mid-term Review Report. In her capacity as the co-ordinator of the Norhed programme at Makerere University, the author had the advantage of her day-to-day monitoring of programme activities and her attendance at the projects' annual planning and monitoring review meetings, where co-ordinators reported to Norad on the progress of their respective projects, with students in attendance. The data from the students' responses were analysed qualitatively and results were disaggregated by sex. Gender issues were highlighted where applicable in what follows in the next section.

Context and description of the student sample

Socio-economic background of the students

Of the total sample of 22 students who completed the questionnaire, 12 were female and ten were male. Seventeen (ten females and seven males) were married, four (two females and two males) were unmarried and one student was widowed. The average age of the sample was 38 years, with the youngest at 29 years of age and the oldest at 52. The age of the females ranged between 34 and 51 years, the average being 38, whereas the average age of the males was 39 years, with the group ranging between 29 and 52 years of age. On average the programme attracted younger female than male students. The average number of children per respondent among the female group was three, as compared to an average of five children among the males. The highest number of children for an individual female was six, with four being the largest number of children for an individual male. On average, nine male as compared to ten female respondents had dependants. The average number of dependants per female respondent was six, whereas for the male students it was five. The overall average for the total sample of 22 students was five dependants per student. It was noted that the programme attracted students in their reproductive age; most of them were married with children and other dependants.

Employment status of students

Of the 22 students, 18 (11 female and seven male) were employed prior to joining the programme, mainly by state departments within the government of South Sudan. Their terms and conditions of service were different, irrespective of their qualification, and salaries differed according to department, qualification and sex. For all of them, however, the salaries were too small to cover their everyday costs and obligations and also support them as students. The highest paid student on this programme earned an equivalent of US$50 per month from the state department. The lowest paid female student earned US$0.4 and the lowest paid male earned US$2.6 per month. In 2017, when the data were collected, the exchange rate of the South Sudan pound (SSP) to the US dollar was SSP180 to US$1. At the time, the average monthly salary the State of South Sudan paid employees was US$19.4 (US$15.9 for females and US$24.8 for males). Four female students on the programme had working spouses. The average salary for their spouses was US$51 per month. The rest of the married students' spouses were not in regular employment. This suggests that on average, students were living on less than US$1 per day, even where both the student and their spouse were in regular employment. Given that the students came to Uganda with their families and dependants, the salaries were inadequate to enable the students to cover their living expenses as well as their academic expenses. Their source of livelihood in Uganda was therefore the stipend from the programme.

Students' monthly stipends

The average student stipend per month was US$539 (US$527 for females and US$557 for males). The lowest stipend paid to female students on the programme was US$340, compared to US$400 for male students – an equivalent of, respectively, 1 156 000 and 1 360 000 Ugandan shillings per month at an exchange rate of US$1 to UGX3 400. The highest stipend paid to female students was US$600 compared to US$1 000 for male students. It is noteworthy that even within the same project, the amount of the student stipend differed according to sex. The stipend was meant to cover the students' costs, such as accommodation, food, transport, stationery, books and photocopying. For the most part, however, the stipend was inadequate to meet the costs of basic student necessities. Jávorka and Church (2017) allude to this in their mid-term report, suggesting that projects appeared to operate in isolation.

Academic and cultural environment at Makerere University

Situated on one of the hills that make up greater Kampala city, the university is less than 20 minutes from the city centre by car. Established by the Government of Uganda in 1922, Makerere University is a secular public university with English as the language of instruction. Luganda is the main language used outside the class environment.

The number of international students at the university has been increasing: from 198 in 2012/13 and 171 in 2013/14, to 232 in 2014/15. Available records for 2015/16 indicate that the enrolment of international students stood at 782, of which 288 were female and 494 were male. The distribution of international students by region of origin in 2012/13 indicates that the vast majority came from East and central Africa (480), followed by 40 from South African countries, 26 from West African countries, 19 from non-African countries, and 17 from various countries in the Horn of Africa (Makerere University 2013b).

With regard to facilities at the university, there is one graduate hall of residence specifically for the graduate students, with a capacity of 101 rooms that can be shared, depending on the need. Saint Francis chapel, St Augustine chapel, the university mosque and two student centres affiliated to the chapels are some of the facilities catering for students' spiritual needs. Games and sports facilities are distributed around the main campus, where the university main library is situated, with specialised libraries distributed across the different college campuses. The university hospital offers treatment and counselling services to teachers and staff. In terms of teaching and learning facilities, there is adequate lecture and laboratory space and a reasonable number of both teaching and non-teaching staff (Makerere University 2013b, 2016).

Student involvement in university governance through active participation of their elected representatives is well enshrined in the Makerere University Guild Constitution. Students are represented on Council and Senate committees, in the hall of residence and at college and school levels, as well as in the student guild. Formal channels for advancing students' governance comprise the heads of departments, who are responsible for academic-related challenges, and the dean of students and wardens in halls of residence, who are responsible for challenges related to social issues. The international office caters for the specific needs of international students. Types of support for international students depend on the student request. Accommodation space to cater for the increasing enrolment has been partially catered for by the privately owned hostels around the university (Makerere University 2013a). This is expected to reduce the level of academic and cultural stress at the university.

Internationalisation is one of the cross-cutting themes of the Makerere University Strategic Plan 2008/09–2018/19. This places the university at the centre of the global arena with respect to teaching and learning, staff and student exchange programmes, joint curriculum development, research and knowledge transfer and international partnerships and collaborative linkages. Although most international graduate students are privately sponsored, some of them come through bilateral arrangements – exchange programmes and/or projects. Sida- (Swedish International Development and Cooperation Agency) and Norad-supported programmes are but two of the Makerere University collaborations/partnerships. The university has long experience in running international development programmes including partnerships with Austria, Italy, the Netherlands, Ethiopia, Kenya, South Africa, Nigeria, Japan, Somalia, the UK and the USA. These aimed at creating a diversity of cultures on campus, with a view to students developing a breadth of knowledge, skills and perspectives across national boundaries, thus enabling them to become more globally aware (Makerere University 2013c). In light of this, Makerere University is clearly multicultural and therefore can provide the ambience, support and academic experience necessary for collaborations and partnerships. However, this is subject to good practices: networking, communicating, collaborating and sharing experiences; ensuring local ownership and securing active support; establishing robust research governance and support structures that promote effective leadership; understanding the local context accurately; evaluating existing research capacity; building strong support, mentorship and supervision structures as well as monitoring and evaluation tools and, equally importantly, thinking long term, learning from experience, being flexible and planning for continuity (Jávorka and Church 2017).

Results and discussion

Foreign students' first impressions of Makerere University

Students held Makerere University in high esteem and were happy to be associated with the university. However, they reported having experienced shock initially, because of the academic pressure that students often feel during the transition phase from undergraduate to graduate studies at Makerere University. Students took time to adjust to this pressure, which later normalised as they settled in and realised that Makerere University was just like any other institution of higher learning, whether in Uganda or South Sudan or elsewhere. They also noted the difference in language: English is the official language of communication in Uganda, as opposed to the Arabic language they were familiar with in South Sudan. Huang (2006), Sun and Chen (1997), and Yan and Berliner (2009) reported similar experiences among Chinese students with respect to English proficiency and vocabulary, resulting in high levels of academic stress and ineffective interactions with foreign lecturers. However, in the context of this research, it must be noted that apart from their Arabic language background, the students' curriculum in South Sudan was also very different from the Ugandan curriculum. This may have influenced their cultural and academic experience at Makerere University.

Efficient and effective communication and shared understanding is key for an effective, well-functioning partnership that delivers benefits to all those involved (Jávorka and Church 2017). South Sudan students reported that Makerere University was welcoming, despite their language limitations. Nonetheless, most students at the university used Luganda as a language of communication outside the class environment, resulting in communication challenges for South Sudan students who had not studied in Uganda before and were therefore not familiar with the language. In addition, the majority of the business community, especially in the accommodation industry, prefer using Luganda as a medium of communication and some do not speak English at all. For the South Sudan students, this translated into difficulties in finding accommodation and other essential amenities due to their limited ability to bargain in Luganda rather than English. They were charged higher rental fees than their Ugandan counterparts, for example. To circumvent being cheated in everyday transactions, they would use fellow Ugandan colleagues to negotiate for them – in the markets, for example – until they learned a few basic words in Luganda.

South Sudan students' life outside Makerere University was also complicated by cultural differences between the students and the local Ugandan population. Apart from difficulties in learning and coping with the local languages, the students found the culture of free interaction between men and women especially difficult. South Sudan culture does not encourage men and women to interact freely; in fact, the separation of the sexes in university hostels is a strictly observed practice. In addition, South Sudan culture is based on a communal lifestyle that emphasises a co-operative spirit, honesty, support for strangers and sharing – whether that is food or academic work. The host culture is permissive and characterised by a degree of liberalism.

South Sudan students reported being called 'baSudany', literally translated as 'those people from South Sudan'. Gudykunst (2005) called this social categorisation by hosts. Applying Kim's (2008) cross-cultural adaptation theory to the students' experiences is helpful. Foreign students are expected to undergo a natural process of dynamic progression that tends towards the restoration of an internal equilibrium as they adapt. In the case of the South Sudan students, it was clear that while some students coped with Ugandan culture, others did not do so well: some, for example, had to move from hostels that were far from the university so that they could avoid seeing 'unpleasant occurrences'. Byram (1997) attributes the former response to attitudes that are pre-conditioned for successful intercultural interaction. Gudykunst (2005) referred to the latter type of response as deriving from excessive anxiety and uncertainty, which sometimes leads to failure in adjustment or communication when the cultural gap is too big. The above notwithstanding, there were good attributes that impressed South Sudan students, as their voices reveal:

> I was impressed to join a high-ranking institution in Africa that produced good brains and leaders in various fields of science ...

> It was an opportunity for me to get a new exposure ... The sys-
> tems of lecturers using projectors during lectures were new to
> me and good, except for the presentation skills ... The built up
> environment – lecture halls, internal roads, and monuments
> impressed me. (Responses to the questionnaire)

In general, the students' perceptions of cultural life outside Makerere University were that this is challenging, the main causes being the language barrier and social liberalism. This might have hampered their ability to integrate effectively with ordinary Ugandans.

Students' perceptions of their academic experience

Analysis of students' perception of their primary role at Makerere University revealed that 19 of the 22 (ten female, nine male) knew that they were at Makerere University in order to achieve an academic award within a given timeframe. Three (two female and one male) were indifferent about this goal. Those who understood their primary reason for being at Makerere University perceived this as requiring that they attend lectures, build a knowledge base through literature searches, develop a concept research paper leading to full proposal development, execute field investigations and finally write a research report. They understood that this required hard work and close supervision, the development of writing and review techniques, team-building and teamwork skills, the development of listening, presentation and organisational skills, participation in cross-cutting courses and the creation of good working relationships with fellow students and academic staff. The female students also believed that they were expected to be role models to other South Sudan female students and, in addition, to attend to their family needs. The male students perceived that they were expected to be leaders. In terms of the collaborative partnership between the two universities, this indicated that the majority of the students understood their mission at Makerere University.

Analysis of the students' level of academic stress revealed that eight of the 22 experienced academic life at Makerere University as very stressful; 11 reported that it was stressful and only three reported that it was not very stressful. A sex-disaggregated analysis of academic stress revealed that four of the 12 females found academic life at Makerere University very stressful, seven found it stressful and only one found it not so stressful. Four of the ten male students found academic life very stressful; another four found it stressful and only two found it not so stressful. Generally, female students were more academically stressed than the male students. This was attributed to the many demands made on them by their families and associated gender roles in addition to the academic demands, but also to the number of their dependants, their employment status, and the differences in their earnings and stipends.

Further analysis revealed that too much was expected of the students by their lecturers/supervisors, exacerbating their levels of academic stress. The students felt detached from their supervisors yet they needed more time and guidance from them. This made the development of the research concept paper and proposal writing a long and arduous process, and their efforts to get help from Ugandan students did not yield much either. This suggests a divergence between the expectations of the students and those of the supervisors. It seems the supervisors might have had the expectation that, at the very minimum, students would be able to navigate through the process of concept and proposal development with minimal support. This misconception was attributed to the absence of a forum where the students and professors met to discuss the progress of research projects.

It was also found that academic stress was caused by the stipend, which was too meager to cater adequately for the students' academic needs, including adequate accommodation facilities, stationery, paying for downloading reference materials, printing and photocopying, in addition to their own personal needs such as food, health insurance and other incidental expenditures. This created financial stress for the students, some of whom had to find work to make ends meet which, in turn, created academic stress since it ate into their study time. In-depth interviews on how students were coping with the situation revealed that students came from an already stressed socio-economic environment, riddled by war and civil strife. Given the state of emergency in South Sudan, and given that the South Sudan social system rests on principles of community sharing, some students had come to Uganda with their families and dependants. In their mid-term review, Jávorka and Church (2017) attributed this stress to external factors, notably the insecurity in South Sudan that influenced project implementation and collaboration among the partners. Nonetheless, although these factors were external to the collaboration, the collaborating partner institutions should have studied the background economic and social conditions of the students recruited onto the programme, in order to identify the likely factors that could create stress not only in their home country, but also in the host country, with a view to offering adequate support.

Students were requested to list all the stressors related to their academic life. The overall analysis of students' academic stressors indicated that the South Sudan students perceived the stipend as the greatest stressor. This was reported by six of the 22 students. This was followed by language difficulties, which five of the 22 students reported as their greatest stressor, and inadequate supervisor interaction, which was reported by five students as their most stressful issue. Five of the 22 students reported supervisor feedback as their greatest stressor, and one response reported difficulties in locating accommodation as a great stressor. Although the students ranked the stipend and language difficulties as among the highest stressors with respect to academic stress, this was overriden by student–supervisor interaction and supervisor feedback combined. Students reported that lecturers were too busy and it was extremely difficult to set up meetings with them, as some of the student voices reveal:

> Too much is given with minor support to us … Too much is expected of us from the professors … Supervisors are difficult to meet; they delay in reading students' scripts, without communication … My supervisor is ever busy, has no time to share/ critique or suggest a way forward and hence you may take more time to deliver your write up … Some supervisors do not co-operate between themselves. (Responses to the questionnaire)

Students coped with the challenges by doing their assignments and then followed up by monitoring lecturers frequently. Some students reported exercising patience and bearing with the situation in the interests of obtaining the 'paper'. Others tried to fit in by joining discussion groups with friends; some struggled individually, coping with the situation on their own. Some students put in extra effort and time to develop reading skills and to co-operate with supervisors. Theoretically, one may view the students' responses in terms of what Kim (2008) alluded to as acculturation, where we keep our sights on our goal. One may also view them in terms of Gudykunst's (2005) anxiety/uncertainty management theory, where moderate levels of anxiety and uncertainty can motivate people to better adjust to the host environment.

From the perspective of the tutoring relationship, we are reminded of what Koskinen and Tossavainen (2003) refer to as the pastoral and clinical rather than academic nature of the relationship. They noted that the pastoral aspect of the relationship was essential in assisting students to adjust to the stress of studying in a foreign country. Our results also echo their (2003) finding that tutors were uncertain about their role and did not integrate the host culture or practice into theory.

In their mid-term report, Jávorka and Church (2017) observed that the lack of funding for staff on the projects represented a challenge as staff took on additional workloads, often with strict deadlines for delivery of the project, and with no additional salary or other incentive. They also pointed to project co-ordinators' inadequate skills in motivating project colleagues to ensure the quality of both academic and administrative deliverables. They also noted that some project co-ordinators were managing big international partnerships for the first time and were ill-equipped to meet the challenges. This constraint was likely to result in asymmetric collaboration and hence limit the potential for effective, equal partnerships as well as sustainability. In addition, the shift to designate global South partners as the agreement partner represented a major shift in programme design, set new expectations and demands and required most organisations to undergo major and often steep learning curves. As a co-ordinator, I observed that the development partner (Norad) conferred unlimited powers on project co-ordinators such that it was difficult, even in supersystems, to supervise, oversee and/or advise them on certain issues. Some co-ordinators assumed that grants had been awarded to them in their individual capacity but not on behalf of the institutions they were serving. Future partnerships and collaborations should trim some of these powers.

The above notwithstanding, there were many positive academic experiences, as some of the student voices reveal:

> The courses offered to us were well organised and constructed in such a way that being a natural resource manager, it will benefit me in my teaching career and policy contributions in South Sudan ... Research is one of the best experiences that I got from Makerere University ... The staff at Makerere University have unique teaching experience, availability of teaching facilities and participatory teaching methods ... I valued the change of academic environment, exchange of knowledge and experience between South Sudanese students and Ugandan students ... The uniqueness in academic programming ... The availability of library and internet services ... The well-organised postgraduate programmes, gender-focused research course and committed lecturers. (Responses to the questionnaire)

In sum, the positive aspects of the students' overall academic experience outweighed the negative attributes. The latter could have been easily addressed in the programme development guidelines and followed up during implementation in annual review meetings. For the future sustainability of partnerships, however, the positive attributes will have to be upheld.

Students' rating of their own proficiency in English

Seven (one female and six male) of the 22 students who participated in this study rated themselves as very proficient in English; 11 (eight female and three male) as proficient and four (three female and one male) as average at English language, indicating that 18 out of the 22 students saw themselves as having above average English proficiency. This is in line with the criteria for admission to any academic programmes at Makerere University. In terms of Arabic (the South Sudan official language), eight students (three female and five male) were very proficient, five (four female and one male) were proficient, six (three female and three male) were average and three (two female and one male) were below average in proficiency. A reasonable number of students were more proficient in English than in Arabic, suggesting that South Sudan students were unlikely to experience communication challenges in English.

Family life and its effects on students' academic experiences

Students were required to explain how they managed family and student life, given that the programme did not cater for spouses and dependants. It was noted that if one had sufficient financial support, family life per se did not have a serious effect on academic life. With adequate financial support, the widows and widowers on the programme could afford to leave their children with a close relative at home and pursue their goals. However, students with dependants were faced with the dual problem of academic development and parenting, within limited financial means. For the married category especially, the female students struggled to cope with the situation. The husband and the children demanded their time. The children needed care, especially when sick and they had to support children with their daily schoolwork in addition to dealing with routine home demands. For the female students, time management was vital to cope with the demands of family life and an academic career. Two female students reported suspending relationships with their spouses in order to concentrate on their study programme.

Some students coped with their stressors by missing lectures in times of crisis, such as when children were ill. Some would challenge their spouses in South Sudan to visit more regularly or to offer moral and financial support. Other coping mechanisms involved cutting back on many activities at home in South Sudan, communicating with families on the phone for those who had left their families in South Sudan, being honest with their family about the challenges they were facing, sharing their future plans with their spouses, and overworking to meet the study requirements. When it was inevitable, students took the risk of travelling by bus if the road was 'safe' to go and visit their families back in South Sudan. This suggests that family ties were a major source of academic stress that students nursed and suppressed, and which, inadvertently, would translate into poor student performance and poor programme outputs with, as a result, negative effects on the sustainability of the collaborative partnership.

Students' experiences with the Ugandan local community

It was noted that Ugandans spoke a wide range of local languages although the most commonly used commercial languages in Kampala are Swahili and Luganda. Some South Sudan students spoke Arabic and socialised more between themselves than with Ugandans. Apart from the common tie of Sudanese culture, some of them were colleagues who had been working in the same universities and spoke the same local language. With respect to coping with social life outside the university, 11 of the 22 students reported that they were doing nothing since they did not feel that anything could make a difference. These were students who were already stressed by war in their country and this was additional stress. Two of the 22 suspended all social activity and put their careers first; they considered expectations of the local community (Uganda) to be a non-issue. Nine of the students tried to assimilate into Ugandan culture to enable them to interact and participate at least in the local market activities. It was noted that differences in the indigenous culture and language were marked, in some cases prohibiting communication and therefore acculturation by either Ugandans or South Sudan students. Some students tried to cope with Ugandan culture; some failed. They engaged with the local communities only for strategic reasons – to find accommodation and to purchase daily necessities, among but a few. This contradicts the assumption that contact between cultures automatically leads to intercultural learning and to the development of positive attitudes towards the target culture (Allport 1979; Coleman 1998; Fischer 1998). However, it does allude to what Kim (2008) noted: that a person's old identity can never be completely replaced by a new one, but it can be transformed into something that contains some of the old and some of the new culture to form a new perspective. In the case of this collaboration/ partnership, it was incumbent on the South Sudan students to learn at least one of the basic languages used, especially in markets – Kiswahili or Luganda.

Implications for the sustainability of partnerships

The issue of replicating and sustaining the Norhed model of partnerships to support higher education was put to students via the questionnaire. All the students' responses were positive:

> The arrangement of the collaborations is excellent, as we have exchange programmes with our partner universities in the South and the North … I recommend more of these collaborations but stipends in the South should be increased … Norad should also plan to bring Ugandans to study and conduct some research in South Sudan … The programme should enhance the efficiency of the collaboration through donor's regular meetings with the students, at annual monitoring and evaluation and academic visits. (Responses to the questionnaire)

Conclusion and recommendations

In this chapter, I have analysed the academic and cultural perceptions of foreign students at Makerere University and implications for the sustainability of international collaborations and partnerships. The methodology was built on a case study of South Sudan students under the Norhed programme at Makerere University. Primary data were drawn from a student questionnaire, in-depth interviews, annual review reports and the personal observations of the co-ordinator of the Norhed programme at Makerere University. The approach to the data analysis was qualitative.

The results pointed to the social and economic background of the students as contributory factors to the academic and cultural stress of the students. The main economic sources of stress were the meagre incomes and limited financial support in the form of a stipend. This was followed by the political instability in South Sudan and the gender roles of the female students. In their mid-term review, Jávorka and Church (2017) pointed out that, in order to facilitate a successful collaboration, project partners need to study the background circumstances of the recruited students not only from an economic perspective, but also from the perspective of their social and political situation at home as compared to in the host country.

In addition, it was found that foreign students' social life outside of the Makerere University precinct was challenging, largely due to the language barrier that prevented effective communication with ordinary Ugandans, especially while negotiating for services outside the university. A broad programme designed to support language learning is recommended.

Students were aware of the ultimate goal, the timeframes and the expectations of the academic programme, yet both male and female students were academically stressed, the female students more so than the male students. Their stress was related to ineffective communication between them and their lecturers and the inability of supervisors to give students timely feedback, especially with regard to their research projects. It seems that South Sudan students in Uganda would have benefited if they had been assigned personal tutors to enhance learning. Their level of academic stress also suggests the need for strong and well-skilled project co-ordinators, equipped to tackle all challenges that arise in the course of programme implementation.

Students' academic achievement depends on their initial perceptions about the host institutional environment and how fast they can adjust to it, as well as how ready the host institution is to handle the students' challenges. Their adjustment process is essential to the success of project implementation. In light of this, it is recommended that students on study programmes in foreign countries undergo a short programme to help them with adjustment to the institutional culture and academic environment of the host institutions and the host country. That said, the foreign students also play a central role in the collaboration. The host institution can plan strategies to facilitate this, but students should also display resilience in acquiring communication skills and competences to enable them to integrate into the cultural norms and practices of the host culture and in addition, actively engage in local social processes.

From the Makerere University perspective, it is vital to prioritise accommodation for foreign students, preferably in the halls of residence within the campus, and to design a language programme for the foreign students in order to shorten the transition and adjustment period. Equally vital is the need to consider providing a skills development training programme for the staff involved, in project management in particular, and in co-ordination in general, with a view to providing an enabling platform for effective, successful project implementation and co-ordination.

Clearly, development partners should study and reflect on the real issues that affect student performance in light of the programme goals, reflecting upon them and considering solutions both during the programme design and during the implementation and monitoring of the programme. Similarly, the hosting institution's capacity should be assessed before the start of the programme, and if necessary some basic training in project implementation and co-ordination of international programmes should be given, with a view to ensuring the efficiency and sustainability of the collaboration.

Overall, the results and conclusions show that international collaborations and partnerships provide a good learning experience for both foreign students and collaborating institutions. They provide an opportunity for students' career growth; they act as a vehicle for cultural fusion and acculturation in the formation of a universal culture and they advance development co-operation and thus development.

About the author and the project

Elizabeth Kaase-Bwanga is a senior lecturer in the School of Women and Gender Studies, Makerere University, Uganda

Project title: Understanding the academic and cultural perceptions of South Sudan students at Makerere University
Partner institutions: Makerere University (Uganda), University of Juba (South Sudan)

References

Allport G (1979) *The Nature of Prejudice*. Reading, MA: Addison-Wesley

Berger CR and Calabrese RJ (1975) Some explanations in initial interaction and beyond: Toward a development theory of interpersonal communication. *Human Communication Research* 1(2): 99–112

Brecht R and Robinson J (1995) On the value of formal instruction in a study abroad context. In BF Freed (ed.) *Second Language Acquisition in a Study Abroad Context*. Amsterdam: John Benjamins Publishing. pp 317–334

Byram M (1997) *Teaching and Assessing Intercultural Communicative Competence*. Bristol: Multilingual Matters

Coleman J (1998) Evolving intercultural perceptions among university language learners in Europe. In: M Byram and M Fleming (eds) *Language Learning in Intercultural Perspective*. Cambridge: Cambridge University Press

Croucher SM and Eric Kramer E (2017) Cultural fusion theory: An alternative to acculturation. *Journal of International and Intercultural Communication* 10(2): 97–114

De La Garza AT and Ono KA (2015) Retheorizing adaptation: Differential adaptation and critical intercultural communication. *Journal of International and Intercultural Communication* 8(4): 269–289

Fischer G (1998) *E-mail in Foreign Language Teaching. Towards the Creation of Virtual Classrooms*. Tübingen: Stauffenburg Medien

Forstat RE (1951) Adjustment problems of international students. *Sociology and Social Research* 26(1): 25–30

Freed BF (1990) Language learning in a study abroad context: The effect of interactive and non-interactive out-of-class context on grammatical achievement on oral proficiency. In: J Alatic (ed.) *Linguistic Language Acquisition: The Interdependence of Theory, Practice and Research*. Washington, DC: Georgetown University Press

Freed BF (1993) Assessing the linguistic impact of study abroad: What we currently know, what we need to learn. *Journal of Asia Pacific Communication* 4(4): 151–166

Freed BF (1998) An overview of issues and research in language learning in a study abroad setting. *Frontiers: The Interdisciplinary Journal of Study Abroad* 4(2): 31–60

Gudykunst WB (1988) Uncertainty and anxiety. In: YY Kim and WB Gudykunst (eds) *Theories in Intercultural Communication.* Thousand Oaks, CA: Sage

Gudykunst WB (2005) An anxiety/uncertainty management (AUM) theory of strangers' intercultural adjustment. In WB Gudykunst (ed.) *Theorizing about Intercultural Communication.* Thousand Oaks, CA: Sage

Guntermann G (1995) The Peace Corps experience: Language and learning in training and in the field. In: BF Freed (ed.) *Second Language Acquisition in a Study Abroad Context.* Amsterdam: John Benjamins

Huang J (2006) English abilities for academic listening: How confident are Chinese students? *College Student Journal* 40(1): 218–226

Huang J and Brown K (2009) Cultural factors affecting Chinese ESL students' academic learning. *Education* 129(4): 643–653

Jávorka Z and Church S (2017) *Mid-term Review of the Norwegian Programme for Capacity Development in Higher Education and Research for Development.* Oslo: Norhed

Kim YY (2008) Toward intercultural personhood: Globalization and a way of being. *International Journal of Intercultural Relations* 32(4): 359–368

Kim YY and Ruben BD (1988) Intercultural transformation: A systems theory. In: YY Kim and WB Gudykunst (eds) *Theories in Intercultural Communication.* Thousand Oaks, CA: Sage

Koskinen L and Tossavainen K (2003) Relationships with undergraduate nursing exchange students: A tutor perspective. *Journal of Advanced Nursing* 41(5): 499–508

Lafford (1995) Getting into, through and out of a survival situation: A comparison of communicative strategies used by students studying Spanish abroad and at home. In BF Freed (ed.) *Second Language Acquisition in a Study Abroad Context.* Amsterdam: John Benjamins

Lee JJ and Rice C (2007) Welcome to America? International student perceptions of discrimination. *Higher Education* 53(3): 381–409

Li MZ and Stodolska M (2006) Transnationals, leisure, and Chinese graduate students in the United States. *Leisure Sciences* 28(1): 39–55

Makerere University (2013a) *Assessment Report: Becoming a Learner-Centered Research University.* Kampala: Makerere University, Directorate of Quality Assurance

Makerere University (2013b) *Fact Book 2012/13,* 4th edition. Kampala: Makerere University

Makerere University (2013c) *Annual Report.* Kampala: Makerere University

Makerere University (2016) *Fact Book 2015/16.* Kampala: Makerere University

Miller E (1993) Cultural shock: A student's perspective of study abroad and the importance of promoting study abroad programs. Paper presented at the Annual Intercultural and International Communication Conference, Miami, FL, 25–27 April

Power L, Millington KA and Bengtsson S (2015) *Building Capacity in Higher Education Topic Guide.* Health and Education Advice and Resource Team for DfID, UK. Available online

Poyrazli S and Lopez MD (2007) An exploratory study of perceived discrimination and homesickness: A comparison of international students and American students. *Journal of Psychology* 141(3): 263–280

Spenader AJ (2011) Language learning and acculturation: Lessons from high school and gap-year exchange students. *Foreign Language Annals* 44(2): 381–398. Available online

Sun W and Chen GM (1997) Dimensions of difficulties mainland Chinese students encounter in the United States. Paper presented at the International Conference in Cross-Cultural Communication, Tempe, AZ. March

Wang CC and Mallinckrodt B (2006) Acculturation, attachment, and psychological adjustment of Chinese/Taiwanese international students. *Journal of Counseling Psychology* 53(4): 422–433. Available online

Wei M, Heppner P, Mallen MJ, Ku T-Y, Liao KY-H and Wu T-F (2007) Acculturative stress, perfectionism, years in the United States, and depression among Chinese international students. *Journal of Counseling Psychology* 54(4): 385–394. Available online

Yan K and Berliner DC (2009) Chinese international students' academic stressors in the United States. *College Student Journal* 43(4): 939–960

Zimmermann S (1995) Perceptions of intercultural communication competence and international student adaptation to an American campus. *Communication Education* 44(4): 321–335. Available online

16

Models of co-operation
between a university in Norway
and two universities in Africa:
An autoethnographic report

Birgit Brock-Utne

This article deals with two different collaborations between the University of Oslo and two universities on the African continent. Since I have been strongly involved in both of the projects on the Norwegian side, it is an autoethnographic account: I describe my own involvement in the projects, the different models of organisation and their strengths and weaknesses as I have experienced them. In the introductory article to a special issue of the *International Review of Education*, I describe *autoethnography* as an approach to research and writing that seeks to describe and systematically analyse (*graphy*) personal experience (*auto*) in order to understand cultural experience (*ethno*).[1] Autoethnography challenges conventional ways of doing research. Research is seen as a political, socially just and socially conscious act that provides an opportunity to explore aspects of our social lives in a deeper and more sustained manner than conventional research methodologies allow. The resulting analysis draws upon personal experiences, which inform our broader social understandings which, in turn, enrich our self-understandings. An autoethnographic approach implies the researcher's own voice describing the research findings (Creswell 2013). According to Ellis et al. (2011) autoethnography is one of the research approaches that acknowledges and accommodates subjectivity, emotionality, and the researcher's influence on research, rather than hiding from these matters or assuming they don't exist.

Teaching at the University of Dar es Salaam and at the University of Oslo

I worked as a professor in the Department (later Faculty) of Education at the University of Dar es Salaam (UDSM) from 1988 to 1992, and from 1989 to 1991 also as the head of the Department of Educational Psychology. Within the first few weeks I had made two critical observations. First, that all my colleagues and my students conversed in Kiswahili in all informal situations. My students also switched to Kiswahili during buzz group discussions of questions I had written in English on the chalkboard. Second, that the curriculum taught and the reading lists students were given had a strong Western bias. The reading lists consisted of books from the US or Canada, often those the professors themselves had used when they studied overseas. These books could not be bought in Tanzania. There were one or two copies (mostly just one) on reserve in the library, which meant that a student could read the book only in the library, usually for just one hour at a time. The books were highly irrelevant for Africa, containing theories that had been built upon empirical research done in the North.

In a study of three of the world's leading journals of educational psychology[2] Yussen (2016) showed their significant bias towards what others have dubbed 'WEIRD' research (conducted with participants from Western, Educated, Industrialised, Rich and Democratic countries). Yussen concludes that a vast majority of high-profile educational psychology research is being conducted on children who represent a small fraction of the world's population. This means that much of what we consider to be 'fact' and 'best practice' in educational psychology may not apply to the vast majority of the world's children. He finds it very likely that we don't know nearly as much as we think we do. Theories are built on the basis of this research and applied to cultures where they do not fit. In an article reflecting on the Western bias of media theory, Denis McQuail (2009) notes that the bias partly comes from the extent to which media theory is dependent on and reflective of the media themselves, who are also very Western, if not American. In seeking a more universal form of media theory, the question arises as to how to combat, avoid or counter the bias. The roots of the Western bias, he claims, lie deeply embedded in Western social science, which is permeated by ideas about the superiority of Western (and Protestant) society.

Part of my work at UDSM involved classroom observation of secondary school student teachers. In the course of doing so, I also observed the secondary school students and noticed the great difficulties they had in coping with English as the language of instruction. In addition, during my time at UDSM I noticed that girls experienced greater challenges in education than boys: parents were more eager to pay school fees for their sons than for their daughters, for example, or how girls were chased out of school and sometimes even from their home if they got pregnant, while the boy could continue his schooling. I was therefore one of the founding members of and the fundraiser for the research group WED (Women, Education, Development) and helped organise research on the gender dimension (see for example Brock-Utne and Katunzi 1991; Brock-Utne and Possi 1990; Sumra and Katunzi 1991).

When I returned to the Faculty of Education at the University of Oslo (UiO) in 1992, I was allowed to use half of my teaching time to organise a weekly three-hour seminar titled 'Education in Africa'. After the first term I had several phone calls from people who wanted very much to attend the seminar. These were not students, and they came from a range of backgrounds: some worked as regular teachers in secondary schools, some in NGOs such as the Refugee Council, Save the Children and the United Nations Association, and there were even a couple from the Norwegian Agency for Development Cooperation (Norad) and the Ministry of Foreign Affairs. After some years, a group of the seminar participants encouraged me to develop a master's programme in Comparative and International Education. I worked on this during 1997 and 1998 and welcomed the first cohort of students in August 1998.

SIU, NUFU and the North–South committees at the Norwegian universities

In 1991 the Royal Norwegian Ministry of Foreign Affairs and the Norwegian Council of Universities (NCU)[3] signed a co-operation agreement, which led to the initiation of the Norwegian Council of Universities' Programme for Development Research and Education (NUFU).[4] The main objectives of the NUFU programme were to contribute to competence building in low- and middle-income countries (LMICs) through co-operation between universities and research institutions in Norway and corresponding institutions in LMICs, and to contribute towards increased South–South co-operation.[5]

Though the money for the NUFU programme came from the development aid budget, the programme was administered by a committee under the NCU, dedicated to research and development in LMICs. The programme had a funding framework of NOK 175 million over five years (Nyborg 2013). The Centre for International Cooperation between Universities (SIU),[6] was established in autumn 1991, with its headquarters at the University of Bergen (Nyborg 2013). The centre ran several programmes, including the NUFU programme. Academics at Norwegian universities, in co-operation with academics at universities in LMICs, could apply for funding for a five-year co-operative project. There were also Norad fellowships for students from LMICs who could come to Norway and get a degree as part of the co-operative project. For some years we also had a 'quota' scheme whereby students from LMICs were given state bank loans (as were Norwegian students) but if they went back to their countries after graduation, the loan was converted into a scholarship and the loan debt cancelled. Between 1994, when the scheme was established, and the academic year 2016/2017, when the scheme was phased out, 4 545 students completed at least one degree under the scheme. Of these, 78.5 per cent (3 567) completed a master's degree; 11.2 per cent (507) completed a PhD and 10.4 per cent (471) completed a bachelor's degree.[7]

In 1979 the Norwegian universities started organising North–South committees. These committees prioritised the applications for funding which came in, peer reviewed the yearly reports from the projects and gave professional advice. The committees comprised one representative from each faculty, appointed for a two-year period. I represented the Faculty of Education on the North–South committee at the University of Oslo from 1 January 2000 to 31 December 2001. When the Dean called me and asked me to take that position, I protested because I wanted to apply for NUFU funding myself and was afraid I would not be eligible to do so if I joined the committee. But she insisted; I should be the representative of the Faculty of Education. When I joined the committee, I found that almost everyone else on the committee had a NUFU project, and of course when our own project application for funding was evaluated and discussed, we had to leave the room.

The committees still exist[8] though the NUFU programme was closed down in 2012. Per Nyborg, who was the secretary general of NCU and chairperson of the SIU Board when NUFU was created, wrote in an e-mail to me (30 October 2018) that in the first years of NUFU's existence,

> its work was characterised by the enthusiastic involvement of engaged professionals both in the NUFU secretariat and in the many NUFU projects. [In] the first five years of NUFU's existence the NUFU secretariat had an agreement with the Foreign Ministry. The professionals worked without any involvement or control by the Ministry whatsoever. The change of personnel in the Foreign Ministry meant more control of NUFU projects. It got worse when Norad took over. They wanted even more of a say.

The LOITASA project

After I returned to Norway I kept contact with my colleagues at UDSM. I went back to Tanzania several times as a consultant and I discussed a co-operative research project with my former colleagues. They wanted, like me, to investigate the situation regarding the language of instruction in Tanzania. At a CIES[9] conference in the US in March 1999, I met the South African professor Harold Herman who told me that at his campus – the University of the Western Cape (UWC) – several staff members were very interested in the language of instruction issue in South Africa. Some of them wanted to do research in Khayelitsha, a township in Cape Town, where the vast majority of the inhabitants are isiXhosa speakers, yet the language of instruction in schools is English from the fourth grade onwards. I met one of his colleagues, Professor Zubeida Desai, at the Oxford conference[10] in September the same year. We were on the same panel on language of instruction in Africa and started talking about a possible co-operation. Together with a group of UDSM and UWC academics, I applied for seed money to develop a co-operative research project. We named the project we came up with LOITASA (Language of Instruction in Tanzania and South Africa). The project began in January 2002 and the first phase continued through to 2006. At the end of that phase we were granted a second round of funding (2007–2011). We also had funding from a Norway–South Africa research programme administered by the Human Sciences Research Council (HSRC) in South Africa and the Norwegian Research Council.

LOITASA was a South–South–North co-operation project, which in this case, involved research co-operation between UWC in South Africa, UDSM in Tanzania and UiO in Norway. We had master's and PhD students from each of these countries involved in the project. Two of the students got their PhDs from UWC with NUFU funding and a doctoral student from UDSM got his PhD degree with a grant from LOITASA. The others were students of the Comparative and International Education master's programme and got their master's and PhD degrees from UiO. The master's programme, with its curricular options, reading lists and courses, had gone through the boards of the Department and Faculty of Education and had been revised a couple of times in response to student evaluations before the students who chose to be connected to the LOITASA project entered the programme. The PhD students also followed the courses in the master's programmes but, in addition, took PhD courses in the theory of science, in qualitative and quantitative research methods when these were given in English.

Both phases of the LOITASA project comprised two main parts. The first included a description and analysis of current language policies and their implementation in Tanzania and South Africa (see Brock-Utne 2005a, 2005b, 2005c, 2012; Desai 2000; Holmarsdottir 2005).

The second involved an experimental design dealing with the language of instruction in South Africa and Tanzania. In South Africa, the empirical research involved a longitudinal study from Grades 4 to 6 at two schools in the Western Cape, with one class at each school being taught Science and Geography in isiXhosa and the other in English, the current medium of instruction. The study started in 2003, with the Grade 4 learners. An isiXhosa-speaking staff member at UWC, Vuyokazi Nomlomo, who was involved in LOITASA, did research for her PhD on this part of the project. She obtained her PhD in 2007, the first year of the new phase of the project (Nomlomo 2007). My research assistant, Halla Holmarsdottir, worked on the same part of the project and obtained her PhD in 2005 (Holmarsdottir 2005).

The Tanzanian part of the project was to take place at secondary school level since that is when Tanzanian schools officially start using English as the medium of instruction. The intention was to focus on Form 1 and Form 2 learners, with one class at each school being taught in Kiswahili and the other in English. However, the empirical part of this study did not take place as planned since the then-minister of education was unwilling to grant the necessary permission for it. Instead, we had to conduct smaller experiments, which could be done through research clearance from UDSM. Two Tanzanian doctoral students, Mwajuma Vuzo and Halima Mwinsheikhe, wrote their doctoral theses on these experiments, both also receiving their doctorates in 2007 (Mwinsheikhe 2007; Vuzo 2007). I worked alongside them, doing research in the same classrooms (Brock-Utne 2007).

During the first phase we had two workshops in Tanzania and two in South Africa, which all resulted in books (Brock-Utne et al. 2003, 2004, 2005, 2006). The fifth workshop was held in Norway in 2006 and took the form of a large conference, the Languages and Education in Africa conference, which involved five NUFU projects at UiO dealing with the language question in Africa. A book, edited by Brock-Utne and Skattum (2009) resulted from that conference. No workshop took place in 2007 as it was a year for summing up, consolidation and planning the new phase.

The first LOITASA workshop in the second phase was held at UiO from 30 April to 1 May 2008 and was followed immediately by an international conference named IMPLAN (Implications of Language for Peace and Development) from 2 to 3 May 2008. This enabled LOITASA researchers to participate in both events. LOITASA Book 5 (Qorro et al. 2008) is based on this workshop. Another book, built on papers presented at the IMPLAN conference, came out the following year (Brock-Utne and Garbo 2009). Several LOITASA researchers are represented in both of these books. At a CIES conference some time later I met a Canadian, Alan Pitman, who had spent some time in Africa and had come across all four of the LOITASA books from the first phase. He praised the books highly but thought it was a great pity that they were difficult to get hold of outside of Africa. It was a deliberate choice on the part of the editors to publish in Africa, the first volume in Tanzania, the next in South Africa, the third in Tanzania and so on, alternating publication between the two countries. Pitman asked if he would be allowed to select chapters from all four of the books published in the first phase, and collate them in a book that would be published in Europe and thus more easily reach an audience in the North. We thought this was a good idea but emphasised that we did not want to have anything to do with the selection of chapters he made since we were not only editors but also authors, all three of us having a chapter in each book. His selection was peer reviewed before being published in 2010 (Brock-Utne et al. 2010).

We continued our research activities during the second phase of LOITASA, and held annual workshops, which resulted in four more books, two published in Tanzania (Qorro et al. 2008, 2012) and two in South Africa (Desai et al. 2010, 2013). In Tanzania we shifted our focus from secondary to primary schools and made a comparison between pupils who were taught in the English-medium private primary schools and those who were taught in the Kiswahili-medium public primary schools. We found that if we strengthened the public schools with textbooks and the teachers were given in-service teacher training, these Kiswahili-medium schools did better than the fee-paying, English-medium private schools (Bakahwemama 2009; Brock-Utne 2012; Vuzo 2012).

The LOITASA project produced ten books, held eight research workshops and organised two international conferences. Eleven students got their PhDs under the project, the last one in 2016 (Bakahwemama 2016). Eight of the students were awarded their PhDs from UiO, two from UWC and one from UDSM. More than 30 students wrote their master's theses based on research connected to the project. The steering committee, consisting of the project leader from each of the three universities, met once a year just before the workshops to write a joint report, discuss the project and plan for the following year's activities. The three of us sat together, physically, to fill in the reporting forms required by the SIU. The economic consultants had a parallel meeting on the same days. The report required was similar to the one we had to do each year for our own universities: naming publications produced and describing workshops and conferences attended. We also reported on the progress of master's and PhD students. There was a wonderful, collegial atmosphere in the steering committee meetings. Apart from the very first meeting, there were no major conflicts. During the first meeting it had become clear that we did not have enough money to do all we wanted. We had to either cut down on activities or deal with only one country in the South. Luckily a new grant, derived from the collaboration between the HSRC and the Norwegian Research Council, rescued our project and we could run it as originally planned. The fact that the steering committee was small, being just one project leader from each country, was a clear advantage.

The students from the LMICs, who were mostly attached to the LOITASA project, especially those who chose the 'Education and Development' master's option, enriched the programme with their experiences. In 1999 there was a celebration of the 20 years of institutionalised co-operation between UiO and the universities in the South. Inger Joanne Røste, who had been central in building up this co-operation, mentioned that although it was important to give LMIC students the opportunity to study in Oslo, it was just as important that researchers and students in the North developed an interest in studying the situation in LMICs (Garbo 1999). Many of the Norwegian students attached to the LOITASA project were later employed in various international NGOs, development organisations or universities, and have been engaged with North–South questions throughout their lives. With the abolishment, first of the Norad fellowship programme and then of the quota programme, there are now fewer students from LMICs in the master's programmes at UiO, which is regrettable from a Norwegian viewpoint.

The TRANSLED project

There is little doubt that the NUFU programme, as I experienced it through the LOITASA project, was very successful. The evaluation of the programme was also positive, especially as seen by those in the South – the students who had had the opportunity to study in Norway. Yet the programme was closed down and a very different programme for co-operation between Norwegian universities and universities in the South was established. The Norwegian Programme for Capacity Development in Higher Education and Research for Development (Norhed) was launched by Norad in 2012.[11] The rationale behind the establishment of Norhed is both idealistic and economic. The more idealistic aspect of this rationale seems to be that it placed the universities in the South in the driver's seat. The evaluation of the NUFU programme had claimed that capacity building in the NUFU projects had been more about individuals than about institutions. The programmes, according to the evaluation, supported primarily the education of individual students and researchers, and only to a limited extent the wider research environment. Thus the joint leadership and administration between North and South, which had been central to the NUFU programme, was dismantled and the responsibility for budgeting and reporting was placed with the institution in the South, on academics already overburdened with heavy teaching loads.

Instead of having students come to Norway to participate in master's and PhD programmes that had been built up over time, new master's and PhD programmes were to be built up in the South, partly with the help of Northern partners. This seemed to be a cheaper alternative to the NUFU model. It was also claimed that it would be cheaper to have Norad administer the Norhed programme than to have the very professional staff at SIU in Bergen with the help of the North–South committees at the various Norwegian universities administer it, as they had done for NUFU. While SIU is an organisation with a close connection to the universities, Norad is an agency with little knowledge of how universities work. Both the application procedure and the reporting had to be done in the language of public management, which is rather unfamiliar to most academics and has little relevance for the way academics write and report.

I applied for seed money and used contacts I had at UDSM, in Tanzania mainland, and at the State University of Zanzibar (SUZA) in Zanzibar, to create an application for Norhed funding. I chose a colleague to work with at UiO and since he had a tenured job, he formally became the co-ordinator and I an assistant co-ordinator. He and I went to SUZA and UDSM to discuss the application with academics there. Several had worked within the LOITASA project and naturally wanted to continue working on the language issue. There were also others at the two universities who were more interested in the gender and youth issue, which also interested the Norwegian co-ordinator. The application our colleagues at SUZA and UDSM worked out together with us envisaged PhD programmes (at UDSM) and master's degree programmes (at both SUZA and UDSM) in both of these areas. We chose SUZA to be the main partner in the South since this university had hardly any master's degree programmes and was more in need of development than UDSM. We defined the question of school drop-outs as a research focus – a question that may involve both the language of instruction and the gender and youth issue. We named our project TRANSLED (Transformation, Language, Education and Development) and sent off our application in November 2012. On 26 June 2013 we received a letter from Norad informing us that our project had been recommended for support under the Norhed programme. We surmised that one of the reasons why our application was successful was that we had placed the main administration of the project at a newly established university in the South, greatly in need of development. Later on, however, Norad suggested that it might be easier for UDSM to handle such a large project. We did not feel that we could change the project leader in the South after the money had been granted, although with the benefit of hindsight Norad's suggestion seems to have been a wise one.

The project aimed to develop curricula and degree programmes at both SUZA and UDSM in the two specialities: Language, Education and

Development, and Youth, Gender and Development. Originally, SUZA planned to host only two master's programmes, while UDSM was to develop two PhD specialities as well as two master's programmes within the same areas. Later on SUZA decided to develop another master's programme: Teaching Kiswahili to Speakers of Other Languages (MEd TEKSOL). TEKSOL was originally supposed to be a speciality within the Language in Education master's programme and not a fully fledged master's degree in itself. Making it into a master's programme had not been discussed and therefore had not been agreed upon in the TRANSLED steering committee meeting. Nonetheless, it became an independent master's programme and was approved by the Tanzania Commission for Universities (TCU), which is the regulatory body mandated to recognise, approve, register and accredit courses offered at universities operating in Tanzania.

We used the whole of 2014, 2015 and 2016 to build up the two PhD specialities at UDSM and the two master's programmes at SUZA and UDSM. This was a frustrating experience, more for our Southern partners than for us in the North. We helped in some small way to prepare the programmes, suggesting modules and reading lists. Suggesting compulsory reading for the prospective students was no easy task since our partners in the South were so used to reading lists naming authors from the North that they even forgot research that they had been part of themselves, such as the WED research and the ten LOITASA books, which largely focused on educational issues in Africa and had been authored by Africans. Universities and their scientific knowledges are often seen to have universal qualities; therefore, capacity building may appear straightforward. Hanne Adriansen et al. (2015) contest such universalistic notions. Inspired by ideas about the 'geography of scientific knowledge' they explore what role specific places and relationships have in knowledge production, and analyse how cultural experiences are included and excluded in teaching and research. Drawing on discussions about the hegemony of Western thought in education and knowledge production, the various contributors to the book examine what constitutes legitimate scientific knowledge and how such knowledge is negotiated and contested. Their own experiences with higher education capacity building and knowledge production are discussed and used to explain the turn to and rise of auto-ethnography.[12] In the TRANSLED project, we in the North could influence the reading lists to a limited extent, but had no influence whatsoever on the work of the committees these programmes had to go through. The programmes were sent back several times with questions from various committees, delaying the start of the new PhD specialities and master's programmes. At SUZA, three new master's programmes were developed in 2015 and approved, at institutional level, at the end of 2016. In 2017 two of the programmes were approved by the TCU. The two approved programmes at SUZA were the MEd in Youth, Gender and Development and the MEd TEKSOL. The approved programmes were offered for the first time in the academic year of 2017/2018. The third programme, namely the MEd in Language in Education, has not yet (November 2018) been approved by the TCU, despite being submitted on the same day as the other two programmes and despite being the master's programme decided on by the TRANSLED group. It seems that the reason for this is that some academics claim that it has too much in common with the TEKSOL master's programme. Institutional politics may also be at play, which easily happens when money comes to an impoverished institution in the South, especially when a relatively young member of staff is placed in charge.

At UDSM, the two master's programmes proposed were Language, Education and Development (MEd LED) and Youth, Gender and Development (MEd YOGEDE). The former commenced in 2017 while the latter is still (November 2018) under revision due to an institutional directive to increase the number of courses in order to improve the programme. These master's programmes were further developed to continue as PhD specialities within the existing PhD in Education programme.

So far there has been only one conference in the TRANSLED project. This conference was held to formally launch the project and took place at SUZA in January 2016. An edited volume of the conference papers has been produced and was launched at a workshop in Bagamoyo in November 2018 (Brock-Utne, Ismail and Vuzo 2018).

The teaching requiring services from UiO could only start in 2017 since none of the programmes had been approved before that. It had been agreed that we would teach a module (five weeks of teaching, including giving and grading of term papers) in both of the specialities. In the spring of 2017, I taught a module of five weeks in Language, Education and Development to both master's and PhD students of that speciality at UDSM. Two of my colleagues spent 14 weeks (seven weeks each) at UDSM and SUZA in October and November 2017, teaching part of the Youth, Gender and Development component.

Though TRANSLED, like LOITASA, is a South–South–North project, it is vastly different in many ways. Research, which was such an important part of LOITASA and encouraged joint work among academics in the North and the South, has played little role in Norhed projects generally, and has played hardly any role at all in TRANSLED. I cite from a paper about the TRANSLED project:

> Joint research is the part on our agenda that has suffered the most. This activity has hardly started. This has partly to do with the fact that there was no meeting between the partners of the North and the South in 2018 – the year that joint research could have started. Joint research has budget implications. It could not take place because we had no funds disbursed from Norad in 2017/2018. In our original application we mentioned the dropout problem and the problem of out-of-school youth as an important research area for PhD and master students, but hardly any research or writing within this area has taken place. (Makame and Brock-Utne 2018)

At the end of 2017, Norad decided to freeze the money to the TRANSLED project because they were not satisfied with reporting from the South. The academic co-ordinator at SUZA claimed that he had answered all the queries from Norad several times, but changes of staff at Norad without adequate handover procedures had caused a problem. The fact that Norad had changed programme officers connected to Norhed several times over the previous three to four years made communication difficult. Freezing grant money for a whole year had never happened in any NUFU project. Moreover, in the NUFU projects the Norwegian partner had had a more decisive role since the money first went to the Norwegian universities and was dispersed from there. In 2018 the TRANSLED partners in the South still had some unused money – which should have been used for equipment, but had not been used because of the lengthy procurement procedures. Norad did not seem to be aware of the fact that the competitive bidding process that the World Bank had forced on poor universities in the South (Brock-Utne 2000) resulted in allocated funds not being used for a prolonged period of time. In this case, where the money for the whole project had been frozen, the unused money in Tanzania was temporarily reallocated for research and for attending conferences, but at UiO there was no money left. This meant that the teaching I should have done in 2018 could not take place. Neither could an important research seminar I had promised to organise with the project leader at UDSM take place. Throughout 2018, there was no money for me to travel to Tanzania. An important international conference I attended in 2018, and where I presented the only joint publication on our research theme (Brock-Utne, Halvorsen and Vuzo 2018), I had to pay for myself, even though my participation had been budgeted for.

In contrast to LOITASA, where the three project co-ordinators had a meeting to share the reporting and budgeting tasks, the main responsibility for reporting and drawing up the budgets in TRANSLED was placed with SUZA. If Norad was not satisfied with the reports they received from SUZA, they froze not only the budgets for our partners in the South, but also those of the Norwegian partner. Neither I nor the project leader at SUZA can see the wisdom of this decision. Had the budget that was supposed to have gone to UiO in 2018 not been frozen, important research on the school drop-out problem could have started.

The fact that curricula have been built up and decided upon in the South does not necessarily make them more 'African'. Much depends on the former training of the staff in the South and the expertise coming to them from the North. While I was teaching at UDSM I was asked to evaluate a textbook called *Social Psychology in Africa*, written by one of my Tanzanian colleagues. The title excited me because I had so long missed a book on exactly that topic. But the content was a great disappointment. There was nothing African about the book except 'Africa' and 'African' being mentioned in some places. All the references were from the North (mostly from the US where my colleague had studied) and even when he wrote about 'the family' it was the US/European ideal of a nuclear family and the gender roles within that family he was discussing, not the African extended family with its gender roles. I could not recommend the book for publication. There are excellent examples of African doctoral students studying in industrialised countries who have been encouraged by their supervisors in these countries to use theories developed in Africa. Suffice it here to mention a doctoral thesis by Elpidus Baganda (2016) from Tanzania, delivered at the University of Newcastle in New South Wales in Australia. Baganda's three Australian supervisors had encouraged him to analyse his data using the educational theory of the educational thinker and statesman Julius Kambarage Nyerere.

With the rise of the 'knowledge for development' paradigm, 'local knowledge' and its importance for transformational processes has become a central theme in the international discourse on development (Koch and Weingart 2016). In the context of development co-operation, 'local knowledge' usually refers to the knowledge generated in LMICs in contrast to Western knowledge. In their study, Koch and Weingart use the term to differentiate knowledge that is locally available in a given society (both scientific and non-scientific) from knowledge that is provided by external (foreign) experts. However, this knowledge can sometimes be more easily appreciated by foreigners who have been living for extended periods in LMICs and have learned to recognise and appreciate ways of thinking that are different from Western modes. For instance, in his book on education and indigenous knowledges, Anders Breidlid (2012) focuses on the hegemonic role of Western epistemology that spread in the wake of colonialism and the capitalist economic system, and its exclusion and othering of other epistemologies. Through a series of case studies Breidlid discusses how the domination of Western epistemology has had a major impact on the epistemological foundation of education systems across the globe. His book queries the sustainability of hegemonic epistemology both in classrooms in the global South and in the face of the imminent ecological challenges of our common earth, and discusses whether indigenous knowledge systems would better serve learners in the global South and help promote sustainable development.

Conclusion

While the LOITASA project led to a very fruitful co-operation between North and South that benefited both partners, led to joint research and many joint publications, the TRANSLED project, so far, has produced few results. In the year 2018, where there has been no money for any joint research or even any physical meetings, our partners in the South have done some research, but we in the North know nothing about it. For our partners in the South, it has been good to receive aid enabling the purchase of items such as new equipment and more books for the library, and making it possible to attend international conferences and to do research. Most of the work building up the new graduate programmes they had to do by themselves. Most of the teaching we have done could have been done locally, provided money had been allocated for that purpose; this is especially true for the gender speciality. For me as the initiator of the TRANSLED project, there has been no professional benefit from the project and it has so far led to a lot of frustration. But it has of course been good to meet again with Tanzanian friends and be back speaking Kiswahili, a language I love.

One of the reviewers of an earlier draft of this chapter asked: since you describe your experience with a project within the NUFU programme as much more successful than your experience with a project within the Norhed programme, is your conclusion that power over the programme should remain in the North? My answer is that the power has all the time remained in the North since the money comes from Norway. The point is that we hardly noticed this in the LOITASA project, since the money that was first sent to UiO was redistributed as soon as possible to the other two universities, according to agreed on budgets. With Norad's capacity and willingness to freeze even the Norwegian budget if they do not get what they want from our Southern partners, the power is much more clearly and visibly located in Norway, specifically in Norad. While the LOITASA project was built up around joint research interests, the TRANSLED project has relied on starting research with students in master's programmes and PhD specialties, which first had to be developed. This took much longer than we anticipated. With the benefit of hindsight we should maybe have started research from the beginning, in parallel with building up the various degree programmes.

Acknowledgements

I would like to thank two anonymous peer reviewers for their important advice, which I have followed in this version of my chapter. I would also like to thank Per Nyborg, who was the Secretary General of NCU and Chair of the SIU Board when NUFU was created, for reading my chapter and giving valuable input and criticism. It is good to have critical friends.

About the author and the project

Birgit Brock-Utne is attached to the Department of Education at the University of Oslo as a professor of education and development. She also works as a visiting professor at the University of Dar es Salaam, Tanzania and the University of Witwatersrand, South Africa. She runs a consultancy firm called EDCON (Education and Development Consulting)

Project title: Transformation, Language, Education and Development
Partner institutions: State University of Zanzibar, University of Dar es Salaam (both Tanzania) and University of Oslo (Norway)

Notes

1   See Brock-Utne (2018b).
2   Namely: the *Journal of Educational Psychology*, *Contemporary Educational Psychology* and the *British Journal of Educational Psychology*.
3   The university council had a steering committee consisting of the rectors of the universities of Oslo, Bergen, Trondheim and Tromsø, two representatives from the university colleges and the leader of the Norwegian Student Union.
4   In Norwegian: *Norsk utvalg for Utviklingsrelatert Forskning og Utvikling* (NUFU). Though it was started in 1991, it really took off only from 1996 (personal communication from Marit Egner, 3 October 2018). Egner administers the North–South Board at UiO.

5   For the last evaluation of the NUFU programme, commissioned by Norad in early 2009, see: https://www.norad.no/om-bistand/publikasjon/2010/ evaluation-of-the-norwegian-programme-for-development-research-and-educa-tion-nufu-and-of-norads-programme-for-master-studies-noma

6   In Norwegian: Senter for Internasjonalt Universitetssamarbeid.

7   See: https://www.regjeringen.no/no/dokumenter/Horing---Evaluering-av-kvoteordningen/id765134/

8   See https://www.uio.no/for-ansatte/nettverk-moter/los-enhetene/ nord-soer-utvalget/

9   CIES refers to the Comparative and International Education Society, in this case the US-based branch, which has annual conferences in the US and surrounding coun-tries like Canada, Jamaica and Brazil.

10   The Oxford conferences are arranged by the United Kingdom Education and Development Forum (UKFIET) every second year in the examination hall of Oxford University and gather researchers from all over the world interested in education in LMICs. See www.ukfiet.org

11   For further information, see www.norad.no/norhed

12   See the following articles in a special issue on autoethnography in research in Africa: Brock-Utne 2018a, 2018b; Vuzo 2018).

References

Adriansen HK, Møller Madsen L and Jensen S (eds) (2015) *Higher Education and Capacity Building in Africa: The Geography of Knowledge*. Routledge Studies in African Development series. London: Routledge

Baganda E (2016) The trajectory of universal primary education and educational decen-tralisation in Tanzania 1961–2015: A Nyererean perspective. PhD thesis, Faculty of Education and Arts, University of Newcastle, Australia

Bakahwemama JB (2009) What is the difference in achievement of learners in selected Kiswahili and English primary schools in Tanzania? MA thesis, Institute for Educational Research, University of Oslo

Bakahwemama JB (2016) Change of language of instruction for science and mathematics in grade five in Zanzibar: What was the reasoning behind the policy change? PhD thesis, Institute for Educational Research, University of Oslo

Breidlid A (2012) *Education, Indigenous Knowledges, and Development in the Global South: Contesting Knowledges for a Sustainable Future*. Routledge Research in Education series. London: Routledge

Brock-Utne B (2000) *Whose Education for All? Recolonization of the African Mind*. New York: Falmer Press

Brock-Utne B (2005a) Globalisation, language and education. In: J Zajda (ed.) *International Handbook on Globalisation, Education and Policy Research*. Dordrecht: Kluwer

Brock-Utne B (2005b) Language-in-education policies and practices in Africa with a special focus on Tanzania and South Africa: Insights from research in progress. In: AMY Lin and P Martin (eds) *Decolonisation, Globalisation: Language-in-Education Policy and Practice*. Clevedon: Multilingual Matters

Brock-Utne B (2005c) The continued battle over Kiswahili as the language of instruction in Tanzania. In: B Brock-Utne and RK Hopson (eds) *Languages of Instruction for African Emancipation: Focus on Postcolonial Contexts and Considerations*. Cape Town and Dar es Salaam: CASAS and Mkuki na Nyota

Brock-Utne B (2007) Learning through a familiar language versus learning through a foreign language: A look into some secondary school classrooms in Tanzania. *International Journal of Educational Development* 27(5): 487–498

Brock-Utne B (2012) Understanding what the teacher is saying: Kiswahili- and English-medium primary schools in Tanzania. In: M Qorro, Z Desai and B Brock-Utne (eds) *Language of Instruction: A Key to Understanding What the Teacher is Saying*. Dar es Salaam: Kad

Brock-Utne B (2018a) Using a narrative approach to researching literacy and non-formal education in Africa and Asia. *International Review of Education* 64(6): 701–711

Brock-Utne B (2018b) Researching language and culture in Africa using an autoethnographic approach. *International Review of Education* 64(6): 713–715

Brock-Utne B, Desai Z and Qorro M (eds) (2003) *Language of Instruction in Tanzania and South Africa (LOITASA)*. Dar es Salaam: E&D

Brock-Utne B, Desai Z and Qorro M (eds) (2004) *Researching the Language of Instruction in Tanzania and South Africa*. Cape Town: African Minds

Brock-Utne B, Desai Z and Qorro M (eds) (2005) *LOITASA Research in Progress: Language of Instruction in Tanzania and South Africa*. Dar es Salaam: K&D

Brock-Utne B, Desai Z and Qorro M (eds) (2006) *Focus on Fresh Data on the Language of Instruction Debate in Tanzania and South Africa*. Cape Town: African Minds

Brock-Utne B, Desai Z and Qorro M with Pitman A (eds) (2010) *Language of Instruction in Tanzania and South Africa: Highlights from a Project*. Boston/Rotterdam: Sense

Brock-Utne B and Garbo G (eds) (2009) *Language and Power: Implications of Language for Peace and Development*. Dar es Salaam: Mkuki na Nyota

Brock-Utne B, Halvorsen T and Vuzo M (2018) The drop-out or rather 'push-out' problem in the South and in the North. Paper presented in the Africa SIG at the 62nd annual meeting of the Comparative and International Education Society (CIES) in Mexico City, Mexico, 25–29 March

Brock-Utne B, Ismail M and Vuzo M (eds) (2018) *Transforming Education for Development in Africa*. Dar es Salaam: Mkuki na Nyota

Brock-Utne B and Katunzi N (eds) (1991) Women and education in Tanzania: Twelve papers from a seminar. WED Report 3, University of Dar es Salaam

Brock-Utne B and Possi M (1990) The expectations of some secondary school students in Tanzania concerning their future life, education and jobs. Paper presented to the Women, Education and Development seminar in Morogoro, Tanzania, 16–20 September. WED Report 1, University of Dar es Salaam

Brock-Utne B and Skattum I (eds) (2009) *Languages and Education in Africa: A Comparative and Transdisciplinary Analysis.* Oxford: Symposium Books

Creswell JW (2013) *Qualitative Inquiry and Research Design: Choosing Among Five Approaches.* London: Sage

Desai Z (2000) Mother tongue education: The key to African language development. A conversation with an imagined South African audience. In: R Phillipson (ed.) *Rights to Language: Equity, Power and Education.* Mahwah, NJ: Lawrence Erlbaum

Desai Z, Qorro M and Brock-Utne B (eds) (2010) *Educational Challenges in Multilingual Societies.* Cape Town: African Minds

Desai Z, Qorro M and Brock-Utne B (eds) (2013) *The Role of Language in Teaching and Learning of Science and Mathematics.* Cape Town: African Minds

Ellis C, Adams TE and Bochner A (2011) Autoethnography: An overview. *Forum: Qualitative Social Research/Sozialforschung* 12(1). Available online

Garbo G L (1999) 20 år med Nord–Sør-samarbeid (20 years with North–South co-operation). *Uniforum* 19. Available online

Holmarsdottir H (2005) From policy to practice: A study of the implementation of the language-in-education policy in three South African primary schools. PhD dissertation, University of Oslo

Koch S and Weingart P (2016) *The Delusion of Knowledge Transfer: The Impact of Foreign Aid Experts on Policy-Making in South Africa and Tanzania.* Cape Town: African Minds

Makame A and Brock-Utne B (2018) Knowledge, identity, culture: The birth and development of the Norhed project called TRANSLED (Transformation, Language, Education and Development). Paper presented at the Norhed workshop held at Oslo Metropolitan University, 15–16 March

McQuail D (2009) Some reflections on the Western bias of media theory. *Asian Journal of Communication* 10(2): 1–13. Available online

Mwinsheikhe HM (2007) Overcoming the language barrier: An in-depth study of Tanzanian secondary school science teachers' and students' strategies in coping with the English/Kiswahili dilemma in the teaching/learning process. PhD dissertation, University of Oslo

Nomlomo VS (2007) Science teaching and learning through the medium of English and isiXhosa: A comparative study of two primary schools in the Western Cape. Unpublished PhD dissertation, University of the Western Cape, Cape Town

Nyborg P (2013) Den sosiale dimensjonen i høyere utdanning (The social dimension in higher education). *Michael* 10, Supplement 14

Qorro M, Desai Z and Brock-Utne B (eds) (2008) *LOITASA: Reflecting on Phase I and entering Phase II*. Dar es Salaam: E&D Vision Publishing

Qorro M, Desai Z and Brock-Utne B (eds) (2012) *Language of Instruction: A key to understanding what the teacher is saying*. Dar es Salam: K&D Associates

Sumra S and Katunzi N (1991) *The Struggle for Education: School Fees and Girls' Education in Tanzania*. WED Report 5, University of Dar es Salaam

Vuzo M (2007) Revisiting the language of instruction policy in Tanzania: A comparative study of geography classes taught in Kiswahili and English. PhD dissertation, University of Oslo

Vuzo M (2012) A comparative analysis of teaching and learning strategies used in government and private primary schools. In: M Qorro, Z Desai and B Brock-Utne (eds) *Language of Instruction: A Key to Understanding What the Teacher is Saying*. Dar es Salaam: K&D Associates

Vuzo M (2018) Towards achieving sustainable development goals: Revisiting language of instruction in Tanzanian secondary schools. *International Review of Education* 64(6): 803–822

Yussen S (2016) The publication gap: Western bias in educational psychology journals. *Improving Lives: CEHD Vision 2020 Blog*, 22 April. Available online

PART FIVE

REFORMING UNIVERSITIES,
REFORMING SOCIETIES

Introduction to Part Five

Tor Halvorsen

Universities are embedded in culture. They reproduce and change the norms and values that hold a society together. Conflicts within a society are explicitly, vividly and at times violently, played out within universities. New generations of students bring with them expectations of change and engage in the transformation of both society and the university. The #FeesMustFall movement in South Africa is just one example (Booysen 2016).

Actors outside the university, often in open conflict with the actors inside the university, find ways of influencing what a university should be through the networks of politics or with the help of the power of money. It is common to cite an almost 100-year-old statement that a university is not outside, but inside 'the general social fabric of an era ... it is an expression of an age, as well as an influence operating upon both present and future' (Flexner 1930 quoted in Kerr 2001: 3).

Universities in all societies represent a push for normative change. They are radical institutions by nature and necessity. They promote human rights, foster attitudes to change, make space for new gender values, promote innovation and new work roles and are arenas for multicultural dialogue and international networking. They may of course also defend conservatism; established authorities, rituals and habits; and justify the legitimacy of traditional powers in family and society, in religious traditions as well as in the patriarchal economy and the working life at large. But if this is the case, it is expected to be with reference to knowledge, not by reference to the value of tradition, established norms or regimes as such.

This cultural embeddedness is thus one of contradiction. The university is part of a society to which it brings critical knowledge, questioning all established norms and institutions. Yet, it is this criticised society that must bring to universities the resources for its work. Securing the material basis of universities activates the debate about the relevance of universities for development: what is there to gain from these investments?

As the saying goes: universities do not grow their own potatoes. If public funding is failing, perhaps due to a lack of belief in academic knowledge or due to a country's authorities resisting its critical role, universities may be forced to show their relevance to the *functioning of society* in order to be supported by sources other than the general public. The World Bank, for example, is focusing on the development of 'human capital' and 'innovations' for the economy and thus, through functional arguments, is pushing privatisation. In many of the countries where the projects described in this book are located, those already dependent on private funding fear the consequences of this functional justification of universities at the cost of their critical public role. This is the case not only in Africa, but also at Harvard, USA, according to a previous university president:

> I worry that commercialization may be changing the nature of academic institutions in ways we will come to regret. By trying so hard to acquire more money for their work, universities may compromise values that are essential to the continued confidence and loyalty of faculty students, alumni, and even the general public. (Bok 2003: x)

The conflict between the usefulness of knowledge for specific purposes in society versus the development of 'knowledge for its own sake', that is, knowledge for society at large, thus how universities are funded, influences what is given priority within a broader culture of a society (Collini 2012; Sander 2009).

Donor-funded universities

Much of the material support of universities, such as those we discuss below, comes from donors. Donors believe in the development potential of knowledge, for both functional and cultural purposes. For example, in the projects presented below, which are supported by the Norwegian Programme for Capacity Development in Higher Education and Research for Development (Norhed), the development of knowledge is seen as a support to women in education, the transformation of patriarchal attitudes and as research relevant for the oppressed in society. Some donors drive universities towards the market, as does the World Bank, mentioned above. The overall impression, however, is that European support for higher education promotes 'public universities' and their critical role in society (Adriansen et al. 2016; Halvorsen and Nossum 2016; Obrecht 2015). In other words, the Norhed programme is but one example.

What holds the university together, the link between functional and cultural values, is the common purpose of truth-telling through critical reflection on what we think we already know as well as what we want to know but have not yet reflected upon. This value again presupposes that universities are part of and promote freedom of expression, that they promote and protect the freedom for the academic profession to search for knowledge wherever they find it worthwhile and encourage them to express their findings in both teaching and publications accordingly. The academic profession, then, cannot be reduced to being functional contributors only (as the World Bank does so eagerly) but must build on ideas of openness and dialogue, with democracy as a basic value. The ideas of academic freedom generally go together with processes of democratisation. In many countries, however, this is a huge normative challenge.

It is worth noting that how universities relate generally to society is crucial for how we solve the 'burning issues' debated in Part Two. As forcefully argued by Melissa Leach in *The Politics of Green Transformations* in a series of books on the 'pathways to sustainability', *at universities, a democratic dialogue is needed* about what knowledge may promote our work towards a sustainable world,[1] and what knowledge we must criticise for not doing this, no matter how 'functional' this knowledge may be. As she notes 'some forms of knowledge and action are clearly incompatible with sustainable futures, and need to be contested strongly'. She continues: 'Fostering a plural, democratic politics of knowledge is therefore key to defining and achieving green transformation' (Leach 2015: 37, 38). We could add that this is also key for social justice.

The Norhed programme and reflexivity

The Norhed programme evolves out of a polity where the belief in academic knowledge is high. The profile of the Norhed programme shows that it believes in the value of universities as critical cultural institutions, but also argues that universities have an important functional role for societal development. And as argued in the programme, these roles are linked. For example, it is possible to be a highly qualified engineer fulfilling functional demands and also an academic capable of understanding how the practical world is normatively embedded in a cultural context. Based on this belief in the role of knowledge *in and for* society, the Norhed programme promotes the role of universities as change agents of society both culturally and functionally.

This duality can be referred to in the term the *'reflexive society'*. The role of the university in a reflexive society is to develop the ability to take part in the world of work but also to reflect on the role taken within this working life. This allows for a critical outside view on the prevailing norms and values (Readings 1996). Being on the inside, one can, through independent analytical training at universities, also learn to see oneself and one's role in society from the outside. This is – and should be– the purpose of both master's- and doctoral-level education, central to many of the presentations in this section.

As a society becomes more differentiated and the division of labour grows, there is institutional variation linked to a diversification of power and authority as well as a demand for more specialised work and often, increasing professionalised knowledge. This creates a demand for higher education and training in specialised disciplines.

The Norhed programme, which focuses on 'growing independent and qualified academics', builds on a belief in academic knowledge. If we believe in knowledge, and the development of a more independent knowledge, then the ability to reflect on both the cultural and personal consequences of the division of labour, the differentiation of society and the institutional values to which university-based education contributes becomes a societal value. This is what we above have called a reflexive society.

The projects in this section are all examples of how university–society relations are played out, given this dialectic between cultural embeddedness and functional expectations.

In Chapter 17, Andrea Felde and I explore the social sciences arena at Makerere University in Kampala, Uganda. For social science, it is a challenge to balance being too involved with the actors of society on the one hand and being too far from the social reality which these disciplines are duty bound to analyse critically. As academic work presupposes the democratic values of freedom of expression and freedom of teaching and learning, the social sciences in addition have to manage their own role in creating or promoting a democracy in which social science has meaning and may be influential. At Makerere University, scholars within these disciplines struggle to find their role. Some actively take part in a political process seeking to promote popular-democratic values while others withdraw either due to repression or under the banner of 'positivism', as expressed in the idea of neutrality of science.

In Chapter 18, Bernt Lindtjørn, Moges Tadesse and Eskindir Loha describe their experiences of a joint PhD programme from southern Ethiopia. The justification for this project is functional – the need for medical help – but also cultural in the sense that the knowledge mediated must be evidence based. In other words, those who learn to use the knowledge (the PhD students) and those who benefit (the clients) must be able to believe in this knowledge as the truth, as evidently so. In this case, the authors argue that truth-telling by the medical profession directly influences ways of acting politically. They therefore seek to demonstrate that in a political and social culture where the belief in knowledge is strong, and where knowledge is legitimised as 'truth-telling', the lives of citizens will improve.

In Chapter 19 on the academic leadership of women, Jeanette H Magnus, Kora Tushune and Abraham Haileamlak introduce a broad strategy for how to use universities and their academics to change societal norms. The authors begin with the question: how do you use knowledge within a knowledge institution to democratise its internal life, in this case the opportunity for women to get jobs according to qualifications, thus also showing society that repressive norms can be changed? The answer they suggest is to start with a leadership programme. For many female academics, being good at their work is not enough, and excellence does not necessarily speak for itself. For this reason, the authors argue that space must be deliberately created for female leaders. Reflecting on their efforts, through which at least two women in the leadership training programme are now university vice-presidents, the authors show how social norms in a university can undermine the democracy that such institutions must build upon if more women are to be respected for their work.

In Chapter 20 on 'Engendering and decolonising legal education', we again see how universities become an important tool for changing societal norms. These changes presuppose change in curriculum, a critique of established knowledge in law, as well as new research to establish a knowledge underpinning the social rights of women, both within universities as well as in society. Patricia Kameri-Mbote, Anne Hellum, Julie Stewart, Ngeyi Kanyongolo and Mulela Munalula show how complex and challenging it is to implement what seems like a simple slogan: 'gender mainstreaming'. To fight discrimination is hard work, particularly since universities are so embedded within societal norms and a culture which resists this mainstreaming. In this chapter, we also see how a cultural transformation may, in addition, change the functional role of a university through how the legal profession changes.

In Chapter 21, on transforming research, teaching and learning of public administration in Malawi, the authors present another angle on how knowledge and society can relate. The role of universities in educating bureaucrats is as old as the university itself. Thus the quality of public administration depends on the universities. It is therefore crucial that those who are to hold executive power in the state receive an excellent education. The ethos of bureaucracy is not automatic. When it comes to improving the knowledge base of future administrators, Happy Kayuni, Dan Banik, Boniface Dulani and Kaja Elise Gresko reveal the value of the Norhed project, demonstrating how reforms of both attitudes and practices within a culture of corruption and mismanagement can start from within the universities.

Chapter 22, on occupational health, is an example of how research-based knowledge can be crucial for the weak and vulnerable in a cultural context where they have little protection and no voice or support. Here, knowledge from the university is transformed into action research through controversial topics raised about workplace environments and a lack of protection for workers. Given that occupational health risks are increasing in low-income countries, particularly for women and children, while the economic actors profiting from this voiceless labour power are increasing, one important contribution for improvement is to mobilise the medical profession as a guardian force. One tool for this is a massive open online course, another is the dissemination of research tools, a third is the more heroic action of seeking access to the workplaces that no one in charge wants you to see. Bente E Moen, Wakgari Deressa and Simon HD Mamuya demonstrate how the power of knowledge challenges the much stronger forces of both economics and politics, but also how actors with access to knowledge become change agents for the better.

In Chapter 23, Mapatano Mala Ali, Christiane Horwood and Anne Hatløy show how university-based research and education can make research visible and accessible in ways that makes a difference for groups in society that need knowledge-based information. As the authors argue, good nutrition is the cornerstone of good health, and a master's programme developing and mediating this insight becomes vital in sharing this awareness. The authors describe how those most victimised by lack of access to healthy food, who most need knowledge about what constitutes nutritious food, can be prioritised by the academic community if the students take their practice into the rural areas. They explain that this is not only a question of developing needed knowledge generally, but also of steering the gaze of the professionals towards the most needy. Knowledge for society creates a knowledge society for the underprivileged.

Notes

1   This is in the broad meaning of the word, see UN 2030 Agenda for Sustainable Development.

References

Adriansen HK, Madsen LM and Jensen S (2016) *Higher Education and Capacity Building in Africa*. Abingdon: Routledge

Bok D (2003) *Universities in the Marketplace. The Commercialization of Higher Education*. Princeton: Princeton University Press

Booysen S (ed.) (2016) *Fees Must Fall: Student Revolt, Decolonisation and Governance in South Africa*. Johannesburg: Wits University Press

Collini S (2012) *What are Universities for?* London: Penguin

Collini S (2017) *Speaking of Universities*. London: Verso

Halvorsen T and Nossum J (2016) (eds) *North-South Knowledge Networks: Towards Equitable Collaboration Between Academics, Donors and Universities*. Cape Town: African Minds. Available online

Kerr C (2001) *The Uses of the University*. Massachusetts: Harvard University Press

Leach M (2015) What is green? Transformation imperatives and knowledge politics. In: I Scoones, M Leach and P Newell (eds) *The Politics of Green Transformations*. London: Earthscan

Obrecht AJ (ed.) (2015) *APPEAR: Participative Knowledge Production Through Transnational and Transcultural Academic Co-operation*. Vienna: Bölaug Verlag

Readings B (1996) *University in Ruins*. Massachusetts: Harvard University Press

Sander H (ed.) (2009) *Fremtidens universiteter*. Copenhagen: Gyldendal

17

Voices from within:
The academic profession and the
social sciences at Makerere University

Andrea Felde & Tor Halvorsen

Introduction

In general, the academic profession is defined by an ability to be objective, detached from specific societal interests and, importantly, to control the realm and scope of its work, including the conditions under which this is performed. Despite this ideal of objectivity, the social sciences are involved in the social processes they study through the process of knowledge creation. Indeed, the history of social science scholarship (which, chronologically, grew out of the emergence of the humanities and law) is arguably about the balance between academic independence and an involvement with other social actors. How involved can social science scholars be on behalf of knowledge and still be considered members of the scientific community? How distant can they be without being irrelevant to the societies they live in? Should the potential for social change (social engineering) related to teaching topics and research focus areas always be pursued? Or should academics detach themselves from the social consequences of their knowledge and abstain from producing or promoting evidence-based facts and/or knowledge-based arguments when powerful social actors contradict, ignore or dismiss these?

The history of the academic profession, and of the social sciences in particular, presupposes the existence of the kinds of institutions and social contexts that make academic freedom possible. By this we mean free speech and open public forums, the protection of individual rights, etc. Accordingly, social science scholarship is generally seen as contributing to deepening and strengthening the practice of democracy. This can involve providing evidence of the workings of liberal representative democracy, but it can also consist of contributing to, and motivating for, the kinds of civil activism or 'deliberative democracy' that involves all actors affected by all political and economic decision-making.

Through its scholars, social science can be used as a repressive force in the hands of the state – often on behalf of wider economic or more brutal forces. In such cases, the formation of citizens involves the normalisation of certain disciplinary forms of behaviour. However, as a general trend, the social sciences have tended to contribute to the formation of increasingly self-reflexive societies; that is, societies in which scholars invite reflection on the powers shaping citizens, on how such powers achieve social legitimacy and on the consequences of this (including unintended and possibly destructive ones). For social scientists, therefore, questions about how close or far away they should be from social actors, and to whom do they want their work to be relevant, are perennial and constantly worth revisiting.

In Uganda, this issue of distance and closeness to actors in society is a particularly burning one for social scientists. Here, a kind of democracy, that has been more or less forced on the country, takes the form of a limited representative system within a neo-patrimonial regime. In this chapter, we discuss how social scientists at Uganda's Makerere University (MU) see the relationship between their disciplinary work and the society they form part of. Our study is based on 25 in-depth interviews and discussions with four academics in a feedback seminar, mainly during 2016 and early 2017. Our aim is to inspire further reflection on the dilemmas that social scientists face in finding a balance between, on the one hand, staying close to societal actors and the issues that affect them and, on the other hand, respecting the requirements of science that they keep their distance and remain 'detached'. In so doing, we try to describe how scholars at MU handle the issue of academic professionalism in a context where doing social science is, in itself, a form of social engagement that, for some, requires navigating beyond the limits of representative democracy.

Where (Western) ideals of academia meet neo-patrimonialism

Our point of reference is an idea of the academic profession as an ideal type, following the way it has evolved within the ambit of the West. The growing division of labour, the differentiation of society and different types of democracy are all linked to the growth of professionalism as an occupational principle. Professionalism implies an ability to control (or at least choose) the kind of work we do. In exchange for this control, we have an implicit contract with society to apply our knowledge for the betterment of the world. The academic profession, as protected and promoted by universities, has been one engine of this evolutionary process.

The academic profession itself, however, does not (ideal-typically) have a contract with society to be relevant for a particular purpose or client but rather to the professions they educate. In general, members of the academic profession see the relevance of their work as related to their duty to interact independently with (any) relevant communities; enlighten the public, whether asked to do so or not; conduct research to gain and disseminate new knowledge; and advise on issues of political practice and governance (or 'speak truth to power') with the aim of using argument to influence better policy and political decisions.

From the start, the social sciences have struggled to find the balance between relevance and independence. Academic freedom is always hard won and difficult to protect. If we look to European history, universities and their disciplines have been integral to the formation of the ruling elites (see Bourdieu 1989; Ringer 1969). With the expansion of industrial capitalism, the widening of liberal democracy (political representation through parties) and the differentiation between political, administrative and economic powers, academic knowledge gained influence over new areas of society. And as economic actors became increasingly dependent on educated professionals, the formation of citizens gradually required state policy. Consequently, academics acquired some distance from the traditional elites of which they were once an integral part.

For contemporary social scientists, being too close to particular actors (economic or political) undermines professional autonomy in terms of the amount of control academics have over their own work (that is, what they choose to study and teach). Since, historically, the role of the social sciences has been to reflect on and critique established social relations, norms, practices and, most importantly, values, regimes that are opposed to democratic values tend to see social science as a threat. Almost inevitably, such regimes try to bind social science to their own hegemonic projects, with the aim of either disciplining or co-opting the masses. For the latter, educational institutions, from preschool to tertiary level, are considered vitally important.

Within the academic profession, the social sciences are particularly dependent on universities to create *and protect* the balance between social engagement and distance. In the ideal model, if universities are to support academic freedom and autonomy, they need to be both embedded in and supportive of a culture of democracy. Under undemocratic regimes, universities turn into theatres of turmoil that throw the academic profession into great struggles over what role it should play. This kind of turmoil is evident at MU, and is part of what we attempt to examine in what follows.

The case study

The Ugandan scholars we describe in this chapter share a number of characteristics that are mentioned here as a frame for readers' interpretations and possible generalisation. Most of the scholars obtained their PhDs abroad, mainly in Western countries. For many, this created an affinity with research universities and with the idea of academia as an international, even global, community. On the other hand, most of the scholars also expressed their emotional identification with Uganda and its developmental challenges, and see themselves primarily as Ugandan citizens (as opposed to 'citizens of the world'). Their experience of different academic cultures has given most relatively flexible ideas about the boundaries of scholarly disciplines; they have first-hand experience of how these can vary at different universities. Accordingly, they also have more understanding of science as a social practice than is common among academics who have experienced less cross-cultural mobility. Most importantly, our impression (based on about 90 interviews done within our broader project) is that most of the scholars would see a popular-democratic cultural current as guiding their role as academics.

As a colonial university, building capacity for the colonial adminis-tration, repeating a colonially mediated curriculum, MU was never going to become a university of the elites, like the French *écoles* or the US's Ivy League campuses. Thus, although touted as a 'flagship' institu-tion, the history of MU is not about how education for the elites was gradually transformed into 'higher education for the many'. Instead, as a university established to educate the employees of a state bureau-cracy, it evolved under a historical burden of double distrust: the distrust of popular leaders who steered the liberation movements into conquering a state filled with colonially trained bureaucrats, and the distrust of society for its part in the imperialists' project of social and psychological domination. After independence, MU's gradual transfor-mation into a donor-funded university only strengthened the notion that knowledge production happens in spheres beyond Uganda's bor-ders and excludes its most important local actors. In the years following independence, the university was still highly dependent on academic input from Western countries. The new educated academic elites who were selected to build the newly independent country came to rely on donors. This is particularly visible in research, where donor money was crucial to keep academic networks going. Most had earned their PhDs from Western countries, and established academic networks during their stays abroad as PhD students. These networks often deteriorated due to lack of research money. Also, on returning, most of the new academics were drawn into development projects defined by external interests, rather than being able to pursue their own as a continuation of their PhDs. To this we can add that donors' trust in the new academic elite tended to be low. This made them donors reply on their own exter-nal experts, leaving Uganda's homegrown 'organic intellectuals' likely to work only as assistants for external consultants. In other words, donors both built Uganda's universities and undermined its academic profession by bringing in their own experts as lead academics.

At the time of writing in 2019, MU still struggles with the legacy of violence, in which social scientists have had to face the guns of a dictator, and a tradition of neo-patrimonial rivalry fuelled by donor money. This strange reality is rendered 'legitimate' by a 'parliament of representation' (inspired by the Westminster model) that, at times, functions as little more than an arena for the redistribution of donor-driven 'income streams'. As a donor-dependent state, Uganda's neo-patrimonial political system is heavily influenced by the neoliberalism of the World Bank, the EU, USAID, etc. Promoting the (failed) notion that economic development and growth is a precondition for liberal democracy, the government and its allies push for economic growth first and the expansion of democracy later. Regardless of all evidence to the contrary, the state propagates the belief that, as long as the economy transforms traditional values and representational democracy remains formally in place, democratic values will gradually deepen and the 'naturally enlightened and tolerant' middle classes will expand.

For those who cling to this belief, (global) market relations must take priority, neoclassical economics must guide development, and the other social sciences must endorse this model. In many universities, this belief system is driving a growing emphasis on those disciplines believed to be the most relevant to economic growth – that is science, technology, engineering and mathematics (the STEM disciplines). Thus, an alliance of global and local state power is strongly backing the expansion of these STEM disciplines to the detriment of the humanities (including law and social science) that were once seen as vital to the formation of national identity and the building of state capacity, etc.

The World Bank often justify their prioritisation of the STEM disciplines by arguing that they are the most relevant to driving economic growth, which they see as being able to solve most problems, and especially poverty. Yet, at MU, academics have to manoeuvre between the wide-ranging and overlapping powers and interests that political and economic actors have created to support one another. Such manoeuvres form the backdrop to this chapter. We limited our study to the College of Humanities and Social Sciences (CHUSS) and to the social science-oriented aspects of the School of Law (SoL), those professors who orient themselves towards social justice. Accordingly, in CHUSS, some of the academics we spoke to are part of the Makerere Institute of Social Research (MISR) and, in SoL, we met several members of the Human Rights and Peace Centre (HURIPEC).

Responses and reactions

We found academics using a variety of strategies to manage the relationship between politics and knowledge in their working lives. Some seek refuge in positivism – accepting the idea that university knowledge finds the one right answer to any question, and that every question can have only one right answer. For them, this is how science works, and they adopt a 'take it or leave it, my job is done' attitude. We chose to call this the *abstractionist position*. These academics seemingly achieve balance by playing the role of 'distant truth-teller' on behalf of science and simply leave any hermeneutic demand for more contextual and/or particular knowledge out of the equation. Others take a hermeneutical commitment as their point of departure, promoting strategies of knowledge creation and dissemination that transgress the boundaries set by liberal democracy. They interact with and engage in civil activism, and even experiment with direct democracy for the sake of promoting change in line with knowledge about what constitutes 'a better life' or 'a good society'. We call this the *hermeneutical position*. Between these two, several other positions are discernible, ranging from fear of the regime to and identification with the state and its model of national development as an expression of the Ugandan nation.

It is in CHUSS's formal mandate to promote democratic values, although this is perhaps a consequence of donor influence or a copying of Western ideals. For example, the College's strategic plan notes that its role is to analyse, guide and inform policy, inform decision-makers and the public at large, and look critically at issues of governance, respect of human rights and ethical matters in society (CHUSS 2011). SoL describes its mission and objective as to 'foster a commitment to justice for all, develop and enhance the legal knowledge necessary for practical application in national development, democratic governance and integrity in public and private institutions, while at the same time reproducing the legal profession as such – that is, educate Ugandan lawyers to ensure they are familiar with the legal system and legal problems in their political context' (SoL 2006: 7; see also MU 2007).

From our interviews, we concluded that two conceptions of the role of knowledge can be found in CHUSS and SoL. The first relates to the influence of British positivist abstractionism and the second to the idea of universities as tools for the development of a liberated colony. Thus, both units understand the relevance of knowledge both for its own sake (the distance model), and as something that should respond to the needs of society. Thus, an imbalance related to being too distant and too close is built into the university's institutional history. This is reflected in the purpose of the units and in their attempts to express their identities.

MU seems to lack a unified voice towards politics which would make the hermeneutical approach more powerful. Independent evaluations of the university, such as *Bringing the Future to the Present* (Visitation Committee on Makerere University 2017), leave readers in no doubt that its academics have the capacity to conduct research and generate new knowledge on issues of relevance for Ugandans. Yet, according to academics at CHUSS, neither the government nor other actors seem to consider these to be relevant to developing knowledge that has legitimacy for decision-making and development. Consequently, considerable tension exists between how the academics and the government conceptualise their relevance to such processes.

A mistrust of evidence-based knowledge and advice

Academics can influence political processes and political systems in various ways. After the Second World War, social scientists in the democratic societies of the industrialised world (mostly in north-western Europe), quickly entered the public service (working side by side with or replacing lawyers), and later took up administrative positions in the bigger private companies. This had an indirect influence on other established professions (particularly in the legal domain, but also among health professionals, educationists, pastors, etc.), which also gradually started to reflect on their role in society. The social sciences, or the so-called 'free disciplines' (Maasen and Weingart 2005: 9), gradually became relevant to political decision-making and to the legitimising of political decisions. Similarly, social science influenced a general process of knowledge dissemination and has led to the transformation of language about how individuals, knowledge and politics relate within society.

The contributions and influence of academics in relation to political and social processes – from shaping notions of citizenship to policy formulation and the monitoring and evaluation of its implementation – can also be understood in terms of two issues (Solberg et al. 2017). The first is the dimension of *time* – in the sense that it often takes time for a completed research project to have a concrete impact on society. The second is the issue of *attribution*. The further one looks for the impact of research on broad and long-term social and political change, the harder it is to establish causal links between the two (Solberg et al. 2017). *Trust* in the social sciences is therefore important for its influence, as relevance can hardly ever be quantified on the spot (despite attempts to do so using models derived from the STEM disciplines).

However, most of the academics at CHUSS and SoL are influenced by the notion of 'knowledge as liberating'. They want their work to be more relevant to the political decision-making process and argue that they should be encouraged to participate as academic experts in policy-making. According to a number of respondents, being close to politics as professors does not imply being co-opted by the state. The positivist tradition inherited from British domination of MU's earlier history seems to underpin this way of thinking. The problem is that the government and public administration have no interest in their views. The academics at CHUSS and SoL are seldom called in as experts, and the regime is uninterested in creating space for academics to offer advice and make recommendations as tends to occur in more democratic societies (Tellmann 2016). Rarely does the government in Uganda accept recommendations from academics and act upon them. Social science is largely seen as irrelevant, even useless. The state does not seem to see CHUSS and SoL as producing 'usable knowledge'. The one exception, as noted below, is when the government set up and helped fund a 'think tank' of economics professors. Here, again, however, the contributions of these academics are remarkable for their positivist justifications of 'disinterest' and 'distance' from the consequences of their work.

Unlike the government, the majority of our respondents do see their research as relevant to social issues, such as the causes of poverty, corruption and patronage; human rights abuses such as unconstitutional laws that violate human rights, police brutality and arbitrary arrests; political party structures and electoral shortcomings that prevent a levelling of the political playing field; as well as other issues related to the decentralisation of governance and the accountability of local government (see also ACFIM 2015; Helle and Rakner 2016; Olum 2010).[1] For this research to be acknowledged and used by state structures requires a change in current practices (ACFIM 2015; Mbazira 2016). Uganda's administrative systems, once in the pocket of the imperialists and later of shifting repressive regimes, have not developed a taste for knowledge or an ethos of using knowledge to benefit society. Although a formal education is a basic requirement for employment in the public service, proof of competency is not.

Generally speaking, Ugandan academics believe that few government officials have much knowledge of or interest in research related to their field of work. Most politicians and bureaucrats are unwilling (and some even unable) to absorb and utilise the range of research being done by, for example, CHUSS and SoL. According to academics we spoke to, one of the root causes for this is the lack of a reading culture in government and state structures. That is, a certain distance from knowledge is culturally embedded and accepted among politicians and public servants. As a result, very few political and policy decisions are based on scientific knowledge or research. Many respondents in our study suggested that politicians' own private motives and perceptions guide their actions, and that policy-makers rely more on the views of the politicians who employ them than on empirical research produced by academics or any other external sources, including consultants. Table 17.1 sums up our findings on relations between state structures and academic research in Uganda.

Table 17.1 The knowledge–politics nexus in Uganda

Variables	Politics	Social science and law
Policy-making	Politicians rarely make knowledge-based decisions, and political statements and policies seldom reference scientific knowledge produced by CHUSS and SoL. *Expertise*: policy-makers use academic expertise to legitimise political decisions (post hoc) *Advisory processes*: government officials control the selection of advisors and the fields of knowledge they represent but they rarely seek the advice of academics *Agenda setting*: the ruling party have almost total control of the political agenda, and it is difficult for other actors in society to contribute	Scientific knowledge is expected to feed into policy-making but this rarely happens *Expertise*: contributing policy-making is not a regular occurrence for academics although some do sit on boards or committees, such as the Ministry of Gender, Labour and Social Development's Technical Committee on Societal Protection *Advisory process*: those who never criticise government practices or the ruling elite are sometimes invited to provide advice *Agenda setting*: academics are rarely able to put social or political issues on policy-makers' agendas
Legitimation	Government officials do not seek assurance or legitimacy from the knowledge produced by CHUSS and SoL The political opposition do not use research to inform their political campaigns or programmes	Inadequate funding and informal methods of control are undermining the legitimacy of academic research
Consultancy work	Rarely does government commission CHUSS and SoL to research issues of political interest, and if they consult these units, they rarely follow the recommendations they receive	There is a strong consultancy culture among academics but very few have clients in government
Outreach and activism	*Outreach*: the head of state criticises humanities and social sciences for being irrelevant to development and to national needs *Activism*: activist academics face threats and informal means of control by government. 'Colonial laws' are used to shut down dissenting voices *Critical research*: formal and informal methods are used to control academics; including the seizing of books, poor remuneration and direct threats)[a]	*Outreach*: a few well-known academics regularly engage in public debates via the media *Activism*: some academics engage in social activism to promote justice and democratisation but few openly oppose the government *Critical research*: HURIPEC and MISR consistently conduct critical research
Translation and bridging	Collaboration, communication and mediation between academics and policy-makers is uncommon	Channels for communication and influence are inadequate

Variables	Politics	Social science and law
Academic freedom	This is restricted in various ways, from direct threats and seizing books to withholding payments during strike action, etc. (see Note a below) No measures are taken to protect academic freedom	Due to uncertainty about restrictions and reprisals, academics engage in self-censorship
Democracy and professionalisation	New members of parliament are trained in workshops organised by SoL	SoL and CHUSS are training and educating future leaders and in this way are contributing to democratisation in the long term by encouraging students to do research on family constellations and sexual rights
Networks of affection	The ruling elite buys off critical voices by offering them positions in government and offering a few consultancy jobs to loyal academics	Academics get positions in government, the civil service or the judicial system if they are loyal to the regime

Note: a. Respondents mentioned being aware of spies who attend certain classes and report back to the regime. They also mentioned instances of the police closing off campus before or during public debates that might be critical of the regime, and of academics receiving threats through text messages or phone calls; some have been arrested and/or prevented from leaving the country (Amnesty International 2017a, 2017b). On publications being seized, see Hitchen (2017) and Kafeero (2017). As a result of intimidation, respondents reported feeling fearful and noted that they perceived a need to play it safe, practising self-censorship.

Some academics have been co-opted into acting as 'advisors' to the regime. Those whose work is perceived as 'irrelevant', or because they are too critical, receive no such requests from government. Those who are repeatedly asked to act in this role are perceived as 'uncritical'. In essence, critical academic voices are not utilised by the state but are instead undermined and silenced.

The question is, do those academics who do sometimes act as advisors to state structures legitimise or delegitimise the role of the academic profession? Do they create social support for, and belief in the value of, the academic profession or are academics always seen as a threat to the political order? Are the advisors playing less of an academic role and instead joining the political game in which only carefully selected views are heard? Is the role of critical intellectuals inevitably threatened by getting too close to government?

It was common knowledge among respondents that some academics have informal patron–client-type relationships with state representatives. Respondents noted that these relationships ensure that such academics avoid conducting research that portrays political actors in a bad light. In return, they apparently receive favours (such as consultancies on government committees, etc). Colloquially, these individuals are referred to as 'official academics', and some have later taken up ministerial or judicial positions.

Our interviews revealed that academics at MU are either co-opted or kept at a distance by the state. This indicates the presence of two parallel stories at MU. One story is about the 'official academics' who are informally connected to the regime; the other is the story of committed and independent academics who are preoccupied with the advancement of knowledge and the pursuit of the truth. Contrary to what one might expect, the latter group receive little respect. Of course, academics who are informally connected to the regime did not speak to us about this in detail.

What was clear, however, is that the work done by CHUSS and SoL is very seldom, if ever, referenced or used by politicians. Regarded as critical institutions, the two units are kept at a distance. When necessary, the government typically legitimises its decisions by referencing international experts from organisations such as the World Bank. Such citations not only operate as a form of tribute to the donor that the regime depends on to build its networks, but also neutralise Uganda's local academic community.

Professional autonomy versus democracy as sources of independence

Sicherman (2005:106) observes that, during Milton Obote's first term as president (1966–1971), MU was seen as one of the three centres of power in Uganda, together with government and commerce. Obote increased state control over Uganda's universities (via the University Act of 1970). Today, the state views academics and their research (especially from CHUSS and SoL) with scepticism, and sees them as likely dissenting and opposing voices. Academics are viewed as having the potential to challenge the power of the ruling elites when teaching students about the concepts of democracy and democratisation, human rights, etc. (Halvorsen 2010b).

Since much of the research conducted at CHUSS and SoL challenges the status quo, their recommendations run counter to the 'deep core' beliefs and values of the political elite (Jenkins-Smith and Sabatier quoted in Owens 2011: 84). It is therefore not surprising that these academics are rarely able to put issues on the political agenda or contribute to policy-making processes. As Meulemann and Tromp (2010: 203) suggest, the Westminster system 'works against' the academic profession in the sense that political decisions are not taken on the basis of available knowledge per se, but on the basis of knowledge that politicians decide is relevant.[2] In Uganda, the political elite tend to see the knowledge that emanates from CHUSS and SoL as critical of the state, and therefore as irrelevant to national needs and development. From the perspective of the regime, the two institutes are failing the developmental project by promoting 'ivory tower' knowledge that is too distant from the needs of society as defined by the state.

Even so, the state's political actors realise that they cannot act completely irrationally, and seek legitimation for their political decision-making. Lentsch and Weingart (2011: 7) argue that governments' 'mandate of rationality' explains why they need expert opinions to support their policies. They know that if they can convey the idea that their policy-making is knowledge-based, they stand to gain legitimacy and authority.

Knowledge and nepotism

Trust in knowledge is usually found where political regimes have some legal and rational basis (see Halvorsen 2010a). Where patrimonial relations predominate, knowledge is, at best, a kind of instrumental expertise, often invoked by imported consultants. Stehr (2003) points out that academic knowledge is vulnerable and risks vanishing entirely unless society exhibits some degree of trust in the academic profession.

In our study, several respondents reported instances in which government committees employed academics as consultants but never used their evidence or recommendations as a basis for subsequent decision-making. Other respondents reported holding seminars for members of parliament and being invited to join committees to provide political actors with scientific knowledge and expert advice. Although such actions can be understood as indicating some level of government trust in academic knowledge and expertise, most of our respondents tended to see these as attempts by the state to co-opt them, thereby legitimising government decisions and policies.

We were informed that academics tend to be employed as advisors or experts in their personal capacities, and not as university professors; that is, they are encouraged to become part of and subject to the patrimonial network. As one respondent put it:

> Some of the professors in this department are strong allies of the ruling party; some are critical of the ruling party. There are those in this department who actually sit on certain committees of government and they serve as advisers to government units. So those tend to carry the view that government is doing the right thing. They appear to lend academic weight even to the mistakes and the misinformation which seem to prevail in government ... In short, our view, our relationship with government, depends on where we stand.

Knowledge hierarchies and politics

The government seems to value knowledge that is 'positively given'. By this they seem to mean information that speaks to government policy in ways that asserts its independence from observer bias and its relevance to the economic framework that multilateral financial institutions (particularly the World Bank) promote as following science or a 'natural law'. Ideally such knowledge or information should also help to link Uganda into global trade networks. The relationship between Uganda's patrimonial regime, which has few democratic checks and balances, and the world's global neoliberal economic institutions has an African equivalent in the ideas about 'development first' (mostly developed by a former MU student who later became president of Tanzania, Julius Nyerere). Mahmood Mamdani (2008) argues that since Uganda's ruling party, the National Resistance Movement (NRM) came to power in

1986, they have pushed a strong developmentalist line in relation to economic and infrastructural development. Mamdani asserts that the NRM see the humanities and the social sciences as an inexcusable luxury that has only marginal significance. Today, these attitudes still prevail as the current president, Yuweri Museveni, follows the World Bank's lead, issuing statements affirming that that only the STEM-disciplines have relevance for the economy, and for development, implying that the other disciplines are little more than 'nice to have' add-ons.[3]

Museveni's support for the hard sciences – and his undermining of the social sciences – can also be understood as a strategy to control the scope of the social sciences in ways that amount to a kind of political control. This move is further legitimised by multilateral organisations that promote economic growth as a necessary precursor to democracy (see Bisaso 2017). As Weiler (2006) points out, creating hierarchies of knowledge is the quintessential manifestation of power over knowledge. At MU, and no doubt at other higher education institutions in Uganda too, knowledge hierarchies have become a pervasive structural characteristic. Different fields of knowledge are endowed with unequal status, value and influence, with the STEM disciplines occupying the leading position.

Maintaining an academic perspective

Contrary to the World Bank and Museveni's position, and in line with our ideal-model, Mamdani (2017) argues that the public interest cannot be equated with the interests of any regime. He argues that the public interest is the interest of society, and any government is only a part of this. Mamdani suggests that this is why no university or group of academics should 'represent' the government, but should instead maintain the distance that makes it possible for them to be representative of the general public and thus also of all their interests. That is, because academics represent all the different interests in society, universities should provide a *forum* in which the public interest can be discussed, debated and formulated (Mamdani 2017). Such forums would reflect on values but not take a position on these, apart from the values made explicit in choice of topics and theories; however, *without the social sciences no such forum can exist.*

In our study, none of the respondents said they see Uganda's political system as democratic or would be supportive of such a forum. As one respondent put it:

> Everyone is talking about democracy in the sense it is practised in the West – in terms of freedom of association, freedom of speech, freedom of opinion, freedom of the press. I think democracy here ... does not exist. But as far as I am concerned, what we have here is authoritarianism, and you cannot be democratic and authoritarian at the same time.

Some respondents pointed out that the checks and balances that are supposed to guarantee the separation of powers in a democracy are completely missing in Uganda. They pointed to the near collapse of almost all key institutions of the state, including the judiciary, the administration and the legislature. They explained that judges are appointed because of their political affiliations and members of parliament owe their positions to the president. Generally, elections are not perceived to be free and fair and government shuts down social media during elections. Several respondents gave examples of police brutality during elections, highlighting how the government used the police and army to prevent opposition parties and organisations from campaigning.

A common view is that the entire political system centres on the president.

> One of the problems is that we have a Head of State who is so occupied with being in power ... He has been in power for so many years, nothing will be done. He does nothing and this is very well known: if you are his supporter you can do anything and you can get away with anything. If you are not his supporter they will look for any chance to throw you out.

On the other hand, one respondent argued that, despite high levels of corruption making the public service intolerably inefficient, Uganda is relatively democratic, and pointed to the fact that elections take place amidst an election race and other political activities. Others noted that there is at least a semblance of democratic practice, and that the High Court is seen as having integrity and enjoys public trust (especially when compared with the police service).

A term often used by respondents to describe Uganda's political system was 'electoral autocracy'. As one academic elaborated,

> In 'a democratic dispensation', the courts work according to set laws and standards, and they are independent of the political system. The media are independent of the state and free to report on any societal and political situation. People are free to criticise government in public, without fear for their lives.

In the experience of our respondents, these conditions have not yet been secured in Uganda. As another respondent noted:

> When it comes to thinking about the deeper meaning of democracy – that deeper or consolidated democracy – it is absent in this country because you have a group of people who control power in here. They control all the political processes. They control the juridical processes, the parliamentary processes, and even elections.

Thus, most indicated that the ruling party uses the politics of fear, and their history of violence, to stay in power. Uganda has never experienced a peaceful regime change, and several respondents expressed doubt that the country's existing democratic processes would ever be able to guarantee this in future elections.

In our view, few academics had a clear understanding of how they could or should contribute to democratisation, and seemed to confuse the study of democratic values with an engagement in promoting such values. Most believed that they could be more relevant to the process of democratisation, and could justify making value judgements if they were less restricted by the many other limitations they face. There were however contrasting views about distance and closeness illustrating the imbalance that value judgements can create. In answering the question of whether or not academics should influence their students' views, some argued that their job as a teacher is to teach students to think critically, to help them to produce sound arguments for their views, and empower them to participate effectively in discussion forums, both within and beyond the limits of representative democracy. We call this the 'study of values' approach. Others said they see the shaping of future democratic leaders and public servants, and teaching them to respect the democratic process, as one of the goals of their teaching. This seemed to imply mediating the 'technical qualifications' or professionalising the management for governance and social control. We call this the 'value judgement approach'. In our view, the latter gets too close to the 'users of knowledge', while the former is defensible only if democratic values allow critical thinking.

One respondent argued that the role of social science education is to develop democratic leadership:

> Certainly, this is part of the teaching, this is part of (what) the university is trying to do. We are preparing these people to go out there, as they say, to be the next leaders of the country. So certainly, as we do the training, part of the mission is to prepare these people to, you know, run the country.

This is a reclaiming of the positivist position in the sense that the role of a teacher is seen as being to put knowledge on the table and give students a theoretically objective interpretation. An alternative and more reflexive position holds that students need freedom to discuss and reflect on the theoretical perspectives they encounter. However, the majority of our respondents were afraid of getting too close to politics. In one respondent's words:

> When it comes to democracy, the teacher should not force this onto the students, but rather, if the students decided that democracy is important, it should be because the students appreciate this method.

A minority of the academics we interviewed resolved this dilemma by excluding themselves. Those who withdrew totally referred to the lack of university support, stating that being able to shape students' views is beyond their capacity, given the meagre salaries they receive and the time pressures they experience. These academics thus give up their professional role not because of political risk, but due to exhaustion and starvation, which they attribute to poor levels of institutional and societal support for their work.

Attempts at democratic practices

Different views were expressed on whether academics should train students to become leaders and bureaucrats, and/or enlightened citizens and public intellectuals. Those opting for the latter were themselves often trying to practise what they preached. Some respondents hold panel discussions and debates to which they invite politicians from outside the university to speak, with the hope of inspiring the students. Others attempt to challenge bourgeois ideas of the relationship between knowledge and politics. For example, SoL's Public Interest Law Clinic offers a programme that ensures that students interact with the community outside of MU. The objective of the programme is to raise students' social awareness of real problems facing poorer communities. Similarly, the Human Rights and Peace Centre also has an outreach element and CHUSS offers courses on ethics and public administration as well as on ethics and international relations. Academics in CHUSS noted that they see this as a way of influencing students' thinking about their future role both in the workplace and as citizens. For the same reason, CHUSS runs a youth leadership programme called the Young Leaders Forum in collaboration with the Friedrich Ebert Stiftung. Also, at CHUSS, some professors have been engaged in running programmes for members of parliament, although we were given no specific examples of where, when and how often this happens. As one staff member noted:

> One of the requirements of this department, one of its missions, would be to [educate] cadres of Ugandan civil servants. That's

why we teach public administration, so it is one of the core missions of the department certainly ... It is one of the core aims of
the department to ... train public administrators.

Similarly, at SoL, academics argued that their role includes providing
training for *democratic* leadership and bureaucrats via the running of
programmes for government officials and policy-makers. In fact, professors at SoL are regularly involved in, and give priority to, training
new members of parliament on international human rights law and on
constitutionalism in Uganda. On occasion, they also provide guidelines
on how certain legal cases should be handled by the judiciary.

In general then, both CHUSS and SoL have some staff members who
are active and others who are inactive in terms of community outreach,
participation in public debates and discussions, and in commenting on
political and social issues via various media. Those that are active see this
as an important part of the many roles they play as academics at MU. The
others do not see this as an important or interesting aspect of their work,
and simply neglected it entirely. One staff member at SoL recalled:

Many of our colleagues have engaged in, you know, public
debates and discussions on different issues, I remember myself,
after the first presidential debate before the elections in
February 2016, I was one of the legal analysts of the debate you
see, [I had to say] what were the issues. So, we also take up a
public role, really, to discuss how is the government of this
country and where could it be better.

Another respondent noted:

There are those that are still teaching and, yes, they are well
known for their writing and their critique of, you know, what is
going on in Uganda – of politics, of human rights, you know of
everything really. So I think professors ... they definitely have
played a quite significant role in critiquing some of the unconstitutional laws, laws that violate human rights, laws that are
not fair. You know, the way elections are conducted, and all

these things. They have definitely played a role, and they continue to play a role through talking, writing, research, and writing opinion pieces in the newspapers.

The academics who regularly engage with the public are also those that other respondents saw as activists. Activism in this context was not understood as partisan political activity but rather as social activism that transcends political ideologies. Within SoL, all respondents we spoke to engage with the public regularly. In addition to being academics, they can also be seen as social activists since they critique illegitimate practices, participate in public discussions, train government officials, conduct critical research, and speak the truth to power.

Academics we met at CHUSS were divided between those who are critical of government and those who were not. The division was apparently quite visible within the university but none of the respondents explicitly indicated to us who belonged to which group. However, some staff are clearly critical of government actions and policies (even though they have faced restrictions at times). The other group prefers to stay passive, and seemingly has no interest in politics or no interest in provoking the regime. While those that we interpreted to be part of the first group often spoke more openly of their roles in relation to politics, few of the academics in the second group revealed their personal opinions in this regard. One of these, however, stated:

> I told you, I am really weak on activism because I am a coward. I don't want to cross the government, and I don't want to be known by them. I prefer to keep a low profile because I don't think the risk is worth it. If something happens to me, it is my kids that will miss me, and who will care for them? You know, which is probably a fallacy because Uganda is for all of us, and if we don't solve them now, we don't leave a better country for our children. So, I know my thinking is wrong and I know I should do more, and I keep telling myself that I will do more, but I always get too busy with life.

We cannot know how many academics have chosen to leave MU rather than work in these conditions, or count the number of 'voices' opposed to the state. The influence of opposition voices seems to be limited. For example, when parliamentary committees draft laws, parliament, as a rule, does not take suggestions from SoL seriously, and in fact, sometimes used these to close legal loopholes. One respondent observed:

> [We make] important submissions but, in fact, sometimes when you propose such things, you see, you can even contribute to make an even worse law because they realise 'this is it'. Then they can tighten it. So, the opportunities are there but the situation might not allow it. In certain cases, proposals have a political problem, not because what is being proposed is not sound, but because parliament is too narrow and too partisan to take it up.

This lack of influence over public debate, despite brave attempts, is also linked to a lack of institutional support. Many said they were demoralised by the imbalance between their heavy workloads and meagre salaries. However, some see this demoralisation as an individual flaw, pointing out that others do manage to maintain their commitment to the work of transformation even though they face the same challenging working conditions. As one respondent put it:

> I hope for change but there are so many things wrong with this university, I don't even know ... Ok, if you feel that you have an obligation to be here and be a part of the change, that might be ok. But the rest are only here to teach and go home, and they don't have time to care about it.

Two important issues that the respondents see as undermining their commitment to this aspect of their work are nepotism and corruption within MU. On this issue, one respondent said:

> I actually considered leaving academia for good. When you work here, you see the ugly side of academia, and you are not sure if you want to be part of it.

Another issue raised in the interviews was what academics can do when they experience challenges or difficulties in contributing to what they see as promoting the 'process of democratisation'. We asked if academics felt that they have the protection they need within MU. Most responded that the alliance between regime and university management means that they do not.

One exception is the Economic Policy Research Center (EPRC). Knowledge that has high legitimacy in relation to the donor-driven development paradigm (economics) is more easily channelled through to Uganda's political structures. Referred to as a think-tank for government at the university, the EPRC also provides an avenue for combining global economic interests and the global push for liberal democracy, with solutions to the issue of how to integrate the masses within the political economy. One respondent noted that channelling research through the EPRC is one efficient way of getting government to listen to the research produced by academics:

> I channel my views through a team of researchers in the EPRC. And when these ideas reach government, the government accepts them, because they are coming from a research institute that is 65 per cent government funded and is in good books of government. So, critical views from EPRC are sometimes toned down, edited, but those views are accepted more directly because EPRC is seen as a think tank of the government.

To sum up: in our view the academics at SoL are the most committed to this role, so are many at CHUSS. Others stay passive, and seem to have no interest in participating in public debate, or lacked commitment to this aspect of work, as they were preoccupied with their traditional roles –focusing primarily on teaching and doing some research, without any explicit aim of contributing to democratisation at MU or in Uganda as a whole.

Social science and wider societal impressions

Unlike the regime's leadership structures, Ugandan citizens generally affirm the value of academic knowledge. A study by the Human Rights and Peace Centre (HURIPEC 2016) found that many Ugandans expect academics to play an active role in shaping politics, and assert that social sciences have both a duty and an opportunity to contribute to public debate and the deepening of democracy. However, some members of society said it is unrealistic for academics to play an active part in political transformation because Uganda's academic institutions are so structurally and organisationally weak. Others find the reason to be that academics are grabbed by apathy or that academics have chosen to partner with the state in order to benefit from state resources thus not being in a position to criticise them (HURIPEC 2016).

Some civil society representatives we spoke to (in less formal interviews) said they thought the academics at CHUSS and SoL should be able to guide government and parliament through their work. One informant stated:

> In a fragile democracy, if you want to call it that, or in a disguised dictatorship, as you see here, academia is supposed to try and guide, in my opinion, to be able to guide the country. For example, if there is no rule of law, they are supposed to say 'this is how things should be done'. If there is an abuse of human rights, they are supposed to come out and guide.

On the work of SoL, a journalist we spoke to said the following:

> So, the silence from the Faculty of Law: okay, they are saying a few things nowadays, but for me I still find it is not enough. The School of Law needs to do much more than they are doing right now. They have to speak out more. They need to engage more.

When linking knowledge to national mobilisation, knowledge/policy actors seem to merge for the general public. Various events and public lectures organised at MU can be understood as contributions to democratisation with this alliance with civil society acting as a kind of 'security' and inspiration. In 2014, for example, the Department of Political Science and Public Administration in CHUSS hosted a session at the East African Uongozi Institute's Summer School (which included students from MU, and the Universities of Nairobi, Dar es Salaam, Burundi and Rwanda) with the aim of inculcating democratic leadership qualities and competencies in the next generation of East African leaders (MU 2014). Several academics and politicians from the region talked to the students on the theme 'African States: Competing Identities and Democratisation'. At one such event, Uganda's education minister noted:

> Such institutions are of great importance at this time when Africa is faced with many leadership challenges that have resulted into suppression of human rights, violent conflicts, and economic deterioration. (MU 2014: 35)

Staff members as CHUSS (MU 2007) argue that the long-term objectives of their master's in Public Administration and Management is to build national capacity in public policy formulation and to promote democratic values and practices in the Ugandan society. It was expected that dissertations completed as part of this master's programme would make a significant contribution to knowledge of public policy and planning. Thus, it was seen as a way of shaping students while simultaneously contributing to democratisation and increasing the level of interaction between the academic profession and the political system for the sake of nation-state development.

Public engagement is reported on several times in MU's annual reports, showing that issues relevant for democratisation are covered in public lectures and dialogues (see MU *Annual Reports* 2013, 2015, 2016). In addition, an inaugural lecture series serves as a platform for academic staff to contribute not only to the academic life of the university, but also a way to engage students and the public more generally (MU 2016).[4]

Concluding remarks

As we have shown, the balancing act required of academics at MU, particularly in the social sciences, to both keep their distance from and participate in daily political realities, while attempting to generate knowledge and expand its influence, is particularly challenging. This is clearly expressed in ongoing debates about democracy, regime change and the influence of power and politics.

Meanwhile, multilateral donor organisations are working with the regime to advocate a limited representative democracy. However, when the social scientists focus their teaching and research on the character and social consequences of the incumbent state, they necessarily reference wider democratic values that imply the possibility of alternatives to the current situation. This is unavoidable but it also puts academics at risk. Their dilemma is exacerbated by the fact that sharing and producing social science knowledge presupposes academic freedom. This, in turn, presupposes that universities are strong enough to be able to defend their academics and the internal ideals of academic freedom. It also presupposes that academic freedom can be used in ways that both convince society of academics' impartiality and justify their acting as public intellectuals in line with their own ethics and values (see Mamdani, this volume) – something that is possible only in countries that have an independent media and in which free speech and (social and political) opposition are protected.

At the time of writing, the forum Mahmood Mamdani proposed was not in evidence, and our impression is that the academic sector (as represented by staff members of CHUSS and SoL) is weak and has found little common ground with other social actors in terms of its role in society. Both units have made numerous attempts to engage with processes of democratisation, and experience gained in these attempts seems to indicate insufficient institutional protection for academic freedom. That is, the balance between engagement and distance that we expect the university to watch over and protect is, at best, still in the making. In the meantime, the university is pushing social science away from social engagement. This leaves academics facing the question of how to contribute to social transformation without being blamed for it.

Given the nature of the incumbent regime in Uganda, and the embeddedness of the university leadership in the ruling elite, it is crucial that academics find (*and reach consensus on*) a balance between analytical distance and engagement, *for which they can win societal support*. Such a forum might gain the autonomy and influence needed to make social science relevant again. Without this, even the most analytically reserved might one day face the guns of the regime and (again) take the blame for value judgements that the regime cannot tolerate.

About the authors and the project

Andrea Kronstad Felde is a PhD student in the Social Science Faculty at the University of Bergen

Tor Halvorsen is a senior researcher at the University of Bergen Global and SDG Bergen, as well as at the Fafo Institute for Labour and Social Research, Oslo

Project title: Building and Reflecting on Interdisciplinary PhD Studies for Higher Education Transformation
Partner institutions: Makerere University (Uganda), University of Bergen (Norway)

Notes

1   See also Human Rights Watch: https://www.hrw.org/africa/uganda
2   This also justifies the notion that knowledge that can be seen as relevant for economic and technical development, such as the research disseminated from the STEM-disciplines, should take priority in terms of funding and support (Meulemann and Tromp, 2010: 203).
3   See D Wandera, Arts courses are useless – Museveni, *Daily Monitor* 18 August 2014; and Museveni concerned about quality of university education, *Daily Monitor* 6 November 2016. Both articles are available online. See also Higgins (quoted in Halvorsen 2016).
4   So far, such forums have included a number of actors from the university colleges, as well as civil society organisations and partner universities, such as Simmons College, the University of Pretoria and the Friedrich Ebert Stiftung). Issues covered so far include: new and emerging issues in social development; the role of the police in

upholding and promoting democracy; human rights and violations of public order; corruption and good governance; promoting human rights awareness (sensitisation) among academics, students and the public; democratic deficits in the courts; the role of money in elections and party politics; nudity, law and protests; and the role of youth in politics and elections.

References

ACFIM (Alliance for Campaign Finance Monitoring) (2015) *ACFIM Second Report Period: October 2015*. Kampala. Available online

Amnesty International (2017a) Uganda: University lecturer must be released. *Amnesty International Campaign* 19 April Index: AFR 59/6060/2017. Available online

Amnesty International (2017b) Uganda: Stella Nyanzi free but ludicrous charges must be dropped. *Amnesty International News*. 10 May 2017. Available online

Bisaso R (2017) Makerere University as a flagship institution: Sustaining the quest for relevance. In: D Teferra (ed.) *Flagship Universities in Africa*. London: Palgrave

Brennan J (2007) The academic profession and increasing expectations of relevance. In: E Kogan, M Teichler and U Kassel (eds) *Key Challenges to the Academic Profession*. Paris: Unesco

Bourdieu P (1989) *La Noblesse d'État: Grandes écoles et esprit de corps*. Paris: Le sens commun

CHUSS (College of Humanities and Social Sciences) (2011) *Makerere University College of Humanities and Social Sciences Strategic Plan, 2011–2018*. Kampala: Makerere University. Available online

Halvorsen T (2010a) Politics and knowledge. In: KB Alemu and T Halvorsen (eds) *Shaping Research Universities in the Nile Basin Countries*. Kampala: Fountain

Halvorsen T (2010b) Between democracy and dictatorship, modernity and tradition: A contribution to the debate about the research university in Africa. In: Nile Basin Research Programme, *Reshaping Research Universities in the Nile Basin Countries*. Kampala: Fountain

Halvorsen T (2016) Higher education in developing countries: Peril and promise a decade and a half later: Development lost? *International Journal of African Higher Education* 3(1). Available online

Helle SV and Rakner L (2016) *The impact of elections: The case of Uganda*. In: J Gerschewski and CH Stefes (eds) *Crisis in Autocratic Regimes*. Boulder, CO: Lynne Rienner. Available online

Hitchen J (2017, 16 June) Book review: Controlling consent: Uganda's 2016 election by J Oloka-Onyango and J Ahikire (eds), LSE blogpost. Available online

HURIPEC (Human Rights and Peace Centre) (2016) *The Road to 2016: Citizens' Perceptions of Uganda's Forthcoming Elections, a Synthesis Report*. Kampala

Kafeero S (2017, 16 March) Book on 2016 polls seized. *Daily Monitor*. Available online

Lentsch J and Weingart P (2011) Introduction: The quest for quality as a challenge to scientific policy advice: An overdue debate? In J Lentsch and P Weingart (eds) *The Politics of Scientific Advice: Institutional Design for Quality Assurance*. Cambridge: Cambridge University Press

Maasen S and Weingart P (2005) What's new in scientific advice to politics? In: S Maasen and P Weingart (eds) *Democratization of Expertise? Exploring Novel Forms of Scientific Advice in Political Decision-Making*. Dordrecht: Springer

Mamdani M (2008) *Scholars in the Marketplace. The Dilemmas of Neo-Liberal Reform at Makerere University, 1989–2005*. Cape Town: HSRC Press

Mamdani M (2017) Undoing the effects of neoliberal reform: The experience of Uganda's Makerere Institute of Social Research. In: T Halvorsen and J Nossum (eds) *North-South Knowledge Networks: Towards Equitable Collaboration Between Academics, Donors and Universities*. Cape Town: African Minds

Mbazira C (2016) *The Road to 2016: Citizens' Perceptions of Uganda's Forthcoming Elections*. Kampala: Kituo Cha Katiba. Available online

Meuleman L and Tromp H (2010) The governance of usable and welcome knowledge: Two perspectives. In: RJ Veld (ed.) *Knowledge Democracy: Consequences for Science, Politics, and Media*. New York: Springer

MU (Makerere University) (2007) *Makerere University Prospectus 2007–2010*. Kampala: Department of the Academic Registrar, Makerere University

MU (2014) *Makerere University Annual Report 2014*. Kampala

MU (2016) *Makerere University Annual Report 2016*. Kampala

Olum Y (2010) The political system and environment in Uganda: Are the checks and balances to power and the political playing field sufficient to consolidate multiparty democracy? in Y Kiranda and M Kamp (eds) *Reality Check: The State of Multiparty Democracy in Uganda*. Bonn: Konrad Adenauer Stiftung

Owens S (2011) Knowledge, advice and influence: The role of the UK Royal Commission on environmental pollution, 1970–2009. In: J Lentsch and P Weingart (eds) *The Politics of Scientific Advice: Institutional Design for Quality Assurance*. Cambridge: Cambridge University Press

Ringer FK (1969) *The Decline of the German Mandarins: The German Academic Community, 1890–1933*. Cambridge, MA: Harvard University Press

Sicherman C (2005) *Becoming an African University: Makerere 1922–2000*. Kampala: Fountain

SoL (School of Law) (2006) *Makerere University School of Law, Strategic Plan 2006–2016: Seizing the Initiative and Fostering Excellence*. Kampala: Makerere University. Available online

Solberg E, Tellmann SM, Aanstad S, Aksnes DW, Ramberg I and Børing P (2017) *Pathways to Global Impact: Tracing the Impacts of Development Research Funded by the Research*

Council of Norway, Report 13. Oslo: Nordic Institute for Studies in Innovation, Research and Education

Stehr N (2003) The social and political control of knowledge in modern societies. *International Social Science Journal* 55(4): 643–655

Tellmann, SM (2016) Bounded deliberation in public committees: The case of experts. *Critical Policy Studies* 11(3): 311–329. Available online

Visitation Committee on Makerere University (2017) *Bringing the Future to the Present: The Report of the Visitation Committee on Makerere University, 2016*. Available online

Weiler HN (2006) Challenging the orthodoxies of knowledge: Epistemological, structural and political implications for higher education. In G Neave (ed.) *Knowledge, Power and Dissent: Critical Perspectives on Higher Education and Research in Knowledge Society*. Paris: Unesco

18

Developing a sustainable PhD programme: Experiences from southern Ethiopia

Bernt Lindtjørn, Moges Tadesse & Eskindir Loha

More than 60 years since most universities in sub-Saharan Africa were founded, a recent review has underlined the poor record of African universities (Fonn et al. 2018). However, the reasons why African research institutions contribute less than 1 per cent of the global expenditures on research and development are complex (Fonn et al. 2018). Whereas countries in sub-Saharan Africa account for 14 per cent of the global population, the same region contributes to less than 1 per cent of the research expenditure. Although the research output may have increased in recent years, in 2007, Ethiopia spent only 0.2 percentage points of its gross national product on research (Tijssen 2007). A recent analysis of research collaboration between European and African universities showed the largest research collaboration is between Europe and South Africa, probably because of the location of research institutions that are both academically good and have adequate research infrastructure (Breugelmans et al. 2015).

The Norwegian Agency for Development Cooperation (Norad) is among the important funders of capacity-building programmes in Africa (Davies and Mullan 2016). In 2012, Norad launched The Norwegian Programme for Capacity Development in Higher Education and Research for Development (Norhed), whose vision is to improve the livelihoods of people in low- and middle-income countries (LMICs) through a programme on higher education. The programme has the following objectives (Jávorka et al. 2018):

- To increase and improve levels of research administered by the countries' own researchers, thereby improving knowledge within each country;
- To produce a more qualified job candidate, enabling a larger and more skilled workforce;
- To enable evidence-based policy and decision making; and
- To enhance gender equality.

Need for evidence-based health policy

Many LMICs experience poverty and high disease burdens, often leading to a vicious cycle where poverty aggravates the disease burden and people with heavy disease burdens exacerbate poverty (Preston 1975). These are some of the reasons why many communities do not have access to good quality basic health services. Public policies that seek to address these challenges will only work if the choices made by decision-makers, technical or political, are informed by the best available evidence. Research is essential in producing sound evidence to inform local, national and international policy that, in turn, has the potential to transform lives for the better.

Policy-making informed by the best available evidence helps to make effective policy decisions. While it may result in changes in legislation, it also occurs in areas such as decisions about resource allocation, regulations and new strategies. Most often, the people making these decisions are government officials and institutional leaders at local, regional and national levels.

Researchers produce evidence that policy makers use for decisions and in return, policy-makers could provide scientists with information and resources that could lead to new research (Choi et al. 2005). However, the way that research findings are implemented into the policy-making process is often complex. It is important that scientists understand this complex process and communicate their findings in a way that policy-makers find acceptable and understandable. Sometimes organisational constraints and lack of appropriate communication channels limit the incorporation of science and technology into policy

(Choi et al. 2005). However, through an interactive process between policy-makers and researchers, it should be possible to build the trust necessary for implementing important scientific findings (Strydom et al. 2010).

Africa, with the largest burden of disease, has few skilled health researchers (Agyepong et al. 2017). In 2013, the World Health Organisation called for renewed efforts in strengthening the health research capacity in African countries as a means towards universal health coverage. Many such initiatives, often originating from high-income countries, have been criticised for failing to strengthen, incorporate, and involve institutions from LMICs in priority setting and publications (Davies and Mullan 2016; Sewankambo et al. 2015). In 2008, the Council on Health Research for Development organised a meeting in Bamako in Mali, West Africa. This was a ministerial meeting and participants included the Global Forum for Health Research, Unesco, the World Health Organization, the World Bank and the Government of Mali. It brought together ministries, researchers, academics, representatives of research-funding agencies, civil society and the private sector. One of the main aims was to focus on the needs of LMICs and give them a stronger voice in the discussion about the requirements for health research in LMICs.

Our South Ethiopia Network of Universities in Public Health (SENUPH) project, supported by Norhed, emerges from the need for the universities to play an important role in educating and training professional staff and future leaders. Therefore, high-level education is important for future health improvements. Strengthening the research capacity in LMICs includes efforts to support individuals' training for PhDs or for postdoctoral training, improving their local institutions' capacity so that they can become high-quality centres in their countries as well as strengthen larger networks. Higher education institutions can share intellectual and social capital with implementing organisations such as ministries of health and NGOs (Agyepong et al. 2017). In such a network, the aim is to provide and enhance evidence-based and informed policy-making for improved health.

PhD training as a means to strengthen development

PhD training strengthens the research capacity of individual universities and their countries. For example, a recent review of externally funded training of postgraduate students in health research at institutions in sub-Saharan Africa showed that most of the master's and PhD grantees were funded by the International Development Research Centre (IDRC) in Canada, Norad and the Wellcome Trust (Abate et al. 2004). Developing quality PhD programmes significantly contributes to improvements in training PhD students and young, local researchers who will become trainers, researchers, political leaders and expert advisers for public decision-making, which contributes to making their countries more competitive on regional, national and international levels.

The need for expanding tertiary-level training in the public health sciences is clear. The burden of health problems, the increasing population pressure and economic challenges suggest the need for effective and efficient programming of both curative and public health interventions (Agyepong et al. 2017). However, the human-resource crisis in present-day Ethiopia has created a major obstacle to implementing the health sector development plan to its fullest extent (Assefa et al. 2017; Girma et al. 2007). After 1991, Ethiopia introduced an ethnic federal governance system made up of regional states and autonomous cities. This restructuring led to the decentralisation of some power to the regions (Bekele and Kjosavik 2016). Decentralisation occurs when the work or activities of an organisation such as a higher education institution or a ministry of health are delegated away from an authoritative, central location. The decentralised governance in the public and private sectors, with a rapid increase in the numbers of universities and health institutions, and the growing number of national and international NGOs, has led to an increasing demand for competent professionals (Assefa et al. 2017).

Ethiopia's government hopes that investing in research and development will promote socio-economic development in the country (FDRE 2016). New PhD programmes have been established to meet Ethiopia's development needs. Thus, doctoral training has become a focus of universities, researchers, policy-makers, governments and donors across Africa and around the world. The Ethiopian government recognises that high-level education is vital for developing the country (FDRE 2016), which aspires to become a middle-income country by 2025. The Ethiopian government's policy and strategic shift to the mass production of high-level professionals and academics to support programme implementation and the expansion of education opportunities have also posed a large challenge to institutions of higher learning (Assefa et al. 2017).

Reliable, sound evidence often comes from studies that involve an intentional change, for example, through introducing preventive or therapeutic regimens. Such intervention studies can be carried out as medical experiments which aim to improve new treatments or public health programmes. The demand for such evidence-based interventions is increasing, which calls for training enough high-level professionals. Also, offering a long-term training opportunity for academics across the country is used as a mechanism to keep PhD holders within the country and at universities.

Research collaboration between Ethiopia and Norway

Ethiopia and Norway have a long-standing collaboration on research, starting with the establishment of the Armauer Hansen Research Institute in 1968 (Miorner and Britton 1999). This was a research collaboration between Ethiopia, Sweden and Norway, but also included researchers from other European countries and the USA. Several examples of outstanding research came from this which led to a better understanding of leprosy that resulted in better treatment or improved public health control of the disease (Bloom and Godal 1983). Since the mid-1980s, Norwegian researchers have developed a close collaboration with Addis Ababa University, and since the mid-1990s, such research has been expanded to universities in southern Ethiopia, mainly at the universities in Hawassa and Arba Minch (Dare 2007; Datiko 2011; Lindtjørn et al. 2014; Shargie 2007; Shumbullo 2013; Ulesido 2017).

This collaborative research was enabled by the Norwegian institution providing both funds for research and scholarships for Ethiopian researchers to do research-based master's and PhD degrees. These candidates either did the PhDs at universities in Norway or they were trained under a so-called sandwich model where the student did the coursework in the North and most of the research in the South.

There are several definitions of a 'sandwich model'. Some define it as when the doctoral student stays in different universities. Others define it as a stay at two institutions as part of joint supervision ('cotutelle'), where the student is registered at both universities. However, as most often occurred in Norway, the doctoral student was registered at a Norwegian university and a supervisor from an Ethiopian university took part in the supervision. Although there were attempts to include both Ethiopian and Norwegian supervisors, the results often showed that the main research supervisor was from the North. Most often, the research topic was decided between the candidate and the supervisor, with limited involvement of the local university and the health authorities in the South.

The joint PhD degree programme

The 'South Ethiopia Network of Universities in Public Health (SENUPH): Improving Women's Participation in Postgraduate Education' project started in 2014. Its vision is to enhance the capacity of universities in southern Ethiopia to train enough staff to carry out necessary public health work and do essential research to improve the health of the people living in southern Ethiopia. These goals were achieved through the setting up of the following activities:

- Strengthening the research capacity through PhD and master's programmes;
- Establishing and strengthening a network of the universities in southern Ethiopia so that the universities and the Ministry of Health could increase their teaching capacity and train enough staff to meet the demands within the public health sector, including evidence-based health research for policy improvement;

- Substantially increasing the number of women with postgraduate education; and
- Increasing the number of teachers in public health at the universities.

This project has four integrated parts:

1. A PhD programme for all universities, located at Hawassa University;
2. A new master's programme in reproductive health at Dilla University;
3. Strengthening an existing master's programme in nutrition at Wolaita Sodo University; and
4. A new master's programme in medical entomology (with the main focus on malaria control) at Arba Minch University.

By closely collaborating with the Ministry of Health and developing a network of the main universities in southern Ethiopia, we address several important areas such as the relevance of research topics, staff development and improving human capacity in higher education, in public health, reproductive health, nutrition and malaria control. In practice, the Ministry of Health and the PhD programme had regular meetings where PhD students presented their research ideas. Through these interactions, the joint PhD programme received valuable feedback from the Ministry of Health that the research questions were relevant and important for southern Ethiopia.

The joint PhD is a doctorate done at two degree-awarding institutions. Students are fully registered at both universities and must comply with both their admission requirements and assessment regulations. This results in one jointly awarded PhD, with the degree certificate showing two university logos, which is equivalent to PhD degrees offered at European universities. The benefits for students are: access to complementary facilities and resources; exposure to two cultural approaches to research; international student mobility; enhanced acquisition of research and transferable skills, such as negotiation skills and adaptability; and better networking opportunities. Such a joint PhD programme provides PhD-level, taught courses in a high-quality

PhD programme while enhancing knowledge and skill transfer for the supervision of PhD students. In addition, such partnerships between universities of LMICs have a major potential to increase research capacity in both settings.

Developing a joint degree: Experiences and lessons learned

Does the joint degree improve the quality of education in the South? This is a difficult question to answer. However, by adhering to the universities' rules and regulations, candidates are ensured a PhD training that adheres to the quality demands of both universities in the South and North, where courses taken in the South are recognised as equivalent to courses taken at a Northern university and vice versa.

An important element of the joint PhD programme is that the 'home university' is in the South. In our example, the home university is Hawassa University. The student is first registered at Hawassa University where (s)he defines the research topic in close collaboration with the regional health authorities and the local university. Regular meetings are held between the PhD students, supervisors and officials in the Ministry of Health to present research ideas and results. Such a mechanism ensures the research topic is relevant for public health in southern Ethiopia and is prioritised by both institutions of higher education and the authorities implementing the future health programmes. This also enables the research to be relevant for future health policy and translated into action. By having regular and interactive meetings between research students and the Ministry of Health, we strengthened the trust necessary for implementing important scientific findings.

A conventional scholarship for PhD studies assumes that a scholarship holder will stay at a Norwegian institution of higher education for several consecutive years and may visit their home country for data collection. Another approach, which our project did not use, is the 'sandwich model'. In this case, the PhD students carry out their research and studies alternately in their home country and in Norway under continual supervision by a Norwegian academic, and sometimes also including a supervisor from the South, but the doctorate is obtained at the Norwegian university. Although the sandwich model was favoured by many PhD students who remained in their home institution after graduating from the university in the North, the model's weakness was that the decision-making and funding were most often directed from the North. To alleviate these shortcomings, a process was started to discuss the possibility of establishing a PhD programme where both the partners from the South and the North had an equal share in decision-making and in the management of funds. The idea was that the PhD training should eventually be carried out in the South using resources from the South.

Based on our work with 20 PhD students, of which over 50 per cent are women, we experienced the following: 16 of these students were selected based on an open competition among staff from the South universities, as Norhed allowed only university staff to take part in the competition. Later four students were admitted without any limitations on their line of work.

The research topics had to be within public health and each student proposed his or her research topic. This was followed by consultancy meetings with the Regional Office of the Ministry of Health to ensure the research topics would be within the ministry's prioritised areas. Representatives from the universities also agreed that the topics would be relevant for the major health problems in southern Ethiopia and would also be within areas needing to improve both the health services and the health policy Thus, the relevance of the proposed research topics was immediately established with the implementing Ministry of Health, which also would employ some of the future graduates. After being admitted to Hawassa University, each student developed his or her research proposal. Later, the students wrote a research protocol, a detailed presentation of the study's methodology, which had to be written in a way that satisfied university PhD requirements. The research protocols were submitted for ethical clearance by the Institutional Ethical Review Board at Hawassa University and later to the Regional Committee for Medical and Health Research Ethics in Norway. Once these procedures were accomplished, the students were admitted to the PhD programme at the University of Bergen.

Three years after starting this programme, students and supervisors were asked what they thought were the strengths and limitations of the joint PhD programme. They were also asked to suggest how to improve the programme. The PhD students found that the joint PhD degree programme was good. They especially appreciated being exposed to a foreign university by taking certain courses at a Norwegian university and having supervisors from the North as well as having the opportunity to present their research results at international scientific conferences. The main weakness that they expressed was the limited supervisory experience in the South. As most of these supervisors had graduated with their PhDs only a few years previously, students advised that the local supervisory and support systems at universities in southern Ethiopia should be strengthened.

Based on these opinions and recommendations from the PhD students, we managed to reallocate some funds to improve the supervisory skills and capacity. This includes supervisors having an opportunity for supervisory skill training in the North, participating in a local supervisory group to exchange experiences, and joining other African supervisors in discussing opportunities and challenges in supervising their PhD students. In addition, supervisors present their research within research groups with peers to exchange experiences, information and learning. Supervisors from the South also present their research at international conferences and publish their own research in peer-reviewed international journals. These efforts will thus resemble postdoctoral work and we believe it will strengthen both their research and supervisory capacities.

All staff and students agreed that this partnership between universities in high- and low-income countries through the joint degree programme, has the potential to increase the capacity and quality at both universities. There has been a great interest from Norwegian researchers to take part in this research collaboration and it has given the University of Bergen the opportunity to collaborate on areas defined by students from the South as important areas of research. This partnership has improved the sharing of scientific ideas and resources between the South and North. In addition, research initiated by individuals from the South will have the first and corresponding authors from the South.

We believe that this collaborative research environment is addressing critical Ethiopian health issues and health system priorities and that it will result in enhancing the research capacity through relevant PhD and master's programmes. Meanwhile, the research done in the region will aid in defining the future health policy. Our programme includes four universities and the collaboration between them has been strengthened. In addition, supervisors from other Ethiopian universities have taken part in this programme, which has strengthened the links between national universities. Through this collaboration, we were also able to establish a molecular laboratory to study infectious diseases such as malaria, as well as a nutritional laboratory. Modern public health studies need laboratory support (Davies et al. 2017; Greenwood et al. 2012). Such infrastructure is important and can contribute to quality research undertakings and attract further research collaborations. A recent and positive development is that other researchers, research groups and potential students with other funding wish to join this research training programme. Several students have asked to join the programme as it would give them international recognition when doing their PhDs.

Future directions

Recently, a World Bank study showed that sub-Saharan Africa has increased the quantity and quality of research output in the past 20 years (Lan et al. 2014). This growth is strongly linked to advances in health sciences research, most of which is externally funded. Today, health science research accounts for 45 per cent of sub-Saharan research. However, unless the funding for such research also comes from the sub-Saharan African nations, it may not be sustainable.

Therefore, it is vital to maintain and expand the quantity and quality of research at universities in countries such as Ethiopia and especially in southern Ethiopia. It is important to strengthen research-intensive universities. Such work would require growing and consistent investments in human capital, research equipment and administrative support.

Our joint PhD programme increases available training opportunities, boosts the quality of relevant research and thus strengthens the research agenda. It fosters partnerships between universities, stimulates international partnerships, and promotes funding to include quality PhD degrees originating from the South. Registering Ethiopian PhD students at a Northern partner institution ensures the participation of experienced supervisors and monitoring of an individual student's progress. Thus, the joint degree programme helps the development of effective postgraduate training programmes at African universities. It can thus also help to prevent the brain drain. In addition, such a scheme is believed to give greater visibility related to the prestige of the universities and promote a new generation of academics.

The project has succeeded in setting up a PhD programme that has a fair balance of sound, relevant PhD research, a fair gender balance, research courses and motivated PhD students. However, the institutional challenges, especially in the South, include the development of functioning research groups, enhancing grant writing skills and strengthening network building both within the universities and between universities in southern Ethiopia. Solving these institutional challenges is important for continued funding on both sides of the partnership.

The universities in southern Ethiopia are young. Although some of the staff members have attained PhDs and have published scientific papers, few have gained adequate supervisory skills. These universities have so far not institutionalised a postdoctoral system that would qualify researchers for more independent research, research group leadership and supervisory capacity. However, based on experience from the North, postdoctoral fellows need support and mentoring in developing their independent research careers.

The long-term commitment of this project is to ensure continued capacity development in the South. In addition, improving essential research infrastructure, such as laboratory space, biobanks to store biological samples, and internet access, is important to ensure the success of the research projects. With satisfactory infrastructure, universities in the South increase their chances to compete for project grants.

For sustainable research training programmes, it is important to provide graduate students with opportunities for postdoctoral positions and career development schemes. In addition, the research projects in the university setting need to address the Ethiopian health sector priorities to translate research findings into policy and practice.

The ultimate goal of the joint PhD degree programme between Hawassa University and the University of Bergen has been to establish a good PhD programme at the University in the South. During 2018 and 2019, Hawassa University set up a committee to develop their own PhD curriculum and revise the coursework of the existing joint degree curriculum. The committee critically evaluated the existing courses that were mainly based on courses available at the University of Bergen and adapted the new coursework to meet the specific needs of Ethiopian PhD students. These courses now include more emphasis on English scientific writing skills and on data analysis as well as a closer follow-up of scholarly articles that the students produce. We appreciate these important developments and believe they will improve the quality of the PhD work. From the autumn of 2019 onwards, this PhD programme will be based only in Hawassa, although some students may still be co-supervised by staff from the University of Bergen. In this way, the joint PhD programme has served as a mechanism to establish a high-quality PhD programme in southern Ethiopia.

About the authors and the project

Bernt Lindtjørn is a professor at the Centre for International Health, University of Bergen
Moges Tadesse is a PhD student at Hawassa University and Dilla University in Ethiopia
Eskindir Loha is an associate professor at the School of Public Health, Hawassa University, Ethiopia

Project title: South Ethiopia Network of Universities in Public Health
Partner institutions: Hawassa University, Arba Minch University, Dilla University and Wolaita Sodo University (all Ethiopia), University of Bergen (Norway)

References

Abate G, Aseffa A, Selassie A, Goshu S, Fekade B, WoldeMeskal D et al. (2004) Direct colorimetric assay for rapid detection of rifampin-resistant Mycobacterium tuberculosis. *Journal of Clinical Microbiology* 42(2): 871–873

Agyepong IA, Sewankambo N, Binagwaho A, Coll-Seck AM, Corrah T, Ezeh A et al. (2017) The path to longer and healthier lives for all Africans by 2030: The Lancet Commission on the future of health in sub-Saharan Africa. *The Lancet* 390(10114): 2803–2859

Assefa T, Mariam DH, Mekonnen W and Derbew M (2017) Health system's response for physician workforce shortages and the upcoming crisis in Ethiopia: A grounded theory research. *Human Resources for Health* 15(1): 86

Bekele YW and Kjosavik DJ (2016) Decentralised local governance and poverty reduction in post-1991 Ethiopia: A political economy study. *Politics and Governance* 4(4): 1–15

Bloom BR and Godal T (1983) Selective primary health care: Strategies for control of disease in the developing world. *Reviews of Infectious Diseases* 5(4): 765–780

Breugelmans JG, Makanga MM, Cardoso AL, Mathewson SB, Sheridan-Jones BR, Gurney KA et al. (2015) Bibliometric assessment of European and sub-Saharan African research output on poverty-related and neglected infectious diseases from 2003 to 2011. *PLoS Neglected Tropical Diseases* 9(8). Available online

Choi BC, Pang T, Lin V, Puska P, Sherman G, Goddard M et al. (2005) Can scientists and policy makers work together? *Journal of Epidemiology & Community Health* 59(8): 632–637

Dare DJ (2007) HIV antiretroviral therapy in Ethiopia: Overcoming implementation challenges. PhD thesis, University of Bergen. Available online

Datiko DG (2011) Improving tuberculosis control in Ethiopia: Performance of TB control programme, community DOTS, and its cost-Effectiveness. PhD thesis, Centre for International Health, University of Bergen. Available online

Davies J, Abimiku A, Alobo M, Mullan Z, Nugent R, Schneidman M et al. (2017) Sustainable clinical laboratory capacity for health in Africa. *Lancet Global Health* 5(3): e248–e249. Available online

Davies J and Mullan Z (2016) Research capacity in Africa: Will the sun rise again? *The Lancet Global Health* 4(5): 287

FDRE (Federal Democratic Republic of Ethiopia) (2016) Growth and Transformation Plan II (GTP II) (2015/16-2019/20). Addis Ababa: National Planning Commission

Fonn S, Ayiro LP, Cotton P, Habib A, Mbithi PMF, Mtenje A et al. (2018) Repositioning Africa in global knowledge production. *The Lancet* 392(10153): 1163–1166

Girma S, AG Yohannes, Y Kitaw, Y Ye-Ebiyo, A Seyoum, H Desta and A Teklehaimanot (2007) Human resource development for health in Ethiopia: Challenges of achieving the Millennium Development Goals. Ethiopian *Journal of Health Development* 21(3): 216–231

Greenwood B, Bhasin A and Targett G (2012) The Gates Malaria Partnership: A consortium approach to malaria research and capacity development. *Tropical Medicine and International Health* 17(5): 558–563

Jávorka Z, Allinson R, Varnai P and Wain M (2018) *Mid-term Review of the Norwegian Programme for Capacity Development in Higher Education and Research for Development (Norhed)*. Available online

Lan G, Blom A, Kamalski J, Lau G, Baas J and Adil M (2014) *A Decade of Development in Sub-Saharan African Science, Technology, Engineering and Mathematics Research*. Washington, DC: World Bank

Lindtjørn B, Loha E, Deressa W, Balkew M, Gebremichael T, Sorteberg A et al. (2014) Strengthening malaria and climate research in Ethiopia. *Malaria Journal* 13(S1): 56

Miorner H and Britton S (1999) 30 years of successful mycobacteriology research: The AHRI in Addis Ababa, a unique research environment in a developing country. *Lakartidningen* 96(6): 585–587

Preston SH (1975) The changing relation between mortality and level of economic development. *Population Studies* 29(2): 231–248

Sewankambo N, Tumwine JK, Tomson G, Obua C, Bwanga F, Waiswa P et al. (2015) Enabling dynamic partnerships through joint degrees between low- and high-income countries for capacity development in global health research: Experience from the Karolinska Institutet/Makerere University partnership. *PLoS Medicine* 12(2). Available online

Shargie EB (2007) Trends, challenges and opportunities in tuberculosis control in rural Ethiopia: Epidemiological and operational studies in a resource-constrained setting. PhD thesis, University of Bergen. Available online

Shumbullo EL (2013) Variation in malaria transmission in southern Ethiopia: The impact of prevention strategies and a need for targeted intervention. PhD thesis, University of Bergen. Available online

Strydom WF, Funke N, Nienaber S, Nortje K and Steyn M (2010) Evidence-based policy-making: A review. *South African Journal of Science* 106(5/6). Available online

Tijssen RJW (2007) Africa's contribution to the worldwide research literature: New analytical perspectives, trends, and performance indicators. *Scientometrics* 71(2): 303–327

Ulesido FM (2017) Malaria vectors in southern Ethiopia: Some challenges and opportunities for vector control. PhD thesis, University of Bergen. Available online

19

From needs assessment to academic leadership training for women in Ethiopia

Jeanette H Magnus, Kora Tushune & Abraham Haileamlak

Introduction

In this chapter, we briefly present the 'Strategic and Collaborative Capacity Development in Ethiopia and Africa (SACCADE)' project, funded by the Norwegian Programme for Capacity Development in Higher Education and Research for Development (Norhed) from 2013 to 2019. We describe the project's setting, the partnership strategy and one selected activity, the Jimma Executive Program for Women in Academic and Educational Leadership (JEWEL). In the main thrust of the paper we place JEWEL in a national and international context related to the imperative of gender equality and women's leadership development in higher education (HE). We also describe the philosophical and educational approach used when developing this special programme.

Strategic and Collaborative Capacity Development in Ethiopia and Africa – SACCADE

Ethiopia, located in East Africa, is the second most populous country in Africa with a diverse ethnic population estimated at 105 million in 2018. Two Ethiopian institutions were selected to participate in this project. The first, Jimma University (JU), is 352km southwest of Addis Ababa and became a fully-fledged university in 1997. It is one of the leading universities in Ethiopia and currently mentors several of the newly established universities and medical schools in the country. JU was previously The College of Health Sciences which was restructured and renamed Jimma University Institute of Health in 2016. It includes the Faculty of Medicine (founded in 1984), the School of Public Health, the Faculty of Allied Health Professionals and Jimma Hospital. In 2012, the College of Health Sciences had 5 472 students enrolled, of which 23.1 per cent were women. Of the 246 academic staff members, only 13.8 per cent were women, compared to about 70 per cent of the administrative staff. The second institution, St Paul's Hospital Millennium Medical College (SPHMMC), is in Addis Ababa and has been a tertiary referral hospital for the whole of Ethiopia since 1947. Since 2007, it has included a medical school with an interdisciplinary modular curriculum. SPHMMC is directly under the Ethiopian Ministry of Health and is key to the strategic plan for healthcare research and health service development in Ethiopia. Its medical school has nearly 50 per cent female students and 30 per cent of all students are from emerging regions. The third participant, the Faculty of Medicine at the University of Oslo (UiO), which is the oldest medical school in Norway, made a strategic decision in 2011 to limit its international institutional partnerships. The intention was to have fewer but more comprehensive, focused initiatives instead of being spread thin across many institutions and countries. Thus, a focus on Ethiopia with JU and SPHMMC as key partner institutions is at the core of this project.

Prior to participation in the Norhed programme, JU and SPHMMC undertook a comprehensive and extensive needs assessment, underscoring the need for capacity building in research and research education in public health, health sciences, and primary healthcare systems as core initiatives to advance higher education in Ethiopia. In addition, administrative capacity and leadership development emerged as important issues. The needs assessment guided the development of the application, anchoring it in the JU, SPHMMC and UiO strategic plans, as well as in the national agenda of Ethiopia. The proposal was discussed at a community stakeholder meeting in Jimma, and the SACCADE project was the operationalisation of a joint roadmap, rather than the implementation of an external agenda. For our purposes, we redefined capacity development to mean capacity exchange between the partners. While the SACCADE project's target group is employees at the Ethiopian partner institutions, and not the students, 12 staff members (50 per cent of whom are women) are currently PhD students at UiO. So far, more than 600 Ethiopian staff members have participated in the UiO-led workshops and courses at JU and at SPHMMC. At the end of the project, most of these activities will be integrated and offered for credit in their ongoing educational programmes.

The Jimma Executive Programme for Women in Academic and Educational Leadership – JEWEL

Women staff are actively encouraged and prioritised, and their participation is facilitated. We have secured a significant participation of female staff from JU and SPHMMC in research and research education activities. Under Norhed, we established JEWEL. This is the only SACCADE activity branching outside JU and SPHMMC. So far, we have had 88 women from 27 different universities across Ethiopia participating in our trainings.

Without female role models, it is challenging to recruit women to various leadership positions. The main purpose of the JEWEL training is to further leadership skills and capacities of women leaders in health and medical education across Ethiopia, ensuring transformational leaders for transforming institutions. This will ultimately be a national programme, dedicated to supporting women faculty at colleges of medical sciences and public health to move into positions of institutional leadership, which potentially will influence and foster sustained positive change. Below we present the status of women in higher education in Ethiopia, international literature related to the training of women in academic leadership, and the JEWEL training strategy, philosophy and next steps, while discussing future implications for the Norhed programme.

Background

Advancement of women in higher education, in research and in society, is at the core of several political documents in Ethiopia, as in Norway. Gender inequality, as described by the United Nations Development Programme (UNDP), refers to the differences in opportunities and achievements between men and women within a nation (UNDP n.d.). The gender inequality index (GII) reflects this difference in achievements, comparing educational attainment, economic status, reproductive health and political representation between men and women (UNDP 2019). The higher the GII value, the greater is the difference in achievements between women and men. In general, European countries have the lowest GII (Norway 4.8 per cent), while nations in central Asia and sub-Saharan Africa have the highest GII. The most recent GII of Ethiopia was 50.2 per cent. It is widely documented that high levels of inequality inhibit the impact of economic growth on poverty reduction (Unesco 2016). The paucity of women occupying major institutional and political leadership positions is stated as both a cause and a result of gender inequality in Ethiopia in official documents (FDRE 2015). At a time when knowledge becomes central to economic prosperity, fair access to knowledge and skills becomes a question of both social justice and economic well-being.

Gender and higher education in Ethiopia

Higher education (HE) is seen as a key driver of the nation's development vision. This is expressed in policy documents as: 'to become a country where democratic rule, good-governance and social justice reign, upon the involvement and free will of its peoples, and once extricating itself from poverty to reach the level of a middle-income economy as of 2020–2023' (FAO 2010). Ethiopia's gross enrolment ratio in HE, just 8 per cent of the relevant age group in 2014, is among the lowest in the world. Approximately 90 per cent of Ethiopian girls enrol in primary school, but this drops to less than 50 per cent in secondary school, and 20 to 30 per cent in college and university.

On their way to and within HE, women face repressive gender norms that impede them from achieving their career or educational aspirations. The problem of gender inequality in Ethiopian HE is reflected in the rates of enrolment, dropout, completion, and graduation (Molla and Cuthbert 2014). It is also illustrated by academic achievements, and the proportion of women in different academic roles and positions compared with their male counterparts (Molla and Cuthbert 2014). The gender inequality in HE is further echoed by reports of unfavourable classroom experiences by female students, the exclusion of female students and academic women from critical decision-making processes, the gendered division of labour, gender violence and sexual harassment (Abebe 2013).

Gender arrangements and relations in a society constitute a social structure. Structural inequality, aligned with a repressive gender culture at societal and institutional levels, creates major barriers for women's advancement in academia. The National Policy on Ethiopian Women,[1] enacted in 1993, identifies the patriarchal system as a key structural factor that exposes women to political, economic, and social discrimination. A repressive gender order is often subtle, but nevertheless expressed, and fills important messages with prejudice and low expectations about the role and responsibility of women in HE institutions (Molla 2013). Understanding gender culture in the context of HE necessitates problematising social interactions and power relations as manifested in the lived experiences of women (Molla 2013). The gender dynamics of society operating in the classroom in various arenas of HE institutions, through representations of women as less capable and weak, socialises them to accept gender-based inequalities as normal (Abebe 2013).

Factors contributing to Ethiopian women's low participation in leadership are complex (Molla 2018). The challenges encountered by women academic staff include negative attitudes towards women in public roles. Strong beliefs, according to which women are not capable of performing and succeeding, undermine affirmative action, as they feed ideas that women are not able to obtain positions on their own merit. Harassment and insecurity, both on campus and in the surrounding communities, pose specific challenges to women and limit their working hours on campus (Molla and Cuthbert 2014). With respect to management and leadership positions, negative attitudes, lower access to information and resources, as well as the late hours of many meetings undermine opportunities for women to participate and succeed. Nomination and voting procedures also affect the likelihood that women take up management positions. Support of senior managers to women in leadership positions is crucial for success, as are other forms of support, unfortunately currently often lacking. Women faculty also face challenges in balancing work and private life; universities have not adapted to the changing composition of their workforce, and the different roles and responsibilities of male and female staff (Molla 2018).

After more than two decades of preferential admission policies for historically disadvantaged groups (including women), gender inequality in HE persists (FDRE 2015). The first full professorship rank given to a woman was in March 2009 by Addis Ababa University (Semela et al. 2017). It has wide-ranging ramifications for policy-making in Ethiopia when HE only managed to produce two women as full professors in its first 60 years of higher education history (Molla 2018). Increasing female leadership in HE is a critical step towards reducing gender inequality in society. Today, HE institutions hold an important role in shaping the future of society. Evidence shows that a strong system of HE institutions is a significant contributor to the country's ability to compete globally in various ways (Samir and Lutz 2017). However, many of the HE institutions are challenged in producing the next generation of leaders. Even though they are few in number, it is evident that women leaders are innovative, productive, and successful (Downs et al. 2014). While women around the world face many common barriers to higher education leadership, low-income countries such as Ethiopia have their own peculiar factors. Therefore, working on increasing female leadership in HE is a critical step towards reducing gender inequality in the society.

Leadership framework

Gender equity and equality in HE requires cultural change, national policies, institutional actions, mentoring and leadership training of female staff (Winchester and Browning 2015). In other words, gender culture refers to both the macro-level, hegemonic cultural beliefs about gender, and the micro-level social relational contexts in which the beliefs are enacted. Gender difference is not a problem in itself. The problem comes when the difference fails to entail a different-but-equal relationship between female and male persons. Often the hegemonic cultural belief about gender is hierarchical in the sense that it presupposes the superiority of men in relation to women as masculine pursuits are given greater value (Molla 2018). Leadership in Ethiopia reflects its masculine culture, so this must be considered while developing and conducting leadership training for women (Abebe 2013). There was limited or no research literature regarding leadership training or career advancement of women in academic medicine or health-related fields in Ethiopia or sub-Saharan Africa available to us in 2012.

The Executive Leadership in Academic Medicine (ELAM) Program for Women was launched in 1995 (Richman et al. 2001). This is a year-long part-time fellowship for women faculty in the schools of medicine, dentistry and public health at Drexel University, USA. More than 1 000 ELAM alumnae hold leadership positions in institutions around the world. This is one of the few academic leadership programmes for women that has been evaluated (Helitzer et al. 2014). The first author of this chapter, Magnus, was a fellow in ELAM in 2010/2011. In order to advance mid-career women academic faculty into leadership roles in HE institutions, selected ELAM elements were used with permission for the development of JEWEL. Magnus has attended several leadership training courses and programmes, and also taught leadership courses at postgraduate level and for professionals in Norway and the USA. The first academic leadership course Magnus taught in Ethiopia was at Mekelle University in February 2012.

JEWEL

The main purpose of this training is to further the leadership skills and capacities of women leaders in health and medical education across Ethiopia. The long-term aim of JEWEL is to be an in-depth, national programme dedicated to preparing senior women faculty at colleges of medical sciences and public health to move into positions of institutional leadership where they can effect sustained, positive change.

Overall objectives

- Establish a training and education programme suiting the needs of women leaders in HE in Ethiopia;
- Facilitate a community of practice of leadership among women leaders in academic medicine and health sciences;
- Enable women leaders in HE in medicine and health sciences to inform the leadership-training curriculum;
- Increase the diversity of role models for the next generation of academic professionals;
- Ensure high-quality pedagogic and participatory methods in the training programme; and
- Achieve high participant satisfaction ratings.

Setting

Participants were solicited from medical and health colleges across Ethiopia. The deans of colleges were each invited to nominate a fellow. We asked the deans to consider the following when nominating their candidate: 'Her academic track record (credentials, training, publications, teaching and leadership experience), her potential as an emerging leader, your institution's commitment to her, your concrete plans for formal or informal leadership roles for her in coming years, her plans for additional advanced academic training'. In addition, they were required to state their personal commitment to being a mentor for her during her time in the training programme. The letter had to address each of these issues and be accompanied by the applicants' academic CV, and a letter from her stating her personal interests in academic and leadership development. The deans were also informed that if the candidate was not approved, another university would be given the opportunity to have the slot. So far, we have had 88 participants from 27 different Ethiopian universities. The SACCADE programme pays for travel and accommodation. We have used a local hotel conducive to such an intense, interactive training. The six-day training, as described below, concentrates on general aspects related to leadership, personal styles and skills relevant to leadership and team development. This has been conducted four times with 16 to 27 participants each time. We aim to do a more advanced follow-up session with the participants in the coming year.

Educational methods

The SACCADE project is grounded in adult learning principles, including andragogy and self-motivated learning. Andragogy also tends to place an emphasis upon learner-centred and not teacher-centred strategies. The JEWEL sessions include brief didactic lectures, interactive plenary seminars, group work (exercises, reflections, case discussions, tasks), individual assessment tools, role-playing, individual interviews, readings and action-based learning (from interviews and action projects). Magnus has used these principles in all her teaching since 1999. For a recent review on andragogy and its use in leadership teaching, see McCauley et al. 2017.

Educational content

Each day builds on the next and addresses three main skills: interpersonal, leadership and networking. Each topic has a short 7 to 12-minute introduction followed by questions, scenarios or tasks posted for brief 10 to 20-minute group discussions. Plenary report-back provided rich reflections and discussions. Sometimes the participants did interviews, crafts, or role-play. They also had homework from one day to the next, presenting their results in plenary sessions. The training was conducted in English, but all group discussions were in their language of preference. The plenary session was often halted to solicit the Amharic word for a term. This frequently initiated discussions on the interpretation and understanding of the use of English terminology related to leadership.

Networking: For the vast majority of the participants, this was the first time any of them were part of a professional women-only event addressing aspects of leadership, working life and gender relations in

---

JEWEL session objectives

Personal competencies

- Facilitate an understanding of the importance of self-awareness
- Foster understanding of and strategies for self-reflection
- Foster and increase understanding of the importance of self-promotion
- Increase understanding of personal attitudes, roles and behaviours in teams

Skills

- Increase knowledge about types, styles and role of communication
- Enhance ability to reflect on leadership skills, traits and styles
- Increase knowledge and perspectives on team-building, teamwork, team culture and team dynamics
- Increase understandings of the importance of mentoring, networks and community of practice participation
- Time management and project planning

Ethiopia. As the trainers, we presented the Eurocentric style of male networking and the group discussed Ethiopian gender styles. Strategies for increasing their personal networks were discussed in small groups and in plenary sessions. The venue itself provided unusual opportunities for networking and forging professional and personal bonds. This was strengthened by the introduction of the concept of a community of practice and several of the groups have continued on social media or with in-person meetings. Personal communications from several of the participants since the training have highlighted their strategic activities in networking and how they have sought out personal mentors.

Leadership: We presented selected theories and perspectives related to leadership skills, traits and styles. As homework, each participant identified her leadership role model and elaborated on why this person was a special leader in their class presentations. Studies on gender differences in leadership based on research in high-income countries prompted discussion on the Ethiopian context and female perspectives on leadership. Various female, Ethiopian role models were identified and presented.

Interpersonal: Leadership starts with self-knowledge and self-awareness. We used the Whole Brain® thinking model as a self-assessment tool. The affirmation of the tool and personal experiences led into discussion and sharing amongst people with similar preferences. This approach facilitates discussion about interpersonal relationships and about working in teams of people with different personal preferences. Communication is more than our words, and the role of non-verbal communication in Ethiopia was also thoroughly discussed in terms of gender differences in communication. The use of various styles in communication, and the link this has to personal thinking preferences, is also addressed.

In addition, participants do a personal SWOT analysis, identifying personal strengths, weaknesses, opportunities and threats in relation to personal advancement in academic leadership at their institution. As we gradually move from the concept of being born as a leader to developing as a leader, the group discussions uncover societal gender norms and solicit personal testimonies throughout the week. The personal, private and institutional characteristics of the stories warrant discretion and respect and this is included in the overall group rules established on the very first day. Increased self-awareness, reflection and understanding of the importance of self-advocacy slowly emerge through the sessions and become more evident in the discussions. We continually reflect back to the societal and cultural context, both at their particular HE institutions as well as in their communities. This is deliberately done using group tasks. Due to the heterogeneity of the participants we also discuss ethnic, regional and religious perspectives during the sessions.

Evaluation

Magnus has developed a self-efficacy instrument related to academic leadership. The level and pace of each day was assessed using a collective 'temperature' tick-off scale to indicate the challenges as well as the relevance of the topics of the day. This facilitated discussion the following day and the presenter modified the sessions. The whole six-day training was evaluated using a standardised evaluation form with Likert scales, used for global assessment of the relevance of a topic, and with places for personal comments. A full evaluation with qualitative and quantitative measures assessing participants' personal reflections has been developed and will be conducted in 2019.

Reflections

As limited literature and assessment of leadership training sessions for women in academia were available when we started, the relevance to the Ethiopian context was continually assessed during the sessions while soliciting feedback from the participants during group sessions and reflections. Based on the experience with JEWEL, Western curricula for women's leadership can be adapted to Ethiopian settings, with beneficial personal and individual outcomes. User participation and adult learning principles ensured active participation and relevance to Ethiopian culture and context. The comprehensiveness of the JEWEL programme has been validated when compared to recent publications (Sonnino 2016). To the best of our knowledge, the JEWEL programme is the largest leadership training programme for women in HE in Ethiopia. A recent study presents interviews with and the perspectives of eight Ethiopian female medical faculty participating in an international fellowship programme on leadership in the USA, expressing increased motivation and sense of skills related to leadership (Kvach et al. 2017).

The Educational Sector Development Programme V (FDRE 2015) in Ethiopia sets objectives to strengthen the representation and leadership of women academics in universities. It aims to have a proportion of 25 per cent female academic staff by 2019 and at least one woman in a top academic position as a university vice-president at each of the 36 public HE institutions. Action items would be: 'Developing and implementing guidelines on composition of university boards and top leadership for greater representation of females' and 'Designing and implementing a female talent cultivation centre for inspiring and assisting females to participate and succeed in leadership and management at all levels' (FDRE 2015). At least two of the JEWEL participants are now university vice-presidents. We see systematic leadership training as imperative, so the lack of knowledge does not set up for failure those pioneering women daring to step forward in line with the Ethiopian ESDP V. The JEWEL programme has caught the interest of the Ministry of Education in Ethiopia and the Norwegian Ministry of Foreign Affairs and a scale-up is currently being discussed.

Way forward

A brain drain, especially related to HE and in medicine and health, is a major national challenge and is discussed in Ethiopian news media.[2] Interestingly, an American study (Chang et al. 2016) demonstrates that leadership training offered a retention advantage to women faculty as, after undergoing a leadership training programme, they were less likely to leave their institutions than other women and men at junior and mid-level ranks. Senior professors of both genders were as likely to change institutions in this study. This could have significant implications for capacity development and faculty retention in HE institutions in Ethiopia. Participation in JEWEL or similar comprehensive, academic leadership training programmes might have material implications for the sustainability of mid-level leadership at the new HEs across the country.

The need to increase the proportion of women in leadership is an urgent global issue (Downs et al. 2014). A few studies have found that women leaders are more likely to focus on issues that directly improve the lives of women, such as access to healthcare, clean water supply, improved education and income generation (Molla 2018). Active participation and inclusion of women in leadership at all levels are related to national advancement. This is also why in 2015 this was included as one of the UN Sustainable Development Goals (SDGs). SDG 5 (Achieve gender equity and empower all women and girls) includes as one target to 'ensure women's full and effective participation and equal opportunities for leadership at all levels of decision-making in political, economic and public life'.

Numerical parity is a proxy for gender equality in HE, but two interesting papers using a case study from South Africa look beyond this and assess if deeper inequalities are overlooked in policy and practice (Loots and Walker 2015, 2016). Employing a capabilities approach to the meaning of gender equality in HE requires promoting individual agency through empowerment, as well as challenging cultural gender roles and the social structure. Loots and Walker conclude that the capability approach provides a framework that could be an evidence-based driver for the development of policy and initiatives for achieving true gender equality.

Interest in African leadership is increasing as illustrated by Fourie et al. (2017) and Hallinger (2017). A host of leadership training pro-grammes, such as 'Leadership Universities' and 'Leadership Academies', have emerged in recent years, some of which include women. The continent needs more women in leadership roles to serve as role models for female students. As culture and context differ, national and regional adaptations will be called for. The JEWEL programme has a built-in reflection cycle conducive to these needs and will thus be malleable and transferable to other countries. Elements of the JEWEL programme have been run as smaller sessions for HE faculty members in Russia with great acceptance and similar success. Magnus has also had mixed gender sessions, where group work is by gender, with favourable outcomes.

Conclusions

The Norhed programme enabled two Ethiopian HE institutions to develop a roadmap to target challenges identified through a needs assessment. Capacity building in research and research education is at the core of the SACCADE project. Development, implementation and advancement of research in core areas within health and medical sciences are essential to Ethiopia. Development of the country's own evidence base through active research is necessary to increase institu-tional, regional and national capacity and to reduce brain drain. Leadership development is crucial to ensure the success of fledgling HE institutions in the country. Women's participation at all levels of aca-demic life in HE institutions is imperative for Ethiopia to reach its national goals as well as the SDG 5. Historically, community and political leaders often grow out of academia and HE institutions. The planned assessment of the JEWEL programme in Ethiopia might demonstrate that leadership training and the increased presence of women as university leaders can be a 'model' for societal changes in terms of how women are able to find their way into leadership positions. The JEWEL programme developed under the Norhed funding scheme could be used as a model for scale-up in Ethiopia, Africa and elsewhere, facilitating the advancement of women leadership.

Acknowledgements

The insights, reflections and support of Bernadette N. Kumar, Serawork Wallelign, Ashresash Demessie, and Bosena Tebeje are appreciated.

About the authors and the project

Jeanette H Magnus is a special advisor to the leadership of the Faculty of Medicine at the University of Oslo in Norway and an adjunct professor at Tulane School of Public Health and Tropical Medicine in New Orleans, USA
Kora Tushune is Vice-President for Development at Jimma University in Ethiopia
Abraham Haileamlak is a professor of paediatric cardiology at Jimma University in Ethiopia

Project title: Strategic and Collaborative Capacity Development in Ethiopia and Africa (SACCADE)
Partner institutions: Jimma University, St. Paul's Hospital Millennium Medical College (both Ethiopia) and the University of Oslo (Norway)

Notes

1   The National Policy on Ethiopian Women is available online at: http://www.mowca. gov.et/-/--9-30?inheritRedirect=true
2   See, for example, The nature of Ethiopia's brain drain: Leaving while productive, returning as retirees, *Ethiopian Herald* 28 July 2017 (text in Amharic, translated by Abraham Haileamlak).

References

Abebe G (2013) Status of women academicians and their perceptions of gender bias vis-à-vis some organizational variables: The case of three public universities in Ethiopia. *The Ethiopian Journal of Education* 33(1): 25–52

Chang S, Morahan PS, Magrane D, Helitzer D, Lee HY, Newbill S et al. (2016) Retaining faculty in academic medicine: The impact of career development programs for women. *Journal of Women's Health (Larchmt)* 25(7): 687–696

Downs JA, Reif LK, Hokororo A and Fitzgerald DW (2014) Increasing women in leadership in global health. *Academic Medicine* 89: 1103–1107

FAO (Food and Agriculture Organization) of the UN (2010) *Ethiopia: Growth and Transformation Plan 2010/11–2014/15.* Available online

FDRE (Federal Democratic Republic of Ethiopia) (2015). *Education Sector Development Programme V (ESDP V) 2015/16-2019/20.* Addis Ababa: Federal Ministry of Education. Available online

Fourie W, Van der Merwe SC and Van der Merwe BJ (2017) Sixty years of research on leadership in Africa: A review of the literature. *Leadership* 13(2): 222–251

Hallinger P (2017) Surfacing a hidden literature: A systematic review of research on educational leadership and management in Africa. *Educational Management Administration and Leadership* 45: 1–23

Helitzer DL, Newbill SL, Morahan PS, Magrane D, Cardinali G, Wu CC et al. (2014) Perceptions of skill development of participants in three national career development programs for women faculty in academic medicine. *Academic Medicine* 89: 896–903

Kvach E, Yesehak B, Abebaw H, Conniff J, Busse H and Haq C (2017) Perspectives of female medical faculty in Ethiopia on a leadership fellowship program. *International Journal of Medical Education* 8: 314–323

Loots S and Walker M (2015) Shaping a gender equality policy in higher education: Which human capabilities matter? *Gender and Education* 27(4): 361–375

Loots S and Walker M (2016) A capabilities-based gender equality policy for Higher Education: Conceptual and methodological considerations. *Journal of Human Development and Capabilities* 17(2): 260–277

McCauley KD, Hammer E and Hinojosa AS (2017) An andragogical approach to teaching leadership. *Management Teaching Review* 2(4): 312–324

Molla T (2013) Higher education policy reform in Ethiopia: The representation of the problem of gender inequality. *Higher Education Policy* 26(2): 193–215

Molla T (2018) *Higher Education in Ethiopia: Structural Inequalities and Policy Responses.* Education Policy and Social Inequality series, vol 2. Singapore: Springer

Molla T and Cuthbert D (2014) Qualitative inequality: Experiences of women in Ethiopian higher education. *Gender and Education* 26(7): 759–775

Richman RC, Morahan PS, Cohen DW and McDade SA (2001) Advancing women and closing the leadership gap: The Executive Leadership in Academic Medicine (ELAM) program experience. *Journal of Women's Health and Gender-Based Medicine* 10: 271–277

Samir KC and Lutz W (2017) The human core of the shared socioeconomic pathways: Population scenarios by age, sex and level of education for all countries to 2100. *Global Environmental Change* 42: 181–192

Semela T, Bekele H and Abraham R (2017) Navigating the river Nile: The chronicle of female academics in Ethiopian higher education. *Gender and Education.* Available online

Sonnino RE (2016) Health care leadership development and training: Progress and pitfalls. *Journal of Healthcare Leadership* 8: 19–29

UNDP (United Nations Development Programme) (n.d.) *People: Gender Equality. Equal Rights: Equal Contributors.* Available online

UNDP (2019) *Human Development Reports.* Gender inequality index (GII). Available online

Unesco (United Nations Educational, Scientific and Cultural Organization) (2016) *World Social Science Report 2016, Challenging Inequalities: Pathways to a Just World.* Available online

Winchester HPM and Browning L (2015) Gender equality in academia: A critical reflection. *Journal of Higher Education Policy and Management* 37(3): 269–281

20

Engendering and decolonising legal education: South–South and South–North co-operation

Patricia Kameri-Mbote, Anne Hellum, Julie Stewart,
Ngeyi Ruth Kanyongolo & Mulela Margaret Munalula

Introduction

The questioning of legal education as gendered and unequal began in African law faculties in earnest in the 1980s. Feminists were seeking to transform the normative tradition of law to recognise what law traditionally treated as "otherness", as central to an understanding of law and society' (Mossman 1985: 214). This was within a context where despite the political decolonisation of African countries, colonial laws remained intact and denied other legal forms recognition and spaces for expression (Ndlovu-Gatsheni 2015). The need for critical examination of the role of law, lawyers and legal institutions in maintaining colonial vestiges formed a significant part of scholarship in the 1970s and 1980s (Dias et al. 1981).

Southern and eastern African and Scandinavian researchers realised that it was not enough to extend Western law into African contexts and challenged law's claim to objectivity through research on family, succession, labour and social insurance laws that took women's lived realities as the starting point (Dahl 1987; Hellum et al. 2007; Stewart and

Armstrong 1990). Their research uncovered how law privileged male life situations, values and interests and, as such, affected men and women in different ways, even when couched in gender-neutral terms. This is compounded by the uncritical importation and privileging of legal notions and values based on Western law originating from the colonising powers. Law courses often focus on state law as is, without interrogating its colonial and gendered context. Research findings led to new courses in women's law, gender and the law, and equality and anti-discrimination law at African, Asian and Scandinavian universities (Mehdi and Shaheed 1997).

Most universities, however, still use a textual or black letter approach to teaching law. This shortcoming was vividly depicted in the description of how family law was taught at Makerere University in Uganda in the early 1980s:

> We were not exposed to the different contexts, historical, polit-
> ical economy, gender relations or even human rights, within
> which the law operated. Instead the professor took us through
> the black letter rules as laid out in the statutes and cases, con-
> structing the 'ideal' family as a natural, ahistorical and God-given
> entity that was beyond questioning. He taught the law with
> various underlying assumptions that were never examined,
> questioned or even challenged in the lecture room. Students
> were left to absorb it all, absent scrutiny and discussion of all
> the inconsistencies, contradictions, double standards and para-
> doxes embedded in the law. (Tamale 2015: 1)

In this chapter we address initiatives to mainstream a gender perspec-
tive in legal education by legal scholars from five partner universities in Zimbabwe, Zambia, Malawi, Kenya and Norway. We focus on a project called 'Master's, PhD and Research Programme for Capacity Building in Law Faculties', funded by the Norwegian Programme for Capacity Development in Higher Education and Research for Development (Norhed).

Gender mainstreaming has been defined as

the process of assessing the implications for women and men of any planned action, including legislation, policies and programmes, in all areas and at all levels. It is a strategy for making women's as well as men's concerns and experiences an integral dimension of the design, implementation, monitoring and evaluation of policies and programmes in all political, economic and societal spheres so that women and men benefit equally and inequality is not perpetuated. (UN 1997: 27)[1]

The overall aim of the Norhed project is to change legal education that discounts the experiences and values of women who are marginalised because of their gender, often in combination with other identity markers, such as ethnicity, sexual orientation, class and disability. Acknowledging the shortcomings of a gender-neutral approach that simply extends men's rights to women, the project sets out to engender legal education (Fredman 2013). Legal engenderment is associated with substantive as opposed to formal equality. It calls for the integration of theories, methods and skills that enable students to critique and recast rights in the light of different groups of women's lived realities, into all areas of legal education.

In the following discussion, we address encounters between gender-specific and seemingly gender-neutral approaches to legal disciplines, such as human rights law, constitutional law, customary law, criminal law, family law and inheritance law, at each of the five partner institutions.

The overall research question is: how, with what results and under what conditions have the measures and activities, which were adopted to engender legal education, resulted in change. These measures were in areas such as curriculum review, staff development, and joint research and publication.

Through qualitative methods, particularly experiential data acquired through participation and observation (Smart 2009), the authors describe, reflect on and compare their experiences in engendering legal education.

The Norhed project on gender mainstreaming in legal education: Background, aims and means

Building women's law through separate research programmes and courses

The Norhed project on gender mainstreaming in legal education emerged from a long-standing co-operation between women's law experts at southern and eastern African universities and experts from the Institute of Women's Law at the University of Oslo. The introduction of the Women's Law Diploma for African lawyers in the University of Oslo's Department of Public Law in the late 1980s coincided with the research on women and law in southern and eastern Africa.[2] The interaction between the two sets of research and education projects raised awareness of methodological approaches in how to analyse the discriminatory aspects of seemingly gender-neutral law in both contexts.

It was felt that the relevance and impact of the diploma course could be enhanced if it moved from Norway to sub-Saharan Africa. This was for several reasons. More students and lecturers from the region could be involved. Fieldwork training, needed to decolonise law through bottom-up perspectives on the position of women in law and society, could be carried out. Empirical research under Women and Law in Southern Africa (WLSA) and Women and Law in Eastern Africa (WLEA) on inheritance, marriage and maintenance demonstrated that extending the application of imported Western law to Africans was not an adequate response to women's actual needs. The diploma programme moved to the University of Zimbabwe in 1990. In 1994, The Southern and Eastern African Regional Centre for Women's Law (SEARCWL) was established. Its master's and PhD programmes drew students and teaching faculty from diverse southern and eastern African and northern European countries. Scholars from southern and eastern Africa, partnering with scholars from Oslo and Copenhagen, published ground-breaking gender analysis that took African legal pluralities (more than one legal system operating within one geographic area or population) and people's social, economic and political realities as a starting point (Ikdahl 2014). This led to an understanding of customary law as a fluid, flexible and living form of law, as opposed to the static approach that had been developed by the colonial courts and applied by the post-colonial courts (Bentzon et al. 1998; Hellum 1999; Hellum et al. 2007; Stewart 1997). This legal pluralist framework was successfully adopted by southern and eastern African researchers and activists who set out to reform the discriminatory customary laws that applied in the field of inheritance and family law (Stewart and Tsanga 2007).

Three decades of research and education in women's law have impacted the entire law, justice, governance and order sector in the southern and eastern African region through the training of personnel from the judiciary, legislature, army and police, among others.[3] Graduates from the diploma course serve as judicial and law enforcement officers, senior government officials and key staff of local, regional, national and international human rights and gender agencies. Academia in all these countries has benefited through staff development, particularly the uptake of academic staff with research and teaching competence in the field of women's law, and equality and anti-discrimination law (Jones et al. 2013). Both the men and women who have completed the diploma programme speak to its transformative effects on their personal and professional lives.

Women's law in a changing legal context

Today, all African countries, except two, have ratified the Convention on the Elimination of All Forms of Discrimination against Women (CEDAW) and the Protocol to the African Charter on Human and Peoples' Rights on the Rights of Women in Africa (the Maputo Protocol). Countries have reformed constitutions and formulated policies to underpin equality. Zimbabwe, Zambia, Malawi and Kenya have ratified CEDAW and the Maputo Protocol and have constitutions that guarantee equality.[4] The eventual recognition of the principle of equality of opportunity has in recent years led to the gradual removal of discriminatory provisions in customary and statutory law. Most constitutional provisions in colonial and immediate post-independence constitutions, which provided for equality of all persons on the one hand while expressly saving customary laws from the application of equality clauses, have been abolished and replaced by equality standards that apply in all areas (Damiso and Stewart 2013; Kameri-Mbote 2018). Despite these provisions, equality is yet to be realised and constitutional reform is yet to deliver benefits for the populace. The disjuncture between constitutional ideals and legal practice has resulted in a public demand that legal education should address the constitutional values and principles, including the right to equality and non-discrimination, clearly and unequivocally. Most post-colonial constitutions have responded by subjecting customary law to the test of constitutional equality and non-discrimination. These constitutions, unlike the colonial ones, also recognise socio-economic rights for all citizens.

These legal and political developments opened space for SEARCWL scholars, calling for new educational approaches that could bridge the knowledge gap between gender-specific, bottom-up and context-oriented disciplines such as women's law and disciplines taught in a top-down and gender-blind fashion, such as human rights law, constitutional law, criminal law and customary law. Scholars realised that more could be achieved by launching programmes that, in addition to offering separate, optional courses in women's law, gender and the law, and equality and anti-discrimination law, would integrate ways of analysing law developed within these disciplines into compulsory courses at the partner universities. Ironically, the University of Zimbabwe, which had hosted the SEARCWL programme since the 1990s, had not fully integrated women, gender and non-discrimination perspectives into the law curriculum. Similarly, the struggle to fully integrate these perspectives was ongoing at the Faculty of Law at the University of Oslo, which had not succeeded in implementing its policy from 2003 on mainstreaming a women, gender and equality perspective in compulsory courses.[5]

Moving on: Engendering law curricula

Against this background, a SEARCWL research and education team from the faculties of law at the University of Nairobi, Chancellor College in Malawi, the University of Zambia, the University of Zimbabwe and the University of Oslo decided to embark on a joint teaching and research project aiming to engender the law school curricula in their respective institutions in 2014. Our application focused on 'capacity building in law faculties to mainstream gender, non-discrimination, human rights and socio-economic rights frameworks and analysis into the application and administration of the law'. In our view, new approaches had to evolve to help students understand how law affected both men and women and how issues of access to law, particularly social constraints on taking legal action in matters such as divorce, impinged on lives. Furthermore, students needed training to understand how law – state law, religious laws and the customary laws on the books – gave preference to and protected male interests and entitlements. Unlike the top-down approach of conventional Western jurisprudence, the grounded theory that took women's lives as the starting point enabled students to challenge the hegemonic, decontextualised colonial laws. Even more so, as Hellum, Kameri Mbote and Van Koppen point out, students needed tools to address the complex relationship between the plurality of international, national and local norms that have a bearing on the social and economic rights of different groups of women in relation to issues such as land, water and sanitation[6] (Hellum et al. 2015). This would help students deal with the doctrinal human rights approach, which lacks grounding in empirical knowledge derived from gendered, classed and ethnicised situations and the plural legalities involved in local struggles as addressed by Hellum, Stewart, Ali and Tsanga (Hellum et al. 2007). To aptly describe, understand and improve women's situations, students need tools, theories and methods to identify and analyse the often complex, ambiguous contentions between women's human rights and legal pluralism (Hellum et al. 2007).

Our proposal fed into new regional and national policies that saw gender mainstreaming, at all levels of legal education in African universities, as critical for development, the rule of law and the realisation of justice (Association of Commonwealth Universities 2011). These new policies entailed a fundamental transformation of the underlying paradigms which inform education (Oladunni 2014). The methodologies to be used for integrating women, gender and equality perspectives in legal education and whether these perspectives should be dealt with as separate, optional or compulsory courses were core issues concerning curriculum development and teaching.

A primary challenge that is faced in mainstreaming a women, gender and equality perspective in compulsory courses is that of academic freedom, which university teachers consider as critical to the performance of their work. The obligations following from the new constitutions in certain African countries have changed the nature of the debate about how to strike a balance between individual academic freedom and the societal responsibility of law schools as institutions of higher learning. Where constitutions include the right to gender equality and non-discrimination, academic freedom can no longer serve as an argument to exclude gender issues from courses on constitutional law, criminal law or family law or avoid public scrutiny and reach (see Evans 2013).

Another challenge regarding educational reform was and still is resource allocation. Institutions unwilling to implement changes can, in the face of new constitutional challenges, cite inadequate financial and other resources as barriers. This is an issue for universities in Africa that have progressively received reduced funding as a result of governments' focused attention on universal primary education (Okebukola 2015). The African universities in this partnership are public universities whose main source of funding is the government. Curriculum review in these law schools, though vital for the implementation of nations' constitutions, could easily be relegated to the back burner due to demands for funding from other institutions such as the executive, the legislature and the judiciary.

The Norhed funding for a five-year programme, which began in 2013 to support capacity development in higher education through South–North and South–South collaboration, constituted a timely platform to stimulate and promote critical aspects of reform in the teaching of law. The proposal, devised jointly by the five partners, sought to broaden their existing co-operation by instilling the approach to women, gender and equality law, developed at SEARCWL, into local law school activities so as to have a bearing on the executive, the national legislature and the judiciary. Norhed's decision to fund this regional research and teaching partnership laid an economic foundation for peer learning, exchange of experiences, strategies, successes and failures in the quest to reform curricula in the respective law faculties. This entailed making gender, sex, human rights, the right to equality and non-discrimination and socio-economic rights core concerns in the teaching of law.

The main activities in this project, aimed at the integration of a women, gender and equality perspective in law curricula in the African law schools on this programme have been:

- Review of undergraduate and postgraduate curricula with a view to whether and how a gender perspective, the right to protection against discrimination and relevant social and economic rights have been included.
- Increased focus on how courses on human rights, socio-economic rights, disability rights and children's rights, which have found space in the curricula as compulsory or elective courses at undergraduate and at postgraduate levels, have integrated these perspectives.
- Capacity building on the complex relationship between the right to gender equality and protection against discrimination in international human rights and constitutional law and the legal pluralities on the ground that affect women's lives. This is facilitated through master's, doctoral and postdoctoral fellowships offered by SEARCWL in co-operation with the Institute of Women's Law in Oslo.
- Staff and student travel to partner universities where capacity on gender and the law and equality and anti-discrimination law was absent and where assistance had been requested.
- Research fellowships geared towards facilitating the generation of research on women, gender and the law and the right to equality and non-discrimination.
- Publication of journal articles, books and teaching modules building the stock of knowledge as well as providing the required materials for teaching.
- Supporting the master's and PhD in the Women's Law programme at SEARCWL conducted in co-operation with the

Institute of Women's Law, which provided a pivotal space for
staff and student mobility throughout the partnership.

- Availing doctoral, postdoctoral fellows and staff under the
partnership with annual opportunities for training in research
methodology, sharing experiences and information, and peer
learning.

- Facilitating staff to attend conferences related to women,
gender and the law and the right to gender equality and non-
discrimination.

- Infrastructure support to enable academics to perform opti-
mally, including the provision of reliable power supply, internet
connectivity, subscription to online resources and the procurement of technology to enhance teaching and learning.

Transformative initiatives in the partner universities

External factors such as international, national and regional law's recognition of women's right to gender equality and protection against
discrimination, and the changing regional and national university policies, along with Norhed funding, opened, as we have seen, space to
embark on a project aimed at engendering legal education at the partner universities in the South. We now turn to the process of change
that was initiated not only at the four individual partner institutions in
the South, but also at the Northern partner university.

Zimbabwe

The Law Faculty at the University of Zimbabwe has had a long-running
postgraduate programme on Women's Law and has, in co-operation
with the University of Oslo, produced master's and PhD graduates in
the field. It therefore would be assumed that the transformation in
undergraduate teaching would have been an easy process.

Although female Zimbabweans currently constitute the largest
number of graduates each year, this is not reflected in the composition
of the Faculty of Law staff, where males are the dominant group, being
18 out of a total of 24 full- and part-time members of staff, yet the

student body is now approximately 70 per cent female. Transforming the undergraduate curriculum as projected in the Norhed project has been met with indifference and, at best, inaction.

Three out of four undergraduate law programmes in universities in Zimbabwe have compulsory courses on Gender and Law, and Human Rights. Paradoxically, the University of Zimbabwe (UZ) remains the odd one out although there is an optional course on Women's Law that was introduced without dispute in the late 1980s.[7] Uptake of the course is low as it is not among the courses that are required for automatic admission as a legal practitioner on completion of a law degree. Ironically, the courses at the other Zimbabwean universities were introduced because of the influence of SEARCWL graduates involved with those programmes and the key lecturers are almost all graduates from the SEARCWL Master's in Women's Law programme.

The last major curriculum reform in the Faculty of Law at UZ took place in 2005, but both Women's Law and Human Rights Law remained as optional subjects. In 2015/16 the International Commission of Jurists (ICJ) provided funding for a thorough review of the curriculum and this was an ideal opportunity to collaborate and engage in further discussions on the Norhed-based proposals to make these courses compulsory.

A workshop was held where extensive discussions on curriculum reform took place. SEARCWL was instrumental in designing the programme, providing documentation and paradigms for reform. During the workshop some syllabi were notionally reformed on paper after discussions on the dynamics of including gender and the law, human rights, and equality and anti-discrimination law in the teaching of courses. It was, or so it seemed at that point, just a matter of consolidation, further development of syllabi for courses, reconfiguring the curriculum and incorporating gender and law and human rights courses as compulsory courses. The workshop ended on the basis that a Faculty Board would be convened within the month to approve the proposal; meanwhile, all syllabi would be reviewed and submitted to the faculty. Despite attempts to restart the matter, its finalisation has been postponed at faculty meeting after meeting, even when formal proposals are presented.

However, curriculum reform does not have to begin in law faculties. The legal profession as a whole has recognised the need for change. The Council for Legal Education, which determines criteria for admission as a legal practitioner, has proposed to the minister of justice, legal and parliamentary affairs new criteria for such automatic recognition of Zimbabwean law degrees. The recommended reforms are comprehensive and directed at bringing all law programmes in line with the human rights and gender equality and non-discrimination provisions of the Constitution of Zimbabwe Amendment (No. 20) Act, 2013. If this process is successfully completed and if the UZ Faculty of Law wishes to retain its status of facilitating automatic registration as a legal practitioner by its graduates, it will have to make courses on gender equality, non-discrimination and human rights compulsory.

Kenya

Until 1988, the University of Nairobi's School of Law (then named the Faculty of Law) had mainly male lecturers, normalising male dominance in law school instruction. The first woman[8] hired was a Women's Law graduate from the University of Oslo who was instrumental in questioning the gender deficit in staff, course content and working conditions. The School has undertaken four major curriculum reviews – in 1978, 1989, 1999 and 2013. The course on Women in the Legal Process was introduced in 1992 after the second review. To build capacity, a staff member pursued the Postgraduate Diploma in Women's Law at the University of Zimbabwe in 1994. The course was offered for the first time to fourth-year students in 1995 and attracted more than half the students in the class.[9]

The course survived the 1999 review and was offered until a radical review was undertaken in 2013 to align the curriculum with the country's 2010 Constitution, which included principles of human rights, gender equality and non-discrimination.[10] Also by then, the number of women on the faculty had grown to about a third of the faculty. This was critical, whether such women taught from a women's law perspective or not, because it contributed to changing the usual situation of having only male lecturers and professors.

The Constitution demanded change in the governance of higher education generally and legal education specifically. The Universities' Act 2012 and the Legal Education Act 2012 were enacted. The latter mandated the Council for Legal Education (CLE) to accredit legal education programmes and providers. CLE, in executing its mandate, prescribed 16 mandatory courses[11] to be included in curricula. Each law school was also expected to identify a specialisation as its core niche (Kameri-Mbote 2014).

The School's stated niche is as a centre of excellence in scholarship and teaching in five thematic areas, one of which is Human Rights Law. Students specialise in one of the five thematic areas in their fourth year. The curriculum has five additional obligatory courses in addition to the 16 CLE ones. These include Human Rights and Equality Law offered in the third and fourth years respectively. Students can also opt for the Gender and Law course[12] under the Human Rights theme.

The implementation of the new curriculum coincided with the Norhed partnership in 2013. A study on gender mainstreaming was carried out by the Kenyan Norhed team and discussed at a 2014 retreat to review undergraduate and graduate curricula. While some members of faculty resisted gender mainstreaming, citing academic freedom, others eagerly supported it. The approach taken has been to identify spaces of least resistance. Norhed funding has helped the School to implement the obligatory course on equality law and consolidate human rights, gender equality and socio-economic rights in the undergraduate and graduate curricula. Staff members have published relevant articles in the School's flagship journal, the *East African Law Journal*. A postdoctoral research framework has also been developed, while teaching materials for the School of Law and the African Women's Studies' Centre were developed through the Open Distance and eLearning (ODeL) Campus. Moreover, capacity has been enhanced through postgraduate training; mentoring gender equality teachers at other Kenyan universities (Strathmore and Egerton); and hosting public debates on topical equality issues such as sexual harassment in the wake of the #Me too campaign.

Malawi

The University of Malawi's Faculty of Law has made notable efforts to promote gender equality, non-discrimination and socio-economic rights through a gradual increase in female student enrolment, along with the recruitment of female faculty. Four of the five female staff members have a background in women's law and gender while two were trained at SEARCWL. The two have further benefited from the Norhed project in studying for PhDs in women and law. The Faculty also made gender equality and human rights part of the law curriculum offered to students in second and third years respectively. Initially, the gender and the law course was optional while Human Rights was a core course. The Norhed project, which coincided with the ongoing process of educational reform, enabled the Malawian team to make significant contributions from a gender and human rights perspective.

A review process, facilitated by the Malawian Norhed team, entailed textual analysis of the policies, legislation, course syllabi and outlines, as well as engagement with students and staff in relation to both the old and revised curricula. The process began with the development of a concept note for mainstreaming gender, non-discrimination and socio-economic rights in curricula. This was presented at a Faculty meeting where members resolved to ensure the mainstreaming of gender and human rights principles in the curriculum. Consultations with students and lecturers were then carried out to inform the content of the curriculum. This was followed by the development of the course syllabi. The process was anchored on obligations under the country's Constitution, national legislation and policies requiring mainstreaming of gender and human rights, in combination with the specific objectives of the Norhed project.

A new curriculum, partly supported under Norhed, was approved in 2017 and uses a competence-based approach to legal education by adopting effective teaching and learning strategies. One of the new curriculum's guiding principles is effective and gender-responsive teaching and learning at all levels of development and delivery.[13] The new curriculum made the gender and the law course offered in the first year compulsory. It also seeks to mainstream gender and human rights in all modules. The course on human rights has been retained as a core module.

The outcomes of the review and new curriculum include: making the course on gender and the law a core stand-alone module; strengthening the civil and political rights, and socio-economic and cultural rights content of the courses; clearly linking courses in the curriculum to specific human rights, especially socio-economic rights, gender equality and the principle of non-discrimination. The curriculum has also adopted innovative delivery methods, such as clinical legal education that keeps law students practically engaged in people's lived realities.

Staff members, through their continued participation in SEARCWL's research and teaching programme, have developed specialist competence and have shared knowledge and lessons learned. One remaining challenge, however, is the knowledge and skills gap in tackling gender issues among lecturers since not all lecturers have a background in gender studies. Those with expertise in the area need to support and assist other colleagues to bridge this gap.

Zambia

The Norhed Programme at the University of Zambia (UNZA) School of Law sought to change the way law is taught and to train lawyers who practise law differently. It used a three-pronged approach: (a) developing a *crop* of staff development fellows and postdoctoral candidates capable of researching and teaching gender law, human rights, particularly socio-economic rights, and non-discrimination; (b) developing frameworks to implement and monitor gender mainstreaming for law teaching and practice; and (c) continually appraising and reshaping curricula and teaching approaches.

The Gender Equity and Equality (GEE) Act,[14] legitimated by the 2016 Constitution of Zambia Amendment Act,[15] enjoins all legislation, institutions and individuals to mainstream and implement gender equality. Notably, it retains a gender-insensitive Bill of Rights despite making gender equality a cornerstone. The UNZA Strategic Plan has also, since 2013, repeatedly called for university-wide curriculum reforms to mainstream gender equality.

Under the Norhed programme, two PHD candidates[16] and two post-doctoral candidates were recruited. Curricula engendering and teaching methodologies took place between 2015 and 2018 but the evidence of the impact of this process on law students and the actual practice of law in Zambia is yet to be seen. It will only be ascertained after the current law students graduate and begin to practise law. The school has changed both undergraduate and postgraduate curricula and raised the aware-ness of the faculty through reforms targeting all courses and programmes. All undergraduate courses now include gender issues in the objectives, the context and topics.

This is a seismic shift at the school where until 2014 there was no appreciation of the fact that so-called gender-neutral teaching of law was in fact male-centred and marginalised women deliberately or inad-vertently. Anecdotal evidence shows that the male perspective that permeated the course curriculum and teaching methods was accepted as normal, neutral and objective. The introduction of the Socratic method of teaching in 2007 and eight years under a female dean had no visible engendering impact, despite the faculty profile attaining two-thirds female members and the number of female law students surpassing that of males.

For many years the school offered only two courses on human rights and gender[17] in the third year of study. They were neither compulsory nor particularly popular. The compulsory foundational courses did not mention gender inequality. When the subject of engendering law teach-ing came up, at the 'buy-in' workshop in 2015, the dean renamed the process 'endangering the law' due to the hostility from faculty mem-bers. It took three years of concerted effort to change the attitudes of many faculty members.

The first effort was the programme launch to publicise it to key stakeholders such as the judiciary, the Law Development Commission and the Law Association of Zambia. This was followed by a baseline survey assessing the extent to which gender issues had already been incorporated in the law curricula, the statutes and cases covered in the courses. The school then organised a curriculum review meeting to engender the undergraduate courses where the staff was introduced to Heather Wishnik's list of questions posed by feminist jurisprudence (Freeman 2001). However, the exercise was suspended due to entrenched beliefs in the infallibility of law and the general lack of gender awareness/sensitivity and engendering skills on the part of most faculty members. A Technical Committee tasked to engender the undergraduate courses presented its report at two review meetings where faculty members validated it. Postgraduate programmes and courses are currently undergoing the same process.

Despite the relative success of the phased engendering process, many faculty members are not fully equipped to employ the new teaching frameworks. Students were therefore recently engaged to create a database of online materials for each course to build the lecturers' capacity to include gender issues in their courses. The Norhed/UNZA programme team is working on the publication of a text documenting the engendering process.

Oslo

The Norhed programme, like most development programmes, is premised on the assumption that the development of higher education in the South is a process that involves the transfer of knowledge from the North through equitable university co-operation. However, on turning attention to the ongoing struggle regarding the implementation of the Oslo Law Faculty's Equality Policy, aiming at gender balance in academic staff and leadership as well as the integration of a women, gender and equality perspective in the compulsory and elective courses, we question this assumption.[18]

The faculty's effort to promote gender justice through teaching and research goes back to 1975 when women's law was introduced as a legal discipline. The initiative came from lecturers and students working in the organisation, Free Legal Advice for Women. Women's law was defined as a legal discipline that seeks to describe, understand and improve the position of women in law and society (Dahl 1986). Taking the lived reality of women as the starting point, a large body of research, which showed how the construction of family law, social welfare law, labour law or criminal law was moulded on the life experiences of men, was produced (Dahl 1986).

The rapidly growing body of research gave rise to new optional courses, one in Equality and Anti-Discrimination Law and one in Women's Human Rights. It also prompted new debates about the place of knowledge about gender, equality and the law in compulsory legal disciplines such as family law, criminal law and social welfare law. In connection with the curriculum reform in 2003, a proposal to integrate a women and gender perspective in all compulsory courses was unanimously approved.[19] An overall framework, which made reference to the right to equality under national and international law, was devised to facilitate the engenderment of legal disciplines such as constitutional law, public administrative law, criminal law, EU law and human rights law.[20]

The faculty's mainstreaming policy was followed up by two evaluations initiated by the Equality Board. The 2008 evaluation report found progress in disciplines such as family law, tax law and social welfare law. However, the perspective was absent in disciplines like human rights law, constitutional law, criminal law and tort law. To ensure its implementation, the evaluation report called for strong leadership and provision of resources (Sørlie 2008). A second evaluation, which was carried out by the Equality Board in 2016, showed that the recommendations had not been followed up. Yet there was some progress in family law and significant progress in areas like human rights law and constitutional law.[21] Progress in these areas was ascribed to two factors. Firstly, the faculty's decision to rotate leadership responsibility changed the gender balance. Secondly, recruitment of staff members with competence in the field of women, human rights and gender equality law opened new spaces for scholars in this field.

The insights provided by the two evaluations have led the Faculty Programme Committee for the Master's in Legal Science (PMR) to adopt new measures for the implementation of required reforms. Firstly, it has commissioned a 'cookbook' on how to integrate a gender perspective from experts in the field of women's law, and equality and anti-discrimination law.[22] Secondly, it has appointed an expert group that will provide individual lecturers with guidance and resources and also facilitate the production of a new textbook with articles that provide a women, gender and equality perspective in areas such as constitutional law, criminal law, social welfare law and commercial law.

These changes were first set off by initiatives from a committed research and teaching environment in the field of women's law, and equality and anti-discrimination law. In Norway, as in the African partner countries, constitutional reform, particularly a new equality standard, was a factor that contributed to change. Furthermore, the rapid process of gender mainstreaming that was taking place at the co-operating law faculties in southern and eastern Africa was an eye-opener and source of inspiration.[23] Another important push factor is the public debate about the role of legal education in preventing gender violence and sexual harassment prompted by the Me Too campaign.[24]

Achievements, lessons and future challenges

The extent and design of gender mainstreaming in the curricula differs from university to university. However, it is evident that the interaction between the law lecturers in the partner faculties with other faculties in their institutions, as well as with other law faculties in the South and the North, has had a multiplier effect through gender mainstreaming being undertaken in the curricula of various other faculties.

A process of mutual learning in the South and the North

In this long-running institutional co-operation in engendering legal education, learning has not flowed only from the North to the South. Southern partners have, as we have seen, been in the forefront of developing new obligatory courses on human rights, gender and the law, and equality and anti-discrimination law. For instance, The Faculty of Law at the University of Malawi and the School of Law at the University of Nairobi have introduced human rights core courses. Malawi has gone further to make their course on gender and the law compulsory. Nairobi has pioneered in making equality and anti-discrimination law a compulsory course along with requiring the adoption of gender perspectives in other obligatory courses such as property law. The methodical approach to engendering the curriculum that started out at the Faculty of Law at the University of Oslo in 2003 was an important source of inspiration for the other partners. It demonstrates the need for systematic evaluations at various junctures to address passive resistance and identify areas that require continued improvement. Zimbabwe's regional influence through the master's and PhD programmes at SEARCWL demonstrates the benefits and the necessity of sustained regional training and research co-operation in the field of women, gender and equality, particularly with a view to research and teaching methodologies.

Getting a foot in the door

In the face of resistance from individual staff members, several internal and external factors contributed towards the successful undertaking of this process. First, all the partner countries, including Norway, had relatively new constitutions with strong provisions on gender equality. The need to align law curricula with the new constitutions provided a cogent basis for the different faculties' decision to mainstream gender equality. Second, regulations in many partner universities require curricula to undergo review at set intervals. The mainstreaming process therefore leveraged on these regulations in some partner universities. In other countries, curriculum review was driven by the requirement of professional regulatory bodies, outside the university, governing legal education. Involvement by stakeholders such as the legal profession and the judiciary also prompted change. Third, against this background, the Norhed funded co-operation played a catalytic role. Most importantly, it laid an economic foundation for the development and implementation of strategies for the mainstreaming process. As such, it facilitated research co-operation resulting in the publication of special issues on gender, equality and the law in regional and national African law journals (Hellum et al. 2015).[25] Furthermore, it provided an accountability framework through reporting, monitoring and evaluation, which made the partners more deliberate in ensuring that gender mainstreaming in law curricula was achieved. Fourth, research and administrative leadership that was supportive of the process played a critical role in obtaining support from faculty members. This was coupled with female leadership with expertise in the field of women, gender and equality law and the hiring of new staff members who had benefited from SEARCWL's postgraduate research and training programmes.[26]

Moving on and making it stick

Partner universities, as we have seen, have used the Norhed partnership as both a catalyst and driver of transformative initiatives that are highly relevant for law's contribution to the realisation of the UN Sustainable Development Goals (SDGs) (UN 2016) and the African Union Agenda 2063: The Africa We Want (African Union 2015). Both these strategies have identified gender equality as a specific goal and a means to enhance the dignity of the individual by reducing poverty and inequalities.

In this regard, we must bear in mind that decolonising and engendering law curricula are not one-off engagements and require sustained momentum. Continued capacity enhancement for staff at universities is critical for educating lawyers who can handle equality issues that arise in relation to the implementation of social and economic rights, such as the right to health, housing, water, land, education, work and democratic participation. This requires research-based education and includes training in pedagogical approaches, research methodologies, development of material for implementation of the curriculum through postgraduate, doctoral and postdoctoral interventions as well as sharing experiences within and between partner universities. The role of SEARCWL, as a regional centre of research and postgraduate training, is instructive in this regard.

Furthermore, while the core mandate of universities is curriculum reform and implementation, competing needs affect these initiatives. Funding for universities has not kept up with the growing needs of the institutions. Gender equality and non-discrimination are constitutional imperatives but investment in their inclusion in curricula is not a priority in most institutions. North–South and South–South initiatives in higher education programmes, such as Norhed, are imperative for the realisation of constitutional ideals such as human rights, gender equality and non-discrimination. Norhed funding has played a catalytic role in the partner universities' process of engendering curricula. By facilitating the exchange of experiences between the universities, it has challenged each institution, including the University of Oslo, to go deeper.

Finally, the gains can be eroded if there is no evaluation and monitoring of the gender mainstreaming process as it evolves. Most importantly, the processes of gender mainstreaming in and decolonisation of law curricula are continual processes intended to impact different justice sectors. Gender-sensitive law graduates who can contribute towards jurisprudence that promotes and protects the right to gender equality are in high demand at the bar and in civil society, in private companies and in other sectors. Partner universities thus need to evaluate the impact of their law curricula's gender component beyond counting the number of female staff members, the numbers of such courses offered and the number of law graduates who have taken them. The effect of these courses must be evaluated with a view to their impact on decisions, policy and practice in their areas of operation. Thus, it is time to shift the focus from the number of women in academia and on the bench, to the need for gender-sensitive legal education and to the question of whether it makes a difference.

Acknowledgements

The authors gratefully acknowledge the contributions of the Norhed country teams in the preparation of the chapter; special thanks go to Dr Sarah Kinyanjui, Ms Theresa Chome, Dr Bernadette Malunga, Dr Ella Siangandu and Prof Ingunn Ikdahl.

About the authors and the project

Patricia Kameri-Mbote is a law professor and former dean of the School of Law at the University of Nairobi

Anne Hellum is a law professor and director of the Institute of Women's Law, Child Law and Equality Law at the Faculty of Law, University of Oslo

Julie Stewart is a law professor and director of the Southern and Eastern African Regional Center for Women's Law, which is housed in the Law Faculty at the University of Zimbabwe

Ngeyi Ruth Kanyongolo is a senior lecturer and former dean of the Faculty of Law at the University of Malawi's Chancellor College

Mulela Margaret Munalula is a former associate professor of human rights law and dean of the School of Law, University of Zambia

Project title: Master's, PhD and Research Programme for Capacity Building in Law Faculties to Mainstream Gender, Non-discrimination, Human Rights and Socio-economic Rights Frameworks and Analysis into the Application and Administration of the Law

Partner institutions: Faculty of Law and the Institute of Women's Law, Child Law, Equality and Anti-Discrimination Law, University of Oslo (Norway), Southern and Eastern African Regional Centre for Women's Law (SEARCWL), University of Zimbabwe (Zimbabwe), Faculty of Law Chancellor College, University of Malawi (Malawi), School of Law, University of Zambia (Zambia) and the School of Law, University of Nairobi (Kenya)

Notes

1   See also the UN General Assembly Resolution A/Res/52/100 of December 1997.

2   The Norwegian Agency for Development Cooperation (Norad) and the Norwegian Ministry of Foreign Affairs (MFA) have funded the Women's Law programme at the University of Zimbabwe from 1987 up to date. The Danish International Development Agency (DANIDA) funded the Women and Law in Southern Africa Research project from 1988 till 2006.

3   Since 1994 there have been 10 doctoral and 260 master's graduates in women's law graduates, a quarter of whom are men from Zimbabwe, Kenya, Uganda, Tanzania, Mozambique, Malawi, Ethiopia, Lesotho, Namibia, Swaziland, Cameroon, South Sudan and Botswana.

4   Articles describing the legal position in Zimbabwe, Malawi and Kenya are to be contained in a forthcoming special issue of the *East African Law Journal* (1965–2017). It is being edited by Prof Garton Kamchedzera and Dr Ngeyi Kanyongolo, both of the Faculty of Law at the University of Malawi; Dr Sarah Kinyanjui and Dr Nkatha Kabira, both of the School of Law at the University of Nairobi; and Dr Edwin Bikundo and Ms Janice Sim, both of Griffith Law School, Griffith University, Australia.

5   See under the heading below on transformative initiatives in the partner universities.

6   The complex relationship between community-based land and water rights and international, constitutional, and national regulations of access, control and ownership of land and water is addressed in Hellum et al. (2015).

7   Mary Maboreke who wrote the first M.Phil thesis in women's law at the University of Zimbabwe introduced the course.

8   Janet Kabeberi Macharia.

9   Patricia Kameri-Mbote taught the course after she completed the Postgraduate Diploma in Women's Law at the University of Zimbabwe.

10   Constitution of Kenya, Article 10.

11   Legal Research; Law of Torts; Law of Contracts; Legal Systems and Methods; Criminal Law; Family Law and Succession; Law of Evidence; Commercial Law; Law of Business Associations; Administrative Law; Constitutional Law; Jurisprudence; Equity and the Law of Trusts; Property Law; Public International Law; and Labour Law.

12   New name for Women in the Legal Process Course.

13   Faculty of Law, LLB (Honours) Programme Document (2017) 21.

14   No. 22 of 2015.

15   Act No. 2.

16   One PhD candidate subsequently dropped out.

17   'Gender Discrimination and the Law' course and course text introduced by MM Munalula in 2005.

18   Equality Policy, Equality Board, Faculty of Law, UiO, 2015–2017.

19   Faculty of Law, Delvedtak 4, 21 January 2003. The proposal came from the Institute of Women's Law and was made by Helga Aune, Anne Hellum and Kirsten Ketscher.

20   Report to the Study Reform Committee of 18.03.03 on 'Integration of a women's and gender perspective in obligatory subject areas' by Professor Hans Jacob Bull (Chair of the Equality Board) and Professor Anne Hellum (Director of the Women's Law Institute).

21   En rapport om kjønnsbalanse blant de fast vitenskapelig ansatte ved Det juridiske fakultet og om integrering av kjønnsperspektiver på masterstudiet i rettsvitenskap, (Report on gender balance and the integration of a gender perspective in legal education) by TR Korsvik and GB Linnet, University of Oslo 2017.

22   Guidance on Gender Mainstreaming in Legal Education, by I Ikdahl and A Hellum, November 2017.

23   Interview with Professor Patricia Kameri-Mbote on gender mainstreaming in legal education at the University of Oslo and at faculties of law in Southern and Eastern Africa, https://khrono.no/samfunn/2017/09/stolt-aeresdoktor-fra-sor

24   Juss, kjønn og metoo, Fortsetter å utdanne jurister som tror loven er lik for alle, Leder artikkel i Dagbladet, 17 January 2018, https://www.dagbladet.no/kultur/fortsetter-a-utdanne-jurister-som-tror-loven-er-lik-for-le/69338297

25   See the *Zambia Law Journal*, Special Issue 46 (2015) edited by M Munalula; see also Note 4 above.

26   Patricia Kameri-Mbote was dean of University of Nairobi School of Law from 2012 to 2016, Ngeyi Kanyongolo was dean of Chancellor College from 2014 to 2016, Margaret

Munalula was dean of University of Zambia Faculty of Law from 2006 to 2014 and Julie Stewart acted as dean at the University of Zimbabwe Faculty of Law intermittently between 2016 and 2018.

References

African Union Commission (2015) *Africa's Agenda 2063: The Africa We Want*. Available online

Association of Commonwealth Universities (2011) Building university partnerships for sustainable development. *ACU Spotlight* No. 2: 1. Available online

Bentzon AW, Hellum A, Stewart J, Ncube W and Agersnap T (1998) *Pursuing Grounded Theory in Law. South-North Experiences in Developing Women's Law*. Harare: Mond Books, Oslo: Tano Aschehoug

Dias CJ et al. (1981) (eds) *Lawyers in the Third World: Comparative and Developmental Perspectives, Studies of Law in Social Change and Development*. Uppsala, Sweden: Scandinavian Institute of African Studies

Dahl TS (1986) (ed.) *Kvinnerett I and II* (Women's Law I and II). Oslo: Norwegian University Press

Dahl TS (1987) *Feminist Jurisprudence*. Oslo: Norwegian University Press

Damiso C and Stewart J (2013) Zimbabwe and CEDAW compliance: Pursuing women's equality in fits and starts. In A Hellum and HS Aasen (eds) *Women's Human Rights: CEDAW in International, Regional and National Law*. Cambridge: Cambridge University Press

Evans J (2013) Adjudicative Independence: Canadian Perspectives. Unpublished paper

Fredman S (2013) Engendering socio-economic rights. In A Hellum and HS Aasen (eds) *Women's Human Rights: CEDAW in International, Regional and National Law*. Cambridge: Cambridge University Press

Freeman MDA (2001) *Lloyd's Introduction to Jurisprudence*, 7th edn. London: Sweet and Maxwell

Hellum A (1999) *Women's Human Rights and Legal Pluralism in Africa: Mixed Norms and Identities in Infertility Management in Zimbabwe*. Harare: Mond Books, Oslo: Tano Aschehoug

Hellum A, Kameri-Mbote P and Van Koppen B (2015) *Water is Life: Women's Human Rights in International, National and Local Water Governance in Southern and Eastern Africa*. Harare: Weaver Press

Hellum A, Stewart J, Ali SS and Tsanga A (2007) (eds) *Human Rights, Plural Legalities and Gendered Realities: Paths are Made by Walking*. Harare: Weaver Press

Ikdahl I (2014) Om rettsvitenskap og internasjonalisering: Fagutvikling ved kvinnerettsmiljøet i Oslo i perioden 1985-2013. *Retfærd* 37: 94–114

Jones P, Bjerkreim Hellevik S and Stefiszyn K (2013) *Evaluation of the Southern and Eastern Africa Regional Centre for Women's Law (SEARCWL)*. Oslo: Norad

Kameri-Mbote P (2014) Legal education and lawyers. In YP Ghai and JC Ghai (eds) *The Legal Profession and the New Constitutional Order*. Nairobi: Strathmore University Press

Kameri-Mbote P (2018) Constitutions as pathways to gender equality in plural legal contexts. *Oslo Law Review* 5(1): 20–40

Mehdi R and Shaheed F (1997) (eds) *Women's Law in Legal Education and Practice in Pakistan. North South Co-operation*. Copenhagen: New Social Science Monographs

Mossman MJ (1985) 'Otherness' and the law school: A comment on teaching gender equality. *Canadian Journal of Women and the Law* 1(1): 213–218

Ndlovu-Gatsheni SJ (2015) Decoloniality as the future of Africa. *History Compass* 13(10) 485–496. Available online

Okebukola P (2015) *Towards Innovative Models for Funding Higher Education in Africa*. Accra: Association of African Universities

Oladunni TM (2014) Best practices in gender mainstreaming in the academia: Lessons from African higher education institutions. *International Journal of Humanities, Social Sciences and Education (IJHSSE)* 1(10): 81–87

Smart C (2009) Shifting horizons: Reflections on qualitative methods. *Feminist Theory* 10(3): 1–14

Sørlie C (2008) Kvinne- og kjønnsperspektivet i master i rettsvitenskap. *Studies in Women's Law* 75. University of Oslo

Stewart J (1997) *Paving A Way Forward, A Review and Research Primer of WLSA Research Methodologies*. Harare: Women and Law in Southern Africa (WLSA)

Stewart J and Armstrong A (1990) (eds) *The Legal Situation of Women in Southern Africa*. Harare: University of Zimbabwe Publications

Stewart J and Tsanga A (2007) The widow's and female child's portion: The twisted path to partial equality for widows and daughters under customary law in Zimbabwe. In: A Hellum, J Stewart, SS Ali and A Tsanga (eds) *Human Rights, Plural Legalities and Gendered Realities: Paths are Made by Walking*. Harare: Weaver Press

Tamale S (2015) The context and content of teaching of family law in Uganda: A feminist analysis. *Zambia Law Journal* 46: 1–51

UN (1997) *Economic and Social Council Report A/52/3*. Available online

UN (2016) *Transforming Our World: The 2030 Agenda for Sustainable Development*

21

Transforming research, teaching and learning of public administration for improved governance and management: The Norhed experience in Malawi

Happy Kayuni, Dan Banik, Boniface Dulani & Kaja Elise Gresko

Since 2014 the University of Malawi and the University of Oslo have undertaken joint research and teaching on ways to improve democratic and economic governance in Malawi. The Norwegian Programme for Capacity Development in Higher Education and Research for Development (Norhed) has made a grant available for a five-year project running from 2014 to 2018, with a cost-extension to carry out activities through 2020. This project has enabled the Department of Political and Administrative Studies (hereafter PAS) at Chancellor College and the University of Oslo's Centre for Development and the Environment (hereafter SUM) to conduct basic research on governance, state legitimacy and public policy formulation and implementation. The two partners have also established a master's programme in Public Administration and Management (MPAM) at the University of Malawi, which is targeted at mid-level and senior civil servants. In this chapter we discuss the experiences and lessons from this collaborative work, focusing mainly on the research and MPAM components, and highlighting both challenges and opportunities. In the first part of the paper, we provide an overview of the whole project as well as our research. We conclude with an exposition of current and ongoing plans for sustaining the various initiatives and opportunities upon completion of the project.

Overview of the project

The two institutions, with a long and productive history of collaboration, conceived a concept for a research project titled 'Strengthening Capacity for Democratic and Economic Governance in Malawi'. In order to develop the research concept into a full proposal, in early 2013 we applied for a seed grant, for several pre-research initiatives that would feed into the development of a full proposal. This was submitted to the Norwegian Agency for Development Cooperation (Norad) under Norhed's 'Democratic and Economic Governance' sub-theme. The aim of the PAS-SUM project was to address the following set of interrelated questions:

- How, and to what extent, can processes related to democratic and economic governance be strengthened in order to make political and administrative authorities more responsive to the development needs of Malawi?
- What characterises the successful implementation of public policy and the effective and timely delivery of basic services in Malawi, and to what extent is gender-based discrimination prevalent in service delivery?
- In what ways can increased citizen participation and dialogue with local government authorities facilitate improved service delivery at the local level?
- What are the critical factors that enable civil society organisations to hold political and administrative officials to account for failing to provide efficient delivery of public services?
- How can research be utilised more effectively to promote better evidence-based policy formulation and implementation, in addition to greater acceptance of gender mainstreaming?

The five-year project, with funding of NOK17.8 million, has had three main components: education, research and institutional capacity building for Chancellor College staff (see Figure 21.1).

Capacity building

Capacity building and theories of change

One of the three major components of the project, capacity building, or development, can be defined as 'the process whereby people, organisations and society as a whole unleash, strengthen, create, adapt and maintain capacity over time' (OECD 2006: 12). Capacity building was one of the key issues highlighted in the Paris Declaration on Aid Effectiveness, and the agreement states that the 'capacity to plan, manage, implement, and account for results ... is critical for achieving development objectives' (OECD 2005: 4). However, despite this recognition of the importance of

Figure 21.1: Thematic focus areas of the PAS-SUM Norhed project

EDUCATION
- Collaborative MA programme in Public Administration and Management (MPAM) at Chancellor College
- Classes jointly taught by PAS and SUM staff (four cohorts of students enrolled by end-2018)

RESEARCH
- PAS and SUM research
- Dissemination of research findings
- Publications based on research (journal articles, book chapters, policy briefs, media coverage)

CAPACITY BUILDING
- PhD fellowships for PAS staff
- Pre- and postdoctoral visits by PAS staff to SUM
- Learning visits by Chancellor College administrative staff to SUM and University of Oslo
- Training for PAS clerical staff and Chancellor College accounts staff

capacity building, Otoo et al. (2009: 1) argue that most initiatives in this field 'are poorly grounded in theory and lack consistent conceptual frameworks' and, more importantly, the link between capacity-building efforts and overall developmental goals is often not clearly spelled out.

The ideas underlying the PAS-SUM project align with two theories about approaches to change. They are the World Bank's Capacity Development Results Framework (CDRF) and a people-focused theory of change for building capacity to use research evidence. The key features of the CDRF include: (a) an emphasis on changes in the use of knowledge and information that empower local agents; (b) focus on change efforts targeting institutional and policy-related constraints and opportunities; (c) use of standardised indicators for needs assessment and results measurement; and (d) integration of monitoring and evaluation (M&E) at all stages of capacity-development programmes to promote adaptive management (Otoo et al. 2009: 5).

CDRF arguably ties together various elements of change theories and also 'addresses several longstanding criticisms of capacity development work' such as a lack of clear definitions and comprehensible conceptual frameworks (Otoo et al. 2009: ii).

In accordance with the CDRF framework, information generated through research has been one of the crucial parameters of the PAS-SUM project. The emphasis on knowledge and information in addition to the focus on institutional and policy-related constraints have both guided our project. It was important that key government institutions that deal with policy matters were at the centre of conceptualising the project. From this basis, the research output was meant to immediately feed into the teaching and outreach activities of the project.

Stewart (2015) is a main proponent of the approach advocating a people-focused theory of change for building capacity to use research evidence. She argues that in order to effectively use public policy for development in Africa, there is a need to strengthen the adoption of research evidence to inform decision-making. There is no 'clear evidence as to how best to encourage evidence-informed decision-making and how to build capacity among decision-makers in the use of research' (Stewart 2015: 547). She calls for a closer interaction between producers and users of research findings. The theory aims to change the behaviour of decision-makers by providing them with relevant research findings. It has the following five main elements (Stewart 2015):

- Building sustainable relationships: the focus of capacity building should be on a network or consortium of policy-makers, research producers and research-use facilitators, rather than on individuals;
- Building relationships specifically with national governments: the emphasis should be on influential government agencies whose activities cut across monitoring and evaluation functions;
- Using relationships to build organisational and systems change, as well as individual capacity: the use of research relies on three key elements: organisational change, systems change and individual capacity. This implies understanding the environment in which decision-makers operate, including the barriers as well as incentives for change at individual, organisational or systems levels;
- Ensuring the right people and agencies are targeted: this implies targeting individuals and organisations that demonstrate the motivation to use the research evidence to change their work habits; and
- Ensuring partner commitment and post-programme sustainability: an important way to achieve sustainability is to incorporate all capacity-building activities 'within existing professional development and human resources systems when possible' (Stewart 2015: 552).

The applicability of this people-focused theory of change (which is being used by the Africa Evidence Network organisation) is highlighted in Figure 21.2. The figure shows that the theory's long-term goal is to enhance the capacity of the civil service to use evidence from research in policy decisions, thus facilitating the effective delivery of development programmes.

There are strong similarities between the World Bank's CDRF and Stewart's people-focused theory of change, which have directly influenced the conceptualisation of the PAS-SUM capacity-building programme. Specifically, both theories highlight the relevance of the

Figure 21.2: Application of people-focused theory of change

STRATEGY	ASSUMPTIONS
To build capacity among civil servants in southern Africa in accessing, appraising and using available research evidence through employing five person-centered approaches.	1. That it is feasible to increase demand and build capacity, leading to increased use of evidence. 2. That we can build the relationships needed between research users, producers and intermediaries.

INFLUENTIAL FACTORS	THE PROBLEM	DESIRED OUTCOME AND IMPACT
We are an experienced, southern-led consortium with the support of high-level champions within key departments. There is a drive for greater use of evidence to demonstrate 'aid effectiveness'. We have strong collaborative partnerships.	Southern Africa includes some of the world's most unequal and impoverished communities, providing an imperative for greater use of research-evidence if decision-making is to contribute to reductions in poverty and inequality. **CURRENT NEEDS** Research-use initiatives have been limited and although capacity-building activities exist they have been narrow in terms of audience, scope and approach.	Enhanced capacity among civil servants to use research-evidence in making policy decisions. Increased use of research-evidence in decision-making contributing to reductions in poverty and inequality.

Source: Stewart (2015)

effective use of research findings, proper targeting of key institutions or individuals and ensuring that results are clearly noted.

The PAS-SUM Norhed project to strengthen capacity: An integrated approach

In tandem with the two overarching theoretical approaches highlighted above, the PAS-SUM project has pursued an integrated approach with three overlapping areas of work as indicated in Figure 21.3. The research and publications feed into the teaching and outreach activities of the project. We expect that with this aspect of the project, there will be an improved capacity in public sector management and service delivery which is sustainable as the foundations are built on solid research-based evidence.

Figure 21.3: The integrated approach of the PAS-SUM Norhed project to strengthen capacity

TEACHING
- Improved public sector management and service delivery capacity
- Improved relations between bureaucrats and political leaders
- MPAM master's programme
- Short courses for both policy-makers and implementers
- Staff capacity building
- PhD supervision
- Specialised refresher courses
- Exchange programmes
- Staff salaries for additional staff
- Infrastructure for course delivery in Zomba and satellite centres

RESEARCH & PUBLICATION
- Build staff capacity to conduct research on key issues of public sector management
- Publish high-quality research in reputable journals
- Produce better teaching materials, textbooks and material for outreach programmes
- Present at relevant conferences

OUTREACH
- Build capacity of civil society organisations to better understand and engage with public institutions and policy processes
- Enhance capacity of citizens to engage with public office holders and service providers

Academic culture

Before this project began, research in the field of economic and democratic governance by the University of Malawi's Chancellor College had been scanty. With the issue of governance as an overarching working theme, we attempted to merge democratic and economic governance themes in the project's research agenda. Governance often refers to 'a government's ability to make and enforce rules, and to deliver services, regardless of whether that government is democratic or not' (Fukuyama 2013: 350). In this context, it implies that political and administrative structures of the state form the central pillars of governance and cannot be ignored. It is also through these structures that engagement with citizens is defined and appraised. Thus, the quality of administrative and political governance is reflected in the mechanisms, processes and institutions through which citizens exercise and articulate their rights and mobilise action based on perceived needs. The crucial role that governance can play in development has also more recently been recognised in the Sustainable Development Goals (SDGs) agenda through SDG 16, which specifically advocates the importance of building 'strong institutions'.

Some of the key questions we addressed in this collaborative project include the following:

- How is statehood perceived and practised in daily life?
- How is the state 'performed' and 'enacted'?
- How have external actors facilitated or constrained the capacity of the state?
- Which 'agents of justice' (political parties, civil society organisations, etc.) speak on behalf of the poor and how do they frame the issues in local and national debates?
- To what extent do ordinary African citizens demand good government and how much do they think is being supplied?
- How do people living in extreme poverty avoid or engage directly or indirectly (through intermediaries) with political actors and institutions?
- What are the complexities, paradoxes, and contradictions in implementing political and administrative governance reforms?
- What insights can be drawn from the African experience, which may have implications for other low- and middle-income countries (LMICs)?

There is evidently a legitimate perception among citizens suggesting the public service has consistently underperformed since the early 1990s. The development literature indicates that while Malawi's public service was among the top three performing in sub-Saharan Africa until the late 1980s, recent observations find it to be among the least performing in the region. And a series of Afrobarometer surveys suggest widespread citizen disappointment with service delivery by the public service. The public service's slippage from the Golden Era of the 1970s and early 1980s can be attributed to, among other challenges, the loss of work ethics and insufficient management and technical knowledge and skills necessary for the modern civil service. The bridging of the gap between economic and democratic themes in governance in this project has thus significantly transformed the understanding of the developmental aspect of governance in the University of Malawi's development discourse.

Research component

The second major component of the PAS-SUM project is research. This support fits directly into the University of Malawi's mission, which highlights the advancement of knowledge and understanding by, among others, enabling its staff to engage in research and public and community engagement. Despite recognising the importance of research, competing demands have meant that there are usually no funds allocated by the university to enable academic staff to undertake research. It is within this context that the inclusion of a research component in the PAS-SUM Norhed project has made it possible for PAS staff to collaborate with their SUM colleagues to undertake research that has contributed towards the generation of empirically based evidence. This, in turn, is being used to inform debates in postgraduate courses and seminars. It is also helping to shape public debates on topical issues through interactions with key stakeholders that range from ordinary citizens to senior public officials and policy-makers in the country. Through a series of research dissemination events and citizen engagement forums that have been an important part of the research exercise, the project is further helping to bridge the gap between academia, policy-makers and local communities. For each of the five years of the Norhed project, dedicated resources are set aside toward research.

The research outputs from PAS highlight the transformative nature of the PAS-SUM Norhed project in reinvigorating a culture of research in the department. This has translated into numerous outputs that include articles in top-rated international journals as well as several policy papers jointly published by the PAS Department and SUM. A major outcome of the Norhed research was the publication in 2016 of an edited volume titled *Political Transition and Inclusive Development in Malawi,* published by Routledge. Reflecting the collaborative nature of the PAS-SUM project, the volume was co-edited by Professor Dan Banik (SUM, University of Oslo) and Professor Blessings Chinsinga (PAS, University of Malawi). The book includes contributions from faculty members from PAS and SUM, focusing on three central themes related to the Norhed project, namely, democratisation and political culture; governance and policy implementation; and activism, aid and accountability.

A related part of the research aspect of the PAS-SUM project has been to disseminate the results of the research projects to a wider audience with a view to inform debates and influence policy change. As a result, PAS and SUM staff have made several presentations on the research findings at workshops in Malawi and Norway and at other global conferences.

Research implementation strategy

Staff members at PAS were previously not keen to work in research groups. However, conducting research alone has had certain problems because such research outputs do not necessarily demonstrate a diversity of skills and analyses. More importantly, it leads to diminished teamwork in other important departmental endeavours, including teaching. To improve the quality and quantity of research outputs – and with inputs from SUM – a new research strategy was devised which grouped PAS academic staff into three research groups. Each of these groups pursued a distinct but related research theme under the broader Norhed project on democratic and economic governance. Due to this, there has been a general improvement in the quality and quantity of research outputs, including a higher number of academic workshops, journal articles, policy briefs and the Norhed book, with an official launch attended by distinguished guests, including the Norwegian ambassador to Malawi and the vice-chancellor of the University of Malawi. A notable impact of these outputs has included news articles about the research findings in national newspapers and websites, which have attracted interest from a broad spectrum of the national social and political arenas. Such attention has, moreover, resulted in heated (and often vociferous) public debate on the major research findings on governance in Malawi. Public debate stimulated by the research findings included an examination of citizen trust of both elected and traditional leaders and an assessment of the effectiveness of the public service reform initiative being implemented by the Malawian government, which will be discussed further below.

Gender mainstreaming efforts and research

It has been observed by various scholars that the gender composition of researchers does matter in order to provide a balanced view of social phenomena (Henderson et al. 2017). However, for many years, PAS had only two female lecturers as against 11 male staff members. This gender imbalance was not acceptable, especially considering several recent national developments aimed at increasing female representation in all key positions of authority. In 2013, the Malawi Parliament approved the Gender Equality Bill (to which the president assented in 2014), which requires a minimum of 60:40 gender representations in all public institutions. PAS had previously tried to recruit more female members but was unsuccessful in retaining their services. However, experience showed that staff members recruited soon after the completion of their studies tend to stay. Using resources from the Norhed project, PAS recruited three recently graduated female students as demonstrators/research assistants as part of the long-term staff development programme to build capacity and enhance gender-balance initiatives at PAS.

For many years, the PAS experience was that very few students were willing to conduct research on gender-related issues. Drawing resources from the gender mainstreaming budget of the programme, a Norhed Gender Research Scholarship programme was designed with the goal of awarding stipends to students with the best gender research proposals, regardless of the author's gender. With the help of a scholarship committee, guidelines were developed to help in the identification of suitable proposals and in the management of the scholarship so as to achieve transparency and fairness in the award process.

Administrative capacity development as part of research support

The project did not ignore the administrative structure of Chancellor College as effective administrative practices enhance delivery of academic programmes and research. In line with this thinking, six administrative staff members from Chancellor College went to the University of Oslo on an educational visit. The team included the vice-principal, the college registrar, the college director of information and communications technology (ICT), a college librarian, a senior finance officer and a procurement officer, who were accompanied by the PAS Norhed project co-ordinator. The team interacted with University of Oslo staff and learned about best practices in their respective professional fields with the view to improve operational systems at Chancellor College. The team also held interactive sessions with staff from the University of Oslo and Norad. An important outcome was the development of a proposal to improve the human resources management (HRM) system and the student registration process at Chancellor College.

Pre- and postdoctoral visits to University of Oslo

The second sub-theme of the capacity-building component focuses on pre- and postdoctoral learning visits to SUM and the University of Oslo. Under this sub-theme, predoctoral and postdoctoral PAS staff have spent several weeks at SUM, utilising the research resources and writing facilities to draft academic articles, some of which were done jointly with their Norwegian counterparts. PAS members drafted manuscripts and made presentations of their work to SUM staff, who provided important critiques and suggestions for refining and revising the papers. In the first four years of the project, two members of PAS staff spent an average of four weeks annually at SUM as part of this staff exchange.

In addition, some PAS staff members have made presentations of their ongoing doctoral research to SUM staff, while others have been assisted in developing and refining their doctoral proposals in Norway.

Contributions of the PAS-SUM Norhed project within and outside of Chancellor College

The success or failure of any project or intervention can be measured by examining the set goals against outputs (Fitz-Gibbon 1996; Streatfield 2009). Before highlighting the contributions that the PAS-SUM project is making within Chancellor College and outside, it is important to recognise that at the time of writing this chapter, the project was in its fourth year with a fifth to come. Thus, in addition to the contributions highlighted below, more will be made and documented in the short- and medium-term. Further, long-term contributions will ensue, for example, those to the nation resulting from the postgraduate pro-grammes at Chancellor College, and the training and capacity building of Chancellor College staff.

Contributions within PAS and Chancellor College

The contributions of the project within PAS can be disaggregated accord-ing to the three focal areas of the project, namely, education, research and capacity building.

The third major component of the project, education, had as its main task the development and launch of a Master of Arts (MA) in Public Administration and Management (MPAM) by the Department of Political and Administrative Studies at Chancellor College. From its conceptual phase, the MPAM was designed to employ a special, collab-orative teaching approach involving joint teaching on all coursework modules at Chancellor College campus in Zomba by faculty from PAS and SUM. The joint teaching of the MPAM programme draws from research demonstrating positive benefits to learners and teachers from such collaboration (Ronfeldt et al. 2015; Vanderbilt University 2014). In the words of Killion (2015: 62), when teachers engage in high-quality collaboration 'there is both an individual and collective benefit, [and it] is associated with increases in ... their students' achievement, their performance, and their peers' students' achievement'.

In keeping with the collaborative nature of the MPAM concept, the modules were developed after an extensive consultative process that involved various stakeholders. This included government officials, members of parliament, the leadership of parastatal organisations, civil society organisations, members of academia, and private sector actors. These consultations were undertaken to generate input towards the development of training modules that are modern, relevant and responsive to the needs of the contemporary public sector in Malawi and beyond. From this exercise, a total of eight modules were identified and jointly developed by PAS and SUM staff as outlined in Table 21.1.

Table 21.1: Modules offered under the MPAM at the University of Malawi's Chancellor College

	Course title	Teaching faculty
1	Theories of Public Administration and Management	PAS and SUM
2	Public Sector Human Resources Management	PAS and SUM
3	Public Policy and Political Economy Analysis	PAS and SUM
4	Leadership and Change Management	PAS and SUM
5	Public Sector Economics	PAS
6	Gender and Development	PAS and SUM
7	Research Methods and Practice	PAS and SUM
8	Public Service Ethics and Governance	PAS and SUM

In order to ensure a balance between faculty and student ratios, the MPAM programme intake was set at 20 students per year. Although it was anticipated that the programme would be launched in 2014, the processing and approval of the programme through the relevant University of Malawi offices meant that the first cohort of MPAM students was enrolled for the 2015/16 academic year. In February 2018, a total of three cohorts had been enrolled (starting in 2015, 2016 and 2017), with a fourth cohort of students selected to start in September 2018. The number of applications received every year shows that despite its relative newness, the MPAM programme has already gained a good reputation and is among the most sought-after postgraduate programmes offered in the PAS Department and within the wider Chancellor College community (see Table 21.2).

Table 21.2: Number of students in the MPAM Programme by year, 2015–2018

Academic year	No. of applicants	No. of students accepted	No. who enrolled
2015/16	95	30	18
2016/17	79	30	18
2017/18	33	30	19
2018/19	34	25	-
Total	241	115	

To highlight the popularity of the MPAM programme, we compared the number of students applying for and accepting places on two other MA programmes within the PAS Department. These were the MA in Political Science and the MA in Human Resources Management and Industrial Relations, launched in 2007 and 2013 respectively. The data in Table 21.3 show that despite being the newest of the three MA programmes, MPAM has quickly established itself both in terms of having the highest number of applications, highest number of students offered places and the highest proportion of students who enrol.

Table 21.3: Student enrolment in MA programmes offered in PAS Department at Chancellor College

Programme	MA Public Administration and Management (launched 2015)	MA Human Resources Management and Development (launched 2013)	MA Political Science (launched 2007)
Number of applicants (2015–2018)	241	117	36
Students offered places (2015–2018)	115	35	18
Total number of students who enrolled (2015–2017)	55	14	10

Note: The 2018 cohorts for all three programmes started in September 2018, so records of the turnout rate were not available at the time of writing.

While the Norhed project has enabled Malawian students to study under the MPAM programme, it has also enabled academics from PAS and SUM to collaborate in teaching and supervising the students. Each module is jointly taught by faculty members from the two institutions and this extends to the supervision of students in conducting research and producing research-based dissertations. The collaborative teaching has brought together a rich variety of the knowledge and skills of all the lecturers in a way that has not been previously done within Chancellor College for an extended period. The joint teaching of MPAM stands to benefit both staff and students in the short, medium and long term. The students are exposed to an expanded number of teaching styles that enable their learning preferences to be more easily met. The lecturers meanwhile benefit by learning from each other and through their class interactions with students as they jointly prepare lesson plans and share teaching resources.

One of the common challenges for postgraduate programmes in the wider University of Malawi system has been delays in student completion rates. This is due to many factors that include challenges in student supervision, an uncertain calendar that is often disrupted, and problems encountered by students due to a failure to pay fees, plus their work and family responsibilities. Through the Norhed programme, several MPAM students have been awarded competitive scholarships towards their fees or to enable them to undertake research. The collaboration between PAS and SUM in delivering the MPAM has meant that the programme has one of the most stable and predictable calendars within Chancellor College. This has allowed MPAM students to complete their coursework in a timely manner and to embark on the research phase according to schedule.

In the joint supervision of students during their research and dissertation writing, PAS has benefited from practices employed at the University of Oslo to facilitate the timely completion of studies. This has included the development of a student–supervisor supervision contract that spells out the student and supervisor obligations. All these initiatives have made it possible for students to make progress in their studies and graduate without long delays. At the end of the 2016/17 academic year, which was the programme's second year, a total of seven students had been cleared for graduation from the MPAM programme. Many more were at advanced stages of their studies and nearing completion.

Contribution of the project outside Chancellor College

In a country where the public sector is the major employer and service provider, the PAS-SUM project has already fulfilled several of its key objectives, including influencing public policy and helping to build and strengthen the research, educational and administrative capacity in Malawi. As noted earlier, the MPAM programme is already graduating students, who have gone on to work in various government, non-governmental as well as private entities. In several cases, graduates from the MPAM programme have assumed jobs in Malawian universities, thus helping to pass on the knowledge gained from the programme to a new generation of public administrators and managers.

As a further illustration of the project's impact in influencing democratic discourse in Malawi, the workshops presenting the project's research results were well attended and received widespread media coverage. For example, the workshop presentation on 'The Paradox of Traditional Leadership in Democratic Malawi' on 17 March 2017 was reported on the front pages of Malawi's two main daily newspapers, *The Nation* and *The Daily Times*, generating debates that eventually resulted in the president commenting on it.

Meanwhile, the PAS-SUM Norhed project has significantly contributed to increasing the profile of the PAS Department and its staff. As a result, its staff members are regularly sought to comment in the media on issues of democracy, governance and development. Such platforms have enabled PAS members to infuse empirical evidence into ongoing public debates on governance issues in the country.

An additional aim of the project is to strengthen administrative and institutional capacity in Malawi. This aim is to be achieved through a set of interrelated activities which include undertaking collaborative research on democratic and economic governance, and training Malawian students in the science of administration and management up to master's and doctoral levels. As a way to achieve this goal, from its inception, the project sought to prioritise and incentivise civil servants and other public officials to enrol on the MA in Public Administration and Management. This is helping to inculcate modern administration and management skills among the top and middle tiers of the Malawian

Figure 21.4: Screenshot from The Nation *newspaper's coverage of PAS-SUM Norhed research findings presentation, 21 March 2017*

public sector so that it is equipped to deal with 21st century challenges. It is expected that this will lead ultimately towards the building of a critical mass of more, and better qualified, Malawians who can engage with political and economic elites and policy-makers, and thereby positively influence decision-making processes related to democratic and economic governance.

One of the novel interventions employed in the PAS-SUM project is the inclusion of Village Consultative Sessions. During these sessions, PAS staff engage local communities to identify issues that require government intervention. These issues are presented to public officials at the local government level and their input sought. Public officials are then brought together face-to-face with the local communities to discuss the issues raised and how government will respond to them. At the time of writing, a total of four such village consultation meetings and feedback sessions had been held in the Zomba district of southern Malawi. Through these sessions, community members in four rural communities in Zomba have been given a platform to air their development needs and frustrations with government, while meeting local government officials who have made commitments to address their needs. Apart from facilitating development interventions, this part of the project is indirectly promoting democratic citizenship while promoting responsive governance and policy-making at the local government level.

Challenges encountered

The programme has faced several challenges over the years, which include the following:

- Increased workload for the project team against stagnant staff establishment at the University of Malawi. The master's programme and its research component were introduced against the background of several other undergraduate and postgraduate programmes the department has offered over the years. Due to financial reasons, the number of established positions has, however, remained the same over the years and this has put much pressure on the available staff.
- Hostility (intimidation and threats) from the political establishment and the Government of Malawi towards some research findings, public policy debates and individual scholars from PAS has become common. Due to the sensitive nature of some of the research outputs, politicians (especially in government) have repeatedly shown hostility towards members of the research team. However, efforts have been made to make sure that the research outputs are objectively received and ultimately applied.
- There is limited physical infrastructure at Chancellor College. Over the past four years, the undergraduate student numbers and the postgraduate programmes have significantly increased, hence putting much pressure on the limited physical infrastructure. As one way of addressing this problem, the department is in the process of constructing offices and a lecture room for the programme. The financial resources for construction have been drawn from the fees that students pay in the master's programme.
- Since the master's programme operates on the logic of financial sustainability, students are expected to pay tuition fees and it has become clear that some students are not able to fulfil their tuition fee commitments. Hence this may on occasion delay their graduation.

Conclusion

The Norhed SUM-PAS collaborative research and training project described in this chapter can be said to have been successful in advancing research and education in Malawi.

In the education component, there has been full, fruitful collaboration in the teaching and supervision of students; however, inadequate infrastructure and lack of scholarships remain critical challenges.

The project has reached out to stakeholders to build a better understanding of public institutions and policy processes and effectively engage with the public sector and public policy processes. It has also improved the capacity of citizens to better engage with public office holders and service providers. However, this effective reaching out has led to the emergence of a major challenge where the political leadership has not received the feedback from the research positively, but has perceived the findings as trying to undermine the state's authority. This has negatively affected the research thrust the project intended to achieve.

While the reaction to certain critical research findings has sometimes been negative, the project has nevertheless helped to raise the profile of the Department of Political and Administrative Studies. This has been to the extent that numerous governance stakeholders, including political and civil society leaders, are increasingly seeking the advice of academic staff from the department to provide insights and advice on how to address emerging political challenges in the country. One such impact was when the department was asked by the United States Agency for International Development (USAID) to undertake a sociological study on traditional leadership in Malawi after becoming aware of the project on 'The Paradox of Traditional Leadership in Democratic Malawi' that was undertaken as part of the Norhed research component.

About the authors and the project

Happy Kayuni is a professor in the Department of Political and Administrative Studies at Chancellor College, University of Malawi

Dan Banik is a professor at the Centre for Development and the Environment, University of Oslo

Boniface Dulani is a senior lecturer in the Department of Political and Administrative Studies, Chancellor College, University of Malawi

Kaja Elise Gresko is a research co-ordinator at the Centre for Development and the Environment, University of Oslo

Project title: Strengthening Capacity for Democratic and Economic Governance in Malawi

Partner institutions: Chancellor College, University of Malawi (Malawi) and University of Oslo (Norway)

References

Fitz-Gibbon CT (1996) *Monitoring Education: Indicators, Quality and Effectiveness*. London: Cassell

Fukuyama F (2013) What is governance? *Governance* 26(3): 347–368

Henderson L, Herring C and Prados S (2017) Gender diversity and the rankings of STEM departments in research universities: Does gender composition matter? *Journal of Women and Minorities in Science and Engineering* 23(4): 323–337

Killion J (2015) High-quality collaboration benefits teachers and students. *The Learning Professional* 36(5): 62–64

OECD (Organisation for Economic Co-operation and Development) (2005) *Paris Declaration on Aid Effectiveness 2005*. Paris. Available online

OECD (2006) *The Challenge of Capacity Development: Working Toward Good Practice*. Development Assistance Committee. OECD Publishing: Paris

Otoo S, Agapitova N and Behrens J (2009) *The Capacity Development Results Framework: A Strategic and Results-oriented Approach to Learning for Capacity Development*. World Bank Institute

Ronfeldt M, Farmer S, McQueen K and Grissom J (2015) Teacher collaboration in instructional teams and student achievement. *American Educational Research Journal* 52(3): 475–514

Stewart R (2015) A theory of change for capacity building for the use of research evidence by decision makers in southern Africa. *Evidence and Policy* 11(4): 547–557

Streatfield D and Markless S (2009) What is impact assessment and why is it important? *Performance Measurement and Metrics* 10(2): 134–141. Available online

Vanderbilt University (2014) Team/Collaborative Teaching. Available online

22

The challenge of capacity building in occupational health: Experiences from Tanzania, Ethiopia and Norway

Bente E Moen, Wakgari Deressa & Simon HD Mamuya

Introduction

In this chapter, we describe our joint scientific and administrative experiences as project leaders in a capacity-building project in Tanzania, Ethiopia and Norway. The project aims to change activities in universities to include the topic of occupational health in both research and curricula related to reducing the burden of injuries and occupational exposures. The purpose of this change is to influence the working life of the countries involved, to improve their working conditions and to be able to reduce adverse health effects caused by environmental factors at work sites. The project began in 2014 and runs until 2019. We have high ideals and have experienced different challenges in the struggle to reach our goals. We reflect here upon our achievements and challenges.

Reforming universities to respond to the need for occupational health competence in society

The relationship between work and health has been of interest to health personnel for centuries. Work is an important factor for promoting health, as we work for our living. Salaries are necessary to pay for our food and housing, and in addition, work gives people status in society. However, work may also have negative side effects, as the workers might become exposed to factors that are harmful for health. For instance, as far back as the fifteenth century Paracelcus documented that work in mines can cause respiratory problems among the miners (Debus 1999). Another person interested in this scientific area was Bernadino Ramazzini (1633–1719), who made an important contribution to medicine with his book on occupational diseases *De Morbis Artificum Diatriba* (Diseases of Workers) (Ramazzini 1703). Since then, we have developed a large body of literature on work and health, or occupational health as this scientific area is called. However, despite this extensive knowledge, millions of men and women still perform paid work under poor and hazardous conditions.

In the Western world, we can easily find knowledge on how to prevent and avoid occupational hazards and how to protect and promote health in the workplace. Still, large gaps exist between and within countries with regard to competence in occupational health, leading to major differences in risks for the workers. In low-income countries (LICs), there is limited knowledge about occupational health and the workers experience very high occupational injury rates. These and similar facts have been summarised clearly by the World Health Organization in their report, *WHO Global Plan of Action on Workers' Health (2008-2017): Baseline for implementation* (WHO 2013).

The need for capacity building in occupational health is obvious in developing countries which is why our project in the Norhed programme was established. The idea of the project is that competence building in occupational health in the universities will lead to higher competence in this scientific area in general in their countries. The project wanted to contribute to the education of staff at universities, so that they would be able to teach students about occupational health. These students would be able to use this knowledge in working life outside the universities and hopefully contribute to improving the working conditions in their countries.

As one of the key functions of higher education institutions, research remains a primary source of knowledge and innovation at national, regional and international levels (Kearney 2009). In order to carry out high-quality research aimed at solving health problems of workers in the LICs, strengthening the capacity for research on occupational health is fundamental (Whitworth et al. 2008). The research community and infrastructure in the LICs is generally weak and there are very few institutions mandated to conduct health research in these countries. Occupational health is rarely a part of the ongoing research programme at any university in LICs (Ethiopian Academy of Sciences 2013). One of our strategies to combat this challenge was to focus on strengthening the research capacity in occupational health at the universities in LICs (Lansang and Dennis 2004; Nchinda 2002).

Occupational health risks are increasing in low-income countries

Ethiopia and Tanzania have shown a remarkable economic growth during the last decade. In addition to improving agricultural production, major industrialisation activities are currently underway in urban and rural areas of both countries. Industrial work is flourishing in various manufacturing sectors. Among these, the manufacture of food and beverage products (such as coffee or beer), textile, cement and flower farms (especially roses), as well as mining, are contributing to the economies of both countries (Moen et al. 2019). The construction industry has also become an important sector for development and is employing large numbers of workers. Despite a clear link between exposure to harmful or hazardous substances at many of these workplaces and adverse health outcomes for the workers, there is a weak commitment by the governments to occupational health research and the enforcement of health and safety regulations (Nuwayhid 2004). This is similar to the situation in many other LICs. Despite the improved economic situations in both Ethiopia and Tanzania, occupational health and safety has received minor attention from their governments so far.

There is an extensive labour force engaged in manufacturing industries, including women and children, and the potential for adverse health impacts is enormous. However, the health and safety at these types of workplaces is weak, particularly in Ethiopia, as there is little knowledge about occupational health among its workers, employers, health personnel and policy-makers. A few studies conducted in the Rift Valley of Ethiopia revealed that 85 per cent of workers in three farming systems did not attain any pesticide-related training and only 10 per cent used a full set of personal protective equipment (Negatu et al. 2016). This contrasts with the requirements, as other studies show that pesticides are in daily use to avoid diseases in the crops, causing a high prevalence of respiratory and dermal symptoms among workers in flower farming (Hanssen et al. 2015; Nigatu et al. 2015).

The resistance against developing a decent and safe work environment might be caused by the fact that preventive and protective measures at these workplaces may interfere with the productivity and income of the factories in the short run. Investments in protective measures and the extra time required to spend on implementing them are seldom welcomed in a growing industry. In the long term, however, injured workers and workers with reduced health can be a problem for employers. However, when establishing new workplaces in a LIC needing low-skilled workers, the number of potential workers is high.

The development of health problems among the workers is seldom a problem for the employers in these situations as the employers can easily find new workers. Lack of competence in occupational health in a country is often the cause of the absence of appropriate rules and regulations to protect the workers. With few workplace regulations and a lack of control systems for the existing ones, employers do not spend time and energy on how to protect the health of their workers.

Our knowledge about the increasing health problems, seen in relation to the workplace in Tanzania and Ethiopia, made us eager to improve the competence in occupational health in these countries.

Building capacity in occupational health

Previous co-operation provided the foundation for the project

In the 1990s, the Norwegian government established a special scholarship programme for students from LICs, called quota scholarships. These scholarships made it possible for students from LICs to study and obtain master's or PhD degrees in Norway. A master's study programme in international health was established at the Centre for International Health (CIH), University of Bergen (UiB) at this time. The programme was especially suited for students from LICs. The programme was a great success, and hundreds of master's degree students have been educated at CIH, most of them from East African countries. The best students continued their studies as PhD candidates. After fulfilling their education, most of the CIH students returned to their home countries and became important in capacity building at universities in the South.

CIH students attending the master's programme at UiB could choose a track in occupational health. The students came to Norway for courses and supervision and performed fieldwork on their relevant topic in their home country. The performance of fieldwork required close co-operation between researchers in Norway and the institutions in the South. This was the start of the co-operation between researchers at CIH and many institutions in Africa, among them, Muhimbili University of Health and Allied Sciences (MUHAS) in Tanzania and Addis Ababa University (AAU) in Ethiopia.

In addition, a specific project called 'Occupational respiratory diseases among workers in dusty industries in Tanzania' started in 2002 and continued until 2010 as a co-operative venture between researchers in Tanzania and Norway. The project was funded by the Norwegian Programme for Development, Research and Education (NUFU), and included capacity-building opportunities for five PhD candidates (Moen 2015). These candidates established a scientific group at MUHAS in occupational health.

However, the funding policy in Norway changed from supporting students in coming to Norway, to supporting competence-building projects taking place in LICs. In 2013, Norhed launched its competence-building programme that supported our study described in this chapter. Our application could not have been written without the solid, previously developed co-operation between the institutions in the North and South. The scientific group in occupational health at MUHAS was essential for the start of this project. At AAU we had no similar group but had a few people educated in occupational health at UiB. These people established contact between UiB and the School of Public Health, AAU.

Building research capacity at the universities

The project aimed to develop research skills in occupational health among the staff. Five postdoctoral candidates and three PhD candidates employed at both MUHAS and AAU were supported by the project. The students were able to work with senior supervisors at UiB on their proposals, data analysis and manuscript writing. In addition, the students have benefited from using the state-of-the-art library at UiB, access to computers, software and other related resources that were not easily affordable or available at their home universities.

Our strategy was to strengthen the research capacity primarily centred in the LIC's institutions. A team of local professionals, who networked among themselves and efficiently tapped into external resources and knowledge to carry out research on relevant occupational health problems, was established both in Ethiopia and Tanzania. Plans for three research programmes were developed based on their relevance to the LICs.

At the same time, colleagues from Ethiopia, Tanzania and Norway were actively working together throughout the research programme, as a large project team. Regular meetings in each country, as well as weekly e-mail or Skype contacts were important to motivate and support each other. The group co-operated in all sub-projects, from the initial conceptualisation of the objectives and research questions to be addressed, through to student recruitment, proposal development, the data collection and management process, supervision, and the dissemination of the findings of a broad range of occupational health topics.

In addition to the specific research performed in the project, the project team established and equipped an Occupational Health and Safety (OHS) laboratory for dust analysis at the premises of the core biomedical laboratory at the College of Health Sciences of AAU during 2014 and 2015 and strengthened the OHS laboratory at MUHAS. This would otherwise not have been possible. The two laboratories, furnished with modern equipment for dust, noise, illumination and hearing loss assessment, and supported by technical training, were finally integrated into the universities and they are now able to be used by students and faculty researchers. To have such instruments available for students is an asset to the universities, attracting motivated students in occupational health. With instruments and laboratories of this type, students know that the courses and curricula are of a high quality.

The current Norhed project is the first of its kind at AAU and MUHAS for occupational health research, and it has made a tremendous contribution to the research capacity of both universities. Because of this research project, the number of occupational health researchers and faculty members has increased from two in 2012 to seven in 2017 at AAU and from four in 2012 to 16 in 2017 at MUHAS. In addition, a great interest has been generated among the postgraduate students to join the field of occupational health at the master's and PhD levels.

At both universities, occupational health has become a visible part of the study programmes. At MUHAS, there is greater activity, with more students and more projects. This is natural, as MUHAS had the advantage of already having a group of skilled scientists when this Norhed project began. At AAU, there were few people available for the project at the start, but activities have increased during the project period. No specific obstacles have been met from the university side to prevent this growth, and, in general, the project has been welcomed both at MUHAS and AAU.

Improved education in occupational health in Ethiopia and Tanzania

The project aimed to educate 50 master's students in occupational health, 35 at MUHAS and 25 at AAU. In 2018, when this chapter was written, this aim had almost been fulfilled. Several of these students were employed at MUHAS and AAU and will be able to contribute to the scientific work there after completing their education. Other students planned to continue their careers at other universities in Tanzania or Ethiopia, or in industry or governmental positions in these countries.

An alumni study is planned and will give us more details about career paths and capacity strengthening. Most of the master's students performed their fieldwork in industry locations and the work they did for their master's theses was of interest to both industry and society.

In addition, the project aimed to educate 60 BSc students in occupational health at MUHAS. This BSc study programme was developed at the start of the project, in close co-operation with the Occupational Safety and Health Agency (OSHA) in Tanzania, representing the Labour Inspectorate. OSHA participated in the project by teaching students and by training them to perform worksite visits. This is an important and useful skill, as there is a need for qualified inspectors in OSHA for the whole of Tanzania. OSHA had been in the process of establishing stronger units in the different parts of the country, and this co-operation between OSHA and MUHAS is of mutual interest. By educating inspectors, Tanzania will be able to control regulations in the world of work and will be able to give advice to the industry and workplaces on how to improve the work environment. This part of the Norhed project was possible due to the participation of the strong scientific group at MUHAS from the project's inception.

At both universities, the project was included in activities at the Schools of Public Health, as we wanted to focus on preventive issues at the workplace. The education of medical students has not been directly involved in the activities of the project. This part of the university education is also important, and it should be a future aim for both universities to include occupational health in the curricula of medical students.

Developing an open online course

The project planned at first to make a web-based introductory book on occupational health, with its management at UiB. At the time of planning, the possibility came up of developing a whole introductory module as a massive open online course (MOOC). The UiB wanted scientific staff to develop MOOCs and gave the project the resources needed to develop a MOOC in occupational health. The course was developed with the co-operation of the three partner institutions and is named 'Occupational Health in Developing Countries: An Introduction'. The course runs twice a year from the technical platform Futurelearn, and attendance is free of charge. As at May 2018, the course has had more than 12 000 students, from more than 150 countries. It is a great success and has been awarded two prizes for Internationalization in Education from the Faculty of Medicine at UiB and the Owl Award for education at UiB, the university's top education prize. It is difficult to measure the effect of this online education, but at the minimum, the course has contributed to increasing awareness of this type of education and has provided important information about occupational health issues. There are numerous positive comments from the students. Many students state that they benefited from the course as there is no education in occupational health in their country. Some students' comments explain that they have experienced the leadership of their country actively inhibiting the possibility of establishing unions or competence-building bodies in occupational health. Because of these problems, an online course is extremely helpful and attracts people interested in improving the working conditions in their countries.

An analysis of the participants shows that more than half of the students attending the course come from LICs. FutureLearn runs a great number of different courses on their platform and does not have a similar country profile in their other courses. In fact, they seldom have participants from LICs. This shows that the course has been of interest for our main target group: people from LICs.

Dissemination of research results – contacts in the society

The Norhed project facilitated research in different areas, including respiratory health among coffee industry workers, noise and hearing loss in metal and steel industries, chemical exposure in horticulture, injuries in gold mines and antimicrobial resistance among meat handlers. The dissemination of research findings to workers was carried out successfully. Dialogue about how to establish communication between researchers and policy-makers, employers and workers was supported by the Norhed project in Ethiopia as well as Tanzania.

In Tanzania, a large workshop was held in 2016, involving participants from the Ministry of Health, the Ministry of Labour, representatives from trade unions, the Workers Compensation Fund, personnel from OSHA, the Dean and people from the School of Public Health at MUHAS, and several NGOs. The workshop was an important networking opportunity for MUHAS and will facilitate the development of co-operation with policy-makers in occupational health. The Norhed project has been important for establishing this type of relationship between the university and society. A lack of resources at the universities makes it difficult to arrange this type of meeting, which is crucial for establishing contacts.

After the workshop, the contact between MUHAS and different governmental bodies and organisations increased. MUHAS is now involved in more activities outside the university and is involved in policy-making in the country. In addition, MUHAS has started to develop 'policy briefs' in occupational health. MUHAS staff organised a workshop for staff and students on how to write policy briefs. They will establish the routine development of such briefs which will make the relationship between MUHAS and the wider society more sustainable and visible.

This activity, in addition to the co-operation between MUHAS and OSHA working together in Tanzania, has been inspiring for AAU. Therefore, a Memorandum of Understanding has been initiated between AAU and the labour inspectorate at the Ministry of Labour and Social Affairs (MOLSA) in Ethiopia. This is a good start for co-operation between these bodies, a co-operation which will benefit the project and the country. This co-operation makes it more likely that there will be improvements in working life.

In Ethiopia, the MOLSA, the Bureaus of Labour and Social Affairs (BOLSA) of Addis Ababa City Administration and the Oromia Regional State have shown interest in working with AAU on occupational health and safety issues, and we have begun formal negotiations to work with them. The terms of reference are currently in the process of being signed by the authorities. This signals increased interest in and demand for stronger and more expanded occupational health research and laboratory capacity in Ethiopia. However, the establishment of co-operation is time consuming, and this is a new kind of relationship for AAU.

In addition to these local activities related to the sub-projects, it has also been important for the project to share its activity via international scientific publications. This Norhed project has been the source of about 15 original international papers so far on different issues within occupational health in LICs. This dissemination of new knowledge is important internationally and can provide inspiration and facts to other universities and researchers. This is important in order to be able to support occupational health activity in LICs. In addition, the staff connected to this Norhed project has presented their research results at several international conferences. This helps to increase the visibility of occupational health problems in LICs. It has also facilitated researchers in the South in establishing networks with researchers from other countries. This is critical for the sustainability of scientific work in occupational health in Tanzania and Ethiopia.

Restricted access to some workplaces

In most of the sub-projects within this Norhed project umbrella, the access to industries has been easy. Most employers have been interested in obtaining more knowledge about their workplaces and have welcomed researchers and students. Also, the teachers responsible for the work have much experience in fieldwork at the work sites and know that it is necessary to have good communication with the employers and employees before a study is planned and started. The experienced mentors and supervisors of this project have been vital for the successful activities conducted at the workplaces.

However, it has been a challenge to conduct occupational health research in the field of floriculture in both Ethiopia and Tanzania. Accessibility to the workers in the field sites is strongly limited by the farm and industry owners in this trade. This project has performed three studies on flower farms, despite this problem. It required multiple visits to the factories and many discussions with the factory or farm owners in order to get permission to conduct the studies, factors which had time and cost implications for the researchers. For example, we faced a significant challenge and resistance at two flower farming sites in Ethiopia in 2013. The plan was for one of our PhD students to collect data from the flower farm workers to study the health effects from exposure to pesticides (Nigatu et al. 2015) but, unfortunately, the researchers were almost thrown out of the plant. At this site, interviews and sample collections were conducted with workers selected by the farm administration, not the researchers. The workers were instructed not to talk about any health problems, and the validity of the data gathered from the interviews at this work site is highly questionable. The environment in the flower farm industry has often been unfriendly and it has been challenging for researchers to independently carry out occupational health research. Thus, it discourages researchers to be engaged in this field of research, requiring strong commitment and dedication by the researchers. This is problematic, as the industry is increasing in several LICs, and there is a need for openness and evaluation of these workplaces. Pesticides are in daily use in this industry. Most of these substances are highly toxic and can have serious implications for the workers' health. Thousands of workers are employed in this industry. Most are young and unexperienced and have no knowledge about the health risks they are being exposed to.

From our experience with this project, we recommend that the authorities of the involved countries ask for studies of work environment and health to be undertaken in such new industries, to avoid serious health problems among large groups of workers. The flower farms often have foreign plant owners, with less interest in the Ethiopian welfare. It might be especially important to control factors in the working environment in industries established by foreigners.

In our project, much time has been spent on discussing this topic. However, the resources available did not make it possible to work more in this resistant and uncooperative industry. In future projects of this type, resources should be allocated to facilitate more thorough dialogue with, for instance, authorities such as the Ministry of Health or Ministry of Labour in Ethiopia on such issues.

Gender balance

One of the aims of the Norhed project was to increase the number of female master's and PhD/postdoctoral candidates to 50 per cent at MUHAS and 33 per cent at AAU. The recruitment of female students was difficult at AAU. At MUHAS this was easier, as the university had developed a gender policy some years previously, and we had a Tanzanian female scientist in our management group with special responsibility for gender issues. This activity was stimulating for the AAU partner, and a one-week short course on scientific writing and communication was developed and provided for 74 female students of AAU during 2015 to 2017. Similar training sessions were conducted in MUHAS where 60 participants were trained. The main content of the training included proposal writing, review of published articles, writing for a scientific journal, writing methods, results, discussion and the referencing methods for research articles, critical appraisals, the submission process to medical journals, as well as peer reviewing and responding to the peer reviews' comments.

At MUHAS, we achieved the aim of 50 per cent female postdoctoral candidates. At AAU, one in four candidates was female. However, there had been no female PhD candidates previously at the School of Public Health at AAU, so we are pleased to register we have broken a barrier. Similarly, there were female master's students registered at MUHAS, but in higher numbers than those at AAU.

Gender issues were also in focus regarding the types of projects chosen at the workplaces. Several typical female work sites were studied, such as textile production and hand picking of coffee in factories.

Political instability

It is not only the availability of funding and trained human resources that determine the proper implementation of health research in countries south of the Sahara. Political stability is also of importance. The political unrest in Ethiopia, particularly during field data collection, was an important contextual point. For instance, such instabilities developed in the Oromia region of Ethiopia in 2015 and 2016 and interrupted the doctoral candidates' field data collection. This was totally beyond the control of the researchers. There were moments in which some of the flower farm sites initially selected for the study were burned down due to protests, forcing the research team to change the study sites. As a result, the data collection was completed after the situation was normalised at the end of 2016 and some of the candidates were delayed in their projects.

Administrative challenges encountered

Administrative challenges are inevitable when operating with complex issues and systems between institutions that are working together. Different institutional cultures and working procedures contribute to challenges in achieving the expected goals (Kok et al. 2017). We describe the administrative challenges encountered in our project below. They are not particularly connected to the topic of occupational health, but they are important in the development and reformation of the universities in the South in general.

Management group

A management group was established, consisting of the project leader from each of the three universities, as well as three more members from these universities and one member from OSHA in Dar es Salaam, Tanzania. Guidelines were written for work procedures in the management group and the group has engaged in joint planning to ensure the proper implementation of the project (Smith et al. 2018). Meetings in the management group were combined with supervision meetings with students and PhD/postdoctoral candidates and were held twice a year. However, we always ended up with too little time. The project managers were busy and although it would have been better if they had been more readily available, the meetings were extremely effective and included many topics. In addition, the meetings were always inspiring.

The key to this successful co-operation was discussed when we met in the management group; no problems were hidden. It was probably important for the project to have project leaders who had important leadership positions at the local universities. This made decisions regarding changes in curricula and new student groups easy. The project had no resistance at the local universities regarding the introduction of new topics in occupational health. In fact, the new competence was appreciated and supported.

Between the physical meetings, it was very difficult for the management group to have contact. We tried Skype meetings, but this did not work very well for more than two, or sometimes more than three, participants. The internet line from MUHAS was not good initially but improved later. AAU and UiB achieved the best Skype communication at first, but this connection stopped due to internet blackouts in Ethiopia in 2015 and 2016. The aim was to have Skype meetings with all three universities and OSHA every month, but it was not possible. The invitation to Skype meetings was normally initiated by the co-ordinator in the North. After some months with unsuccessful Skype conversations, we decided to have Skype calls with two persons only and inform the others by e-mail. This kept the project members together and the co-operation alive between the universities.

The project co-ordinator was located in Tanzania; this was preferred by Norad. The co-ordinator had competence in leadership and administration, which is clearly necessary to manage such a large project. The project manager was able to reinforce the need for co-operation and mutual support and kept the group together. This was important for the participants' motivation.

Postdoctoral scholarships

Postdoctoral positions were something new at both universities in the South. Several such positions have been included in this project. We have struggled to find a way to organise the work for the postdoctoral candidates. In both universities, the postdoctoral scholars have been teaching a great deal, have supervised many master's students and have participated in different university activities. This has left them with little time for research. The management group discussed this and several times suggested interventions, such as reducing teaching and the administrative load.

The intervention was not successful for all candidates. With a clearer structure, the candidates would have contributed more to the research results. At AAU it was not possible to pay the salaries for postdoctoral positions, as this type of position did not exist at the institution. The solution was to pay the postdoctoral scholars' salaries directly from

Norway. This worked out well in our project, but administrative systems should be developed for this type of position in the South.

All in all, the postdoctoral positions seem not to be the best solution for the universities in the South, and other types of scholarships or affiliations might be better. This is something to take into consideration when planning future projects.

Access to library services in the North

During the visit of Ethiopian students and staff to UiB in 2015, it became clear that students and staff at AAU needed better access to scientific books and journals. During their stay at UiB, this access was extremely useful for them, and they wished for similar access after returning to Ethiopia. In response to this, a library project group was established at UiB, consisting of a North co-ordinator, two people from the administration at the Centre for International Health, UiB and a librarian. The group's work has made it possible to register project members as guest students at UiB for one year at a time. This gives them access to the UiB library via the internet, with its search functions, electronic books and journals.

We recommend that electronic library services should be developed in the South. The solution found in our project is not sustainable, as it requires a contact with the individual researcher to continue the access to the Norwegian library. This is a topic for future projects.

Reporting problems

This project required that various reports had to be written and sent to Norad. We were always asked by Norad to revise the delivered products, resulting in the final reports being delivered too late several times. The project co-ordinators found the Norad reporting system unclear and time consuming, with very many details being asked for. As this was the first time with co-ordination of this type of project from the South, it was a major challenge for the project manager at MUHAS. The reports were circulated from MUHAS to both AAU and UiB, with new versions and short deadlines, which led to a number of different versions of reports, and this again led to several mix-ups of reports, with again more delays. Our project group would have clearly benefited from clearer reporting structures and simple guidelines to follow regarding reporting. The problem related to reporting was solved by extra travel from UiB to MUHAS, which included the North project leader as well as administrative staff working with the project economy at the CIH, UiB.

The problems related to the reporting were very negative for the project. A lot of time was spent on unimportant details and the researchers could have used this time for useful research instead. If a new project should be developed, much greater resources must be allocated to the performance of these administrative tasks.

Financial issues

Both AAU and MUHAS have struggled to be able to report the financial issues related to the project back to Norad. These two universities have traditions for accounting that are different from the Norwegian system. Dealing with these issues has been very difficult. For instance, Norad required a separate account for the project at both universities. This requirement took a very long time but was finally a reality in 2015 for MUHAS, while it was not possible for AAU. In that case, AAU continued using their own financial system. Also, it was difficult to understand how to perform the accounting to match the Norhed format. UiB helped by using one of the accountants at CIH and arranged and paid for extra travel to, and meetings in, the South for every year of the project. It is clear that administrative assistance and support is very important in this type of project, and the project should have put more resources into these aspects.

The transfer of funding from MUHAS to AAU was extremely slow initially. This led to a joint wish for funding to go directly from Norad to AAU; this was implemented in the second year of the project. The bank transactions in the South are too slow for our purposes.

Norad asked for audit reports and this was also new for the universities in the South. There were delays in the audit reporting from

AAU by MUHAS, and delays of the audit report from MUHAS to Norad. A decision to start procurement of an auditing firm one month before the end of the financial year minimised the problem.

Many problems in the project have been related to the delay in reporting. Delayed reports led to delayed disbursements on several occasions and made many problems for students, especially those who had been out for fieldwork.

Theft has been a problem. One student had a computer with field work data stolen while she was in the field. Also, we had a burglary at MUHAS in 2015, losing instruments and computers, and a PhD candidate lost instruments while traveling from Norway to Tanzania.

New instruments and computers were purchased by the project. After the burglary in 2015, the follow-up was for the project to pay for burglar-proofing, while backups of data at UiB facilitated the retrieval of the data.

All these obstacles were not related to the topic of occupational health itself. We were fortunate that they were solved in the end. However, the universities in the South need to learn from these experiences to be better able to host future projects.

Networking in new directions

The North–South co-operation was good at all times in this project. However, we had two countries in the project in the South. The relationship between the two universities in the South has improved during the project. For instance, one postdoctoral researcher from MUHAS and one PhD candidate from AAU worked together on the same topic of coffee dust and respiratory health, together with a supervisor from AAU and two supporting supervisors from UiB. This gave an opportunity for close co-operation, but the co-operation was not well developed. The South–South co-operation could probably have been developed more. This would have been possible with better planning. This is a lesson learned for future projects: to allocate more resources and time for the development of South–South co-operation. Strengthening this relationship would make the scientific environment in both countries stronger and more sustainable.

Conclusion

Has this project reduced the burden of injuries and occupational expo-sures through capacity building in LICs, as the main aim of the project stated? It is difficult to answer this question clearly. Although we have not been able to measure these specific outcomes fully, we have meas-ured indicators related to this main aim. The project has clearly developed new research in occupational health and disseminated these results to the industry, stakeholders and policy-makers, as well as pub-lished the results internationally. Staff at the two universities in the South have improved their scientific competence in occupational health, and a number of students have been educated. Many of these students have jobs that will influence and probably reduce the occur-rence of occupational injuries and diseases in the future. Gradually, their competence in occupational health will influence society, and political support for occupational health issues will grow.

This project is the first one on capacity building in occupational health in the South being co-ordinated from the South. Although the project has experienced challenges related to certain industries, we think that our strategy for building competence has been good. Developing competence in occupational health by increasing competence at the universities is crucial. This competence leads to an understanding of the problems we see in working life, and rules and regulations will be developed when stakeholders, policy-makers and the authorities also become educated. We think the activity from the project will contribute to reduce the burden of injuries and diseases in LICs. However, it is critical that the universities continue to perform their work in co-operation with the industry and political stakeholders in their countries. This co-operation will lead to improvements in occupational health at the workplaces and in the society.

Acknowledgements

We are most grateful to Norad for financing this project through Norhed. We would like to acknowledge Muhimbili University of Health and Allied Sciences (MUHAS), Addis

Ababa University (AAU) and the University of Bergen (UiB) for contributing human resources, time and energy to the success of this initiative. OSHA in Tanzania and MOLSA in Ethiopia are also acknowledged for their co-operation and technical linkages to the training and research industries. We also want to express our thanks to the language editor Elinor Bartle at UiB.

About the authors and the project

Bente Elisabeth Moen is professor and director of the Centre for International Health, University of Bergen, Norway

Wakgari Deressa is an associate professor in the School of Public Health, Addis Ababa University, Ethiopia

Simon Henry David Mamuya is a senior lecturer at the School of Public Health and Social Sciences, Muhimbili University of Health and Allied Sciences, Tanzania

Project title: Reduction of the Burden of Occupational Diseases and Injuries in Developing Countries

Partner institutions: Addis Ababa University (Ethiopia) Muhimbili University of Health and Allied Sciences(Tanzania) and the University of Bergen (Norway)

References

Debus AG (1999) Paracelsus and the Medical Revolution of the Renaissance: A 500th Anniversary Celebration. Paracelsus, Five Hundred Years: Three American Exhibits. National Library of Medicine, Washington, DC. Available online, see also: https://www.brmi.online/paracelsus#!

Ethiopian Academy of Sciences (2013) *Report on Mapping the Health Research Landscape in Ethiopia*. Addis Ababa: Eclipse Printing Press

Hanssen VM, Nigatu AW, Zeleke ZK, Moen BE and Bråtveit M (2015) High prevalence of respiratory and dermal symptoms among Ethiopian flower farm workers. *Archives of Environmental and Occupational Health* 70(4): 204–213

Kearney M-L (2009) Higher education, research and innovation: Charting the course of the changing dynamics of the knowledge society. In: VL Meek, U Teichler and M-L Kearney (eds) *Higher Education, Research and Innovation: Changing Dynamics: Report on the Unesco Forum on Higher Education, Research and Knowledge, 2001-2009*. Kassel: International Centre for Higher Education Research Kassel

Kok MO, Gyapong JO, Wolffers I, Ofori-Adjei D and Ruitenberg EJ (2017) Towards fair and effective North–South collaboration: realising a programme for demand-driven and locally led research. *Health Research Policy and Systems* 15(1): 96

Lansang MA and Dennis R (2004) Building capacity in health research in the developing world. *Bulletin of the World Health Organization* 82: 764–770

Moen BE (2015) Training occupational health personnel in developing countries. *The Barents Newsletter* 18: 40–41

Moen BE, Nyarubeli IP, Tungu AM, Ngowi AV, Kumie A, Deressa W and Mamuya SHD (2019) The challenge of obtaining a decent work environment in sub-Saharan Africa. In M Ramutsindela and D Mickler (eds) *Africa and the Sustainable Development Goals.* Berlin: Springer

Nchinda TC (2002) Research capacity strengthening in the South. *Social Science and Medicine* 54: 1699–1711

Negatu B, Kromhout H, Mekonnen Y and Vermeulen R (2016) Use of chemical pesticides in Ethiopia: A cross-sectional comparative study on knowledge, attitude and practice of farmers and farm workers in three farming systems. *The Annals of Occupational Hygiene* 60: 551–566

Nigatu AW, Bråtveit M, Deressa W and Moen BE (2015) Respiratory symptoms, fractional exhaled nitric oxide and endotoxin exposure among female flower farm workers in Ethiopia. *Journal of Occupational Medicine and Toxicology* 10:8. Available online

Nuwayhid IA (2004) Occupational health research in developing countries: A partner for social justice. *American Journal of Public Health* 94: 1916–1921

Ramazzini B (1703) *De Morbis Artificum Diatriba.* Available online

Smith LM, Keiser M, Turkelson C, Yorke AM, Sachs B and Berg K (2018) Simulated inter-professional education discharge planning meeting to improve skills necessary for effective interprofessional practice. *Professional Case Management* 23(2): 75–83. Available online

Whitworth JAG, Kokwaro G, Kinyanjui S, Snewin VA, Tanner M, Walport M et al. (2008) Strengthening capacity for health research in Africa. *Lancet* 372: 1590–1593

WHO (World Health Organization) (2013) *WHO Global Plan of Action on Workers' Health (2008-2017): Baseline for Implementation.* Available online

23

Building a new master's and PhD programme in nutritional epidemiology in Kinshasa: How to face obstacles beyond the control of the project

Mapatano Mala Ali, Christiane Horwood & Anne Hatløy

Background

Capacity building in health research in low-income countries (LICs) to improve the skills and competencies of local scientists is crucial for improving the availability of evidence-based, effective health interventions and health service delivery systems in resource-poor settings. Developing the capacity to carry out essential health research is a priority focus identified by the World Health Organization (WHO) (Lansang and Dennis 2004). Overall, African countries, such as the Democratic Republic of the Congo (DRC), have small numbers of skilled researchers, and these researchers are under-represented as authors on research publications. The aims of capacity building in research are that individuals and organisations become adaptable and achieve sustainability by identifying problems, seeking and evaluating solutions and disseminating findings (Bates et al. 2011). Both long-term and short-term strategies are required to achieve this, aimed at all levels including individual scientists, organisations and governments (Lansang and

Dennis 2004). Partnerships between research institutions are an important mechanism for developing capacity for researchers in all participating institutions. Partners in LICs gain access to skills, new ideas, technical expertise, a wider audience for their research findings and increased leverage for ongoing research, while partners in high-income countries also gain opportunities to improve their skills and experience. However, such partnerships are difficult to build as they require trust, joint ownership and decision-making, and may be expensive to maintain. At the same time, however, due to the small number of scientists in LICs, it is crucial for longer-term sustainability that the links with outside research communities are maintained.

Good nutrition, with adequate intake of energy and micronutrients, is the cornerstone of good health. Therefore, the study of nutrition and nutritional epidemiology, including factors associated with sub-optimal nutrition, the impact of this on communities, and the identification and evaluation of possible interventions in nutrition is a crucial field of study. This is particularly important for resource-limited countries such as the DRC, where poor nutrition is a primary reason for individuals, particularly children, failing to reach their potential. The GrowNut project aims to develop nutritional epidemiology as a sustainable field of study at master's and PhD level at the Kinshasa School of Public Health (KSPH), at the University of Kinshasa. In this way, we aim to create a pool of senior scientists and researchers with strong skills to provide leadership in the field and contribute to a knowledge base and policy development for nutrition in the DRC.

GrowNut is a collaboration between KSPH, the Centre for Rural Health at the University of KwaZulu-Natal (UKZN) in South Africa, and the Centre for International Health at the University of Bergen (UiB), Norway. It is funded by the Norwegian Programme for Capacity Development in Higher Education and Research for Development (Norhed). GrowNut started in 2014 and was designed in collaboration with the National Nutrition Programme (PRONANUT) under the Ministry of Health in the DRC, with the vision of facilitating the translation of research data into nutrition policy, particularly through the establishment of a rural research site to allow the integration of the nutrition policy into routine activities. A key project aim was to

Developing scientists and staff in nutritional epidemiology

promote sustainability and build institutional capacity by providing opportunities for skills development for junior members of staff at KSPH, and opportunities for research collaborations between participating institutions. As a result, a number of joint scientific articles have been published in international journals. Students have been accepted into the nutritional epidemiology study programme based on their performance in the entrance examinations, including their competence in English. In addition, in each year, five students have received a GrowNut scholarship to cover their costs. One of these scholarships has been earmarked for a student based at KSPH with the aim of internal capacity building, and the four remaining scholarships have been given to students from vulnerable groups, such as people from war-prone areas, people originating from the study site and, to avoid strong gender bias, as many as 10 out of 13 vulnerability scholarships have been given to female candidates.

The intention at the heart of the GrowNut project is to build research capacity in nutrition in the DRC that will continue to grow, building on the foundation of skilled human resources developed among the GrowNut students. The project is designed to support staff and students from KSPH to identify and prioritise problems, develop and evaluate solutions and disseminate the knowledge acquired in order to translate new knowledge into policy. The project aims to combine academic degrees with a 'learning by doing' approach, taking the students to a rural research site to get hands-on experience, in line with the principles of adult learning. In addition to individual development, institutional development is key to the success and sustainability of capacity building in research, and GrowNut includes a strong development component for teaching and research staff at KSPH. Another important attribute of successful approaches to capacity building in research is the building of linkages with partner organisations in developing and developed countries (Lansang and Dennis 2004). GrowNut is founded on strong linkages with the Universities of Bergen, KwaZulu-Natal and Kinshasa. Hence, the GrowNut vision is a combination of short-term and long-term strategies at individual and institutional levels to develop research capacity.

The establishment of a rural research site is essential for the vision of the GrowNut master's and PhD programmes to ensure that students have the opportunity to learn practical skills in nutrition and research and are exposed to the real problems of rural communities in the DRC. Considerable resources were required to support the development of the infrastructure in order to provide students with facilities including accommodation, transport and study facilities. All students were required to undertake an internship at the rural site, which includes data collection. This was to ensure that the project research agenda had a strong focus on under-resourced rural communities, and to provide opportunities for collaborative research projects at the site. Popokabaka in Kwango province was identified for the rural site. In Popokabaka, master's students undertake a three-month internship for practical teaching and learning. Every two to three weeks a supervisor visits the students for a week for interactive teaching. This field training gives the students the opportunity to interact with communities where they can assess nutritional problems and see the whole spectrum of malnutrition, ranging from acute and chronic malnutrition to vitamin and mineral deficiencies. Students are also able to observe malnutrition in the local health facilities. During the fourth month of the site training, students are expected to collect data for their theses, as Popokabaka also serves as the research site for the project.

In this chapter we focus on our experiences in developing the master's programme in nutritional epidemiology, which is the fifth master's programme to be established at KSPH. It will focus on three areas. The first is what is needed to integrate a new programme in an existing structure. The second dimension is the challenge of integrating traditions from three different institutes in three countries into one programme, including challenges that were met, both in teaching and in supervision. A third dimension is how to undertake such a collaboration in an area where political unrest led to challenges and delays in planning project activities and resulted in travel restrictions for project partners.

Progress so far

GrowNut was launched on 15 November 2014 by the Rector's Representative, a sign of acceptance and recognition by the University of Kinshasa.

The programme experienced various unexpected challenges during the set-up period, including the untimely deaths of two of the senior collaborators, one in Norway and one in South Africa. There were also challenges in establishing the rural site because the first research site selected was Bwamanda, but due to the loss of the two senior staff members who had the contacts in that area, and problems with getting a collaboration agreement with the local NGO, it was not possible to continue.

Popokabaka was therefore selected as an alternative research site, based on recommendations from PRONANUT. A memorandum of understanding was signed between KSPH and the Diocese of Popokabaka, and the Popokabaka site has been functioning since 2015. GrowNut is housed in a compound owned by the church; however, a fair amount of renovation to the building was required. Students from all four cohorts have undertaken their internships and collected data in

Professor Mapatano, KSPH, at the official opening of GrowNut, November 2014

the Popokabaka area. A mini-conference was held in Popokabaka in February 2019 to provide feedback on research findings to local stakeholders and the local community. It was attended by 70 participants, including key international agencies working in the area.

We are now moving towards the end of the project in December 2019, and a total of 42 students have been enrolled in the master's programme supported by the GrowNut project. Teaching the modules for the master's programme was conducted in KSPH and for the first two years this teaching was supported by visiting facilitators from partner institutions. However, from 2016 it was no longer possible for international staff to travel to Kinshasa due to security constraints, and teaching was undertaken by facilitators from KSPH. In contrast to other teaching at KSPH, the medium of instruction for GrowNut was English. All students have been co-supervised, with the main supervisor from KSPH and with a co-supervisor from UKZN or UiB. As of July

Research site in Popokabaka

2019, 31 students have graduated from the master's programme and one student from previous cohorts is preparing to submit his thesis. The last seven are planning to graduate in early 2020. Two students have dropped out and one is uncertain. In addition, six PhD students have been enrolled, two have graduated, two have dropped out and two are planning to defend their theses in 2020.

Annual meetings have been held each year since 2014, attended by representatives from all participating institutions and from the Norwegian Agency for Development Cooperation (Norad). These meetings have intentionally alternated between the three partner institutions. At the annual meetings, activities have been reviewed and plans for future activities discussed. A level of flexibility in planning was required as the project team worked to mitigate the threats to the project that arose with the political unrest and travel restrictions.

In terms of visibility, one can point out that GrowNut has allowed for several scientific articles that were published in international journals. These articles have been authored jointly with contributions from UKZN, KSPH and CIH/UiB. In 2016, GrowNut was represented at the World Public Health Nutrition Conference in Cape Town with three posters and one oral presentation, as well as representatives from each of the three collaborating partners. In 2018, nine graduates of the GrowNut master's programme in nutritional epidemiology attended the African Nutritional Epidemiology Conference in Addis Ababa, contributing five oral presentations and five posters.

Integration of a new project into existing structure: What is needed?

GrowNut brought together senior academics from three diverse institutions in different geographical locations with the aim of developing an academic programme at the KSPH, the most under-resourced of the three settings. Each institution had different expectations of students, access to different resources, and different established practices for teaching and supervision. A key challenge for KSPH was to set the academic calendar so that it did not overlap with the other four existing master's programmes. In addition, academic requirements for the completion of master's-level studies were not consistent, and while the language of instruction at KSPH is French, the GrowNut students were expected to learn and write in English. A shared vision of the academic processes to be implemented in the project was a key requirement for integration.

GrowNut delegates to the 8th African Nutrition and Epidemiology Conference in Addis Ababa, October 2018

Good communication is key to developing a shared vision and developing integration; this is more challenging when collaborators are in separate geographical locations. Throughout the planning and implementation of the GrowNut project, senior project staff have communicated frequently via Skype calls and e-mail. Regular calls are scheduled between project leaders at the three sites to monitor progress with project activities, develop common understandings of planned activities, and address challenges as these arise. Minutes of these meetings are circulated to provide an ongoing record of the discussions. However, there is no substitute for face-to-face meetings, particularly to address challenges and develop common understandings of complex issues such as curriculum development or master's-level supervision.

Another important requirement was to develop a strong team and trusting relationships between colleagues at the three institutions. Regular face-to-face meetings strengthened the communication developed at a distance and provided opportunities to build closer relationships with colleagues. Project leaders from all three sites met at least once per year, for the annual meeting with Norad, the senior academic leaders at KSPH and PRONANUT. In addition, team members also met during teaching and supervision in the DRC and at conferences where GrowNut results have been presented. As a result of the continuing positive communication over the project period, and the commitment to working together towards a common vision, a productive working environment with a strong team has been developed.

The aim of the project was for resources and skills to be shared amongst the institutions, with each providing support to project activities according to their strengths and resources. This could be understood to mean that the more highly resourced institutions share their resources and expertise with the University of Kinshasa. However, it was important to the vision of the project that resources and opportunities should flow in both directions and that the collaboration would provide opportunities for all participating institutions to share experiences and benefit from each other's skills. In particular, the project aimed to provide a shared platform for research between the three institutions to allow long-term collaboration to strengthen the research portfolios of all three institutions.

Different institutions are different:
Challenges of integrating

The first challenge faced in establishing the master's programme was a lack of access to study resources in the DRC, particularly library facilities, which were inadequate in providing students with up-to-date literature to support their studies. In addition, there were the challenges of interrupted electricity supplies and internet access was slow and unavailable in areas outside the university. As a result, it was not always possible to maintain communication with colleagues and with students. This was addressed by accessing books and journals and physically taking these to KSPH so that there is a small library for GrowNut students to use. In addition, students were given access to the online library at UiB, but this was not well utilised. Students reported that the lack of internet connectivity was the key reason for this but a lack of skills in accessing literature was also a factor.

Another key challenge throughout the project has been to develop a common understanding of the different aspects of the master's supervision, including the curriculum, timelines and deadlines, academic requirements, and administrative processes. Despite efforts to maintain good communication, collaborating at a distance remained a challenge. Thus, practical aspects of the master's programme undertaken by students in Kinshasa was not always clearly understood by colleagues at other institutions, with the result that misunderstandings arose and external facilitators were not always able to comply with giving timeous feedback and support to students. In addition, it was difficult at times to reconcile the expectations of each institution. In order to address these issues, a workshop was held in 2017 where team members met with the objective of developing common understandings and clear guidelines for the GrowNut master's students. This workshop was facilitated by an external facilitator and participants agreed to a common list of requirements for the scope of the students' research for the master's programme, as well as the proposal and thesis write-ups. The primary responsibility for the quality of the work, especially the timing of submission for theses, remained with the local-level supervisors.

Although the DRC is primarily a francophone country and most of the courses taught at the KSPH are conducted in French, the GrowNut academic programme is taught in English. This allowed for the participation of the Norwegian and South African partners and provided KSPH students with opportunities to study in English and to have access to English-speaking academic facilities and resources. However, this has added further complexity to an already challenging process, particularly in preparing academic work. It has sometimes been difficult to determine whether students' failure to achieve high quality work was related to a lack of performance or their inability to engage with learning activities conducted in English, or poor skills in written English. This challenge was addressed by including an assessment in speaking English in the requirements for entry to the master's programme, introducing an English class at the beginning of the academic year, and using language editing to improve English written work. However, a few students were requested to prepare their theses in French.

The establishment of the rural site was a challenge; travel to the site was difficult, time-consuming and expensive. The journey to Popokabaka took 11 hours over very rough roads using expensive, four-wheel drive vehicles. Thus, the area was hardly accessible for students and staff, and travel to and from Popokabaka during the period of internship was sometimes impossible. In some cases, students were unable or unwilling to make this journey due to health issues or other responsibilities in Kinshasa, and research was conducted closer to Kinshasa. However, despite the challenges, the majority of students have successfully completed their internship in Popokabaka, and a mini-conference was held in Popokabaka.

Challenge of political violence

During 2016, the third year of the project, political violence arose in the DRC and travel recommendations were that travel to the DRC should be limited to emergency travel only. As a consequence, there was no travel by GrowNut partners to the DRC from 2016 to December 2018. This has resulted in problems maintaining good communication between role players and made it impossible for the collaborating institutions to provide the support to the KSPH that was proposed in the project plan. Some members of the team did not have the opportunity to travel to the DRC at all.

As a result, project activities had to be re-conceptualised, with the aim of maximising the benefit to the colleagues and students at KSPH, during the period that travel was impossible. This was addressed in workshops and meetings held at UKZN in Durban with all role players coming together, including students who travelled from the DRC, to continue with the development of the academic programme.

Responding to these challenges required flexibility from partners, openness to changing responsibilities, particularly for the team member from the DRC who had to take on additional tasks, as well as flexibility from the funders. As a result of the good teamwork and communication built up over the period of project implementation, and with the support of Norad, the project was able to adapt to new challenges and continue to support the students.

Conclusion

This project provides a framework for integration between academic institutions with very different backgrounds. Developing common understandings, sharing ideas and building long-term partnerships can lead to a rich collaboration providing opportunities for staff and students at all partner universities to enrich their experiences; enable meaningful research; improve leadership for policy change; and link policy to practice.

However, substantial challenges were experienced by the GrowNut team; many of these were the result of the severe political, resource and infrastructure challenges experienced in the DRC and should, therefore, provide strong motivation for continuing and strengthening such collaborations. Challenges were overcome through strong communication and teamwork, the flexibility and commitment of GrowNut collaborators, and support from funders. It is crucial that such partnerships continue to provide support to institutions with the greatest need, and that challenges do not lead to defeat with resources being withdrawn and redirected to settings where it is easier to work, but where there is less need for support. Facing challenges and overcoming these to achieve the goals set out for the programme, is the most important measure of success.

About the authors and the project

Mapatano Mala Ali is a professor at the Kinshasa School of Public Health, University of Kinshasa. *Christiane Horwood*, is deputy director of the Centre for Rural Health at the University of KwaZulu-Natal

Christiane Horwood is deputy director of the Centre for Rural Health at the University of KwaZulu-Natal

Anne Hatløy is an associate professor at the University of Bergen's Centre for International Health

Project title: GrowNut: *Growing Partnership for Higher Education and Research in Nutritional Epidemiology in DR Congo*

Partner institutions: University of Kinshasa (DR Congo), University of KwaZulu-Natal (South Africa), University of Bergen (Norway)

References

Bates I, Taegtmeyer M, Squire SB, Ansong D, Nhlema-Simwaka B, Baba A and Theobald S (2011) Indicators of sustainable capacity building for health research: Analysis of four African case studies. *Health Research Policy and Systems* 9(14). Available online

Lansang MA and Dennis R (2004) Building capacity in health research in the developing world. *Bulletin of the World Health Organization* 82(10): 764–770

POSTSCRIPT

24

Higher education institutions and transformational development: Ways forward

Kristin Skare Orgeret

Norhed was born of Norad's wish to share the broader socio-economic benefits of higher education with low- to middle-income countries (LMICs), and the relevance of knowledge production for sustainable development lies at Norhed's core. Consequently, the research and educational projects it supports are expected to impact on broader economic, social and environmental development in the partner countries. In this process, Norhed has attempted to encourage partner institutions in LMICs to take the lead in defining project proposals and be responsible for project implementation, management and co-ordination. Partner institutions were also asked to ensure that the needs and priorities they identified were in line with their own governments' national and regional policies and priorities. By combining education, research, institutional development and administrative management in a holistic approach, Norhed aimed to strengthen the academic sector generally and foster research relevant for transformational development.

A growing scholarly opus refuses to accept that any narrowly defined neoliberal and technical process of poverty eradication linked only to economic benefits can be seen as development. For example, Naila Kabeer (2015) points out that a narrow focus on economic growth has often proven to worsen the living standards of the poor, not least women. She argues that vertical and horizontal inequalities[1] render people, and particularly women from poor and socially marginalised groups, desperate for income, and notes that women tend to be concentrated in the occupations that are simultaneously the lowest paid as well as the most precarious, exploitative, and stigmatised (Kabeer 2015).

A fully articulated gender and development perspective demands a degree of structural change that most national and international development organisations have found difficult to incorporate into their programmes and strategies. As a result, development programmes have largely failed to investigate substantive gender equality and women's empowerment (Struckmann 2017). The Women Major Group (2014) argue that it is not sufficient merely to *include* women in projects, but that truly transformative projects should present strategies that focus on *increasing* women's and girls' *agency and autonomy* so as not only to end discrimination and violence against women, but also to guarantee gender justice and sustainable development. As the group points out, structural and underlying causes, combined with social norms that influence and perpetuate gender inequality, make it difficult to see how isolated initiatives can succeed in delivering the gender-transformative agenda that is essential to end the current status quo which ensures that half of humanity is held back (Women Major Group 2014).

While the mere inclusion of women is, indeed, insufficient to guarantee fair and sustainable development, the active participation of growing numbers of women in higher education and research is certainly a good start. Ndaruhutse and Thompson (2016, citing Sifuna 2006) show how widely low levels of participation by women in higher education are reported as a key constraint to national development. A comprehensive review of the obstacles women face in entering higher education in Kenya (Sifuna 2006) found that, in the existing policy framework, gender is a determinant of educational provision. That is, the legacies of colonial and/or cultural economic structures restrict women to subordinate positions and tend to prevent their participation in education. This reality is replicated globally to a greater or lesser extent. To overcome such challenges, development and knowledge-production projects have to be highly cognisant of the contextual factors that impede women, and governments must transform legislative and policy frameworks so as to promote the education of females.

The politics of knowledge: Democratisation of access

Adriansen et al. (2016) show how the deepening of geographical and spatial knowledge in the humanities and social sciences led to the emergence of new interdisciplinary fields. That is,

> By using a spatial approach for exploring the current and future development of knowledge production in Africa, we ... [can] explore how scientific knowledge is negotiated and contested in parallel to societal changes in general and capacity building in particular, and thus how scientific knowledge becomes local. (2016: 3)

The ownership of knowledge production is central to what the Norhed project seeks to achieve. This includes ownership of teaching (what is taught and how) and research (what is researched and why). Strengthening and establishing robust research environments in the LMICs and creating transnational networks of co-operation across borders and regions is important, not least since most of the global challenges we face – from climate change to terrorism, migration and corruption – cannot be addressed solely at a national level.

If we acknowledge the relationships between our spatial positions and perspectives on any given issue, the need to diversify the sources we engage in our scholarship becomes obvious. It is interesting to note that in March 2015, about the same time as Norhed projects began to take shape across 36 countries, a decolonial battle began at the University of Cape Town (UCT) in South Africa, highlighting the problematic legacy of one of the university's major donors, Cecil Rhodes. Rhodes (1853–1902) was a British businessman, mining magnate, politician and ardent imperialist who helped entrench apartheid-style colonial rule throughout southern Africa. The 'Rhodes Must Fall' campaign gained traction when it set out to remove a huge statue of Cecil Rhodes that stood in a prominent spot at the centre of UCT's main campus. In fact, however, the campaign signalled that the time had come for many of the assumptions, beliefs and ideologies which had characterised South Africa's historically white universities since the days of Rhodes and his ilk, to be systematically challenged by an upcoming generation of black students and academics. The campaign was an example of what often happens when institutions face the need for a shift in institutional culture, and the resulting conflict raised a range of identity markers, including race, gender, class and sexual orientation. Although decolonisation, in the words of author, film maker and sociologist, Zethu Matebeni (2015), is 'often misrecognised as the new buzz word next to "transformation", its content is often not so easily embraced'. Nevertheless, the campaign spread quickly, inspiring debates throughout the region and internationally about the need to decolonise universities and knowledge regardless of institutions' specific historic trajectories. By October 2015, the campaign had morphed into #FeesMustFall, a student-led protest movement that continues to campaign for reduced student fees and increased government funding for students.

Epistemic liberation, to use an expression with Latin American roots, is necessarily a long process. According to the *Stanford Encyclopedia of Philosophy*, Latin America's 'philosophy of liberation' has practical aims, and therefore defines itself as

> a counter-philosophical discourse, whether it be as a critique of colonialism, imperialism, globalisation, racism, and sexism, which is articulated from out of the experience of exploitation, destitution, alienation and reification, in the name of the projects of liberation, autonomy and authenticity. (Mendieta 2016)

Similarly, epistemic liberation aims to critique and challenge the basic assumptions and research priorities defined in the global North. Perhaps more importantly, it aims to make higher education and research institutions more responsible, particularly for the sociopolitical situation in which humankind finds itself.

In his article, 'Decolonizing the university', Achille Mbembe sets out the following questions: 'What are the limits placed on the decolonisation project by the forces of neoliberalism? How are the latter affecting the future of the university? Is "decolonisation" the same as "Africanisation?"' In responding to these, Mbembe writes about the democratisation of access – a topic that is relevant to many Norhed partner countries – and argues that the doors of higher learning must be opened. He then qualifies this as follows:

> But when we say access, we are not simply thinking in demographic terms, although these are crucial. When we say access, we are also saying the possibility to inhabit a space to the extent that one can say, 'This is my home. I am not a foreigner. I belong here.' (Mbembe 2016: 30)

Mbembe argues that the Rhodes Must Fall campaign was important and necessary, and notes that the movement won a tactical battle. But, he continues,

> The struggle is only starting. It has revealed numerous lines of fracture within South African society and has brought back on the agenda the question of de-racialization of the country's institutions and public culture ... We all seem to agree that there is something anachronistic, something entirely is wrong with a number of institutions of higher learning in South Africa. There is something profoundly wrong when, for instance, syllabuses designed to meet the needs of colonialism and Apartheid should continue well into the liberation era ... So today the consensus is that part of what is wrong with our institutions of higher learning is that they are 'Westernized'. (2016: 32)

In his seminal work, *Decolonising the Mind* (1981), Ngũgĩ Wa Thiong'o describes how 'the sword and the bullet' affected Berlin in 1884, noting that:

> The night of the sword and bullet was followed by the morning of the chalk and the blackboard. The physical violence of the battlefield was followed by the psychological violence of the classroom. (1981: 9)

Over 35 years later, Thiong'o continues to explain the need for linguistic and academic decolonisation:

> Unfortunately, African scholarship has achieved this great visibility in the world by the tremendous feat of making itself invisible to Africa. African scholarship wears a linguistic mask with the magic quality of making it invisible to the majority in Africa and simultaneously visible to those with the key made in Europe ... We can only see ourselves through European eyes, at the minimum. This makes us look at Africa with the eyes of an outsider, thus in effect giving up on our responsibility to secure the continent for African people ... Are we sure that after fifty years of modern African scholarship we are in touch with the nation, the continent, African peoples? Or more basic and consequential, is the independent African state, now in existence for the same fifty years, in touch with its people? (Thiong'o 2017)

Linking the role of scholarship and the universities clearly to the democratic role that higher education should play, Thiong'o goes on to suggest that African universities should be full of scholars who know and work in African languages. We should 'use English instead of English using us' he declared. In his view, a knowledge of African languages should matter in how teachers from abroad are evaluated within in African institutions, and it ought to be 'both cool and clever' to know an African language.

> This does not and should never mean retreating into linguistic self-isolation. If you know all the languages of the world, and you don't know your mother tongue or the language of your culture, that is enslavement; but if you know your mother tongue or the language of your culture, and add all the other languages of the world to it, that is empowerment. And surely we want an Africa economically, politically, culturally and psychologically empowered, an Africa secure in its base, even as it engages with other peoples and continents. (Thiong'o 2017)

Of course, Thiong'o acknowledges that objections to the adoption of African languages in teaching and learning in higher education are based not only on the fear that it will disunite nations, but that it might hamper students' participation in the globalised world. Indeed, Africanisation can be seen as a counter discourse to calls for the internationalisation of African universities (see Adriansen et al. 2016). And it is precisely within this field of opposing trends that many interesting discussions of higher education and capacity building in the global South take place.

In Norhed, English (and to a small degree Portuguese and Spanish) is the *lingua franca* and, for the time being, it is hard to imagine an international programme of this scale using smaller local languages (including Norwegian) in its work. At the same time, discussions in the programme have often touched on the need to acknowledge that curricula and knowledge production can be 'improved' in several ways. An analysis of reading lists, for example, can provide a fairly good impression of what kind of research is (and isn't) being done and by whom. Similarly, an awareness of the realities of each research context encourages researchers to question the status quo and seek new approaches to what defines a good curriculum.

At this point, through the Norhed programme, analyses and reconstruction of curricula, as well as support for the publication and dissemination of more scientific and scholarly material stemming from, and focusing on, the global South, have contributed to a decolonisation of the academics involved. To what degree this decolonisation is 'real' is too early to tell. As the chapters in this book illustrate, some projects tended to perpetuate academic colonisation (in the sense that some research projects closely followed paths laid out by colleagues in the North) *and* yet simultaneously provided new platforms from which researchers are able to co-operate across countries and regions.

The politics of knowledge

As Roy Krøvel (2017) reminds us, according to indigenous leaders all over Latin America, 'Westernised' or 'Northern' ways of producing knowledge exclude by default many forms of indigenous knowledge.

Their indigenous universities believe conventional research methodologies relegate indigenous knowledges to a zone of non-being. Consequently, Krøvel explains, indigenous leaders do not subscribe to Northern concepts of 'equality' or 'inclusion':

> The rectors of the indigenous universities do not want to be 'equal' or 'included' in dominant society, they tell me. Instead, the indigenous leaders I know struggle for the right to remain different. The indigenous struggles cannot easily be captured with concepts such as 'equality', especially when the understandings of 'equality' originate from the Global North. Instead, the indigenous movement seek to preserve diversity confronted by a perceived process of cultural homogenization. (2017: 60)

However, as Meera Sabaratnam (2017) makes clear, contestations over the politics of knowledge are as old as universities themselves and, in this sense, attempting to decolonise universities is, in itself, a manifestation of a 'fusty old tradition' of challenging received wisdom, asking questions about society and generating the insights needed to change the world.

A greater representation of 'non-European' thinkers in revised curricula, as well as better historical awareness of the contexts in which scholarly knowledge has been produced is important. Co-operation across cultures, traditions and histories may expose dogmas – the 'taken for granted' assumptions about how our world is. Where these are not shared, discussing them may offer us golden opportunities to interrogate conventions, models and frameworks for specific biases. In this sense, Norhed can be said to have proven itself to be a project with much potential as a tool of decolonisation.

Norhed's successes are closely linked to the invaluable dedication, enthusiasm and hard work of its unit within Norad, which despite being short-staffed and caught up in Norad's own institutional changes, guided, discussed and dialogued with Norhed project partners in 35 countries in Africa, Asia, the Middle East, Latin America and in Norway.

Is any knowledge universal?

Another noteworthy axis of scholarly tension is the one between seeing scientific knowledge as universal, neutral and objective on the one hand and as 'situated' on the other. 'Science', argues Nicolaas Rupke, 'is not just a collection of abstract theories and general truths but a concrete practice with spatial dimensions' (2011: 439). Rupke echoes David Livingstone's (2005) argument that space matters in the production of science even though this goes against the widely accepted perception that scientific knowledge is universal. From a universalistic perspective, access to higher education is seen as key to modernity, whereas from a post-colonial perspective, much of what occurs in higher education globally is perceived as just another form of Western imperialism (Adriansen et al. 2016).

In the final chapter of their book, *The Delusion of Knowledge Transfer*, Koch and Weingart discuss their findings from an empirical review of aid-related advisory processes in South Africa and Tanzania. They conclude that providing developing countries with outside experts will not achieve desired changes, 'irrespective of the commitment and goodwill of individual actors or attempts to refine approaches' (2016: 344). Koch and Weingart's findings suggest that donors

> should be dissuaded from continuing to supply advice to countries that lack the absorptive capacity to adequately deal with it ... [and that] it would probably be more constructive to use the available means to support the knowledge communities in developing countries so that these become able to produce a critical mass of local experts who qualify as producers and critical scrutinisers of expertise. (2016: 344)

This points to the core of Norhed's main objective, which is to strengthen the capacity of higher education institutions in LMICs to better educate higher numbers of students (of all genders), and to improve the quality and quantity of research conducted by these countries' own researchers.

Whereas earlier development projects in the higher education sector focused largely on *knowledge transfer*, Norhed's aim is to *produce knowledge* through collaboration. In its first phase, Norhed bravely called for innovative forms of South–South–North co-operation. This opens the way for a more multifaceted approach to what is defined as 'local' and 'foreign' than, for instance, the approaches that Koch and Weingart (2016) critique, and highlights the fact that future discussions might need to focus on how to de-essentialise the 'foreign'.

Reflections for future programmes on higher education

The Norhed programme was founded on the idea of knowledge for development and introduced a holistic approach to capacity development in higher education. The role of universities and higher education institutions in finding solutions that address development challenges has, therefore, been seen as central to the programme, as the chapters in this volume illustrate. Although less often explicitly expressed, the work of universities and research institutions is also seen as central to achieving the UN's Sustainable Development Goals (SDGs).

The SDGs are more ambitious than the earlier Millennium Development Goals (MDGs) that they replaced. Unlike the MDGs, which (according to *The Guardian*, 19 January 2015) were drawn up by a group of men in the basement of UN headquarters, for the SDGs, the UN conducted the largest consultation programme in its history to gauge opinion on what the SDGs should include. They also acknowledged that governments cannot achieve the SDGs alone, and that collaboration with the private sector, civil society, and educational institutions at all levels is crucial.

At a conference on the SDGs held in Bergen, Norway, in February 2018, Norway's prime minister, Erna Solberg, noted that responsibility for the SDGs is global, and usefully pointed out that 'in this context, we are all developing countries'.[2]

The SDGs focus, directly and indirectly, on inequalities within and between countries. Gender inequalities, poverty, global economic, social and environmental problems, are all of concern. Although the SDGs mention a triad of economic, social and environmental issues, a closer analysis of Agenda 2030 – such as that carried out by Koulaouzides and Popović (2017) – reveals that it is dominated by an economic paradigm that is aiming for economic growth. As Koulaouzides and Popović argue, the focus on inequalities is not necessarily reflected in the SDGs' educational aspects. On the contrary, educational goals, especially those dealing with adult education, 'give the impression that lack of vocational and technical skills of adults is the main global problem, and leads to the most efficient solutions for all other problems' (Koulaouzides and Popović (2017: 5).

A central aim of the SDGs is that they become an integral part of research and education. Increasing access to higher education institutions is seen as essential for promoting equitable and sustainable growth and attaining the goals. Furthermore, higher education must pursue the goals of equity, relevance and quality simultaneously. Gender equality in higher education and research is also seen to be of fundamental importance in achieving the SDGs and, as noted, is central in all Norhed programmes (see also Norad 2015). So far, Norhed projects seem to have succeeded in actively including women. A next phase could be to set up mentoring systems that support women as they climb the steep academic ladders and ensure that women's active participation is soon also found at decision-making level in higher education and research institutions and in potential future projects run in co-operation with the industry.

As emphasised by Halvorsen and Nossum (2016: xiii), Norhed's goals build on a relatively *organic* idea of development.

> Compared to a number of other donor programmes, Norhed's goals build on ideas about development rarely seen today. Other programmes have, for example, *political* goals such as building better leaders, *functional* goals relating to promoting economic growth, *pedagogical* goals for producing better students or *social* goals of spreading enlightenment and promoting middle-class values.

By accepting that knowledge is embedded within a social context, the Norhed programme aims to shape this context through the ways in which knowledge networks are built and, through these, to ensure that new and shared theory develops. Several chapters in this book speak to the challenges that such an idealistic vision presents, but also show how knowledge and skills can develop and be shared where academic openness prevails. In addition, several Norhed projects provide evidence that knowledge-based capacity exchange is key in the shift towards sustainable development.

The programme has furthermore shown a great deal of procedural independence and innovation. For example, from an early stage, Norhed opened the door to narrative reporting from projects. This is important as numerical or quantitative indicators, such as improved curricula, increasing numbers of research publications and further research projects, are often used to establish if a higher education partnership has been effective. However, such evidence does not always reflect the complex processes that underpin effective partnerships (Ndaruhutse and Thompson 2016). Processes that increase academic openness, knowledge and skills networks cannot solely be measured in numbers.

In a possible future round, it might be a good idea to take this organic approach even further. For instance, regular, mandatory forums for discussing pedagogical perspectives could be introduced as arenas for sharing experiences and strengthening the didactic competencies of all partners. This could be part of a more process-based methodology, wherein continuous learning and adjustments of project goals are consciously considered throughout project life spans.

A core question raised by this book is how to produce knowledge that resonates as universally relevant or true *and* derives from the context within which it is developed, including from societies marked by structural inequalities of different kinds. In attempting to find answers to this question, I and my co-editors of this volume suggest that future Norhed projects should be able to develop and demonstrate strategic partnerships with relevant sectors in their specific field of interest, and show how their research has direct bearing on the SDGs and the massive environmental challenges facing the world.

Our hope is that the Norhed programme will continue to strengthen links between academics and society to promote respect for scholarship, academic freedom and freedom of expression. We also hope that Norwegian politicians continue to be relatively independent, and remain willing to chart their own course where necessary when making decisions about support to higher education. Norhed's ambitious approach requires time and a strong commitment to building academic partnerships and promoting capacity and sustainability over the long term so that rigorous and independent research on issues relating to education for work and for democracy can thrive and aspire to being the best, not *in* but *for* the world.

Notes

1   Vertical inequalities refer to class-based inequalities, while horizontal inequalities address discrimination based on marginalised social identities, such as gender, race, and caste.
2   Prime Minister Erna Solberg's Key Note Address at SDG Conference Bergen, University of Bergen, 9 February 2018. Available online.

References

Adriansen HK, Madsen LM and Jensen S (eds) (2016) *Higher Education and Capacity Building in Africa*. New York: Routledge

Halvorsen T and Nossum J (eds) (2016) Preface. In: *North–South Knowledge Networks: Towards Equitable Collaboration Between Academics, Donors and Universities*. Cape Town: African Minds. Available online

Kabeer N (2015) Gender, poverty, and inequality: A brief history of feminist contributions in the field of international development. *Gender and Development* 23(2): 189–205

Koch S and Weingart P (2016) *The Delusion of Knowledge Transfer: The Impact of Foreign Aid Experts on Policy-Making in South Africa and Tanzania*. Cape Town: African Minds. Available online

Koulaouzides GA and Popović K (eds) (2017) *Adult Education and Lifelong Learning in Southeastern Europe*. Rotterdam: Springer

Krøvel R (2017) Indigenous perspectives on researching indigenous peoples. *Social Identities* 24(1): 58–65

Livingstone D (2005) Science, text and space: Thoughts on the geography of reading. *Transactions of the Institute of British Geographers* 30(4): 391–401

Matebeni Z (2015, 11 September) The more things change, the more they stay the same. Blogpost to *Mail & Guardian's Thoughtleader*. Available online

Mbembe AJ (2016) Decolonizing the university: New directions. *Arts and Humanities in Higher Education* 15(1): 29–45. Available online

Mendieta E (2016, Winter Edition) Philosophy of Liberation. In: EN Zalta (ed.) *Stanford Encyclopedia of Philosophy*. Available online

Ndaruhutse S and Thompson S (2016) *Literature Review: Higher Education and Development*. Norad Report 7/16, Oslo

Norad (2015) *The Norwegian Programme for Capacity Development in Higher Education and Research for Development: Results 2015*. Oslo. Available online

Rupke N (2011) Afterword: Putting the geography of science in its place. In: DN Livingstone and CWJ Withers (eds) *Geographies of Nineteenth-Century Science*. Chicago, IL: University of Chicago Press

Sabaratnam M (2017, 18 January) Decolonizing the curriculum: What is all the fuss about? *SOAS Blog*. Available online

Sifuna DN (2006) A review of major obstacles to women's participation in higher education in Kenya. *Research in Post-Compulsory Education* 11(1): 85–105

Struckmann C (2017) A postcolonial feminist critique of the 2030 Agenda for Sustainable Development. MA thesis, University of Stellenbosch, South Africa

Thiong'o NW (1981) *Decolonising the Mind: The Politics of Language in African Literature*. London: Heinemann

Thiong'o NW (2017) Decolonise the mind: Secure the base. Public lecture, 2 March, University of the Witwatersrand. Available online

Women Major Group (2014) *The Women Major Group's Vision and Priorities for the Sustainable Development Goals*, Major Group Position Paper, March. Available online

Printed in the United States
By Bookmasters